BTEC First Travel Atlas
UK & Europe Edition

ISBN: 1-84690-005-0

First published in 2006

© 2006 Columbus Travel Publishing
Pages 6-12, 15-21 & 144 © Edexcel Limited 2006

Distributed by:
Pearson Education Limited
Edinburgh Gate
Harlow
Essex CM20 2JE
www.longman.co.uk

• Cartographic Editor: *David Burles*.

• Production Editor: *Brian Quinn*.

• Additional Cartography: *Anderson Geographics Ltd, Berkshire*.

• Contributors: *Patrick Fitzgerald, Tony Peisley, Patrick Thorne, Penny Locke, Graeme Payne, Jon Gillaspie, Bill la Violette, Ned Middleton, Sachiko Burles, Carol Spencer, Hayley Dalton, Lucy Stewart*.

• Continental Introductions: *Brian Quinn*.

• Cover Design: *Antonio Manuel of Nexus Media Communications*.

• Printed by: *Croxsons, Chesham*.

• Founding Editor: *Mike Taylor of the University of Brighton*.

• Publisher: *Pete Korniczky*.

This publication has been created from a wide range of sources and where appropriate these have been credited on the relevant maps, charts or articles. The publishers would like to thank all the many organisations and individuals who have helped in the preparation of this edition, with particular thanks to Ian Alexander of Battlefiels Tours; Bill Adams of Safari Consultants; Isobel Falk of JLA; Keith Wright of Amusement Business; Brad Smith of Foremost West; John Knighton of African Pride; Maria Hinayon of ACI; Kate Pirie and Natalie de la Porte of Southern Skies Marketing; John Douglas of Malawi Tourism; John Haycock of Africa Explorer; David Ezra of the Saltmarsh Partnership; Maria Polk of Tours.com; Cathy Keefe of Travel Industry Association of America; Graham Johnson; Dirk Triep of the German National Tourist Office; Theresa Mancini of IACO; Olaf Schoonhoven of the World Travel School; Ivo Siebens of KHM; Ann Tack of Spermalie Hotel & Tourism School; Jeff Bertus of Bertus Leisure; Elliot Frisby of Visit Britain; Simon Hampton and Anne-Marie Hansen of Kuoni; Jane Voss; Dan Josty; Steve Jackson; Leila Carlyle; and Michael Knop. Apologies to organisations or individuals omitted from this list in error.

General Contents

This General Contents provides a summary of the main subjects and areas covered in this atlas. For clarity, many of the individual countries and topics covered are not listed separately here. Many countries have focus maps which give detailed coverage of areas of particular importance. For further help with locating countries or topics, see the Country Contents (3), the Thematic Contents (4-5) and the navigation panels which appear at the top of every page and which refer to a selection of related themes.

Country Contents

This section lists the countries in Europe as they have been defined for the purposes of this book. For more information on what is and what is not a country – a less clear-cut matter than might be supposed – please see the World Pointers section on page 24, the introduction to the Countries A-Z section on page 108 or the Columbus *World Travel Dictionary*. Countries are here prefixed with a dot. Only one page number has been given per entry and this generally refers to where a map of the entire country can be found; more detailed maps may appear on the subsequent page/s. A selection of other names is also given here, in *italics*. If preceding ≈, this is not, or no longer, the official name of the country: the official or current name follows the symbol. If preceding >, this is politically part of another country: the 'mother' country follows the symbol. (For ease of reference, the page number has been given where this is different from that of the 'mother' country). If preceding Δ, this is a geographical area or informal term: the countries it comprises follow the symbol. The list of such ambiguities could be many times longer and only those regarded as being the most important for the purposes of this atlas have been included here. For further help with locating places, see the General Contents (2), the Thematic Contents (4-5), the World Political map (28-29), Appendix 1: Geographical Definitions (100), Countries A-Z (108-116), the Index (117-143) and the navigation panels which appear at the top of every page and which refer to a selection of related themes.

Names preceded by > are politically part of another country; by ≈ are old/unofficial titles; by Δ are geographical areas. *See also introduction above.*

4 Contents

Country Contents

▶ *See also...* General Contents (2-3); Thematic Contents (6-7); World Pointers (10); Countries A-Z (202-210); Index (211-256)

The listings above refer to a selection of related themes.

Thematic Contents

This Thematic Contents gives page references for a selection of the topics covered in the Atlas. The abbreviations SIs and CSs mean that the theme is covered in the section introductions or the country sections. For further help with locating topics, please see the General Contents (2), the Country Contents (3), the Index (117-143) and the navigation panels which appear at the top of every page and which refer to a selection of related themes.

KEY TO TOPOGRAPHIC MAPS

Communications

✈ Airport *main international gateways and domestic hubs*

Motorway/expressway or equivalent *focus maps only*

Main road • Road in tunnel

Main passenger railway, with station • Railway in tunnel

Dedicated high-speed rail line *focus maps only*

Ferry route *selected passenger routes; focus maps only*

Boundaries & boxes

International boundary • Disputed international boundary

Internal administrative boundary *sometimes shown as solid line for clarity*

National park, wildlife reserve

Area featured in a focus map

Settlement

● ● ○ ○ ○ Towns and cities *size of dot is determined by population; darkest red indicates a city with over one million inhabitants*

■ ■ □ □ □ National capital/capital of overseas territory *named in CAPITAL LETTERS*

Built-up area *larger scale focus maps only*

∴ ⌂ Archaeological site, ruins • Important building/s (e.g castle, temple)

◆ Other place of interest (e.g. park, reserve, natural feature) *focus maps only*

Physical features (see individual map pages for elevation tints)

△ ▽ Mountain peak • Land depression *with altitude in metres*

= Pass, canyon *with altitude in metres*

River, with waterfall, with dam • Seasonal river

Lake • Seasonal lake • Salt lake

Canal

Coral reef

Introduction

The BTEC First Atlas: UK and Europe edition is an invaluable resource for teaching and assessing students working towards BTEC First Certificate and Diploma in Travel and Tourism.

The UK and Europe edition of the BTEC First Atlas has been specifically designed for *Unit 3: UK Travel and Tourism Destinations* and *Unit 4: European Holiday Destinations*. The following teaching sessions are for planning and developing lessons, enabling students to get full use out of the atlas. The sessions also show how activities can be combined to develop students' knowledge and understanding of UK and European geography. Blank maps of the UK and Europe have been provided for use in the teaching sessions and are found on pages 13 and 14 of this atlas. 'Test yourself' quizzes are also included, starting at page 15. The answers can be found on page 144.

Important note: The sessions published in this supplement have not been designed to form part of the assessment for the units mentioned and should not be used in this way. These sessions do not cover all of the content that has been set out in the specification. When teaching and assessing students for these units, please refer to guidance published in the specification for this qualification with the publication code BF017274. This and other support materials for this qualification can be obtained from the Edexcel website www.edexcel.org.uk.

Teaching sessions

> United Kingdom

• Teaching topic:
The UK and its regions

Session objectives:

- To understand the location of the UK nations, their capitals and their regions
- To check understanding with *UK Quiz 1 – UK regions*

Guidance

An interactive session is recommended using large-scale blank outline maps displayed to encourage group participation. Students' own UK holiday experiences should be shared and locations plotted on a map.

Students can then move on to structured map work, using the atlas to determine the location of significant tourist destinations in the UK. On a blank UK map, and using the map on pages 58/59, ask students to identify England, Scotland, Wales and Northern Ireland and their capital cities. Using the same, or a new blank map, ask students to identify and locate the regions of the UK that attract high numbers of tourists. The maps on page 61 are a good starting point.

TV travel programmes can be used for additional visual and factual input. Some tourist boards are able to provide promotional videos for educational purposes and may also be willing to offer guest speakers. Details of tourism regions can be found on page 60 of this atlas

• Teaching topic:
Tourist destinations: UK towns and cities

Session objectives:

- To understand the factors affecting the appeal of historical and cultural towns and cities (including spa towns)
- To understand what is on offer in UK towns and cities for tourists
- To find out the location of key UK towns and cities which attract tourists

Guidance

Devise practical activities to help students become proficient and independent in using brochures, leaflets, guidebooks, trade manuals and websites to locate information on UK destinations. These tools should be used specifically to examine the factors affecting the appeal of historical, cultural and spa towns or cities for different types of visitors.

Get students to investigate specific locations, taking into account visitor attractions, topography, facilities, arts and entertainment, sightseeing and transport links. Initial focus should be on a tourist town or city in the locality. This should be followed by paired work to investigate different town or city destinations across the UK, culminating in short presentations.

Using the map on pages 58/59, ask students to identify

towns and cities that appeal to tourists. For each location students should summarise what the main appeal is for inbound and domestic tourists.

The following is an example list of UK towns and cities with appeal to tourists:

Bath, Belfast, Buxton, Canterbury, Cardiff, Cheltenham, Edinburgh, Glasgow, Harrogate, Inverness, Liverpool, London, Londonderry, Manchester, Oxford, Stirling, Stratford-upon-Avon, York

Many UK towns and cities have their own marketing teams that may be able to provide guest speakers or additional information.

• Teaching topic:
Tourist destinations: UK seaside resorts

Session objectives:

- To understand the factors affecting the appeal of UK seaside resorts
- To find out what UK seaside resorts have to offer tourists
- To design posters to promote a UK seaside resort
- To find out the locations of popular UK seaside resorts
- To check understanding with *UK Quiz 2 – UK seaside resorts*

Guidance

Develop research activities, using the internet, guidebooks, holiday brochures and leaflets, to examine the factors affecting the appeal of UK seaside resorts for different types of visitors. This should take into account visitor attractions, topography, facilities, arts and entertainment, sightseeing and transport links. The group will benefit from individual students selecting different seaside resorts for investigation.

Ask students to design and display posters to promote the appeal of a seaside resort for a specific type of visitor.

Using the map on page 60 ask students to locate popular seaside resorts. For each one located students should state their appeal (this could include areas of natural beauty, built visitor attractions, events and festivals).

The following are examples of UK seaside resorts:

Aberdour, Aberystwyth, Ballycastle, Barmouth, Blackpool, Brighton, Llandudno, Margate, Newquay, Portrush, Scarborough, South Wold, Tenby

Many seaside resorts have their own marketing teams who can provide guest speakers or additional information.

• Teaching topic:
Tourist destinations: UK islands, countryside and coastal areas

Session objectives:

- To understand factors affecting the appeal of islands, countryside and coastal areas

- To understand what islands, countryside and coastal areas have to offer tourists

- Design fact sheets about islands, countryside and coastal areas

- Check understanding with *UK Quiz 3 – Transport links to islands, the countryside and coastal areas* and *UK Quiz 4 – National Parks of England Scotland and Wales*

Guidance

Develop research activities, using the internet, guidebooks, holiday brochures and leaflets, to examine the factors affecting the appeal of islands, countryside and coastal areas, for different types of visitor. This should take into account visitor attractions, topography, facilities, arts and entertainment (where applicable), sightseeing and transport links. Additional activities could be organised to investigate accessibility of tourist islands from the mainland.

Compile fact sheets to make up a display on a wide variety of islands, countryside and coastal areas.

Use maps on pages 58/59 to locate islands. Ask students to note what features each island has that might help its appeal to inbound and domestic tourists. *The following are examples of UK islands:*

Arran, Guernsey, Isle of Wight, Mull, Skye, St. Marys

Use maps on pages 58, 59, 60, 61 and 64 to locate countryside and coastal areas that appeal to tourists *The following are examples of UK countryside areas:*

Cadir Idris, Chiltern Hills, Forest of Dean, Lake District, Loch Lomond, Loch Ness, Mourne Mountains, New Forest

The following are examples of UK coastal areas:

Chesil Bay, Gower Peninsula, Lizard Heritage Coast

Many National Parks have visitor centres which may be able to provide videos for educational purposes, guest speakers or additional information.

• Teaching topic:
Transport: UK airports

Session objectives:

- To locate major international air gateways for inbound tourists

- To understand locations of UK airports and their 3-letter codes

- To check understanding with *UK Quiz 5 – Airports and their 3-letter codes*

Guidance

Using the map on page 62, locate the major international air gateways into the UK for inbound tourists. Although almost every airport has international flights, students could focus on Heathrow, Gatwick, Manchester, Glasgow International and Belfast International. Using a variety of sources students should identify where inbound tourists may arrive from into these airports.

Students can then locate on a blank map all the airports in the UK, with their 3-letter codes. Ask students to make observations about the locations of the airports and how this could affect the appeal for both inbound and domestic tourists in specific areas.

• Teaching topic:
Transport: UK seaports

Session objectives:

- To know locations of major seaports in the UK

- To know the names of ferry operators and types of vessels operating to, from and within the UK

- To check understanding with UK Quiz 6 – UK seaports and their destinations

Guidance

Using the map on page 62, ask students to identify major seaports in the UK on a blank map.
The following are examples of UK seaports:

Aberdeen, Dover, Fishguard, Harwich, Holyhead, Liverpool, Portsmouth, Ryde, Stranraer, Troon

For six of these seaports ask students to research the number and names of the ferry services operating, and their destinations. Ask them to find out what type of vessel operates (for example, car carrying, high speed) and how they think this might affect the appeal for inbound and domestic tourists.

There should be at least one example of:

1. a route within the UK (for example, Portsmouth to Ryde),

2. a route from mainland UK to the Republic of Ireland (for example, Fishguard to Rosslare),

3. a route from the UK to continental Europe (for example, Harwich to Hook of Holland).

> Europe

For the purposes of this unit, Europe is considered to be all of continental Europe west of the Urals and including the Republic of Ireland, the Canary Islands, the Azores and Cyprus. It does not include any part of the United Kingdom including the Channel Islands or the Isle of Man.

The term 'holiday destination' can refer to a specific city or town that is an established holiday destination, such as Madrid, St. Moritz or Benidorm. It could also be a small island or a distinct area, for example Ibiza or Côte d'Azur, or a specific city or town within that area, for example San Antonio or Nice. Countryside areas can include lakes and mountains such as the Italian Lakes or the Black Forest.

• Teaching topic:
Countries of Europe

Session objectives:

- To gain a general overview of the geography of Europe

- To gain an understanding of the variety of resorts in Europe

- To develop skills in using an atlas and other types of reference material

Guidance

Using a blank map of Europe ask students to locate European countries, noting which ones are in the EU and which are in the Eurozone. The maps on pages 44 and 46 may be helpful in this exercise.

Using statistics, brochures or other sources ask students to identify which countries are popular with ex-UK tourists and why.

Working in groups, students can then be allocated different European countries to investigate using tour operators' brochures, websites and the atlas. This enables different groups to produce and present annotated maps to identify a wide range of holiday destinations within different European countries. The maps should highlight the variety of holiday destinations and transport gateways within individual countries. A wide range of destinations should be located within each country chosen, including (where appropriate) at least one each of summer sun, winter sun, winter sport, countryside, city break and cruise areas. Airports and passenger ferry ports should also be identified.

• Teaching topic:
Summer and winter sun destinations

Session objectives:

- To identify and locate summer and winter sun destinations
- To find out about natural attractions and how they might affect the popularity and appeal of summer and winter sun destinations
- To check understanding with *Europe Quiz 1 – Summer sun destinations*

Guidance

Ask students to research popular summer and winter sun destinations using brochures. *The following are examples of summer sun destinations:*

Algarve, Croatia, Gumbet, Ibiza, Limassol, Salou, Santorini

The following are examples of winter sun destinations:

Gran Canaria, Lanzarote, Tenerife

Students can locate summer and winter sun destinations on a blank map, using maps found on pages 76-95.

Ask students to research natural attractions (for example beaches and lakes) and climate (for example average temperature and rainfall) and say how these affect the popularity of winter and summer sun destinations. The climate map on page 45 might be useful.

• Teaching topic:
Winter sports and countryside destinations

Session objectives:

- To find out about significant geographical features in Europe and activities that might be associated with these
- To know locations for winter sports in Europe and the physical factors that affect their appeal
- To find out about countryside areas and their appeal to ex-UK tourists
- To check understanding with *Europe Quiz 2 – Areas of European countryside*

Guidance

On a blank map ask students to identify significant geographical features in Europe (for example forests, lakes, volcanic areas, areas of wilderness, sub-tropical forests and glacial lakes). The maps on pages 44 and 54 identify some of the most significant ones. Ask students to identify what types of activities may be popular in these areas.

Using brochures, students should identify and locate popular European winter sport destinations. The map on page 57 might be helpful in this exercise. *The following are examples of winter sports destinations:*

Are, Flaine, Meribel, Poiana Brasov, Soldeu, Vogel

Ask students to explain what physical factors might affect the appeal of winter sport destinations (for example altitude, number of runs or distance from airport).

Using the map on page 54 identify and research six countryside areas in Europe. For each one they should locate them on a map and describe the natural features that would appeal to ex-UK tourists.

• Teaching topic:
City breaks

Session objectives:

- To find out the locations of city break destinations in Europe

- To learn about how low-cost airlines and flight times can contribute to the popularity of city break destinations

- To understand the importance of arts and culture on the appeal of city breaks

- To learn about the negative impacts of too much tourism on European cities

- To check understanding with *Europe Quiz 3 – Low-cost carriers and their destinations*

Guidance

Students should locate major European city break destinations on a blank map. *The following are examples of major European city break destinations:*

Brussels, Krakow, Madrid, Paris, Prague, Rome, Tallinn

Using route maps of low-cost airlines, and other sources, ask students to identify popular European city breaks that are served by low-cost carriers.

Develop research activities using the internet, guidebooks, *World Travel Guide*, holiday brochures and leaflets to examine the traditions, culture and image of a variety of European holiday destinations.

Ask students to use guidebooks (such as the *Rough Guides*) to find out about traditions, arts and culture that cities are famous for. They should imagine they are making a bid to have the city named as European City of Culture 2014. What are the main highlights of the city they would like to bring to the judges attention? TV travel programmes can be used for additional visual and factual input.

Newspaper articles, especially bad press (for example, about crime level, loutish behaviour or sporting clashes) should be reviewed to prompt discussions about image. Ask students to consider which cities have a negative image because of crime or too much tourism.

The map on page 39 indicates flying times from London. Students should note which of the destinations they have found are within two hours flying time of London. Ask students to consider how far people would be willing to travel for a city break, and which city breaks are popular with UK tourists and why.

• Teaching topic:
European cruise areas

Session objectives:

- To find out about the European cruise areas and their appeal to tourists

- To check understanding with *Europe Quiz 4 – Cruise areas: ports of call*

Guidance

Using the map on page 40/41, ask students to locate the major European cruise areas on a blank map. Using cruise brochures, ask students to explain how cruises in major European areas might appeal to different types of tourists.

• Teaching topic:

Transport: European airports

Session objectives:

- To know the location of major air gateways in Europe

- To check understanding with *Europe Quiz 5 – Airports and their 3-letter codes*

Guidance

On a blank map, ask students to locate key airports in Europe with flights to and from the UK, noting their 3-letter codes. The map on page 38 locates some of these.

Using airport websites, ask students to identify scheduled and charter routes to and from these airports to the UK.

• Teaching topic:

Transport: European sea ports

Session objectives:

- To know the locations of major seaports and ferry routes from the UK to Europe

- To check understanding with *Europe Quiz 6 – European seaports and their destinations*

Guidance

Using the map on page 62, ask students to identify major seaports in Europe with links to the UK on a blank map. *The following are examples of European sea ports which link to the UK:*

Calais, Bilbao, Esbjerg, Rotterdam, Zeebrugge

For six of these seaports ask students to research the number and names of the ferry services which operate from the port, and their destinations. Ask them to find out what type of vessel operates (for example car carrying, high speed) and how they think this might affect the appeal to ex-UK tourists.

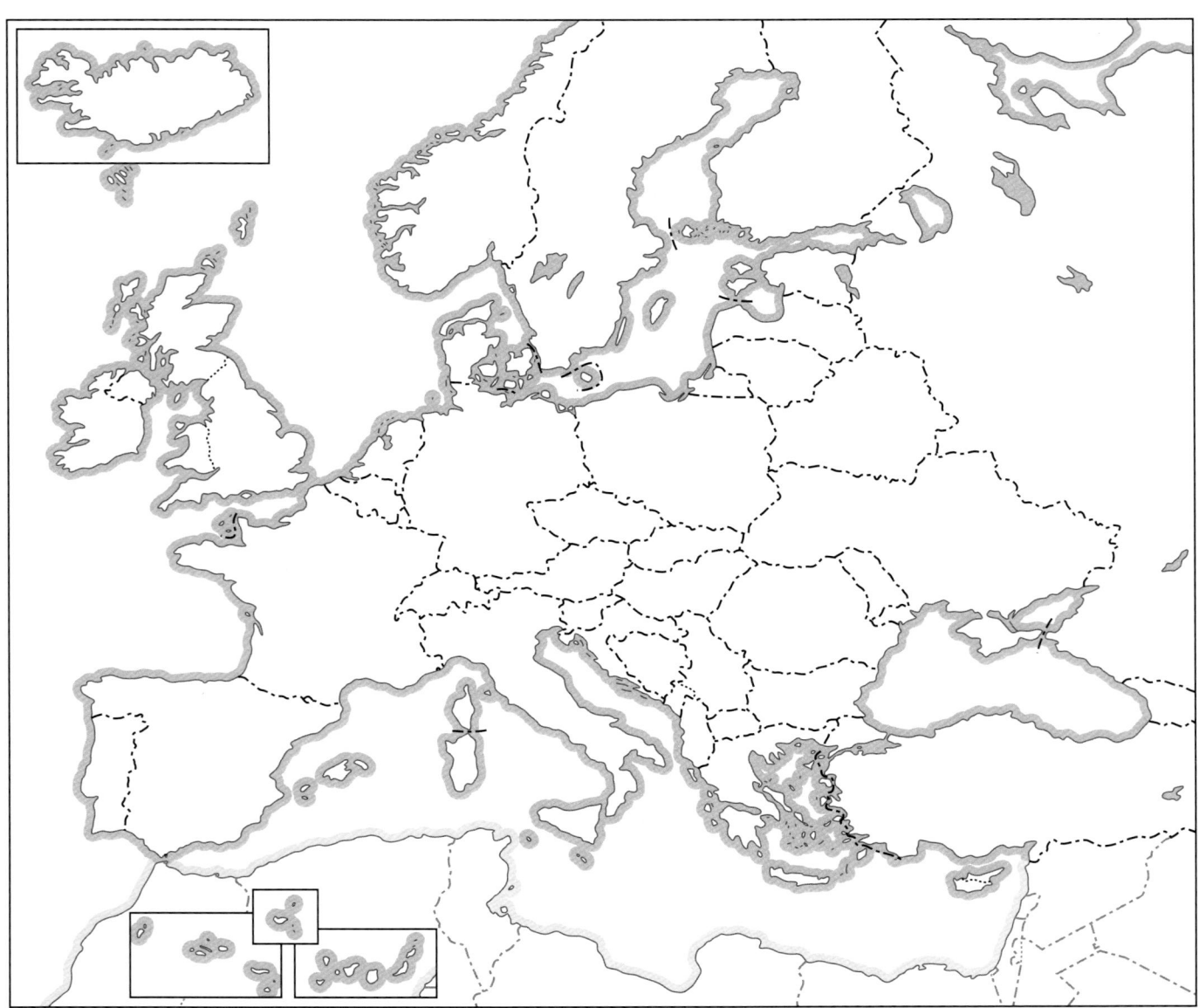

Quizzes

Answers to all UK and European quizzes can be found on page 144

> United Kingdom

■ UK Quiz 1 – UK regions

Match the description to the region it describes.

	Question	**Answer**
1	This area of England is home to two National Parks and the UK's surfing capital.	☐
2	These are all islands that are part of the Inner Hebrides.	☐
3	This Northern Ireland county is home to the Giants Causeway.	☐
4	The Heart of England is the birthplace of which famous English playwright?	☐
5	Gatwick, Heathrow and Stansted are all located in this region.	☐
6	Glamorgan and Pembrokeshire are counties in which area of the UK?	☐
7	Loch Lomond and Loch Tay are two of the many lochs found in this area of the UK.	☐
8	Lowestoft, South Wold and Cromer are all in this English Tourist Board region.	☐
9	This county is home to the Mourne Mountains.	☐
10	Although nearer France these islands are British dependencies.	☐

A	Shakespeare	D	East of England	G	South Wales	J	County Down
B	Scottish Lowlands	E	Southeast England	H	The Channel Islands		
C	Antrim	F	West Country	I	Mull, Jura and Islay		

■ UK Quiz 2 – UK seaside resorts

Name the seaside resort to which the fact relates.

Fact   **Resort**

1   This English seaside resort is home to a famous pavilion built for King George IV.   _____

2   Dolphins are often spotted near this Welsh seaside resort in Cardigan Bay.   _____

3   This Cornish seaside resort is home to the China Clay Trials and near to
    the Eden Project.   _____

4   This seaside resort is home to the famous 'pleasure beach' amusement park.   _____

5   This seaside resort is home to the world's longest pier.   _____

6   This Welsh beach is sometimes referred to as the unofficial capital of the
    Llyn Peninsula.   _____

7   This seaside resort in Northern Ireland is well known for its Ould Lammas Fair.   _____

8   This seaside resort has its own Tate gallery.   _____

9   This popular Isle of Wight beach has a pier, a small airport and its own
    dinosaur museum.   _____

10 This Yorkshire seaside resort is famous for its fair held each May.   _____

■ UK Quiz 3 – Transport links to islands, the countryside and coastal areas

What is the closest city, and therefore transport gateway to these areas?

1   Peak District   ☐

2   New Forest   ☐

3   Lough Neagh   ☐

4   The Trossachs   ☐

5   Jersey   ☐

6   Gower Peninsula   ☐

7   Lake District   ☐

8   Norfolk Broads   ☐

9   Isle of Wight   ☐

10 Land's End   ☐

A	Lancaster	D	Sheffield	G	Southampton	J	Penzance
B	Stirling	E	Lowestoft	H	Swansea		
C	St. Helier	F	Ryde	I	Belfast		

■ UK Quiz 4 – National Parks of England, Scotland and Wales

Label the National Parks on the map.

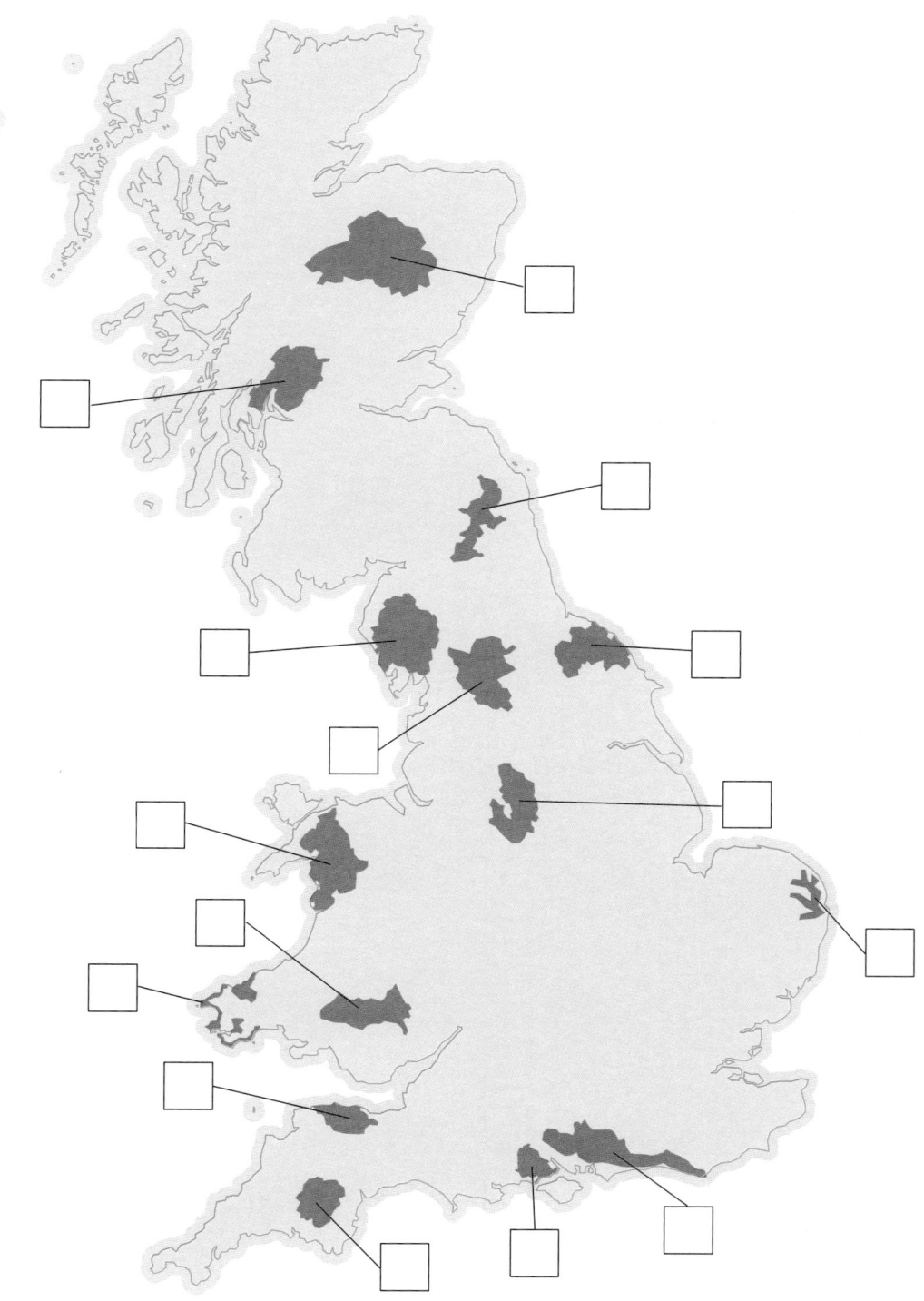

A Cairngorms National Park	I Pembrokeshire Coast National Park
B Loch Lomond National Park	J Brecon Beacons National Park
C Northumberland National Park	K Exmoor National Park
D Lake District National Park	L Dartmoor National Park
E Yorkshire Dales National Park	M New Forest National Park
F North York Moors National Park	N Broads Authority National Park
G Peak District National Park	O South Downs Proposed National Park
H Snowdonia National Park	

■ UK Quiz 5 – Airports and their 3-letter codes

Complete the table.

	Airport	3-letter code
1	London Heathrow	_____
2	Londonderry	_____
3	Edinburgh	_____
4	London Stansted	_____
5	Leeds Bradford	_____
6	_____	BHX
7	_____	CWL
8	_____	GLA
9	_____	BHD
10	_____	BOH

■ UK Quiz 6 – UK seaports and their destinations

Match the UK seaport with its destination.

Seaport

1 Dover ☐

2 Harwich ☐

3 Portsmouth ☐

4 Holyhead ☐

5 Ullapool ☐

6 Belfast ☐

7 Southampton ☐

8 Liverpool ☐

9 Newhaven ☐

10 Plymouth ☐

A	Stranraer	D	Roscoff	G	Stornoway	J	East Cowes
B	Bilbao	E	Dun Laoghaire	H	Douglas		
C	Dieppe	F	Calais	I	Esbjerg		

> Europe

■ Europe Quiz 1 – Summer Sun Destinations

The following summer sun destinations are all located on islands. Name the island, the country to which it belongs and the sea that it is in.

Resort	Island	Country	Sea/Ocean
1 Lindos			
2 Kavos			
3 Paphos			
4 Kyrenia			
5 Alcudia			
6 Funchal			
7 Sliema			
8 Alghero			
9 Porto Vecchio			
10 Molyvos			

■ Europe Quiz 2 – European Countryside Areas

Describe the natural features of these European countryside areas and suggest activities that tourists could do while they are there. The first one has been done for you.

Area	Natural features	Activities
1 The Dolomites, Italy	*Mountains and lakes, with snow in winter*	*Skiing in winter, walking, cycling in summer*
2 The Black Forest, Germany		
3 Gauja, Latvia		
4 Mount Teide, Tenerife, Spain		
5 Trakai, Lithuania		
6 The Pyrenees, Spain		
7 Wolinski, Poland		
8 Sumava, Czech Republic		
9 Hamra, Sweden		
10 Wicklow Mountains, Ireland		

■ Europe Quiz 3 – Low-cost carriers and their destinations

The following are airports served by low-cost carriers. For each one, identify the major town or city nearby and which airlines operate there.

Airport	Nearby town or city	Airlines
1 Ciampino		
2 Bratislava		
3 Sabiha Gokcen		
4 Brescia		
5 Beauvais		
6 Reus		
7 Mulhouse		
8 Schonefeld		
9 Treviso		
10 Torp		

■ Europe Quiz 4 – Cruise areas: Ports of call

In which body of water are the following ports?

Port	Body of water
1 Bergen	
2 Crete	
3 Dubrovnik	
4 Porto	
5 Palma de Mallorca	
6 Istanbul	
7 Stockhlom	
8 Tromso	
9 Tallinn	
10 Gibraltar	

■ Europe Quiz 5 – Airports and their 3-letter codes

Complete the table.

	Airport	3-letter code
1	Paris Orly	
2	Faro	
3	Palma, Majorca	
4	Cork	
5	Mikinos	
6		AGP
7		ADB
8		LCA
9		PRG
10		KRK

■ Europe Quiz 6 – European seaports and their UK destinations

Match the European seaport with its UK destination.

1	Cuxhaven	☐
2	Bergen	☐
3	Cork	☐
4	Kristiansand	☐
5	St. Malo	☐
6	Cherbourg	☐
7	Zeebrugge	☐
8	Dunkirk	☐
9	Santander	☐
10	Granville	☐

A Swansea	D Kingston upon Hull	G Plymouth	J Poole
B Weymouth	E Harwich	H Newcastle	
C Dover	F Lerwick	I St. Helier	

▶ **See also...** World Political (28-29); Travel Indicators (34-35); Europe Introduction (42-43)

The listings above refer to a selection of related themes. For more information, see the Contents (2-5).

Key facts

Number of Countries	226
Area ('000 sq km)	135,477
Population ('000)	6,450,988
Population Density (per sq km)	48
Gross National Income (US$m)	39,659,845
Visitor Arrivals ('000)	766,000
Visitor Receipts (US$m)	601,726

GNI figures are for 2004. Population figures are taken from the most recent reliable source. Travel figures (UNWTO) are based on overnight stays, not same-day visitors, and are for 2004. For more information see the Countries A-Z section from page 202.

World

There are many opinions as to how big the worldwide travel business really is. Like all service-based sectors it has no physical product that can be weighed or counted. Many problems of definition follow from this – an airline pilot or a travel agent is clearly part of the industry; but what about a small-town taxi driver, or the owner of a convenience store that also sells local souvenirs? Different countries and organisations will take different views on such points. Despite such challenges, widely accepted estimates are produced by several respected bodies. One such, the World Travel and Tourism Council, suggests that 10.6% of the world's GDP and 8.3% of the world's jobs depend directly or indirectly on travel and tourism, making it the world's largest industry: in the 1960s it was not even in the top ten. The World Tourism Organisation further suggests that travel is the world's fastest growing one, with an annual average increase in receipts of 9% between 1984 and 2000. Various projections put the real growth per year at around 4 to 5% between 2006 and 2015. By any estimate, travel is clearly big business – a multi-trillion dollar industry, driven by people's frequent desire to be elsewhere.

The *World Travel Atlas*, now in its tenth edition, provides a unique overview of the travel industry in the early 21st century. The focus maps which complement the conventional regional and country plates offer detailed, travel-specific coverage of the most-visited areas. A large number of themes, ranging from economic indicators to UNESCO World Heritage Sites and from ski resorts to time zones, are covered throughout the book, supplemented with detailed appendices. There are also six continental introductions, which provide an overview of each region, a discussion of some of the key travel-related issues, a summary of the main travel destinations and a selection of statistics. Themes covered here include low-cost airlines, the cruise industry, intra-regional travel patterns, the changing role of the travel agent, responsible tourism, regional economic change, the internet, the problems of the major airlines, globalisation and niche markets. Many of the maps and charts are new to this edition and all pre-existing ones have been updated. Another first-time feature is the navigation aid panel at the top of each page which refers to maps or charts of related interest. There is also are also two additional contents providing thematic and country-by-country overviews of the numerous topics that the *World Travel Atlas* addresses. Overall, the book's aim is to provide a clear, balanced and accurate picture of the world for a wide range of readers in the travel industry and elsewhere.

Past, present and future

Apart from 1982 (due mainly to the Gulf War) and 2001 (due mainly to the 11 September terrorist attacks), visitor numbers and travel receipts have risen in every year since accurate records began in 1950. Aviation figures go back even further than that: in 1926 the US domestic air travel market involved some 8,000 passengers, about the number that took to the skies for domestic flights in America every seven minutes in 2005. As for international flights from the USA in 1926, there were none recorded. It was not until 1946 that US international departures broke through the one million mark. They have increased by an average of about one million per year ever since.

By whatever means of transport, Europe remained comfortably the most-visited continent in 2005. What is encouraging for the global health of the industry is that, while Europe's market is still growing, arrivals to other regions – notably Asia – are growing at a faster pace. The WTO's Tourism 2020 Vision forecasts that worldwide international arrivals are likely to exceed 1.56 billion by 2020. Under this model, Europe will remain the most-visited region, but with a market share reduced from 60% in 1995 to 46% in 2020. As regards outbound travel, Europe will continue to dominate, but Asia will, by 2020, have doubled its number of visitors compared to 1995 whereas those of the Americas will only have increased by 50%. The report goes on to predict that long-haul travel will grow at a faster rate than regional travel during this period.

The leading countries in the travel-numbers league seem to have their positions assured, for the next few years at least. The six top countries in terms of visitor arrivals were the same in 2004 as in 1997, with France comfortably in the lead and the chasing pack bunched some way behind them, occasionally changing their positions from year to year. On the other three basic indicators, the Germans travel more and (having recently overtaken the USA) spend the most, while the Americans receive the most money. The most significant medium-term change is likely to be the emergence of China, not only as a destination but also as a source of travellers. The increase in number of countries being granted Approved Destination Status, the relaxation of travel restrictions and China's rapidly growing prosperity have already led to international departures more than doubling between 2000 and 2004. By many estimates, China will be supplying more tourists than any other country by 2010.

Travel remains something of an exclusive market: the 11 most visited countries accounted for over 50% of all tourist arrivals in 2004. It is also something of a crowded one: in 41 of the world's countries the annual visiting population in 2004 exceeded the native one, on four occasions (Andorra, Macau, the British Virgin Islands and Aruba) by a factor of more than 10.

Prospects for 2006 and beyond appear good on the basis of recent performance and medium-term trends,

although there are several potential problems ahead. The WTO has identified terrorism, rising oil prices and the spread of the H5N1 avian flu virus as three of the most important factors which could disrupt the industry during the coming years.

Travel trends

2005 was another record year for the travel industry with visitor arrivals reaching 808 million according to the WTO, an increase of 5.5% and over 40 million travellers compared to 2004's 766 million. All this was despite a catalogue of problems including natural disasters, health scares, terrorism and oil price rises, all seemingly striking at the very heart of the industry. The strongest continental growth was recorded in the less mature markets, with Africa (10% up) leading the way: further good news for an industry which, like any other, is seeking to diversify its appeal. Even the airlines prospered better than many would have predicted a couple of years ago, with RPKs (revenue passenger kilometres) of IATA members up by nearly 8%. Still more surprisingly, many observers predict that the aviation industry as a whole will return to profit by the end of 2007. It was another excellent year for many niche markets: cruising, for example, attracted double the number of travellers in 2005 than ten years earlier. New holiday options are constantly being offered and new ways of doing business developed. In addition, a new ethical dimension is being added, with an increased emphasis on responsible and sustainable tourism. All things considered, the travel business is clearly both very adaptable and very robust.

An important area of the industry, but one that is often overlooked, is domestic tourism. The extent of this is for obvious reasons very hard to quantify. Although this generates no new revenue from foreign countries, it at least keeps money flushing through a national economy and keeps travel-related businesses healthy even at times when people are, for whatever reason, disinclined to venture abroad. Around 95% of all trips taken by Americans are domestic, according to TIA – 'See America First' was first used as a slogan by the National Parks Service in 1906 and has been popular ever since – while the UK Tourism Survey estimates that over 126 million such journeys were made in Britain in 2004. Many national tourist offices now devote a good part of their budget to encouraging their own citizens not to travel abroad.

Special-interest holidays have been growing steadily in recent years and the trend shows no sign of slowing. Adventure holidays, cruising, winter sports and city

▪ Visitor arrivals

The world's 25 most visited countries in 2004 (millions)
Source: WTO

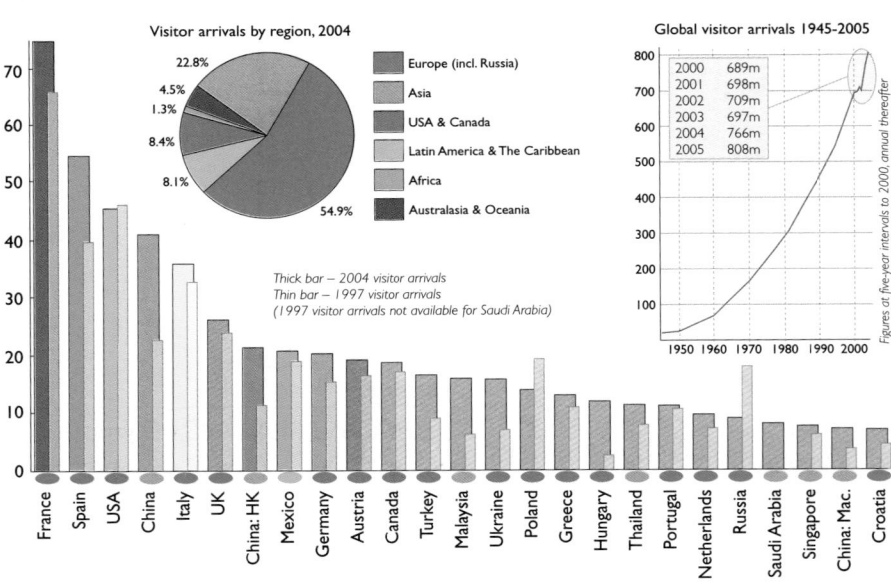

Visitor arrivals by region, 2004

- 22.8% Europe (incl. Russia)
- 4.5% Asia
- 1.3% USA & Canada
- 8.4% Latin America & The Caribbean
- 8.1% Africa
- 54.9% Australasia & Oceania

Thick bar – 2004 visitor arrivals
Thin bar – 1997 visitor arrivals
(1997 visitor arrivals not available for Saudi Arabia)

Countries: France, Spain, USA, China, Italy, UK, China: HK, Mexico, Germany, Austria, Canada, Turkey, Malaysia, Ukraine, Poland, Greece, Hungary, Thailand, Portugal, Netherlands, Russia, Saudi Arabia, Singapore, China: Mac., Croatia

Global visitor arrivals 1945-2005

2000	689m
2001	698m
2002	709m
2003	697m
2004	766m
2005	808m

Figures at five-year intervals to 2000, annual thereafter

- In economic terms, international travel and tourism receipts are classified as exports, and international tourism expenditure as imports. According to the WTO, travel and tourism is one of the top five export categories for over 80% of countries.
- In 2004, Air France-KLM carried 47,190,000 international passengers, more than any other airline. Delta carried the most domestic passengers (79,289,000).
- 19 countries received over 10 million international visitors in 2004. 60 others received over 1 million.
- 17 countries supplied more than 10 million international travellers in 2004. 40 others supplied more than 1 million.
- 17 countries received in excess of US$10billion from international travel in 2004. 46 others received in excess of US$1billion.
- 14 countries spent in excess of US$10billion on international travel in 2004. 28 others spent in excess of US$1billion.
- The biggest travellers, the Germans, have, on average, 35 vacation days a year: Americans have only 13.
- The world's population grew from 1.6 billion to 6.1 billion during the 20th century and is expected to exceed 7 billion by 2015.
- In an average year, Carnival Cruise lines puts 10 million chocolate mints on their guests' pillows.
- Saudi Arabia is the most generous aid donor measured by contributions as a proportion of national income.
- 41 countries (including France, Hong Kong, Portugal, UAE, Ireland, Singapore and many Caribbean states) receive annually more visitors than their population.
- According to ACI, the world's airlines carried 6.7% more passengers in June 2005 than in June 2004.
- Over 55% of cruises in 2005 were in the Caribbean or the Mediterranean.
- The first commercial flight took place in 1914.
- More people are killed on the roads of the USA in an average six-month period than have been in all commercial aviation accidents since 1960.
- The WTO predicts that international travel arrivals will exceed 1.5 billion by 2020.
- And finally, a few thoughts from some other travellers:

> 'Like all travellers, I have seen more than I remember and remembered more than I have seen.'
> (Benjamin Disraeli)

> 'Maps encourage boldness. They're like cryptic love letters. They make everything seem possible.'
> (Mark Jenkins)

> 'The traveller sees what he sees – the tourist sees what he has come to see.'
> (GK Chesterton)

> 'The destination is never a place, but a new way of seeing things.'
> (Henry Miller)

> 'Everywhere I go, I find a poet who has been there before me.'
> (Sigmund Freud)

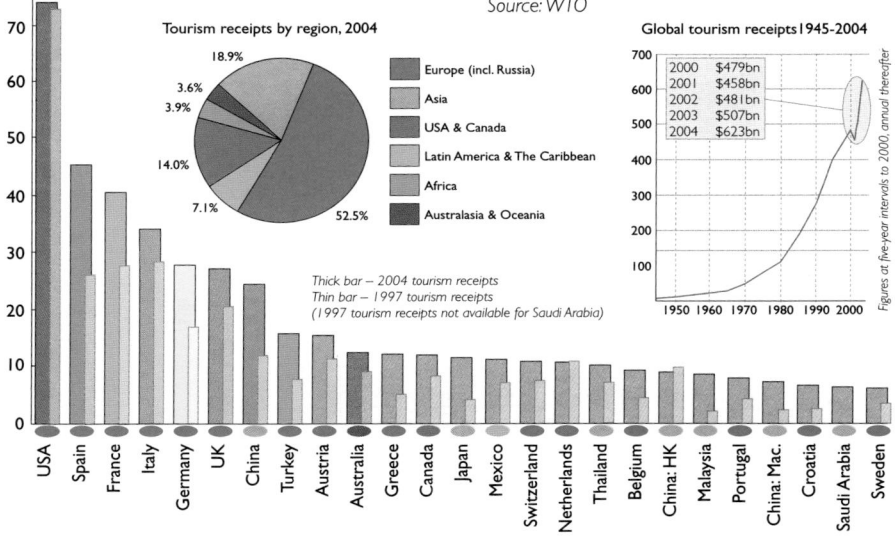

■ Visitor receipts

The 25 countries that received the most from international travel in 2004 (US$ millions)
Source: WTO

Tourism receipts by region, 2004

- Europe (incl. Russia) — 52.5%
- Asia — 18.9%
- USA & Canada — 14.0%
- Latin America & The Caribbean — 7.1%
- Africa — 3.9%
- Australasia & Oceania — 3.6%

Thick bar – 2004 tourism receipts
Thin bar – 1997 tourism receipts
(1997 tourism receipts not available for Saudi Arabia)

Global tourism receipts 1945-2004

2000	$479bn
2001	$458bn
2002	$481bn
2003	$507bn
2004	$623bn

Figures at five-year intervals to 2000, annual thereafter

breaks are four of the most important and travel agencies able to offer specialist advice and services in these areas have benefited. Travellers are also becoming more discriminating, demanding and adventurous, a trend fuelled by the internet. In Europe, for example, the low-cost airlines are offering a complete one-stop range of short-break options – flights, hotels, car-hire and insurance – through their web-sites. Many of these involve destinations that ten years ago would have been almost unknown, and the list is growing. The number of European city breaks doubled between 2000 and 2004, and many cities have seen year-on-year growth of over 30% in this period.

The low-cost airlines are one sign of change, and of a kind that few would have predicted 15 years ago. In fact, the distinction between low-cost and other kinds of airlines is already starting to blur. With varying degrees of success, many traditional carriers now compete on cost, and some have started up their own low-cost operations. The business model of successful entrants into any market is usually based on a mixture of addressing the failings of the incumbents and utilising new technology, and the new breed of airlines have exploited both. Furthermore, it is easier to start with a blank slate, free of long-established and possibly outdated labour contracts, marketing perceptions and partnership arrangements, than it is to adapt an

existing business. Low-cost airlines have been highly successful in re-defining the travel business.

So to has the internet, the other major force for change of recent years. Numerous statistics, some of which are reported elsewhere in this book, testify to the internet's dramatic growth as a medium for travel information and bookings, and appear to suggest an irreversible trend towards direct sales. The reality is rather more complex. The more successful agencies are now making use of the internet as a 24-hour marketing and sales tool, while at the same time ensuring that their levels of knowledge (often in specialist areas) and customer service keep pace with consumers' increasing expectations. In the same way, many on-line companies are looking to provide a human face to their services by using retail outlets. In time, these developments are likely to blur the distinction between 'on-line' and 'traditional' travel suppliers. Throughout the travel industry, as in others, the companies that thrive will do so because they manage to provide the best and most cost-effective service to their customers.

■ Big spenders

The 20 countries whose residents spent the most on international travel in 2004.
Source: WTO/IMF/World Bank

	Expenditure (US$ millions)	GNI (US$ millions)	Expenditure as % of GNI
Germany	72,271	2,488,974	2.9%
USA	65,635	12,150,931	0.5%
UK	55,930	2,016,393	2.8%
Japan	38,129	4,749,910	0.8%
France	28,636	1,858,731	1.5%
Italy	20,544	1,503,562	1.4%
China	19,100	1,676,846	1.1%
Netherlands	16,539	515,148	3.2%
Canada	16,017	905,629	1.8%
Russia	15,730	487,335	3.2%
Belgium	13,954	322,837	4.3%
China: HK	13,258	183,516	7.2%
Spain	12,156	875,817	1.4%
Austria	11,416	262,147	4.4%
Sweden	10,123	321,401	3.1%
Korea, Rep.	9,499	673,036	1.4%
Australia	9,407	541,173	1.7%
Switzerland	8,797	356,052	2.5%
Norway	8,428	238,398	3.5%
Taiwan	8,170	317,070	2.6%

The reasons for travelling, the means by which the arrangements are made, the choice of possible destinations and the activities to engage in one arrived are all more numerous than ever before. Business trips or beach holidays, cruises or kayaking, safaris or skiing – they are all available somewhere, as long as one has the necessary leisure time and disposable income.

Travel and wealth

Sadly, many people in the world are currently no more than spectators of this glamorous industry. According to the World Bank, the percentage of the population in developing countries who live on a purchasing power parity of less than US$2 a day (defined as describing what US$2 will actually buy in that country, rather than what it will buy in the USA) was 62.1% in 1990 and had only fallen to 55.6% by 2000 and 52.9% in 2004. This is over 3.4 billion people. In subsistence economies, leisure time as it is understood in the developed world is non-existent. For such people, international leisure travel is an impossibility.

As beneficiaries, directly or otherwise, of the leisure time and spending of others, however, travel and tourism becomes rather more relevant. For many countries, incoming travel represents a large, if not the largest, source of foreign exchange and jobs. The infrastructure required is generally less damaging or divisive than that needed for an industrial operation, there is less danger of its being sold out to a foreign government or corporation and at least as good a chance of the wealth it creates reaching the local economy. Moreover, the 'product' itself is generally already in place, in the shape of beaches, jungles, temples or local culture. The demands of tourism have in many cases reversed trends of destruction and development; without tourists, many national parks and game reserves would not be financially viable. The world's number-one industry may have its share of faults and cause its share of problems, but it also has much to be proud of.

Ethical tourism

All forms of travel have an impact on the planet, as do the creation and maintenance of what visitors expect on arrival: while mass tourism can cause change and disruption to the destination societies, and not always for the better. All sectors have been forced to become more aware of the effects of their transient presence. A number of organisations such as the The International Ecotourism Society, The Pro-Poor Partnership, Tourism Concern, The Travel Foundation and Just a Drop, sometimes in conjunction with major airlines and bodies as the WWF, ABTA, PATA, AITO

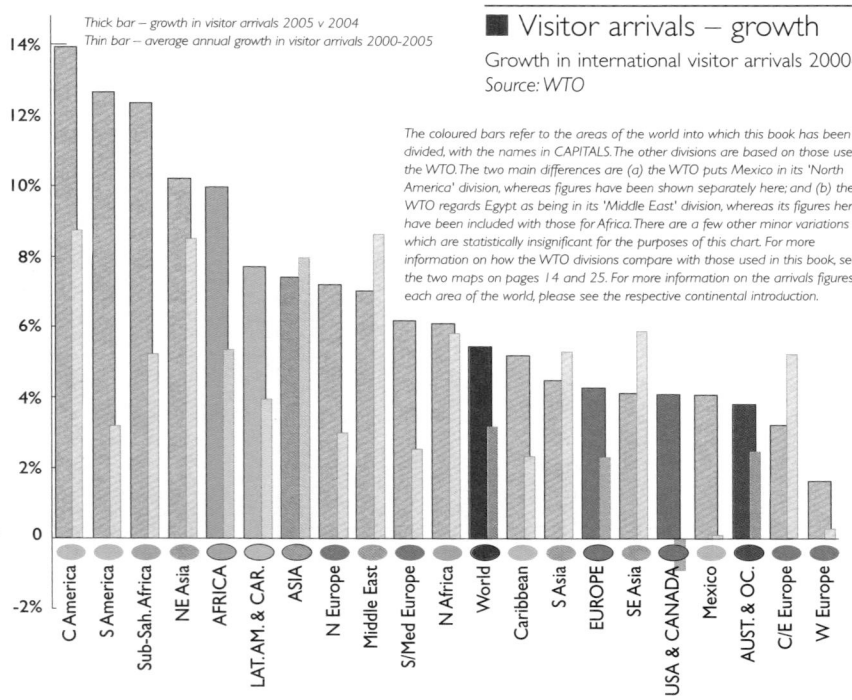

Thick bar – growth in visitor arrivals 2005 v 2004
Thin bar – average annual growth in visitor arrivals 2000-2005

■ Visitor arrivals – growth

Growth in international visitor arrivals 2000-2005
Source: WTO

The coloured bars refer to the areas of the world into which this book has been divided, with the names in CAPITALS. The other divisions are based on those used by the WTO. The two main differences are (a) the WTO puts Mexico in its 'North America' division, whereas figures have been shown separately here; and (b) the WTO regards Egypt as being in its 'Middle East' division, whereas its figures here have been included with those for Africa. There are a few other minor variations which are statistically insignificant for the purposes of this chart. For more information on how the WTO divisions compare with those used in this book, see the two maps on pages 14 and 25. For more information on the arrivals figures for each area of the world, please see the respective continental introduction.

and the EU, have emerged in recent years, all in their different ways dedicated to the idea of improving, or at least mitigating, the impact of travel. An increasing number of awards, such as Tourism for Tomorrow, are designed to motivate good practice, and newspaper travel supplements frequently devote their entire edition to the subject of ethical tourism. In a world dominated by globalisation, it is increasingly hard to be know how much expenditure will benefit the community, or even the country, being visited. To pick but one example, in 2005 nearly 75% of Kenyan hotels were foreign-owned, as were all of the charter airlines serving the country. Such statistics suggest that the benefit of tourism is not being equally shared.

Fortunately, steps are being taken to address these problems. Many operators have become involved in projects ranging from water conservation to sponsorship of schools. Local bodies, like ASSET in the Gambia, have emerged in recent years to offer representation, business training and marketing advice to small local businesses such as local guides and restaurants which depend on visitors. Bodies ranging from national tourist offices to small hotels are increasingly keen to stress their ethical credentials. There is certainly no shortage of innovative ideas in this area. The challenge for the industry as a whole is to reconcile growth with sustainability and responsibility, in all the ways these terms are now used, while at the same time offering value for money. So far, the signs are encouraging, but much still remains to be done.

World pointers ▶

This section provides information or definitions for a selection of the global events, industry trends and technical terms which are directly or indirectly relevant to today's travel business, many of which are referred to throughout this Atlas. This list is not intended to be exhaustive, but merely an Editor's selection. More information on these and many other points may be explored in more detail elsewhere in this book, or in the *World Travel Guide* and the *World Travel Dictionary*, also published by Columbus Travel Guides.

11 Sept 2001 • The date on which Islamic terrorists hijacked four planes in the USA and destroyed the twin towers of the World Trade Centre in New York and damaged the US Defense Pentagon building in Virginia with the loss of around 3,000 lives. Often referred to as 9/11. For the travel business not least, the scars have been psychological as much as physical and plunged airlines in particular into a sharp decline. On a wider level, the event has served to redefine the nature and focus of US foreign policy.

Adventure travel • Originally, this was a general terms for a type of holiday, such as trekking, white-water rafting or jungle expeditions, which involved a fairly high level of physical exertion and often an element of danger. Increasingly, the term covers a wider field: skiing, diving, cycling and walking holidays are now often referred to in this way.

AIDS • Acquired Immune Deficiency Syndrome, a loss of cellular immunity as a result of viral infection generally through sexual fluids and blood, which leaves the body vulnerable to a wide range of often fatal infections. The first reported case was in December 1980. Estimates as to how many people are, or will be, infected vary greatly, but many experts predict over 40 million worldwide by 2007. The majority of cases are in sub-Saharan Africa.

Bird flu • The common name for avian influenza, a viral disease believed until 1997 not to be transmittable to people. The H5N1 strain of the disease has

been identified as causing human deaths initially in south-east Asia and increasingly elsewhere. The first confirmed avain case in the UK was in April 2006. The World Health Organization has warned of the risk of a global pandemic.

Climate change • The effects of industrial pollution and in particular the burning of fossil fuels has, according to most estimates, caused measurable increases in average global temperatures and sea levels. Travel and tourism, along with many other industries, is now taking some steps to redress these potentially very serious problems. Most remedies are, however, seemingly incompatible with economic growth.

Concorde • The world's first and, to date, only supersonic passenger aircraft. An Anglo-French co-operative venture, it made its maiden flight in March 1969: regular trans-Atlantic services started in May 1976. Only 20 were ever built, though the original plan was for over 300. On 25 July 2000, an Air France Concorde crashed on take-off from Paris with the loss of 113 lives. Services were resumed the following November. British Airways and Air France announced in April 2003 that all Concordes would be withdrawn from service and the last scheduled flight landed at London Heathrow on 24 October 2003.

Continents • There are anything between five and eight of these depending on which source one consults. The six divisions used in this

atlas have been created to make the title easy to use and have no political or other significance.

Countries • As with continents (qv), there is no clear definition as to how many countries there are in the world. Many 'countries' have varying degrees of connection with an independent state which might in some cases amount to practical independence. In other cases, a conflict has created differing views as to the 'country's' status. French Guiana, Gibraltar, Jersey, Guam, Palestine, the Cook Islands, Taiwan, Western Sahara and Bonaire all provide different examples of this ambiguity. For travel purposes the distinction is often unimportant but can lead to confusions with paperwork such as visas. The most important examples are Hong Kong and Macau which, though now part of China, are still regarded as separate destinations by, for example, the World Tourism Organization for statistical purposes.

Cruising • One of the fastest-growing sectors within the travel business, and one of the areas which has shown continued growth throughout the problematic years of the early 21st century. In 1985 there were 2.75 million worldwide cruise passengers: this had risen to 4.5 million in 1990, to 11 million in 2000 and to 14 million in 2005. The industry is developing additional itineraries and introducing new ports of call, particularly in the Indian sub-continent and the Far East.

Eco-tourism • Tourism which respects the environment being visited. (The term is often used in conjunction with the overlapping concepts of 'fairtrade tourism' and 'responsible tourism' (qv) and also other more general terms such as 'ethical tourism' (qv).)

Ethical tourism • The increasingly popular type of, and attitude to, travel which seeks to ensure that tourism development and activity respects the geographical and social environment. This includes involving local communities in

the creation and management of tourism projects, sharing the socio-economic benefits fairly with them, and ensuring that any development makes as much use as possible of sustainable local resources. (The term is often used in conjunction with the overlapping concepts of 'responsible tourism' and 'fairtrade tourism' (qv) and also other terms such as 'ethical tourism' (qv). Such terms are often used interchangeably, but all convey a similar attitude.)

Euro • The common currency of 12 of the members of the European Union, introduced in January 2002 and replacing the previously used local currencies. Other countries, notably the UK, may join in the future.

European Capital of Culture • An initiative, formerly known as the European City of Culture, run by the EU since 1985 to reflect, promote and celebrate Europe's cultural diversity. Until 1999, one city a year was selected, but in the millennium year of 2000 there were nine (Avignon, Bergen, Bologna, Brussels, Cracow, Helsinki, Prague, Reykjavik & Santiago de Compostela). Since then, the cities have been/will be: 2001 – Oporto & Rotterdam; 2002 – Bruges & Salamanca; 2003 – Graz; 2004 – Genoa & Lille; 2005 – Cork; 2006 – Patras; 2007 – Luxembourg & Sibiu; 2008 – Liverpool & Stavanger. The UK's only previous representative was Glasgow in 1990.

European Union expansion • In 1957, there were six founding members of the then-European Economic Community: from mid-2004 the European Union had 25 members and now, for the first time, has a frontier with Russia. Several other countries including Bulgaria, Romania and Turkey are waiting to join.

Fair-trade tourism • Tourism which is developed and operated in partnership with local communities, and which is designed to be at least partly for their social and economic benefit. This will include ensuring a fair remuneration for

Conclusion

Change, renewal and growth appear to be the three words that best sum up the prospects for the travel business. The world is changing fast, and the best companies are adapting to it. Few industries have such a solid record of performance stretching back several decades to help underpin their future. The desire for new destinations and new experiences seems to be insatiable. Public demand for new ethical standards is growing and will shape future supply. The industry has long since shifted away from its traditional commission-driven pattern of package holidays and monopolistic airlines. It is also shifting away from its well-established Europe-North America axis. To a certain extent, every traveller has become their own travel planner. Do any certainties remain?

Quite possibly not. It seems more than likely that entrepreneurial companies and new technology will continue to challenge all our current preconceptions about travel. So – what's next? Space tourism? In fact, it already exists. Denis Tito was the first (in 2001). Others have followed since, and many more plan to boldly go in the future. Low-cost space tourism, booked through the internet? Now there's a thought…

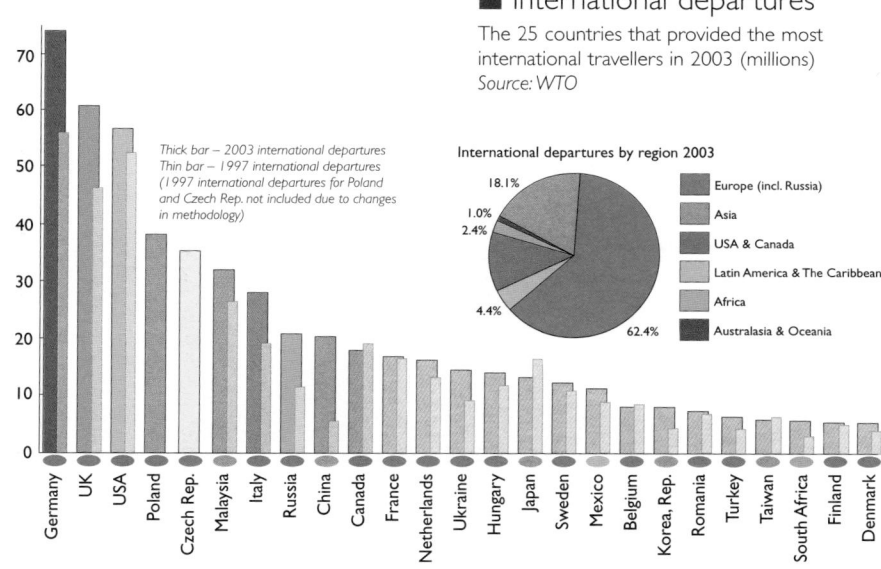

■ International departures

The 25 countries that provided the most international travellers in 2003 (millions)
Source: WTO

Thick bar – 2003 international departures
Thin bar – 1997 international departures
(1997 international departures for Poland and Czech Rep. not included due to changes in methodology)

International departures by region 2003

- Europe (incl. Russia) — 62.4%
- Asia — 18.1%
- USA & Canada — 4.4%
- Latin America & The Caribbean — 2.4%
- Africa — 1.0%
- Australasia & Oceania

---

workers, maximising the level of local (rather than foreign) ownership of the tourism facility, encouraging the use of local suppliers of products and services (such as food and tour guides) and establishing sustainable relations between all parties involved. (The term is often used in conjunction with the overlapping concepts of 'responsible tourism' and 'ecotourism' (qv) and also other terms such as 'ethical tourism' (qv).)

GDP and GNI • In crude terms, GDP (Gross Domestic Product) is the value of the wealth produced by a nation – 'the gross value of all resident producers in the economy' as the part of the World Bank's definition puts it. GNI (Gross National Income) is increasingly used in many publications, including this one. The two measures are broadly comparable: in essence, GNI also includes income derived by residents of the country in question from abroad, such as from external investments.

High-speed rail • Many countries, particularly in Western Europe and Japan, have invested massive sums in dedicated high-speed lines and trains offering city-to-city services at speeds in excess of 200 kph. The network is constantly expanding and major projects are being planned in many countries, including China and the USA. New Maglev (magnetic levititation) trains represent the new generation, and should run at over 550kph. In Europe, the low-cost airlines have provided considerable competition.

Indian Ocean tsunami • The devastating tidal wave resulting from an undersea earthquake near Northern Indonesia on 26 December 2004. Over 200,000 people were killed and 500,000 left homeless, mainly in Thailand, Indonesia, Sri Lanka, India, the Maldives and the coastal regions of East Africa.

Internet • On-line sales and information services have revolutionised the travel business in recent years, and the trend is increasing. There are countless statistics to illustrate this, and the growth in web usage generally. It took radio 38 years and TV 13 years to build an audience of 50 million in the US: the internet

achieved this in three and a half years. The internet had over one billion worldwide users in April 2006.

Iraq war • After years of diplomatic stand-off and unsuccessful UN attempts to locate Iraq's alleged weapons of mass destruction, US-led coalition forces began attacking the country on 20 March 2003. The war itself, and in particular its protracted count-down, caused a slump in the travel industry worldwide, although the relatively quick resolution of the initial phase of the conflict saw a fairly quick recovery in airline bookings. Despite elections in 2005, the long-term future of Iraq and the nature of its government remains uncertain, as does the question as to whether the intervention will have calmed or inflamed the volatile situation in the Middle East.

Long-haul charters • The introduction of medium-sized wide-body aircraft such as the Boeing 767 and Airbus A300 in the 1990s facilitated the growth of package holidays to destinations further afield such as Goa, Sri Lanka and the Maldives. These areas suddenly became very affordable and, as a consequence, have rapidly developed as a result of the arrival of charter flights from Europe. Many local authorities are currently reviewing the desirability of receiving such flights.

Low-cost airlines • The terms 'budget' and 'no-frills' are also often used. The concept began in the USA in 1971 when Southwest Airlines started services between Dallas and San Antonio. Numerous other airlines have since followed suit, including Jet Blue, Ryanair and easyJet. Their low prices and commercial flexibility result from following very precise and efficient business models.

Mega cruise ships • Any ship with a gross registered tonnage of 100,000 is regarded as mega. The first of these arrived in the late 1990s as *Voyager of the Seas* owned by Royal Caribbean Line at GRT 142.000 GRT: it took 21 million man-hours to build and is (so far) the only cruise vessel with its own zip-code (33132-2028). These massive ships of up to 22 decks high have become resorts at

sea opening the cruise market to a much wider audience. On 12 January 2004, Cunard Lines' 150,000 GRT *Queen Mary 2* entered service on the traditional transatlantic scheduled route. RCI's 156,000 GRT *Freedom of the Seas* made its maiden voyage in June 2006.

MICE • 'Meetings, incentives, conferences and exhibitions', which have in recent years become a distinct and increasingly important part of the the global travel business.

Olympic Games • Last held in Athens in August 2004. The next Olympics (the 29th) will be in 2008 in Beijing.

Pets Travel Scheme • Introduced in 2000, this allows cats and dogs to travel between the UK and a number of European and long-haul destinations (though currently not North America) without the need for quarantine on arrival back in the UK. Pets must be micro-chipped, be issued with an appropriate pet passport, and have a valid vet's certificate certifying vaccination against rabies.

Responsible Tourism • The increasingly important principle that guides touristic development and behaviour, particularly in respect of developing countries, with the aim of ensuring that its impact is as positive as possible. Exact definitions vary, but the Cape Town Declaration of 2002 provides possibly the most comprehensive summary. Its key points are that responsible tourism should: minimise negative economic, environmental, and social impacts; involve local people positively and generate economic benefits for them; contribute to the conservation of natural and cultural heritage; offer more rewarding experiences for tourists through more connections with local people and a greater understanding of local cultural, social and environmental issues; and provide access for physically challenged people. (The term is often used in conjunction with the overlapping concepts of 'fairtrade tourism' and 'eco-tourism' (qv) and also other more general terms such as 'ethical tourism'(qv).)

SARS • Severe Acute Respiratory Syndrome, an air-borne virus which causes flu-like symptoms and sometimes

death. The first reported case was in Hanoi in February 2003 and it rapidly spread to other parts of Asia, and to Canada, causing havoc in the travel industry for several months.

Set Jetter • A person who makes holiday destination decisions based wholly or partly on being able to visit the sets or locations of films or novels. By some estimates, up to one in four outbound travellers from the UK could be so described.

Travel statistics • There are a multitude of these available. organisations, cities, states, countries and regions all produce their own, for a variety of purposes; while the most authoritative global figures are compiled by the World Tourism Organization (WTO or, more formally, UNWTO to distinguish it from the Would Trade Organization), which is based in Madrid. Statistics concerning movement of people and money as a result of travel can most conveniently be divided into inbound and outbound, of which the former are generally more complete and reliable. Because of the time spent collating and analysing them, many statistics are not published for months or even years after the period to which they refer and historical data is often revised retrospectively. Comparisons between figures produced by different organisations may be misleading due to possible different methodologies used or time periods covered.

USSR • The Union of Soviet Socialist Republics (also known as the Soviet Union). Dominated by Russia, it came into being in 1922 in the aftermath of the Russian Revolution and Civil War. During the early 1990s it fragmented into 15 independent states in Eastern Europe and Central Asia. All of the former states apart from the three Baltic republics formed the Commonwealth of Independent States in 1991 which still retains some co-ordinating powers.

World Cups • Many sports, notably rugby, cricket and football, organise regular international tournaments, usually every four years. Flights and accommodation for such events may need to be booked months or even years in advance.

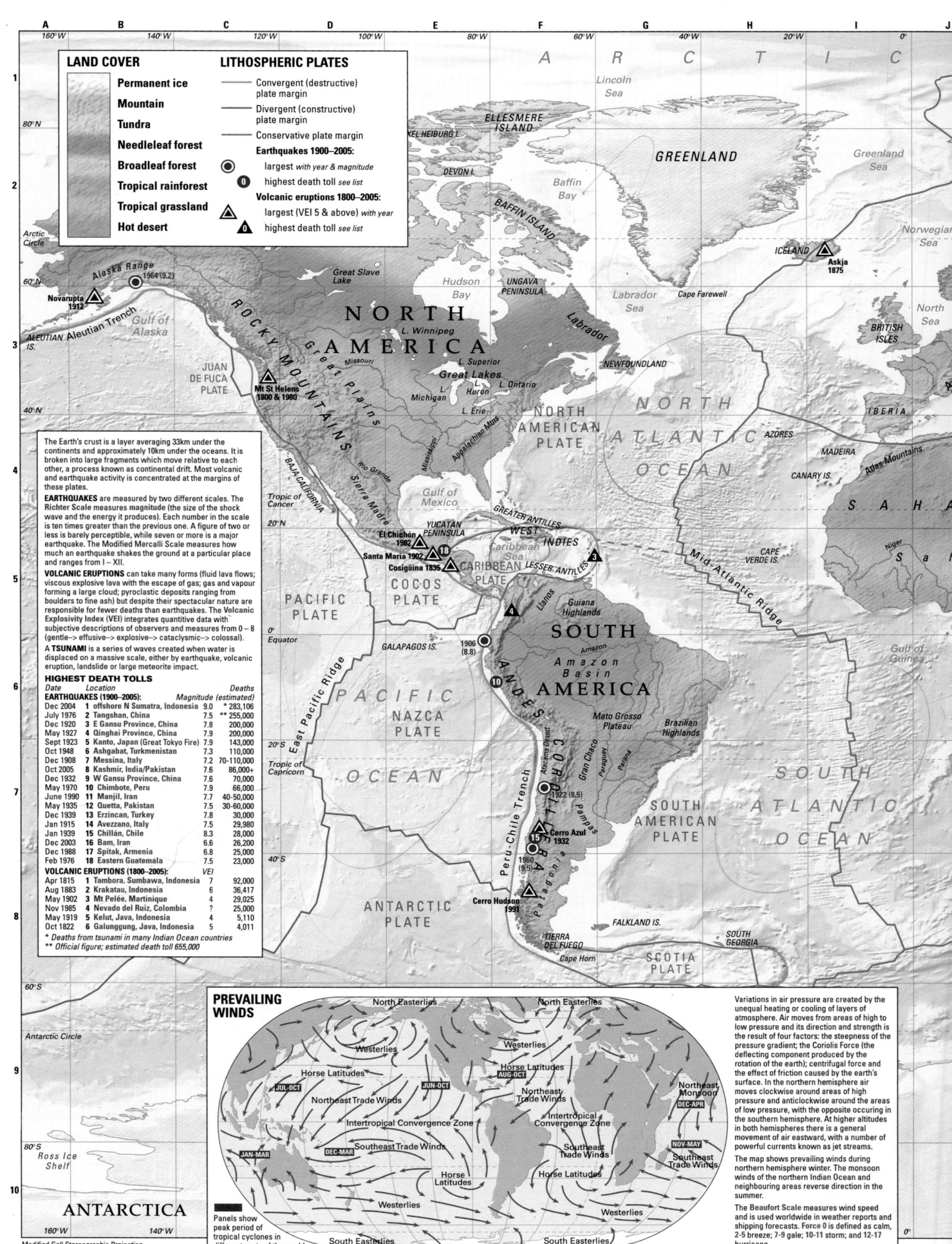

LAND COVER

- Permanent ice
- Mountain
- Tundra
- Needleleaf forest
- Broadleaf forest
- Tropical rainforest
- Tropical grassland
- Hot desert

LITHOSPHERIC PLATES

- Convergent (destructive) plate margin
- Divergent (constructive) plate margin
- Conservative plate margin

Earthquakes 1900–2005:
- ◉ largest *with year & magnitude*
- ⓪ highest death toll *see list*

Volcanic eruptions 1800–2005:
- △ largest (VEI 5 & above) *with year*
- ▲ highest death toll *see list*

The Earth's crust is a layer averaging 33km under the continents and approximately 10km under the oceans. It is broken into large fragments which move relative to each other, a process known as continental drift. Most volcanic and earthquake activity is concentrated at the margins of these plates.

EARTHQUAKES are measured by two different scales. The Richter Scale measures magnitude (the size of the shock wave and the energy it produces). Each number in the scale is ten times greater than the previous one. A figure of two or less is barely perceptible, while seven or more is a major earthquake. The Modified Mercalli Scale measures how much an earthquake shakes the ground at a particular place and ranges from I – XII.

VOLCANIC ERUPTIONS can take many forms (fluid lava flows; viscous explosive lava with the escape of gas; gas and vapour forming a large cloud; pyroclastic deposits ranging from boulders to fine ash) but despite their spectacular nature are responsible for fewer deaths than earthquakes. The Volcanic Explosivity Index (VEI) integrates quantitive data with subjective descriptions of observers and measures from 0 – 8 (gentle→ effusive→ explosive→ cataclysmic→ colossal).

A **TSUNAMI** is a series of waves created when water is displaced on a massive scale, either by earthquake, volcanic eruption, landslide or large meteorite impact.

HIGHEST DEATH TOLLS

EARTHQUAKES (1900–2005):

Date	Location		Magnitude	Deaths (estimated)
Dec 2004	1	offshore N Sumatra, Indonesia	9.0	* 283,106
July 1976	2	Tangshan, China	7.5	** 255,000
Dec 1920	3	E Gansu Province, China	7.8	200,000
May 1927	4	Qinghai Province, China	7.9	200,000
Sept 1923	5	Kanto, Japan (Great Tokyo Fire)	7.9	143,000
Oct 1948	6	Ashgabat, Turkmenistan	7.3	110,000
Dec 1908	7	Messina, Italy	7.2	70-110,000
Oct 2005	8	Kashmir, India/Pakistan	7.6	86,000+
Dec 1932	9	W Gansu Province, China	7.6	70,000
May 1970	10	Chimbote, Peru	7.9	66,000
June 1990	11	Manjil, Iran	7.7	40-50,000
May 1935	12	Quetta, Pakistan	7.5	30-60,000
Dec 1939	14	Erzincan, Turkey	7.8	30,000
Jan 1915	14	Avezzano, Italy	7.5	29,980
Jan 1939	15	Chillán, Chile	8.3	28,000
Dec 2003	16	Bam, Iran	6.6	26,200
Dec 1988	17	Spitak, Armenia	6.8	25,000
Feb 1976	18	Eastern Guatemala	7.5	23,000

VOLCANIC ERUPTIONS (1800–2005):

Date	Location		VEI	Deaths
Apr 1815	1	Tambora, Sumbawa, Indonesia	7	92,000
Aug 1883	2	Krakatau, Indonesia	6	36,417
May 1902	3	Mt Pelée, Martinique	4	29,025
Nov 1985	4	Nevado del Ruiz, Colombia	?	25,000
May 1919	5	Kelut, Java, Indonesia	4	5,110
Oct 1822	6	Galunggung, Java, Indonesia	5	4,011

* *Deaths from tsunami in many Indian Ocean countries*
** *Official figure; estimated death toll 655,000*

PREVAILING WINDS

Variations in air pressure are created by the unequal heating or cooling of layers of atmosphere. Air moves from areas of high to low pressure and its direction and strength is the result of four factors: the steepness of the pressure gradient; the Coriolis Force (the deflecting component produced by the rotation of the earth); centrifugal force and the effect of friction caused by the earth's surface. In the northern hemisphere air moves clockwise around areas of high pressure and anticlockwise around the areas of low pressure, with the opposite occurring in the southern hemisphere. At higher altitudes in both hemispheres there is a general movement of air eastward, with a number of powerful currents known as jet streams.

The map shows prevailing winds during northern hemisphere winter. The monsoon winds of the northern Indian Ocean and neighbouring areas reverse direction in the summer.

The Beaufort Scale measures wind speed and is used worldwide in weather reports and shipping forecasts. Force 0 is defined as calm, 2-5 breeze; 7-9 gale; 10-11 storm; and 12-17 hurricane.

Panels show peak period of tropical cyclones in different parts of the world

Modified Gall Stereographic Projection

The listings above refer to a selection of related themes.
For more information, see the Contents (2-5).

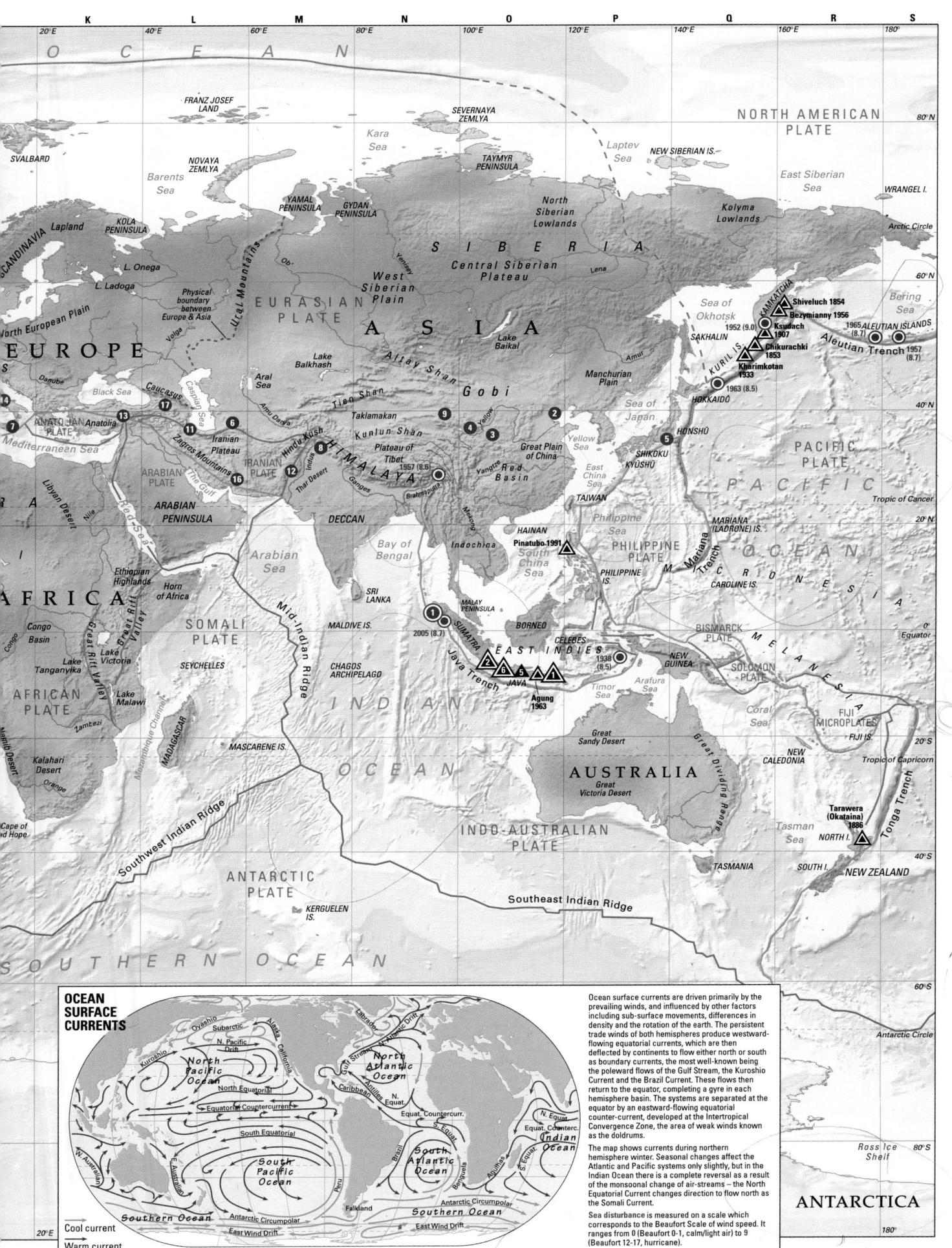

OCEAN SURFACE CURRENTS

Ocean surface currents are driven primarily by the prevailing winds, and influenced by other factors including sub-surface movements, differences in density and the rotation of the earth. The persistent trade winds of both hemispheres produce westward-flowing equatorial currents, which are then deflected by continents to flow either north or south as boundary currents, the most well-known being the poleward flows of the Gulf Stream, the Kuroshio Current and the Brazil Current. These flows then return to the equator, completing a gyre in each hemisphere basin. The systems are separated at the equator by an eastward-flowing equatorial counter-current, developed at the Intertropical Convergence Zone, the area of weak winds known as the doldrums.

The map shows currents during northern hemisphere winter. Seasonal changes affect the Atlantic and Pacific systems only slightly, but in the Indian Ocean there is a complete reversal as a result of the monsoonal change of air-streams – the North Equatorial Current changes direction to flow north as the Somali Current.

Sea disturbance is measured on a scale which corresponds to the Beaufort Scale of wind speed. It ranges from 0 (Beaufort 0-1, calm/light air) to 9 (Beaufort 12-17, hurricane).

→ Cool current
→ Warm current

▶ **See also...** World Physical (26-27); City Nicknames (106-107); Countries A-Z (108-116)

The listings above refer to a selection of related themes.
For more information, see the Contents (2-5).

ALB. - ALBANIA
AUS. - AUSTRIA
AZ. - AZERBAIJAN
B-H. - BOSNIA-HERZEGOVINA
BELG. - BELGIUM
CRO. - CROATIA
HUNG. - HUNGARY
LIE. - LIECHTENSTEIN
LUX. - LUXEMBOURG
MAC. - FORMER YUGOSLAV REPUBLIC OF MACEDONIA
MO. - MONTENEGRO
NETH. - THE NETHERLANDS
PAL. - PALESTINE NATIONAL AUTHORITY REGION
(West Bank & Gaza)
S. - SAN MARINO
SLOV. - SLOVENIA
SWITZ. - SWITZERLAND
UAE - UNITED ARAB EMIRATES
V. - VATICAN CITY
SE. - SERBIA MONTENEGRO

Map labels (selected):

ARCTIC

ELLESMERE ISLAND
AXEL HEIBURG I.
DEVON I.
BAFFIN ISLAND
PARRY IS.
BANKS I.
VICTORIA I.

Greenland (Denmark)
Nuuk

Jan Mayen (Nor.)
ICELAND
Reykjavik
Faroe Is. (Den.)
DENM

Arctic Circle
Alaska (US)
Anchorage
60° N

CANADA
Edmonton
Calgary
Vancouver
Seattle
Winnipeg
Québec
Ottawa
Montreal
Toronto
Boston
Halifax
St-Pierre et Miquelon (Fr.)
New York
Philadelphia
Washington DC

UNITED KINGDOM
Dublin IRELAND
London
Amsterdam NE
BELG.
Brussels
Paris
FRANCE
MONACO
ANDORRA

NORTH ATLANTIC OCEAN

40° N
UNITED STATES OF AMERICA
San Francisco
Los Angeles
San Diego
Phoenix
Denver
Dallas
Houston
Chicago
Detroit
New Orleans

Bermuda (UK)

PORTUGAL
Lisbon
Madrid
SPAIN
Gibraltar (UK)
Ceuta (Sp.)
Algiers
Rabat
Melilla (Sp.)
Azores (Port.)
Madeira (Port.)
Casablanca
MOROCCO
TUN

Tropic of Cancer
Hawaii (US)
20° N
Monterrey
Gulf of Mexico
MEXICO
Guadalajara
Mexico City
Havana
CUBA
Nassau
BAHAMAS
Miami

Canary Is. (Sp.)
Laâyoune
WESTERN SAHARA
ALGERIA

MAURITANIA
Nouakchott
MALI
NIG
Dakar
SENEGAL
Bamako
Niamey
CAPE VERDE
GAMBIA
Banjul
GUINEA-BISSAU
Bissau
GUINEA
BURKINA
Ouagadougou
NIGE
Freetown
SIERRA LEONE
CÔTE D'IVOIRE
Conakry
Yamoussoukro
Abuja
Monrovia
LIBERIA
Accra
TOGO
EQUATORIAL GUI
São Tomé E PRÍNCIPE
Malab
Libreville

Belmopan
BELIZE
GUATEMALA
Guatemala City
HONDURAS
Tegucigalpa
San Salvador
EL SALVADOR
NICARAGUA
Managua
San José
COSTA RICA
PANAMA
Panama City
JAMAICA
Kingston
HAITI
DOMINICAN REPUBLIC
Cayman Is. (UK)
Turks & Caicos (UK)
British Virgin Is. (UK)
Virgin Is. (US)
Puerto Rico (US)
Anguilla (UK)
St Maarten (Neths.) & St-Martin (Fr.)
St-Barthélemy (Fr.)
ANTIGUA & BARBUDA
Guadeloupe (Fr.)
DOMINICA
Martinique (Fr.)
ST KITTS & NEVIS
Netherlands Antilles
Aruba (Neths.)
Montserrat (UK)
ST LUCIA
BARBADOS
GRENADA
ST VINCENT & THE GRENADINES
TRINIDAD & TOBAGO

Caribbean Sea

Medellín
Bogotá
COLOMBIA
Caracas
VENEZUELA
Georgetown
GUYANA
Paramaribo
SURINAM
Cayenne
French Guiana (Fr.)

São Pedro e São Paulo (Brazil)

ECUADOR
Quito
Galápagos Is. (Ec.)
PERU
Lima
Manaus
Belém
BRAZIL
Fortaleza
Recife
Fernando de Noronha (Brazil)
Ascension (UK)

La Paz
BOLIVIA
Sucre
PARAGUAY
Asunción
Brasília
Belo Horizonte
Rio de Janeiro
São Paulo
Porto Alegre
Salvador
Trindade e Martin Vaz (Brazil)

St Helena (UK)

SOUTH ATLANTIC OCEAN

Santiago
CHILE
Córdoba
ARGENTINA
URUGUAY
Buenos Aires
Montevideo

Juan Fernández Is. (Chile)
Easter I. (Chile)

Tristan da Cunha (UK)
Gough I. (UK)

Tropic of Capricorn
20° S

PACIFIC OCEAN

KIRIBATI
INTERNATIONAL DATE LINE
Tokelau (NZ)
American Samoa (US)
Cook Islands (NZ)
Niue (NZ)
French Polynesia (Fr.)
Pitcairn Is. (UK)

0° Equator

Falkland Is. (UK)
South Georgia (UK)
South Sandwich Is. (UK)

Antarctic Circle
ALEXANDER I.
ANTARCTIC PENINSULA
BERKNER I.
ANTARCTICA

■ Capital city
■ Other city
○ For reasons of space, capital cities for some smaller countries have not been show here: see the respective country maps or the Countries A-Z section on pages 108-116.
For more information on the symbols used on other political and physical maps, see the Key to Topographic Maps on page 5.

Modified Gall Stereographic Projection

See also... World Physical (26-27); City Nicknames (106-107); Countries A-Z (108-116)

The listings above refer to a selection of related themes. For more information, see the Contents (2-5).

▶ See also... Europe Climate (45); Regional Climate Terms (104)

The listings above refer to a selection of related themes. For more information, see the Contents (2-5).

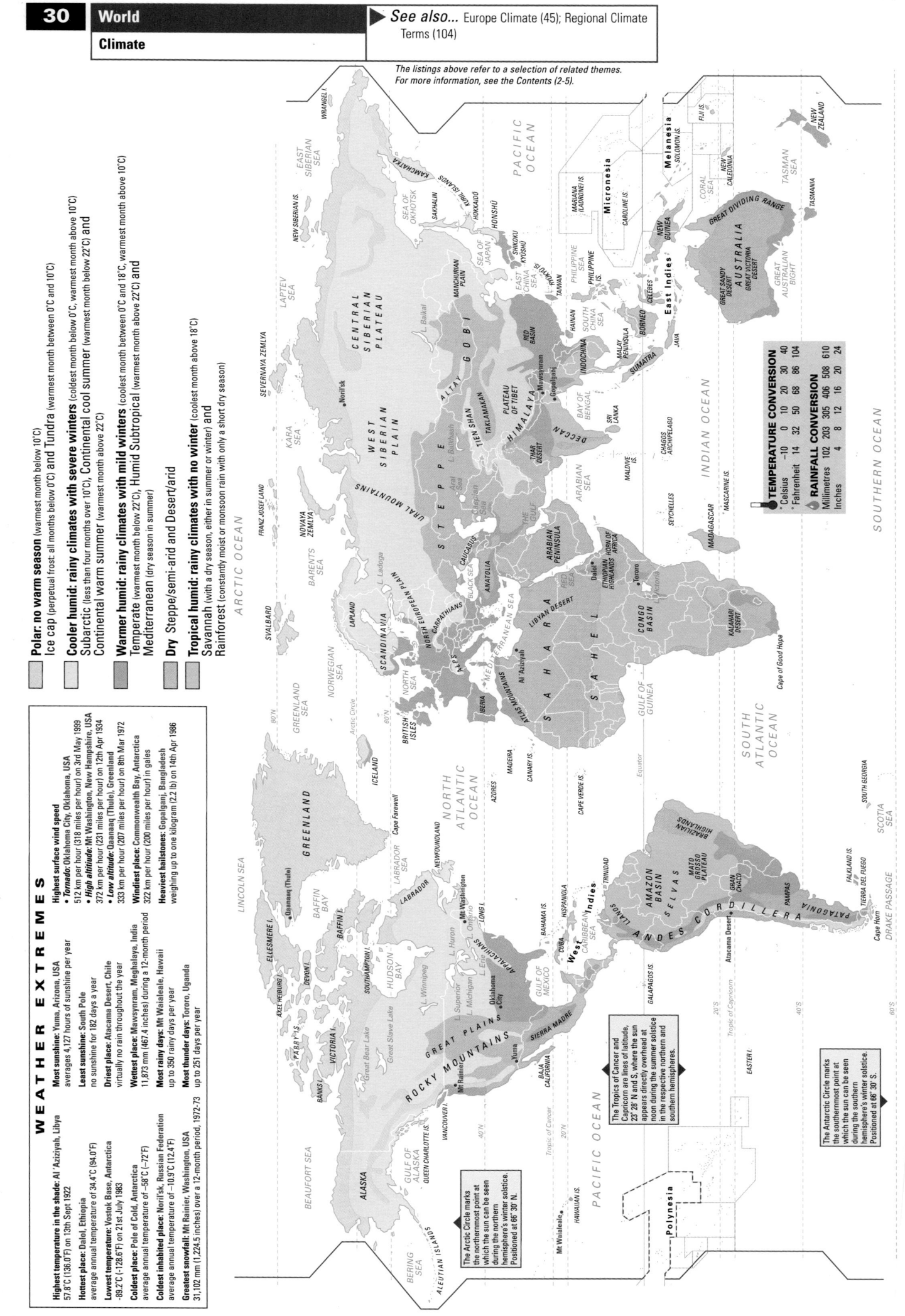

Polar: no warm season (warmest month below 10°C)
Ice cap (perpetual frost: all months below 0°C) and Tundra (warmest month between 0°C and 10°C)

Cooler humid: rainy climates with severe winters (coldest month below 0°C, warmest month above 10°C)
Subarctic (less than four months over 10°C), Continental cool summer (warmest month below 22°C) and Continental warm summer (warmest month above 22°C)

Warmer humid: rainy climates with mild winters (coolest month between 0°C and 18°C, warmest month above 10°C)
Temperate (warmest month below 22°C), Humid Subtropical (warmest month above 22°C) and Mediterranean (dry season in summer)

Dry Steppe/semi-arid and Desert/arid

Tropical humid: rainy climates with no winter (coolest month above 18°C)
Savannah (with a dry season, either in summer or winter) and Rainforest (constantly moist or monsoon rain with only a short dry season)

TEMPERATURE CONVERSION

°Celsius	-10	0	10	20	30	40
°Fahrenheit	14	32	50	68	86	104

RAINFALL CONVERSION

Millimetres	102	203	305	406	508	610
Inches	4	8	12	16	20	24

The Tropics of Cancer and Capricorn are lines of latitude, 23° 28' N and S, where the sun appears directly overhead at noon during the summer solstice in the respective northern and southern hemispheres.

The Arctic Circle marks the northernmost point at which the sun can be seen during the northern hemisphere's winter solstice. Positioned at 66° 30' N.

The Antarctic Circle marks the southernmost point at which the sun can be seen during the southern hemisphere's winter solstice. Positioned at 66° 30' S.

W E A T H E R   E X T R E M E S

Highest temperature in the shade: Al 'Aziziyah, Libya
57.8°C (136.0°F) on 13th Sept 1922

Hottest place: Dalol, Ethiopia
average annual temperature of 34.4°C (94.0°F)

Lowest temperature: Vostok Base, Antarctica
-89.2°C (-128.6°F) on 21st July 1983

Coldest place: Pole of Cold, Antarctica
average annual temperature of -58°C (-72°F)

Coldest inhabited place: Noril'sk, Russian Federation
average annual temperature of -10.9°C (12.4°F)

Greatest snowfall: Mt Rainier, Washington, USA
31,102 mm (1,224.5 inches) over a 12-month period, 1972-73

Most sunshine: Yuma, Arizona, USA
averages 4,127 hours of sunshine per year

Least sunshine: South Pole
no sunshine for 182 days a year

Driest place: Atacama Desert, Chile
virtually no rain throughout the year

Wettest place: Mawsynram, Meghalaya, India
11,873 mm (467.4 inches) during a 12-month period

Most rainy days: Mt Waialeale, Hawaii
up to 350 rainy days per year

Most thunder days: Tororo, Uganda
up to 251 days per year

Highest surface wind speed
• **Tornado:** Oklahoma City, Oklahoma, USA
512 km per hour (318 miles per hour) on 3rd May 1999
• **High altitude:** Mt Washington, New Hampshire, USA
372 km per hour (231 miles per hour) on 12th Apr 1934
• **Low altitude:** Qaanaaq (Thule), Greenland
333 km per hour (207 miles per hour) on 8th Mar 1972

Windiest place: Commonwealth Bay, Antarctica
322 km per hour (200 miles per hour) in gales

Heaviest hailstones: Gopalganj, Bangladesh
weighing up to one kilogram (2.2 lb) on 14th Apr 1986

The listings above refer to a selection of related themes.
For more information, see the Contents (2-5).

MAJOR INTERNATIONAL SPORTING EVENTS

SUMMER OLYMPICS
The first modern Olympic Games, founded by Frenchman Baron de Coubertin, were first held at Athens in 1896. They are held every four years, and a Paralympic Games is held in conjunction with the main Games. An extra Olympics held in 1906 celebrated the tenth anniversary of the 1896 Games. The next Games, the 29th Olympiad, will be held in Beijing in 2008 and the 2012 Games will be in London.

WINTER OLYMPICS
The first separate Winter Games took place in 1924 at Chamonix, France. The Games originally took place in the same year as the Summer Olympics, but are now held every four years in between. The next Winter Olympics are due to be held in Vancouver in 2010.

COMMONWEALTH GAMES
Originally the British Empire Games, first held in 1930 at Hamilton, Ontario. Renamed the British Empire and Commonwealth Games in 1954, the British Commonwealth Games in 1970 and the Commonwealth Games in 1978. Held every four years, the next Games are due to be held in New Delhi in 2010.

WORLD ATHLETICS CHAMPIONSHIPS
The World Athletics Championships were first held in Helsinki in 1983, and at four-year intervals until 1991. They are now held every two years. The next Championships are due to be held in Osaka in 2007 and Berlin in 2009.

FOOTBALL WORLD CUP
Association Football's premier event. Brazil kept the Jules Rimet Trophy after winning it for the third time in 1970. The teams now compete for the FIFA World Cup. Held every four years, the next competition is due to be hosted by South Africa in 2010.

CRICKET WORLD CUP
The venue of the first Cricket World Cup in 1975 was England. Played every three to five years, it was not until 1987 that the competition was held outside England. The next World Cup is due to be held in the West Indies in 2007.

RUGBY UNION WORLD CUP
The first Rugby Union World Cup was held in 1987 and is now held every four years, with the next competition in France in 2007.

FOOTBALL WORLD CUP FINAL RESULTS
1930	Uruguay 4	Argentina 2
1934	Italy 2	Czechoslovakia 1
1938	Italy 4	Hungary 2
1950	Uruguay 2	Brazil 1
1954	FR Germany 3	Hungary 2
1958	Brazil 5	Sweden 2
1962	Brazil 3	Czechoslovakia 1
1966	England 4	FR Germany 2
1970	Brazil 4	Italy 1
1974	FR Germany 2	Netherlands 1
1978	Argentina 3	Netherlands 1
1982	Italy 3	FR Germany 1
1986	Argentina 3	FR Germany 2
1990	FR Germany 1	Argentina 0
1994	Brazil 0	Italy 0
	(Brazil won 3-2 on penalties)	
1998	France 3	Brazil 0
2002	Brazil 2	Germany 0

RUGBY UNION WORLD CUP FINAL RESULTS
1987	New Zealand 29	France 9
1991	Australia 12	England 6
1995	South Africa 15	New Zealand 12
1999	Australia 35	France 12
2003	England 20	Australia 17

FIFA WORLD RANKINGS
	May, 2003	May, 2004	May, 2005	May, 2006
1	Brazil	Brazil	Brazil	Brazil
2	France (2=)	France	Czech Rep.	Czech Rep.
3	Spain (2=)	Spain	France	Netherlands
4	Germany	Netherlands	Spain	Mexico
5	Netherlands	Argentina	Netherlands	Spain
6	Argentina	Mexico	England	USA
7	England	England	Mexico	Portugal
8	Turkey	USA	Spain	France
9	Mexico	Czech Rep.	Portugal	England
10	USA (10=)	Mexico	Italy	England
11	Denmk. (10=)	Italy	USA	Denmark
12	Italy	Cameroon (12=)	Greece	Nigeria
13	Czech Rep.	Italy	Turkey	Nigeria
14	Portugal	England (12=)	Sweden	Italy
15	Ireland	Denmark	Ireland	Turkey
16	Belgium	Ireland	Uruguay	Cameroon
17	Cameroon	Nigeria	Japan	Sweden
18	Iran	Iran	Iran	Egypt
19	Paraguay	Rep. of Korea	Germany (19=)	Japan
20	Sweden	Portugal	Germany (19=)	Greece

CRICKET WORLD CUP FINAL RESULTS
1975	West Indies (291-8) beat Australia (274) by 17 runs
1979	West Indies (286-9) beat England (194) by 92 runs
1983	India (183) beat West Indies (140) by 43 runs
1987	Australia (253-5) beat England (246-8) by 7 runs
1992	Pakistan (249-6) beat England (227) by 22 runs
1996	Sri Lanka (245-3) beat Australia (241) by 7 wickets
1999	Australia (133-2) beat Pakistan (132) by 8 wickets
2003	Australia (359-2) beat India (234) by 125 runs

SOME OTHER SPORTS: ANNUAL EVENTS

CYCLING
Major tours:
Giro d'Italia (Tour of Italy); Tour de France; Tour DuPont, USA; Vuelta d'España (Tour of Spain).
Classics:
Belgium:
Flèche Wallonne;
Liège-Bastogne-Liège;
Tour of Flanders.
France:
Grand Prix des Nations;
Paris-Nice;
Paris-Roubaix.
Italy:
Milan-San Remo;
Tour of Lombardy.
Paris-Brussels.

HORSE RACING
English Classics:
1,000 & 2,000 Guineas, Newmarket;
St Leger, Doncaster;
Derby & Oaks, Epsom.
Triple Crown, USA:
Belmont Stakes, NY;
Kentucky Derby, Louisville;
Preakness Stakes, Baltimore.
Other major races:
Cheltenham Gold Cup, UK;
Dubai World Cup;
Grand National, Aintree, UK;
Irish Derby, The Curragh;
Japan Cup, Tokyo;
Melbourne Cup, Australia;
Prix de l'Arc de Triomphe,

GOLF
Majors:
British Open; US Open;
US Masters; US PGA Championship.
Principal international tournament:
Ryder Cup (every 2 yrs.)

MOTOR RACING
Circuits which have held a Formula One race since 1990 are marked ℉:
Other major races:
Indianapolis 500, USA;
Le Mans 24-hour, France.
Major rallies:
Lombard RAC, UK;

Paris, France;
Monte Carlo;
Safari Rally, Kenya.

MARATHON
Major marathons Ⓜ:
Athens, Berlin, Boston, Chicago, London, Moscow, NY, Prague, Rotterdam.

TENNIS
Grand Slam:
Australian Open, Melbourne;
French Open, Roland Garros, Paris;
US Open, Flushing Meadow, New York;
Wimbledon, UK.
Principal international tournament:
Davis Cup.

ASIA
Asian Cup *(football)*
Held every 3/4 years
Last held: China, 2004
Next: Indonesia/Malaysia/Thailand/Vietnam, 2007
Asian Games
Held every 4 years
Last held: Busan, Rep. of Korea, 2002
Next: Doha, Qatar, 2006; Guangzhou, China, 2010

EUROPE
European Championships *(athletics)*
Held every 4 years
Last held: Munich, Germany, 2002
Next: Gothenburg, Sweden, 2006
European Championships *(football)*
Held every 4 years
Last held: Portugal, 2004
Next: Austria & Switzerland, 2008

AFRICA
African Cup of Nations *(football)*
Held every 2 years
Last held: Egypt, 2006
Next: Ghana, 2008
All-Africa Games
Held every 4 years
Last held: Abuja, Nigeria, 2003
Next: Algiers, Algeria, 2007

WORLDWIDE
Pan-Arab Games
Held every 4 years
Last held: Algeria, 2004
Next: Libya, 2007
Universiade
(World University Games)
Held every 2 years
Last held: Izmir, Turkey, 2005
Next: Bangkok, Thailand, 2007

AMERICAS
Copa América *(football)*
Held every 2/3 years
Last held: Peru, 2004
Next: Venezuela, 2007
Pan-American Games
Held every 4 years
Last held: Santo Domingo, Dominican Rep., 2003
Next: Rio de Janeiro, Brazil, 2007

The listings above refer to a selection of related themes.
For more information, see the Contents (2-5).

Country	Time	(DST time)	DST change
Afghanistan	+4.30		
Albania	+1	(+2)	LSuM-LSuO
Algeria	+1		
American Samoa	-11		
Andorra	+1	(+2)	LSuM-LSuO
Angola	+1		
Anguilla	-4		
Antigua & Barbuda	-4		
Argentina	-3		
Armenia	+4	(+5)	LSuM-LSuO
Aruba	-4		
Australia – Western	+8		
– Central	+9.30	(+10.30)	LSuO-LSuM (SA)
– Eastern	+10	(+11)	1SuO-1SaM (not QL)
Austria	+1	(+2)	LSuM-LSuO
Azerbaijan	+4	(+5)	LSuM-LSuO
Bahamas	-5	(-4)	LSuM-LSuO
Bahrain	+3		
Bangladesh	+6		
Barbados	-4		
Belarus	+2	(+3)	LSuM-LSuO
Belgium	+1	(+2)	LSuM-LSuO
Belize	-6		
Benin	+1		
Bermuda	-4	(-3)	LSuM-LSuO
Bhutan	+6		
Bolivia	-4		
Bonaire	-4		
Bosnia-Herzegovina	+1	(+2)	LSuM-LSuO
Botswana	+2		
Brazil – Western	-5		
– Central	-4	(-3)	3SuO-3SaF
– Eastern	-3	(-2)	3SuO-3SaF
– Fernando de Noronha	-2		
British Virgin Islands	-4		
Bulgaria	+2	(+3)	LSuM-LSuO
Burkina	UTC		
Burundi	+2		
Cambodia	+7		
Cameroon	+1		
Canada – Newfoundland	-3.30	(-2.30)	1SuA-LSuO
– Atlantic	-4	(-3)	1SuA-LSuO
– Eastern	-5	(-4)	1SuA-LSuO
– Central	-6	(-5)	1SuA-LSuO (not SK)
– Mountain	-7	(-6)	1SuA-LSuO
– Pacific	-8	(-7)	1SuA-LSuO
Cape Verde	-1		
Cayman Islands	-5		
Central African Republic	+1		
Chad	+1		
Channel Islands	UTC	(+1)	LSuM-LSuO
Chile – incl. Juan Fernandez	-4	(-3)	2SuO-2SaM
– Easter Island	-6	(-5)	2SuO-2SaM
China – incl. HK & Macau	+8		
Colombia	-5		
Comoros	+3		
Congo (DR) – Western	+1		
– Eastern	+2		
Congo, Republic	+1		
Cook Islands	-10		
Costa Rica	-6		
Côte d'Ivoire	UTC		
Cuba	-5	(-4)	LSuM-LSuO
Curaçao	-4		
Cyprus	+2	(+3)	LSuM-LSuO
Czech Republic	+1	(+2)	LSuM-LSuO
Denmark – Mainland	+1	(+2)	LSuM-LSuO

Country	Time	(DST time)	DST change
– Faroes	UTC	(+1)	LSuM-LSuO
Djibouti	+3		
Dominica	-4		
Dominican Republic	-4		
East Timor	+9		
Ecuador – Mainland	-5		
– Galapagos	-6		
Egypt	+2	(+3)	LFrA-LThS
El Salvador	-6		
Equatorial Guinea	+1		
Eritrea	+3		
Estonia	+2	(+3)	LSuM-LSuO
Ethiopia	+3		
Falkland Islands	-3	(-4)	3SuA-1SaS
Fiji Islands	+12		
Finland	+2	(+3)	LSuM-LSuO
France	+1	(+2)	LSuM-LSuO
French Guiana	-3		
Fr. Polynesia – Gambier	-9		
– Marquesas	-9.30		
– Papeete	-10		
Gabon	+1		
Gambia, The	UTC		
Georgia	+4		
Germany	+1	(+2)	LSuM-LSuO
Ghana	UTC		
Gibraltar	+1	(+2)	LSuM-LSuO
Greece	+2	(+3)	LSuM-LSuO
Greenland – Eastern	-1	(UTC)	LSuM-LSuO
– Central	-3	(-2)	LSuM-LSuO
– Western	-4	(-3)	LSuM-LSuO
Grenada	-4		
Guadeloupe	-4		
Guam	+10		
Guatemala	-6		
Guinea	UTC		
Guinea-Bissau	UTC		
Guyana	-4		
Haiti	-5		
Honduras	-6		
Hungary	+1	(+2)	LSuM-LSuO
Iceland	UTC		
India	+5.30		
Indonesia – Western	+7		
– Central	+8		
– Eastern	+9		
Iran	+3.30	(+4)	A-O; dates vary
Iraq	+3	(+4)	A-O; dates vary
Ireland	UTC	(+1)	LSuM-LSuO
Israel	+2	(+3)	M-O; dates vary
Italy – incl. San Marino, Vat.	+1	(+2)	LSuM-LSuO
Jamaica	-5		
Japan	+9		
Jordan	+2	(+3)	M-O; dates vary
Kazakhstan – Western	+5		
– Central	+5		
– Eastern	+6		
Kenya	+3		
Kiribati – Christmas Is.	+14		
– Phoenix Is.	+13		
– Gilbert Is. (incl. Tarawa)	+12		
Korea, DPR (North)	+9		
Korea, Republic (South)	+9		
Kuwait	+3		
Kyrgyzstan	+6		
Laos	+7		
Latvia	+2	(+3)	LSuM-LSuO

Country	Time	(DST time)	DST change
Lebanon	+2	(+3)	LSuM-LSuO
Lesotho	+2		
Liberia	UTC		
Libya	+2		
Liechtenstein	+1	(+2)	LSuM-LSuO
Lithuania	+2	(+3)	LSuM-LSuO
Luxembourg	+1	(+2)	LSuM-LSuO
Macedonia, FYR	+1	(+2)	LSuM-LSuO
Madagascar	+3		
Malawi	+2		
Malaysia	+8		
Maldives	+5		
Mali	UTC		
Malta	+1	(+2)	LSuM-LSuO
Marshall Islands	+12		
Martinique	-4		
Mauritania	UTC		
Mauritius	+4		
Mexico – Central	-6	(-5)	1SuA-LSuO
– Mountain	-7	(-6)	1SuA-LSuO
– Pacific	-8	(-7)	1SuA-LSuO
Micronesia – Yap, Chuuk	+10		
– Kosrae, Pohnpei	+11		
Moldova	+2	(+3)	LSuM-LSuO
Monaco	+1	(+2)	LSuM-LSuO
Mongolia – Central/Eastern	+8	(+9)	LSuM-LSuO
– Western	+7	(+8)	LSuM-LSuO
Montenegro	+1	(+2)	LSuM-LSuO
Montserrat	-4		
Morocco	UTC		
Mozambique	+2		
Myanmar (Burma)	+6.30		
Namibia	+1	(+2)	1SuS-1SuA
Nauru	+12		
Nepal	+5.45		
Netherlands	+1	(+2)	LSuM-LSuO
New Caledonia	+11		
New Zealand – N & S Is.	+12	(+13)	1SuO-3SuM
– Chatham Island	+12.45	(+13.45)	1SuO-3SuM
Nicaragua	-6		
Niger	+1		
Nigeria	+1		
Niue	-11		
Northern Mariana Is.	+10		
Norway	+1	(+2)	LSuM-LSuO
Oman	+4		
Pakistan	+5		
Palau	+9		
Palestine NAR	+2	(+3)	M-O; dates vary
Panama	-5		
Papua New Guinea	+10		
Paraguay	-4	(-3)	3SuO-2SuM
Peru	-5		
Philippines	+8		
Poland	+1	(+2)	LSuM-LSuO
Portugal – incl. Madeira	UTC	(+1)	LSuM-LSuO
– Azores	-1	(UTC)	LSuM-LSuO
Puerto Rico	-4		
Qatar	+3		
Réunion	+4		
Romania	+2	(+3)	LSuM-LSuO
Rwanda	+2		
Russian Fed. – Kaliningrad	+2	(+3)	LSuM-LSuO
– Moscow, St Pet, Astrakh.	+3	(+4)	LSuM-LSuO
– Samara, Izhevsk	+4	(+5)	LSuM-LSuO
– Perm, Yekater'g, Surgut	+5	(+6)	LSuM-LSuO
– Omsk, Novosibirsk	+6	(+7)	LSuM-LSuO

Country	Time	(DST time)	DST change
– Tuva, Norilsk, Abakan	+7	(+8)	LSuM-LSuO
– Bratsk, Irkutsk, Ulan-Ude	+8	(+9)	LSuM-LSuO
– Yakutsk, Tynda, Mirny	+9	(+10)	LSuM-LSuO
– Vladiv'k, Khab'k, Sak'n	+10	(+11)	LSuM-LSuO
– Magadan, Chirskiy	+11	(+12)	LSuM-LSuO
– Kamchatka, Anadyr	+12	(+13)	LSuM-LSuO
St Eustatius	-4		
St Kitts & Nevis	-4		
St Lucia	-4		
St Maarten	-4		
St Pierre et Miquelon	-3	(-2)	1SuA-LSuO
St Vincent & the Gren.	-4		
Saba	-4		
Samoa	-11		
São Tomé e Príncipe	UTC		
Saudi Arabia	+3		
Senegal	UTC		
Serbia	+1	(+2)	LSuM-LSuO
Seychelles	+4		
Sierra Leone	UTC		
Singapore	+8		
Slovak Republic	+1	(+2)	LSuM-LSuO
Slovenia	+1	(+2)	LSuM-LSuO
Solomon Islands	+11		
Somalia	+3		
South Africa	+2		
Spain – incl. Balearic Is.	+1	(+2)	LSuM-LSuO
– Canary Islands	UTC	(+1)	LSuM-LSuO
Sri Lanka	+5.5		
Sudan	+3		
Surinam	-3		
Swaziland	+2		
Sweden	+1	(+2)	LSuM-LSuO
Switzerland	+1	(+2)	LSuM-LSuO
Syria	+2	(+3)	A-O; dates vary
Taiwan	+8		
Tajikistan	+5		
Tanzania	+3		
Thailand	+7		
Togo	UTC		
Tonga	+13		
Trinidad & Tobago	-4		
Tunisia	+1		
Turkey	+2	(+3)	LSuM-LSuO
Turkmenistan	+5		
Turks & Caicos Islands	-5	(-4)	LSuM-LSuO
Tuvalu	+12		
Uganda	+3		
Ukraine	+2	(+3)	LSuM-LSuO
United Arab Emirates	+4		
United Kingdom	UTC	(+1)	LSuM-LSuO
United States – Eastern	-5	(-4)	see note*
– Central	-6	(-5)	see note*
– Mountain	-7	(-6)	see note* (not AZ)
– Pacific	-8	(-7)	see note*
– Alaska	-9	(-8)	see note*
– Aleutian/Hawaii	-10		
US Virgin Islands	-4		
Uruguay	-3	(-2)	2SuO-2SuM
Uzbekistan	+5		
Vanuatu	+11		
Venezuela	-4		
Vietnam	+7		
Yemen	+3		
Zambia	+2		
Zimbabwe	+2		

*1SuA-LSuO (2006 only); 2SuM-1SuN from 2007.

This table provides time differences compared to the Universal Time Co-ordinate (UTC), now the generally accepted term for Greenwich Mean Time (GMT). Time differences, in hours and (sometimes) minutes, are coloured by whether the 'normal' (non Daylight Saving) time in the main part of the country is ahead (red) or behind (blue) UTC. Countries that use UTC are in green.

Several countries span more than one time zone. In some cases (such as the USA) these zones have names which are widely understood. In others (such as Russia) a list of the main cities within each zone has been considered more useful. The names used to describe these zones here do not necessarily follow any official term, even where one exists. Countries may change their time arrangements without reference to any international body, although alterations usually only affect Daylight Saving Time (see below) rather than the 'normal' time. One exception to this was in 2000 when part of Kiribati moved its time forward to UTC+14 in order to be the first place on earth to see in the new millennium.

Daylight Saving Time (DST) was first introduced in some European countries during the First World War, but the idea did not become firmly or widely accepted until the 1960s. Today it is used in some or all of about 70 states, generally outside the tropics. Clocks are advanced by one hour in spring and put back one hour in autumn. While many countries change their clocks on predictable days from year to year, others do not. There is no universal agreement on the subject and countries, or regions within them, may make any arrangements they see fit, often at short notice. Some countries, most notably the USA, have extended the period of DST as an energy-saving measure, and others may follow suit. All information may thus be subject to change.

The dates between which DST is effective are shown in the 'DST change' column. For the reasons described above, these may alter from year to year. The letters M, A, S, O and N refer to March, April, September, October and November. The abbreviations Su, Th, etc refer to the day of the week. The initial number (or L for last) refers to the incidence of that day in the month. Thus LSuM-LSuO (by far the most common period, and one which applies throughout Europe) means the Last Sunday in March to the Last Sunday in October. In some cases, particularly countries in the Middle East which use different calendars, dates cannot accurately be predicted and so more general ranges have been given. Sometimes DST is not observed throughout all of the area in question. The more important of these exceptions are referred to in this column.

For reasons of space, information has not been included on several minor dependencies and overseas territories.

The listings above refer to a selection of related themes.
For more information, see the Contents (2-5).

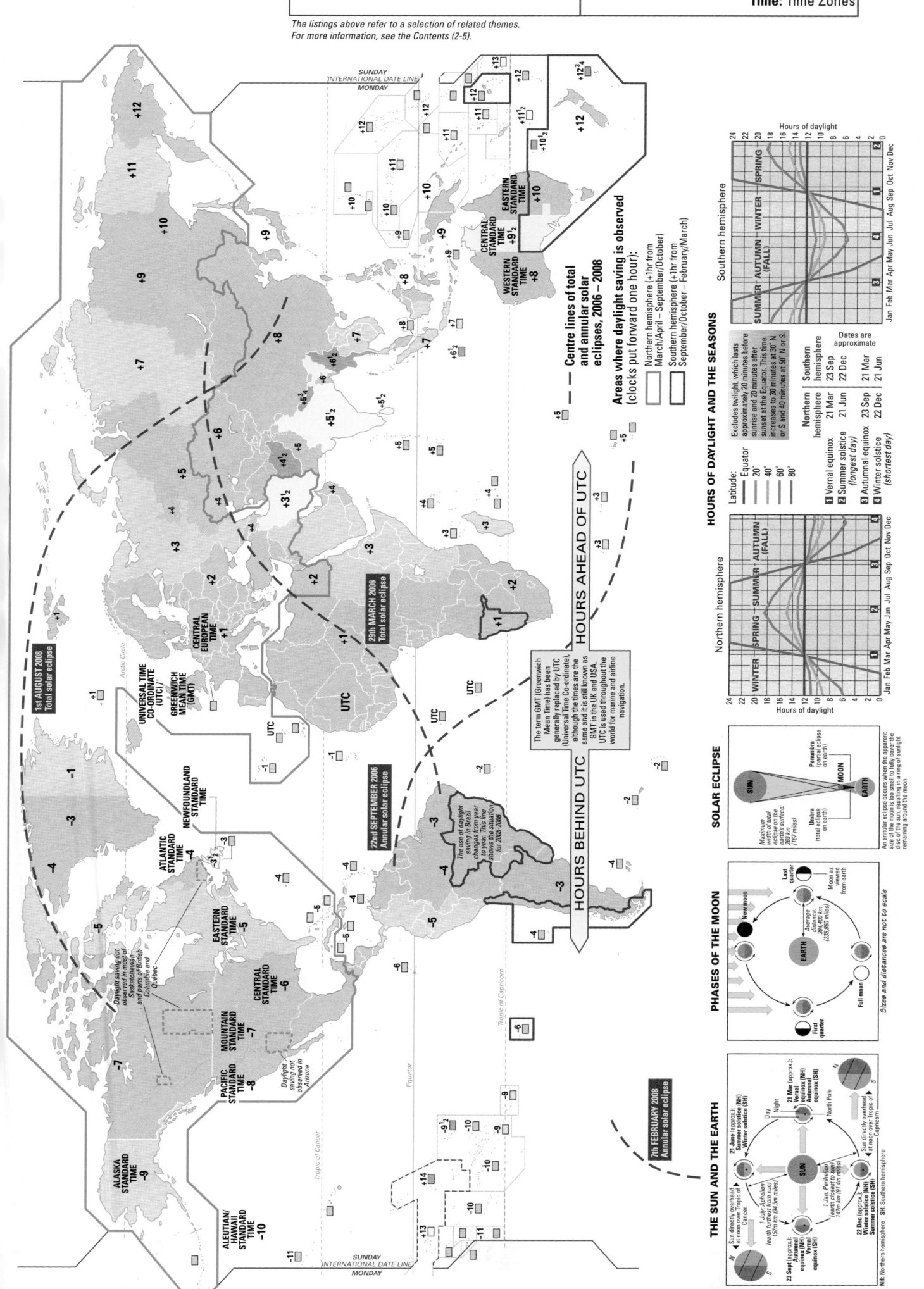

The listings above refer to a selection of related themes. For more information, see the Contents (2-5).

VISITOR RECEIPTS

Statistics for Portugal include Azores and Madeira, statistics for Spain include Canary Is. and statistics for the US include Alaska and Hawaii.

'International arrivals' are defined as people staying at least one night and exclude people arriving and departing on the same day; however in a few countries separate figures are not available and so total arrivals are shown. **This applies to all international arrivals charts in this atlas.**

Visitor receipts, 2004
(money received from international visitors)

▨ US$10,000 million and over	▨ US$100m – $499m	▨ No data available
▨ US$2,000m – $9,999m	▨ US$30m – $99m	
▨ US$500m – $1,999m	▨ Less than US$30m	

Excludes international transport   *Source:* World Tourism Organisation

Countries with more than 200,000 international arrivals in 2004 are named on the map. Those with over four million arrivals are shown in **BOLD CAPITALS**. *See note on left.*

VISITOR EXPENDITURE

Statistics for Portugal include Azores and Madeira, statistics for Spain include Canary Is. and statistics for the US include Alaska and Hawaii.

Consistent statistics for outbound travel are unavailable for a number of countries. Countries which indicate significant levels of expenditure but for which departures figures are unavailable, an * is shown. In some instances, departures figures are available but not expenditure.

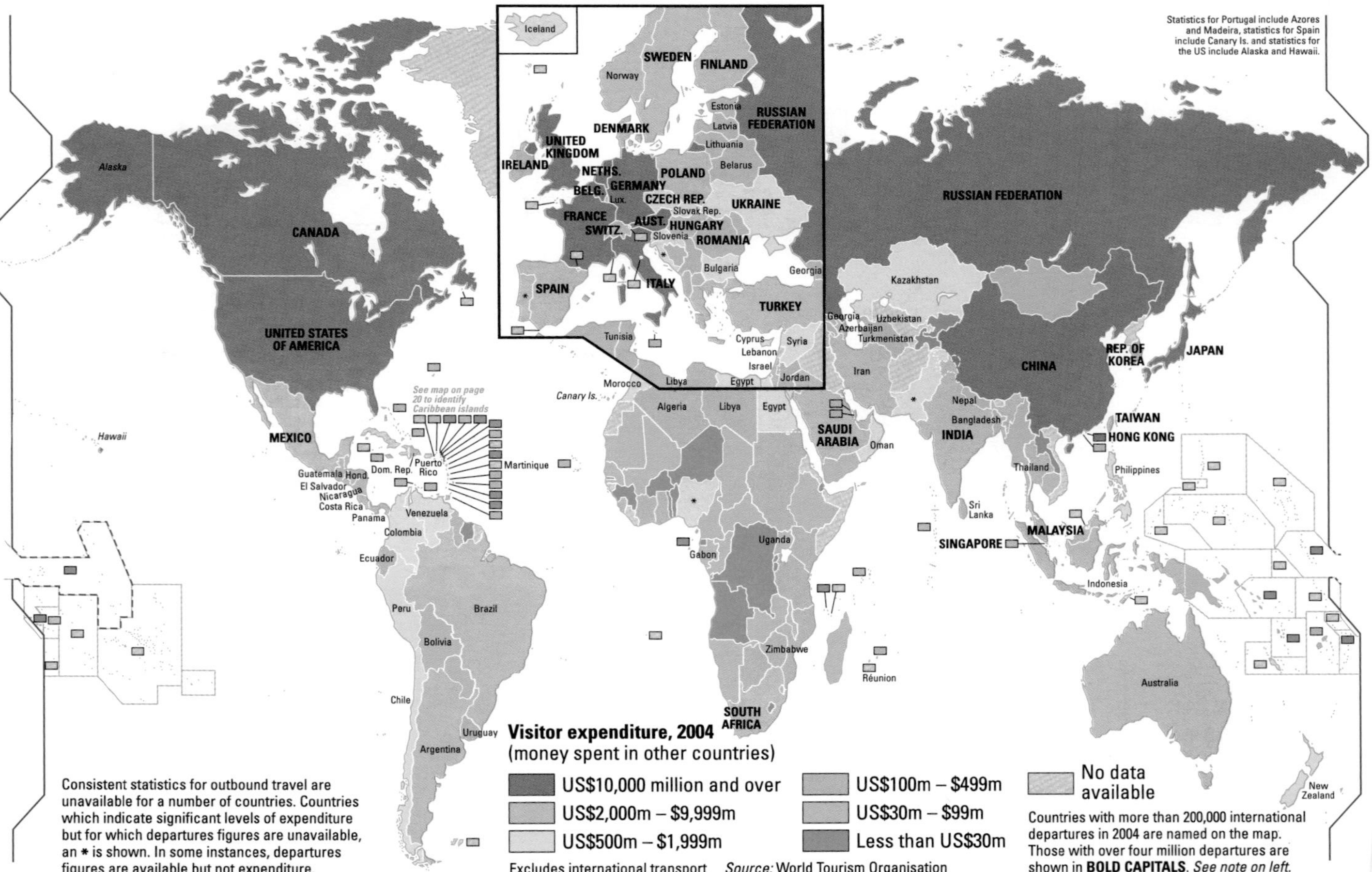

Visitor expenditure, 2004
(money spent in other countries)

▨ US$10,000 million and over	▨ US$100m – $499m	▨ No data available
▨ US$2,000m – $9,999m	▨ US$30m – $99m	
▨ US$500m – $1,999m	▨ Less than US$30m	

Excludes international transport   *Source:* World Tourism Organisation

Countries with more than 200,000 international departures in 2004 are named on the map. Those with over four million departures are shown in **BOLD CAPITALS**. *See note on left.*

The listings above refer to a selection of related themes.
For more information, see the Contents (2-5).

UNITED STATES TOURISM

UNITED KINGDOM TOURISM

Total arrivals in USA
(millions)

% change on previous year
+5.7 | −8.4 | −7.1 | −5.4 | +11.8
2000 | 2001 | 2002 | 2003 | 2004

Canada
13,849
(30.1%)

Japan **3,748** (8.1%)

Rep. of Korea **627** (1.4%)

Australia **520** (1.1%)

Rest of world
8,134 (17.7%)

Mexico
11,906
(25.8%)

INTERNATIONAL ARRIVALS, 2004
(top ten countries of origin, thousands)
Width of bar is proportional to number of travellers

UK **4,303** (9.3%)**

Netherlands **425** (0.9%)

Germany **1,320** (2.9%)

France **775** (1.7%)

Italy **471** (1.0%)

Canada **740** (2.7%)

USA **3,616** (13.0%)*

Ireland **2,578** (9.3%)

Rest of world
8,275 (29.8%)

Spain
1,465
(5.3%)

France
3,254
(11.7%)

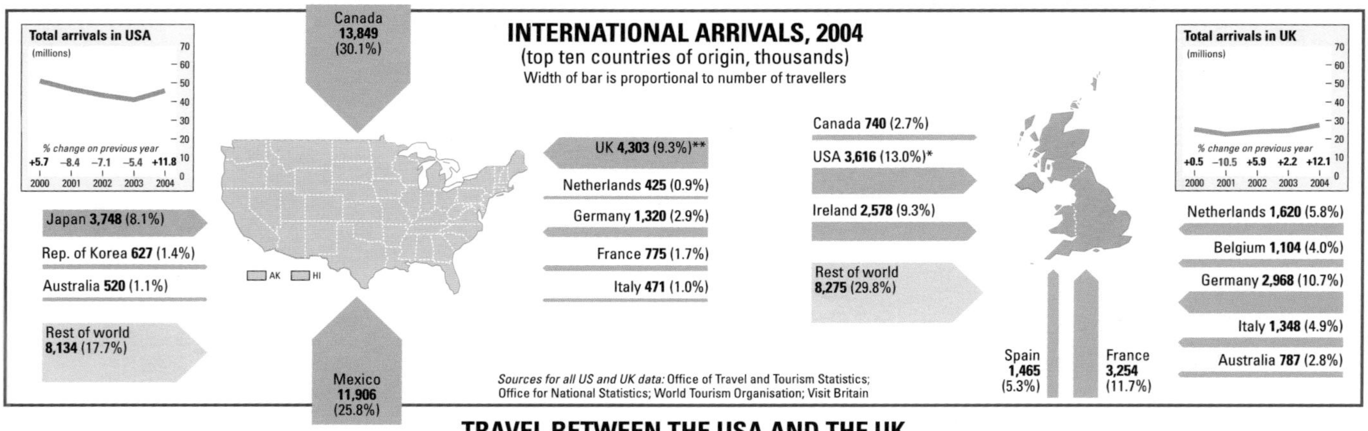

Sources for all US and UK data: Office of Travel and Tourism Statistics;
Office for National Statistics; World Tourism Organisation; Visit Britain

Total arrivals in UK
(millions)

% change on previous year
+0.5 | −10.5 | +5.9 | +2.2 | +12.1
2000 | 2001 | 2002 | 2003 | 2004

Netherlands **1,620** (5.8%)

Belgium **1,104** (4.0%)

Germany **2,968** (10.7%)

Italy **1,348** (4.9%)

Australia **787** (2.8%)

TRAVEL BETWEEN THE USA AND THE UK

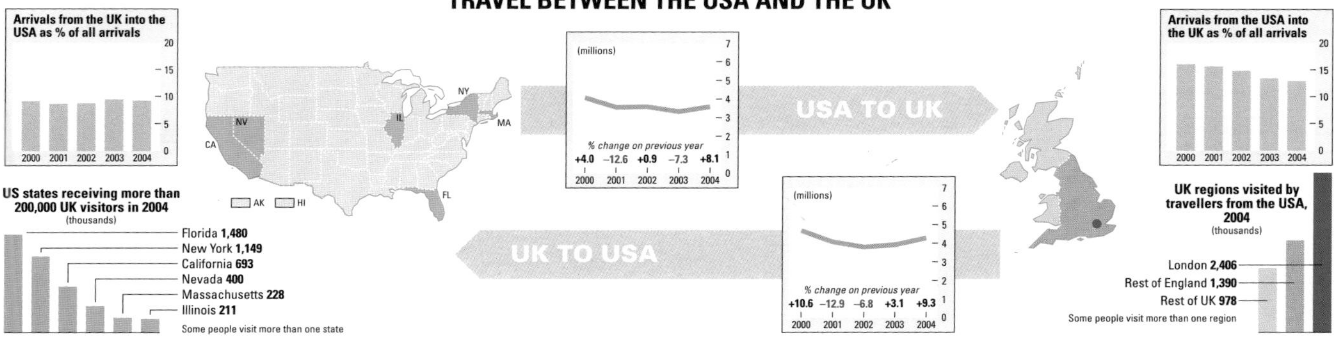

Arrivals from the UK into the USA as % of all arrivals

2000 | 2001 | 2002 | 2003 | 2004

US states receiving more than 200,000 UK visitors in 2004
(thousands)

Florida **1,480**
New York **1,149**
California **693**
Nevada **400**
Massachusetts **228**
Illinois **211**

Some people visit more than one state

USA TO UK

(millions)

% change on previous year
+4.0 | −12.6 | +0.9 | −7.3 | +8.1
2000 | 2001 | 2002 | 2003 | 2004

UK TO USA

(millions)

% change on previous year
+10.6 | −12.9 | −6.8 | +3.1 | +9.3
2000 | 2001 | 2002 | 2003 | 2004

Arrivals from the USA into the UK as % of all arrivals

2000 | 2001 | 2002 | 2003 | 2004

UK regions visited by travellers from the USA, 2004
(thousands)

London **2,406**
Rest of England **1,390**
Rest of UK **978**

Some people visit more than one region

INTERNATIONAL DEPARTURES, 2004
(top ten destinations, thousands)
Width of bar is proportional to number of travellers

Total departures from USA
(millions)

% change on previous year
+7.0 | −3.1 | −2.3 | −3.2 | +10.0
2000 | 2001 | 2002 | 2003 | 2004

Canada
15,056 (24.4%)

Japan **1,067** (1.7%)

China **1,067** (1.7%)

Rest of world
13,183 (21.3%)

Mexico
19,369 (31.4%)

Jamaica **1,258** (2.0%)

Bahamas **1,012** (1.6%)

UK **3,692** (6.0%)*

Germany **1,750** (2.8%)

France **2,407** (3.9%)

Italy **1,915** (3.1%)

USA **4,331** (7.6%)**

Ireland **3,961** (7.0%)

Rest of world
12,683 (22.3%)

Spain
11,154
(19.6%)

France
11,903
(20.9%)

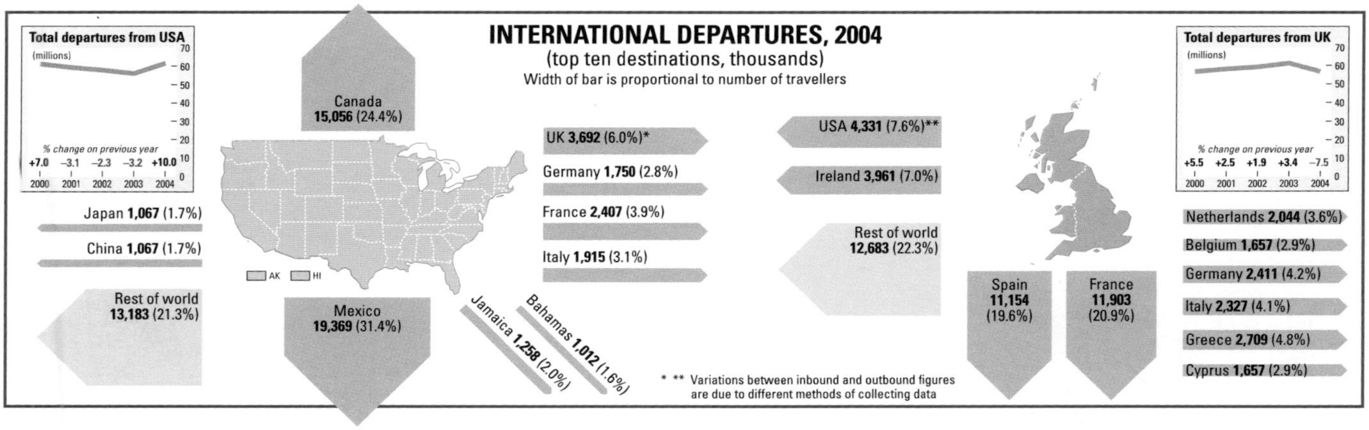

* ** Variations between inbound and outbound figures
are due to different methods of collecting data

Total departures from UK
(millions)

% change on previous year
+5.5 | +2.5 | +1.9 | +3.4 | −7.5
2000 | 2001 | 2002 | 2003 | 2004

Netherlands **2,044** (3.6%)

Belgium **1,657** (2.9%)

Germany **2,411** (4.2%)

Italy **2,327** (4.1%)

Greece **2,709** (4.8%)

Cyprus **1,657** (2.9%)

WORLDWIDE TOURISM

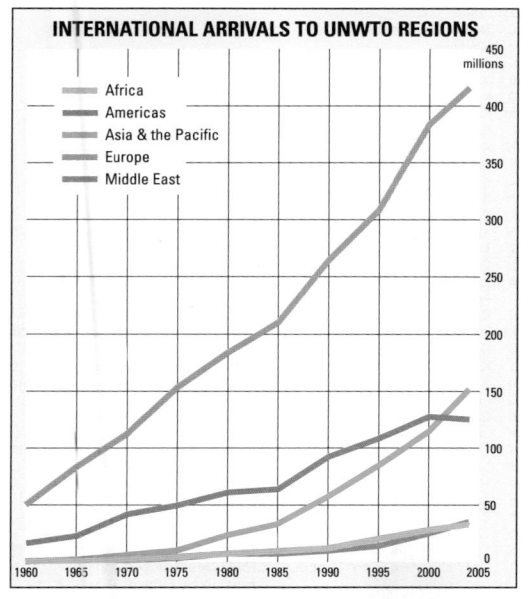

INTERNATIONAL ARRIVALS TO UNWTO REGIONS

450 millions
400
350
300
250
200
150
100
50

— Africa
— Americas
— Asia & the Pacific
— Europe
— Middle East

1960 | 1965 | 1970 | 1975 | 1980 | 1985 | 1990 | 1995 | 2000 | 2005

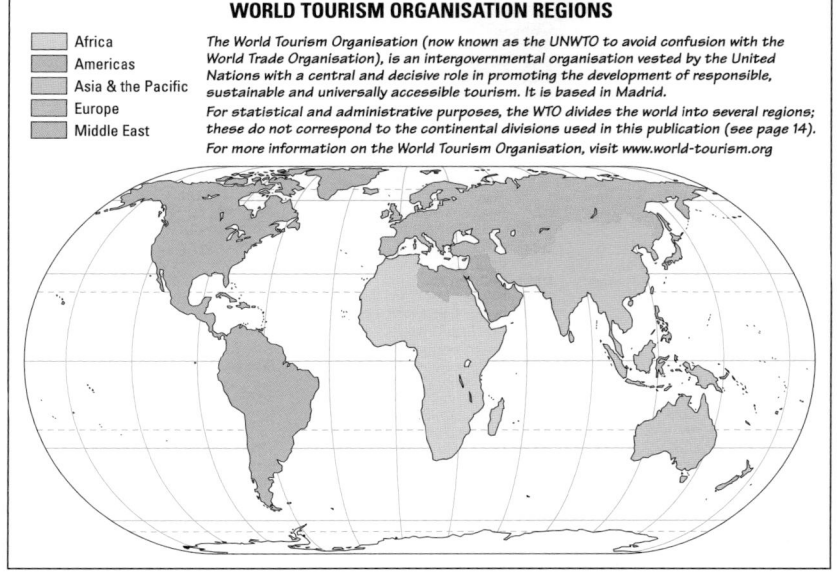

WORLD TOURISM ORGANISATION REGIONS

Africa
Americas
Asia & the Pacific
Europe
Middle East

The World Tourism Organisation (now known as the UNWTO to avoid confusion with the World Trade Organisation), is an intergovernmental organisation vested by the United Nations with a central and decisive role in promoting the development of responsible, sustainable and universally accessible tourism. It is based in Madrid.

For statistical and administrative purposes, the WTO divides the world into several regions; these do not correspond to the continental divisions used in this publication (see page 14). For more information on the World Tourism Organisation, visit www.world-tourism.org

▶ *See also...* Time (32-33); Flight Times (39); Cruising (40-41); Europe Transport (50-53); London Airports (63); Berlin Airports (71); Paris Airports (75)

The listings above refer to a selection of related themes. For more information, see the Contents (2-5).

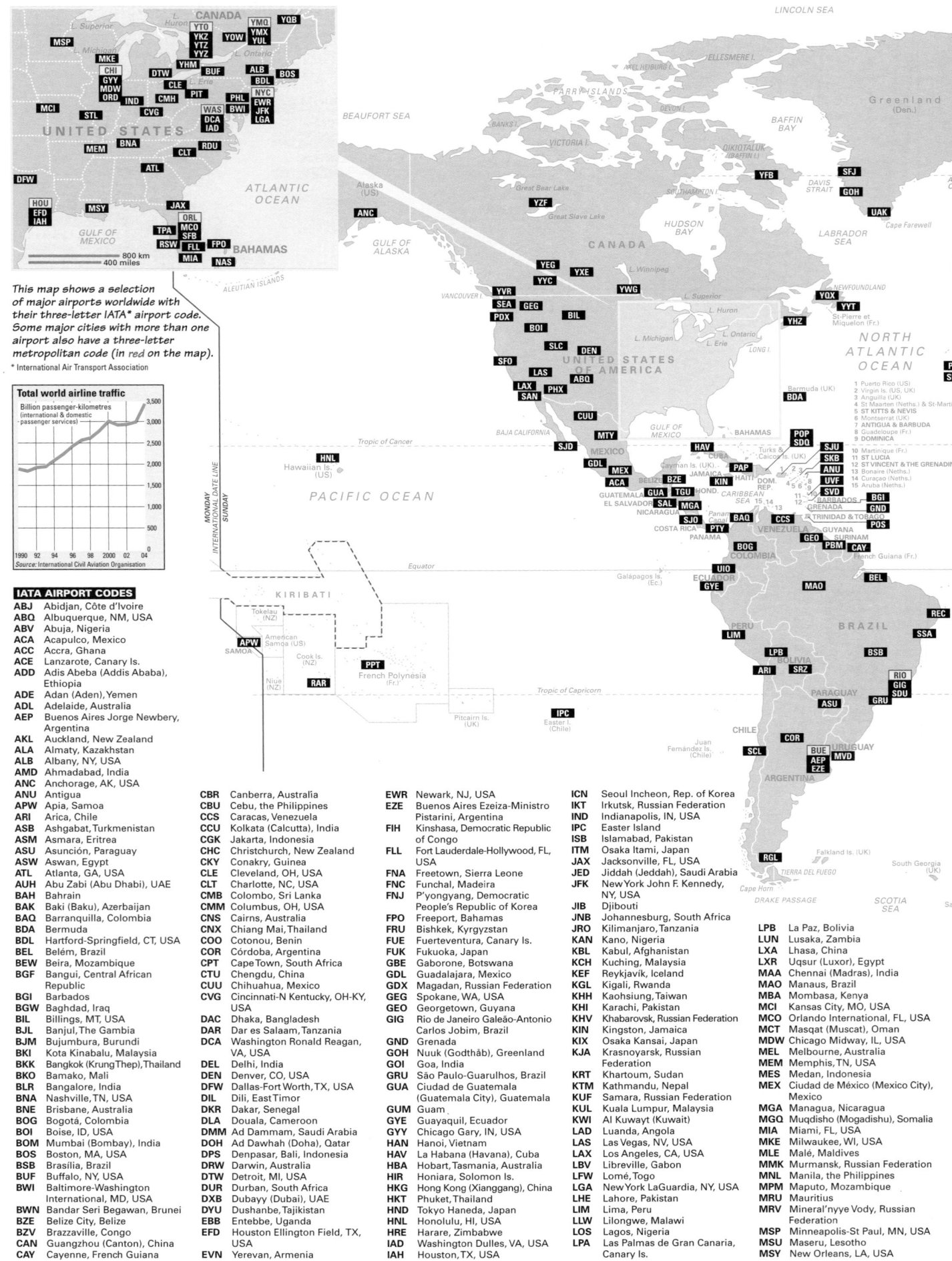

This map shows a selection of major airports worldwide with their three-letter IATA* airport code. Some major cities with more than one airport also have a three-letter metropolitan code (in red on the map).

* International Air Transport Association

Total world airline traffic

Billion passenger-kilometres (international & domestic passenger services)

Source: International Civil Aviation Organisation

IATA AIRPORT CODES

ABJ	Abidjan, Côte d'Ivoire
ABQ	Albuquerque, NM, USA
ABV	Abuja, Nigeria
ACA	Acapulco, Mexico
ACC	Accra, Ghana
ACE	Lanzarote, Canary Is.
ADD	Adis Abeba (Addis Ababa), Ethiopia
ADE	Adan (Aden), Yemen
ADL	Adelaide, Australia
AEP	Buenos Aires Jorge Newbery, Argentina
AKL	Auckland, New Zealand
ALA	Almaty, Kazakhstan
ALB	Albany, NY, USA
AMD	Ahmadabad, India
ANC	Anchorage, AK, USA
ANU	Antigua
APW	Apia, Samoa
ARI	Arica, Chile
ASB	Ashgabat, Turkmenistan
ASM	Asmara, Eritrea
ASU	Asunción, Paraguay
ASW	Aswan, Egypt
ATL	Atlanta, GA, USA
AUH	Abu Zabi (Abu Dhabi), UAE
BAH	Bahrain
BAK	Baki (Baku), Azerbaijan
BAQ	Barranquilla, Colombia
BDA	Bermuda
BDL	Hartford-Springfield, CT, USA
BEL	Belém, Brazil
BEW	Beira, Mozambique
BGF	Bangui, Central African Republic
BGI	Barbados
BGW	Baghdad, Iraq
BIL	Billings, MT, USA
BJL	Banjul, The Gambia
BJM	Bujumbura, Burundi
BKI	Kota Kinabalu, Malaysia
BKK	Bangkok (Krung Thep), Thailand
BKO	Bamako, Mali
BLR	Bangalore, India
BNA	Nashville, TN, USA
BNE	Brisbane, Australia
BOG	Bogotá, Colombia
BOI	Boise, ID, USA
BOM	Mumbai (Bombay), India
BOS	Boston, MA, USA
BSB	Brasília, Brazil
BUF	Buffalo, NY, USA
BWI	Baltimore-Washington International, MD, USA
BWN	Bandar Seri Begawan, Brunei
BZE	Belize City, Belize
BZV	Brazzaville, Congo
CAN	Guangzhou (Canton), China
CAY	Cayenne, French Guiana

CBR	Canberra, Australia
CBU	Cebu, the Philippines
CCS	Caracas, Venezuela
CCU	Kolkata (Calcutta), India
CGK	Jakarta, Indonesia
CHC	Christchurch, New Zealand
CKY	Conakry, Guinea
CLE	Cleveland, OH, USA
CLT	Charlotte, NC, USA
CMB	Colombo, Sri Lanka
CMM	Columbus, OH, USA
CNS	Cairns, Australia
CNX	Chiang Mai, Thailand
COO	Cotonou, Benin
COR	Córdoba, Argentina
CPT	Cape Town, South Africa
CTU	Chengdu, China
CUU	Chihuahua, Mexico
CVG	Cincinnati-N Kentucky, OH-KY, USA
DAC	Dhaka, Bangladesh
DAR	Dar es Salaam, Tanzania
DCA	Washington Ronald Reagan, VA, USA
DEL	Delhi, India
DEN	Denver, CO, USA
DFW	Dallas-Fort Worth, TX, USA
DIL	Dili, East Timor
DKR	Dakar, Senegal
DLA	Douala, Cameroon
DMM	Ad Dammam, Saudi Arabia
DOH	Ad Dawhah (Doha), Qatar
DPS	Denpasar, Bali, Indonesia
DRW	Darwin, Australia
DTW	Detroit, MI, USA
DUR	Durban, South Africa
DXB	Dubayy (Dubai), UAE
DYU	Dushanbe, Tajikistan
EBB	Entebbe, Uganda
EFD	Houston Ellington Field, TX, USA
EVN	Yerevan, Armenia

EWR	Newark, NJ, USA
EZE	Buenos Aires Ezeiza-Ministro Pistarini, Argentina
FIH	Kinshasa, Democratic Republic of Congo
FLL	Fort Lauderdale-Hollywood, FL, USA
FNA	Freetown, Sierra Leone
FNC	Funchal, Madeira
FNJ	P'yongyang, Democratic People's Republic of Korea
FPO	Freeport, Bahamas
FRU	Bishkek, Kyrgyzstan
FUE	Fuerteventura, Canary Is.
FUK	Fukuoka, Japan
GBE	Gaborone, Botswana
GDL	Guadalajara, Mexico
GDX	Magadan, Russian Federation
GEG	Spokane, WA, USA
GEO	Georgetown, Guyana
GIG	Rio de Janeiro Galeão-Antonio Carlos Jobim, Brazil
GND	Grenada
GOH	Nuuk (Godthåb), Greenland
GOI	Goa, India
GRU	São Paulo-Guarulhos, Brazil
GUA	Ciudad de Guatemala (Guatemala City), Guatemala
GUM	Guam
GYE	Guayaquil, Ecuador
GYY	Chicago Gary, IN, USA
HAN	Hanoi, Vietnam
HAV	La Habana (Havana), Cuba
HBA	Hobart, Tasmania, Australia
HIR	Honiara, Solomon Is.
HKG	Hong Kong (Xianggang), China
HKT	Phuket, Thailand
HND	Tokyo Haneda, Japan
HNL	Honolulu, HI, USA
HRE	Harare, Zimbabwe
IAD	Washington Dulles, VA, USA
IAH	Houston, TX, USA

ICN	Seoul Incheon, Rep. of Korea
IKT	Irkutsk, Russian Federation
IND	Indianapolis, IN, USA
IPC	Easter Island
ISB	Islamabad, Pakistan
ITM	Osaka Itami, Japan
JAX	Jacksonville, FL, USA
JED	Jiddah (Jeddah), Saudi Arabia
JFK	New York John F. Kennedy, NY, USA
JIB	Djibouti
JNB	Johannesburg, South Africa
JRO	Kilimanjaro, Tanzania
KAN	Kano, Nigeria
KBL	Kabul, Afghanistan
KCH	Kuching, Malaysia
KEF	Reykjavík, Iceland
KGL	Kigali, Rwanda
KHH	Kaohsiung, Taiwan
KHI	Karachi, Pakistan
KHV	Khabarovsk, Russian Federation
KIN	Kingston, Jamaica
KIX	Osaka Kansai, Japan
KJA	Krasnoyarsk, Russian Federation
KRT	Khartoum, Sudan
KTM	Kathmandu, Nepal
KUF	Samara, Russian Federation
KUL	Kuala Lumpur, Malaysia
KWI	Al Kuwayt (Kuwait)
LAD	Luanda, Angola
LAS	Las Vegas, NV, USA
LAX	Los Angeles, CA, USA
LBV	Libreville, Gabon
LFW	Lomé, Togo
LGA	New York LaGuardia, NY, USA
LHE	Lahore, Pakistan
LIM	Lima, Peru
LLW	Lilongwe, Malawi
LOS	Lagos, Nigeria
LPA	Las Palmas de Gran Canaria, Canary Is.

LPB	La Paz, Bolivia
LUN	Lusaka, Zambia
LXA	Lhasa, China
LXR	Uqsur (Luxor), Egypt
MAA	Chennai (Madras), India
MAO	Manaus, Brazil
MBA	Mombasa, Kenya
MCI	Kansas City, MO, USA
MCO	Orlando International, FL, USA
MCT	Masqat (Muscat), Oman
MDW	Chicago Midway, IL, USA
MEL	Melbourne, Australia
MEM	Memphis, TN, USA
MES	Medan, Indonesia
MEX	Ciudad de México (Mexico City), Mexico
MGA	Managua, Nicaragua
MGQ	Muqdisho (Mogadishu), Somalia
MIA	Miami, FL, USA
MKE	Milwaukee, WI, USA
MLE	Malé, Maldives
MMK	Murmansk, Russian Federation
MNL	Manila, the Philippines
MPM	Maputo, Mozambique
MRU	Mauritius
MRV	Mineral'nyye Vody, Russian Federation
MSP	Minneapolis-St Paul, MN, USA
MSU	Maseru, Lesotho
MSY	New Orleans, LA, USA

See also... Time (32-33); Flight Times (39);
Cruising (40-41); Europe Transport (50-53); London
Airports (63); Berlin Airports (71); Paris Airports (75)

World **37**

Airports

The listings above refer to a selection of related themes.
For more information, see the Contents (2-5).

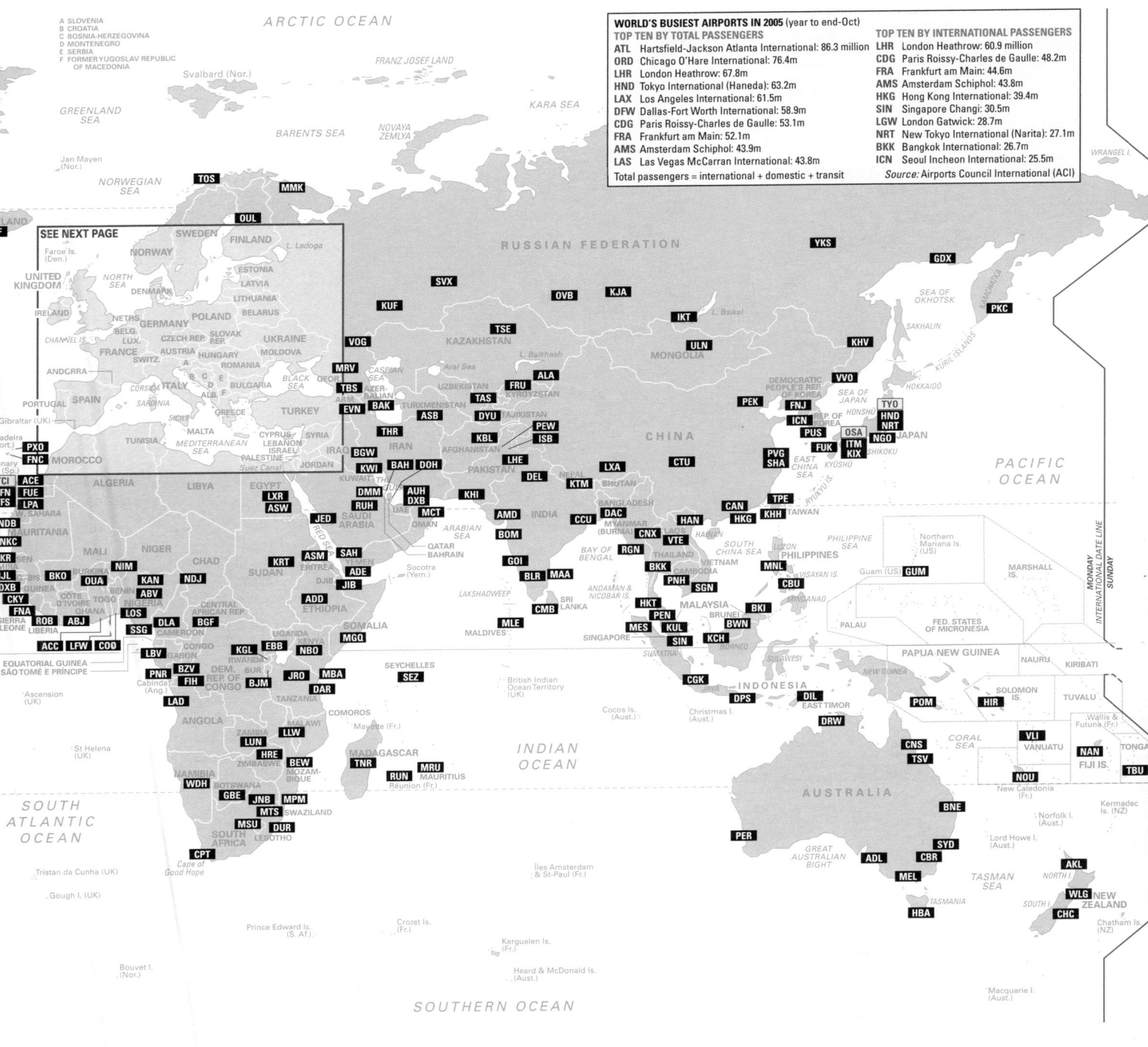

WORLD'S BUSIEST AIRPORTS IN 2005 (year to end-Oct)

TOP TEN BY TOTAL PASSENGERS	
ATL	Hartsfield-Jackson Atlanta International: 86.3 million
ORD	Chicago O'Hare International: 76.4m
LHR	London Heathrow: 67.8m
HND	Tokyo International (Haneda): 63.2m
LAX	Los Angeles International: 61.5m
DFW	Dallas-Fort Worth International: 58.9m
CDG	Paris Roissy-Charles de Gaulle: 53.1m
FRA	Frankfurt am Main: 52.1m
AMS	Amsterdam Schiphol: 43.9m
LAS	Las Vegas McCarran International: 43.8m

TOP TEN BY INTERNATIONAL PASSENGERS	
LHR	London Heathrow: 60.9 million
CDG	Paris Roissy-Charles de Gaulle: 48.2m
FRA	Frankfurt am Main: 44.6m
AMS	Amsterdam Schiphol: 43.8m
HKG	Hong Kong International: 39.4m
SIN	Singapore Changi: 30.5m
LGW	London Gatwick: 28.7m
NRT	New Tokyo International (Narita): 27.1m
BKK	Bangkok International: 26.7m
ICN	Seoul Incheon International: 25.5m

Total passengers = international + domestic + transit

Source: Airports Council International (ACI)

A SLOVENIA
B CROATIA
C BOSNIA-HERZEGOVINA
D MONTENEGRO
E SERBIA
F FORMER YUGOSLAV REPUBLIC OF MACEDONIA

MTS	Manzini, Swaziland	PHX	Phoenix, AZ, USA	SCL	Santiago, Chile	TBS	T'bilisi, Georgia	YKZ Toronto Buttonville, ON, Canada
MTY	Monterrey, Mexico	PIT	Pittsburgh, PA, USA	SDQ	Santo Domingo, Dominican Republic	TBU	Tongatapu, Tonga	YMX Montréal Mirabel, QC, Canada
MVD	Montevideo, Uruguay	PKC	Petropavlovsk-Kamchatskiy, Russian Federation	SDU	Rio de Janeiro Santos Dumont, Brazil	TER	Terceira, Azores	YOW Ottawa, ON, Canada
NAN	Nadi, Fiji Is.					TFN	Tenerife Norte, Canary Is.	YQB Québec, QC, Canada
NAS	Nassau, Bahamas	PNH	Phnom Penh, Cambodia	SEA	Seattle-Tacoma, WA, USA	TFS	Tenerife Sur, Canary Is.	YQX Gander, NL, Canada
NBO	Nairobi, Kenya	PNR	Pointe-Noire, Congo	SEZ	Mahé, Seychelles	TGU	Tegucigalpa, Honduras	YTZ Toronto City Centre, ON, Canada
NDB	Nouadhibou, Mauritania	POM	Port Moresby, Papua New Guinea	SFB	Orlando Sanford, FL, USA	THR	Tehran, Iran	YUL Montréal Dorval, QC, Canada
NDJ	N'djamena, Chad			SFJ	Kangerlussuaq, Greenland	TNR	Antananarivo, Madagascar	YVR Vancouver, BC, Canada
NGO	Nagoya Centrair, Japan	POP	Puerto Plata, Dominican Rep.	SFO	San Francisco, CA, USA	TOS	Tromsø, Norway	YWG Winnipeg, MB, Canada
NIM	Niamey, Niger	POS	Port of Spain, Trinidad	SGN	Ho Chi Minh City (Saigon), Vietnam	TPA	Tampa, FL, USA	YXE Saskatoon, SK, Canada
NKC	Nouakchott, Mauritania	PPT	Papeete, Tahiti, French Polynesia			TPE	Taipei, Taiwan	YYC Calgary, AB, Canada
NOU	Nouméa, New Caledonia	PTY	Ciudad de Panamá (Panama City), Panama	SHA	Shanghai Hongqiao, China	TSE	Astana, Kazakhstan	YYT St John's, NL, Canada
NRT	Tokyo Narita, Japan			SIN	Singapore	TSV	Townsville, Australia	YYZ Toronto Lester B. Pearson, ON, Canada
ORD	Chicago O'Hare, IL, USA	PUS	Busan, Republic of Korea	SJD	San José del Cabo, Mexico	UAK	Narsarsuaq, Greenland	YZF Yellowknife, NT, Canada
OUA	Ouagadougou, Burkina	PVG	Shanghai Pudong, China	SJO	San José, Costa Rica	UIO	Quito, Ecuador	
OUL	Oulu, Finland	PXO	Porto Santo, Madeira	SJU	San Juan, Puerto Rico	ULN	Ulaanbaatar (Ulan Bator), Mongolia	**METROPOLITAN CODES**
OVB	Novosibirsk, Russian Federation	RAI	Praia, Cape Verde	SKB	St Kitts			BUE Buenos Aires, Argentina
		RAR	Rarotonga, Cook Is.	SLC	Salt Lake City, UT, USA	UVF	Hewanorra, St Lucia	CHI Chicago, IL, USA
OXB	Bissau, Guinea-Bissau	RDU	Raleigh-Durham, NC, USA	SMA	Santa Maria, Azores	VLI	Port-Vila, Vanuatu	HOU Houston, TX, USA
PAP	Port-au-Prince, Haiti	REC	Recife, Brazil	SRZ	Santa Cruz, Bolivia	VOG	Volgograd, Russian Federation	NYC New York City, NY, USA
PBM	Paramaribo, Surinam	RGL	Río Gallegos, Argentina	SSA	Salvador, Brazil	VTE	Viangchan (Vientiane), Laos	ORL Orlando, FL, USA
PDL	Ponta Delgada, São Miguel, Azores	RGN	Yangon (Rangoon), Myanmar	SSG	Malabo, Equatorial Guinea	VVO	Vladivostok, Russian Federation	OSA Osaka, Japan
		ROB	Monrovia, Liberia	STL	St Louis, MO, USA	WDH	Windhoek, Namibia	RIO Rio de Janeiro, Brazil
PDX	Portland, OR, USA	RSW	Southwest Florida, FL, USA	SVD	St Vincent	WLG	Wellington, New Zealand	TCI Tenerife, Canary Is.
PEK	Beijing (Peking), China	RUH	Ar Riyad (Riyadh), Saudi Arabia	SVX	Yekaterinburg, Russian Federation	YEG	Edmonton, AB, Canada	TYO Tokyo, Japan
PEN	Pinang (Penang), Malaysia	RUN	Réunion			YFB	Iqaluit, NU, Canada	WAS Washington, DC, USA
PER	Perth, Australia	SAH	Sana'a (Sana), Yemen	SYD	Sydney, Australia	YHM	Hamilton, ON, Canada	YMQ Montréal, QC, Canada
PEW	Peshawar, Pakistan	SAL	San Salvador, El Salvador			YHZ	Halifax, NS, Canada	YTO Toronto, ON, Canada
PHL	Philadelphia, PA, USA	SAN	San Diego, CA, USA	TAS	Toshkent (Tashkent), Uzbekistan	YKX	Yakutsk, Russian Federation	

▶ **See also...** Time (32-33); Flight Times (39);
Cruising (40-41); Europe Transport (50-53); London
Airports (63); Berlin Airports (71); Paris Airports (75)

The listings above refer to a selection of related themes.
For more information, see the Contents (2-5).

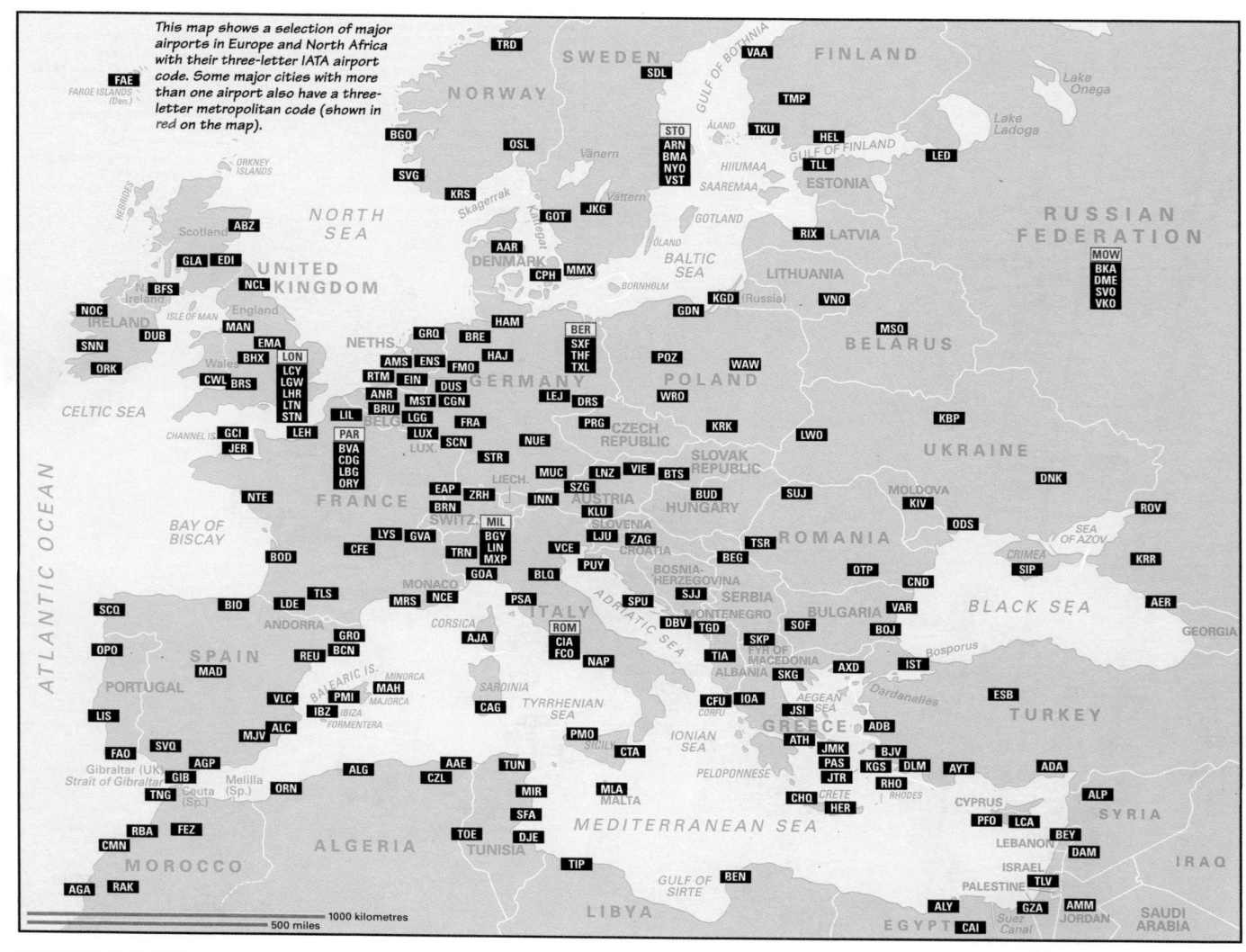

This map shows a selection of major airports in Europe and North Africa with their three-letter IATA airport code. Some major cities with more than one airport also have a three-letter metropolitan code (shown in red on the map).

IATA AIRPORT CODES

AAE	Annaba, Algeria
AAR	Århus, Denmark
ABZ	Aberdeen, Scotland
ADA	Adana, Russian Federation
ADB	Izmir (Smyrna), Turkey
AER	Adler-Sochi, Russian Federation
AGA	Agadir, Morocco
AGP	Málaga, Spain
AJA	Ajaccio, France
ALC	Alacant (Alicante), Spain
ALG	Alger (Algiers), Algeria
ALP	Halab (Aleppo), Syria
ALY	Al Iskandariyah (Alexandria), Egypt
AMM	Amman, Jordan
AMS	Amsterdam, The Netherlands
ANR	Antwerpen (Antwerp), Belgium
ARN	Stockholm Arlanda, Sweden
ATH	Athína (Athens), Greece
AXD	Alexandroúpoli, Greece
AYT	Antalya, Turkey
BCN	Barcelona, Spain
BEG	Beograd (Belgrade), Serbia
BEN	Banghazi (Benghazi), Libya
BEY	Bayrut (Beirut), Lebanon
BFS	Belfast, Northern Ireland
BGO	Bergen, Norway
BGY	Milano (Milan) Bérgamo, Italy
BHX	Birmingham, England
BIO	Bilbao, Spain
BJV	Bodrum-Milas, Turkey
BKA	Moskva (Moscow) Bykovo, Russian Federation
BLQ	Bologna, Italy
BMA	Stockholm Bromma, Sweden
BOD	Bordeaux, France
BOJ	Burgas, Bulgaria
BRE	Bremen, Germany
BRN	Bern (Berne), Switzerland
BRS	Bristol, England
BRU	Bruxelles/Brussel (Brussels), Belgium
BTS	Bratislava, Slovak Republic
BUD	Budapest, Hungary
BVA	Paris Beauvais-Tille, France
CAG	Cágliari, Italy
CAI	Al Qahirah (Cairo), Egypt
CDG	Paris Roissy-Charles de Gaulle, France
CFE	Clermont-Ferrand, France
CFU	Kérkira (Corfu), Greece
CGN	Köln (Cologne)-Bonn, Germany
CHQ	Haniá (Canea), Greece
CIA	Roma (Rome) Ciampino, Italy
CMN	Casablanca, Morocco
CND	Constanta, Romania
CPH	København (Copenhagen), Denmark
CTA	Catánia, Italy
CWL	Cardiff, Wales
CZL	Constantine, Algeria
DAM	Dimashq (Damascus), Syria
DBV	Dubrovnik, Croatia
DJE	Jerba, Tunisia
DLM	Dalaman, Turkey
DME	Moskva (Moscow) Domodedovo, Russian Federation
DNK	Dnipropetrovs'k, Ukraine
DRS	Dresden, Germany
DUB	Dublin, Ireland
DUS	Düsseldorf, Germany
EAP	EuroAirport (Basel (**BSL**)-Mulhouse (**MLH**)-Freiburg), France/Germany/Switzerland
EDI	Edinburgh, Scotland
EIN	Eindhoven, The Netherlands
EMA	Nottingham East Midlands, England
ENS	Enschede, The Netherlands
ESB	Ankara, Turkey
FAE	Vágar, Faroe Islands
FAO	Faro, Portugal
FCO	Roma (Rome) Fiumicino/Leonardo da Vinci, Italy
FEZ	Fès, Morocco
FMO	Münster-Osnabrück, Germany
FRA	Frankfurt am Main, Germany
GCI	Guernsey
GDN	Gdansk, Poland
GIB	Gibraltar
GLA	Glasgow, Scotland
GOA	Génova (Genoa), Italy
GOT	Göteborg (Gothenburg), Sweden
GRO	Girona, Spain
GRQ	Groningen, The Netherlands
GVA	Genève (Geneva), Switzerland
GZA	Gaza, Palestine Nat. Auth. Region
HAJ	Hannover (Hanover), Germany
HAM	Hamburg, Germany
HEL	Helsinki-Vantaa, Finland
HER	Iráklio (Herakleion), Greece
IBZ	Eivissa (Ibiza), Spain
INN	Innsbruck, Austria
IOA	Ioánina, Greece
IST	Istanbul, Turkey
JER	Jersey
JKG	Jönköping, Sweden
JMK	Míkonos, Greece
JSI	Skíathos, Greece
JTR	Thíra, Greece
KBP	Kyiv (Kiev), Ukraine
KGD	Kaliningrad, Russian Federation
KGS	Kós (Cos), Greece
KIV	Chisinau (Kishinev), Moldova
KLU	Klagenfurt, Austria
KRK	Kraków (Cracow), Poland
KRR	Krasnodar, Russian Federation
KRS	Kristiansand, Norway
LBG	Paris Le Bourget, France
LCA	Larnaca, Cyprus
LCY	London City, England
LDE	Lourdes-Tarbes, France
LED	Sankt-Peterburg (St Petersburg), Russian Federation
LEH	Le Havre, France
LEJ	Leipzig-Halle, Germany
LGG	Liège, Belgium
LGW	London Gatwick, England
LHR	London Heathrow, England
LIL	Lille, France
LIN	Milano (Milan) Linate, Italy
LIS	Lisboa (Lisbon), Portugal
LJU	Ljubljana, Slovenia
LNZ	Linz, Austria
LTN	London Luton, England
LUX	Luxembourg
LWO	L'viv (L'vov), Ukraine
LYS	Lyon (Lyons), France
MAD	Madrid, Spain
MAH	Maó (Mahón), Spain
MAN	Manchester, England
MIR	Monastir, Tunisia
MJV	Murcia, Spain
MLA	Malta
MMX	Malmö, Sweden
MRS	Marseille (Marseilles), France
MSQ	Minsk, Belarus
MST	Maastricht, The Netherlands
MUC	München (Munich), Germany
MXP	Milano (Milan) Malpensa, Italy
NAP	Nápoli (Naples), Italy
NCE	Nice, France
NCL	Newcastle, England
NOC	Horan (Knock), Ireland
NTE	Nantes, France
NUE	Nürnberg (Nuremberg), Germany
NYO	Stockholm Skavsta, Sweden
ODS	Odesa (Odessa), Ukraine
OPO	Porto (Oporto), Portugal
ORK	Cork, Ireland
ORN	Oran, Algeria
ORY	Paris Orly, France
OSL	Oslo, Norway
OTP	Bucuresti (Bucharest), Romania
PAS	Páros, Greece
PFO	Pafos (Paphos), Cyprus
PMI	Palma de Mallorca, Spain
PMO	Palermo, Italy
POZ	Poznan, Poland
PRG	Praha (Prague), Czech Republic
PSA	Pisa, Italy
PUY	Pula, Croatia
RAK	Marrakech, Morocco
RBA	Rabat, Morocco
REU	Reus, Spain
RHO	Ródos (Rhodes), Greece
RIX	Riga, Latvia
ROV	Rostov-na-Donu, Russian Federation
RTM	Rotterdam, The Netherlands
SCN	Saarbrücken, Germany
SCQ	Santiago de Compostela, Spain
SDL	Sundsvall, Sweden
SFA	Sfax, Tunisia
SIP	Simferopol, Ukraine
SJJ	Sarajevo, Bosnia-Herzegovina
SKG	Thessaloníki (Salonika), Greece
SKP	Skopje, Former Yugoslav Republic of Macedonia
SNN	Shannon, Ireland
SOF	Sofiya (Sofia), Bulgaria
SPU	Split, Croatia
STN	London Stansted, England
STR	Stuttgart, Germany
SUJ	Satu Mare, Romania
SVG	Stavanger, Norway
SVO	Moskva (Moscow) Sheremetyevo, Russian Federation
SVQ	Sevilla (Seville), Spain
SXF	Berlin Schönefeld, Germany
SZG	Salzburg, Austria
TGD	Podgorica, Montenegro
THF	Berlin Tempelhof, Germany
TIA	Tiranë (Tirana), Albania
TIP	Tarabulus (Tripoli), Libya
TKU	Turku, Finland
TLL	Tallinn, Estonia
TLS	Toulouse, France
TLV	Tel Aviv-Yafo, Israel
TMP	Tampere, Finland
TNG	Tanger (Tangier), Morocco
TOE	Tozeur, Tunisia
TRD	Trondheim, Norway
TRN	Torino (Turin), Italy
TSR	Timisoara, Romania
TUN	Tunis, Tunisia
TXL	Berlin Tegel, Germany
VAA	Vaasa, Finland
VAR	Varna, Bulgaria
VCE	Venézia (Venice), Italy
VIE	Wien (Vienna), Austria
VKO	Moskva (Moscow) Vnukovo, Russian Federation
VLC	València, Spain
VNO	Vilnius, Lithuania
VST	Stockholm Västerås, Sweden
WAW	Warszawa (Warsaw), Poland
WRO	Wroclaw, Poland
ZAG	Zagreb, Croatia
ZRH	Zürich, Switzerland

METROPOLITAN CODES

BER	Berlin, Germany
LON	London, England
MIL	Milano (Milan), Italy
MOW	Moskva (Moscow), Russian Federation
PAR	Paris, France
ROM	Roma (Rome), Italy
STO	Stockholm, Sweden

► *See also...* Time (32-33); Airports (36-38); Cruising (40-41); Europe Transport (50-53); London Airports (63); Berlin Airports (71); Paris Airports (75)

World **39**

Flight Times

The listings above refer to a selection of related themes. For more information, see the Contents (2-5).

Average flight times from London, New York and Singapore to other major destinations. Hours do not include stopover time, when necessary, from one destination to another.

Less than 2 hours
2 hours – 4 hours 59 mins
5 hours – 8 hours 59 mins
9 hours – 14 hours 59 mins
15 hours – 24 hours 59 mins
25 hours and over

LONDON

NEW YORK

SINGAPORE

The main ocean and river cruise areas are highlighted along with the most visited ports (red dots). Follow the green line for a typical three-month world cruise route. The Mediterranean and the Caribbean, the two most popular cruising regions, are shown in extra detail below.

Not all ships can dock alongside all ports. On these occasions, ship's launches are used to tender passengers ashore. In some remote regions such as Antarctica, passengers can only travel ashore by Zodiac boats.

Cruises are year-round except in the following regions, where climate or sea conditions limit the season:
Alaska: cruises scheduled between May and September;
US East Coast May – Sep;
Baltic May – Sep;
South Africa Nov – Mar;
Antarctica & South America (Cape Horn) Nov – Feb

Cruise passengers (millions)

(graph 1980–2005, 0 to 14 millions)

Estimated regional breakdown, 2005 (millions)

- Caribbean/Florida (incl. Panama Canal) 6.3
- Mediterranean Sea/ Black Sea/Red Sea 2.0
- Alaska/W Canada 0.9
- Norwegian Fjords/ Baltic 0.9
- Mexican Riviera 0.85
- Asia 0.75
- US East Coast/ E Canada 0.7
- Hawaiian Is. 0.6
- South America/ Antarctica 0.4
- Bermuda 0.2
- Other regions 0.8

PORTS OF CALL: THE BALTIC

400 km
200 miles

NORWAY
SWEDEN
FINLAND
Oslo
Stockholm
Luleå
Kemi
Vaasa (Vasa)
Helsinki (Helsingfors)
ÅLAND
HIIUMAA
SAAREMAA
Tallinn
Sankt-Peterburg (St Petersburg)
GULF OF BOTHNIA
GULF OF FINLAND
ESTONIA
RUSSIAN FED.
Visby
GOTLAND
Rïga
LATVIA
DENMARK
København (Copenhagen)
ÖLAND
BORNHOLM
BALTIC SEA
Klaipêda
LITHUANIA
Kaliningrad (Russia)
BELARUS
Nord-Ostsee (Kiel) Kanal
Kiel
Warnemünde
Gdynia
Gdańsk
Hamburg
Travemünde
GERMANY
POLAND

McKINLEY SEA

BEAUFORT SEA
Barrow

BERING SEA

GULF OF ALASKA
Anchorage
Valdez
Skagway & Haines
Seward
Whittier
Juneau
Glacier Bay
Sitka
Ketchikan
Misty Fjords
Prince Rupert
Vancouver
Victoria
Seattle

Alaska/Canada (Voyage to the Glaciers) cruise area

NORTH PACIFIC OCEAN

Mexican Riviera cruise area
San Francisco
Los Angeles
Long Beach
San Diego
Ensenada
La Paz
Cabo San Lucas
Mazatlán
Puerto Vallarta
Manzanillo
Acapulco

Tropic of Cancer

MONDAY — INTERNATIONAL DATE LINE — SUNDAY

Waimea, Lihue & Nawiliwili, Kauai
Honolulu, Oahu
Kahului, Maui
Hilo & Kailua Kona, Hawaii I.

Hawaiian Islands cruise area

Polynesia

Pago Pago, Tutuila

Bora Bora
Moorea
Papeete, Tahiti

South Pacific cruise area

SOUTH PACIFIC OCEAN

Equator

Easter I.

HUDSON BAY

LABRADOR SEA

Uummannaq
Ilulissat
Sisimiut
Nuuk (Godthåb)
Narsarsuaq
Arctic Circle
Cape Farewell

NORTH ATLANTIC OCEAN

US East Coast (New England/Canada) cruise area
Québec
Saint John
Montréal
Charlottetown
Halifax
Portland
Bar Harbor
Boston
Cape Cod
New York
Nantucket
Philadelphia
Martha's Vineyard
Newport
Cape Hatteras
Charleston
Natchez
Baton Rouge
New Orleans
Miami
Hamilton, St George's & Royal Dockyard, Bermuda

Europe – New York
Europe – Florida
Transatlantic
Europe – Caribbean

GULF OF MEXICO

BERMUDA TRIANGLE

SARGASSO SEA

Caribbean/Florida cruise area
Greater Antilles
CARIBBEAN SEA
Lesser Antilles

Sã
Vice

CARIBBEAN & CENTRAL AMERICA INSET

Panama Canal

Esmeraldas
Galápagos Is.
Guayaquil
Callao [for Lima]
Pebas
Iquitos
Vendeval
Leticia
Santarém & Alter do Chão
Manaus & Boca de Valeria
Mouths of the Amazon
Belém
Fortaleza
Recife
Salvador de Bahia

Íles du Salut / Devil's Island

South America cruise area

Rio de Janeiro
Santos [for São Paulo]

Tropic of Capricorn

Valparaíso [for Santiago]
Isla Mocha
Montevideo
Buenos Aires
Rio de la Plata
Puerto Montt
Puerto Madryn
Puerto Natales
Punta Arenas
Strait of Magellan
TIERRA DEL FUEGO
Cape Horn
Ushuaia
DRAKE PASSAGE
SCOTIA SEA

PORTS OF CALL: CARIBBEAN & CENTRAL AMERICA

UNITED STATES
Houston
Galveston
Jacksonville
New Orleans
Mississippi Delta
Tampa
Port Canaveral
GRAND BAHAMA ISLAND
Palm Beach
Freeport / Lucaya
Port Everglades, Fort Lauderdale
GREAT ABACO
Miami
NEW PROVIDENCE
ELEUTHERA
Key West
FLORIDA KEYS
Nassau
BAHAMAS
CAT I.
ANDROS
SAN SALVADOR
Straits of Florida
GREAT EXUMA
LONG I.
ACKLINS I.
CROOKED I.
MAYAGUANA

GULF OF MEXICO

Tropic of Cancer

Tampico
La Habana (Havana)
CUBA
Greater Antilles
GREAT INAGUA
TURKS & CAICOS IS. (UK)
Progreso
Playa del Carmen & Calica
ISLA DE LA JUVENTUD
Guantánamo Bay (US)
Cap-Haïtien
DOMINICAN REPUBLIC
Cozumel
CAYMAN IS. (UK)
HAITI
ÎLE DE LA GONÂVE
HISPANIOLA
Puerto Plata
MEXICO
Costa Maya
George Town
Montego Bay
JAMAICA
Ocho Rios
Port-au-Prince
Santo Domingo
PUERTO RICO (US)
San Juan
VIRGIN IS. (US & UK)
Ixtapa-Zihuatanejo
Belize City
BELIZE
GULF OF HONDURAS
Roatán
Santo Tomás de Castilla
Acapulco
GUATEMALA
HONDURAS
Basseterre
ST KITTS
Charlestown
Plymouth
Huatulco
GOLFO DE TEHUANTEPEC
Volcanic activity currently prevents cruise visits
DOMINICA
Puerto Limón
EL SALVADOR
Costa de Mosquitos
NICARAGUA
CARIBBEAN SEA
Lesser Antilles
ST VINCENT
THE GRENADINES
Puerto Caldera
COSTA RICA
Oranjestad
ARUBA (Neths.)
BONAIRE (Neths.)
Willemstad
CURAÇAO (Neths.)
St George's
GRENADA
Bridgetown
BARBADOS
PACIFIC OCEAN
Colón
PANAMA
Balboa
Panama Canal
COLOMBIA
Cartagena
GOLFO DE VENEZUELA
La Guaira [for Caracas]
ISLA MARGARITA
LA TORTUGA
LAGO DE MARACAIBO
VENEZUELA
TOBAGO
TRINIDAD & TOBAGO
Port of Spain
Ciudad Guayana
Orinoco Delta

Charlotte Amalie, St Thomas
Tortola
Virgin Gorda
Frederiksted & Christiansted, St Croix
Philipsburg, St Maarten
Road Bay
ANGUILLA (UK)
ST MAARTEN (Neths.) & ST-MARTIN (Fr.)
SABA (Neths.)
ST EUSTATIUS (Neths.)
ANTIGUA & BARBUDA
Heritage Quay, St John's
MONTSERRAT (UK)
Pointe-à-Pitre
GUADELOUPE (Fr.)
Prince Rupert Bay, Portsmouth
Woodbridge Bay, Roseau
Fort-de-France
MARTINIQUE (Fr.)
Pte Seraphine, Castries
ST LUCIA
Kingstown

ATLANTIC OCEAN

1000 kilometres
500 miles

PORTS OF CALL: BRITISH ISLES

300 km
150 miles

SHETLAND IS.
Lerwick
FAIR ISLE
ORKNEY IS.
Kirkwall
Invergordon
NORTH
ATLANTIC
OCEAN
HEBRIDES
Scotland
NORTH
SEA
Leith
[for Edinburgh]
Greenock
Newcastle
upon Tyne
N. IRELAND
IRELAND
ISLE OF MAN
ANGLESEY
UNITED
KINGDOM
Dublin
Liverpool
Wales
England
Harwich
Waterford
Milford
Haven
London
Tilbury
Cork
Bristol
Dover
Plymouth
Portland
Southampton
CELTIC
SEA
Falmouth
Fowey
English Channel
FRANCE
ISLES OF SCILLY
Guernsey
CHANNEL IS.

PORTS OF CALL: THE GULF

IRAQ
KUWAIT
IRAN
AFGHANISTAN
QATAR
THE
GULF
QESHM
Strait of Hormuz
Bandar-e
'Abbās
Al Manāmah
BAHRAIN
Al Khaṣab
OMAN
Ad Dawhah
(Doha)
Sharjah
Dubai
Khawr Fakkan
Fujairah
GULF OF
OMAN
SAUDI
ARABIA
UNITED ARAB
EMIRATES
Trucial
Coast
OMAN
JAZĪRAT
MAṢĪRAH
Masqaṭ
(Muscat)
ARABIAN
SEA

400 km
200 miles

ARCTIC OCEAN

GREENLAND
SEA
Longyearbyen,
Spitsbergen

Norwegian Fjords
(North Cape/Land of
the Midnight Sun)
cruise area

BARENTS SEA

BALTIC
INSET

Baltic
(Northern Capitals)
cruise area

DENMARK
STRAIT

Hammerfest
Tromsø
Honningsvåg
Narvik
North Cape
NORWEGIAN
SEA
reykjavik
Tórshavn
Ålesund & Geiranger
Molde
Trondheim
Andalsnes
Flåm & Gudvangen
Måløy & Olden
Bergen
Stockholm
Oslo
Helsinki
(Helsingfors)
Eidfjord & Hardangerfjord
Stavanger
København
(Copenhagen)
Sankt-Peterburg
(St Petersburg)
BRITISH
ISLES
INSET
NORTH SEA
Uglich
Amsterdam
Hamburg
Moskva
(Moscow)
Southampton
Dover

Black Sea
cruise area

Volga

CASPIAN
SEA

(Western)

Mediterranean cruise area
(Eastern)

MEDITERRANEAN
SEA

THE GULF INSET

The Gulf
cruise area

Funchal,
Madeira
Tanger (Tangier)
Valletta
Casablanca
SOUTHERN
EUROPE INSET
Al Iskandarīyah
(Alexandria)
Elat
(Eilat)
Arrecife
Puerto del Rosario
Las Palmas de Gran Canaria
Santa Cruz de Tenerife
La Palma
As Suways (Suez)
Sharm ash Shaykh
Uqṣur (Luxor)
Al Aqabah
Būr Safājah
Isnā (Esna) & Idfū (Edfu)
Aswān & Kawm Umbū
Dubai
GULF OF
OMAN
Strait of Hormuz

Atlantic Islands/
West Africa
cruise area

Red Sea
cruise area

Bāb al
Mandab

Mumbai
(Bombay)

NORTH
PACIFIC
OCEAN

Dakar
Banjul
Freetown
Monrovia
Grain
Coast
Ivory Coast
Gold Coast
Slave Coast
GULF OF
GUINEA
Ṣalālah
Al Mukallā
ARABIAN
SEA
Goa
GULF OF
ADEN
Djibouti
Kochi
(Cochin)
Chennai
(Madras)
Colombo
Malé
BAY OF
BENGAL

Vladivostok
Hakodate
SEA OF
JAPAN
Tianjin
[for Beijing]
Dalian
Incheon
[for Seoul]
Yantai
Tōkyō
Yokohama
Nanjing
Wusong
Shanghai
Ningbo
Kobe
Nagasaki
Busan
Chongqing
Wuhan
Yangzi
Guangzhou
(Canton)
Xiamen
E.CHINA
SEA
Haiphong
Macau
Hong Kong
(Xianggang)
Far East
cruise area
PHILIPPINE
SEA
Yangon
(Rangoon)
Da
Nang
Manila
Micronesia
Bangkok
(Krung Thep)
Nha Trang
Port Blair,
S. Andaman
Pattaya
Ho Chi Minh City
Cebu
Phuket
Kuantan
SOUTH
CHINA
SEA
Pinang (Penang)
Melaka
(Malacca)
Kota Kinabalu
Bandar Seri Begawan
Belawan
Kuching
Port Kelang
[for Kuala
Lumpur]
Nias
Singapore
Ternate
Padang
Parepare
Palopo
Ambon
Jakarta
Ujung Pandang
JAVA SEA
Rabaul
Pulau Panjang/
Krakatau
Semarang
Surabaya
Bali
Larantuka,
Flores
Melanesia

Africa-India
(Passage to India)
cruise area

Mombasa
Zanzibar
Victoria,
Mahé
Nosy Bé
Port Louis,
Mauritius
MOZAMBIQUE CHANNEL
INDIAN
OCEAN
Christmas I.
Darwin
Port
Moresby
Honiara
Port Vila,
Éfaté
Yasawa
Suva,
Viti Levu
Nouméa
Nuku'alofa,
Tongatapu
CORAL
SEA

Australasia/
South Pacific
cruise area

SOUTH
ATLANTIC
OCEAN
Durban
Cape
Town
Cape of
Good Hope
Cape
Agulhas
ROUND-
THE-WORLD
SOUTHERN OCEAN

Cairns
Townsville
Whitsunday Is.
Great Barrier Reef
GREAT
AUSTRALIAN
BIGHT
Perth
Sydney
Melbourne
Hobart
TASMAN
SEA
Bay of Islands
Auckland
Tauranga
[for Rotorua]
Napier
Wellington
Picton
Christchurch
Milford Sound
Dusky Sound
Dunedin

Antarctic
cruise area
Auckland I.
Campbell I.
Macquarie I.

MONDAY
INTERNATIONAL DATE LINE
SUNDAY

Grytviken, Bay of Isles & Elsehul,
South Georgia
Port Stanley
& West Point,
Falkland Is.
Signy & Coronation
Is., S. Orkney Is.
King George I.
Hope Bay & Paulet I.
Ushuaia
Yankee Harbour & Half Moon I.
Paradise Harbour & Port Lockroy
Adelaide & Stonington Is.
Drake
Passage
Cape
Horn
ANTARCTIC
PENINSULA
Ronne Ice Shelf
South Pole
SOUTHERN
OCEAN
WEDDELL
SEA
SOUTHERN
OCEAN
Marie
Byrd
Land
Ross Ice Shelf
McMurdo Station
& Scott Base
Cape Evans
Cape Hallet
Cape Adare
ROSS SEA
Wilkes
Land
Antarctic Circle

Antarctic
cruise area

PORTS OF CALL: SOUTHERN EUROPE

Berching
Regensburg
Dürnstein
GERMANY
Linz
Wien
(Vienna)
Budapest
AUSTRIA
HUNGARY
SLOVENIA
CROATIA
MOLDOVA
UKRAINE
Odesa
(Odessa)
Danube
Delta
SEA
OF AZOV
CRIMEA
RUSSIAN
FEDERATION
Venèzia
(Venice)
Danube
ROMANIA
Constanţa
Sevastopol'
Yalta
BAY OF
BISCAY
FRANCE
Bordeaux
Savona
Gènova
(Genoa)
Monte Carlo
Nice
Marseille
(Marseilles)
Toulon
Riviera
Livorno
(Leghorn)
BOSNIA-
HERZEGOVINA
SERBIA
Dubrovnik
MONTENEGRO
BULGARIA
Varna
BLACK
SEA
Sochi
GEORGIA
Bat'umi
A Coruña
Vigo
Porto
(Oporto)
GOLFE
DU LION
LIGURIAN
SEA
Civitavècchia
[for Rome]
Nàpoli
(Naples)
Bari
FYR OF
MACEDONIA
ALBANIA
Istanbul
Çanakkale [for Troy]
Trabzon
SPAIN
ANDORRA
CORSICA
Ajaccio
ITALY
Capri
Sorrento
Kèrkira
(Corfu)
Piraeus
(Piraeus)
[for Athens]
Kuşadası
TURKEY
Lisboa
(Lisbon)
Barcelona
BALEARIC IS.
MINORCA
Maó (Mahón)
SARDINIA
TYRRHENIAN
SEA
Catània
Stretto
di Messina
IONIAN
SEA
Katàkolo
GREECE
Ròdos
(Rhodes)
Antalya
PORTUGAL
Praia da
Rocha
Palma de Mallorca
Eivissa (Ibiza)
MAJORCA
FORMENTERA
Sicily
Githio
PELOPONNESE
CRETE
RHODES
CYPRUS
Bayrūt
(Beirut)
Cádiz
Alacant
(Alicante)
Almería
Tunis
Valletta
MALTA
Iràklio
(Herakleion)
Lemesos
(Limassol)
SYRIA
Màlaga
Gibraltar
LEBANON
Lisboa
Praia da Rocha
Tanger
(Tangier)
Ceuta
Melilla (Sp.)
Strait of Gibraltar
MEDITERRANEAN SEA
Hefa (Haifa)
ISRAEL
Al Iskandarīyah
(Alexandria)
Būr Sa'īd
(Port Said)
IRAQ
Casablanca
MOROCCO
ALGERIA
Tarābulus
(Tripoli)
GULF OF
SIRTE
Banghāzī
(Benghazi)
Nile
Delta
PALESTINE
JORDAN
Agadir
TUNISIA
LIBYA
EGYPT
Suez
Canal
SAUDI
ARABIA

1000 kilometres
500 miles

▶ *See also...* World Introduction (22-25); Tourism (34-35); Countries A-Z (108-116)

The listings above refer to a selection of related themes. For more information, see the Contents (2-5).

Key facts	
Number of Countries	48
Area ('000 sq km)	25,926
Population ('000)	799,763
Population Density (per sq km)	31
Gross National Income (US$m)	13,200,398
Visitor Arrivals ('000)	409,570
Visitor Receipts (US$m)	322,678

GNI figures are for 2004. Population figures are taken from the most recent reliable source. Travel figures (UNWTO) are based on overnight stays, not same-day visitors, and are for 2004. For more information see the Countries A-Z section from page 202.

Europe (including the Russian Federation)

Europe's travel and tourism industry continues to dominate the world and it remains comfortably the world's most visited continent. It has numerous natural and man-made attractions, a generally excellent transport network and a wide range of cities, landscapes and climates. These factors helped draw over 435 million international visitors in 2005, over half the world's total and an increase of some 20 million over 2004. Global recession and the struggle against terrorism depressed the travel industry in 2001 and 2003, but many European travel patterns are well established and impervious to all but the very worst catastrophes. Stability has been vital to this.

That is not to say that Europe has stood still. The political map has altered many times since 1989, as has the membership and influence of the EU (which now rivals the USA as the world's largest economy). Most importantly, these changes have generally been effected peacefully. Given Europe's violent history between 1914 and 1945, this is a considerable achievement.

In general, European states are wealthy, stable, secular, liberal, multi-cultural democracies. Despite linguistic differences, national economies and societies are closely integrated, frontier formalities (for surface travel at any rate) are simple or non-existent and intra-regional trade is high. Apart from some intermittent separatist movements, there is little violent conflict. This inter-dependence, security and stability underpins Europe's vast travel and tourism industry.

Travel overview

Europe's visitor numbers have increased on average by about 2.3% a year since 2000. Although this is below the world average of 3.2%, Europe is a mature market and thus offers less easy opportunities for growth. Intra-regional travel has underpinned Europe's pre-eminence: with so many attractions within easy reach, it is not surprising so many Europeans holiday in their own continent. Nearly nine out of every ten journeys, which start in Europe also finish there. Indeed, trips made by Europeans within Europe account for around half of all international journeys worldwide.

More good news for Europe is that the US market seems to be bouncing back to pre-2001 levels, with an estimated 12.6 million visitors reported in 2005. This is despite the US dollar having lost 6% of its value against the euro in the 12 months up to May 2005, to say nothing of other price increases such as airline fuel and security surcharges.

Whilst the low-cost carriers in Europe continue their seemingly inexorable growth –100 million passengers in 2005 compared to around 50 million in 2003 – the performance of Europe's airlines overall has been encouraging, with a 6% increase in 2005. All of Europe's 25 busiest airports recorded an increase in passenger numbers in year ending October 2005 compared to the previous 12 months (5.25% on average), led by Istanbul with a rise of over 23%. A further 13 airports with one

million-plus passengers saw growth of over 35% in this period. In mature markets, such as the UK, low-cost traffic is expected to continue to grow at around 30% a year, while in newer markets the figure is even higher – 35% in Hungary, for instance. In 2005, low-cost airlines accounted for about 20% of European air travel, as opposed to 5% in 2000. Many observers expect them to account for between a quarter and a third of the continent's market by 2010.

Over 20 European countries now have their own low-cost carriers with more emerging. While not all will survive, the business model has radically changed the face of aviation and has caused major carriers to re-evaluate their pricing, routes and service levels.

Set against this growth is the issue of rising fuel prices which will continue to eat into profitability, particularly for long-haul flights. Fuel surcharges have been imposed by many of the flag-carriers since early 2004 but have so far been resisted by their low-cost rivals. With over half of international journeys in Europe being taken by car, however, the continent's travel industry is much less reliant on air travel than in other parts of the world. With so many countries offering different attractions, history and cultures in such close proximity, touring by rail or road remains popular. Travellers can cover huge swathes of Europe by utilising the continent's integrated transport network.

The seemingly relentless rise of the internet has been another significant feature of the European travel scene. As the preferred booking method for low-cost airlines it has also helped open up many previously under-visited areas of the continent. According to the Centre for Regional and Tourism Research, European online travel sales increased by over 80% between 2003 and 2005 and now accounts for sales of 24 billion euros. This is nearly 10% of the total market: in 1998, online travel was responsible for just 0.1%. The UK, followed by Germany, are the countries with the highest share of internet bookings, although the fastest growth is occurring in the new EU members of Eastern Europe. The internet is increasingly used to research holiday options, even if many may then book through more conventional methods. The continued roll-out of high-speed broadband access across the continent and the increasing willingness of consumers to trust the web for on-line payments are likely to increase this trend. One major hotel chain believes that 50% of all hotel bookings will be online by 2010: at present, the figure is closer to 10%. In the UK, 54% of holidays abroad were pre-paid packages in 2000. By 2004, this had fallen to 45%.

The movement from northern to southern Europe, traditionally in the summer but increasingly at other times, has been happening for decades. Nearly half of all British trips abroad in 2004 were for holidays to the EU15 countries, mainly France and Spain.

Increasingly affordable travel has led to a constant demand for new destinations. Most of the northern Mediterranean coastal region is now seen as a holiday area. To the long-established favourites, one must add Turkey, Croatia, Slovenia and Serbia & Montenegro, all of which saw arrivals increase in 2004 by more than the European average.

■ Economies

The region's 10 largest economies
Source: World Bank/International Monetary Fund

	GNI US$m 2004	GNI/cap US$ 2004	GDP growth av p/a 2004	'97-'06
Germany	2,488,974	30,194	1.6	1.2
UK	2,016,393	33,361	2.7	2.3
France	1,858,731	30,644	1.4	1.7
Italy	1,503,562	25,878	0.4	1.2
Spain	875,817	21,710	2.5	3.1
Netherlands	515,148	31,397	1.7	2.3
Russia	487,335	3,398	7.2	4.7
Switzerland	356,052	47,541	1.8	1.5
Belgium	322,837	31,149	2.6	2.2
Sweden	321,401	35,704	3.6	2.7

■ Big spenders

Expenditure on foreign travel (excluding international transport), 2004 – top ten countries (US$ billions) *Source: WTO*

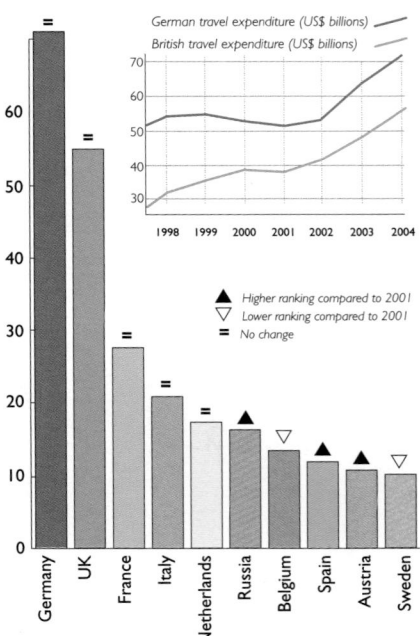

German travel expenditure (US$ billions)
British travel expenditure (US$ billions)

▲ Higher ranking compared to 2001
▽ Lower ranking compared to 2001
= No change

To add to the variety, activities such as camping, city-breaks, skiing and rural holidays are also increasing. Many provide separate holiday options, but sometimes are combined with traditional beach holidays: even skiing, which can be enjoyed in Spain's Sierra Nevada only an hour's drive from the Costa del Sol. Many people take more than one holiday a year to experience more of these ever-increasing alternatives. These factors combined to boost the number of beach holidays taken by Europeans within Europe in 2004 compared to 2003 by 5%, an increase of 3.6 million visits.

According to Eurostat, Europe's economy grew by around 2.2% in 2005. This was below the world average, but – as with visitor arrivals – the continent is generally highly developed and thus offers less opportunity for spectacular increases. Mirroring the performance of the travel industry, the largest growth (in most cases exceeding the world average) is to be found in the east of the continent. Rising fuel costs may have an effect on consumer confidence, but there are few signs that the travel business is going to suffer as a result. Even the spectre of terrorism has not tarnished Europe's appeal. In April 2005, the European Travel Commission commented that 'people are growing more accustomed to living in an unsafe world', and many travellers seem to agree: two weeks after the July 2005 attacks in London, the city's hotel occupancy rates were only slightly down

■ Heading south

European sunshine destinations ex-UK (000s)
Source: BTA/Visit Britain

	1997	2004
to Spain	8,281	13,833
to France	11,149	11,602
to Greece	1,512	2,709
to Italy	1,801	2,974
to Portugal	1,304	1,804
TOTAL	24,047	32,922
% of all outbound trips	52.3%	51.3%

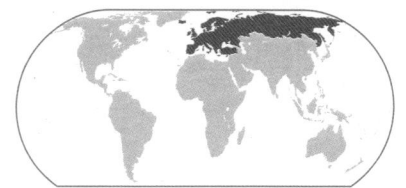

- Europe occupies 18.9% of the world's land area and is home to 12.4% of the world's population. 65% of the area and 18.0% of the population is provided by Russia.
- Europe accounts for 50.3% of global travel departures and 50.0% of arrivals.
- International travel and tourism contributed over US$320 billion to Europe's economy in 2004.
- 17 countries in Europe received more than US$5 billion from travel and tourism in 2004 and ten received more than US$10 billion.
- Europe has six of the ten most visited countries in the world and seven of the top ten travel earners.
- Germans continue to spend more money on foreign travel than any other nationality.
- 12 European countries received more than 10 million visitors in 2004.
- The most popular destination, France, on its own received about one in eleven of the world's international travellers.
- There were 410 million international tourist arrivals in Europe in 2004, an increase of 100 million since 1997.
- The budget of the EU (approx US$135bn) is only slightly less than the GNI of Argentina.
- The most significant growth in tourist arrivals in 2004 compared to 2003 was in Central and Eastern Europe which showed a rise of 13.8%.
- Europe had over 5.5 million hotel rooms in 2003.
- The Leningrad Metro has the world's longest escalator.
- Russia spans 11 time zones.
- Luxembourg has the highest per capita income of any country in the world.
- Italy is the only country that completely surrounds two other countries (the Vatican City and San Marino).
- The Hermitage in St Petersburg has over 3 million works of art.
- Over 100 tons of tomatoes are thrown during the La Tomatina festival in Buñol in Spain.
- Istanbul is the only city which spans two continents.
- Finland has over 81,000 islands and over 187,000 lakes.
- Andorra is the only country with two heads of state.
- Over 24% of Italians are over 60, the highest percentage in the world.
- Switzerland is the only country with a square flag.
- Lake Baikal in Russia is the deepest lake in the world and holds an estimated 20% of the world's liquid fresh water.

across the continent are now taking steps to respond to this increasingly important aspect of travellers' requirements.

- The sun-migration pattern reverses into a dash to the mountains for winter sports. The central Alps remain ever-popular, but Slovenia, Romania and Bulgaria are fast-emerging destinations.
- The recent opening up of Eastern Europe has led to an increase of travel not only between these countries but also from other parts of Europe. Poland, Hungary and the Czech Republic have been in the forefront.
- The states of the former Yugoslavia, particularly Slovenia, Croatia and – increasingly – Serbia & Montenegro have shown solid growth in recent years and are likely to continue to do so.
- Health and spa holidays are also on the increase: again, Eastern Europe is helping to lead the way.
- Golf holidays in Spain and Portugal, have long been popular, while France's uncrowded courses make it a strengthening force in the market.
- The Mediterranean and the Baltic are, after the Caribbean, the most popular cruise areas in the world.
- No-frills hotels are now competing with deluxe brands for the attention of business and leisure travellers who, having invested little in their air fare, are frequenting higher grade hotels and restaurants than in the past.
- EU enlargement is leading to the ten most recent members being further assimilated into Europe's travel patterns. They are also likely to be offer value for money when compared with many traditional destinations.

Destination overview

- **France** – comfortably Europe's, and the world's, most visited country, accounting for nearly one in five of the continent's international arrivals. Paris is the city-break destination *par excellence* and the Côte d'Azur one of the world's most famous playgrounds. From gastronomy to golf and from adventure breaks to fine art, France's highly varied holiday products cater for virtually all tastes.
- **Spain** – the continent's second most popular destination, and the favourite amongst Europeans (with a 13% market share in 2004 compared to France's 12%). The traditional image of beach holidays on the Mediterranean coast is fast changing, spearheaded by the city-breaks to its many magnificent cities, mainly Madrid, Seville and Barcelona.
- **Italy** – Europe's third most visited country has an enviable blend of climate, culture, natural beauty and urban sophistication. *Benessere* (well-being) and *agriturismi* (farm-stay) holidays are increasingly important niche markets. It is hoped the 2006 Winter Olympics in Turin will boost travel to Piedmont.
- **UK** – with estimates from Visit Britain putting growth in tourist arrivals and receipts at about 4.4%, the UK is expected to break the 30 million visitors mark in 2006. The country has long benefitted from its 'heritage' appeal, particularly in the North American market.
- **Germany** – the country's tourism profile has been raised through an effective series of national and regional marketing campaigns emphasising Germany's diversity. It was one of the first countries to be granted Approved Destination Status by China, which has contributed to a growth of nearly 2 million visitors to bring total arrivals up above the 20 million mark. Germany's vibrant cities have also proved popular.
- **Greece** – with around 1,400 islands, Greece can boast a coastline of some 15,000km, and it is upon this, together with its incomparable heritage sites, that its tourism appeal has largely been founded.
- **Turkey** – one of the consistent star performers of the European travel scene in recent years, Turkey's visitor numbers have risen steadily from 9 million in 1997 to nearly 17 million in 2004. Turkey's appeal has been built on the solid foundations of its beaches and cultural sites, as well as value-for-money.
- **Scandinavia** – a mature market with healthy intra-

Big earners

Receipts from foreign travel (excluding international transport), 2004 – top ten countries (US$ billions) *Source: WTO*

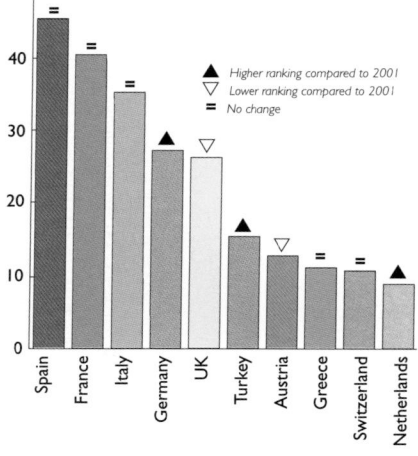

regional trade. Increasing numbers of visitors are drawn by the area's pristine environment and stunning scenery. Short-breaks to the major Scandinavian cities have increased as a result of the rise of the low-cost airlines.

- **Benelux** – these three countries attract around 16 million visitors. Cities such as Amsterdam, Brussels and Bruges are prime short-break destinations.
- **Eastern Europe** – the eight countries in this region that joined the EU in 2004 have benefited from improved air links, reduced border formalities and a favourable rate against the euro. Arrivals to the region grew by 11% in 2004, more than twice the European average. The strong Russian outbound market and well-established patterns of intra-regional travel have also played their part in this increase.

Problem areas

- Further terrorist attacks cannot be ruled out.
- Until the UK adopts the euro (if it does), its imports and exports, including travel, will remain at the mercy of euro/sterling exchange rate fluctuations.
- Although away from the European mainstream, instability is a risk in Russia and some of the former Russian republics. The newly expanded EU's relations with these countries will be of great importance.
- Traffic congestion in some cities has reduced average driving speeds to near walking-pace.
- Air travel has increased more quickly than the investment in air traffic control and airport infrastructure, which can cause delays at peak times, particularly at major hubs: 70% of the air traffic delays in 2004 took place at 30% of Europe's airports.
- Europe's wealth is attracting migrants from poorer parts of the world, which is fuelling social tensions and the growth of right-wing political parties.

on the same period the year before, while Madrid's visitor figures increased in the first nine months of 2004 compared to 2003. In common with other parts of the world, the European travel industry has shown itself to be remarkably resilient. Times are certainly changing; but change is not always for the worse. Certainly, those who value choice, flexibility and value-for-money have never had it so good.

Travel trends

The more extreme tastes in adventure holidays are best satisfied in other continents but, that aside, Europe has something for everyone, from castles to clubs, scuba-diving to ski resorts and golf courses to art galleries. Major patterns or possible future trends, in addition to those discussed above, are as follows.

- In general, people are tending to take more shorter trips rather than one long summer holiday (although this option still remains popular). City breaks are the main examples of this trend, and in 2004 12% more Europeans took city breaks within the continent compared to 2003. Urban fashions come and go, but the main capitals are ever-popular, as are cities such as Bruges, St Petersburg, Istanbul, Tallinn, Dresden, Venice, Barcelona, Munich, Milan, Dubrovnik and Cracow.
- Short breaks to beach destinations such as Majorca, the Côte d'Azur and the Algarve are on the increase.
- Travellers are increasingly looking for holidays that will challenge them and provide new experiences. Adventure holidays fill part of this desire, but educational and foreign-language tourism are growing, as are holidays involving an element of voluntary work.
- The phrases 'responsible tourism' and 'ethical tourism' are in some ways more relevant to other parts of the world than Europe, but numerous resorts

Visitors

Visitor arrivals 2004: top ten countries *Source: WTO*

	Visitors (thousands)	Change since 1997
France	75,121	11.4%
Spain	53,599	27.1%
Italy	37,071	6.0%
United Kingdom	27,755	9.1%
Germany	20,137	23.4%
Austria	19,373	14.3%
Turkey	16,826	58.4%
Ukraine	15,629	64.5%
Poland	14,290	-38.1%
Greece	13,787	26.6%

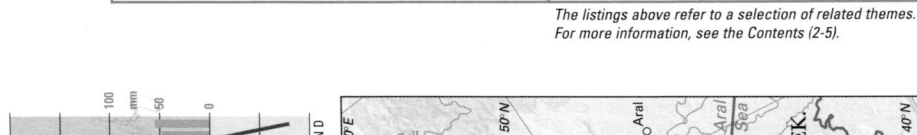

▶ *See also...* World Physical (26-27); World Political (28-29), World Climate (30)

The listings above refer to a selection of related themes.
For more information, see the Contents (2-5).

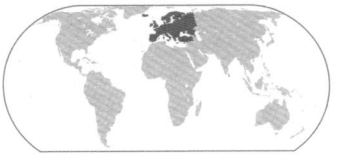

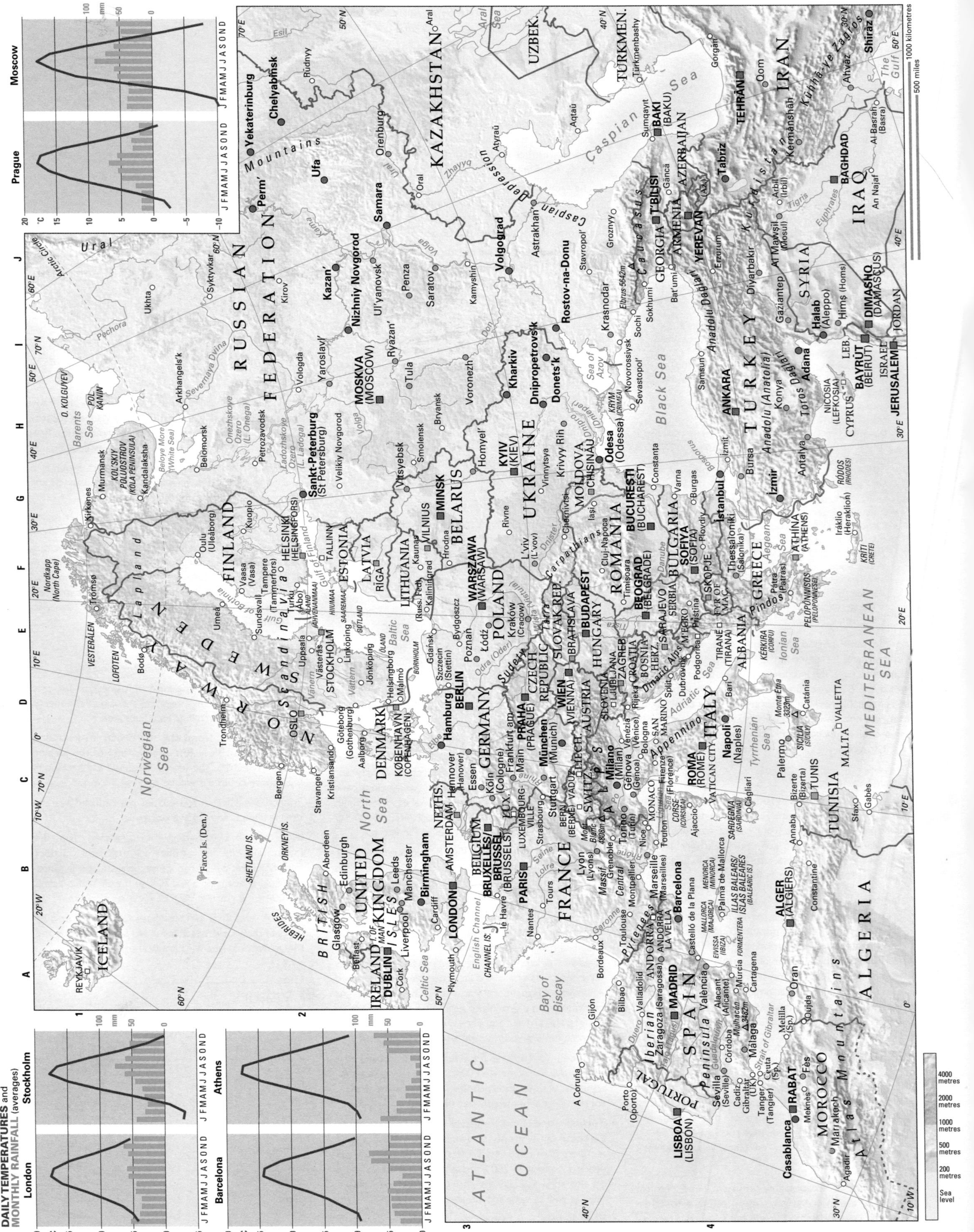

DAILY TEMPERATURES and
MONTHLY RAINFALL (averages)

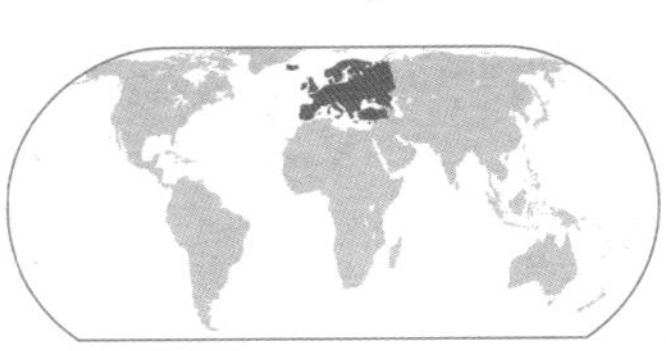

The listings above refer to a selection of related themes. For more information, see the Contents (2-5).

WINTER

TEMPERATURE
(January average, degrees Celsius)
- 10° – 19°
- 0° – 9°
- Minus 10° – minus 1°
- Below minus 10°

PREVAILING WIND shown as white arrows

RAINFALL
(November to April total)
- 500mm and over
- 250 – 499mm
- Less than 250mm

TEMPERATURE CONVERSION

°Celsius	−10	0	10	20	30	40
°Fahrenheit	14	32	50	68	86	104

RAINFALL CONVERSION

Millimetres	102	203	305	406	508	610
Inches	4	8	12	16	20	24

NORTH ATLANTIC DRIFT
An extension of the Gulf Stream which helps to maintain relatively mild winters in the British Isles and along the coast of Norway

FÖHN
A wind which blows down Alpine valleys, warming as it descends, and melts snow rapidly

MISTRAL
A strong cold dry wind from the north

BORA
A cold dry wind which blows from the N and NE, affecting the Adriatic coastline

LEVECHE
A hot, dry and dusty wind which blows from the Sahara

Columbus Travel Guides' *World Travel Guide* contains detailed climate charts for every country in the world, including temperature, rainfall, sunshine and humidity

SUMMER

TEMPERATURE
(July average, degrees Celsius)
- 30° and over
- 20° – 29°
- 10° – 19°
- 0° – 9°

PREVAILING WIND shown as white arrows

RAINFALL
(May to October total)
- 500mm and over
- 250 – 499mm
- Less than 250mm

SIROCCO
A hot dusty wind which blows from north Africa; after crossing the Mediterranean the wind is often very humid

ETESIAN WIND / MELTEMI
A wind blowing from the N and NW, often creating rough seas

The listings above refer to a selection of related themes.
For more information, see the Contents (2-5).

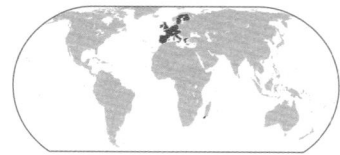

Greenland exercised its autonomy under the Danish Crown and withdrew from the EEC in 1985. The territory now has an Association Agreement with the EU.

The European Union has its origin in the European Coal and Steel Community, established in 1951. It was originally designed to ensure peace in Europe by combining the essential economic interests of its six member countries. These countries became the founding members of the European Economic Community (EEC) in 1957 under the Treaty of Rome. A gradual process of expansion and economic and political integration led in November 1993 to the creation of the 12-member European Union (EU).

The EU has developed far beyond its original design of a free-trade bloc, embracing not only a single currency and a European Central Bank, but also common measures in justice, policing, immigration, transport, environment, security and foreign policy. The EU is also the world's single largest provider of aid to developing countries. As a result, the EU has a complicated structure, in which both individual national governments and pan-EU bodies play a role. The most important of the latter are: the Council of the EU, which comprises senior representatives of the constituent national governments; the European Commission which operates, in effect, as the 'government' or executive of the EU; and the elected European Parliament which serves as its legislature.

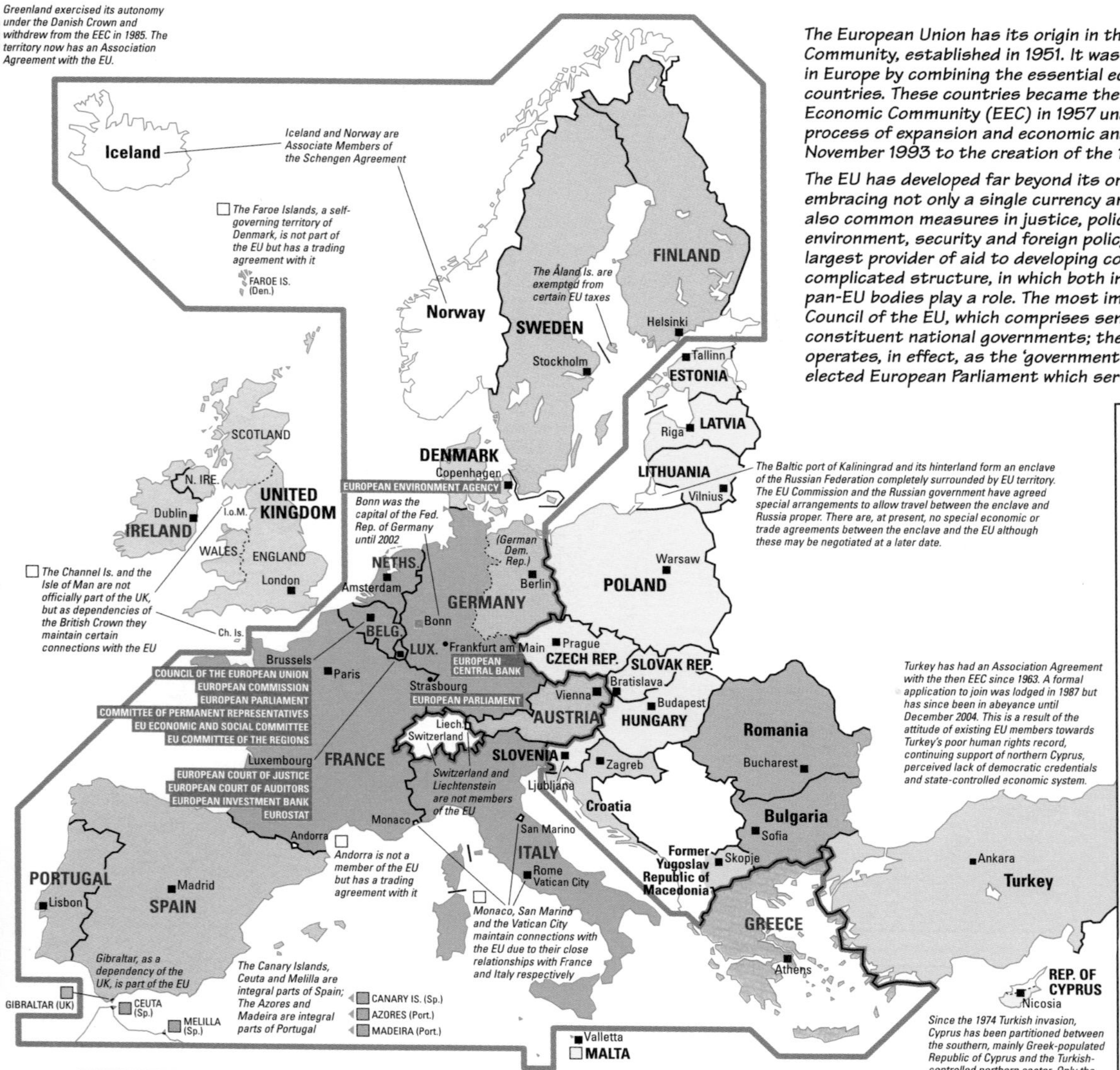

Iceland and Norway are Associate Members of the Schengen Agreement

The Faroe Islands, a self-governing territory of Denmark, is not part of the EU but has a trading agreement with it

The Åland Is. are exempted from certain EU taxes

Bonn was the capital of the Fed. Rep. of Germany until 2002

The Channel Is. and the Isle of Man are not officially part of the UK, but as dependencies of the British Crown they maintain certain connections with the EU

The Baltic port of Kaliningrad and its hinterland form an enclave of the Russian Federation completely surrounded by EU territory. The EU Commission and the Russian government have agreed special arrangements to allow travel between the enclave and Russia proper. There are, at present, no special economic or trade agreements between the enclave and the EU although these may be negotiated at a later date.

Switzerland and Liechtenstein are not members of the EU

Turkey has had an Association Agreement with the then EEC since 1963. A formal application to join was lodged in 1987 but has since been in abeyance until December 2004. This is a result of the attitude of existing EU members towards Turkey's poor human rights record, continuing support of northern Cyprus, perceived lack of democratic credentials and state-controlled economic system.

Andorra is not a member of the EU but has a trading agreement with it

Monaco, San Marino and the Vatican City maintain connections with the EU due to their close relationships with France and Italy respectively

Gibraltar, as a dependency of the UK, is part of the EU

The Canary Islands, Ceuta and Melilla are integral parts of Spain; The Azores and Madeira are integral parts of Portugal

☐ CANARY IS. (Sp.)
☐ AZORES (Port.)
☐ MADEIRA (Port.)

Since the 1974 Turkish invasion, Cyprus has been partitioned between the southern, mainly Greek-populated Republic of Cyprus and the Turkish-controlled northern sector. Only the Republic of Cyprus, which enjoys full international recognition, has been admitted to the EU. The 'Turkish Republic of Northern Cyprus' is not recognised by the EU.

Principal EU institutions (map labels): COUNCIL OF THE EUROPEAN UNION, EUROPEAN COMMISSION, EUROPEAN PARLIAMENT, COMMITTEE OF PERMANENT REPRESENTATIVES, EU ECONOMIC AND SOCIAL COMMITTEE, EU COMMITTEE OF THE REGIONS, EUROPEAN COURT OF JUSTICE, EUROPEAN COURT OF AUDITORS, EUROPEAN INVESTMENT BANK, EUROSTAT, EUROPEAN ENVIRONMENT AGENCY, EUROPEAN CENTRAL BANK.

Legend:

▨	**1957 Founder members** (6)

Subsequent members:

- **1973** (3)
- **1981** (1)
- **1986** (2) **EU-15**
- **1990** Following the reunification of Germany in 1990, the former German Democratic Republic was automatically admitted to the EEC.
- **1995** (3)
- **2004** (10) **EU NEW 10**

▨ **Accession countries** (to join in 2007?)

▨ **Candidate countries** (to join in 2012/13?)

There are no formal limits on the ultimate boundaries of the EU and other nations may apply to join in future. These include countries which have previously opted out (Norway, Iceland, Switzerland), the Balkan countries yet to be candidates (Bosnia-Herzegovina, Serbia, Montenegro, Albania) and perhaps others beyond Europe in the former Soviet Union, the Levant and North Africa.

The process of joining the EU begins with the signing of an Association Agreement, essentially a free trade accord. The next stage is to become a Candidate country by meeting three conditions (The Copenhagen Criteria):
- Democracy, human rights and the rule of law;
- A market economy;
- The adoption of the EU's acquis, which lay down the precepts and standards for all member states and cover almost every aspect of government.

Once a timetable has been agreed for the acquis, the Candidate country is certain to join the EU and becomes an Accession country.

EURO ZONE Members which have adopted monetary union are shown in RED

The single European currency, the euro, came into being in 1999 along with the European Central Bank which supervises the eurozone and sets interest rates. Since 2002, the euro has been the sole legitimate currency in the 12 (out of 25) EU countries which have adopted it. Eurozone membership requires that a country meets various economic criteria covering inflation, interest and exchange rates, and government finances (although these can be somewhat flexible). The UK and Denmark have derogations under the 1992 Maastricht Treaty while Sweden appears to have no intention to join. Of the 10 countries which joined the EU in 2004, all wish to enter the eurozone and all should be admitted by 2012; at present, they have either pegged their currencies to the euro or allow them to float within a fixed range.

Several countries outside the EU, mostly former colonies and associated territories, have linked their currencies to the euro which is now a major force in international finance.

☐ **Schengen countries**

The Schengen Agreement allows for the removal of most frontier controls and the harmonisation of procedures governing the movement of people and goods between signatory countries. It also provides for co-operation between law enforcement agencies in specified areas including immigration, terrorism and serious crime. Two non-EU countries, Iceland and Norway, are associate members of the Schengen Agreement.

The United Kingdom and Ireland subscribe only to some parts of the Schengen Agreement.

Most of the Schengen conditions have now been incorporated into the acquis which comprise the basic conditions for entry into the EU. As such, all new EU members will necessarily adopt the Schengen measures in due course.

▨ **Principal EU institutions**

■ **Capital cities**

SUMMARY TABLE

For more country statistics, including tourism, energy and health, see the Countries A-Z section in the Appendices

The provisions and conditions of EU membership also apply to the following territories which are integral parts of member states: Canary Is., Ceuta and Melilla (Spain); Azores and Madeira (Portugal) and (both not Schengen) French Guiana, Guadeloupe, Martinique and Réunion (France);

Country	Exchange rate, 1st Feb 2006 One euro=	Currency	Central Bank interest rate, 1st Feb 2006 (%)	Standard VAT rate 2005 (%)	Inflation, 2005 average (%)	Unemployment, 2005 average (% of workforce)	Gross National Income (GNI), 2004 (US$ billion)	GDP growth, 2003-2004 (%)	Balance of payments, 2004 (m euros)	Government debt, 2004 (% of GDP)	Gov't expenditure, 2004 (% of GDP)
EUROZONE Central Bank interest rate in the Eurozone is set by the European Central Bank, Frankfurt											
Austria	1		3.25	[1] 20	1.6	5.2	262.2	2.4	+573	64.3	49.9
Belgium	1		3.25	21	2.4	8.4	322.8	2.6	+9,513	96.2	49.5
Finland	1		3.25	[2] 22	1.0	8.3	171.0	3.6	+7,667	45.1	51.1
France	1		3.25	[3] 19.6	1.8	9.2	1,858.7	2.3	−6,760	65.1	53.4
Germany	1		3.25	[4] 16	2.3	9.3	2,489.0	1.6	+83,509	66.4	46.9
Greece	1		3.25	[5] 19	3.4	10.5	183.9	4.7	−8,800	109.3	49.8
Ireland	1		3.25	21	2.2	4.3	137.8	4.5	−1,181	29.8	33.7
Italy	1		3.25	[6] 20	2.4	8.0	1,503.6	1.2	−12,054	106.5	48.6
Luxembourg	1		3.25	15	3.6	5.6	25.3	4.5	+2,851	6.6	45.3
Netherlands	1		3.25	19	1.6	4.7	515.1	1.7	+44,163	53.1	46.6
Portugal	1		3.25	[7] 21	2.5	7.5	149.8	1.2	−8,603	59.4	46.1
Spain	1		3.25	[8] 16	3.4	8.5	875.8	3.1	−44,451	46.9	38.8
NON-EUROZONE											
Cyprus, Rep.of	0.57	Cyprus Pound	4.25	15	2.0	7.9	13.6	3.8	−716	72.0	43.6
Czech Republic	28.41	Koruna	2.00	[9] 19	2.2	7.9	93.2	4.4	−4,518	36.8	44.3
Denmark	7.46	Krone	2.40	[10] 25	1.9	4.5	219.4	2.1	4,493	43.2	55.1
Estonia	15.65	Kroon	3.80	18	4.0	6.6	9.4	7.8	−1,148	5.5	36.4
Hungary	252.55	Forint	6.00	25	3.3	7.3	83.3	4.6	−7,132	57.4	49.7
Latvia	0.70	Lats	4.00	18	7.5	8.6	12.6	9.8	−1,445	14.7	35.8
Lithuania	3.45	Litas	3.25	18	2.8	7.0	19.7	7.0	−1,393	19.6	33.2
Malta	0.43	Maltese Lira	3.25	18	4.3	7.7	4.9	0.1	−431	75.9	48.8
Poland	3.83	Zloty	4.50	22	1.1	17.4	232.4	5.3	−8,406	43.6	43.0
Slovak Republic	37.35	Koruna	3.00	19	3.6	16.0	34.9	5.5	−1,156	42.5	40.6
Slovenia	239.51	Tolar	6.25	20	2.1	5.9	29.6	4.2	−542	29.8	47.4
Sweden	9.24	Krona	1.75	25	1.2	6.4	321.4	3.7	+22,594	51.1	56.7
United Kingdom	0.68	Sterling	4.50	[11] 17.5	2.1	4.7	2,016.4	3.1	−34,563	41.5	43.7

[1] 16% in Junghol z & Mittelberg. [2] Excluding Åland Is. [3] 8.5% in Guadeloupe, Martinique & Réunion. [4] Excluding Helgoland & Busingen. [5] 13% on many of the Greek islands. No VAT applies to Mount Athos. [6] Excluding Livigno, the Italian enclave of Campione d'Italia & territorial waters of Lake Lugano. [7] 15% in the Azores & Madeira. [8] Excluding Canary Is., Ceuta & Melilla. [9] Including UK Sovereign Base Areas. [10] Excluding Faroe Is. & Greenland. [11] Excluding Channel Is.

Sources: European System of Central Banks; Eurostat; European Commission; World Bank; oanda.com

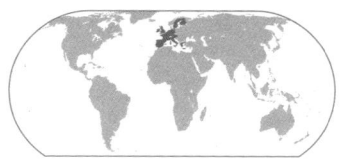

The listings above refer to a selection of related themes.
For more information, see the Contents (2-5).

POPULATION DENSITY

People per square kilometre, 2004

Statistics for Denmark include the Faroe Is.

- 400 and over
- 250 – 399
- 150 – 249
- 80 – 149
- 30 – 79
- Less than 30

Source: Eurostat

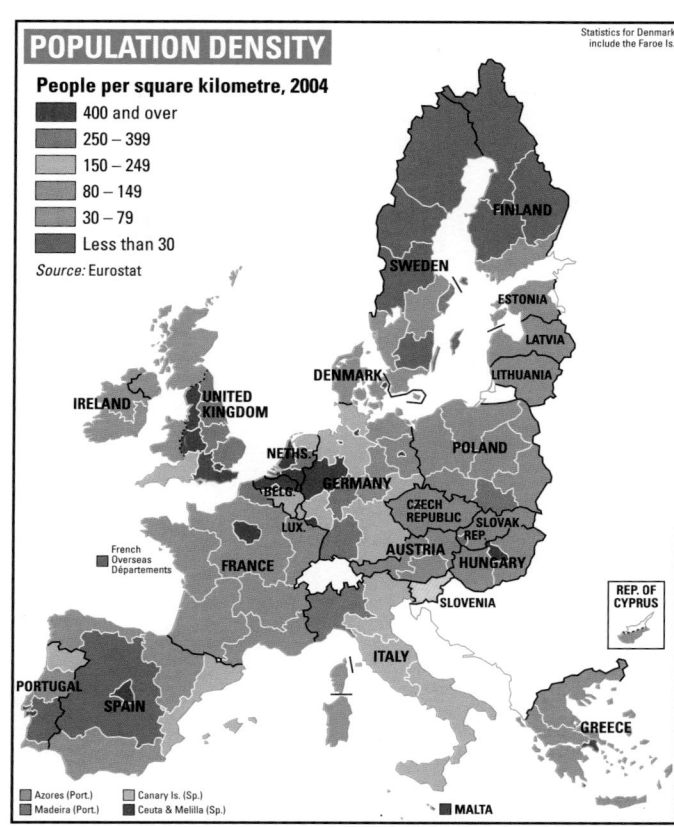

Azores (Port.) Canary Is. (Sp.)
Madeira (Port.) Ceuta & Melilla (Sp.) ■ MALTA

THE EU'S LARGEST URBAN AREAS, 2005

Estimated populations in thousands *Source:* UN

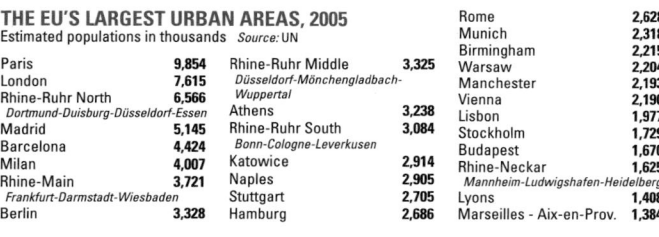

Paris	**9,854**	Rome	**2,628**
London	**7,615**	Munich	**2,318**
Rhine-Ruhr North	**6,566**	Birmingham	**2,215**
Dortmund-Duisburg-Düsseldorf-Essen		Warsaw	**2,204**
Madrid	**5,145**	Rhine-Ruhr Middle	**3,325**	Manchester	**2,193**
Barcelona	**4,424**	*Düsseldorf-Mönchengladbach-Wuppertal*		Vienna	**2,190**
Milan	**4,007**	Athens	**3,238**	Lisbon	**1,977**
Rhine-Main	**3,721**	Rhine-Ruhr South	**3,084**	Stockholm	**1,729**
Frankfurt-Darmstadt-Wiesbaden		*Bonn-Cologne-Leverkusen*		Budapest	**1,670**
Berlin	**3,328**	Katowice	**2,914**	Rhine-Neckar	**1,625**
		Naples	**2,905**	*Mannheim-Ludwigshafen-Heidelberg*	
		Stuttgart	**2,705**	Lyons	**1,408**
		Hamburg	**2,686**	Marseilles - Aix-en-Prov.	**1,384**

THE EU BUDGET

Contributions by member states to the EU, 2006
(Total: 110,160 million euros)

The UK receives an annual rebate (5,685m euros in 2006) due to earlier over-payments

- Germany € **22,650m** (20.6%)
- France € **18,105m** (16.4%)
- Italy € **15,089m** (13.7%)
- United Kingdom € **13,618m** (12.4%)
- Spain € **9,847m** (8.9%)
- Netherlands € **5,735m** (5.2%)
- Belgium € **4,428m** (4.0%)
- Sweden € **2,994m** (2.7%)
- Poland € **2,584m** (2.4%)
- Austria € **2,371m** (2.2%)
- Denmark € **2,216m** (2.0%)
- Greece € **2,031m** (1.8%)
- Finland € **1,631m** (1.5%)
- Ireland € **1,522m** (1.4%)
- Portugal € **1,495m** (1.4%)
- Czech Republic € **1,128m** (1.0%)
- Other countries* € **2,716m** (2.5%)

* Hungary 999m euros
Slovak Rep. 423m
Slovenia 314m
Luxembourg 262m
Lithuania 237m
Cyprus 171m Latvia 144m
Estonia 112m Malta 54m

EU budget expenditure, 2006
(Total: 111,421 million euros)

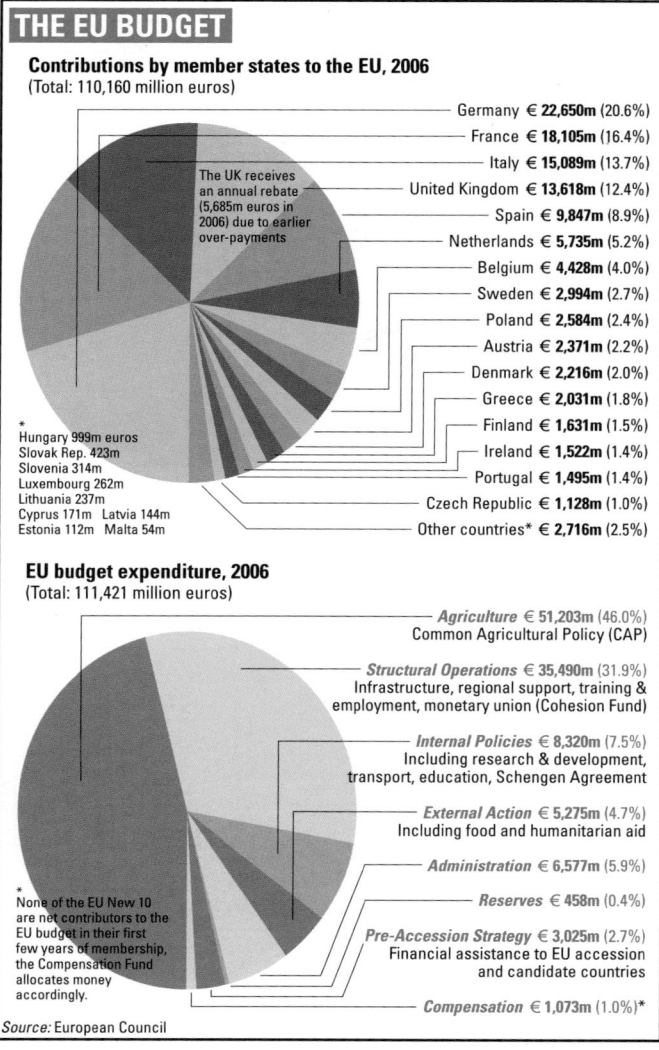

- *Agriculture* € **51,203m** (46.0%)
  Common Agricultural Policy (CAP)
- *Structural Operations* € **35,490m** (31.9%)
  Infrastructure, regional support, training & employment, monetary union (Cohesion Fund)
- *Internal Policies* € **8,320m** (7.5%)
  Including research & development, transport, education, Schengen Agreement
- *External Action* € **5,275m** (4.7%)
  Including food and humanitarian aid
- *Administration* € **6,577m** (5.9%)
- *Reserves* € **458m** (0.4%)
- *Pre-Accession Strategy* € **3,025m** (2.7%)
  Financial assistance to EU accession and candidate countries
- *Compensation* € **1,073m** (1.0%)*

* None of the EU New 10 are net contributors to the EU budget in their first few years of membership, the Compensation Fund allocates money accordingly.

Source: European Council

INCOME

Gross domestic product per person, 2004

Statistics for Denmark include the Faroe Is.

- 26,000 euros (€) and over
- € 21,000 – 25,999
- € 16,000 – 20,999
- € 13,000 – 15,999
- € 9,000 – 12,999
- € 5,000 – 8,999
- Less than € 5,000

Source: Eurostat

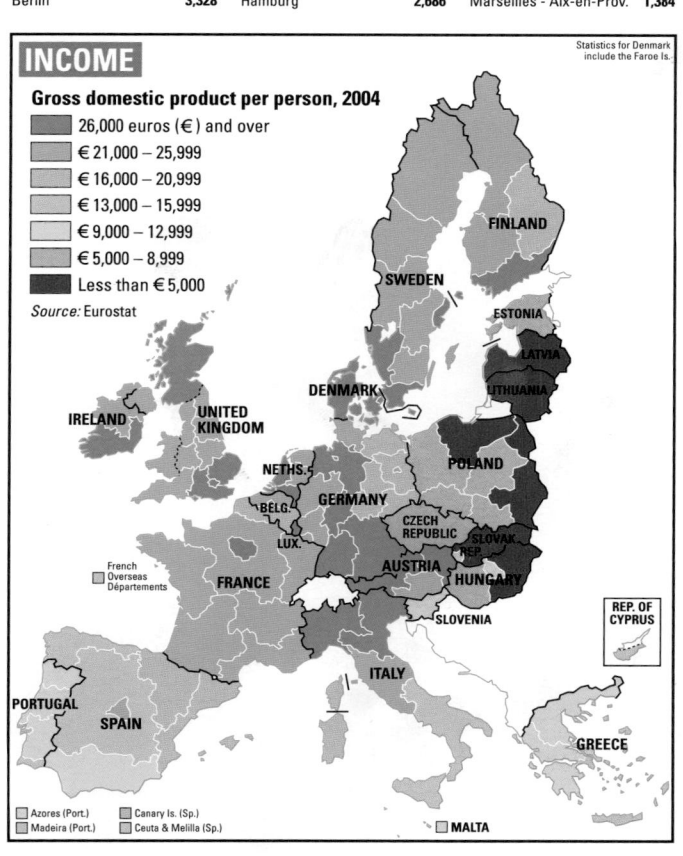

Azores (Port.) Canary Is. (Sp.)
Madeira (Port.) Ceuta & Melilla (Sp.) ■ MALTA

UNEMPLOYMENT

Unemployed as a percentage of the workforce, 2004

Statistics for Denmark include the Faroe Is.

- 20% and over
- 15.0% – 19.9%
- 11.0% – 14.9%
- 8.0% – 10.9%
- 5.0% – 7.9%
- Less than 5.0%

Source: Eurostat

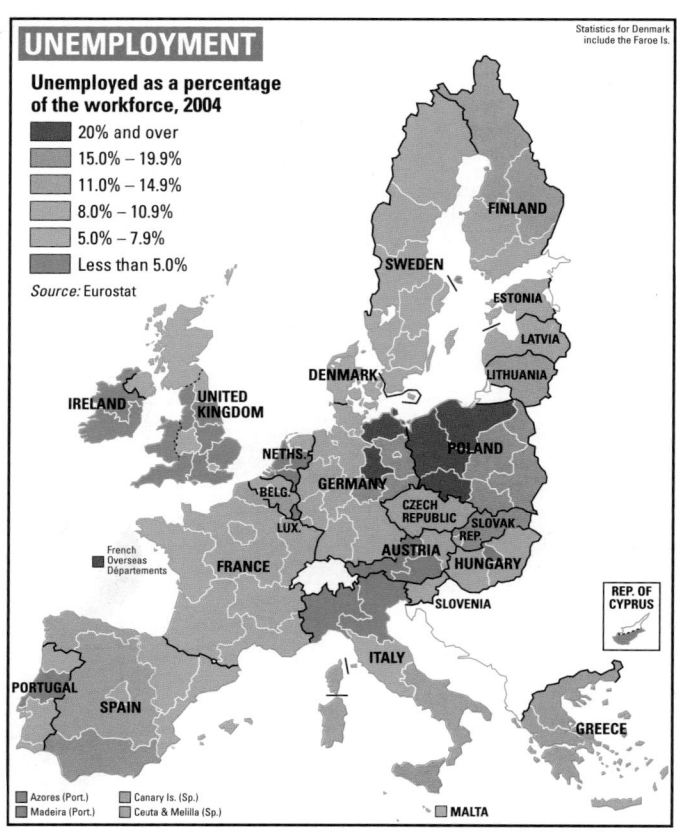

Azores (Port.) Canary Is. (Sp.)
Madeira (Port.) Ceuta & Melilla (Sp.) ■ MALTA

See also... Europe National Parks (54); World Monuments Fund (105)

The listings above refer to a selection of related themes. For more information, see the Contents (2-5).

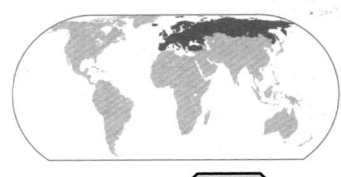

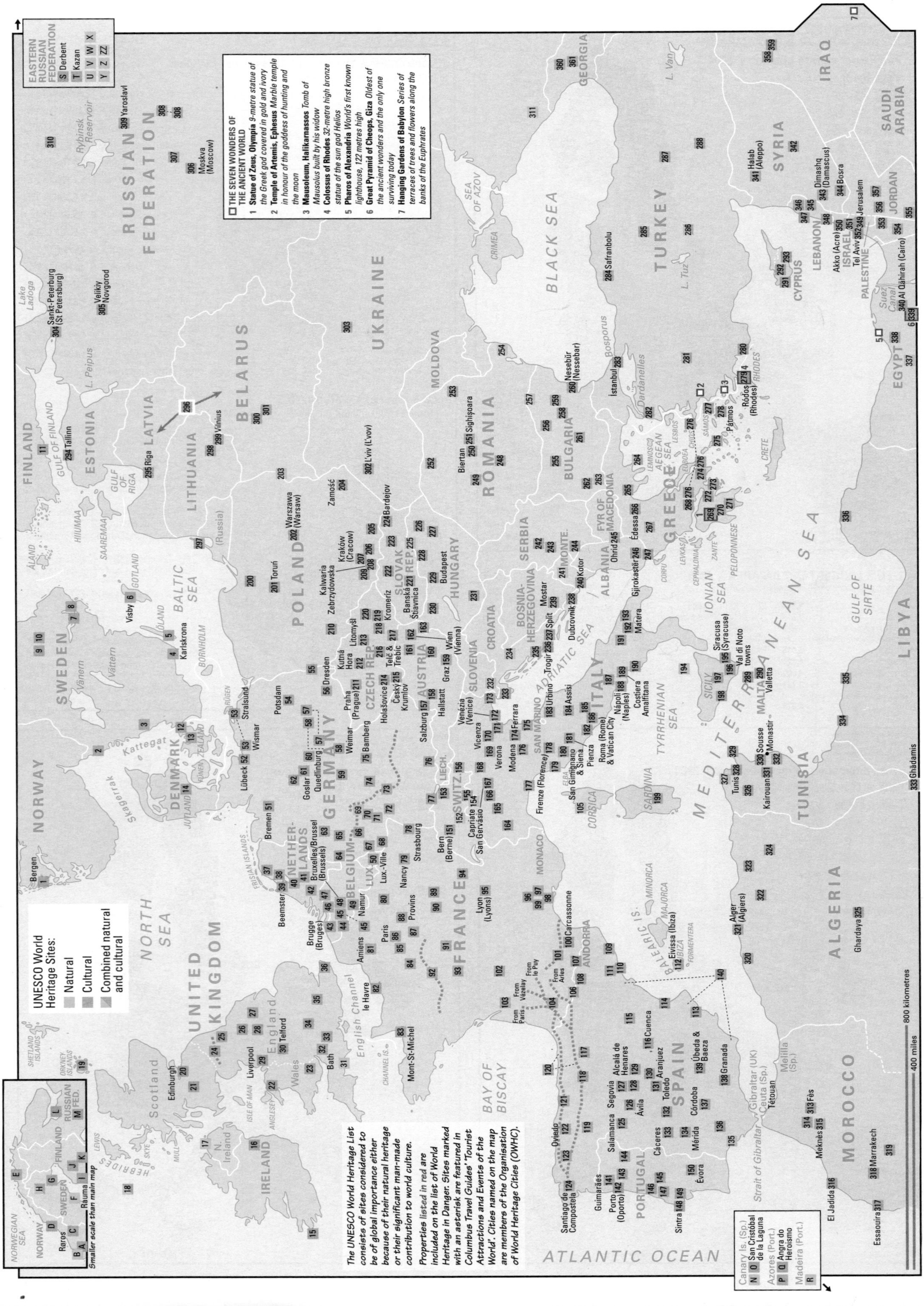

EASTERN RUSSIAN FEDERATION
S Derbent
T Kazan
U V W X
Y Z ZZ

☐ **THE SEVEN WONDERS OF THE ANCIENT WORLD**
1 **Statue of Zeus, Olympia** 9-metre statue of the Greek god covered in gold and ivory
2 **Temple of Artemis, Ephesus** Marble temple in honour of the goddess of hunting and the moon
3 **Mausoleum, Halikarnassos** Tomb of Mausolus built by his widow
4 **Colossus of Rhodes** 32-metre high bronze statue of the sun god Helios
5 **Pharos of Alexandria** World's first known lighthouse, 122 metres high
6 **Great Pyramid of Cheops, Giza** Oldest of the ancient wonders and the only one surviving today
7 **Hanging Gardens of Babylon** Series of terraces of trees and flowers along the banks of the Euphrates

UNESCO World Heritage Sites:
■ Natural
■ Cultural
■ Combined natural and cultural

The UNESCO World Heritage List consists of sites considered to be of global importance either because of their natural heritage or their significant man-made contribution to world culture.

Properties listed in red are included on the list of World Heritage. Sites marked with an asterisk are featured in Columbus Travel Guides' 'Tourist Attractions and Events of the World'. Cities named on the map are members of the Organisation of World Heritage Cities (OWHC).

Canary Is. (Sp.) N O San Cristóbal de la Laguna
Azores (Port.) P Q Angra do Heroísmo
Madeira (Port.) R

Smaller scale than main map

400 miles
800 kilometres

ATLANTIC OCEAN

NORWEGIAN SEA
NORTH SEA
BALTIC SEA
BLACK SEA
MEDITERRANEAN SEA
TYRRHENIAN SEA
ADRIATIC SEA
AEGEAN SEA
IONIAN SEA
SEA OF AZOV

RUSSIAN FEDERATION
NORWAY
SWEDEN
FINLAND
DENMARK
UNITED KINGDOM
IRELAND
NETHERLANDS
BELGIUM
LUX.
FRANCE
GERMANY
SWITZ.
LIECH.
AUSTRIA
ITALY
SPAIN
PORTUGAL
ANDORRA
POLAND
CZECH REP.
SLOVAK REP.
HUNGARY
SLOVENIA
CROATIA
BOSNIA-HERZEGOVINA
SERBIA
MONTE.
ALBANIA
FYR OF MACEDONIA
ROMANIA
BULGARIA
GREECE
MOLDOVA
UKRAINE
BELARUS
LITHUANIA
LATVIA
ESTONIA
TURKEY
CYPRUS
GEORGIA
SYRIA
LEBANON
ISRAEL
PALESTINE
JORDAN
IRAQ
SAUDI ARABIA
EGYPT
LIBYA
TUNISIA
ALGERIA
MOROCCO
MONACO
SAN MARINO
MALTA
SARDINIA
CORSICA
SICILY
CRETE

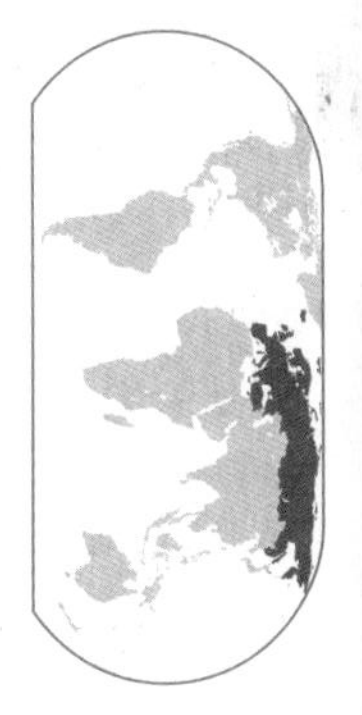

▶ *See also...* Europe National Parks (54); World Monuments Fund (105)

UNESCO: Natural & Cultural Heritage

The listings above refer to a selection of related themes. For more information, see the Contents (2-5).

Numbers: main map Letters: insets

EUROPE (including Turkey & Cyprus)

1 Bergen: Bryggen wharf*, Norway
A Urnes: stave church, Norway
B Geirangerfjorden and Nærøyfjorden, Norway
C Røros: mining town, Norway
D Vega Archipelago, Norway
E Alta: rock drawings, Norway
2 Tanum: rock carvings, Sweden
3 Grimeton: Varberg radio station, Sweden
4 Karlskrona: naval city, Sweden
5 Southern Öland: agricultural landscape, Sweden
6 Visby: Hanseatic town and former Viking site, Sweden
7 Birka and Hovgården: archaeological sites, Sweden
8 Stockholm: Skogskyrkogården cemetery, Sweden; Drottningholms Slot (Drottningholm Royal Palace)*, Sweden
9 Falun: mining area of the Great Copper Mountain, Sweden
10 Engelsberg: ironworks, Sweden
F High Coast, Sweden
G Luleå: Gammelstad church village, Sweden
H Lapponian area, Sweden
I Rauma: old town, Finland; Sammallahdenmäki: Bronze Age burial site, Finland
J Petäjävesi: old church, Finland
K Verla: groundwood and board mill, Finland
11 Helsinki (Helsingfors): Suomenlinna Sea Fortress*, Finland
12 Helsingør (Elsinore): Kronborg Slot (Kronborg Castle)*, Denmark
13 Roskilde: cathedral, Denmark
14 Jelling: mounds, runic stones and church, Denmark
15 Skellig Michael: monastic complex, Ireland
16 Brú Na Bóinne: Newgrange, Knowth and Dowth prehistoric sites, Ireland
17 Giant's Causeway* and its coast, Northern Ireland
18 St Kilda, Scotland
19 Orkney: Neolithic monuments, Scotland
20 Edinburgh: old and new towns (incl. Castle*, Palace of Holyroodhouse*, Royal Mus. & Mus. of Scotland*, Scotch Whisky Heritage Centre & Royal Mile* and Scottish Parliament Building*), Scotland
21 New Lanark: industrial village*, Scotland
22 Castles and town walls of King Edward (incl. Caernarfon Castle* and Conwy Castle*), northwest Wales
23 Blaenavon: industrial landscape (incl. Big Pit National Mining Museum of Wales*), Wales
24 Frontiers of the Roman Empire (1): Hadrian's Wall*, England
25 Durham: castle and cathedral*, England
26 Studley Royal Park and Fountains Abbey ruins, England
27 Derwent Valley mills, England
28 Saltaire: industrial village, England
29 Liverpool: maritime mercantile city (incl. Albert Dock*), England
30 Ironbridge Gorge, England
31 Dorset and East Devon coast, England
32 Bath (incl. Roman baths and pumproom*), England
33 Stonehenge*, Avebury and associated Megalithic sites, England
34 Blenheim Palace, England
35 London: Tower of London*, England; London: Westminster Palace*, Westminster Abbey* and St Margaret's Church, England; Kew: Royal Botanic Gardens, England; Maritime Greenwich*, England
36 Canterbury: cathedral*, St Augustine's Abbey and St Martin's Church, England
37 Wouda steam pumping station, The Netherlands
38 Schokland: prehistoric settlements, The Netherlands
39 Droogmakerij de Beemster (Beemster Polder), The Netherlands
40 Amsterdam: defence line, The Netherlands
41 Utrecht: Rietveld Schröderhuis, The Netherlands
42 Kinderdijk-Elshout: mill network, The Netherlands
43 Brugge (Bruges): historic centre, Belgium
44 Tournai: Cathédrale Notre-Dame, Belgium
45 Belfries of Belgium and France (incl. Onze Lieve Vrouwekathedraal, Antwerpen (Antwerp)*), Belgium/France
46 Antwerpen (Antwerp): Plantin-Moretus Museum, Belgium
47 Flemish Begijnhoven (Béguinages), Belgium
48 Bruxelles/Brussel (Brussels): Grand-Place*, Belgium; Bruxelles/Brussel (Brussels): four town houses of architect Victor Horta, Belgium
49 Canal du Centre: four boat-lifts and environs, la Louvière and le Rœulx, Belgium; Mons: Spiennes Neolithic flint mines, Belgium
50 Luxembourg-Ville: old quarters and fortifications
51 Bremen: town hall and statue of Roland, Germany
52 Lübeck: Hanseatic city, Germany
53 Stralsund and Wismar: historic centres, Germany
54 Berlin: Museumsinsel (incl. Pergamonmuseum*), Germany; Potsdam and SW Berlin: palaces and parks (incl. Schloss Sanssouci*), Germany
55 Muskauer Park, Germany, and Park Muzakowski, Poland
56 Dresden Elbe valley: cultural landscape, Germany
57 Eisleben and Wittenberg: Luther memorials, Germany
58 Dessau-Wörlitz: Garden Kingdom, Germany; Dessau and Weimar: Bauhaus buildings, Germany; Weimar: classical city, Germany
59 Schloss Wartburg, Germany
60 Quedlinburg: collegiate church, castle and old town, Germany
61 Goslar: historic town and Rammelsberg mines, Germany
62 Hildesheim: cathedral and St Michaeliskirche, Germany
63 Essen: Zollverein coal mine industrial complex, Germany
64 Aachen (Aix-la-Chapelle): cathedral, Germany
65 **Köln (Cologne): cathedral***, Germany; Brühl: Schloss Augustusburg & Jagdschl. Falkenlust, Germany
66 Upper Middle Rhine Valley, Germany
67 Trier: Roman monuments, cathedral and Liebfrauenkirche, Germany
68 Völklingen: ironworks, Germany
69 Messel Pit fossil site, Germany
70 Lorsch: abbey and Altenmünster, Germany
71 Speyer: cathedral, Germany
72 Maulbronn: Cistercian monastery complex, Germany
73 Frontiers of the Roman Empire (2): Roman Limes, Germany
74 Würzburg: Residenz with gardens and square, Germany
75 Bamberg, Germany
76 Wies: pilgrimage church, Germany
77 Reichenau: monastic island, Germany
78 Strasbourg: Grand Île, France
79 Nancy: Place Stanislas, Pl. de la Carrière and Pl. d'Alliance, France
80 Reims: Cathédrale Notre-Dame, Abbaye St-Remi and Palais du Tau, France
81 Amiens: cathedral, France
82 Le Havre: city rebuilt after Second World War, France
83 Mont-St-Michel* and its bay, France
84 Chartres: cathedral, France
85 Versailles: palace and park*, France
86 Paris: banks of the Seine (incl. Tour Eiffel*, Musée du Louvre*, Musée d'Orsay* and Cathédrale de Notre-Dame*), France
87 Fontainebleau: palace and park, France
88 Provins: fortified medieval town, France
89 Fontenay: Cistercian abbey, France
90 Vézelay: church and hill, France
91 Bourges: cathedral, France
92 Loire Valley between Chalonnes & Sully-sur-Loire, including Château de Chambord, France
93 St-Savin-sur-Gartempe: church, France
94 Arc-et-Senans: royal saltworks, France
95 Lyon (Lyons): historic city, France
96 Orange: Roman theatre and its surroundings and the triumphal arch, France
97 Avignon: historic centre (incl. Palais des Papes*), France
98 Arles: Roman and Romanesque monuments (incl. Roman amphitheatre*), France
99 Remoulins: Pont du Gard Roman aqueduct, France
100 Carcassonne: historic fortified city*, France
101 Canal du Midi, France
102 Vallée du Vézère: Lascaux* and other decorated caves, France
103 St-Émilion: vineyard landscape, France
104 Way of St James pilgrimage route: four routes through France
105 Golfe de Girolata, Golfe de Porto, Piana Calanches and Réserve naturelle Scandola, Corsica, France
106 Mont Perdu/Monte Perdido, France/Spain
107 Madriu-Perafita-Claror valley: cultural landscape, Andorra
108 Vall de Boí: Catalan Romanesque churches, Spain
109 Barcelona: works of Antonio Gaudí (incl. Parque Güell* and Sagrada Familia*), Spain; Barcelona: Palau de la Música Catalaña and the Hospital de Sant Pau: art nouveau buildings, Spain
110 Tarragona: Roman city of Tárraco, Spain
111 Poblet: Cistercian monastery, Spain
112 Eivissa (Ibiza): biodiversity and culture, Spain
113 Elx (Elche): Palmeral (date palm) landscape, Spain
114 València: La Lonja de la Seda (Silk Exchange), Spain
115 Aragón: Mudéjar architecture, Spain
116 Cuenca: historic walled town, Spain
117 San Millán de la Cogolla: Suso and Yuso monasteries, Spain
118 Burgos: cathedral, Spain; Cuevas de Atapuerca: archaeological site, Spain
119 Las Médulas: Roman gold workings, Spain
120 Camino de Santiago: Way of St James pilgrimage route*, Spain
121 Cuevas de Altamira: archaeological site, Spain
122 Oviedo: churches of the Asturias Kingdom and La Foncalada hydraulic structure, Spain
123 Lugo: Roman walls, Spain
124 Santiago de Compostela: old town (incl. cathedral*), Spain
125 Salamanca: old city, Spain
126 Ávila: old town with extra-muros churches, Spain
127 Segovia: old town and Roman aqueduct*, Spain
128 El Escorial: monastery*, Spain
129 Alcalá de Henares: university and historic precinct, Spain
130 Aranjuez: cultural landscape, Spain
131 Toledo: historic city, Spain
132 Guadalupe: Real Monasterio de Santa María, Spain
133 Cáceres: old town, Spain
134 Mérida: archaeological ensemble, Spain
135 Parque Nacional Doñana, Spain
136 Sevilla (Seville): cathedral*, Alcazar and Archivo de Indias, Spain
137 Córdoba: mosque and historic centre, Spain
138 Granada: Alhambra*, Generalife & Albaicín quarter, Spain
139 Úbeda and Baeza: Renaissance monumental ensembles, Spain
140 Mediterranean seaboard prehistoric rock-art sites, Spain
N Parque Nacional de Garajonay, Gomera, Canary Is.
O San Cristóbal de la Laguna, Tenerife, Canary Is.
P Pico: vineyard landscape, Azores
Q Angra do Heroísmo: central area, Terceira, Azores
R Madeira: Laurisilva (laurel forest)
141 Guimarães: historic centre, Portugal
142 Porto (Oporto): historic centre, Portugal
143 Alto Douro wine region, Portugal
144 Vale do Côa: prehistoric rock-art sites, Portugal
145 Tomar: Convent of Christ, Portugal
146 Batalha: Dominican monastery, Portugal
147 Alcobaça: Cistercian monastery, Portugal
148 Sintra: cultural landscape, Portugal
149 Lisboa (Lisbon): Mosteiro dos Jerónimos* and Torre de Belém*, Portugal
150 Évora: historic centre, Portugal
151 Bern (Berne): old city, Switzerland
152 Jungfrau*-Aletsch-Bietschhorn, Switzerland
153 St Gallen (St Gall): convent, Switzerland
154 Monte San Giorgio, Switzerland
155 Bellinzona: group of fortifications, Switzerland
156 Müstair: Benedictine convent of St John, Switzerland
157 Salzburg: historic centre (incl. Mozart's birthplace and residence*), Austria
158 Hallstatt-Dachstein-Salzkammergut: cultural landscape, Austria
159 Graz: historic centre, Austria
160 Semmering Railway, Austria
161 Wachau: cultural landscape, Austria
162 Wien (Vienna): historic centre (incl. Belvedere*), Austria; Wien (Vienna): Schloss Schönbrunn and gardens*, Austria
163 Neusiedlersee, Austria / Fertő, Hungary: cultural landscape
164 Torino (Turin) and surrounding area: Residences of the Royal House of Savoy, Italy
165 Sacri Monti ('Sacred Mountains') of Piedmont and Lombardy, Italy
166 Milano (Milan): church and convent of Santa Maria delle Grazie with 'The Last Supper' by Leonardo da Vinci, Italy
167 Crespi d'Adda: industrial workers' town, Italy
168 Val Camónica: rock drawings, Italy
169 Verona: historic city, Italy
170 Vicenza: city and the Palladian villas of the Veneto, Italy
171 Pádova (Padua): botanical garden, Italy
172 Venézia (Venice) and its lagoon (incl. Basilica di San Marco*, Palazzo Ducale* and Ponte di Rialto*), Italy
173 Aquileia: archaeological site incl. Patriarchal Basilica, Italy
174 Ferrara: Renaissance city and Po delta, Italy
175 Ravenna: early Christian monuments and mosaics, Italy
176 Modena: cathedral, Torre Civica and Piazza Grande, Italy
177 Portovénere, Cinque Terre (Corniglia, Manarola, Monterosso, Riomaggiore, Vernazza) and the islands (Ísola Palmária, Í. del Tino and Í. del Tinetto), Italy
178 Firenze (Florence): historic centre (incl. Duomo Santa Maria del Fiore*, Galleria degli Uffizi*, Ponte Vecchio*), Italy
179 Pisa: Piazza del Duomo (incl. Torre Pendente: The Leaning Tower*), Italy
180 San Gimignano: historic centre, Italy; Siena: historic centre (incl. Piazza del Campo*), Italy
181 Pienza: historic centre, Italy; Val d'Orcia: Renaissance agricultural landscape, Italy
182 Cervéteri and Tarquínia: Etruscan necropolises, Italy
183 Urbino: historic centre, Italy
184 Assisi: Basilica di San Francesco and other Franciscan sites, Italy
185 Tivoli: Villa d'Este, Italy; Tivoli: Villa Adriana (Hadrian's Villa), Italy
186 Vatican City (incl. Basilica di San Pietro*, Musei Vaticani & Capella Sistina*); Roma (Rome): historic centre and extraterritorial properties of the Holy See & San Paolo fuori le Mura (incl. Colosseo*, Fontana di Trevi*, Foro Romano* and Pantheon*), Italy
187 Caserta: Palazzo Reale & gardens, Vanvitelli aqueduct & San Leucio complex, Italy
188 Nápoli (Naples): historic centre, Italy; Herculaneum, Pompeii* and Torre Annunziata: archaeological areas, Italy
189 Costiera Amalfitana, Italy
190 Cilento area: cultural landscape including Parco Nazionale del Cilento e Vallo di Diano, Certosa di San Lorenzo in Padula and the archaeological sites of Paestum and Vélia, Italy
191 Castel del Monte: medieval castle, Italy
192 Matera: I Sassi di Matera troglodyte settlement, Italy
193 Alberobello: Trulli limestone houses, Italy
194 Ísole Eólie (Lípari Is.), Italy
195 Siracusa (Syracuse) and necropolis of Pantalica, Sicily, Italy
196 Val di Noto: late Baroque towns (Caltagirone, Catánia, Militello in Val di Catánia, Módica, Noto, Palazzolo, Ragusa and Scicli), Sicily, Italy
197 Villa Romana del Casale, Sicily, Italy
198 Agrigento: archaeological area, Sicily, Italy
199 Su Nuraxi di Barúmini, Sardinia, Italy
200 Malbork: Teutonic fortified monastery, Poland
201 Torun: medieval town, Poland
202 Warszawa (Warsaw): historic centre (incl. Warsaw Royal Castle*), Poland
203 Bialowieza Forest, Poland, and Belovezhskaya Puscha, Belarus
204 Zamosc: Renaissance city, Poland
205 Wooden churches of southern Little Poland
206 Wieliczka: salt mines, Poland
207 Kraków (Cracow): historic centre (incl. Market Square* and Wawel Royal Castle*), Poland
208 Kalwaria Zebrzydowska: Mannerist architectural and park landscape complex and pilgrimage park, Poland
209 Oswiecim (Auschwitz): Auschwitz-Birkenau concentration camp*, Poland
210 Jawor and Swidnica: Churches of Peace, Poland
211 Praha (Prague): historic centre (incl. Charles Bridge*, Castle & St Vitus Cathedral* and Old Town Square*), Czech Rep.
212 Kutná Hora*: historical centre, Church of Santa Barbara and Cathedral of Our Lady at Sedlec, Czech Rep.
213 Litomysl Castle, Czech Rep.
214 Holasovice: historical village reservation, Czech Rep.
215 Cesky Krumlov: historic centre, Czech Rep.
216 Telc: historic centre, Czech Rep.; Trebic: Jewish quarter and St Procopius' Basilica, Czech Rep.
217 Lednice-Valtice: cultural landscape, Czech Rep.
218 Brno: Tugendhat Villa, Czech Rep.
219 Zelená Hora: St John of Nepomuk church, Czech Rep.; Kromeríz: castle and gardens, Czech Rep.
220 Olomouc: Holy Trinity column, Czech Rep.
221 Banská Stiavnica: city and mining landscape, Slovak Rep.
222 Vlkolinec: traditional village, Slovak Rep.
223 Spisské Pohradie: Spissky Hrad* and associated monuments, Slovak Rep.
224 Bardejov: fortified medieval town, Slovak Rep.
225 Aggtelek karst caves, Hungary, & Slovak karst caves*, Slovak Rep.
226 Tojaki wine region: cultural landscape, Hungary
227 Hortobágyi National Park, Hungary
228 Hollokö: traditional village, Hungary
229 Budapest: banks of the Danube, Buda Castle* area (incl. Fisherman's Bastion*), Andrássy Avenue and the Millennium Underground, Hungary
230 Pannonhalma: millenary Benedictine monastery and its natural environment, Hungary
231 Pécs: early Christian cemetery of Sopianae, Hungary
232 Skocjan Caves, Slovenia
233 Porec: Episcopal complex, Croatia
234 Plitvice Lakes National Park*, Croatia
235 Sibenik: St James cathedral, Croatia
236 Trogir: historic city, Croatia
237 Split: historic centre with Diocletian's Palace*, Croatia
238 Dubrovnik: old city*, Croatia
239 Mostar: old bridge area, Bosnia-Herzegovina
240 Kotor and its gulf, Montenegro
241 Durmitor National Park, Montenegro
242 Stari Ras: medieval buildings and monuments, Serbia; Sopocani Monastery, Serbia
243 Studenica: monastery, Serbia
244 Decani: monastery*, Serbia
245 Ohrid and its region, FYR of Macedonia
246 Gjirokastër: Ottoman town, Albania
247 **Butrint (Buthrotum): archaeological site**, Albania
248 Horezu: monastery, Romania
249 Orastie Mountains: Dacian fortresses, Romania
250 Southern Transylvania: fortified churches, Romania
251 Sighisoara: historic centre, Romania
252 Maramures: wooden churches, Romania
253 Moldavian churches, Romania
254 Danube Delta, Romania
255 Boyana: church, Bulgaria
256 Sveshtari: Thracian tomb, Bulgaria
257 Srebarna Nature Reserve, Bulgaria
258 Ivanovo: rock-hewn churches, Bulgaria
259 Madara Rider: horseman stone relief, Bulgaria
260 Nesebur (Nessebar): ancient city, Bulgaria
261 Kazanluk: Thracian tomb, Bulgaria
262 Rila: monastery*, Bulgaria
263 Pirin National Park, Bulgaria
264 Athos ('Holy Mountain'), Greece
265 Thessaloníki (Salonika): Palaeochristian and Byzantine monuments, Greece
266 Vergina: archaeological site of Aigai, Greece
267 Metéora: monasteries, Greece
268 Delfí (Delphi): archaeological site*, Greece
269 Olimbía (Olympia): archaeological site*, Greece
270 Bassae: Temple of Apollo Epicurius, Greece
271 Mistrás: medieval ruins, Greece
272 Mycenae* and Tiryns: archaeological sites, Greece
273 Epídavros (Epidaurus): archaeological site*, Greece
274 Athína (Athens): Acropolis*, Greece
275 Delos: archaeological site, Greece
276 Daphni, Hossios Luckas and Néa Moni monasteries, Greece
277 Sámos: Pythagoreion port and Heraion temple remains, Greece
278 Pátmos: historic centre (chorá) with the monastery of St John the Theologian and Cave of the Apocalypse, Greece
279 Ródos (Rhodes): medieval city, Greece
280 Xanthos-Letoon: archaeological site, Turkey
281 Hierapolis-Pamukkale, Turkey
282 Truva (Troy): archaeological site*, Turkey
283 Istanbul: historic areas (incl. Blue Mosque*, Hagia Sophia* and Topkapi Palace*), Turkey
284 Safranbolu: historic city, Turkey
285 Hattusha: Hittite archaeological site, Turkey
286 Göreme National Park* and Cappadocia rock sites, Turkey
287 Divrigi: Great Mosque and hospital, Turkey
288 Nemrut Dag: archaeological site, Turkey
289 Megalithic temples: Ggantija, Hagar Qim*, Mnajdra, Tarxien, Ta'Hagrat and Skorba, Malta
290 Valletta: old city, Malta; Hal Saflieni Hypogeum, Malta
291 Pafos (Paphos): historic city*, Cyprus
292 Troodos region: painted churches, Cyprus
293 Choirokoitia: archaeological site, Cyprus
294 Tallinn: historic centre (incl. Town Hall Square*), Estonia
295 Riga: historic centre*, Latvia
296 Struve Geodetic Arc: a chain of survey triangulations stretching from northern Norway to the Black Sea
297 Curonian Spit, Lithuania/Russian Federation
298 Kernavé Cultural Reserve: archaeological site, Lithuania
299 Vilnius: historic centre, Lithuania
300 Mir: castle complex, Belarus
301 Nyasvizh: architectural, residential and cultural complex of the Radziwill family, Belarus
302 L'viv (L'vov): historic centre, Ukraine
303 Kyiv (Kiev): St Sophia Cathedral*, related monastic buildings and Lavra of Kyiv-Pechersk, Ukraine

RUSSIAN FEDERATION

L Solovetskiye Ostrova: cultural and historic ensemble
M Kizhi Pogost: wooden churches and clock tower
304 Sankt-Peterburg (St Petersburg): historic centre (incl. State Hermitage Museum*)
305 Velikiy Novgorod: historic monuments and surroundings
306 Moskva (Moscow): Kremlin*, Red Square* and St Basil's Cathedral*; Moskva (Moscow): Novodevichy Convent; Kolomenskoye: Church of the Ascension
307 Sergiyev Posad: Trinity Sergius Lavra architectural ensemble
308 Vladimir and Suzdal: White Monuments
309 Yaroslavl: historic centre
310 Ferapontov Monastery
311 Western Caucasus mountain area
S Derbent: citadel, ancient city and fortress
T Kazan: Kremlin
U Komi virgin forests
V Golden Mountains of Altay
W Uvs Nuur basin, Mongolia/Russian Federation
X Lake Baikal
Y Central Sikhote-Alin mountain range
Z Kamchatka volcanoes
ZZ Wrangel Island reserve

AFRICA

312 Tétouan: medina, Morocco
313 Fès: medina*, Morocco
314 Volubilis: archaeological site, Morocco
315 Meknès: historic city, Morocco
316 El Jadida: Portuguese fortified city of Mazagan, Morocco
317 Essaouira: medina, Morocco
318 Marrakech: medina (incl. Djemaa el Fna square* and Saadian Tombs*), Morocco
319 Aït Benhaddou: fortified village, Morocco
320 **Tipasa: archaeological park**, Algeria
321 Alger (Algiers): kasbah, Algeria
322 Benî Hammâd: Al Qal'a, Algeria
323 Djemila: Roman ruins, Algeria
324 Timgad: Roman ruins, Algeria
325 M'Zab Valley: fortified towns, Algeria
326 Dougga (Thugga): archaeological site, Tunisia
327 **Ichkeul National Park**, Tunisia
328 Tunis: medina*, Tunisia; Carthage: archaeological site*, Tunisia
329 Kerkouane: Punic town and its necropolis, Tunisia
330 Sousse: medina, Tunisia
331 Kairouan: holy city, Tunisia
332 El Jem: Roman amphitheatre ruins, Tunisia
333 Ghadamis: old town, Libya
334 Sabratha: archaeological site, Libya
335 Leptis Magna: archaeological site, Libya
336 Cyrene: archaeological site, Libya
337 Wadi Al-Hitan (Whale Valley), Egypt
338 **Abu Mina: Christian ruins**, Egypt
339 Memphis: Pyramid fields from Giza to Dahshur and its necropolis*, Egypt
340 Al Qahirah (Cairo): Islamic city, Egypt

ASIA

341 Halab (Aleppo): ancient city of Aleppo*, Syria
342 Tadmur: archaeological site of Palmyra*, Syria
343 Dimashq (Damascus): ancient city, Syria
344 Bosra: ancient city, Syria
345 Anjar: archaeological site, Lebanon; Baalbek: archaeological site of Heliopolis, Lebanon
346 Holy Valley: early Christian monastic settlements, and Forest of the Cedars of God, Lebanon
347 Byblos: archaeological site, Lebanon
348 Soûr (Tyre): archaeological site of Tyre*, Lebanon
349 **Jerusalem: old city and walls** (incl. Temple Mount*, Western (Wailing) Wall*), site proposed by Jordan
350 Akko: old city of Acre, Israel
351 Biblical tels: Megiddo, Hazor and Beer Sheba, Israel
352 Tel Aviv: White City, Israel
353 Masada: fortress and Roman siege works*, Israel
354 The Incense and Spice Route: desert cities in the Negev, Israel
355 Petra: archaeological site*, Jordan
356 Umm ar Rasas (Kastron Mefa'a): archaeological site, Jordan
357 Qasr Amra: desert castle, Jordan
358 Hatra: fortified city remains, Iraq
359 **Ash Sharqat: ancient city of Ashur**, Iraq
360 Upper Svaneti area, Georgia
361 K'ut'aisi: Bagrati Cathedral and Gelati Monastery, Georgia

▶ **See also...** World Airports (36-38); World Flight Times (39); Europe Railways & Ferries (52-53); London Airport Connections (63) • cont >

The listings above refer to a selection of related themes. For more information, see the Contents (2-5).

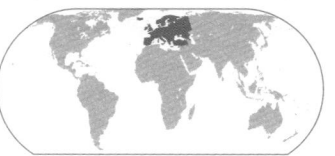

Faced with stern competition from the ever-expanding high-speed rail services and the need to utilise precious runway slots for the more lucrative long-haul routes, several European airlines have been forced into co-operation with rail companies. As a result, many previously prestigious air routes, such as Air France's Paris–Brussels and Lufthansa's Stuttgart–Frankfurt, are now run by, or in conjunction with, high-speed rail operators offering city-centre to city-centre services. As the European rail network expands, as its standards of safety, speed and comfort improve and as the continent's airports become more overcrowded, this development is likely to become more widespread. Increasingly, a consideration of Europe's air routes thus also requires an appreciation of these complementary high-speed rail services.

Note: the airports shown are selected, on the basic of international passenger movements, from those which report to Airports Council International (ACI). Some airports in some countries are therefore not shown.

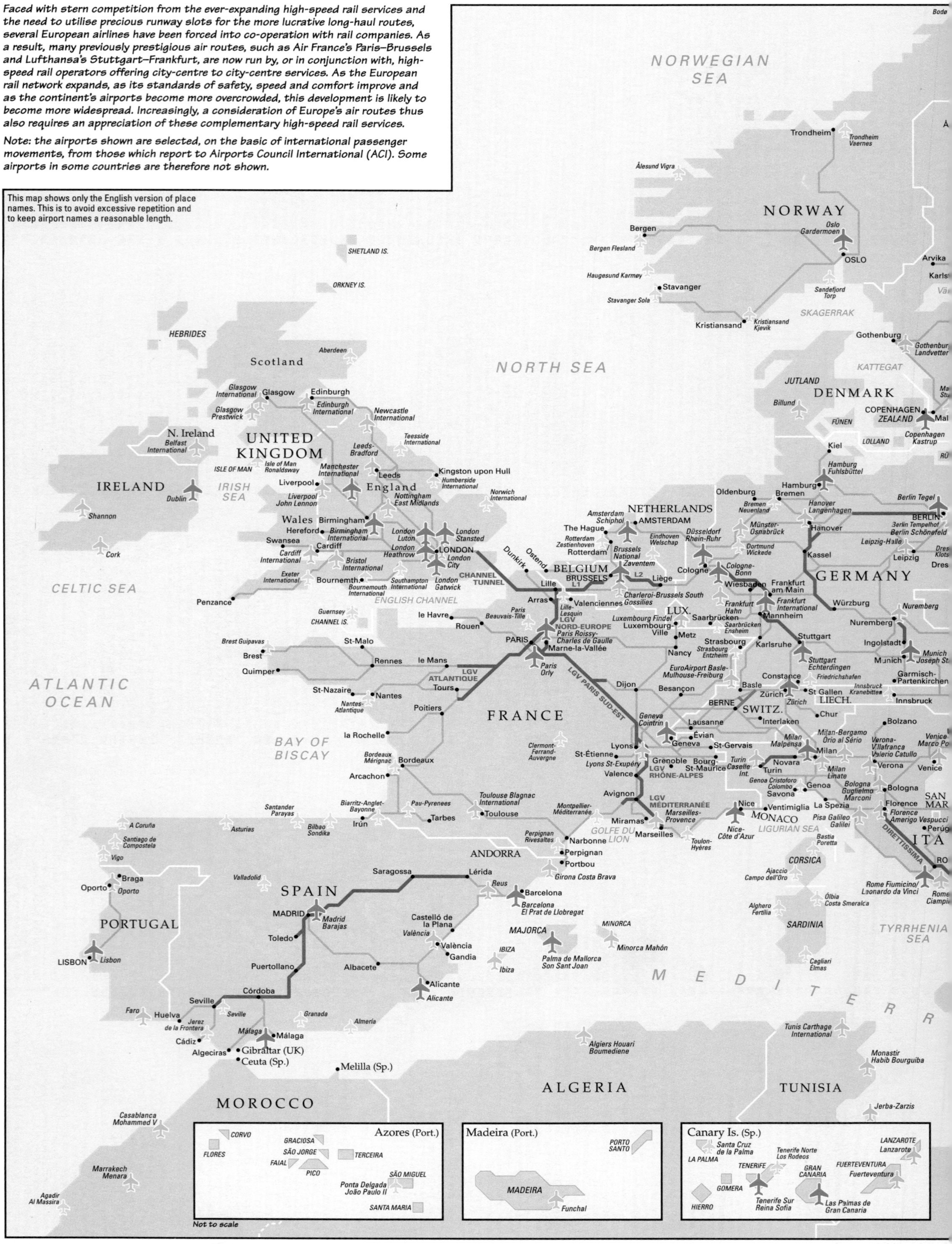

This map shows only the English version of place names. This is to avoid excessive repetition and to keep airport names a reasonable length.

Bode

NORWEGIAN SEA

NORWAY

Trondheim · Trondheim Vaernes

Ålesund Vigra

Bergen · Bergen Flesland

Haugesund Karmøy

Stavanger · Stavanger Sola

Kristiansand · Kristiansand Kjevik

Oslo Gardermoen · OSLO

Arvika

Karlst

Sandefjord Torp

SKAGERRAK

Gothenburg · Gothenburg Landvetter

Vä

SHETLAND IS.

ORKNEY IS.

NORTH SEA

JUTLAND

DENMARK

Billund

COPENHAGEN ZEALAND

FÜNEN

Copenhagen Kastrup

Mal

Mal Stu

LOLLAND

Kiel

HEBRIDES

Scotland

Aberdeen

Glasgow International · Glasgow · Edinburgh · Edinburgh International

Newcastle International

Glasgow Prestwick

N. Ireland · Belfast International

UNITED KINGDOM

ISLE OF MAN · Isle of Man Ronaldsway

Leeds-Bradford

Teesside International

KATTEGAT

Hamburg Fuhlsbüttel

Berlin Tegel

BERLIN

Berlin Tempelhof · Berlin Schönefeld

IRELAND

Dublin

IRISH SEA

Shannon

Cork

Manchester International

Liverpool · Liverpool John Lennon

Leeds

England

Kingston upon Hull · Humberside International

Oldenburg

Bremen Neuenland

Hamburg · Bremen

Hanover Langenhagen

Hanover

Leipzig-Halle

Leipzig

Dres Klots

Dres

Wales · Birmingham · Birmingham International

Swansea · Cardiff · Cardiff International

Nottingham East Midlands

Norwich International

Amsterdam Schiphol · NETHERLANDS · AMSTERDAM

The Hague

Düsseldorf Rhein-Ruhr

Münster-Osnabrück

Dortmund Wickede

Kassel

GERMANY

Würzburg

Nuremberg

CELTIC SEA

Hereford

Bristol · Bristol International

Exeter International

Bournemth.

Bournemouth International

London Luton · London Stansted

London Heathrow · LONDON · London City

Southampton International · London Gatwick

Rotterdam Zestienhoven · Rotterdam

Eindhoven Welschap

Brussels National Zaventem

Cologne

Liège

Cologne-Bonn

Frankfurt am Main

Wiesbaden · Frankfurt Hahn · Frankfurt International

Mannheim

Penzance

Guernsey CHANNEL IS.

ENGLISH CHANNEL

Dunkirk · Ostend

Lille · BELGIUM · BRUSSELS

L1

Arras

CHANNEL TUNNEL

le Havre

Rouen

Beauvais-Tille

Lille-Lesquin LGV

Valenciennes

Charleroi-Brussels South Gosselies

LUX.

Luxembourg Findel · Luxembourg Ville

Saarbrücken · Saarbrücken Ensheim

Metz

L2

Strasbourg

Karlsruhe

Stuttgart

Stuttgart Echterdingen

Ingolstadt

Munich · Munich Joseph St.

Garmisch-Partenkirchen

ATLANTIC OCEAN

Brest Guipavas · Brest

Quimper

St-Malo

Rennes · le Mans

Nantes · Nantes Atlantique

St-Nazaire

Poitiers

LGV ATLANTIQUE

Tours

PARIS

Paris Beauvais-Tille

NORD-EUROPE

Paris Roissy-Charles de Gaulle · Marne-la-Vallée

Paris Orly

FRANCE

Dijon

Nancy

Strasbourg Entzheim

EuroAirport Basle-Mulhouse-Freiburg

LGV PARIS SUD-EST

Besançon

Basle

Zürich

BERNE · SWITZ.

Constance

St Gallen Kranebitten

Innsbruck · Innsbruck Kranebitten

LIECH. · Chur

Nuremberg

BAY OF BISCAY

la Rochelle

Bordeaux Mérignac · Bordeaux

Arcachon

Clermont-Ferrand-Auvergne

St-Étienne

Lyons · Lyons St-Exupéry

Valence

LGV RHÔNE-ALPES

Geneva Cointrin · Lausanne

Évian · Geneva · St-Gervais

Grenoble · Bourg-St-Maurice

Turin Caselle Int.

Turin

Bolzano

Milan-Bergamo Orio al Serio

Milan · Milan Malpensa

Milan Linate

Verona-Villafranca Valerio Catullo · Verona

Venice Marco Po

Venice

Santander Parayas

Biarritz-Anglet-Bayonne

Pau-Pyrenees

Toulouse Blagnac International

Irún

Bilbao Sondika

Montpellier-Méditerranée

Avignon

LGV MÉDITERRANÉE

Marseilles-Provence

Nice

Miramas · Marseilles

Toulon-Hyères

Nice-Côte d'Azur

MONACO

LIGURIAN SEA

Ventimiglia

Genoa Cristoforo Colombo · Savona

Genoa

La Spezia

Bologna Guglielmo Marconi · Bologna

Florence

Florence Amerigo Vespucci

SAN MAR

ITA

DIRETTISSIMA

A Coruña

Santiago de Compostela

Vigo

Asturias

Tarbes · Toulouse

Perpignan Rivesaltes

Narbonne

GOLFE DU LION

Perpignan

Portbou

Ajaccio Campo dell'Oro

CORSICA

Bastia Poretta

Olbia Costa Smeralda

Alghero Fertilia

SARDINIA

TYRRHENIA SEA

Rome Fiumicino/ Leonardo da Vinci

Rome Ciampi

RO

Braga

Oporto · Oporto

PORTUGAL

LISBON · Lisbon

Faro

Huelva

Cádiz

Algeciras · Gibraltar (UK)

Ceuta (Sp.)

Valladolid

Saragossa · Lérida

SPAIN

MADRID · Madrid Barajas

Toledo

Puertollano

Córdoba

Seville · Seville

Jerez de la Frontera

Málaga · Málaga

Granada

Almería

Melilla (Sp.)

Reus

Girona Costa Brava

Barcelona

Barcelona El Prat de Llobregat

Castelló de la Plana

València · València

Gandia

Albacete

Alicante · Alicante

MAJORCA

IBIZA · Ibiza · Ibiza

Palma de Mallorca Son Sant Joan

MINORCA

Minorca Mahón

ANDORRA

Cagliari Elmas

M E D I T E R R

Algiers Houari Boumediene

Tunis Carthage International

Monastir Habib Bourguiba

Jerba-Zarzis

Casablanca Mohammed V

MOROCCO

ALGERIA

TUNISIA

Marrakech Menara

Agadir Al Massira

Azores (Port.)

CORVO · GRACIOSA

FLORES · SÃO JORGE · TERCEIRA

FAIAL

PICO

SÃO MIGUEL

Ponta Delgada João Paulo II

SANTA MARIA

Madeira (Port.)

PORTO SANTO

MADEIRA

Funchal

Canary Is. (Sp.)

Santa Cruz de la Palma · Tenerife Norte Los Rodeos

LA PALMA

TENERIFE

GRAN CANARIA

GOMERA

HIERRO

Tenerife Sur Reina Sofía

LANZAROTE · Lanzarote

FUERTEVENTURA · Fuerteventura

Las Palmas de Gran Canaria

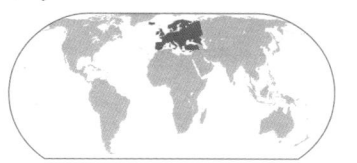

▶ *See also... cont <* • Berlin Airport Connections
(71); Paris Airport Connections (75)

The listings above refer to a selection of related themes.
For more information, see the Contents (2-5).

AIRPORTS (passengers handled, year to end-Oct 2005):

✈ **Over five million international** passengers

✈ **Between one and five million international** passengers

✈ Less than one million international passengers,
but **more than 400,000 total passengers**

HIGH-SPEED TRAINS:

High-speed trains are defined by the International Union of Railways (UIC) as trains able to achieve a minimum of 200 km/hour in western Europe and 160 km/hr (eventually 200 km/hr) in eastern Europe.

Although many run on dedicated high-speed track, most services include stretches on conventional rails, much of which is being upgraded to accommodate greater speeds.

With frequent introductions of new high-speed rolling stock, services are constantly expanding to new destinations

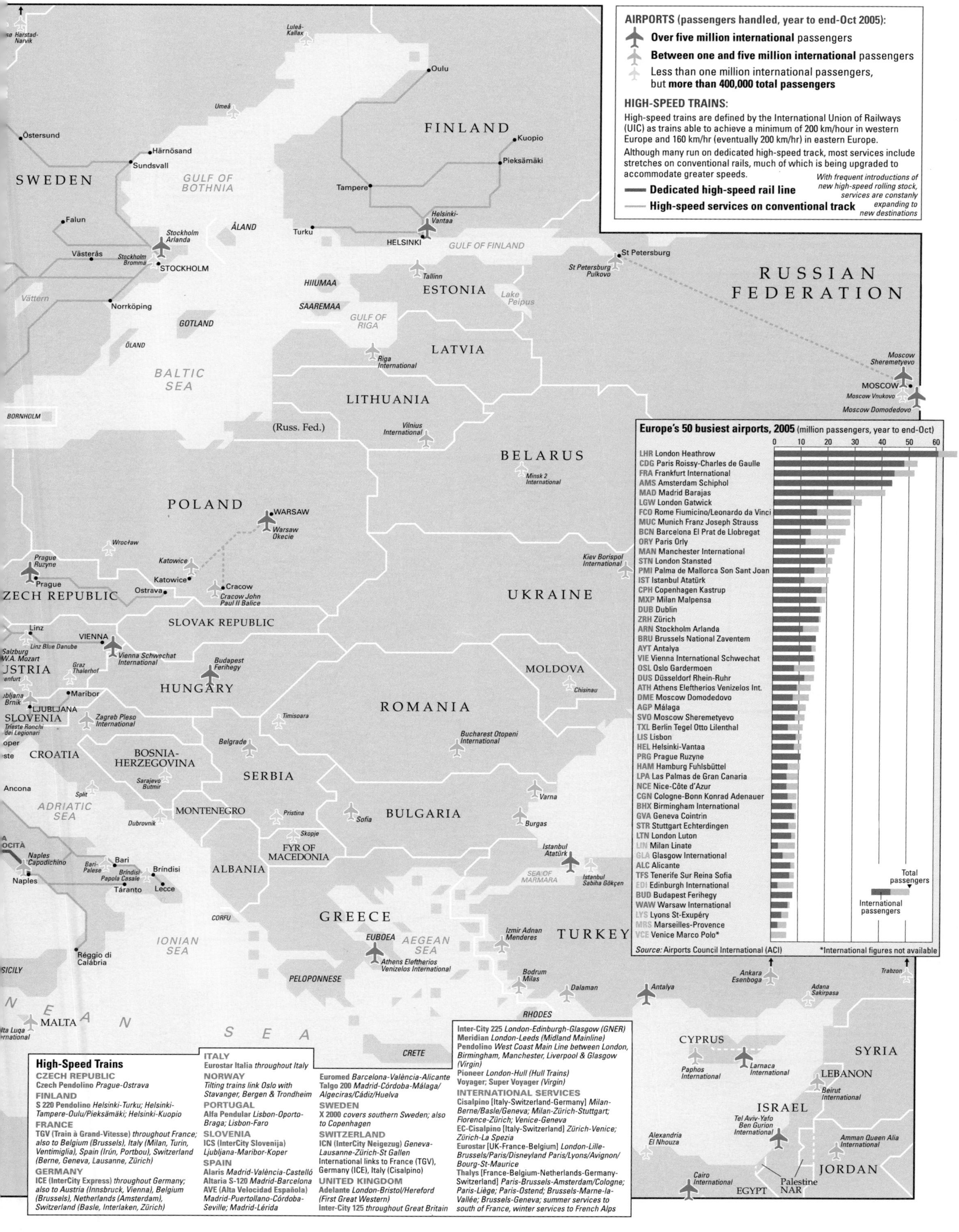

━━━ **Dedicated high-speed rail line**

─── **High-speed services on conventional track**

Europe's 50 busiest airports, 2005 (million passengers, year to end-Oct)

Scale: 0 10 20 30 40 50 60

- LHR London Heathrow
- CDG Paris Roissy-Charles de Gaulle
- FRA Frankfurt International
- AMS Amsterdam Schiphol
- MAD Madrid Barajas
- LGW London Gatwick
- FCO Rome Fiumicino/Leonardo da Vinci
- MUC Munich Franz Joseph Strauss
- BCN Barcelona El Prat de Llobregat
- ORY Paris Orly
- MAN Manchester International
- STN London Stansted
- PMI Palma de Mallorca Son Sant Joan
- IST Istanbul Atatürk
- CPH Copenhagen Kastrup
- MXP Milan Malpensa
- DUB Dublin
- ZRH Zürich
- ARN Stockholm Arlanda
- BRU Brussels National Zaventem
- AYT Antalya
- VIE Vienna International Schwechat
- OSL Oslo Gardermoen
- DUS Düsseldorf Rhein-Ruhr
- ATH Athens Eleftherios Venizelos Int.
- DME Moscow Domodedovo
- AGP Málaga
- SVO Moscow Sheremetyevo
- TXL Berlin Tegel Otto Lilenthal
- LIS Lisbon
- HEL Helsinki-Vantaa
- PRG Prague Ruzyne
- HAM Hamburg Fuhlsbüttel
- LPA Las Palmas de Gran Canaria
- NCE Nice-Côte d'Azur
- CGN Cologne-Bonn Konrad Adenauer
- BHX Birmingham International
- GVA Geneva Cointrin
- STR Stuttgart Echterdingen
- LTN London Luton
- LIN Milan Linate
- GLA Glasgow International
- ALC Alicante
- TFS Tenerife Sur Reina Sofia
- EDI Edinburgh International
- BUD Budapest Ferihegy
- WAW Warsaw International
- LYS Lyons St-Exupéry
- MRS Marseilles-Provence
- VCE Venice Marco Polo*

Total passengers

International passengers

Source: Airports Council International (ACI)

*International figures not available

High-Speed Trains

CZECH REPUBLIC
Czech Pendolino Prague-Ostrava

FINLAND
S 220 Pendolino Helsinki-Turku; Helsinki-Tampere-Oulu/Pieksämäki; Helsinki-Kuopio

FRANCE
TGV (Train à Grand-Vitesse) throughout France; also to Belgium (Brussels), Italy (Milan, Turin, Ventimiglia), Spain (Irún, Portbou), Switzerland (Berne, Geneva, Lausanne, Zürich)

GERMANY
ICE (InterCity Express) throughout Germany; also to Austria (Innsbruck, Vienna), Belgium (Brussels), Netherlands (Amsterdam), Switzerland (Basle, Interlaken, Zürich)

ITALY
Eurostar Italia throughout Italy

NORWAY
Tilting trains link Oslo with Stavanger, Bergen & Trondheim

PORTUGAL
Alfa Pendular Lisbon-Oporto-Braga; Lisbon-Faro

SLOVENIA
ICS (InterCity Slovenija) Ljubljana-Maribor-Koper

SPAIN
Alaris Madrid-València-Castelló
Altaria S-120 Madrid-Barcelona
AVE (Alta Velocidad Española) Madrid-Puertollano-Córdoba-Seville; Madrid-Lérida

SWEDEN
X 2000 covers southern Sweden; also to Copenhagen

SWITZERLAND
ICN (InterCity Neigezug) Geneva-Lausanne-Zürich-St Gallen
International links to France (TGV), Germany (ICE), Italy (Cisalpino)

UNITED KINGDOM
Adelante London-Bristol/Hereford (First Great Western)
Inter-City 125 throughout Great Britain
Inter-City 225 London-Edinburgh-Glasgow (GNER)
Meridian London-Leeds (Midland Mainline)
Pendolino West Coast Main Line between London, Birmingham, Manchester, Liverpool & Glasgow (Virgin)
Pioneer London-Hull (Hull Trains)
Voyager; Super Voyager (Virgin)

INTERNATIONAL SERVICES
Cisalpino [Italy-Switzerland-Germany] Milan-Berne/Basle/Geneva; Milan-Zürich-Stuttgart; Florence-Zürich; Venice-Geneva
EC-Cisalpino [Italy-Switzerland] Zürich-Venice; Zürich-La Spezia
Eurostar [UK-France-Belgium] London-Lille-Brussels/Paris/Disneyland Paris/Lyons/Avignon/Bourg-St-Maurice
Thalys [France-Belgium-Netherlands-Germany-Switzerland] Paris-Brussels-Amsterdam/Cologne; Paris-Liège; Paris-Ostend; Brussels-Marne-la-Vallée; Brussels-Geneva; summer services to south of France, winter services to French Alps

SPAIN (other)
Euromed Barcelona-València-Alicante
Talgo 200 Madrid-Córdoba-Málaga; Algeciras/Cádiz/Huelva

Map labels (selection):

SWEDEN, FINLAND, RUSSIAN FEDERATION, ESTONIA, LATVIA, LITHUANIA, BELARUS, POLAND, CZECH REPUBLIC, SLOVAK REPUBLIC, AUSTRIA, HUNGARY, UKRAINE, MOLDOVA, ROMANIA, SLOVENIA, CROATIA, BOSNIA-HERZEGOVINA, SERBIA, MONTENEGRO, FYR OF MACEDONIA, ALBANIA, BULGARIA, GREECE, TURKEY, CYPRUS, SYRIA, LEBANON, ISRAEL, JORDAN, EGYPT, MALTA

GULF OF BOTHNIA, ÅLAND, GULF OF FINLAND, BALTIC SEA, GULF OF RIGA, GOTLAND, ÖLAND, BORNHOLM, HIIUMAA, SAAREMAA, Lake Peipus, ADRIATIC SEA, IONIAN SEA, AEGEAN SEA, SEA OF MARMARA, MEDITERRANEAN SEA, CORFU, EUBOEA, PELOPONNESE, CRETE, RHODES, SICILY, VÄTTERN

Oslo area cities: Östersund, Härnösand, Sundsvall, Falun, Västerås, Norrköping, Stockholm Arlanda, Stockholm Bromma, STOCKHOLM, Luleå-Kallax, Umeå, Oulu, Kuopio, Pieksämäki, Tampere, Turku, Helsinki-Vantaa, HELSINKI, Tallinn, Riga International, St Petersburg Pulkovo, St Petersburg, Moscow Sheremetyevo, MOSCOW, Moscow Vnukovo, Moscow Domodedovo, Minsk 2 International, Vilnius International, Kiev Borispol International, WARSAW, Warsaw Okecie, Wrocław, Katowice, Cracow, Cracow John Paul II Balice, Ostrava, Prague Ruzyne, Prague, Linz Blue Danube, Linz, VIENNA, Vienna Schwechat International, Salzburg W.A. Mozart, Graz Thalerhof, Maribor, LJUBLJANA, Ljubljana Brnik, Zagreb Pleso International, Budapest Ferihegy, Chisinau, Timisoara, Bucharest Otopeni International, Belgrade, Sarajevo Butmir, Split, Dubrovnik, Pristina, Skopje, Sofia, Varna, Burgas, Istanbul Atatürk, Istanbul Sabiha Gökçen, Izmir Adnan Menderes, Bodrum Milas, Dalaman, Antalya, Ankara Esenboga, Adana Sakirpasa, Trabzon, Athens Eleftherios Venizelos International, Paphos International, Larnaca International, Beirut International, Tel Aviv-Yafo Ben Gurion International, Amman Queen Alia International, Alexandria El Nhouza, Cairo International, Palestine NAR, Harstad-Narvik

Italy: Naples Capodichino, Naples, Bari Palese, Bari, Brindisi Papola Casale, Brindisi, Táranto, Lecce, Réggio di Calábria, Ancona, Trieste Ronchi dei Legionari, Koper

Railways & Ferries

See also... Cruising (40-41); Europe Airports & High-Speed Rail (50-51); UK Airports, Motorways & Ferries (62)

The listings above refer to a selection of related themes. For more information, see the Contents (2-5).

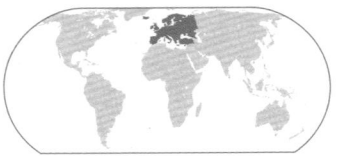

This map shows principal passenger rail and shipping routes in Europe. Some of the railways marked have limited services but are included because of their significance (such as connection to resort or international crossing).

A number of European rail passes are available, offering free travel on many rail and ferry services.

The Eurailpass is valid for first-class rail travel in the countries shown on the map. For those under 26, the Eurailpass Youth is valid in the same countries for second-class rail travel. The pass is not available to European residents or to visitors from Algeria, Morocco, Tunisia, Turkey or the Russian Federation.

European residents are eligible for the Inter-Rail pass, offering train travel in the area shown on the map, excluding the country of purchase.

Passes are available for one or more zones within the validity area.

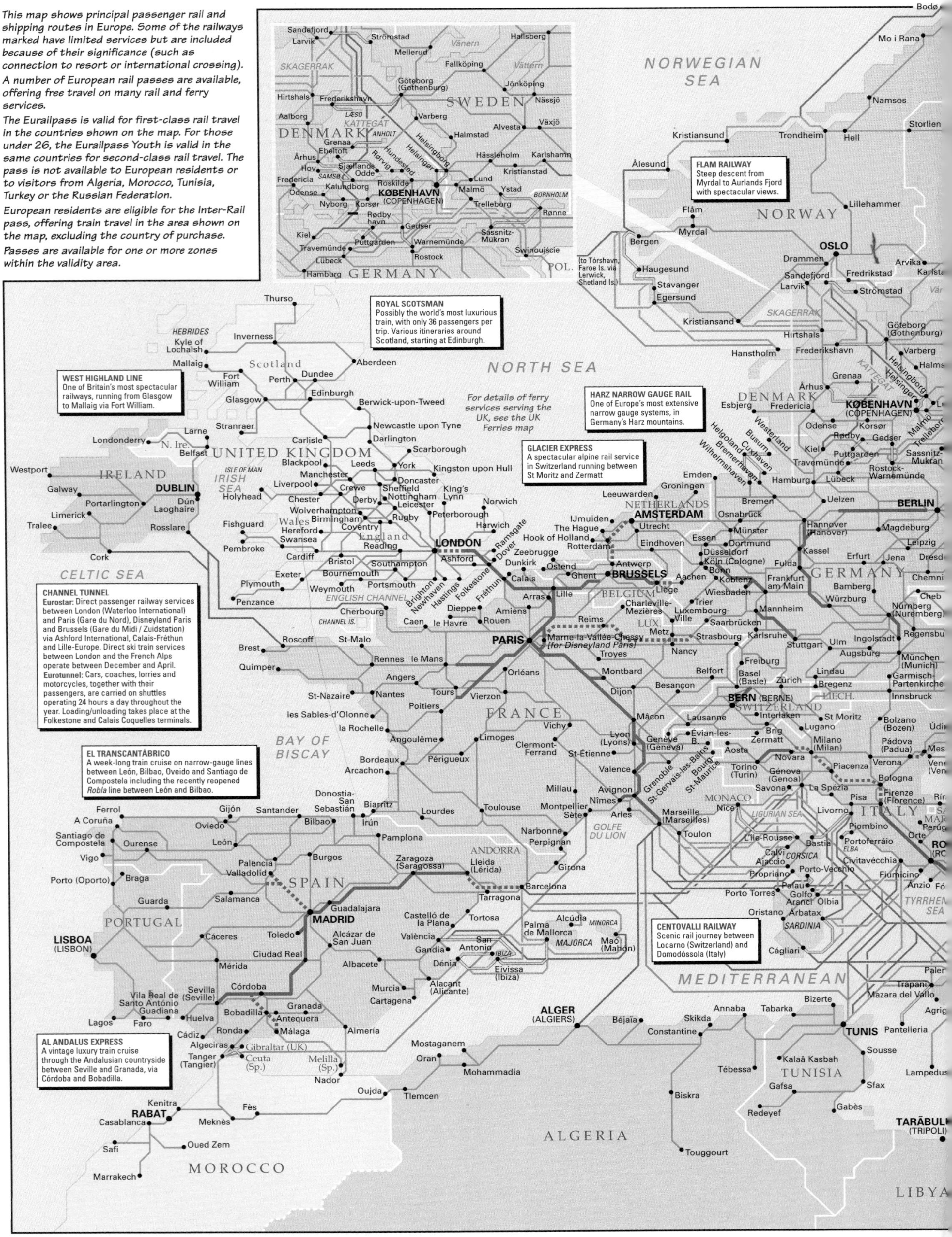
NORWEGIAN SEA
NORTH SEA
CELTIC SEA
BAY OF BISCAY
MEDITERRANEAN
NORWAY
SWEDEN
DENMARK
UNITED KINGDOM
IRELAND
NETHERLANDS
BELGIUM
LUX.
GERMANY
FRANCE
SWITZERLAND
LIECH.
ITALY
SPAIN
PORTUGAL
ANDORRA
MONACO
MOROCCO
ALGERIA
TUNISIA
LIBYA
OSLO
KØBENHAVN (COPENHAGEN)
LONDON
DUBLIN
AMSTERDAM
BRUSSELS
BERLIN
PARIS
BERN (BERNE)
MADRID
LISBOA (LISBON)
ALGER (ALGIERS)
TUNIS
RABAT
ROYAL SCOTSMAN
Possibly the world's most luxurious train, with only 36 passengers per trip. Various itineraries around Scotland, starting at Edinburgh.
WEST HIGHLAND LINE
One of Britain's most spectacular railways, running from Glasgow to Mallaig via Fort William.
FLAM RAILWAY
Steep descent from Myrdal to Aurlands Fjord with spectacular views.
HARZ NARROW GAUGE RAIL
One of Europe's most extensive narrow gauge systems, in Germany's Harz mountains.
GLACIER EXPRESS
A spectacular alpine rail service in Switzerland running between St Moritz and Zermatt
For details of ferry services serving the UK, see the UK Ferries map
(to Tórshavn, Faroe Is. via Lerwick, Shetland Is.)
Marne-la-Vallée-Chessy [for Disneyland Paris]
CHANNEL TUNNEL
Eurostar: Direct passenger railway services between London (Waterloo International) and Paris (Gare du Nord), Disneyland Paris and Brussels (Gare du Midi / Zuidstation) via Ashford International, Calais-Fréthun and Lille-Europe. Direct ski train services between London and the French Alps operate between December and April.
Eurotunnel: Cars, coaches, lorries and motorcycles, together with their passengers, are carried on shuttles operating 24 hours a day throughout the year. Loading/unloading takes place at the Folkestone and Calais Coquelles terminals.
EL TRANSCANTÁBRICO
A week-long train cruise on narrow-gauge lines between León, Bilbao, Oveido and Santiago de Compostela including the recently reopened Robla line between León and Bilbao.
CENTOVALLI RAILWAY
Scenic rail journey between Locarno (Switzerland) and Domodóssola (Italy)
AL ANDALUS EXPRESS
A vintage luxury train cruise through the Andalusian countryside between Seville and Granada, via Córdoba and Bobadilla.

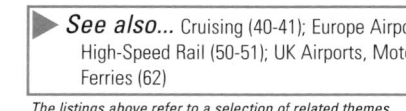

▶ *See also...* Cruising (40-41); Europe Airports & High-Speed Rail (50-51); UK Airports, Motorways & Ferries (62)

The listings above refer to a selection of related themes. For more information, see the Contents (2-5).

RAILWAYS:

———— Dedicated high-speed rail line — *High-speed rail services also run on many normal lines*

·········· High-speed line under construction

———— Other railway

SHIPPING SERVICES (with average shortest journey times):
Times may vary depending on the operator, vessel and weather conditions. Night sailings usually take longer.

———— 3 hours or less

–––––– 3 hours 1 min – 10 hours — *Pecked lines are used to identify particular ferry routes and do **not** represent a different type of service.*

–––––– 10 hours 1 min – 20 hours

–––––– Over 20 hours

EURAIL PASS AND INTER-RAIL PASS:

Inter-Rail pass *and* Eurailpass valid in these countries

Inter-Rail pass valid, Eurailpass not valid

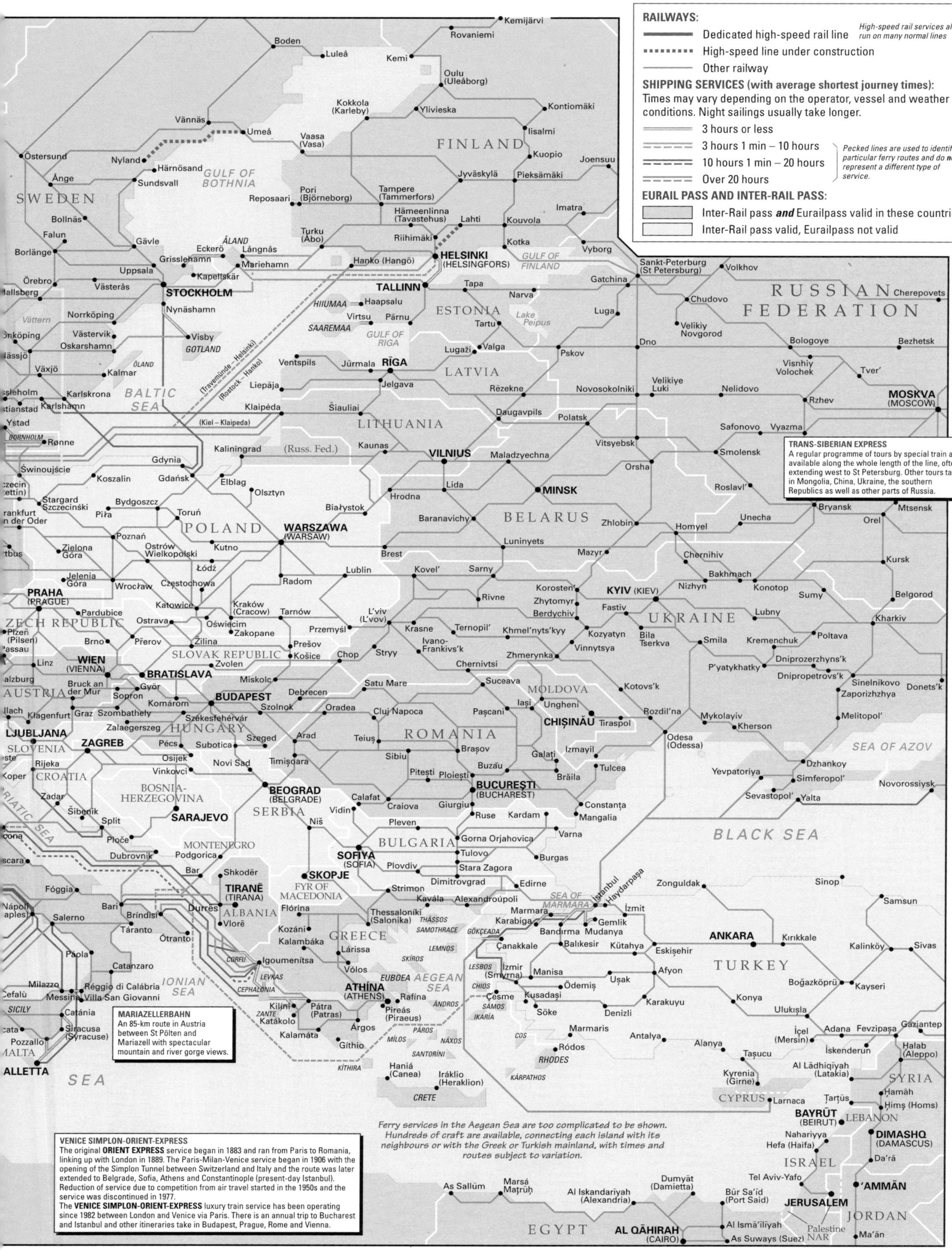

TRANS-SIBERIAN EXPRESS
A regular programme of tours by special train are available along the whole length of the line, often extending west to St Petersburg. Other tours take in Mongolia, China, Ukraine, the southern Republics as well as other parts of Russia.

MARIAZELLERBAHN
An 85-km route in Austria between St Pölten and Mariazell with spectacular mountain and river gorge views.

VENICE SIMPLON-ORIENT-EXPRESS
The original **ORIENT EXPRESS** service began in 1883 and ran from Paris to Romania, linking up with London in 1889. The Paris-Milan-Venice service began in 1906 with the opening of the Simplon Tunnel between Switzerland and Italy and the route was later extended to Belgrade, Sofia, Athens and Constantinople (present-day Istanbul). Reduction of service due to competition from air travel started in the 1950s and the service was discontinued in 1977.
The **VENICE SIMPLON-ORIENT-EXPRESS** luxury train service has been operating since 1982 between London and Venice via Paris. There is an annual trip to Bucharest and Istanbul and other itineraries take in Budapest, Prague, Rome and Vienna.

Ferry services in the Aegean Sea are too complicated to be shown. Hundreds of craft are available, connecting each island with its neighbours or with the Greek or Turkish mainland, with times and routes subject to variation.

▶ **See also...** UNESCO Heritage (48-49);

The listings above refer to a selection of related themes. For more information, see the Contents (2-5).

This map shows the most important areas that have been designated as National Parks throughout Western and Central Europe.

Sites marked with an asterisk (*) are featured in Columbus Travel Guides' *Tourist Attractions and Events of the World*

Iceland
1. Jökulsárgljúfur Spectacular glacial canyon landscape
2. Skaftafell Example of active glacial landscape
3. Thingvellir Broad forested plain, home of historic Iceland parliam't

Norway
4. Øvre Pasvik Forest & tundra
5. Stabbursdalen Arctic landscape: tundra, lakes, gravel plains & forest
6. Øvre Anarjokka Undulating tundra with woodland & lakes
7. Reisa Mixed mountain country
8. Øvre Dividal Mountainous country with tundra & woodland
9. Ånderdalen Mixed mountain country
10. Saltfjellet-Svartisen Varied landscape; fjords, mountains & glacier
11. Børgefjell Remote mountain area with varied habitats
12. Gressåmoen Mountainous country & spruce forest
13. Dovrefjell Mountainous tundra & snowfields; famous for its flora
14. Rondane Mixed mountain country
15. Jostedalsbreen Europe's largest mainland glacier
16. Jotunheimen Mountainous area with tundra, bogs & forest
17. Hardangervidda Large mountain plateau, a popular walking area

Sweden
18. Vadvetjåkka Wild terrain with karst caves
19. Abisko Mountain & forest with tundra, lakes & rivers
20. Muddus Forest, tundra & bog
21. Padjelanta, Sarek and Stora Sjöfallet 3 parks protect Europe's largest wilderness area; mixed landscape
22. Pieljekaise Wooded mountain country with tundra, open water & bogs
23. Skuleskogen Coastal forest landscape
24. Töfsingdalen Woodland, tundra & bog
25. Sånfjället Woodland, tundra & bog
26. Hamra Woodland, tundra & bog, noted for its insects
27. Garphyttan Forest & meadows
28. Tiveden Hilly forest, lakes & bogs
29. Store Mosse Predominantly boggy, with lakes & forest
30. Gotska Sandön Sand & gravel island

Finland
31. Pallas-ja-Ounastunturin Upland plateau & taiga, with lakes, tundra, gorges & forest
32. Lemmenjoen Wilderness mountain area; gold rush in 1940's
33. Urho Kekkosen Large wilderness area with fells, forest & peatlands
34. Pyhätunturin Mountainous area with tundra, bogs & forest
35. Oulangen Varied tundra landscape
36. Petkeljärven Typical Finnish lakeland scenery
37. Linnansaaren Lake & islands
38. Pyhä-Häkin Mainly forest & bog
39. Seitsemisen Typical S Finland landscape with forest & bog
40. Liesjärven Lakes, previously cultivated land & forest
41. Saaristomeren Extensive island group with mixed habitats

Denmark
42. Rebild Bakker Glacial valleys, hills & woodland; home to largest 4th July celebrations outside US

Ireland
43. Glenveagh Mixed upland area
44. Connemara Typical W Ireland mountain area
45. Killarney* Ancient woodland with moorland, lakes, bogs, wetland & mountains
46. Wicklow Mountains Partly wooded mountains with upland moorland & grassland

United Kingdom
47. Cairngorms Mountain region with ski resorts
48. Loch Lomond & The Trossachs Lakes & wooded valley with literary associations
49. Northumberland Mainly upland grassy moorland; Hadrian's Wall in S
50. Lake District Mountain & lakeland; very popular all year
51. Yorkshire Dales Varied upland country
52. North York Moors Hilly uplands with heather moorland
53. Peak District Limestone in the south, with many caves; high peat moors in the north
54. Snowdonia* Mountain country with moorland, grassland & woodland
55. Pembrokeshire Coast Scenic coastline; varied seabird habitats
56. Brecon Beacons* Mainly grass-covered mountain area
57. Exmoor High heather moorland & wooded valleys, with dramatic coastline
58. Dartmoor Granite uplands with heather & grassland
59. New Forest Woodland & heath; famous for wild ponies

Netherlands
60. Dwingelderveld Heathland, fen & woodland with lakes
61. De Hoge Veluwe Variety of habitats: heathland, dunes, fens, wet heath & woodland
Veluwezoom Heath & mixed woodland
62. De Biesbosch Confluence of Maas & Waal

Germany
63. Niedersächsisches Wattenmeer East Frisian Islands; mudflats & saltmarsh
64. Hamburgisches W'meer & Schleswig-Holsteinisches W'meer Mudflats & saltmarsh
65. Vorpommersche Boddenlandschaft Mudflats & saltmarsh with dunes, lagoons, lakes & woodland
66. Jasmund Varied landscape with cliffs, lakes & woodland
67. Müritz Woodland & lakes with heath, marsh & pasture
68. Unteres Odertal Floodplain of the Oder; park shared with Poland
69. Sächsische Schweiz Numerous rock towers; lower slopes wooded; deep valleys
70. Hoch Harz Wooded mountains with moorland, bogs & lakes
71. Bayerischer Wald Wooded mountain area
72. Berchtesgaden Mountain landscape with Alpine pastures, small glaciers, cliffs, lakes & varied woodland

France
73. Vanoise & Écrins High mountain scenery
74. Mercantour Some of the best parts of the Maritime Alps
75. Port-Cros Small wooded island
76. Cévennes Varied mountain & forest
77. Pyrénées-Occidentales Diverse mountain landscape; snowfields, pastures & woodland

Spain
78. Aigües Tortes-Sant Maurici Characteristic glacial landscape of high Pyrenees
79. Ordesa Spectacular mountain & gorge scenery; forests & Alpine pastures
80. Covadonga Mountain area with mixed woodlands, pasture & glacial lakes
81. Tablas de Daimiel Small wetland
82. Doñana Guadalquivir delta; important wildlife site
83. Caldera de Taburiente Volcanic landscape
84. Garajonay Sub-tropical forests
85. Cañadas del Teide Volcanic landscape
86. Timanfaya Volcanic landscapes

Portugal
87. Peneda-Gerês Mountain & forest area; cliffs & rock formations

Switzerland
88. The Swiss National Park Strictly controlled mountainous area; forests, pastures, lakes, cliffs & snowfields

Austria
89. Hohe Tauern High Alpine scenery; forests in lower areas
90. Nockberge Forested mountain area with bogs & moors
91. Donau-auen Danube flood plain E of Vienna

Italy
92. Stelvio Typical Alpine scenery & large glacier
93. Gran Paradiso High Alpine country; famous for the Ibex
94. Monti Sibillini Upspoilt mountain area with folklore connections
95. Gran Sasso e Monti della Laga Varied landscape of mountains, rivers & lakes
96. Abruzzo Wooded mountainous area Maiella Group of high peaks with karst plains
97. Circeo Coastal marsh & rocky promontory
98. Calábria Three areas of wooded mountainous landscape

Poland
99. Wolinski Woodland, lakes and sea cliffs; white-tailed sea eagle the main attraction
100. Slowinski Coastal landscape with shifting sand dunes
101. Kampinoski Landscape nr. Warsaw
102. Mazurski & Wigierski Numerous lakes and extensive forests
103. Biebrzanski Central Europe's largest area of natural peat bogs
104. Bialowieski Europe's largest original lowland forest; principal attraction the European bison

Slovak Republic
105. Bieszczadzki Remote wooded mountain area in E Carpathians
106. Babiogórski, Tatrzanski, Gorczanski & Pieninski Four parks in the spectacular High Tatra mountains
107. Ojcówski Hilly landscape with many rock pinnacles
108. Gory Stolowe & Karkonoski Dramatic mountain scenery of the Sudety Mountains

Czech Republic
109. Krkonose Wooded mountain area with Alpine pastures, meadows, bogs & lakes
110. Sumava Forested slopes, ancient mountains & peat bogs

Slovak Republic
111. Vysoké Tatry* (High Tatras) Nizke Tatry* (Low Tatras) Spectacular mtn area: forests, lakes, grassland & bogs
112. Pieninsky Limestone mountains with mixed forests
113. Slovenský raj Karst plateau with extensive caves

Hungary
114. Aggtelek Important karst scenery Bukk Hilly forested region
115. Hortobágyi Varied steppe landscape with rich birdlife
116. Kiskunság Wide range of lowland habitats

Slovenia
117. Triglav Limestone mountain scenery & mixed forest

Croatia
118. Risnjak Limestone mountain scenery & mixed forest
119. Plitvice Lakes* Scenic lakes linked by waterfalls formed by limestone deposition Paklenica Limestone peaks, gorges & mixed forest
120. Kornati Limestone islands, karst scenery
121. Krka Park follows the route of the Krka river; lakes, dams, gorges, falls & woodland
122. Mljet Western part of island

Bosnia-Herzegovina
123. Sutjeska Wooded mountainous area; mixed landscape & reserve of virgin forest

Serbia
124. Fruska Gora Wooded hilly valley
125. Djerdap Gorge of the Danube; dam has created a long thin lake
126. Tara Mixed upland

Montenegro
127. Durmitor Mountain area in the west, Tara Gorge in east; mixed landscape & karst Biogradska Gora Mountain area with high grasslands & five lakes
128. Lovcen Wooded limestone mountains Skadarsko jezero Montenegran part of Lake Scutari

Former Yugoslav Rep. of Macedonia
129. Mavrovo Mountain area, partly wooded
130. Galicica S end of Dinaric Alps; mostly natural forest Pelister Wooded mountain area with Alpine pastures

Albania
131. Divjaka Dunes & coastal woodland with rich birdlife on neighbouring lagoon

Romania
132. Retezat Mountain country with extensive forests

Bulgaria
133. Rusenski Lom Deciduous woodland
134. Central Balkan Widely varied landscape; thick forests
135. Vitosa Varied mountain area
136. Pirin High mountains; forest & mixed landscape Rila Alpine basin & many small lakes: the 'Eyes of the Rila'

Greece
137. Préspa Shallow lakes with reed- & sedge-beds
138. Olimbos (Olympus) Mountain area with maquis & forest; home of the gods in ancient Greek mythology
139. Pindos Wooded mountain area Vikos-Aóos Wooded mountain area; Vikos & Aóos gorges
140. Aínos Area around Mt Aínos
141. Iti Óros Wooded mountain area Parnassós Wilderness mountain area; mixed habitats
142. Párnitha Limestone area; maquis Soúnion Typical Greek coastline

Turkey
143. Manyas-Kuscenneti Bird reserve, part of large lake
144. Sipil Dagi Home of the famous 'crying rock' of Niobe

Estonia
145. Lahemaa Wooded area & scenic coast
146. Soomaa Marsh & forest, severe annual flooding
147. Karula Forested area with glacial debris

Latvia
148. Gauja River & gorge scenery; the 'Switzerland of Latvia'

Lithuania
149. Kursiv Nerija Long sand spit with popular beaches; ice fishing in winter
150. Zemaitija Forest with popular Lake Plateliai
151. Aukstaitija (Ignalina) Forest & lakes; great diversity of wildlife
152. Trakai 5 lakes; Trakai Castle as centrepiece
153. Dzukija Confluence of Nemunas & Merkys rivers

Neusiedler See Europe's largest steppe lake, over half is thick reedbeds

800 kilometres
400 miles

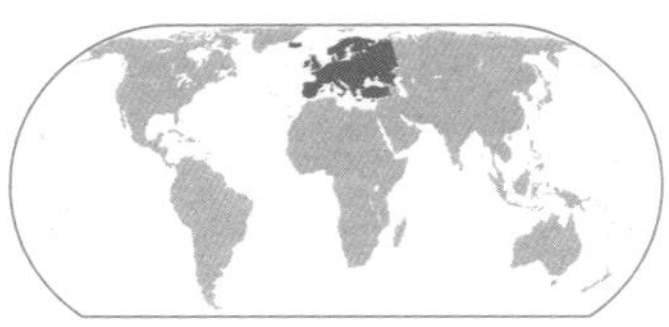

See also... Attractions in UK (64), Belgium (67), Netherlands (69), Germany (73), France (77), Iberia (79) and Italy (86)

The listings above refer to a selection of related themes. For more information, see the Contents (2-5).

This map shows a selection of theme and amusement parks in Europe. Most of these are members of either the International Association of Amusement Parks and Attractions (IAAPA) or the various national associations of amusement parks. For more information see www.ticketforfun.com

Parks marked with an asterisk (*) are featured in Columbus Travel Guides' *Tourist Attractions and Events of the World.*

Thanks to Jeff Bertus Leisure for help in compiling this section.

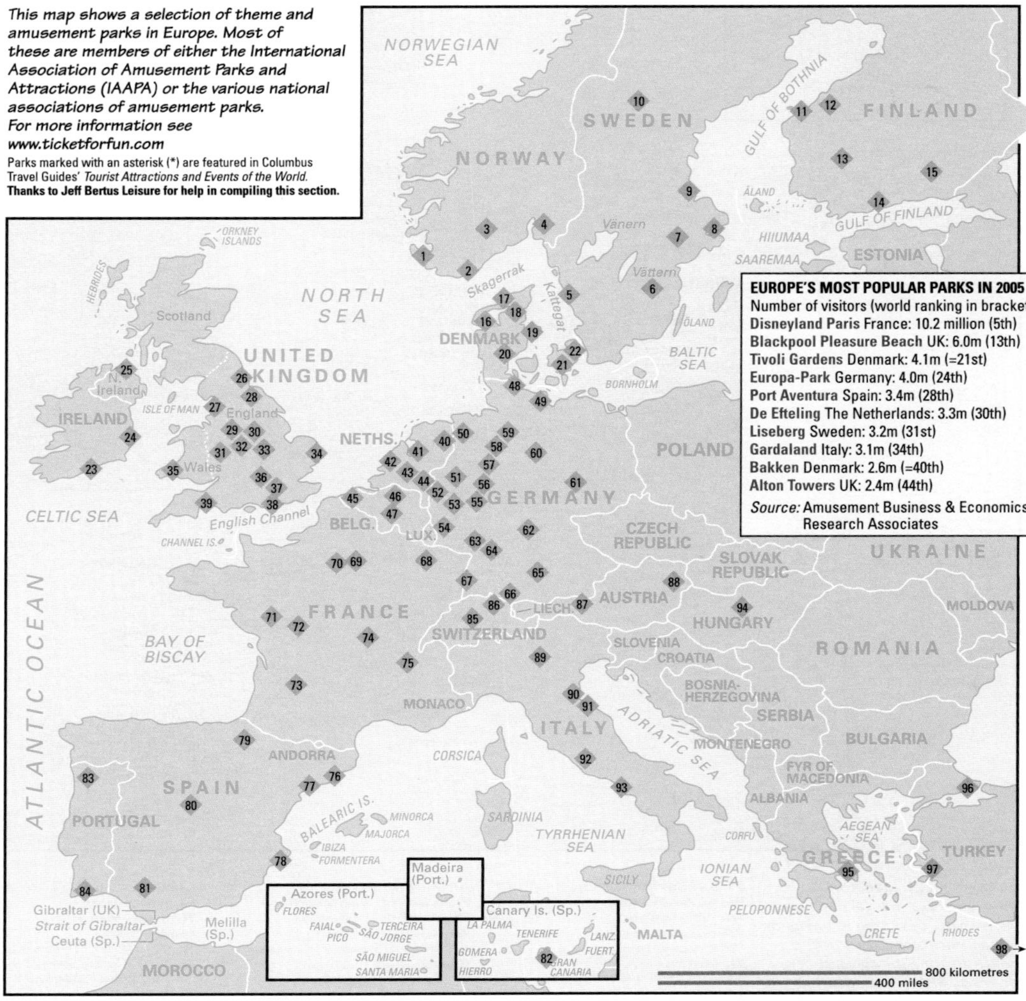

EUROPE'S MOST POPULAR PARKS IN 2005
Number of visitors (world ranking in brackets)
Disneyland Paris France: 10.2 million (5th)
Blackpool Pleasure Beach UK: 6.0m (13th)
Tivoli Gardens Denmark: 4.1m (=21st)
Europa-Park Germany: 4.0m (24th)
Port Aventura Spain: 3.4m (28th)
De Efteling The Netherlands: 3.3m (30th)
Liseberg Sweden: 3.2m (31st)
Gardaland Italy: 3.1m (34th)
Bakken Denmark: 2.6m (=40th)
Alton Towers UK: 2.4m (44th)
Source: Amusement Business & Economics Research Associates

Norway
1 **Lunds Tivoli**, Ålgård
Amusement park
2 **Kristiansand Dyrepark**
Norway's largest zoo and amusement park
3 **Bo Sommarland**, Bø
Combined waterpark and theme park
4 **TusenFryd & VikingLandet**, Vinterbro
Theme park and a small water park; VikingLandet is a re-enactment of the Viking Age

Sweden
5 **Liseberg**, Gothenburg
Large theme park with convention facilities and harbour
6 **Astrid Lindgren's World**, Vimmerby
Park dedicated to the world-famous childrens' author
7 **Parken Zoo i Eskilstuna**
Zoo, amusement park and waterpark
8 **Gröna Lunds Tivoli**, Stockholm
Amusement park in the centre of Stockholm, founded 1883
9 **Furuviksparken**, Gavle
Amusement park and zoo
10 **Jamtli Historieland**, Östersund
Combined indoor and outdoor museum

Finland
11 **Wasalandia**, Vaasa
Family theme park with Tropical Spa Tropiclandia
12 **Lillbacka Powerpark**, Alahärmä
Large amusement park with karting circuit, hotel & conference centre
13 **Tampereen Sarkanniemi Oy**, Tampere
City-centre amusement park and entertainment centre; includes an art museum, dolphinarium and planetarium
14 **Linnanmäki***, Helsinki
Finland's most popular amusement park with live stage shows and a Sea Life Centre
15 **Tykkimäki**, Kouvola
Large amusement park with reptile zoo and dance pavilion

Denmark
16 **Jesperhus Blomstherpark**, Nykøbing, Mors
Animal and flower parks; family entertainment centre
17 **Fårup Aquapark & Sommerland**, Saltum
Amusement park with more than 30 activities and Scandinavia's largest waterpark
18 **Tivoliland**, Aalborg
Large amusement park
19 **Djurs Sommerland**, Nimtofte
Amusement park with more than 60 activities and shows and a waterpark
20 **LEGOLAND Billund***
Theme park based on LEGO toy products; interactive attractions, building challenges, *Driving School* & *Miniland*
21 **BonBon-Land**, Holme-Olstrup
Fourth-largest amusement park in Denmark with over 60 attractions and activities
22 **Dyrehavsbakken ('Bakken')**, Klampenborg
The world's oldest amusement park, over 100 attractions
Tivoli Gardens*, Copenhagen
Large amusement park in the centre of Copenhagen, opened in 1843; a mixture of new and old rides; the famous Copenhagen Christmas Market is held here in Nov & Dec

Ireland
23 **Perks Pleasure Park**, Youghal
Seaside amusement park with neighbouring wildlife park
24 **Clara Lara Fun Park**, Wicklow
Park and amusement centre plus a junior playground

United Kingdom
25 **Barry's Amusement Park**, Portrush
Family amusement park with rides for all ages
26 **The New Metroland**, Gateshead
Europe's largest indoor funfair with many rides
27 **Blackpool Pleasure Beach***
Opened in 1896, over 145 attractions and rides classified according to their 'terror factor'; one of the biggest collections of white-knuckle rides in the world, plus spectacular shows & Ripley's Believe It or Not! Odditorium
Camelot Theme Park, Chorley, Lancashire
A medieval world with over 100 attractions and rides
28 **Flamingo Land and Holiday Village***, Malton
Amusement park and zoo with eight coaster rides and many extreme rides in White Knuckle Valley
Lightwater Valley, Ripon
Theme park with unique attractions including the world's first suspended hang-glider ride
29 **Alton Towers***, near Stoke-on-Trent
One of the UK's most popular theme parks with 125 rides and attractions in a number of different kingdoms: *Ugland, Forbidden Valley, Towers Street* and *Cred Street*
Gullivers Kingdom, Matlock Bath
Theme park with over 35 rides and hot-air balloon flights
30 **American Adventure World**, Ilkeston
Adventure park with a American theme
31 **West Midland Safari Park**, Bewdley
Drive-around safari park; leisure area with over 25 rides
32 **Drayton Manor Park***, Tamworth
Theme park with over 100 rides and attractions, plus a zoo, parkland, lakes and walks
33 **Wicksteed Park**, Kettering
UK's oldest theme park, opened in 1921
34 **Pleasurewood Hills**, Lowestoft
50 rides, sea lion and parrot shows, a castle and theatre
35 **Oakwood***, Narberth
Theme park with over 40 attractions including stage shows
36 **LEGOLAND Windsor***
Over 50 interactive rides, building workshops and driving schools in beautiful parkland
37 **Chessington World of Adventures***
Amusement park and zoo with gorillas and large cats
Thorpe Park, Chertsey
The UK's fastest changing thrill park with many white-knuckle rides
38 **Harbour Park**, Littlehampton
Seaside amusement park with extensive undercover facilities and arcades
39 **Crealy Adventure Park**, Exeter
A re-creation of a country childhood; with six different realms combining magic, adventure, action, animals, farming and nature

The Netherlands
40 **Attractiepark Slagharen**, Slagharen
Theme park with Wild West shows and over 40 rides
Avonturenpark Hellendoorn
Amusement park with many rides and animal attractions
41 **Dolfinarium Harderwijk**
Europe's largest marine theme park featuring six different shows with animals plus a dolphin rehabilitation centre, an open-air dolphin lagoon and a research centre
Walibi World, Dronten
Family amusement park famous for its rollercoasters
42 **Drievliet**, Rijswijk
Family park with over 30 major attractions, shows and playgrounds
Duinrell, Wassenaar
Family park with educational exhibitions; over 50 rides and water attractions
43 **De Efteling**, Kaatsheuvel
One of Europe's leading family leisure parks; a full range of attractions includes spectacular shows and PandaVision, an educational 3D journey through the world of nature
44 **BillyBird Park Hemelrijk**, Volkel
Artificial lake with nature area, beaches, restaurants, pools and an educational playground
Toverland, Sevenum
Large indoor and outdoor amusement park

Belgium
45 **Bellewaerde Park**, Ypres
Mix of attractions and exotic animals in a natural setting
Boudewijn Seapark, Bruges
Family park, famous for its dolphinarium; with rides, skating, boating, Seal Island and other animals
Plopsaland, De Panne
Theme park for families with children up to 12 years old
46 **Bobbejaanland**, Lichtaart
Amusement and theme park with 45 major rides, including *The Revolution* and *Arcade 2000*; also includes *Kinderland*, a covered children's play area with 20 rides
47 **Bruparck**, Brussels
Includes Mini-Europe, cinemas and IMAX, tropical swimming pool and saunaland
Walibi Belgium, Wavre
Over 50 attractions and shows; includes Aqualibi, a tropical waterpark

Germany
48 **Familien-Freizeitpark Tolk-Schau**, Tolk
Amusement park situated in a scenic landscape
49 **Hansapark**, Sierksdorf
Theme park with many rides and attractions including water circus and 3,000-seat Hansapark Theatre
50 **Ferienzentrum Schloss Dankern**, Haren
Family entertainment centre with many water facilities
51 **Movie Park Germany**, Bottrop
Movie theme park with over 40 attractions and shows including stunt shows and a free-fall tower
52 **Kernwasser Wunderland**, Kalkar
Unique amusement park for children up to 12 years old on the site of a former nuclear power station
53 **Phantasialand**, Brühl
Theme park divided into six areas: *China Town, Old Berlin, Fantasy, Mystery, Mexico* and *Silver City*; attractions include shows and culinary delicacies
54 **Eifelpark**, Gondorf bei Bitburg
Wild animal park and amusement park with open-air theatre
55 **Panoramapark Sauerland**, Kirchhundem
Wild animal park and amusement park with its own 500-kilowatt windpower station
56 **Fort Fun Abenteuerland**, Bestwig
Indoor and outdoor children's amusement park; offers facilities for corporate events
57 **Safari & Hollywood-Park**, Schloss Holte-Stukenbrock
Combined safari park and amusement park
58 **Dinosaurier Park Münchehagen**, Rehburg-Loccum
Dinosaur park
59 **Heide-Park**, Soltau
Amusement park with shows and 40 major rides
Serengeti Safaripark, Hodenhagen
Animal park with over 1,000 animals and three themed areas: *Monkey Land, Leisure Land* and *Water Land*
60 **Autostadt**, Wolfsburg
Theme park of the automobile: Volkswagen distribution centre combined with car museum, displays, go-kart track and rides
61 **BELANTIS**, Leipzig
Attractions and live shows in six BELANTIS Worlds: *Castle BELANTIS, Beach of the Gods, Valley of the Pharoahs, Country of the Counts, Island of the Knights* and *Coast of the Discoverers*
62 **Freizeit-Land**, Geiselwind
Theme park and zoo, including four rollercoasters
63 **Holiday-Park**, Hassloch
Theme park with many attractions and rides including a 180-degree cinema and a live show parade
64 **Erlebnispark Tripsdrill**, Cleebronn
Germany's oldest amusement park with rides and animals
65 **LEGOLAND Deutschland**, Günzburg
Unique blend of entertainment and learning by play for families with children up to 13 years old
66 **Ravensberger Spieleland**, Meckenbeuren
Largest playground in the world with over 40 attractions
67 **Europa-Park**, Rust
One of Europe's major parks, close to France & Switzerland

France
68 **Walibi Lorraine**, Maizières-les-Metz
Amusement park with over 30 attractions and shows
69 **Disneyland Resort Paris***, Marne-la-Vallée
Disneyland Paris is divided into five areas: *Main Street USA, Frontierland, Adventure-land, Fantasyland* and *Discoveryland. Walt Disney Studios Park*, opened in 2002, takes visitors back to the golden age of Hollywood and also behind the scenes of movie-making. *Disney Village* is Europe's largest entertainment complex.
La Mer de Sable, Ermenonville
Amusement park developed into themed areas: *China, Wild West* and *Morocco*; includes *Babagattau Village*
Parc Astérix*, Plailly
Theme park offering visitors a 3D trip into comic strip Asterix's universe, spread out over six neighbourhoods
70 **Le Jardin d'Acclimatation**, Paris
Amusement park with family rides and a zoo
71 **Grand Parc du Puy du Fou**, Les Espesses
Historical park with live shows and other attractions
72 **Futuroscope**, Jaunay-Clan, near Poitiers
Space-age park with advanced visual-image technology including an IMAX screen, virtual reality and Cyberspace
73 **Walibi Aquitaine**, Roquefort
With an 18th century castle and 20 attractions and shows
74 **Le Pal**, Dompierre sur Besbre
Animal and amusement park; shows feature sea lions, parrots and birds
75 **Walibi Rhône-Alpes**, Les Avenières
Regional amusement park with more than 30 rides and a waterpark area

Spain
76 **Parc d'Atraccions Tibidabo**, Barcelona
Urban amusement park, founded 1899, renovated 1988
77 **Port Aventura***, Salou
Includes Costa Caribe waterpark and Zona de Playa beach
78 **Terra Mítica***, Benidorm
Five areas: *Egypt, Iberia, Greece, Rome* and *The Islands*, illustrate the past, present and future of Mediterranean culture
79 **Txiki Park**, Pamplona
Family entertainment centre designed for children
80 **Parque de Atracciones Casa de Campo**, Madrid
Urban amusement park, Madrid's main entertainment centre
Warner Brothers Movie World, Madrid
Movie theme park with live shows and numerous attractions including Superman and Batman rides
81 **Parque Isla Mágica**, Seville
Theme park based upon exploration of the New World by 16th century Spanish adventurers
82 **Sioux City**, San Agustín, Gran Canaria
Western-themed park with stage shows and concerts

Portugal
83 **Bracalândia**, Braga
Theme park with various themed areas and attractions
84 **Zoomarine**, Albufeira
Zoo and marine park taking its theme from the Algarve's links with the sea

Switzerland
85 **Mystery Park**, Interlaken
Theme parks presenting unexplained mysteries of the world
86 **Conny-Land**, Lipperswil
Amusement park with underwater and animal shows

Austria
87 **Freizeitpark Familienland**, St Jakob in Haus
Amusement park with over 40 attractions
88 **Wiener Prater**, Vienna
Amusement park for over 100 years

Italy
89 **Gardaland**, Castelnuovo del Garda
Huge multifunctional amusement park with many attractions; four themed villages; profusion of plants and flowers
90 **Mirabilandia**, Ravenna
Amusement park with rides, stage shows and concerts
91 **Fiabilandia**, Rimini
Amusement park and funfair
92 **Luneur**, Rome
Traditional amusement park and funfair, 30 years old
93 **Edenlandia**, Naples
One of Italy's largest amusement parks

Hungary
94 **Budapesti Vidam Park**, Budapest
Amusement park with 33 games and rides; more than one million visitors per year

Greece
95 **Luna Park 'Ta Aidonakia'**, Athens
20 family and children's rides

Turkey
96 **Tatilya Turizm**, Avcilar, Istanbul
Largest indoor entertainment centre in Europe and the Middle East, Tatilya is a holiday and amusement republic with its own president, citizens and constitution
97 **Aqua Fantasy**, Selçuk
Turkey's largest water park

Cyprus
98 **WaterWorld**, Ayia Napa
Cyprus' largest waterpark and most popular attraction

The listings above refer to a selection of related themes.
For more information, see the Contents (2-5).

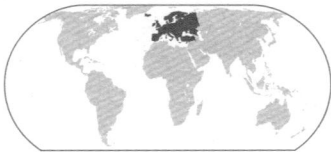

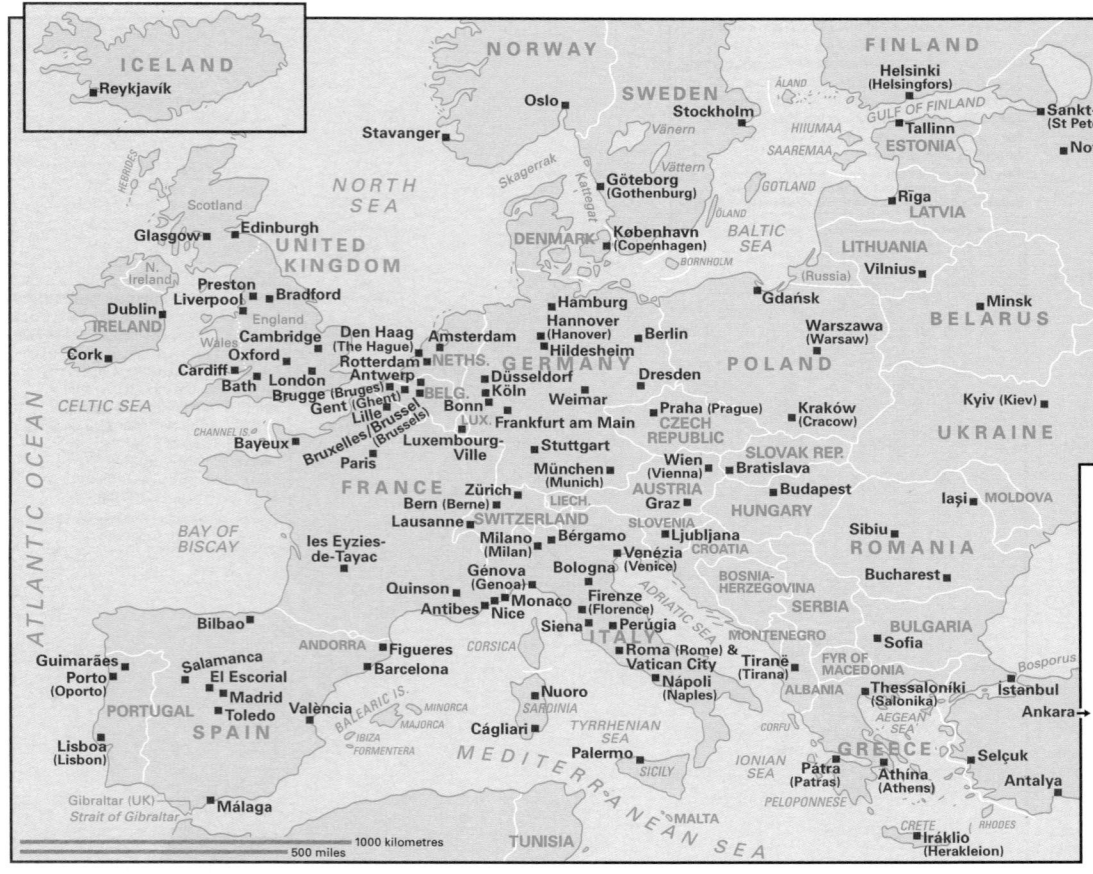

Principal museums and art galleries in the Russian Federation east of Moscow are included on the Asian map, p.129

EUROPEAN CAPITALS/CITIES OF CULTURE

1985	Athens	1999	Weimar
1986	Florence	2000	Avignon, Bergen,
1987	Amsterdam		Bologna, Brussels,
1988	Berlin		Cracow, Helsinki,
1989	Paris		Prague, Reykjavík,
1990	Glasgow		Santiago de Compostela
1991	Dublin	2001	Oporto, Rotterdam
1992	Madrid	2002	Bruges, Salamanca
1993	Antwerp	2003	Graz
1994	Lisbon	2004	Genoa, Lille
1995	Luxembourg	2005	Cork
1996	Copenhagen	2006	Patras
1997	Thessaloniki	2007	Luxembourg-Ville, Sibiu
1998	Stockholm	2008	Liverpool, Stavanger

Pátra (Patras) GREECE
AR Archaeological Museum of Patras
Perúgia ITALY
AR Museu Archeologico Nazionale dell'Umbria
Porto (Oporto) PORTUGAL
AA FA Museu Nacional Soares dos Reis
Praha (Prague) CZECH REPUBLIC
AA Jewish Museum; Museum of Decorative Arts (UPM)
FA Museum of Modern and Contemporary Czech Art;
 Mucha Museum; Museum of Modern Czech
 Sculpture (Zbraslav); National Gallery of Old
 Bohemian Art (St George Convent)
NH National Museum
ST National Museum of Technology
Preston ENGLAND
H National Football Museum
Quinson FRANCE
AR Musée de Préhistoire
Reykjavík ICELAND
W Thjódminjasafn Íslands (National Museum)
Riga LATVIA
AA Museum of Decorative and Applied Arts
Roma (Rome) ITALY & **Vatican City**
W Capitoline museums includes:
AR Museo Capitolino
W Museo del Palazzo dei Conservatori
AR Museo Nazionale di Villa Giulia; Museo Naz. Romano
FA Galleria Borghese; Gall. Doria Pamphili; Pal. Barberini
W Musei Vaticani
Rotterdam THE NETHERLANDS
FA Museum Boymans-van Beuningen
Salamanca SPAIN
AA Museo Art Nouveau y Art Deco
Sankt-Peterburg (St Petersburg) RUSSIAN FED.
W State Hermitage Museum
FO Museum of Anthropology and Ethnography
AR Russian Museum
Selçuk TURKEY
AR Archaeological Museum
Sibiu ROMANIA
FO ASTRA museums
AA FA The Brukenthal Museum
Siena ITALY
W Ospedale di Santa Maria della Scala
Sofia BULGARIA
FO Ethnographic Museum
FA National Art Gallery
AR H National Historical Museum
Stavanger NORWAY
AR Arkeologist Museum
W Stavanger Museum and Maritime Museum
Stockholm SWEDEN
FA Modernamuséet
AA Nationalmuseum
H Statens Historiska Museum
AR Vasamuseet
Stuttgart GERMANY
FA Staatsgalerie
Tallinn ESTONIA
FA National Art Museum
Thessaloníki (Salonika) GREECE
AR Archaeological Museum
FO Folklore Museum
Tiranë (Tirana) ALBANIA
AR National Archaeology Museum
FA National Art Gallery
W National Historical Museum
Toledo SPAIN
AR Museo de Arte Visigótico
FA Museo de Santa Cruz
València SPAIN
ST Ciutat de les Arts i les Ciències
FA Museo de Bellas Artes San Pio V
Venézia (Venice) ITALY
FA Collezione Guggenheim; Galleria dell'Accademia
W Museo Correr
AA Museo Vitrario di Murano
Vilnius LITHUANIA
AA Lithuanian History and Ethnographic Museum
Warszawa (Warsaw) POLAND
W National Museum
Weimar GERMANY
FA Schlossmuseum
Wien (Vienna) AUSTRIA
FA Albertina; Kunsthistorisches Museum
 Österreichische Galerie, Belvedere
W MuseumsQuartier includes:
FA MUMOK (Museum moderner Kunst); Leopold Mus.
Zürich SWITZERLAND
FA Kunsthaus
W Schweizerisches Landesmuseum

Europe's most important museums and art galleries are listed here. Selection is based on importance and depth of the collection and its cultural diversity within a geographic spread.

Most cities named will also offer the visitor a number of smaller museums of specialist interest. Many single great works of art may also be housed in local cathedrals and churches.

Compiled by Jon A. Gillaspie
email: let@sarastro.com

Principal contents of institution:

AA Applied & decorative art
AR Archaeology / ancient art
FA Fine art (paintings, sculpture)
FO Folk art & culture / ethnography
H History / historical site / reconstruction
NH Natural history
ST Science / technology
W Wide range of subjects

Amsterdam THE NETHERLANDS
AA FA Hermitage ann de Amstel
W Rijksmuseum
FA Stedelijk Museum; Van Gogh Museum
Ankara TURKEY
AR Museum of Anatolian Civilizations
Antalya TURKEY
AR Archaeological Museum
Antibes FRANCE
FA Musée Picasso
Antwerpen (Antwerp) BELGIUM
FA Museum voor Schone Kunsten
Athína (Athens) GREECE
AR Acropolis Museum; National Archaeological
 Museum
W Benáki Museum
AR Museum of Cycladic and Ancient Greek Art
Barcelona SPAIN
AR Museu Arqueològic
FA Museu d'Art Contemporani; Museu Nacional
 d'Art de Catalunya; Museu Picasso
Bath ENGLAND
AA Museum of Costume
AR Roman Baths and Museum
Bayeux FRANCE
AA Bayeux Tapestry
Bérgamo ITALY
FA Accademia Carrara
Berlin GERMANY
AR Ägyptisches Museum; Antiken Museum
W Dahlem museums

ST Deutsches Teknikmuseum
W Kulturforum includes:
FA Gemäldegalerie
AA Kunstgewerbemuseum
NH Museum für Naturkunde
W Museumsinsel includes:
FA Alte Nationalgalerie
AR Bodemuseum; Pergamonmuseum
Bern (Berne) SWITZERLAND
FA Kunstmuseum
Bilbao SPAIN
FA Museo de Bellas Arte; Museo Guggenheim
Bologna ITALY
AR Museo Civico Archeologico
Bonn GERMANY
NH Alexander-Koenig-Museum
FA Kunstmuseum
Bradford UNITED KINGDOM
ST National Museum of Photography, Film & TV
Bratislava SLOVAK REPUBLIC
FA National Gallery
W National Museum
Brugge (Bruges) BELGIUM
FA Groeningemuseum
Bruxelles/Brussel (Brussels) BELGIUM
FA Musées Royaux des Beaux-Arts
Bucharest ROMANIA
FA National Art Museum
AR H National History Museum
Budapest HUNGARY
H Holocaust Museum
FA Museum of Fine Arts; National Gallery
AA National Jewish Museum
Cágliari SARDINIA, ITALY
AR Museo Nazionale Archeologico
Cambridge ENGLAND
W Fitzwilliam Museum
Cardiff WALES
FO Museum of Welsh Life [St Fagans]
W National Museum and Gallery of Wales
Cork IRELAND
AA FA Crawford Municipal Art Gallery
Den Haag (The Hague) THE NETHERLANDS
W Gemeentemuseum
FA Mauritshuis
Dresden GERMANY
AA Gemäldegalerie Alte Meister
Dublin IRELAND
FA National Gallery
AR National Museum
Düsseldorf GERMANY
FA Kunstmuseum
FA Kunstsammlung Nordrhein-Westfalen
Edinburgh SCOTLAND
W Royal Museum and Museum of Scotland
FA Scottish National Portrait Gallery
El Escorial SPAIN
FA Monasterio de El Escorial
Les Eyzies-de-Tayac FRANCE
AR Musée national de Préhistoire
Figueres SPAIN
FA Teatre-Museu Dalí
Firenze (Florence) ITALY
FA Bargello; Uffizi

AR Museo Archeologico
Frankfurt am Main GERMANY
FA Museum für Moderne Kunst
W Museumsufer includes:
AA FA Städel; Museum für Kunsthandwerk
Gdansk POLAND
W National Art Museum
Génova (Genoa) ITALY
FA Galleria Nazionale di Palazzo Spinola; Palazzo
 Bianco; Palazzo Rosso
Gent (Ghent) BELGIUM
FA Museum voor Schone Kunsten
Glasgow SCOTLAND
W Burrell Collection
FA Gallery of Modern Art (GOMA); Hunterian Art
 Gallery and Museum
Göteborg (Gothenburg) SWEDEN
FA Konstmuseet
AR Röhsska Konstlöjdmuseet
Graz AUSTRIA
FA Alte Galerie; Kunsthaus
W Landesmuseum Joanneum
Guimarães PORTUGAL
AA Museu Alberto Sampaio
AA Museu Martins Sarmiento
AA Sé (Cathedral museum) [Braga]
Hamburg GERMANY
FA Kunsthalle
AA Museum für Kunst und Gewerbe
Hannover (Hanover) GERMANY
FA Sprengel Museum
Helsinki (Helsingfors) FINLAND
FA Helsinki kaupingin museo
W Kansallismuseo; Kiasma
Hildesheim GERMANY
AR Roemer-Pelizaeus Museum
Iasi ROMANIA
W Palace of Culture
Iráklio (Herakleion) CRETE, GREECE
AR Archaeological Museum
Istanbul TURKEY
W Museum of Turkish and Islamic Art
København (Copenhagen) DENMARK
AR Nationalmuseet
W Ny Carlsberg Glyptotek
FA Statens Museum for Kunst
Köln (Cologne) GERMANY
FA Ludwig Museum; Wallraf-Richartz Museum
AR Römisch-Germanisches Museum
Kraków (Cracow) POLAND
W Czartoryski Museum
Kyiv (Kiev) UKRAINE
H Historical Treasures Museum
FA Russian Art Museum
Lausanne SWITZERLAND
H Musée Olympique
Lille FRANCE
FA Musée des Beaux-Arts
Lisboa (Lisbon) PORTUGAL
FA Museu Nacional de Arte Antiga
W Museu Calouste Gulbenkian
Liverpool ENGLAND
FA Walker Art Gallery
W World Museum

Ljubljana SLOVENIA
FA National Gallery
W National Museum
London ENGLAND
W British Museum; Museum of London
FA National Gallery; National Portrait Gallery;
 Tate Britain; Tate Modern
NH Natural History Museum
ST Science Museum
AA Victoria and Albert Museum
Luxembourg-Ville LUXEMBOURG
W Musée national d'Histoire et d'Art
NH Musée national d'Histoire naturelle
Madrid SPAIN
FA Centro de Arte Reina Sofia; Museo del Prado;
 Museo Thyssen-Bornemisza
AR Museo Arqueológico Nacional
W Museo de América
Málaga SPAIN
FA Museo Picasso
Milano (Milan) ITALY
FA Civico Museo di Arte Contemporanea; Pina-
 coteca Ambrosiana; Pinacoteca di Brera
AR Museo Civico di Archeologico
Minsk BELARUS
FA Belarusian State Art Museum
W National Museum of History and Culture
Monaco
NH ST Musée Océanographique
Moskva (Moscow) RUSSIAN FEDERATION
AA Kremlin
FA Mus. of Private Collections; Tretyakov Gallery
W Pushkin Museum of Fine Arts
München (Munich) GERMANY
FA Alte Pinakothek; Neue Pinakothek;
 Pinakothek der Moderne
AA Bayerisches Nationalmuseum
ST Deutsches Museum
AR Glyptothek und Antikensammlungen
Nápoli (Naples) ITALY
AR Museo Archeologico Nazionale
Nice FRANCE
FO Fondation Maeght [St-Paul-de-Vence]
FA Musée Marc-Chagall; Musée Matisse
Novgorod RUSSIAN FEDERATION
AA Museum of History, Architecture and Art
Nuoro SARDINIA, ITALY
FO Museo Etnografico
Oslo NORWAY
FA Nasjonalgalleriet
FO Norsk Folkemuseum
AR Vikingskiphuset
Oxford ENGLAND
W Ashmolean Museum
FA Museum of Modern Art (MOMA)
Palermo SICILY, ITALY
AR Museo Archeologico Regionale
FO Museo Etnografico Pitrè
Paris FRANCE
ST Cité des Sciences et de l'Industrie
W Institut du Monde Arabe; Louvre
FA Musée d'Orsay; Musée Marmottan; Musée
 national Picasso (Centre Georges
 Pompidou); Musée national du Moyen-Âge;
 Musée national Picasso; Musée Rodin

The listings above refer to a selection of related themes.
For more information, see the Contents (2-5).

A symbol next to a resort's name in the listing below indicates that it is an outstanding example in that category. This is the publisher's selection, and is by its nature subjective. The lack of a symbol does not necessarily mean that the resort does not possess this quality or facility.

▲ **THE MOST BEAUTIFUL RESORTS**
Ski areas with spectacular scenery

❄ **SNOWSURE**
The best reputations for season-long snow cover

▲ **SUMMER SKIING DESTINATIONS**
Resorts where lifts stay open for skiing or boarding during the summer

◆ **EXPERT**
Best of the black diamond destinations

▥ **BEGINNER SKI AREAS**
Best choices for first timers

● **FAMILY FRIENDLY**
Ideal choices for family ski holidays

● **PARTY TOWNS**
Après ski centres

▼ **SNOWBOARDER HEAVEN**
Best bets for boarders

★ **NOT JUST SKIING**
Plenty to do if you don't want to slide

✔ **ECO-FRIENDLY REPUTATION**
(not all resorts have been graded in this category)

Information supplied by Snow24 plc
www.snow24.com

THE LARGEST LINKED RESORT AREAS △

Portes du Soleil (650 km of ski piste) *France/Switz.*
9 Châtel
10 Avoriaz
11 les Gets
11 Morzine
54 Torgon
55 Champéry-Planachaux / Val-d'Illiez / Les Crosets

Grand Massif (265 km) *France*
12 Morillon les Essert
13 Samoëns
14 Sixt
15 Flaine

Paradiski (425 km) *France*
23 les Arcs
24 Peisey / Nancroix-Vallandry
27 la Plagne / les Coches / Montchavin / Plagne Montalbert
28 Champagny-en-Vanoise

Espace Killy (300 km) *France*
25 Tignes
26 Val d'Isère

Trois Vallées (600 km) *France*
29 Courchevel
29 la Tania
30 Méribel
31 Val Thorens
32 les Menuires
33 St-Martin-de-Belleville

Les Sybelles (350 km) *France*
35 le Corbier
35 la Toussuire
36 St-Jean d'Arves

Grand Serre-Chevalier (250 km) *France*
45 Briançon
45 Serre-Chevalier

Milky Way (400 km) *France/Italy*
46 Montgenèvre
117 Clavière
117 San Sicário / Cesana
118 Sestriere
119 Sàuze d'Oulx

4 Valleys (412 km) *Switzerland*
56 Verbier
57 la Tzoumas (Mayens-de-Riddes)

International (350 km) *Italy/Switzerland*
65 Zermatt
123 Breuil-Cervínia
124 Valtournenche

TopCard (308 km) *Switzerland*
79 Davos
80 Klosters / Fideris

KiWest (400 km) *Austria*
99 Hopfgarten im Brixental
99 Westendorf
100 Söll
101 Kitzbühel

Sella Ronda (510 km) *Italy*
142 Arabba
143 Campitello di Fassa
143 Canazei
144 Santa Cristina / Pranauron
144 Selva Gardena (Wolkenstein)
145 Ortisei (St Ulrich)
146 Alta Badia [Colfosco / Corvara / La Villa (Stern) / San Cassiano (St Kassian) / Pedráces / San Leonardo (St Leonhard)]

Germany
1 Feldberg ▥★
2 Oberstdorf ▲●▥●
3 Garmisch-Partenkirchen ▲❄▲◆●★▼
4 Bayrischzell ▥
5 Reit im Winkl ▲▥★

France
6 la Bresse-Hohneck ▥▼
7 Métabief / le Mont d'Or ❄★
8 Abondance / la Chapelle d'Abondance ▲▥●
9 Châtel ▲▥●▼
10 Avoriaz ❄▲▥●▼
11 les Gets ▲▥✔▼
11 Morzine ▲◆▲▥●▼
12 Morillon les Essert ▲▥
13 Samoëns ▲▥▲
15 Flaine ❄▲▥▼✔
16 les Carroz ▼
17 la Clusaz ●▼
18 Notre-Dame-de-Bellecombe ▲
19 Praz-sur-Arly ❄
20 Megève ▲▥▲●▲
21 Chamonix-Mont-Blanc ▲❄●▼
22 les Contamines-Montjoie ▲▥●▼
22 St-Nicolas-de-Véroce ▲▥
23 les Arcs ❄▲▥●▼
25 Tignes ❄▲◆▼
26 Val d'Isère ❄▲◆●▼✔
27 la Plagne / les Coches / Montchavin / Plagne Montalbert ❄★▼
28 Champagny-en-Vanoise ▲▼
29 Courchevel ❄▲●▼
29 la Tania ❄▲✔
30 Méribel / Brides-les-Bains ▲◆●▼★
31 Val Thorens ❄▲◆▲▼
32 les Menuires ◆▥▲▼
33 St-Martin-de-Belleville ▲▥▲
34 Valmorel ▥▲▼
35 le Corbier ▥
35 la Toussuire ▼
36 St-Jean d'Arves ▲
37 Villard-de-Lans / Cote 2000 ▥▼
38 Corrençon-en-Vercors ▥
39 les Sept Laux (le Pleiney / Prapoutel) ▲▥
40 Vaujany / Oz-en-Oisans ▲▲
41 Alpe d'Huez / Auris-en-Oisans / Villard-Reculas ▲❄▲▥◆●▼★
42 les Deux-Alpes ❄▲▥▲●▼★
43 la Grave ▲❄▲◆

Switzerland
44 Valloire ❄★
45 Briançon ▲★
45 Serre-Chevalier ▲▥●▼▲✔★
46 Montgenèvre ❄▥▲▼
47 Risoul ▥★▼
48 Vars ▥▲▼
49 les Orres ▥▲▼
50 Pra-Loup ▥▲★
51 Val d'Allos-la Foux ▲
52 Auron / St-Étienne-de-Tinée ▲●
53 Beuil-les-Launes ▲
53 Valberg ▲
55 Champéry-Planachaux / Val-d'Illiez / Les Crosets ▲▥▲
56 Verbier ❄▲▥●▼◆
57 la Tzoumas (Mayens-de-Riddes) ❄▲
58 Villars-sur-Ollon / Gryon ❄▲▥▲▼◆
59 les Diablerets ▲❄▲◆▲▼✔
60 Château-d'Oex ▲▥▼
61 Gstaad-Saanenland ▲▲●▼✔▲
62 Adelboden ▲▥●▼
63 Lenk ▲▥▲●▼★
65 Crans-Montana ❄▲◆▼★✔
65 Zermatt ▲❄▲◆●▼✔
66 Saas-Fee ▲❄▲▥▲●▼✔
67 Bettmeralp ▲
67 Fiesch ★
67 Mörel-Breiten ▥
68 Sörenberg ▲
69 Mürren / Stechelberg ▲❄▲▥▲
69 Wengen ▲❄▲●▼✔
70 Riederalp ▲
71 Interlaken ▲
71 Wilderswil bei Interlaken ▲▥●★
72 Grindelwald ▲❄▲◆▲★✔
73 Engelberg ❄▲▥▲●▼★
74 Laax ▲❄▲●▼
75 Flims ▲▥✔
75 Flumserberg ▲▥●▼
77 Lenzerheide-Valbella ❄▲▥●▼
77 Parpan ▲▥
78 Arosa ▲❄❄★
79 Davos ▲❄▲◆▼▲✔
80 Klosters / Fideris ▲◆▥▲
81 Celerina ❄
81 Samedan ❄
82 St Moritz ❄▲◆●▼★✔
83 Sils-Maria ❄
85 Maloja ❄
85 Pontresina ❄▲▥✔
86 Samnaun ●★

Austria
87 St Gallenkirch ▲▼
88 Kleinwalsertal [Hirschegg /Mittelberg / Riezlern] ▲
89 Lech / Oberlech ❄▲▥●▼✔
89 Zürs ❄◆
90 St Anton am Arlberg / St Jakob am Arlberg ▲◆●✔
90 St Christoph am Arlberg ▲◆
91 Ischgl / Silvretta ❄▲●▼✔
92 Ehrwald ▲❄▲▥
92 Lermoos ▲▥
93 Obergurgl / Hochgurgl ▲❄▲

94 Sölden ❄▲▲●▼✔
95 Hintertux ▲▲▼
96 Mayrhofen ▲▥▲●▼★✔
97 Zell am Ziller ▲▥▲●
98 Alpbach ▲▥▲✔
99 Hopfgarten im Brixental ▥▲▼
99 Westendorf ▲▥▲●▼
100 Söll ▥●▼
101 Kitzbühel ▲▲▲●▼★
102 Fieberbrunn ◆●▼
102 St Johann im Tirol ▲▥▲●▼
103 Saalbach Hinterglemm ◆▥●▼★✔
104 Leogang ▲▥▲▼
105 Kaprun ▲▥▲●
106 Zell am See ▲●◆★✔
107 Badgastein ▲❄▲●▼
108 Bad Hofgastein ▥▲●▼
109 Grossarl ▲
110 Flachau ◆●▼
111 Altenmarkt-Zauchensee ★
112 Annaberg im Lammertal ▲
113 Ramsau am Dachstein ▲❄▲▼
113 Schladming ▲▲▲●▼✔
114 St Michael im Lungau ▲
115 Bad Kleinkirchheim ▲●▼▲

Italy
116 Limone Piemonte ▥●
117 Clavière ❄▥
118 Sestriere ❄●▼
119 Sàuze d'Oulx ▥▲●
120 Bardonécchia ❄▥●
121 la Thuile ❄▲●
122 Courmayeur ◆●★
123 Breuil-Cervínia ❄▲▥▲●▼
124 Valtournenche ❄
125 Champoluc / Antagnod ❄▥
126 Gressoney / Antagnod / Gressoney-St Jean ❄
127 Alagna-Valsésia ❄◆
128 Livigno ❄▥
129 Bormio ❄●★
130 Folgárida ▼
131 Passo Tonale ❄▲▥★
132 Madonna di Campíglio ▲●▼▲✔
133 Andalo ▲
134 Folgaría ★
135 Lavarone / Luserna ▲
136 Asiago / Canove ▲★
137 Cavalese ❄★
138 Obereggen ▥
139 Bellamonte ▥
140 San Martino di Castrozza ▲●▼★
141 Alleghe ▥
142 Arabba ❄▲◆▥▼
143 Campitello di Fassa / Canazei ▲●
144 Santa Cristina / Pranauron / Selva Gardena (Wolkenstein) ▲▲●
146 **Alta Badia** [Colfosco / Corvara / La Villa (Stern) / San Cassiano (St Kassian) / Pedráces / San Leonardo (St Leonhard)] ▲▥●★
147 Cortina ▲❄▲●▼
148 San Vigilio di Marebbe ▲❄
149 Versciaco (Vierschach) ❄▲

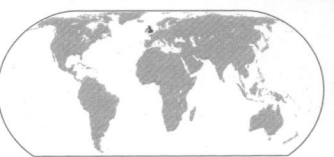

For more information, see the Contents (2-5).

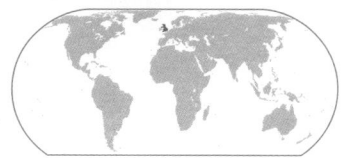

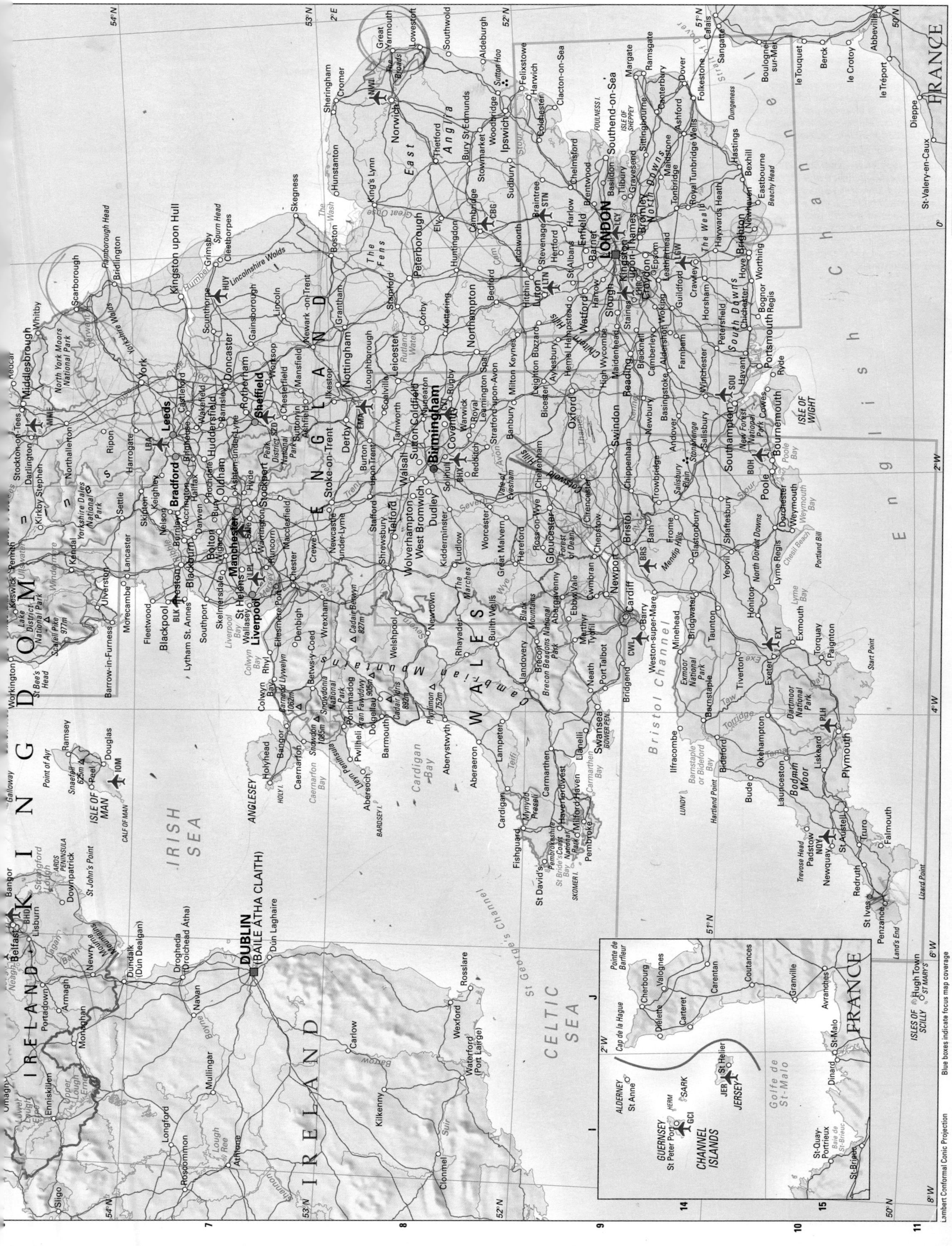

► See also... Europe National Parks (54); UK Attractions (64)

The listings above refer to a selection of related themes. For more information, see the Contents (2-5).

The European Blue Flag Campaign is an environmental awareness raising activity by the Foundation for Environmental Education in Europe (FEEE).

To qualify for a Blue Flag, a beach has to fulfil a number of strict criteria regarding water quality (compliance with the EU Bathing Water Directive), environmental education and information, environmental management and safety and services. The Blue Flag is awarded annually and is valid for one year. The map shows beaches awarded the Blue Flag in 2005. For more information visit: www.seasideawards.org.uk

The UK maps show geographical counties, and not the administrative counties and unitary authorities which have, for administrative purposes, replaced them. Geographical counties give a more familiar picture of the divisions of the UK: they are also of a more consistent size, as they do not reflect the growth of urban populations over the last 200 years. For more information on geographical countries, visit: www.abcounties.co.uk

Scotland
1 Montrose Seafront
2 Broughty Ferry
3 St Andrews: East Sands
  St Andrews: West Sands
4 Elie Harbour
5 Burntisland
6 Aberdour: Silver Sands

Northumbria
7 Whitley Bay South
  Tynemouth: King Edward's Bay
  Tynemouth: Longsands South
8 South Shields: Sandhaven
  Whitburn North: Seaburn

Yorkshire
9 Whitby
10 Scarborough: North Bay
11 Bridlington North
12 Hornsea
13 Cleethorpes Central

Heart of England
14 Mablethorpe Central
  Sutton on Sea Central

15 Skegness: Tower Esplanade

East of England
16 Sheringham
17 Cromer
18 Mundesley
19 Sea Palling
20 Great Yarmouth: Gorleston on Sea
21 Lowestoft North
  Lowestoft South
22 Southwold Pier
23 Felixstowe South
24 Dovercourt
25 Brightlingsea
26 Shoeburyness East
  Shoebury Common
  Southend-on-Sea: Jubilee Beach

South East England
27 Birchington: Minnis Bay
  Westgate-on-Sea: West Bay
28 Margate: Westbrook Bay
29 Eastbourne: Pier to Wish Tower
30 Littlehampton: Coastguards
31 Bognor Regis: East of Pier
32 West Wittering

Southern England
33 Hayling Island: Beachlands Central
  Hayling Island: Beachlands West
34 Bournemouth: Alum Chine
  Bournemouth: Durley Chine
  Bournemouth: Fisherman's Walk
  Bournemouth: Southbourne

35 Poole: Branksome Chine
  Poole: Canford Cliffs Chine
  Poole: Sandbanks
  Poole: Shore Road
36 Swanage Central

Isle of Wight
37 Ryde East
38 Sandown
  Shanklin

South West
39 Dawlish Warren
40 Torquay: Oddicombe
  Torquay: Meadfoot
41 Brixham: Shoalstone Breakwater
42 Blackpool Sands
43 Bigbury-on-Sea North
  Challaborough
44 Falmouth: Gyllyngvase
45 Sennen Cove
46 St Ives: Porthmeor
  St Ives: Porthminster
47 Porthtowan
48 Polzeath
49 Westward Ho!
50 Croyde Bay
  Woolacombe
51 Ilfracombe: Tunnels Beaches

Wales
52 Southerndown
  Porthcawl: Rest Bay
53 Swansea: Bracelet Bay
  Swansea: Caswell Bay
  Swansea: Langland Bay
54 Port-Eynon
55 Pembrey Country Park: Cefn Sidan
56 Amroth
  Saundersfoot
57 Tenby Castle
  Tenby North
  Tenby South
58 Lydstep
59 Dale
60 Broad Haven North
61 Newgale
62 St David's: Whitesands
63 Cardigan: Poppit Sands
64 Aberporth
65 New Quay: Traeth y Harbwr
66 Aberystwyth North
67 Borth
68 Tywyn
69 Fairbourne: Ffriog
70 Barmouth: Abermaw
71 Criccieth
72 Pwllheli: Marian y De
73 Abersoch
74 Dinas Dinlle
75 Penmaenmawr
76 Rhos-on-Sea
77 Prestatyn Central

Anglesey
78 Newborough: Llanddwyn
79 Holy Island: Porth Dafarch
  Holy Island: Trearddur Bay
80 Benllech
81 Llanddona

Northern Ireland
82 Magilligan: Benone Strand
  Downhill Strand
83 Portstewart Strand
  Portrush: East Strand
  Portrush: West Strand
  Portrush: White Rocks
84 Tyrella
85 Cranfield West

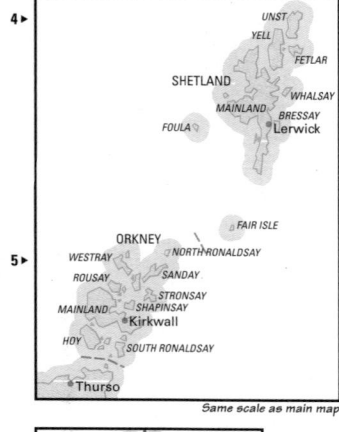

International arrivals (millions)

Source: World Tourism Organisation

0 Blue Flag beach 2005
- - - Geographical county boundary
── English Tourist Board boundary
National Park

100 kilometres
50 miles

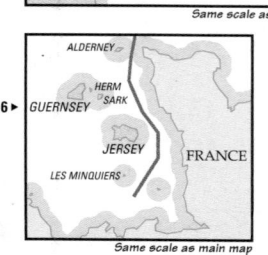

Same scale as main map

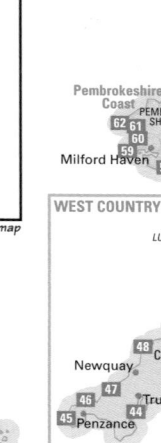

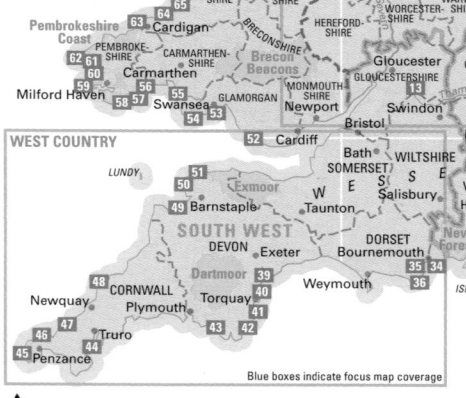

Same scale as main map

Blue boxes indicate focus map coverage

► **See also...** Contents (2-5) – this country features in many thematic and regional maps throughout the *BTEC First Travel Atlas*.

Europe **61**

United Kingdom

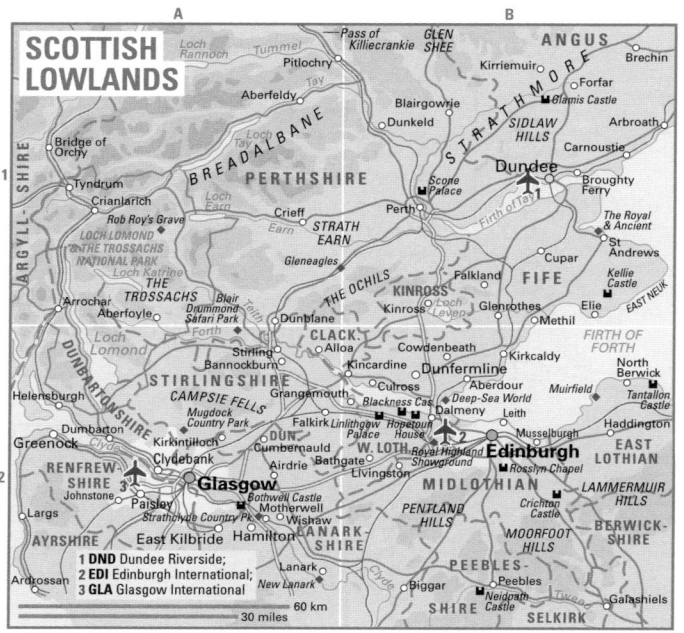

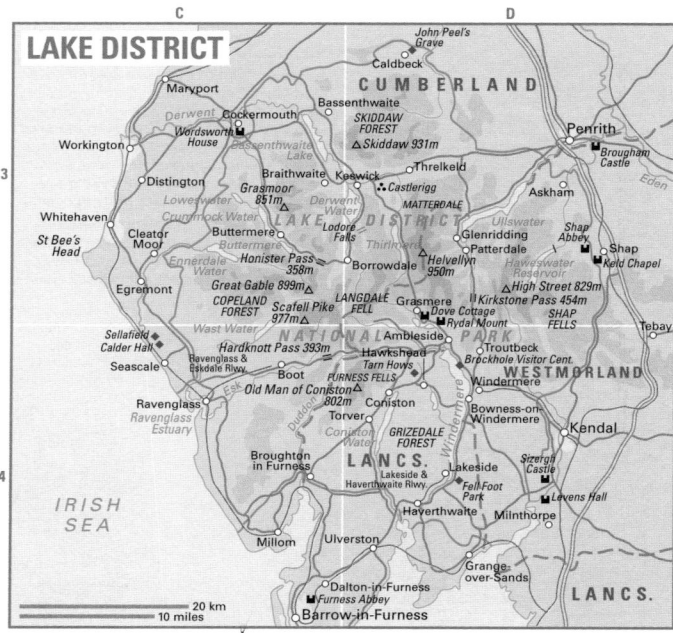

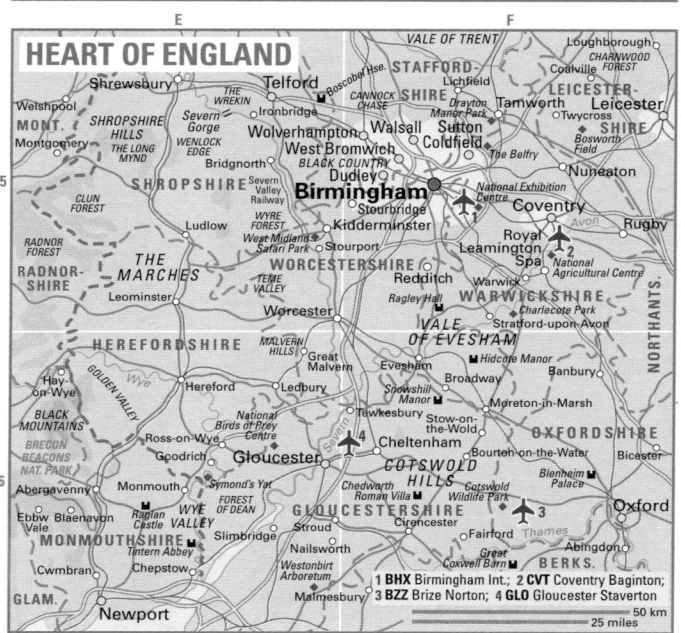

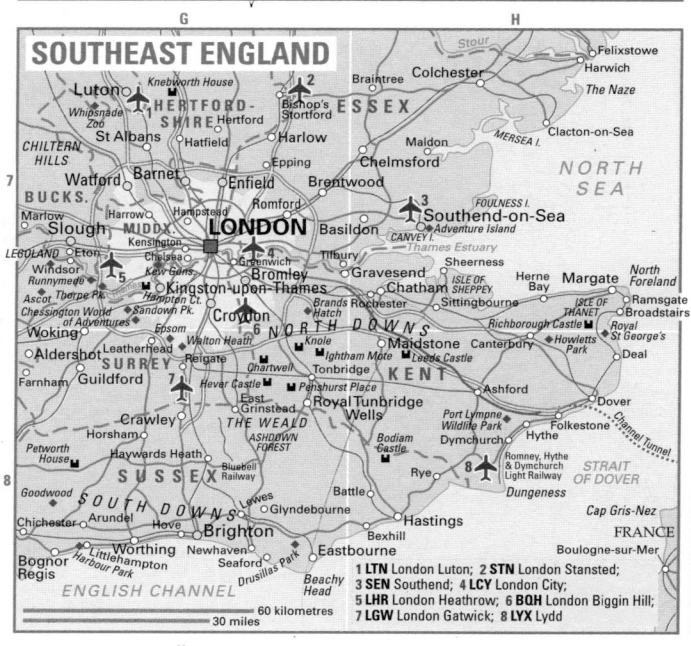

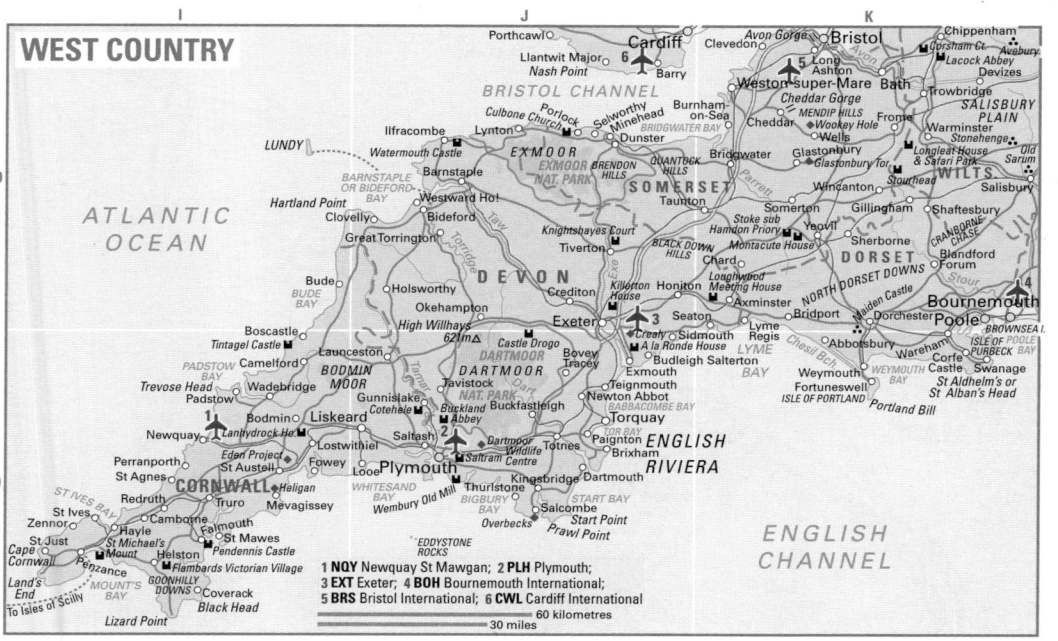

NEW YEAR Hogmanay (**Edinburgh**)
JAN 1st New Year's Day Parade (**London**)
JAN Celtic Connections (**Glasgow**)
JAN 25th Burns Night (**Scotland**)
late JAN Up Helly Aa (**Lerwick, Shetland**)
MAR-APR Ideal Home Show (**London**)
APR **London** Marathon
APR Oxford-Cambridge Boat Race (**London**)
APR Edinburgh International Science Festival
APR 30th Beltane: Celtic Fire Festival
MAY 1st Hobby Horse (**Minehead & Padstow**)
MAY Furry Dance (**Helston**) MAY Mayfest (**Glasgow**)
end MAY Chelsea Flower Show (**London**)
MAY-JUN **Bath** International Festival
MAY-AUG Glyndebourne Opera Festival
early JUN Queen's Birthday parade: Trooping The Colour (**London**)
JUN Royal Highland Show (**Ingliston**)
JUN Aldeburgh Festival late JUN Glastonbury Festival
JUN-JUL York Mystery Plays; 2004 and every four years
JUN-JUL Lawn Tennis Championships (**Wimbledon**)
JUN-AUG Riding of the Marches (**England-Scotland borders**)
JUN-AUG **Cardiff** Festival JUL Henley Royal Regatta
JUL Llangollen International Music Eisteddfod
JUL/AUG WOMAD World Music Festival (**Reading**)
JUL/AUG Highland Games (various places in **Scotland**)
JUL-SEP Promenade Concerts 'Proms' (**London**)
early AUG Royal National Eisteddford (**Wales**: venue changes)
AUG Three Choirs Festival (**Gloucester/Hereford/Worcester**)
AUG Edinburgh International Festival & Fringe; Military Tattoo
AUG Brecon Jazz Festival
AUG Great British Beer Festival (**London**)
AUG Bank Holiday Notting Hill Carnival (**London**)
SEP Royal Highland Gathering (**Braemar**)
SEP-NOV Blackpool Illuminations
NOV 5th Guy Fawkes Night
early NOV London-Brighton Veteran Car Rally
NOV **London** Film Festival; **London** Jazz Festival
NOV **Cardiff** Screen Festival
NOV State Opening of Parliament (**London**)
NOV Lord Mayor's Procession and Show (**London**)

62 Europe
UK: Airports, Motorways & Ferries

▶ **See also...** Flight Times (39); Europe Airports & High-Speed Rail (50-51); Europe Railways & Ferries (52-53); London Airport Connections (63)

The listings above refer to a selection of related themes. For more information, see the Contents (2-5).

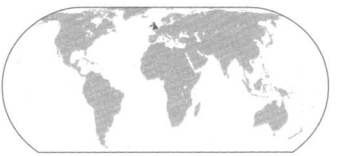

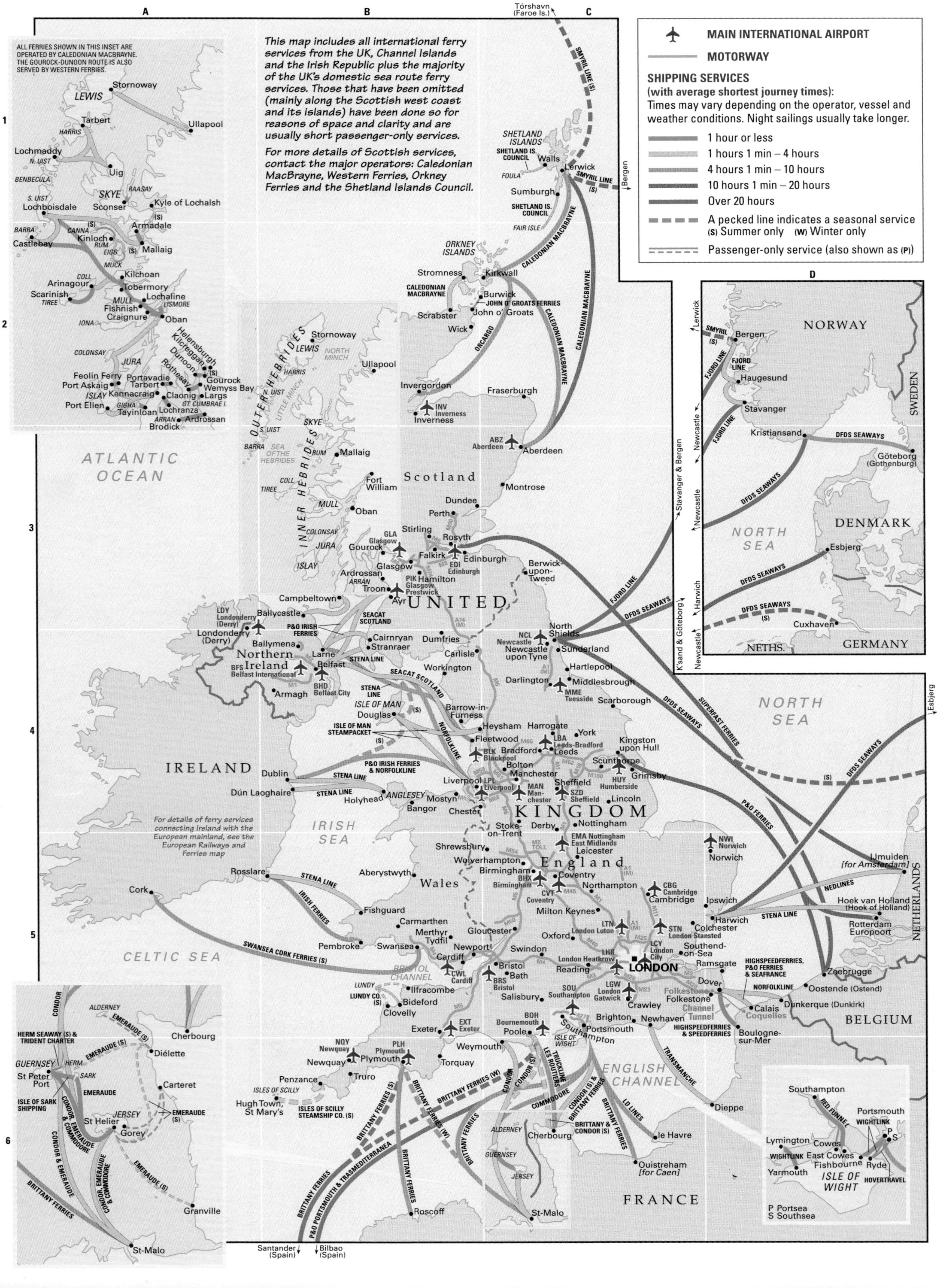

This map includes all international ferry services from the UK, Channel Islands and the Irish Republic plus the majority of the UK's domestic sea route ferry services. Those that have been omitted (mainly along the Scottish west coast and its islands) have been done so for reasons of space and clarity and are usually short passenger-only services.

For more details of Scottish services, contact the major operators: Caledonian MacBrayne, Western Ferries, Orkney Ferries and the Shetland Islands Council.

ALL FERRIES SHOWN IN THIS INSET ARE OPERATED BY CALEDONIAN MACBRAYNE. THE GOUROCK-DUNOON ROUTE IS ALSO SERVED BY WESTERN FERRIES.

Legend

✈ MAIN INTERNATIONAL AIRPORT

— MOTORWAY

SHIPPING SERVICES
(with average shortest journey times):
Times may vary depending on the operator, vessel and weather conditions. Night sailings usually take longer.

— 1 hour or less
— 1 hours 1 min – 4 hours
— 4 hours 1 min – 10 hours
— 10 hours 1 min – 20 hours
— Over 20 hours

- - - A pecked line indicates a seasonal service
(S) Summer only (W) Winter only
····· Passenger-only service (also shown as (P))

For details of ferry services connecting Ireland with the European mainland, see the European Railways and Ferries map.

P Portsea   S Southsea

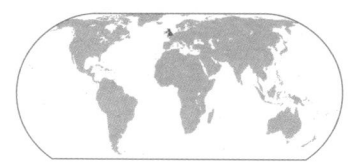

▶ **See also...** Flight Times (39); Europe Airports & High-Speed Rail (50-51); Europe Railways & Ferries (52-53); UK Airports, Motorways & Ferries (62)

The listings above refer to a selection of related themes. For more information, see the Contents (2-5).

This diagram shows the main public transport connections to London's airports from central London and the links between the airports. It is not drawn to scale and many incidental transport links – including the vast majority of the London Underground – have been omitted to improve legibility. Note that all information (particularly bus routes) is subject to change.

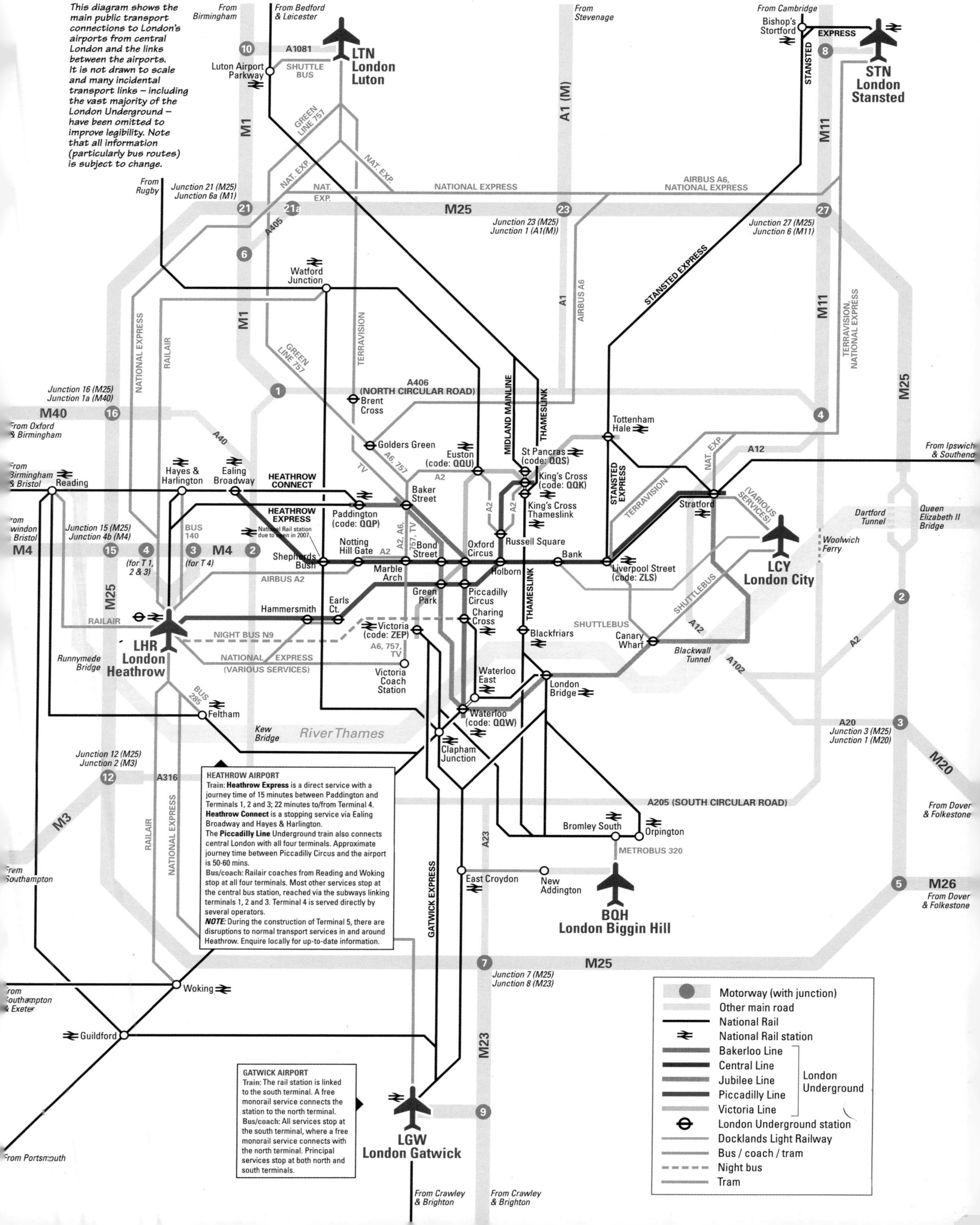

HEATHROW AIRPORT
Train: **Heathrow Express** is a direct service with a journey time of 15 minutes between Paddington and Terminals 1, 2 and 3; 22 minutes to/from Terminal 4. **Heathrow Connect** is a stopping service via Ealing Broadway and Hayes & Harlington.
The **Piccadilly Line** Underground train also connects central London with all four terminals. Approximate journey time between Piccadilly Circus and the airport is 50-60 mins.
Bus/coach: Railair coaches from Reading and Woking stop at all four terminals. Most other services stop at the central bus station, reached via the subways linking terminals 1, 2 and 3. Terminal 4 is served directly by several operators.
NOTE: During the construction of Terminal 5, there are disruptions to normal transport services in and around Heathrow. Enquire locally for up-to-date information.

GATWICK AIRPORT
Train: The rail station is linked to the south terminal. A free monorail service connects the station to the north terminal.
Bus/coach: All services stop at the south terminal, where a free monorail service connects with the north terminal. Principal services stop at both north and south terminals.

Map labels

From Birmingham; From Bedford & Leicester; From Stevenage; From Cambridge; Bishop's Stortford; EXPRESS; STANSTED

LTN London Luton; **STN London Stansted**

Luton Airport Parkway; SHUTTLE BUS; A1081; 10; M1; GREEN LINE 757; A1 (M); M11; 8

From Rugby; Junction 21 (M25) Junction 6a (M1); 21; 21a; A405; NAT. EXP.; NAT. EXP.; NATIONAL EXPRESS; M25; 23; Junction 23 (M25) Junction 1 (A1(M)); AIRBUS A6, NATIONAL EXPRESS; 27; Junction 27 (M25) Junction 6 (M11)

6; Watford Junction; M1; GREEN LINE 757; TERRAVISION; NATIONAL EXPRESS; RAILAIR; STANSTED EXPRESS; M11; TERRAVISION, NATIONAL EXPRESS; M25

Junction 16 (M25) Junction 1a (M40); 16; M40; A40; A406 (NORTH CIRCULAR ROAD); Brent Cross; A1; MIDLAND MAINLINE; THAMESLINK; Tottenham Hale; 4; A12; From Ipswich & Southend

From Oxford & Birmingham; From Birmingham & Bristol; Reading; Hayes & Harlington; Ealing Broadway; **HEATHROW CONNECT**; Golders Green; Euston (code: QQU); St Pancras (code: QQS); King's Cross (code: QQK); STANSTED EXPRESS; AIRBUS A6; Stratford; (VARIOUS SERVICES); Dartford Tunnel; Queen Elizabeth II Bridge

From Swindon & Bristol; Junction 15 (M25) Junction 4b (M4); 15; 4; M4; 3; 2; **HEATHROW EXPRESS**; National Rail station due to open in 2007; Paddington (code: QQP); Baker Street; A2; King's Cross Thameslink; Russell Square; TERRAVISION; Woolwich Ferry

From Southampton & Exeter; (for T1, 2 & 3); (for T4); BUS 140; Shepherds Bush; Notting Hill Gate; A2, A6; Bond Street; Oxford Circus; Bank; Liverpool Street (code: ZLS); **LCY London City**; 2; A2

M25; RAILAIR; AIRBUS A2; Marble Arch; A2; Holborn; SHUTTLEBUS; Canary Wharf; SHUTTLEBUS; A12; Blackwall Tunnel; A102

LHR London Heathrow; Hammersmith; Earls Ct.; Green Park; Piccadilly Circus; Charing Cross; THAMESLINK; Blackfriars; 3; A20; Junction 3 (M25) Junction 1 (M20); M20

Runnymede Bridge; NIGHT BUS N9; Victoria (code: ZEP); NATIONAL EXPRESS (VARIOUS SERVICES); A6, 757, TV; Waterloo East; London Bridge

BUS 285; Feltham; Kew Bridge; River Thames; Victoria Coach Station; Waterloo (code: QQW)

Junction 12 (M25) Junction 2 (M3); 12; A316; M3; Clapham Junction; A205 (SOUTH CIRCULAR ROAD); Bromley South; Orpington; METROBUS 320; 5; M26; From Dover & Folkestone

From Southampton; NATIONAL EXPRESS; RAILAIR; Woking; East Croydon; New Addington; A23; **BQH London Biggin Hill**; 7; Junction 7 (M25) Junction 8 (M23); M25

From Portsmouth; Guildford; GATWICK EXPRESS; M23; 9; **LGW London Gatwick**; From Crawley & Brighton

Legend

●	Motorway (with junction)
	Other main road
	National Rail
	National Rail station
	Bakerloo Line
	Central Line
	Jubilee Line
	Piccadilly Line
	Victoria Line
⊖	London Underground station
	Docklands Light Railway
	Bus / coach / tram
	Night bus
	Tram

London Underground

UK: Attractions

See also... Attractions in Belgium (67), Netherlands (69), Germany (73), France (77), Iberia (79) and Italy (86)

The listings above refer to a selection of related themes. For more information, see the Contents (2-5). See also the Columbus Tourist Attractions & Events of the World.

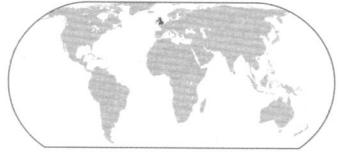

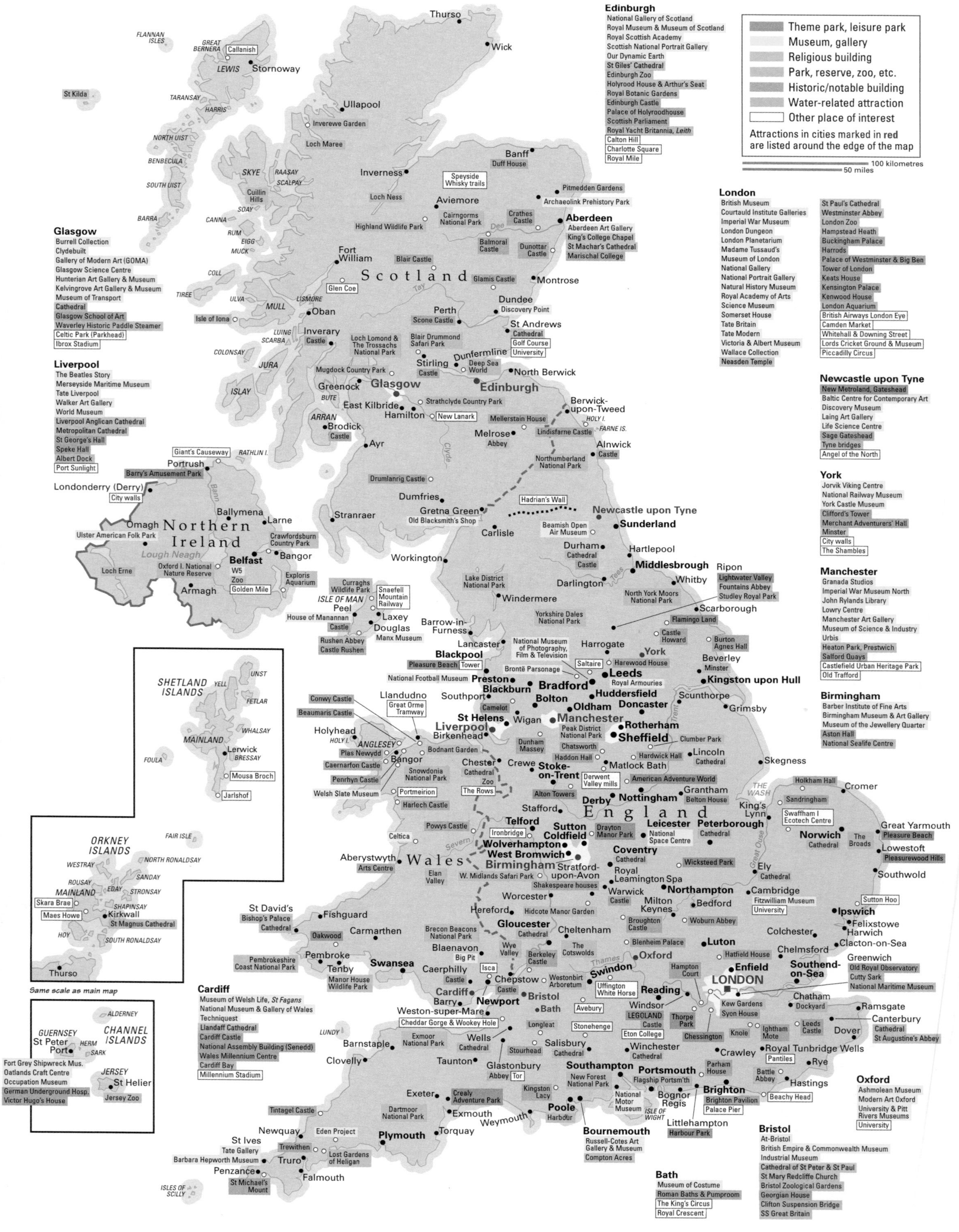

Theme park, leisure park
Museum, gallery
Religious building
Park, reserve, zoo, etc.
Historic/notable building
Water-related attraction
Other place of interest
Attractions in cities marked in red are listed around the edge of the map
100 kilometres
50 miles
Edinburgh
National Gallery of Scotland
Royal Museum & Museum of Scotland
Royal Scottish Academy
Scottish National Portrait Gallery
Our Dynamic Earth
St Giles' Cathedral
Edinburgh Zoo
Holyrood House & Arthur's Seat
Royal Botanic Gardens
Edinburgh Castle
Palace of Holyroodhouse
Scottish Parliament
Royal Yacht Britannia, Leith
Calton Hill
Charlotte Square
Royal Mile
Glasgow
Burrell Collection
Clydebuilt
Gallery of Modern Art (GOMA)
Glasgow Science Centre
Hunterian Art Gallery & Museum
Kelvingrove Art Gallery & Museum
Museum of Transport
Cathedral
Glasgow School of Art
Waverley Historic Paddle Steamer
Celtic Park (Parkhead)
Ibrox Stadium
Liverpool
The Beatles Story
Merseyside Maritime Museum
Tate Liverpool
Walker Art Gallery
World Museum
Liverpool Anglican Cathedral
Metropolitan Cathedral
St George's Hall
Speke Hall
Albert Dock
Port Sunlight
London
British Museum
Courtauld Institute Galleries
Imperial War Museum
London Dungeon
London Planetarium
Madame Tussaud's
Museum of London
National Gallery
National Portrait Gallery
Natural History Museum
Royal Academy of Arts
Science Museum
Somerset House
Tate Britain
Tate Modern
Victoria & Albert Museum
Wallace Collection
Neasden Temple
St Paul's Cathedral
Westminster Abbey
London Zoo
Hampstead Heath
Buckingham Palace
Harrods
Palace of Westminster & Big Ben
Tower of London
Keats House
Kensington Palace
Kenwood House
London Aquarium
British Airways London Eye
Camden Market
Whitehall & Downing Street
Lords Cricket Ground & Museum
Piccadilly Circus
Newcastle upon Tyne
New Metroland, Gateshead
Baltic Centre for Contemporary Art
Discovery Museum
Laing Art Gallery
Life Science Centre
Sage Gateshead
Tyne bridges
Angel of the North
York
Jorvik Viking Centre
National Railway Museum
York Castle Museum
Clifford's Tower
Merchant Adventurers' Hall
Minster
City walls
The Shambles
Manchester
Granada Studios
Imperial War Museum North
John Rylands Library
Lowry Centre
Manchester Art Gallery
Museum of Science & Industry
Urbis
Heaton Park, Prestwich
Salford Quays
Castlefield Urban Heritage Park
Old Trafford
Birmingham
Barber Institute of Fine Arts
Birmingham Museum & Art Gallery
Museum of the Jewellery Quarter
Aston Hall
National Sealife Centre
Cardiff
Museum of Welsh Life, St Fagans
National Museum & Gallery of Wales
Techniquest
Llandaff Cathedral
Cardiff Castle
National Assembly Building (Senedd)
Wales Millennium Centre
Cardiff Bay
Millennium Stadium
Bath
Museum of Costume
Roman Baths & Pumproom
The King's Circus
Royal Crescent
Bristol
At-Bristol
British Empire & Commonwealth Museum
Industrial Museum
Cathedral of St Peter & St Paul
St Mary Redcliffe Church
Bristol Zoological Gardens
Georgian House
Clifton Suspension Bridge
SS Great Britain
Oxford
Ashmolean Museum
Modern Art Oxford
University & Pitt Rivers Museums
University
Scotland
Northern Ireland
England
Wales
Thurso
Wick
FLANNAN ISLES
GREAT BERNERA
Callanish
LEWIS
Stornoway
St Kilda
TARANSAY
HARRIS
Ullapool
Inverewe Garden
Loch Maree
NORTH UIST
BENBECULA
SKYE
RAASAY
SCALPAY
SOUTH UIST
Cuillin Hills
SOAY
BARRA
CANNA
RUM
EIGG
MUCK
COLL
TIREE
ULVA
MULL
LISMORE
Isle of Iona
COLONSAY
LUING
SCARBA
JURA
ISLAY
BUTE
ARRAN
Banff
Duff House
Inverness
Speyside Whisky trails
Loch Ness
Aviemore
Pitmedden Gardens
Archaeolink Prehistory Park
Aberdeen
Cairngorms National Park
Highland Wildlife Park
Crathes Castle
Balmoral Castle
Dunottar Castle
Fort William
Blair Castle
Glen Coe
Glamis Castle
Montrose
Dundee
Discovery Point
Oban
Perth
Scone Castle
St Andrews
Cathedral
Golf Course
University
Inverary
Castle
Loch Lomond & The Trossachs National Park
Blair Drummond Safari Park
Dunfermline
Deep Sea World
Stirling
Castle
Mugdock Country Park
Greenock
Glasgow
Edinburgh
North Berwick
East Kilbride
Strathclyde Country Park
Hamilton
New Lanark
Brodick
Castle
Ayr
Berwick-upon-Tweed
HOLY I.
FARNE IS.
Mellerstain House
Melrose
Abbey
Lindisfarne Castle
Alnwick
Castle
Northumberland National Park
Drumlanrig Castle
Dumfries
Gretna Green
Old Blacksmith's Shop
Hadrian's Wall
Stranraer
Giant's Causeway
RATHLIN I.
Portrush
Barry's Amusement Park
Londonderry (Derry)
City walls
Ballymena
Larne
Omagh
Ulster American Folk Park
Crawfordsburn Country Park
Lough Neagh
Belfast
W5
Zoo
Golden Mile
Bangor
Loch Erne
Oxford I. National Nature Reserve
Armagh
Exploris Aquarium
Newcastle upon Tyne
Sunderland
Beamish Open Air Museum
Carlisle
Durham
Cathedral
Castle
Hartlepool
Middlesbrough
Workington
Lake District National Park
Darlington
Whitby
Ripon
Lightwater Valley
Fountains Abbey
Studley Royal Park
Curraghs Wildlife Park
Snaefell Mountain Railway
ISLE OF MAN
Peel
Laxey
House of Manannan
Castle
Douglas
Manx Museum
Rushen Abbey
Castle Rushen
Windermere
North York Moors National Park
Scarborough
Flamingo Land
Yorkshire Dales National Park
Barrow-in-Furness
Castle Howard
Burton Agnes Hall
Lancaster
National Museum of Photography, Film & Television
Harrogate
York
Beverley
Minster
Blackpool
Pleasure Beach
Tower
Saltaire
Harewood House
Brontë Parsonage
Leeds
Kingston upon Hull
National Football Museum
Preston
Royal Armouries
Blackburn
Bradford
Huddersfield
Scunthorpe
Grimsby
Llandudno
Great Orme Tramway
Southport
Camelot
Bolton
Oldham
Doncaster
Conwy Castle
Beaumaris Castle
St Helens
Wigan
Manchester
Rotherham
Liverpool
Birkenhead
Peak District National Park
Sheffield
Clumber Park
Holyhead
HOLY I.
ANGLESEY
Plas Newydd
Bangor
Bodnant Garden
Dunham Massey
Chatsworth
Haddon Hall
Hardwick Hall
Lincoln
Cathedral
Skegness
Caernarfon Castle
Snowdonia National Park
Chester
Cathedral
Zoo
Crewe
Stoke-on-Trent
Matlock Bath
Penrhyn Castle
Derwent Valley mills
American Adventure World
Welsh Slate Museum
Portmeirion
The Rows
Alton Towers
Derby
Nottingham
Grantham
Belton House
THE WASH
Holkham Hall
Cromer
Harlech Castle
Stafford
King's Lynn
Sandringham
Telford
Sutton Coldfield
Drayton Manor Park
Leicester
National Space Centre
Peterborough
Cathedral
Swaffham Ecotech Centre
Great Yarmouth
Pleasure Beach
Powys Castle
Ironbridge
Norwich
Cathedral
The Broads
Celtica
Wolverhampton
West Bromwich
Coventry
Cathedral
Lowestoft
Pleasurewood Hills
Aberystwyth
Arts Centre
Birmingham
Wicksteed Park
Ely
Cathedral
Elan Valley
W. Midlands Safari Park
Stratford-upon-Avon
Royal Leamington Spa
Shakespeare houses
Southwold
Warwick
Castle
Northampton
Cambridge
Fitzwilliam Museum
University
Worcester
Milton Keynes
Bedford
Sutton Hoo
Ipswich
St David's
Bishop's Palace
Cathedral
Fishguard
Hereford
Hidcote Manor Garden
Broughton Castle
Woburn Abbey
Felixstowe
Harwich
Gloucester
Cathedral
Cheltenham
Colchester
Carmarthen
Brecon Beacons National Park
Oakwood
Blenheim Palace
Luton
Clacton-on-Sea
Wye Valley
The Cotswolds
Pembrokeshire Coast National Park
Pembroke
Blaenavon
Big Pit
Berkeley Castle
Oxford
Hatfield House
Chelmsford
Greenwich
Old Royal Observatory
Cutty Sark
National Maritime Museum
Tenby
Swansea
Manor House Wildlife Park
Caerphilly
Castle
Isca
Chepstow
Castle
Westonbirt Arboretum
Swindon
Hampton Court
Enfield
Southend-on-Sea
LONDON
Cardiff
Barry
Newport
Bristol
Uffington White Horse
Reading
Chatham
Dockyard
Bath
Avebury
Windsor
LEGOLAND
Castle
Thorpe Park
Kew Gardens
Syon House
Ramsgate
Canterbury
Cathedral
St Augustine's Abbey
Weston-super-Mare
Cheddar Gorge & Wookey Hole
Longleat
Stonehenge
Eton College
Chessington
Knole
Ightham Mote
Leeds Castle
Dover
LUNDY
Barnstaple
Exmoor National Park
Wells
Cathedral
Stourhead
Salisbury
Cathedral
Winchester
Cathedral
Crawley
Royal Tunbridge Wells
Pantiles
Rye
Clovelly
Taunton
Glastonbury
Abbey
Tor
Southampton
New Forest National Park
Portsmouth
Flagship Portsm'th
Parham House
Battle Abbey
Hastings
Exeter
Crealy Adventure Park
Kingston Lacy
National Motor Museum
Bognor Regis
Brighton
Brighton Pavilion
Palace Pier
Beachy Head
Tintagel Castle
Dartmoor National Park
Exmouth
Poole
Harbour
ISLE OF WIGHT
Littlehampton
Harbour Park
Weymouth
Newquay
Eden Project
Torquay
Plymouth
Bournemouth
Russell-Cotes Art Gallery & Museum
Compton Acres
St Ives
Tate Gallery
Barbara Hepworth Museum
Trewithen
Lost Gardens of Heligan
Truro
Penzance
Falmouth
St Michael's Mount
ISLES OF SCILLY
SHETLAND ISLANDS
UNST
YELL
FETLAR
MAINLAND
WHALSAY
Lerwick
BRESSAY
FOULA
Mousa Broch
Jarlshof
ORKNEY ISLANDS
FAIR ISLE
NORTH RONALDSAY
WESTRAY
ROUSAY
SANDAY
MAINLAND
EDAY
STRONSAY
Skara Brae
SHAPINSAY
Maes Howe
Kirkwall
St Magnus Cathedral
HOY
SOUTH RONALDSAY
Thurso
Same scale as main map
ALDERNEY
GUERNSEY
St Peter Port
HERM
SARK
CHANNEL ISLANDS
JERSEY
St Helier
Fort Grey Shipwreck Mus.
Oatlands Craft Centre
Occupation Museum
German Underground Hosp.
Victor Hugo's House
Jersey Zoo
Dee
Tay
Clyde
Bann
Tees
Trent
Severn
Thames
Great Ouse

See also... Contents (2-5) – this country features in many thematic and regional maps throughout the *BTEC First Travel Atlas*.

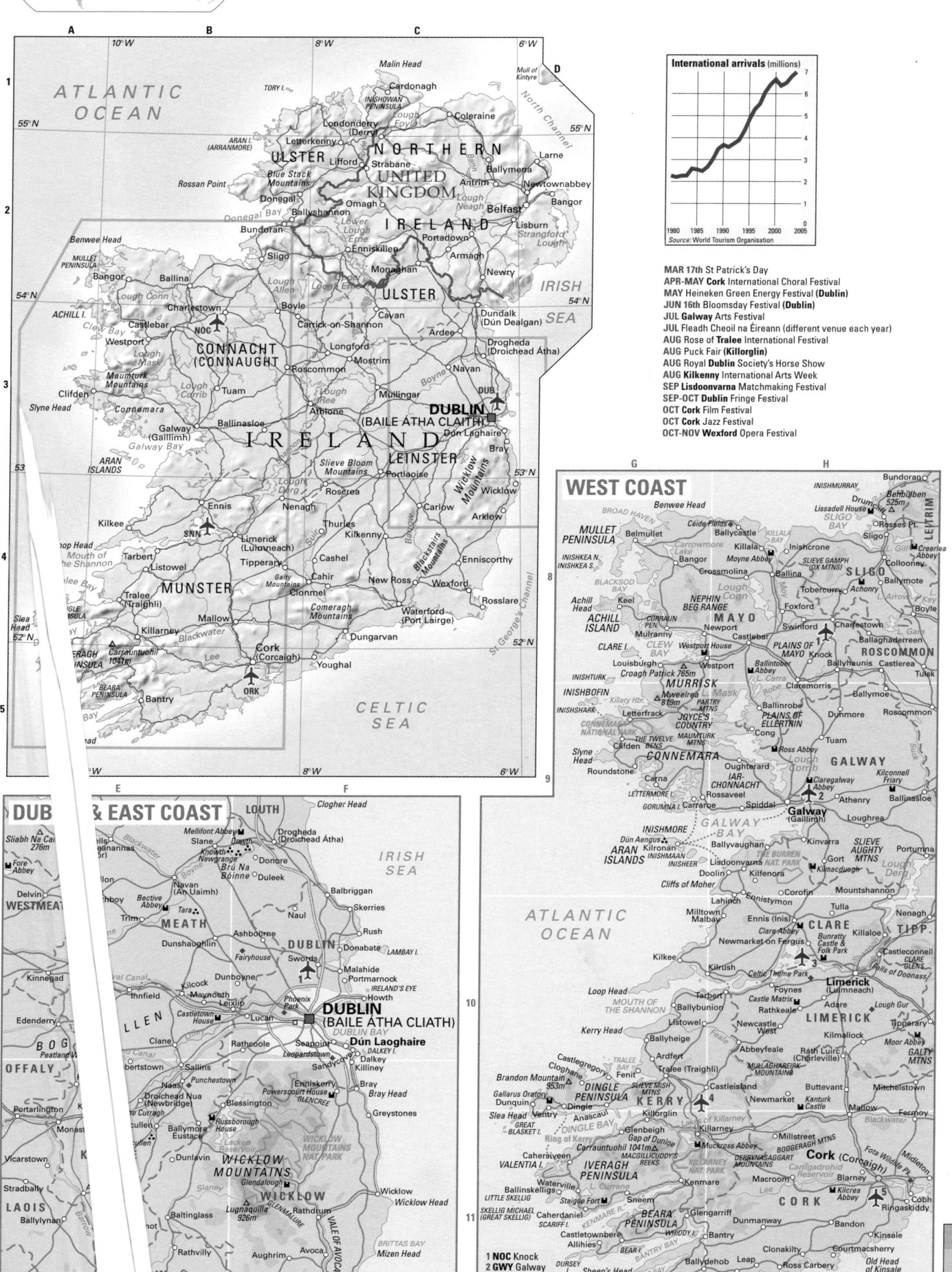

International arrivals (millions)

1980 1985 1990 1995 2000 2005
Source: World Tourism Organisation

MAR 17th St Patrick's Day
APR-MAY **Cork** International Choral Festival
MAY Heineken Green Energy Festival (**Dublin**)
JUN 16th Bloomsday Festival (**Dublin**)
JUL **Galway** Arts Festival
JUL Fleadh Cheoil na Éireann (different venue each year)
AUG Rose of **Tralee** International Festival
AUG Puck Fair (**Killorglin**)
AUG Royal **Dublin** Society's Horse Show
AUG **Kilkenny** International Arts Week
SEP **Lisdoonvarna** Matchmaking Festival
SEP-OCT **Dublin** Fringe Festival
OCT **Cork** Film Festival
OCT **Cork** Jazz Festival
OCT-NOV **Wexford** Opera Festival

The listings above refer to a selection of related themes.
For more information, see the Contents (2-5).

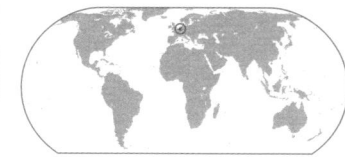

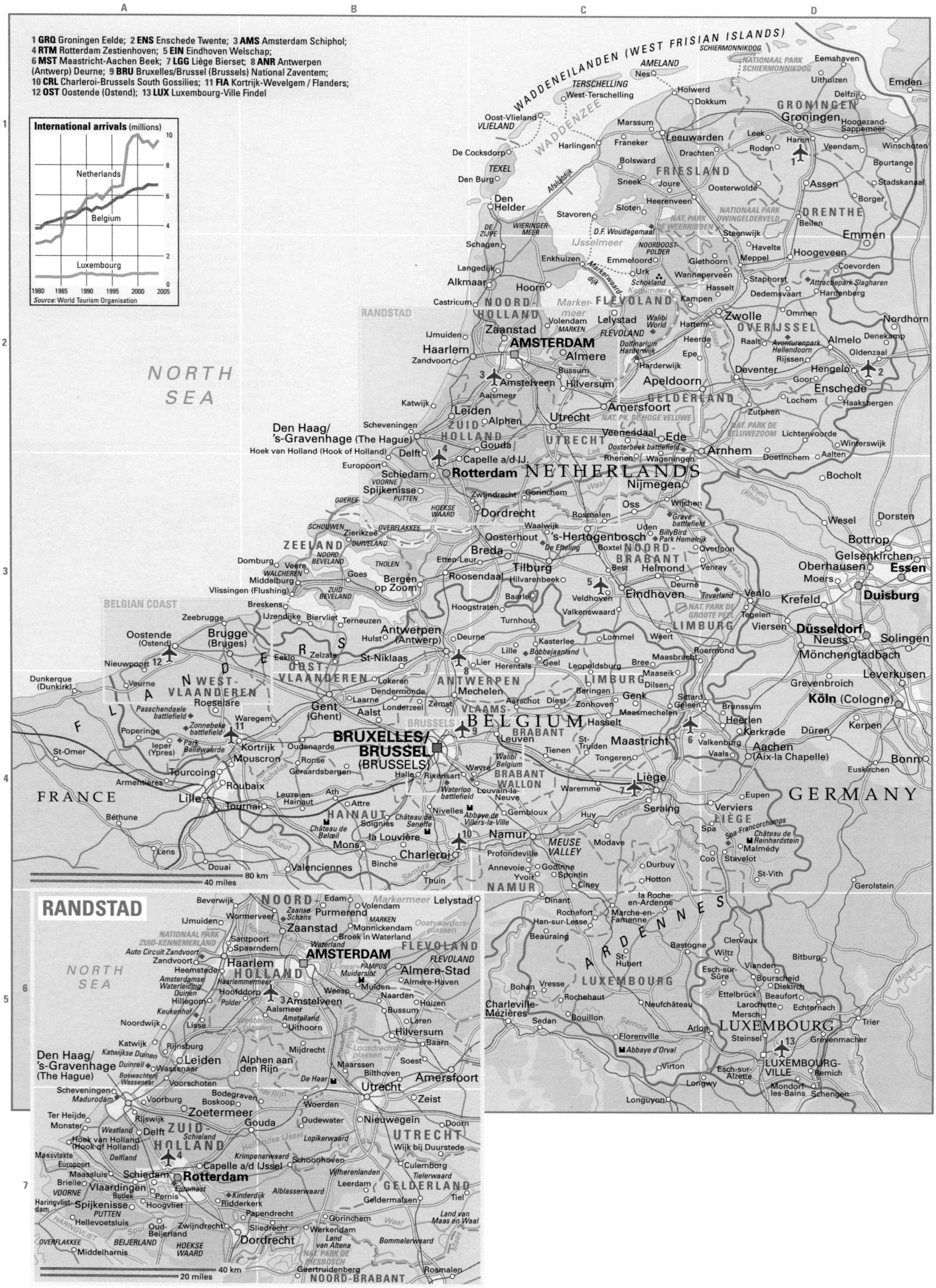

1 **GRQ** Groningen Eelde; 2 **ENS** Enschede Twente; 3 **AMS** Amsterdam Schiphol;
4 **RTM** Rotterdam Zestienhoven; 5 **EIN** Eindhoven Welschap;
6 **MST** Maastricht-Aachen Beek; 7 **LGG** Liège Bierset; 8 **ANR** Antwerpen
(Antwerp) Deurne; 9 **BRU** Bruxelles/Brussel (Brussels) National Zaventem;
10 **CRL** Charleroi-Brussels South Gossilies; 11 **FIA** Kortrijk-Wevelgem / Flanders;
12 **OST** Oostende (Ostend); 13 **LUX** Luxembourg-Ville Findel

International arrivals (millions)

Netherlands

Belgium

Luxembourg

1980 1985 1990 1995 2000 2005
Source: World Tourism Organisation

WADDENEILANDEN (WEST FRISIAN ISLANDS)

NORTH SEA

NETHERLANDS

BELGIUM

LUXEMBOURG

GERMANY

FRANCE

Bruxelles/Brussel (BRUSSELS)

AMSTERDAM

ARDENNES

RANDSTAD

NORTH SEA

NOORD HOLLAND

ZUID HOLLAND

UTRECHT

GELDERLAND

NOORD-BRABANT

AMSTERDAM

Rotterdam

Den Haag/'s-Gravenhage (The Hague)

40 km
20 miles

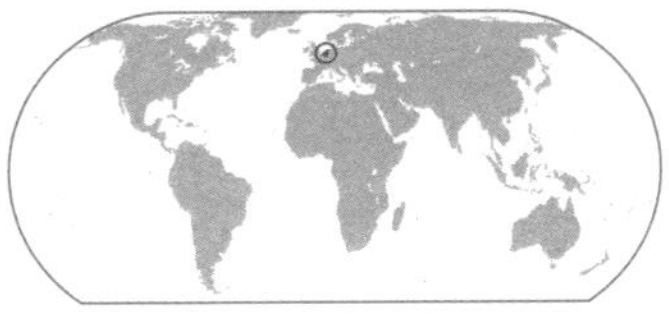

▶ *See also...* Attractions in UK (64), Netherlands (69), Germany (73), France (77), Iberia (79) and Italy (86)

The listings above refer to a selection of related themes. For more information, see the Contents (2-5). See also the Columbus *Tourist Attractions & Events of the World.*

Region boundary
Province boundary
● Province capital
Language areas:
Flemish
French
German
Bilingual (Flemish-French)

80 km
40 miles

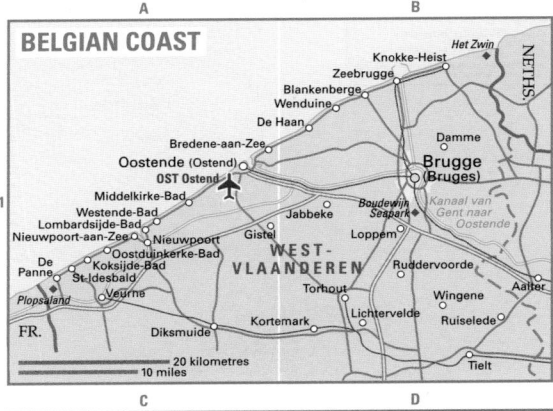

BELGIAN COAST

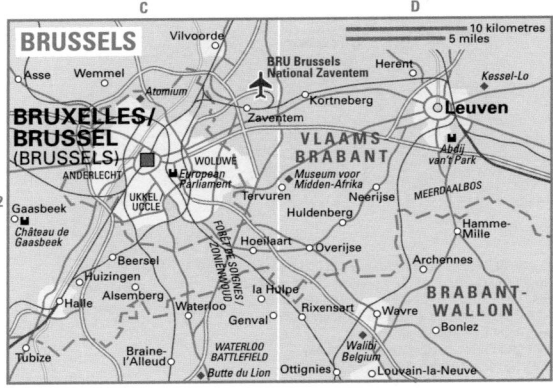

BRUSSELS

FEB Eu…s Festival Musica Antiqua
MAR …es Rats Morts: Dead Rats Ball **(Ostend)**
before…T Carnival **(Binche, Eupen, Malmédy,** and countr…e)
LENT L…re: street parade **(Stavelot)**
APR Fe…al van Vlaanderen **(Flanders)**
MAY Ka…festival: cat festival **(Ypres)**, with a parade of giant cats eve…years
MAY Ku…aFESTIVALdesArts: international cultural festival **(Brusse…)**
MAY Bru…s Jazz Marathon
MAY Har…processie: Procession of Our Lady **(Mechelin)**
MAY Heil… bedprocessie: Holy Blood Procession **(Bruges)**
TRINITY S…DAY Ducasse: Chariot of Gold procession; and …ombat d…agon: St George killing the dragon **(Mons)**
JN-OCT …val de Wallonie **(Wallonia)**
JN Coule…afé: world music event **(Brussels)**

JUN/JUL Ommegang: medieval-style procession **(Brussels)**
JUL Rock Werchter: rock festival **(Leuven)**
JUL De Gentse Feesten: multicultural festival **(Ghent)**
JUL Kroningsfeesten: Virgin Mary procession **(Tongeren)**; 2009 and every seven years
JUL 21st Belgian National Day
JUL Boetprocessie: penitents' procession **(Veurne)**
AUG Tapis des Fleurs: floral carpet (Grand Place, **Brussels**); even years
AUG Ducasse: parade of giants **(Ath)**
AUG Breugel Festival **(Wingene)**
SEP Belgian Beer Weekend **(Brussels)**
SEP Combat de l'Échasse d'Or: Fight for the Golden Stilt **(Namur)**
OCT Hasseltse Jeneverfeesten **(Hasselt)**
DEC Marché de Noël: Christmas market (Grand Place, **Brussels**)

Brugge (Br…es)
B…dewijn Se…
G…ningemuseum
Memlingmuseum
On…Lieve Vro…werk
Beg…nhof
Bel…rt
Can…s
Mar…

Ge…(Ghen…)
Museum voor Sch…Kunsten
Sted…k Museum…
Actu… Kunst Ge… (S…AK)
St-B…skathedra…
Belfort… Lakenha…
Grave…teen
Grasl…
St-Mi…elsbrug

Theme p…k, leisure park
Museum g…llery
Religio…building
Park, re…ve, zoo, etc.
Historic…able building
Water-r…ed attraction
Other pl…of interest

Attraction…in citie…marked in red are listed …round th…map

40 km
20 miles

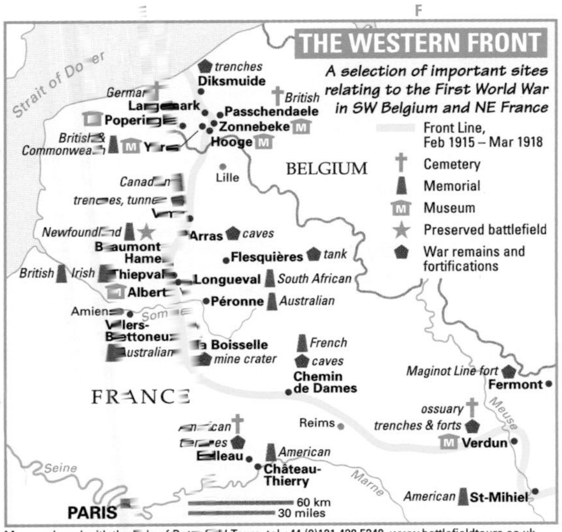

THE WESTERN FRONT

A selection of important sites relating to the First World War in SW Belgium and NE France

━━ Front Line, Feb 1915 – Mar 1918
✝ Cemetery
🅼 Memorial
Ⓜ Museum
★ Preserved battlefield
Ⓕ War remains and fortifications

60 km
30 miles

Liège
Musée Curtius
Musée de la Vie Wallonne
Cathédrale St-Paul
Église St-Barthélemy
Église St-Jacques
Palais des Princes-Évêques

Antwerpen (Antwerp)
Etnografisch Museum
Koninklijk Museum voor Schone Kunsten
Modemuseum (MOMU)
Museum Mayer van den Bergh
Museum Plantin-Moretus
Rubenshuis
Onze Lieve Vrouwkathedraal
St-Pauluskerk
Dierentuin van Antwerpen
Stadhuis
Grote Markt
Wijk Zurenborg

Mechelen
Speelgoedmuseum
Technopolis
St-Romboutskathedraal
Parc Zoologique de Plankendael
Stadhuis

Bruxelles/Brussel (Brussels)
Bruparck
Autoworld
Centre Belge de la Bande Dessinée
Musées Bellevue
Musée David et Alice van Buuren
Musée Horta
Musée Magritte
Musée des Instruments de Musique (MIM)
Musées Royaux des Beaux-Arts
Musées Royaux d'Art et d'Histoire
Musée des Sciences Naturelles

Abbaye Notre-Dame-de-la-Cambre
Basilique nationale du Sacré-Cœur
Cathédrale des Sts-Michel-et-Gudule
Palais Royale
Stadhuis
Serres royales de Laeken
Atomium
Grand Place
Mannekin Pis

▶ **See also...** UNESCO Heritage (48-49); Benelux (66)

The listings above refer to a selection of related themes.
For more information, see the Contents (2-5).

Map legend

– – – Province boundary
● Province capital

60 km / 30 miles

WADDENEILANDEN (WEST FRISIAN ISLANDS)

Waddenzee

FRIESLAND
Leeuwarden

GRONINGEN
● Groningen
GRQ Groningen
● Assen

DRENTHE
● Emmen

Den Helder

IJsselmeer

Alkmaar

FLEVOLAND
● Zwolle

NOORD-HOLLAND
Lelystad

Apeldoorn

OVERIJSSEL

ENS Enschede
● Enschede

AMSTERDAM
Haarlem
AMS Amsterdam

RANDSTAD

Amersfoort

GELDERLAND

Den Haag/ 's-Gravenhage (The Hague)
● Leiden
ZUID-HOLLAND
Utrecht
UTRECHT

Lek
● Arnhem

Hoek van Holland (Hook of Holland)
RTM Rotterdam
● Rotterdam

Waal
● Nijmegen

THE DELTA
Dordrecht

's-Hertogenbosch

Middelburg
ZEELAND
Breda
NOORD-BRABANT
● Tilburg

Vlissingen (Flushing)

Maas

● Eindhoven
EIN Eindhoven

Schelde

LIMBURG

MST Maastricht
Heerlen
● Maastricht

FEB/MAR Carnaval (**Breda, Maastricht** & **'s-Hertogenbosch**)
MAR Stille Ommegang: silent procession (**Amsterdam**)
MAR-MAY National Floral Exhibition (**Keukenhof**)
APR Floral Procession (**Haarlem** to **Noordwijk**)
APR **Rotterdam** Marathon
APR 30th Koninginnedag: Queen's Birthday
MAY National Windmill & Pumping Station Day
MAY-SEP Passion Plays (**Tegelen**): 2005 and every five years
JUN Holland Festival & Amsterdam Roots Festival (**Amsterdam**)
JUL North Sea Jazz Festival (**Rotterdam**)
AUG International Fireworks Festival (**Scheveningen**)
AUG Boekenmarkt (**Deventer**)
AUG **Amsterdam** Gay Pride
AUG-SEP Festival of Ancient Music (**Utrecht**)
SEP Bloemen Corso: floral procession (**Aalsmeer** to **Amsterdam**)
SEP Jordaan Festival (**Amsterdam**)
OCT 3rd Leidens Ontzet: historical procession (**Leiden**)
mid NOV St Nicholas' official entrance (**Amsterdam**)
DEC Candle Festival (**Gouda**)

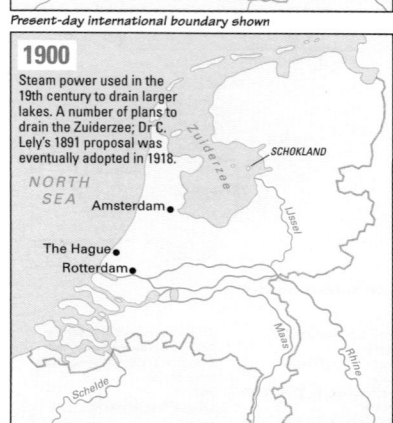

1650

The 17th century: the Dutch 'Golden Age'. Coastal dykes protected low-lying land; windmills used to drain inland lakes.

NORTH SEA
Amsterdam
The Hague
Rotterdam
Zuiderzee
IJssel
Maas
Schelde
Rhine

Present-day international boundary shown

1900

Steam power used in the 19th century to drain larger lakes. A number of plans to drain the Zuiderzee; Dr C. Lely's 1891 proposal was eventually adopted in 1918.

NORTH SEA
Amsterdam
Zuiderzee
SCHOKLAND
The Hague
Rotterdam
IJssel
Maas
Rhine

THE DUTCH vs THE SEA

Without damming or dyking:

Altitude (metres)

20 / 5 / 0	Safe from flooding
	Subject to river flooding
	Subject to almost continual sea flooding
	Totally submerged

60 km / 30 miles

Waddenzee
Leeuwarden
Groningen
Assen
Emmen

Den Helder
IJsselmeer
Alkmaar
Zwolle
Lelystad

AMSTERDAM
Haarlem

LOW NETHERLANDS
VELUWE
HIGH NETHERLANDS

Den Haag/ 's-Gravenhage (The Hague)
Leiden
Apeldoorn
Amersfoort
Utrecht

Hoek van Holland (Hook of Holland)
Lek
Arnhem
▽ *Lowest point: Nieuwerkerk aan den IJssel −6.7m*
Rotterdam
Waal
Nijmegen

DE PEEL

Dordrecht
's-Hertogenbosch
Middelburg
Breda
Tilburg
Vlissingen (Flushing)
Eindhoven
Schelde

Heerlen
Maastricht
Highest point: Vaalserberg 321m

The **IJSSELMEER SCHEME** was begun in 1918, following the 1916 floods. Its aims were to provide protection against flooding in the Zuiderzee, create more land for agriculture and help combat soil salinity in the area by the creation of a freshwater lake, the IJsselmeer.
1 Amsteldiep Dyke, 1919-24 & **Wieringermeer**, 1927-30
2 Afsluitdijk (enclosing dam), 1927-32
3 Noordoostpolder, 1937-42
4 Oostelijk Flevoland, 1950-57
5 Zuidelijk Flevoland, 1959-68
6 Markerwaard, 1963- (abandoned 1986)

The sand islands enclosing the Waddenzee provide an important barrier against North Sea storms.

The Dutch have waged a constant battle against the waters of the North Sea. Nearly one third of The Netherlands is below sea level and every major storm and flood has redrawn the landscape. Dyke building and reclamation has continued for centuries and the two major projects undertaken in the 20th century have provided some degree of security as well as increasing the land area. The engineering achievement is staggering – 'God created the world but the Dutch created the Netherlands' – but opinion is divided as to how long these defences will be able to last without serious modification.

DYKES have been built on the coast and along many rivers to prevent flooding. In creating polders (land reclaimed from the sea, a lake or marshland), a dyke is first built to enclose the area before the water is pumped out. Principal sea dykes are shown here.

Coastal **SAND DUNES**, planted with marram grass to increase stability, provide an important defence against high tides.

● Principal places of interest connected with land reclamation

---

SCHIERMONNIKOOG
AMELAND
TERSCHELLING
VLIELAND
Waddenzee
TEXEL

GRONINGEN
● Groningen
Leeuwarden
FRIESLAND
● Assen
DRENTHE
● Emmen
● Hoogeveen

Den Helder
NOORD-
Alkmaar
IJsselmeer
2
1
Wouda Steam Pumping Station 1920
3 Emmeloord
Zuiderzee Museum
Hoorn
Schokland Former island in the Zuiderzee
Beemster Polder Drained 1612
Markermeer
FLEVOLAND
● Lelystad
● Zwolle
OVERIJSSEL
Noordzee Kanaal
6
Zaanstad
Almere
4
Haarlem
Hengelo
AMSTERDAM
5
Deventer
Enschede
Cruquius Steam Pumping Station 1849
Hilversum
Apeldoorn
Amersfoort
Leiden
Den Haag/ 's-Gravenhage (The Hague)
UTRECHT
Utrecht
GELDERLAND
Hoek van Holland (Hook of Holland)
Delft
Ede
Arnhem
ZUID-HOLLAND
A
Rotterdam
K
Kinderdijk 1738-1761
B
J
Lek
Nijmegen
C
Dordrecht
Waal
D
H I
's-Hertogenbosch
Delta Expo
E F
Bergen op Zoom
Breda
NOORD-BRABANT
Tilburg
Helmond
Middelburg
G
Vlissingen (Flushing)
ZEELAND
Eindhoven
Breskens
Venlo
Terneuzen
Maas
Schelde
LIMBURG

60 km / 30 miles

The Dutch have utilised wind power for many purposes and in the low-lying coastal areas **WINDMILLS** have become synonymous with the draining of the land. No typical Dutch landscape is complete without the inclusion of a windmill – at one time there were over 10,000 in the country. Today there are still approximately 1,000 windmills; the most famous being at Kinderdijk, where a group of 19 drained the Alblasserwaard until 1950.

The **DELTA WORKS** were undertaken after flooding on 1st February 1953 killed nearly 2,000 people. The dams and barriers provide security from inundation and improve the infrastructure of the region. The Delta Works and Afsluitdijk (IJsselmeer dam) together are considered one of the 'seven wonders of the modern world'.
A Maeslantkering: Nieuwe Waterweg Storm Surge Barrier (S.S.B.)
B Haringvlietdam
C Brouwersdam
D Oosterschelde S.S.B.
E Veerse Gatdam
F Zandkreekdam
G Oesterdam
H Grevelingendam & Philipsdam
I Volkerakdam & Haringvlietbrug
J Hartelkering
K Hollandse IJssel S.S.B.

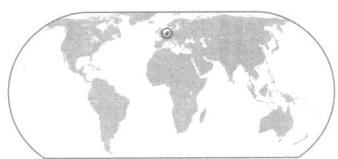

The listings above refer to a selection of related themes.
For more information, see the Contents (2-5). See also the Columbus
Tourist Attractions and Events of the World.

Legend

- Theme park, leisure park
- Museum, gallery
- Religious building
- Park, reserve, zoo, etc.
- Historic/notable building
- Water-related attraction
- Other place of interest

Attractions in cities
marked in red are listed
on the left of the map

Amsterdam
Museum Amstelkring
Amsterdams Historisch Museum
Anne Frankhuis
Hermitage aan de Amstel
Joods Historisch Museum
Madame Tussaud Scenerama
Museum Het Rembrandthuis
Nederlands Scheepvaart Museum
NeMo (New Metropolis)
Rijksmuseum
Stedelijk Museum
Tropenmuseum
Van Gogh Museum
Esnoga Synagogue
Nieuwe Kerk
Westerkerk
Artis
Bloemenmarkt
Begijnhof
Koninklijk Paleis
Amsterdam canals (grachten)

Haarlem
Frans Halsmuseum
Teylers Museum
St Bavokerk
Vleeshal
Grote Markt

Leiden
Museum Boerhaave
Molenmuseum De Valk
Naturalis
Stedelijk Museum De Lakenhal
Rijksmuseum van Oudheden
Rijksmuseum voor Volkenkunde
De Burcht

Den Haag (The Hague)
Madurodam
Museum voor Communicatie
Gemeentemuseum
Mauritshuis
Museum Mesdag; Panorama Mesdag
Museon
Schilderijengalerij Prins Willem V
Binnenhof
Paleis Noordeinde

Delft
Koninklijk Nederlands
Leger- en Wapenmuseum
Prinsenhof
Nieuwe Kerk
Oude Kerk

Rotterdam
Kunsthal
Historisch Museum
Het Schielandshuis
Museum Boymans-Van Beuningen
Museum De Dubbelde Palmboom
Nederlands Architectuurinstituut
Diergaarde Blijdorp
Boat trips to the port
Erasmusbrug
Maritiem Museum
Euromast

Gouda
Stedelijk Museum Het
Catharina Gasthuis
Sint Jan
Stadhuis

Utrecht
Centraal Museum
Museum Het Catharijneconvent
Nationaal Museum van
Speelklok Tot Pierement
Nederlands Spoorwegmuseum
Domkirk; Domtoren
Pieterskerk
Rietveld Schröderhuis

Map labels:

ROTTUMERPLAAT ROTTUMEROOG
SCHIERMONNIKOOG Nationaal Park
Eemshaven
AMELAND HET RIF Menkemaborg
Expozee Lauwersoog Delfzijl
De Boschplaat Appingedam
TERSCHELLING **Groningen** GRONINGEN
Dokkum Groninger Museum
Noordelijk Scheepvaart Museum
Martinikerk
RICHEL GRIEND Goudkantoor
VLIELAND **Leeuwarden** Sappemeer
Fries Museum Leek Haren Hoogezand Winschoten
Museum Het Princessehof, Borg Nienoord Veendam
Vliehors Nederlands Keramiek Museum **Assen**
Franeker Roden Verkeerspark Bourtange
Harlingen Planetarium Drachten Drents Museum Stadskanaal
Noorderhaven Stadhuis FRIESLAND
Slufter Bolsward Oosterwolde Hondsrug
Sneek Attractiepark Duinenzathe Borger
TEXEL Sneeker- Miniatuurpark Noord-Nederland Hunebed Informatiecentrum
Den Burg meer Friese Meren Heerenveen Beilen Hunebedden
Fluessen Slotermeer Speelstad Oranje
Afsluitdijk Friese Meren Nationaal Park Orvelte DRENTHE
NOORDER HAAKS Stavoren Sloten Dwingelderveld Emmen
Lemmer Tjeukemeer Noorder Dierenpark
Den Helder NOORDDOOST- Steenwijk
WIERINGER- POLDER Nationaal Park Hoogeveen Coevorden
MEER Beulaker De Weerribben
Medemblik IJsselmeer Wijde Giethoorn Meppel
Kasteel Radboud Emmeloord Havelte Hardenberg
Schagen Urk Staphorst Dedemsvaart
NOORD- Museum Zwartemeer Attractiepark Slagharen
HOLLAND Schokland Kampen Hasselt Ommen
Enkhuizen Ketelmeer **Zwolle** OVERIJSSEL
Heerhugowaard Drommedaris Zuiderzeemuseum Ecodrome
Alkmaar **Hoorn** Markerwaarddijk De Stadshof Ootmarsum
Kaasmarkt Rode Steen **Lelystad** Stedelijk Museum Denekamp
Heiloo Bataviawerf OOSTELIJK Salland **Almelo**
DROOGMAKERIJ Nieuwland Poldermuseum FLEVOLAND Aventurenpark Oldenzaal
Castricum DE BEEMSTER Markermeer Dronten Nijenhuis Hellendoorn Wierden
Edam FLEVOLAND Heerde Rijssen **Hengelo**
Beverwijk Zaanse Walibi World Epe Goor **Enschede**
IJmuiden **Purmerend** Schans Oostvaardersplassen **Deventer** Rijksmuseum Twenthe
Beeckestein Volendam ZUIDELIJK Textielmuseum Jannink
Nationaal Park **Zaanstad** MARKEN Almere- FLEVOLAND Harderwijk Haaksbergen
Zuid-Kennemerland Buiten Dolfinarium Lochem
Zandvoort **AMSTERDAM** Muiderslot **Almere-Stad** Rijksmuseum **Apeldoorn**
Heemstede **Haarlem** Almere-Haven Ermelo Paleis Het Loo Zutphen
Linnaeushof Amstelveen Weesp Harderwijk Koninklijk Juliana Toren GELDERLAND
Hoofddorp Westeinder- Naarden **Amersfoort** Apenheul Dieren
Noordwijk Aalsmeer plassen Vestingmuseum Kröller-Müller National Park
Space Expo Bloemenveiling **Hilversum** Museum De Veluwezoom
Lisse Uithoorn Baarn Dierenpark Lichtenvoorde Winterswijk
Katwijk Keukenhof Vinkeveense Soest Amersfoort National Park Doetinchem
Leiden **Alphen** plassen Leusden De Hoge Veluwe Aalten
Zeist Jachtslot
Archeon aan den Rijn Loosdrechtse Slot Zeist St Hubertus
Scheveningen Vogelpark Avifauna plassen Utrechtse **Arnhem**
Sea Life Maarssen Heuvelrug Nederlands Openluchtmuseum
Pier Noordwijk Kasteel Woerden Huis Doorn Museum voor Moderne Kunst
Zoetermeer De Haar UTRECHT Burgers' Zoo, Bush en Safari
Rijswijk Bodegraven **Utrecht** Veenendaal
Den Haag/ Drievliet Gouda Kasteel Elst
's-Gravenhage ZUID- Oudewater Vianen Ameringen **Nijmegen**
(The Hague) Delft HOLLAND Heksenwaag Duwehands Amusementspark Tivoli
Hoek van Holland **Nieuwegein** Culemborg Dierenpark Nationaal Fietsmuseum Velorama
Maasvlakte **Capelle** Schoonhoven Valkhof
Het Keringhuis **Rotterdam** aan den IJssel Leerdam Tiel Wijchen
Europoort **Schiedam** Kinderdijk Geldermalsen
Stormvloedkering **Vlaardingen** 19 Windwatermolens Gorinchem Waal **Oss** Grave
Nieuwe Waterweg VOORNE Kasteel Rosmalen Boxmeer
Haringvlietdam **Spijkenisse** Zwijndrecht Loevestein Autotron Overloon
Haringvliet Expo PUTTEN **Dordrecht** Papendrecht Kasteel **'s-Hertogenbosch** Nationaal Oorlogs-
Hellevoetsluis Dordrechts Museum Dussen Noordbrabants Museum en Verzetsmuseum
GOEREE Nationaal Park Het Land van Ooit St Janskathedraal
Brouwersdam Stellendam De Biesbosch Uden Venray
Haringvlietbrug Nationaal NOORD-BRABANT BillyBird Park
Burgh-Haamstede HOEKSE WAARD Automobielmuseum Hemelrijk
Slot Haamstede Zevenbergen Oosterhout De Efteling Kasteeltuinen
SCHOUWEN Grevelingendam Arcen
Stormvloedkering OVERFLAKKEE Philipsdam **Helmond** Kasteel
Oosterschelde Zierikzee DUIVELAND Etten-Leur **Eindhoven** Deurne
Waterland Delta ZEELAND **Breda** **Tilburg** Oirschot Stedelijk Museum
Expo Neeltje Jans Schelde- Grote Kerk Nederlands Abbemuseum Toverland **Venlo**
Veersegatdam Rijnkanaal Steenbergen Textielmuseum Geldrop Blerick
NOORD Zeelandbrug Halsteren **Roosendaal** Safari Beekse Bergen Asten Panningen
BEVELAND THOLEN Bergen op Zoom Veldhoven Kasteel Nationaal Park
Veere Markiezenhof Heeze De Groote Peel
Schotse Huizen Goes Bladel Valkenswaard LIMBURG
Oude Stadhuis Osterschelde ZUID BEVELAND Weert **Roermond**
Vlissingen WALCHEREN Bergeyk Budel Thorn
(Flushing) Miniatuur Walcheren Maasbracht
Arsenaal Middelburg Westerschelde
Zeeuws Museum Susteren
Breskens Abdij Sittard **Geleen**
Stadhuis Terneuzen Hoensbroek
't Zwin ZEEUWS-VLAANDEREN Kasteel Brunssum
Oostburg Hulst Landgraaf
Axel Thermenmuseum **Heerlen** Kerkrade Industrion
Maastricht Valkenburg
Bonnefantenmuseum Pretpark De Valkenier
Onze Lieve Vrouwebasiliek Steenkolenmijnmuseum
St Servaasbasiliek Vaals
St Pieterskerk Drielandenpunt
en Labyrint

NORTH

30 km
15 miles

See also... 71-73 for more on Germany

For more information, see the Contents (2-5).

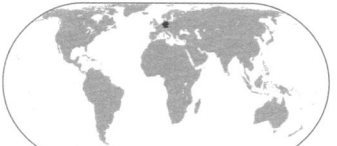

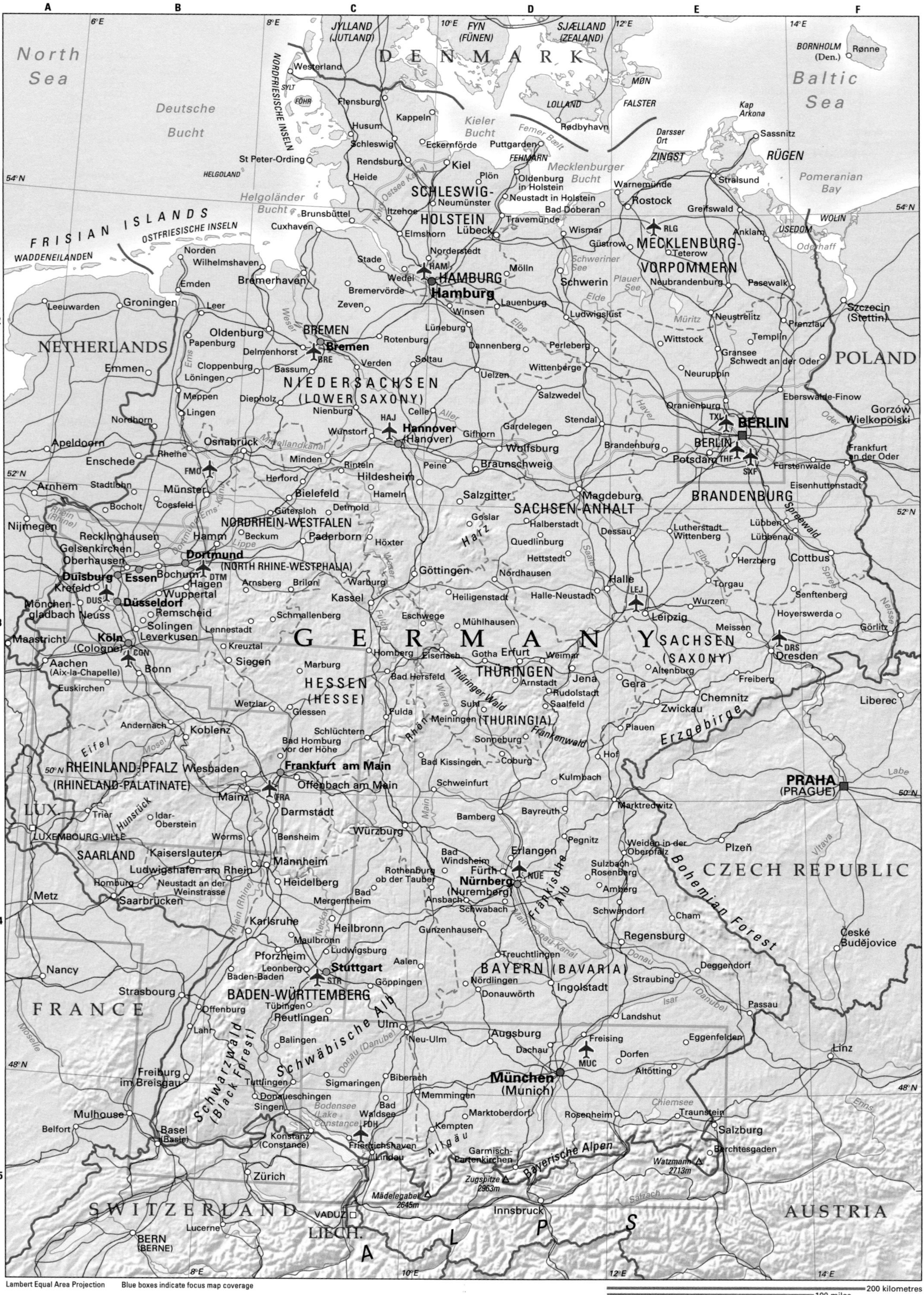

Lambert Equal Area Projection
Blue boxes indicate focus map coverage

200 kilometres
100 miles

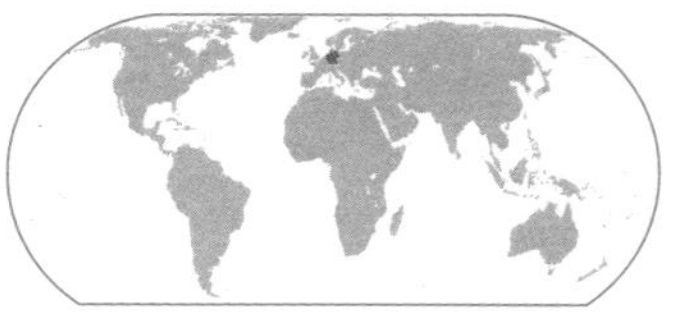

▶ **See also...** Europe Airports & High-Speed Rail (50-51); Europe Railways & Ferries (52-53)

The listings above refer to a selection of related themes. For more information, see the Contents (2-5).

JAN-FEB Fasching: Carnival (**Munich**)
FEB Berliner Filmfestspiele: **Berlin** International Film Festival
APR Walpurgisnacht: witches' sabbath festival (**Harz** region)
MAY-SEP Rattenfängerspiele: Ratcatcher's Play (**Hameln**)
MAY-SEP Passionspiele: Passion Play (**Oberammergau**); 2010 and every ten years
JUN Karneval der Kulturen: Carnival of the Cultures (**Berlin**)
JUN 14th City Foundation Day (**Munich**)
JUN Christopher Street Day (**Berlin**)
JUN Corpus Christi Procession (**Hüfingen**; **Cologne** & **Munich**)
JUN Kieler Woche: regatta (**Kiel**)
JUN-JUL Fürstenhochzeit: royal marriage (**Landshut**); 2005 and every four years
JUN-AUG Meistertrunk: 'Long Drink' history play (**Rothenburg ob der Tauber**)
JUL Love Parade (**Berlin**)
JUL-AUG Bayreuther Festspiele: Wagner opera festival (**Bayreuth**)
AUG Der Rhein in Flammen: The Rhine in Flames (**Braubach to Koblenz**)
AUG Schlossfest: castle festival (**Heidelberg**)
SEP Dürkheimer Wurstmarkt: sausage & wine festival (**Bad Dürkheim**)
SEP **Berlin** Marathon
SEP-OCT Oktoberfest (**Munich**); Cannstatter Volksfest (**Stuttgart**)
OCT Weinlesefest: wine fair & Queen of Wine (**Neustadt an der Weinstrasse**)
OCT **Frankfurt** Book Fair
NOV Hamburger Dom: festival (**Hamburg**)
NOV-DEC Weihnachtsmarkt: Christmas markets (**Munich, Nuremberg** & countrywide)

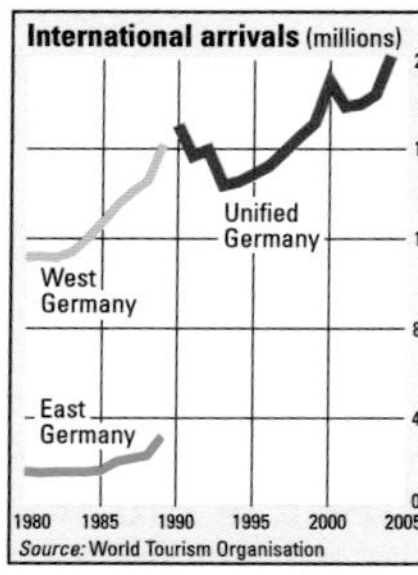

Legend (map A/B)
- - - Land boundary
○ Land capital
- - - Former boundary between East and West Germany
100 km
50 miles

International arrivals (millions)
Unified Germany
West Germany
East Germany
20
16
12
8
4
1980 1985 1990 1995 2000 2005
Source: World Tourism Organisation

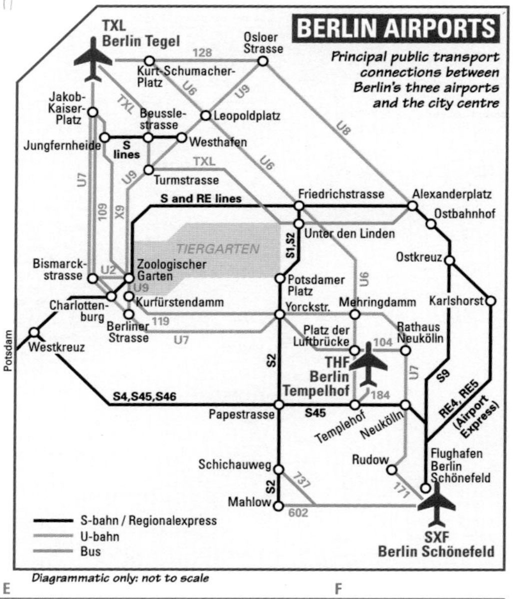

BERLIN AIRPORTS
Principal public transport connections between Berlin's three airports and the city centre

TXL Berlin Tegel
128
Osloer Strasse
Kurt-Schumacher-Platz
Jakob-Kaiser-Platz
Leopoldplatz
U8
U9
Beusselstrasse
Westhafen
Jungfernheide
Turmstrasse
S lines
TXL
U6
Friedrichstrasse
Alexanderplatz
Ostbahnhof
S and RE lines
S1 S2
Unter den Linden
Ostkreuz
Bismarck-strasse
Zoologischer Garten
Potsdamer Platz
Mehringdamm
Karlshorst
Charlottenburg
Berliner Strasse
Kurfürstendamm
Yorckstr.
U9
119
U2
U7
Platz der Luftbrücke
Rathaus Neukölln
THF Berlin Tempelhof
104
RE4 RE5 (Airport Express)
Westkreuz
S4, S45, S46
Papestrasse
S45
Templehof
Neukölln
Rudow
S9
Flughafen Berlin Schönefeld
Schichauweg
S2
Mahlow
602
SXF Berlin Schönefeld
TIERGARTEN

Legend:
▬ S-bahn / Regionalexpress
▬ U-bahn
▬ Bus

Diagrammatic only: not to scale

RUHR BASIN (RUHRGEBIET)

1 **NRN** Niederrhein; 2 **MGL** Düsseldorf Mönchengladbach 3 **DUS** Düsseldorf Rhein-Ruhr; 4 **ESS** Essen; 5 **DTM** Dortmund Wickede
30 km
15 miles

BERLIN

1 **TXL** Berlin Tegel; 2 **THF** Berlin Tempelhof; 3 **SXF** Berlin Schönefeld
20 km
10 miles

1000 metres
500 metres
Sea level

See also... Contents (2-5) – this country features in many thematic and regional maps throughout the *BTEC First Travel Atlas*.

The listings above refer to a selection of related themes. For more information, see the Contents (2-5).

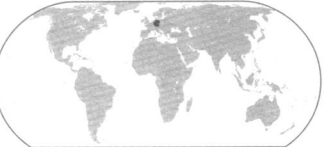

ROMANTIC ROAD

Germany has a well-developed network of tourist routes passing through areas of scenic or historic interest. They include the Coastal Road, the Lakes Road (in Mecklenburg-Vorpommern), the Harz Mountains Road, the Martin Luther Road (Leipzig, Magdeburg, Erfurt), the Saxon Road, the Fairy-Tale Road (Bremen, Hameln, Kassel), the River Road (Rhine & Mosel), the Black Forest Road, the Castle & Thuringia Road, the Alpine Road and the Alpine-Baltic Road.

The Romantische Strasse (Romantic Road) is Germany's most famous tourist route, running 350km from Würzburg to the Austrian border. The unspoilt gently rolling countryside and towns which evoke the medieval and chivalric German past bring many tourists: Rothenburg is the most visited medieval town in Germany.

Würzburg
Tauber Bischofsheim
Weikersheim
Bad Mergentheim
Rothenburg ob der Tauber
Castle & Thuringia Road
Feuchtwangen
Dinkelsbühl
Alpine-Baltic Road
Wallerstein
Nördlingen im Reis
Harburg
Donau (Danube)
Donauwörth
Augsburg
Landsberg am Lech
Schongau
Steingaden
Alpine Road
Wieskirche
Oberammergau
Schloss Linderhof
Füssen
Königschlosser

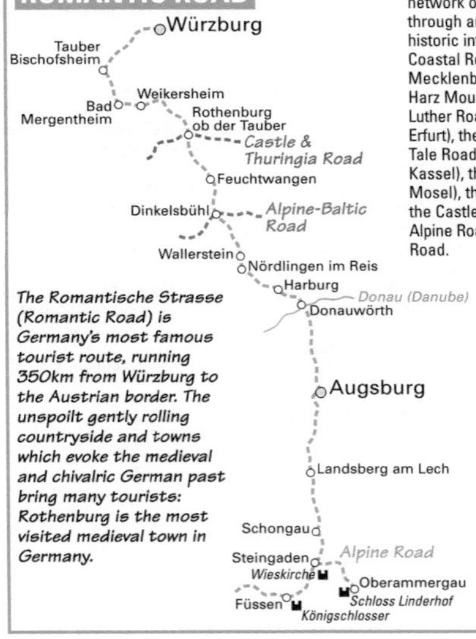

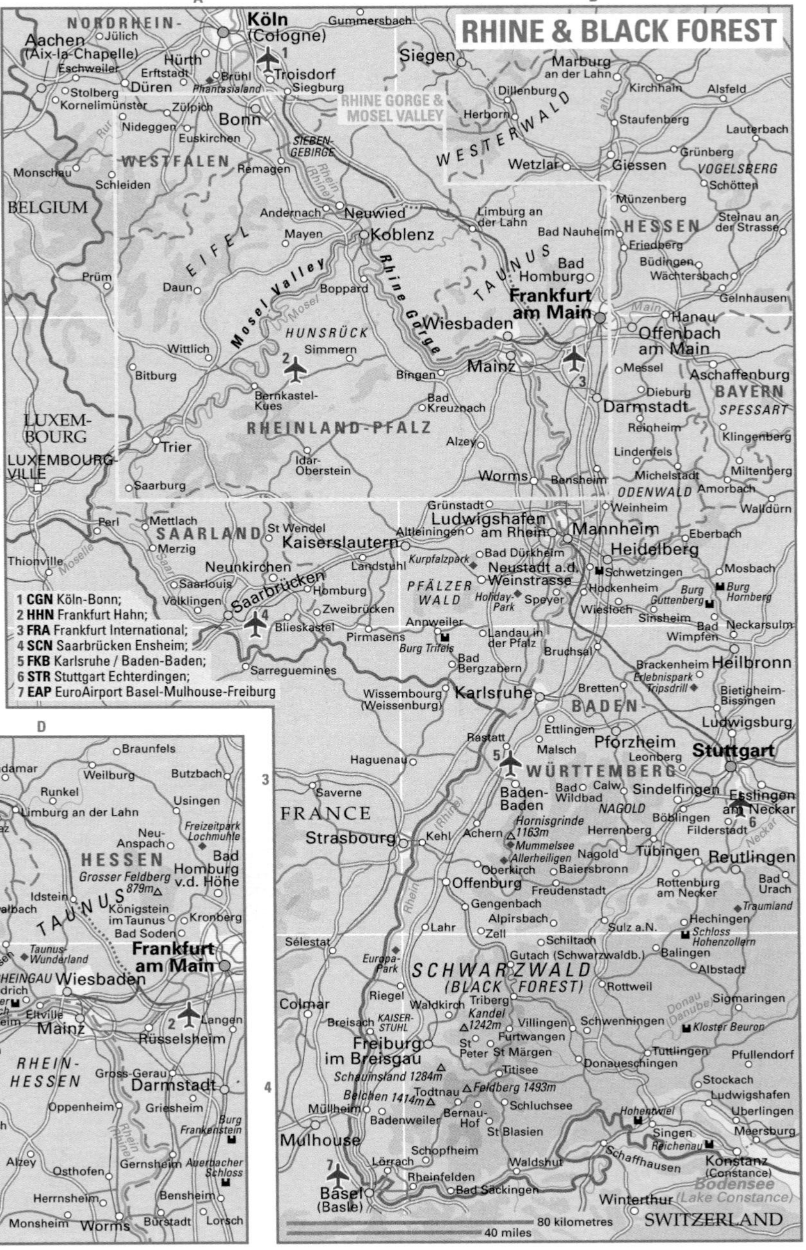

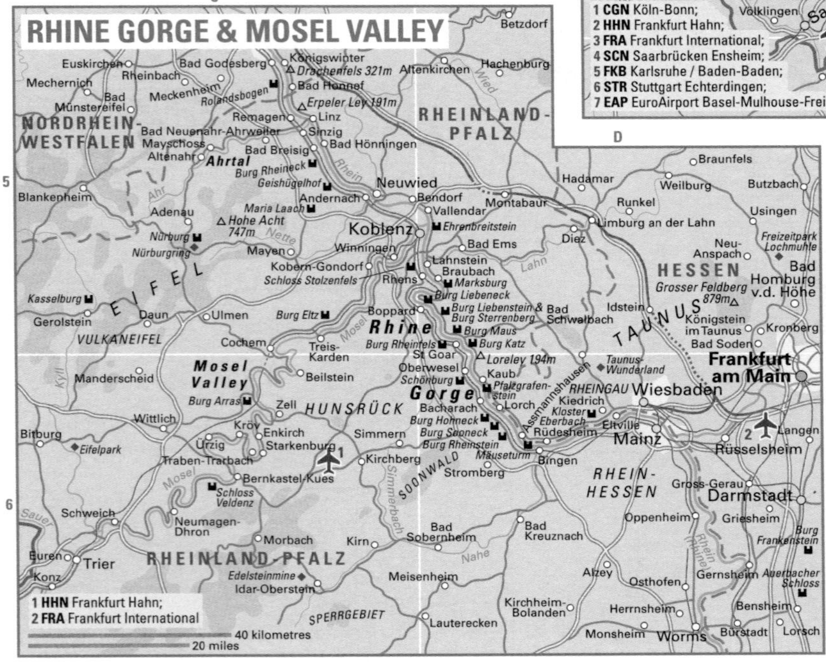

RHINE & BLACK FOREST
RHINE GORGE & MOSEL VALLEY
1 CGN Köln-Bonn;
2 HHN Frankfurt Hahn;
3 FRA Frankfurt International;
4 SCN Saarbrücken Ensheim;
5 FKB Karlsruhe / Baden-Baden;
6 STR Stuttgart Echterdingen;
7 EAP EuroAirport Basel-Mulhouse-Freiburg
80 kilometres
40 miles
Köln (Cologne)
Frankfurt am Main
Stuttgart
Karlsruhe
Mannheim
Heidelberg
Strasbourg
Freiburg im Breisgau
Basel (Basle)
SCHWARZWALD (BLACK FOREST)
FRANCE
LUXEMBOURG
BELGIUM
SWITZERLAND

RHINE GORGE & MOSEL VALLEY
1 HHN Frankfurt Hahn;
2 FRA Frankfurt International
40 kilometres
20 miles
Koblenz
Mosel Valley
Rhine Gorge
Wiesbaden
Mainz
Frankfurt am Main
Darmstadt
Trier
EIFEL
HUNSRÜCK
TAUNUS
RHEINLAND-PFALZ
NORDRHEIN-WESTFALEN
HESSEN

SOUTHERN BAVARIA
1 FDH Friedrichshafen; 2 AGB München (Munich) Augsburg
3 MUC München (Munich) Franz Joseph Strauss
80 kilometres
40 miles
München (Munich)
Augsburg
Ulm
Salzburg
Konstanz (Constance)
Bodensee (Lake Constance)
BAYERN
OBERBAYERN
ALLGÄU
BAYERISCHE ALPEN
AUSTRIA
SWITZERLAND
1000 metres
500 metres
Sea level

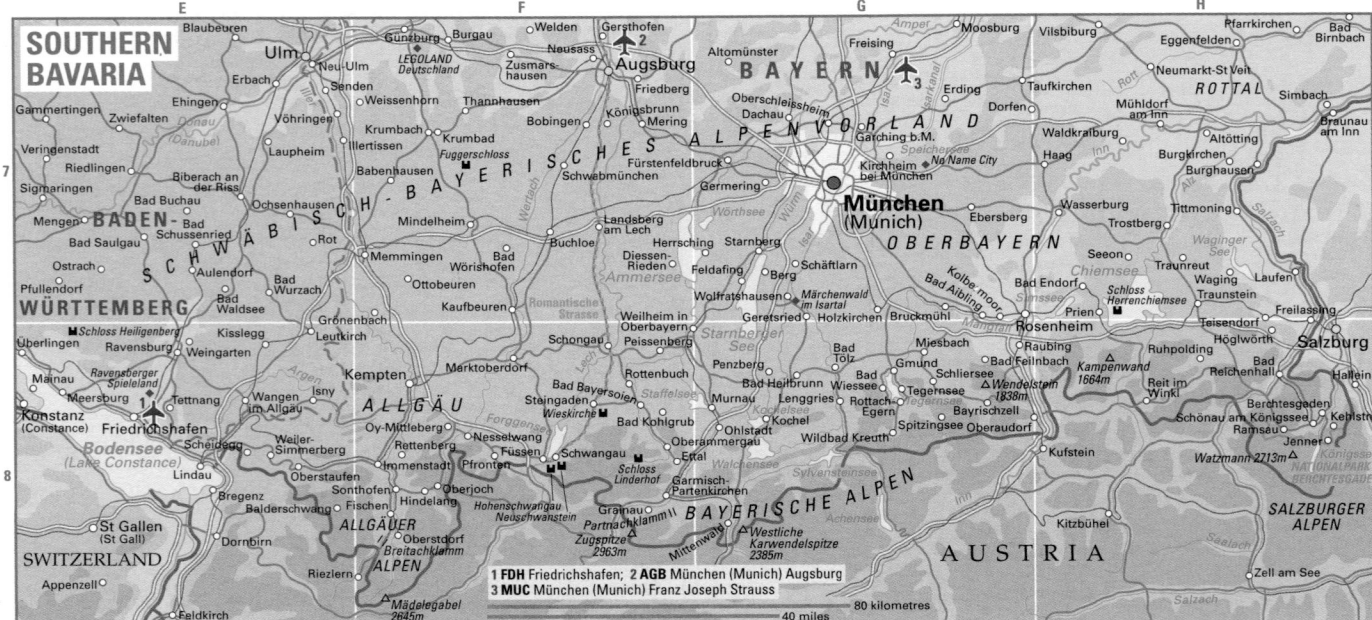

See also... Attractions in UK (64), Belgium (67), Netherlands (69), France (77), Iberia (79) and Italy (86)

The listings above refer to a selection of related themes. For more information, see the Contents (2-5). See also the Columbus Tourist Attractions and Events of the World.

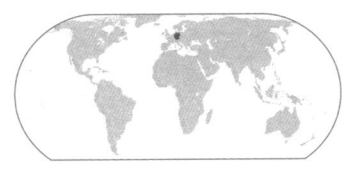

- Theme park, leisure park
- Museum, gallery
- Religious building
- Park, reserve, zoo, etc.
- Historic/notable building
- Water-related attraction
- Other place of interest

Attractions in cities marked in red are listed around the edge of the map

100 kilometres
50 miles

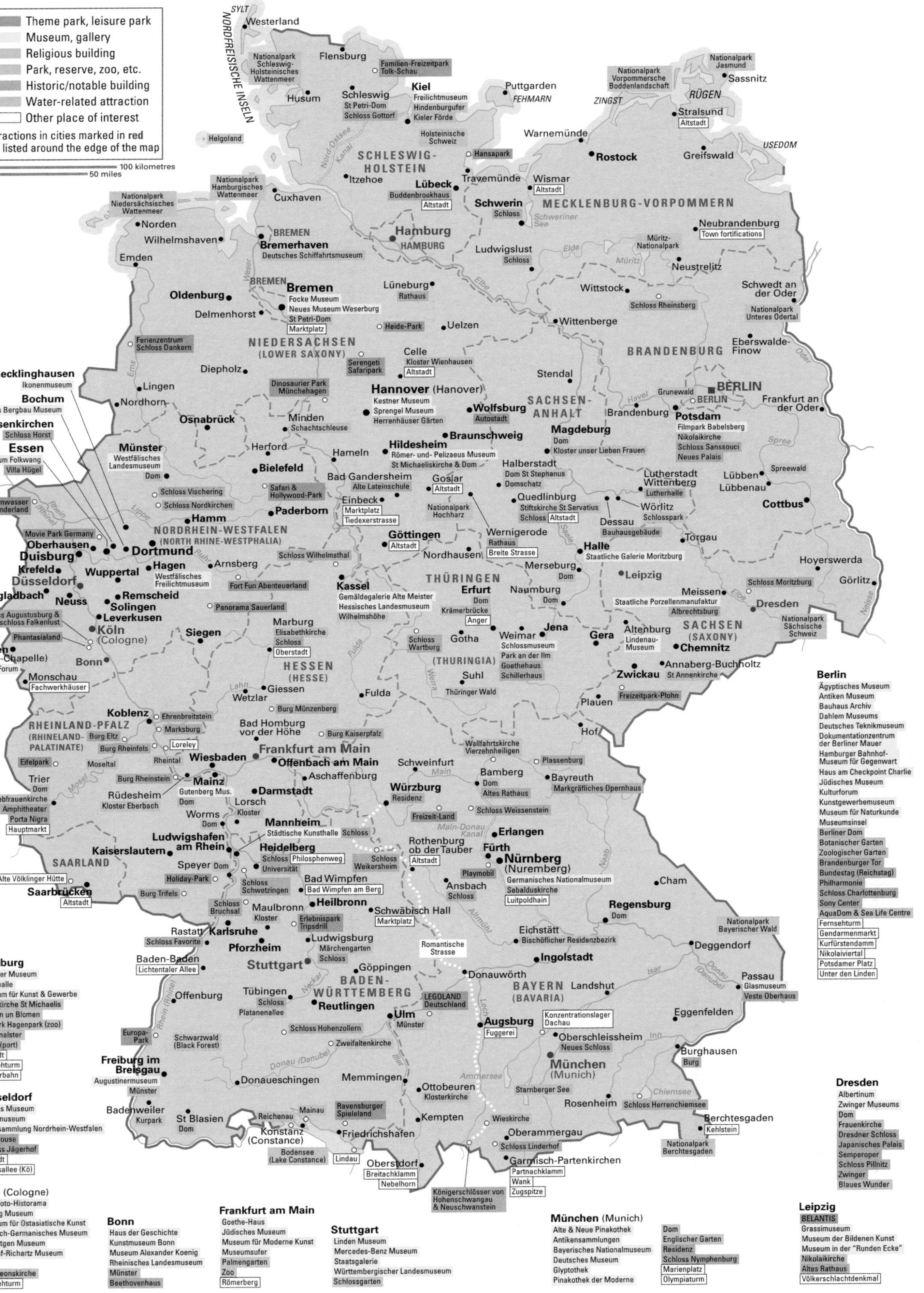

SYLT
Westerland
NORDFRIESISCHE INSELN
Nationalpark Schleswig-Holsteinisches Wattenmeer
Flensburg
Familien-Freizeitpark Tolk-Schau
Husum
Schleswig
St Petri-Dom
Schloss Gottorf
Kiel
Freilichtmuseum
Hindenburgufer
Kieler Förde
Puttgarden
FEHMARN
Nationalpark Vorpommersche Boddenlandschaft
ZINGST
Nationalpark Jasmund
Sassnitz
RÜGEN
Stralsund
Altstadt
Helgoland
Holsteinische Schweiz
Warnemünde
Rostock
Greifswald
USEDOM
SCHLESWIG-HOLSTEIN
Hansapark
Itzehoe
Lübeck
Buddenbrookhaus
Altstadt
Travemünde
Wismar
Altstadt
Nationalpark Hamburgisches Wattenmeer
Nationalpark Niedersächsisches Wattenmeer
Cuxhaven
Schwerin
Schloss
Schweriner See
MECKLENBURG-VORPOMMERN
Norden
Wilhelmshaven
BREMEN
Bremerhaven
Deutsches Schiffahrtsmuseum
Hamburg
HAMBURG
Neubrandenburg
Town fortifications
Müritz-Nationalpark
Müritz
Emden
Ludwigslust
Schloss
Elde
Neustrelitz
BREMEN
Bremen
Focke Museum
Neues Museum Weserburg
St Petri-Dom
Marktplatz
Oldenburg
Delmenhorst
Lüneburg
Rathaus
Elbe
Wittstock
Schloss Rheinsberg
Schwedt an der Oder
Nationalpark Unteres Odertal
Heide-Park
Uelzen
Wittenberge
Ferienzentrum Schloss Dankern
NIEDERSACHSEN (LOWER SAXONY)
Celle
Kloster Wienhausen
Altstadt
Serengeti Safaripark
BRANDENBURG
Eberswalde-Finow
Recklinghausen
Ikonenmuseum
Diepholz
Stendal
Lingen
Dinosaurier Park Münchehagen
Hannover (Hanover)
Kestner Museum
Sprengel Museum
Herrenhäuser Gärten
Wolfsburg
Autostadt
Bochum
Deutsches Bergbau Museum
Nordhorn
Osnabrück
Minden
Schachtschleuse
SACHSEN-ANHALT
Havel
Grunewald
BERLIN
BERLIN
Frankfurt an der Oder
Brandenburg
Potsdam
Filmpark Babelsberg
Nikolaikirche
Schloss Sanssouci
Neues Palais
Spree
Gelsenkirchen
Schloss Horst
Braunschweig
Magdeburg
Dom
Kloster unser Lieben Frauen
Münster
Westfälisches Landesmuseum
Dom
Herford
Hildesheim
Römer- und Pelizaeus Museum
St Michaeliskirche & Dom
Hameln
Essen
Museum Folkwang
Villa Hügel
Bielefeld
Halberstadt
Dom St Stephanus
Domschatz
Lutherstadt Wittenberg
Lutherhalle
Lübben
Spreewald
Lübbenau
Bad Gandersheim
Alte Lateinschule
Goslar
Altstadt
Schloss Vischering
Schloss Nordkirchen
Safari & Hollywood-Park
Kernwasser Wunderland
Rhein (Rhine)
Lippe
Einbeck
Marktplatz
Tiedexerstrasse
Paderborn
Nationalpark Hochharz
Quedlinburg
Stiftskirche St Servatius
Schloss
Altstadt
Wörlitz
Schlosspark
Dessau
Bauhausgebäude
Cottbus
Hamm
NORDRHEIN-WESTFALEN (NORTH RHINE-WESTPHALIA)
Movie Park Germany
Oberhausen
Dortmund
Göttingen
Altstadt
Wernigerode
Rathaus
Breite Strasse
Saale
Halle
Staatliche Galerie Moritzburg
Torgau
Duisburg
Krefeld
Hagen
Westfälisches Freilichtmuseum
Ruhr
Arnsberg
Schloss Wilhelmsthal
Nordhausen
Merseburg
Dom
Hoyerswerda
Düsseldorf
Wuppertal
Fort Fun Abenteuerland
Kassel
Gemäldegalerie Alte Meister
Hessisches Landesmuseum
Wilhelmshöhe
THÜRINGEN
Leipzig
Schloss Moritzburg
Görlitz
Mönchengladbach
Neuss
Remscheid
Solingen
Erfurt
Dom
Krämerbrücke
Anger
Naumburg
Dom
Meissen
Staatliche Porzellanmanufaktur
Albrechtsburg
Elbe
Dresden
Neisse
Schloss Augustusburg & Jagdschloss Falkenlust
Leverkusen
Panorama Sauerland
Marburg
Elisabethkirche
Schloss
Oberstadt
Nationalpark Sächsische Schweiz
SACHSEN (SAXONY)
Köln (Cologne)
Phantasialand
Siegen
Gotha
Schloss Wartburg
Weimar
Schlossmuseum
Park an der Ilm
Goethehaus
Schillerhaus
Jena
Gera
Altenburg
Lindenau-Museum
Chemnitz
Aachen (Aix-la-Chapelle)
Ludwig Forum
Dom
Bonn
HESSEN (HESSE)
(THURINGIA)
Fulda
Werra
Suhl
Thüringer Wald
Annaberg-Buchholz
Zwickau
St Annenkirche
Monschau
Fachwerkhäuser
Lahn
Giessen
Wetzlar
Fulda
Freizeitpark-Plohn
Plauen
Koblenz
Ehrenbreitstein
Marksburg
Burg Münzenberg
RHEINLAND-PFALZ (RHINELAND-PALATINATE)
Burg Eltz
Burg Rheinfels
Loreley
Bad Homburg vor der Höhe
Burg Kaiserpfalz
Hof
Frankfurt am Main
Wallfahrtskirche Vierzehnheiligen
Eifelpark
Moseltal
Rheintal
Wiesbaden
Offenbach am Main
Schweinfurt
Main
Plassenburg
Trier
Dom
Liebfrauenkirche
Amphitheater
Porta Nigra
Hauptmarkt
Mosel
Burg Rheinstein
Mainz
Gutenberg Mus.
Dom
Rüdesheim
Kloster Eberbach
Aschaffenburg
Darmstadt
Bamberg
Dom
Altes Rathaus
Bayreuth
Markgräfliches Opernhaus
Würzburg
Residenz
Lorsch
Kloster
Worms
Dom
Freizeit-Land
Schloss Weissenstein
Mannheim
Städtische Kunsthalle
Schloss
Main-Donau Kanal
Erlangen
Ludwigshafen am Rhein
Kaiserslautern
SAARLAND
Heidelberg
Schloss
Philosphenweg
Universität
Rothenburg ob der Tauber
Altstadt
Schloss Weikersheim
Fürth
Nürnberg (Nuremberg)
Germanisches Nationalmuseum
Sebalduskirche
Luitpoldhain
Speyer
Dom
Alte Völklinger Hütte
Holiday-Park
Bad Wimpfen
Bad Wimpfen am Berg
Playmobil
Ansbach
Schloss
Naab
Cham
Saarbrücken
Altstadt
Burg Trifels
Schloss Schwetzingen
Schloss Bruchsal
Maulbronn
Kloster
Heilbronn
Schwäbisch Hall
Marktplatz
Regensburg
Dom
Altmühl
Nationalpark Bayerischer Wald
Rastatt
Schloss Favorite
Karlsruhe
Erlebnispark Tripsdrill
Pforzheim
Ludwigsburg
Märchengarten
Schloss
Romantische Strasse
Eichstätt
Bischöflicher Residenzbezirk
Deggendorf
Baden-Baden
Lichtentaler Allee
Stuttgart
Göppingen
Ingolstadt
Donauwörth
Isar
Donau (Danube)
Passau
Glasmuseum
Veste Oberhaus
BADEN-WÜRTTEMBERG
Offenburg
Tübingen
Schloss
Platanenallee
Neckar
Reutlingen
LEGOLAND Deutschland
BAYERN (BAVARIA)
Landshut
Lech
Ulm
Münster
Augsburg
Fuggerei
Konzentrationslager Dachau
Eggenfelden
Rhein (Rhine)
Europa-Park
Schwarzwald (Black Forest)
Schloss Hohenzollern
Zweifaltenkirche
Oberschleissheim
Neues Schloss
Inn
Burghausen
Burg
Freiburg im Breisgau
Augustinermuseum
Münster
Donau (Danube)
Iller
München (Munich)
Donaueschingen
Memmingen
Ammersee
Ottobeuren
Klosterkirche
Starnberger See
Chiemsee
Badenweiler
Kurpark
St Blasien
Dom
Reichenau
Mainau
Ravensburger Spieleland
Kempten
Rosenheim
Schloss Herrenchiemsee
Wieskirche
Berchtesgaden
Kehlstein
Konstanz (Constance)
Friedrichshafen
Oberammergau
Schloss Linderhof
Nationalpark Berchtesgaden
Bodensee (Lake Constance)
Lindau
Oberstdorf
Breitachklamm
Nebelhorn
Garmisch-Partenkirchen
Partnachklamm
Wank
Zugspitze
Königsschlösser von Hohenschwangau & Neuschwanstein

Berlin
Ägyptisches Museum
Antiken Museum
Bauhaus Archiv
Dahlem Museums
Deutsches Teknikmuseum
Dokumentationszentrum der Berliner Mauer
Hamburger Bahnhof-Museum für Gegenwart
Haus am Checkpoint Charlie
Jüdisches Museum
Kulturforum
Kunstgewerbemuseum
Museum für Naturkunde
Museumsinsel
Berliner Dom
Botanischer Garten
Zoologischer Garten
Brandenburger Tor
Bundestag (Reichstag)
Philharmonie
Schloss Charlottenburg
Sony Center
AquaDom & Sea Life Centre
Fernsehturm
Gendarmenmarkt
Kurfürstendamm
Nikolaiviertal
Potsdamer Platz
Unter den Linden

Hamburg
Altonaer Museum
Kunsthalle
Museum für Kunst & Gewerbe
Hauptkirche St Michaelis
Planten un Blomen
Tierpark Hagenpark (zoo)
Aussenalster
Hafen (port)
Altstadt
Fernsehturm
Reeperbahn

Düsseldorf
Hetjens Museum
Kunstmuseum
Kunstsammlung Nordrhein-Westfalen
EKO-House
Schloss Jägerhof
Altstadt
Königsallee (Kö)

Dresden
Albertinum
Zwinger Museums
Dom
Frauenkirche
Dresdner Schloss
Japanisches Palais
Semperoper
Schloss Pillnitz
Zwinger
Blaues Wunder

Köln (Cologne)
Agfa Foto-Historama
Ludwig Museum
Museum für Ostasiatische Kunst
Römisch-Germanisches Museum
Schnütgen Museum
Wallraf-Richartz Museum
Dom
St Gereonskirche
Fernsehturm

Bonn
Haus der Geschichte
Kunstmuseum Bonn
Museum Alexander Koenig
Rheinisches Landesmuseum
Münster
Beethovenhaus

Frankfurt am Main
Goethe-Haus
Jüdisches Museum
Museum für Moderne Kunst
Museumsufer
Palmengarten
Zoo
Römerberg

Stuttgart
Linden Museum
Mercedes-Benz Museum
Staatsgalerie
Württembergischer Landesmuseum
Schlossgarten

München (Munich)
Alte & Neue Pinakothek
Antikensammlungen
Bayerisches Nationalmuseum
Deutsches Museum
Glyptothek
Pinakothek der Moderne
Dom
Englischer Garten
Residenz
Schloss Nymphenburg
Marienplatz
Olympiaturm

Leipzig
BELANTIS
Grassimuseum
Museum der Bildenen Kunst
Museum in der "Runden Ecke"
Nikolaikirche
Altes Rathaus
Völkerschlachtdenkmal

For more information, see the Contents (2-5).

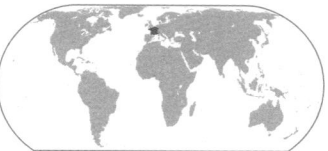

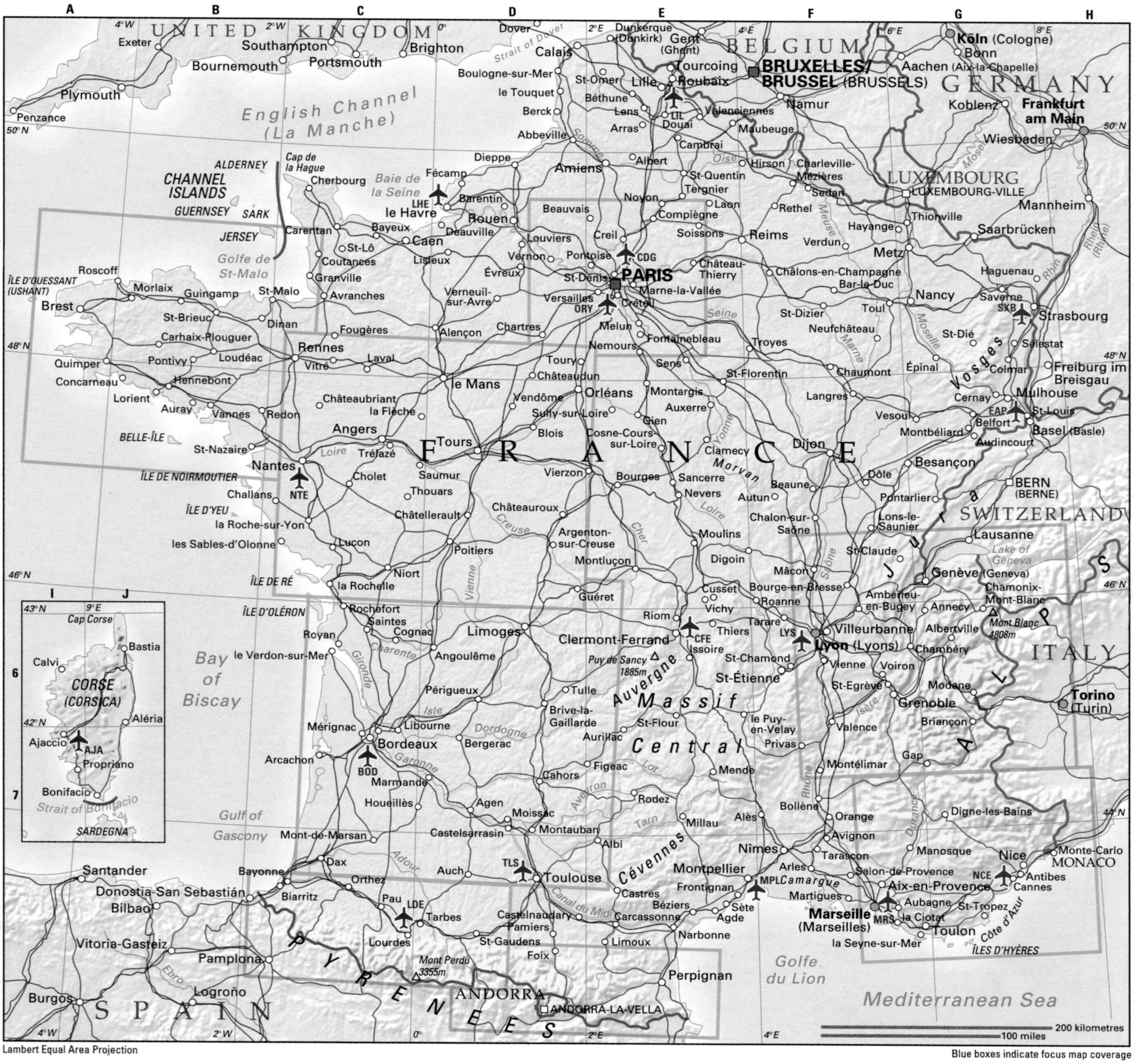

Lambert Equal Area Projection

Blue boxes indicate focus map coverage

WINE REGIONS

Some of the more important vin de pays areas are shown in *BLUE TYPE*. Numbers indicate the month when important wine festivals occur in each region (1=Jan., 12=Dec., E=Easter)

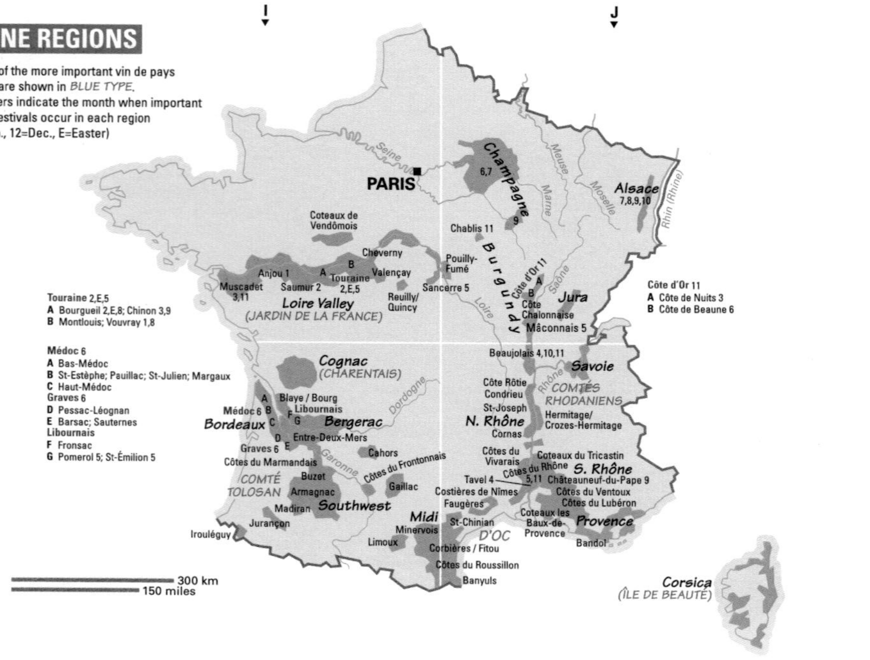

Touraine 2,E,5
A Bourgueil 2,E,8; Chinon 3,9
B Montlouis; Vouvray 1,8

Médoc 6
A Bas-Médoc
B St-Estèphe; Pauillac; St-Julien; Margaux
C Haut-Médoc
Graves 6
D Pessac-Léognan
E Barsac; Sauternes
Libournais 6
F Fronsac
G Pomerol 5; St-Émilion 5

Côte d'Or 11
A Côte de Nuits 3
B Côte de Beaune 6

JAN 1st La Grande Parade de Montmartre (**Paris**)
JAN International Circus Festival (**Monaco**)
JAN 22nd St Vincent Festival: patron saint of wine (**Burgundy**)
FEB Fête des Citrons: Lemon Festival (**Menton**)
before LENT Carnaval de **Nice**
MAY La Fête des Mais: The Feasts of May (**Nice**)
MAY **Cannes** Film Festival
MAY Annual Gypsy gathering (**les Saintes-Maries-de-la-Mer**)
MAY/JUN French Tennis Open (Roland Garros) (**Paris**)
WHIT MONDAY Procession of the Giants of France and Belgium (**Lille**)
JUN **Paris** Air Show
JUN Fête de la Musique: Festival of Music (**Paris** and countrywide)
JUN 24th Fête de St-Jean
JUN-JUL Festival International d'Art Lyrique (**Aix-en-Provence**)
JUL Gypsy and World Music Festival (**Arles**)
JUL Festival of the Giants (**Douai**)
JUL **Nantes** Quinzane Celtique
JUL 14th Bastille Day, Fête Nationale
JUL La Festival de Cornouaille: folklore festival (**Quimper**)
JUL Festival de **Marseille**
JUL Tour de France (finishes in **Paris**)
JUL **Nice** Jazz Festival
JUL-AUG Quartier d'Été: Summer Arts Festival (**Paris**)
JUL-AUG International Fireworks Festival (**Monaco**)
JUL-AUG Festival d'**Avignon**
AUG Basque festivals (**Bayonne** & **Biarritz**)
AUG Festival Inter-Celtique (**Lorient**)
AUG Haute-Provence Festival (**Forcalquier**)
AUG 15th Assumption of the Blessed Virgin Mary
SEP Festival du Livre Vivant: historical pageant (**Fougères**)
SEP Côtes du Rhône Grape Harvest (**Avignon**)
SEP German-French Festival (**Strasbourg** and Germany)
SEP Coupe Icarus: unpowered flight festival (**St-Hilaire-du-Touvet**)
SEP-DEC Festival d'Automne: Autumn Festival (**Paris**)
OCT Festival des Chants Sacrés en Méditerranée; Fiesta des Suds (**Marseille**)
NOV Mondial du Snowboard (**les Deux Alpes**)
NOV Les Trois Glorieuses: wine festival (**Cote d'Or**)
NOV Les Sarmentelles: Beaujolais Nouveau
DEC Festival of Lights (**Lyons**)
DEC Marché de Noël: Christmas market (**Strasbourg**)

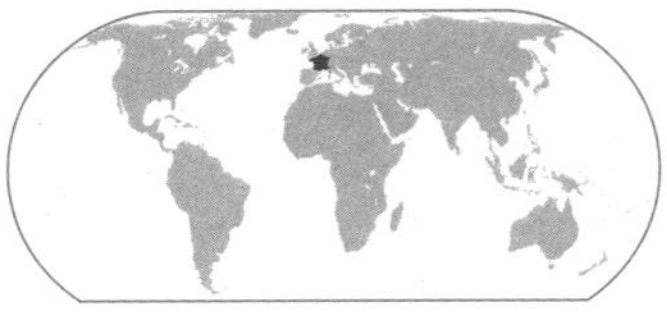

See also... Europe Airports & High-Speed Rail (50-51); Europe Railways & Ferries (52-53)

The listings above refer to a selection of related themes. For more information, see the Contents (2-5).

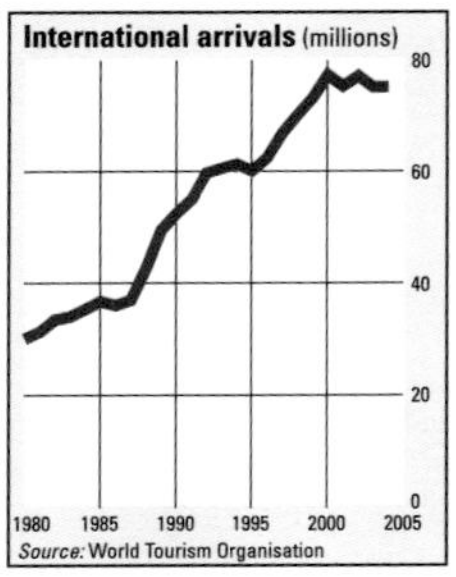

Europe | **75**

France

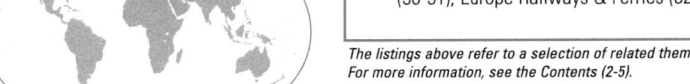

International arrivals (millions)

Source: World Tourism Organisation

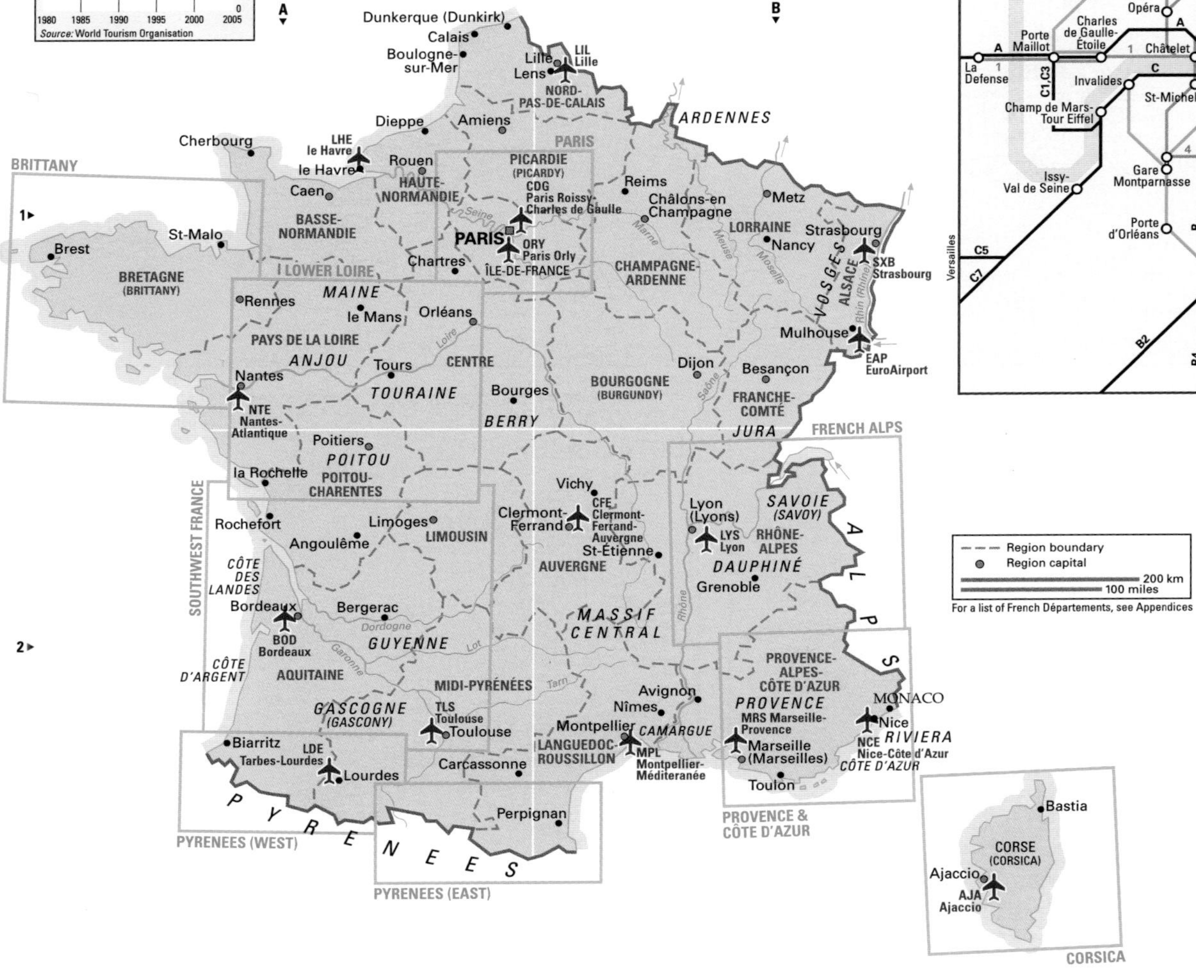

80
60
40
20
0

1980 1985 1990 1995 2000 2005

PARIS AIRPORTS

Principal public transport connections between CDG, ORY and the city centre

- ▨▨▨ High-speed rail (TGV, Thalys)
- ——— RER (Réseau Express Régional)
- ····· Orlyval light rail
- ═══ Metro
- Air France bus
- Other bus

CDG Paris Roissy-Charles de Gaulle

Lille
Lyon
ROISSYBUS
B3
B5
350
351

Gare du Nord
Opéra
Gare de l'Est
Charles de Gaulle-Étoile
Châtelet-Les Halles
Porte Maillot
Châtelet
A
B
La Défense
C1,C3
Invalides
C
St-Michel
St-Michel-Nôtre Dame
Nation
Champ de Mars-Tour Eiffel
Gare de Lyon
Gare d'Austerlitz
Issy-Val de Seine
Denfert-Rochereau
C
Gare Montparnasse
4
Villejuif-Louis Aragon
Porte de Choisy
Porte d'Orléans
B
183
285
Pont de Rungis
C5
C7
B2
B4
Antony
ORY Paris Orly
C4,C6
Versailles
Seine
Disneyland Resort Paris
ORLYVAL
ORLYBUS
N31

Diagrammatic only: not to scale

BRITTANY

Dunkerque (Dunkirk)
Calais
Boulogne-sur-Mer
Dieppe
Amiens
Lille LIL Lille
Lens
ARDENNES
NORD-PAS-DE-CALAIS
PARIS
PICARDIE (PICARDY)
Reims
Metz
Châlons-en-Champagne
LORRAINE
Strasbourg
Nancy
SXB Strasbourg
ALSACE
VOSGES
Mulhouse
EAP EuroAirport

Cherbourg
le Havre LHE
le Havre
Rouen
Caen
BASSE-NORMANDIE
HAUTE-NORMANDIE
Seine
CDG Paris Roissy-Charles de Gaulle
PARIS
ORY Paris Orly
ÎLE-DE-FRANCE
Chartres
Marne
CHAMPAGNE-ARDENNE
Besançon
FRANCHE-COMTÉ
JURA
FRENCH ALPS

St-Malo
Brest
BRITTANY
BRETAGNE (BRITTANY)
LOWER LOIRE
Rennes
MAINE
le Mans
Orléans
Nantes NTE
Nantes-Atlantique
PAYS DE LA LOIRE
ANJOU
TOURAINE
Tours
CENTRE
BERRY
Bourges
Dijon
BOURGOGNE (BURGUNDY)

Poitiers
POITOU
POITOU-CHARENTES
la Rochelle
Rochefort
SOUTHWEST FRANCE
Angoulême
Limoges
LIMOUSIN
Vichy
CFE Clermont-Ferrand-Auvergne
Clermont-Ferrand
St-Étienne
AUVERGNE
Lyon (Lyons)
LYS Lyon
RHÔNE-ALPES
SAVOIE (SAVOY)
DAUPHINÉ
Grenoble
A L P S

CÔTE DES LANDES
Bordeaux
BOD Bordeaux
Bergerac
GUYENNE
Dordogne
MASSIF CENTRAL
Rhône
AQUITAINE
CÔTE D'ARGENT
Lot
Garonne
MIDI-PYRÉNÉES
GASCOGNE (GASCONY)
TLS Toulouse
Toulouse
Tarn
Nîmes
Avignon
Montpellier
LANGUEDOC-ROUSSILLON
CAMARGUE
MPL Montpellier-Méditeranée
PROVENCE-ALPES-CÔTE D'AZUR
PROVENCE
MRS Marseille-Provence
Marseille (Marseilles)
CÔTE D'AZUR
MONACO
Nice
NCE Nice-Côte d'Azur
RIVIERA
Toulon

Biarritz
LDE Tarbes-Lourdes
Lourdes
Carcassonne
Perpignan
P Y R E N E E S
PYRENEES (WEST)
PYRENEES (EAST)
PROVENCE & CÔTE D'AZUR

Bastia
CORSE (CORSICA)
Ajaccio
AJA Ajaccio
CORSICA

- - - Region boundary
- ● Region capital
200 km
100 miles

For a list of French Départements, see Appendices

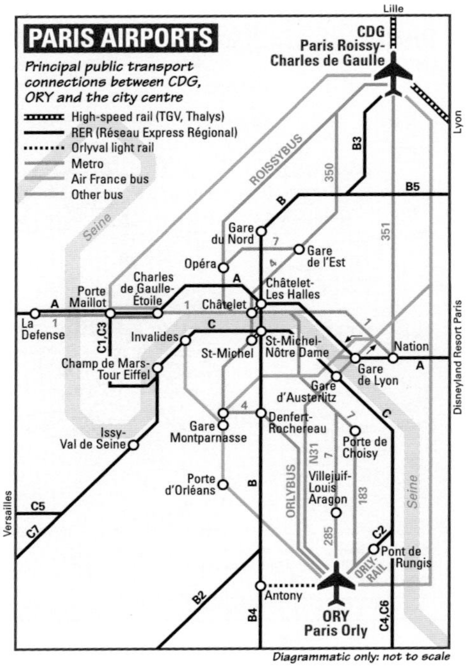

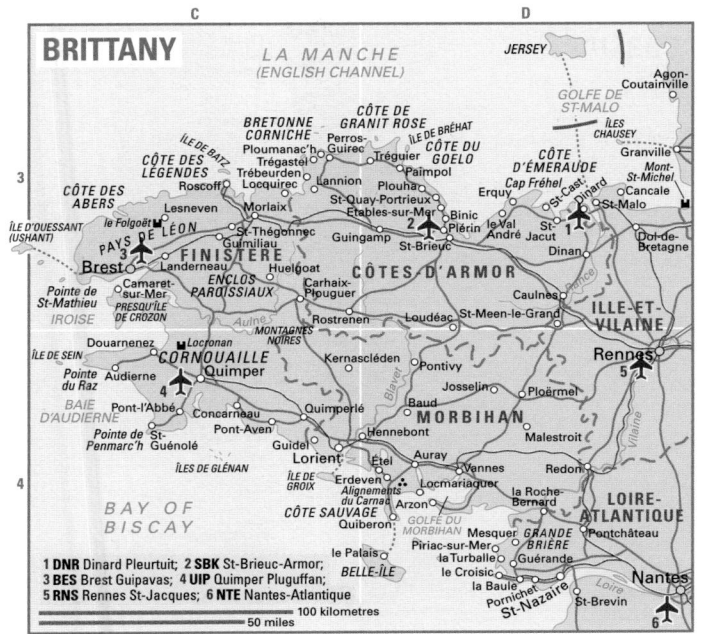

BRITTANY

LA MANCHE (ENGLISH CHANNEL)
JERSEY
GOLFE DE ST-MALO
Agon-Coutainville
ÎLES CHAUSEY
Granville
Mont-St-Michel
Cancale
St-Malo
Dol-de-Bretagne

CÔTE DE GRANIT ROSE
BRETONNE CORNICHE
Perros-Guirec
ÎLE DE BRÉHAT
CÔTE DU GOELO
Paimpol
CÔTE D'ÉMERAUDE
Cap Fréhel
St-Cast
Dinard
ÎLE DE BATZ
Ploumanac'h
Trégastel
Tréguier
Plouha
Erquy
Trébeurden
Locquirec
Lannion
St-Quay-Portrieux
Binic
le Val André
St-Jacut
St-Brieuc
Roscoff
CÔTE DES LÉGENDES
le Folgoët
Plérin
Dinan
CÔTE DES ABERS
ÎLE D'OUESSANT (USHANT)
St-Thégonnec
Morlaix
Guingamp
St-Brieuc
CÔTES D'ARMOR
PAYS DE LÉON
Lesneven
Gumiliau
Huelgoat
Caulnes
ÎLE DE SEIN
Brest
Landerneau
ENCLOS PAROISSIAUX
Carhaix-Plouguer
Rostrenen
St-Meen-le-Grand
ILLE-ET-VILAINE
Pointe de St-Mathieu
IROISE
PRESQU'ÎLE DE CROZON
Camaret-sur-Mer
MONTAGNES NOIRES
Loudéac
Rennes
Douarnenez
Pointe du Raz
Locronan
Audierne
CORNOUAILLE
Quimper
Kernascléden
Pontivy
Josselin
Ploërmel
BAIE D'AUDIERNE
Pointe de St-Penmarc'h
Guénolé
Pont-l'Abbé
Concarneau
Quimperlé
Guidel
MORBIHAN
Baud
Malestroit
ÎLES DE GLÉNAN
Pont-Aven
Lorient
Hennebont
Auray
Vannes
Redon
Étel
ÎLE DE GROIX
Locmariaquer
Erdeven
Alignements du Carnac
LOIRE-ATLANTIQUE
GOLFE DU MORBIHAN
Arzon
Mesquer
GRANDE BRIÈRE
Pontchâteau
CÔTE SAUVAGE
Quiberon
la Turballe
le Croisic
Guérande
la Baule
St-Nazaire
St-Brevin
BELLE-ÎLE
le Palais
Piriac-sur-Mer
Pornichet
Nantes
BAY OF BISCAY

1 **DNR** Dinard Pleurtuit; 2 **SBK** St-Brieuc-Armor;
3 **BES** Brest Guipavas; 4 **UIP** Quimper Pluguffan;
5 **RNS** Rennes St-Jacques; 6 **NTE** Nantes-Atlantique

100 kilometres
50 miles

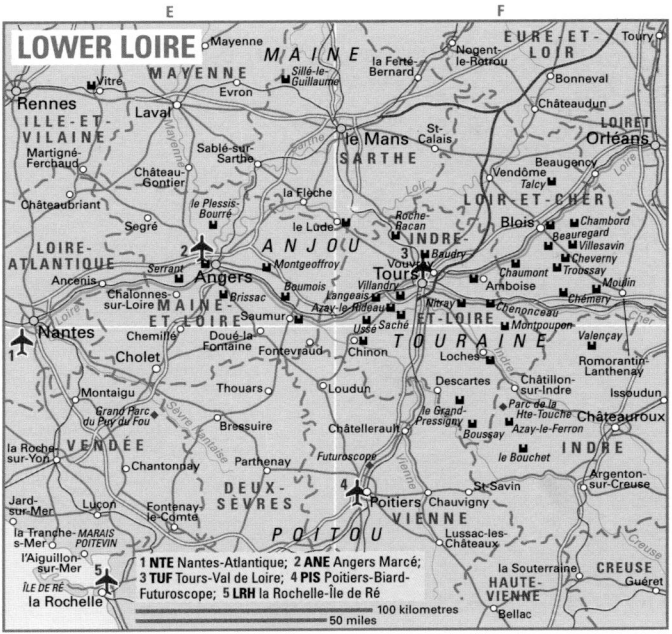

LOWER LOIRE

Mayenne
MAINE
MAYENNE
EURE-ET-LOIR
Nogent-le-Rotrou
Toury
Bonneval
la Ferté-Bernard
Sillé-le-Guillaume
Vitré
Rennes
Châteaudun
LOIRET
Orléans
ILLE-ET-VILAINE
Laval
Evron
Beaugency
Talcy
Vendôme
St-Calais
le Mans
SARTHE
Martigné-Ferchaud
Sablé-sur-Sarthe
LOIR-ET-CHER
Châteaubriant
Château-Gontier
Blois
Chambord
Beauregard
Villesavin
Segré
la Flèche
le Lude
le Plessis-Bourré
Cheverny
ANJOU
Ancenis
Serrant
Montgeoffroy
Angers
Vouvray
Amboise
Chaumont
Chenonceau
Chémery
Valençay
Nantes
MAINE-ET-LOIRE
Chalonnes-sur-Loire
Brissac
Baugé
Langeais
Azay-le-Rideau
Saché
Usse
Villandry
Tours
TOURAINE
INDRE-ET-LOIRE
Montpoupon
Montrésor
Loches
Romorantin-Lanthenay
Issoudun
Cholet
Chemillé
Doué-la-Fontaine
Fontevraud
Saumur
Chinon
Châtillon-sur-Indre
INDRE
Montaigu
Grand Parc du Puy du Fou
Thouars
Loudun
Descartes
Châteauroux
Argenton-sur-Creuse
VENDÉE
la Roche-sur-Yon
Chantonnay
Parthenay
Châtellerault
Hte-Touche
Parc de la
le Grand-Pressigny
Azay-le-Ferron
le Bouchet
Jard-sur-Mer
Luçon
Fontenay-le-Comte
Bressuire
DEUX-SÈVRES
Futuroscope
Chauvigny
St Savin
la Souterraine
la Tranche-sur-Mer
MARAIS POITEVIN
l'Aiguillon-sur-Mer
POITOU
Poitiers
VIENNE
Lussac-les-Châteaux
ÎLE DE RÉ
la Rochelle
CREUSE
HAUTE-VIENNE
Guéret
Bellac

1 **NTE** Nantes-Atlantique; 2 **ANE** Angers Marcé;
3 **TUF** Tours-Val de Loire; 4 **PIS** Poitiers-Biard-Futuroscope; 5 **LRH** la Rochelle-Île de Ré

100 kilometres
50 miles

2000 metres
1000 metres
Sea level

▶ *See also...* Winter Sports (57); The Alps (88-89);
The Mediterranean (94)

The listings above refer to a selection of related themes.
For more information, see the Contents (2-5).

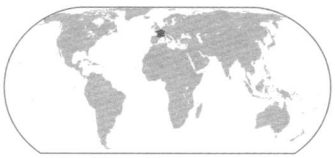

PARIS

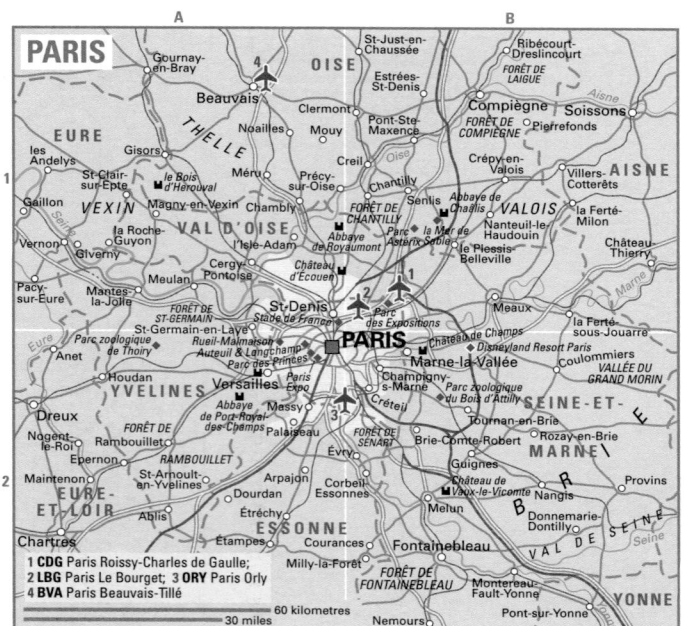

1 **CDG** Paris Roissy-Charles de Gaulle;
2 **LBG** Paris Le Bourget; 3 **ORY** Paris Orly
4 **BVA** Paris Beauvais-Tillé

FRENCH ALPS

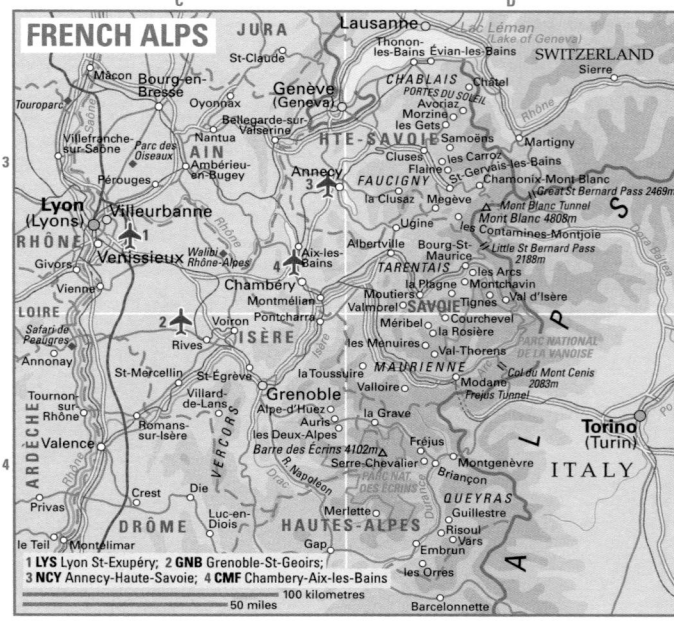

1 **LYS** Lyon St-Exupéry; 2 **GNB** Grenoble-St-Geoirs;
3 **NCY** Annecy-Haute-Savoie; 4 **CMF** Chambery-Aix-les-Bains

SOUTHWEST FRANCE

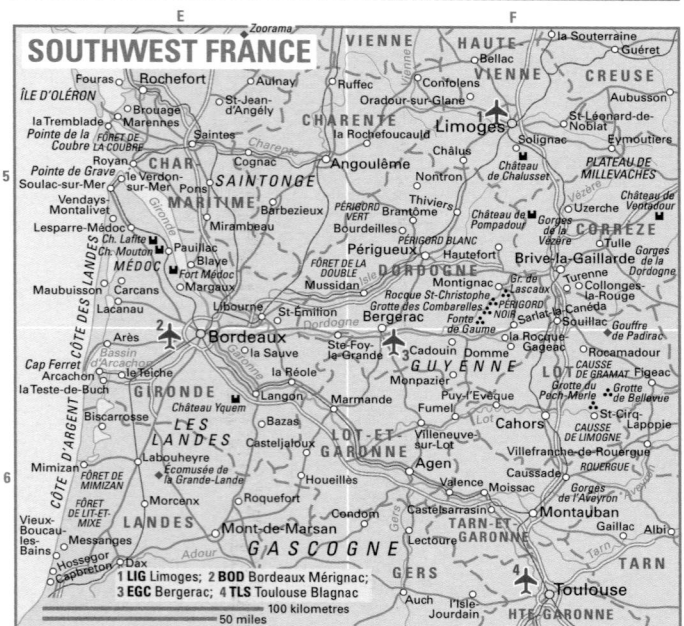

1 **LIG** Limoges; 2 **BOD** Bordeaux Mérignac;
3 **EGC** Bergerac; 4 **TLS** Toulouse Blagnac

PROVENCE & CÔTE D'AZUR

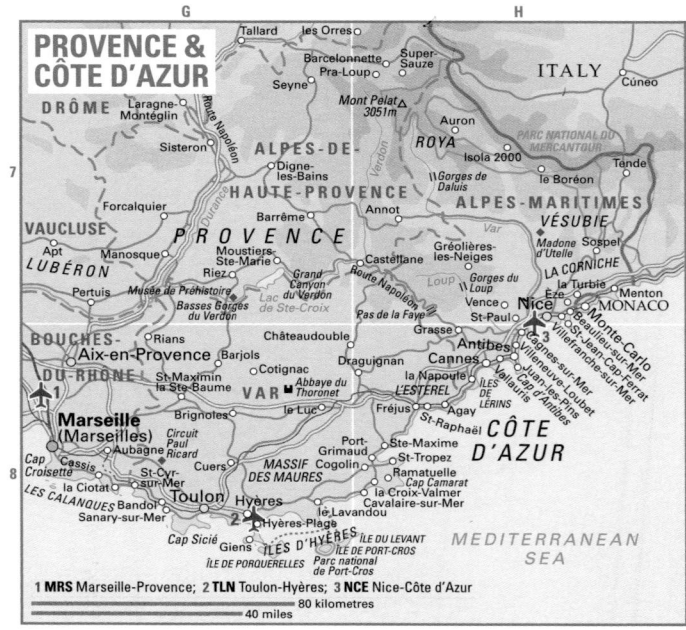

1 **MRS** Marseille-Provence; 2 **TLN** Toulon-Hyères; 3 **NCE** Nice-Côte d'Azur

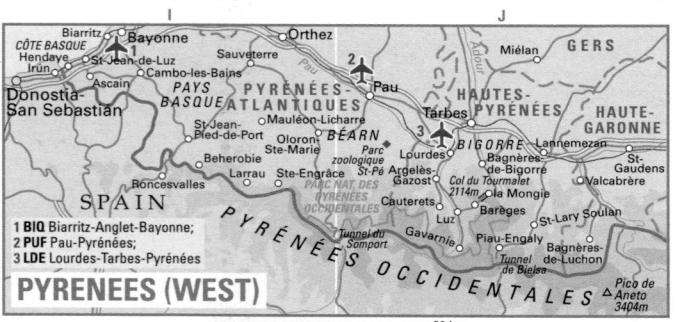

1 **BIQ** Biarritz-Anglet-Bayonne;
2 **PUF** Pau-Pyrénées;
3 **LDE** Lourdes-Tarbes-Pyrénées

PYRENEES (WEST)

CORSICA

1 **BIA** Bastia Poretta;
2 **CLY** Calvi Ste-Catherine;
3 **AJA** Ajaccio Campo dell'Oro;
4 **FSC** Figari-Sud Corse

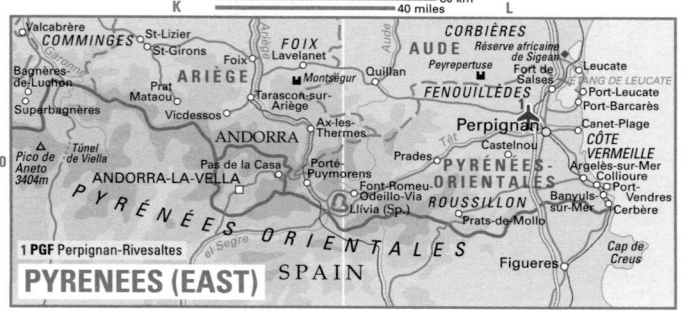

1 **PGF** Perpignan-Rivesaltes

PYRENEES (EAST)

The listings above refer to a selection of related themes. For more information, see the Contents (2–5). See also the Columbus Tourist Attractions & Events of the World.

Theme park, leisure park
Museum, gallery
Religious building
Park, reserve, zoo, etc.
Historic/notable building
Water-related attraction
Other place of interest

Attractions in cities marked in red are listed above and below the map

200 kilometres
100 miles

Paris
Le Jardin d'Acclimatation
Centre Georges-Pompidou
Cité des Sciences et de l'Industrie
Institut du Monde Arabe
Louvre
Musée d'Orsay
Musée Marmottan Monet
Musée national du Jeu de Paume
Musée national du Moyen-Âge
Musée national de l'Orangerie
Musée national Picasso
Musée Rodin
Basilique Royale de St-Denis
Cathédrale de Notre-Dame
Église du Dôme
Panthéon
Sacré-Cœur
Ste-Chapelle
Jardin de Luxembourg
La Grande Arche de la Défense
Hôtel des Invalides
Opéra Garnier
Palais de Chaillot
Arc de Triomphe de l'Étoile
Champs-Élysées
Cimetière de Montmartre
Cimetière du Père-Lachaise
Le Marais
Montmartre
Place de la Concorde
Place des Vosges
Tour Eiffel

Orange
Théâtre Antique
Arc de Triomphe

Avignon
Musée Calvet
Musée du Petit Palais
Palais des Papes
Pont St-Bénézet

Nîmes
Jardin de la Fontaine
Les Arènes
Maison Carrée

Lyon (Lyons)
Musée d'Art contemporain
Musée des Beaux-Arts
Musée de la Civilisation Gallo-Romaine
Musée Henri-Malartre
Centre d'histoire de la Résistance
Musée historique des Tissus
Basilique du Fourvière
Maison des Canuts
Quartier St-Jean

Nice
Fondation Maeght, St-Paul-de-Vence
Musée Picasso
Musée d'Art moderne et d'Art contemporain
Musée Marc Chagall
Musée Matisse
Promenade des Anglais
Riviera Corniche roads

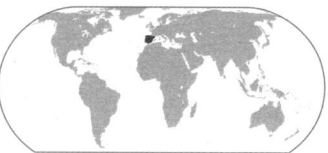

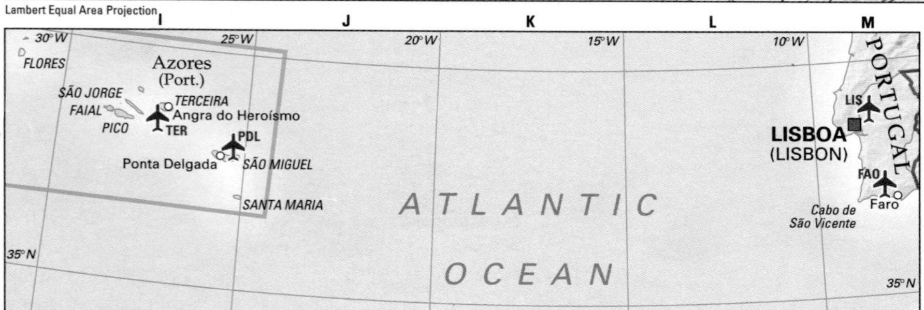

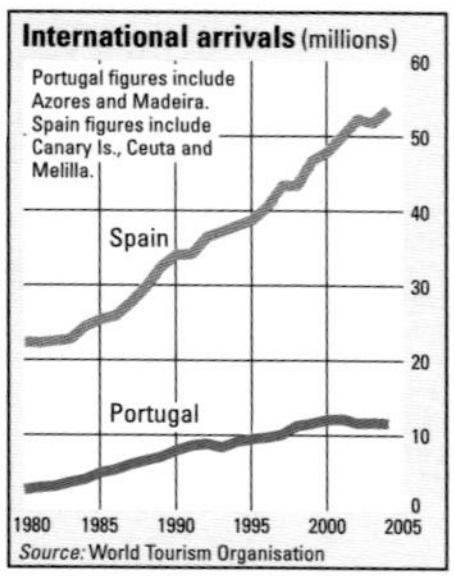

SPAIN
JAN 5th Cabalgata de los Reyes Magos: Three Kings Parade (**Barcelona**)
JAN Festividad de **San Sebastián**: drum parades
before Lent Carnaval (**Cádiz**, **Madrid** and countrywide)
MAR Las Fallas de **València**
EASTER Semana Santa: Holy Week (**Seville** and countrywide)
APR La Feria de **Sevilla**
APR Moros y Cristanos mock battle: St George's Festival (**Alcoy**)
APR 23rd La Diada de Sant Jordi: Day of St George 'Day of Lovers' (**Barcelona**)
MAY Cruces de Mayo and national flamenco competition (**Córdoba**)
MAY Feria del Caballo: horse fair (**Jeréz de la Frontera**)
MAY Festimad Alternative Music Festival (**Madrid**)
MAY-JUN Fiestas de San Isidro (**Madrid**)
WHIT SUNDAY Romería del Rocío: pilgrimage (near **Huelva**)
JUN Sonar: electronic music festival (**Barcelona**)
JUN Haro: Wine war (**La Rioja**)
JUN 23-24th Festes de Sant Joan (**Barcelona** and Catalonia)
JUN 24th Xiquets de Valls: human towers (**Valls**)
JUN-JUL GREC: **Barcelona** Summer Festival
JUN-JUL International Festival of Music and Dance (**Granada**)
JUL Los Sanfermines: running of the bulls (**Pamplona**)
JUL Jazzaldia: Festival de Jazz de **San Sebastián**
JUL Santa Marta de Ribarteme: 'near-death' pilgrimage (**Las Nieves, Pontevadra**)
JUL 22nd Cuesta de los Danzadores: stilt dancers (**Anguiano**, La Rioja)
JUL 25th Feast of St James (**Santiago de Compostela**)
AUG Semana Grande, includes Basque Herri Kilorak: traditional sports (**Bilbao**)
AUG Moros y Cristanos mock battle and mystery play (**Elx**)
AUG La Tomatina: Tomato Battle (**Buñol**)
SEP **San Sebastián** International Film Festival
SEP 19th Americas Day (**Oviedo**)
SEP 24th Festa de la Mercè: Our Lady of Mercy Festival (**Barcelona**)
OCT-NOV **Madrid** Autumn Festival
PORTUGAL
before Lent **Lisbon** Carnival APR Lisbon Half Marathon
MAY 13th Pilgrimage to the Shrine of Our Lady of **Fátima**
MAY Queimade Fitas: academic celebrations (**Coimbra**)
JUN Festas de Lisboa: festivities in honour of three saints (**Lisbon**)
JUL Festa do Colete Encarnado: Festival of the Red Waistcoat (**Vila Franca de Xira**)
AUG Romaria de Nossa Senhora de Agonía: fair & pilgrimage (**Viana do Castelo**)
OCT Fiera do Outubro: October Festival (**Vila Franca de Xira**)
OCT 13th Pilgrimage to the Shrine of Our Lady of **Fátima**
NOV Feira Nacional do Cavalo: National Horse Fair (**Golegã**)
NEW YEAR's EVE Noite Mágica: Magic Night (**Lisbon**)

International arrivals (millions)

Portugal figures include Azores and Madeira.
Spain figures include Canary Is., Ceuta and Melilla.

Spain

Portugal

1980 1985 1990 1995 2000 2005
Source: World Tourism Organisation

Blue boxes indicate focus map coverage
Lambert Equal Area Projection

See also... Attractions in UK (64), Belgium (67), Netherlands (69), Germany (73), France (77) and Italy (86)

The listings above refer to a selection of related themes.
For more information, see the Contents (2-5). See also the Columbus Tourist Attractions & Events of the World.

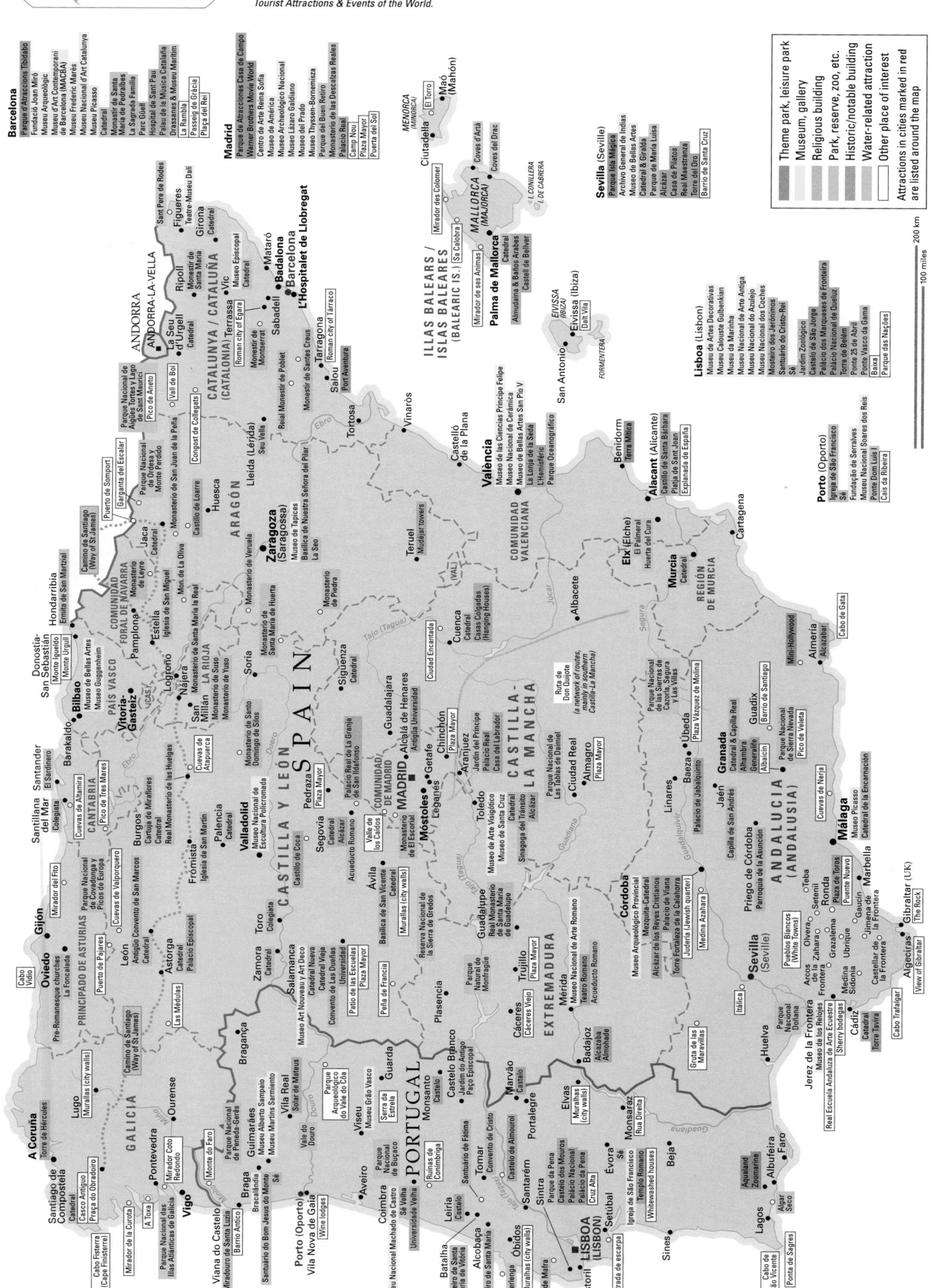

The listings above refer to a selection of related themes.
For more information, see the Contents (2-5).

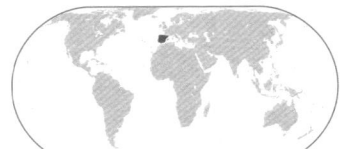

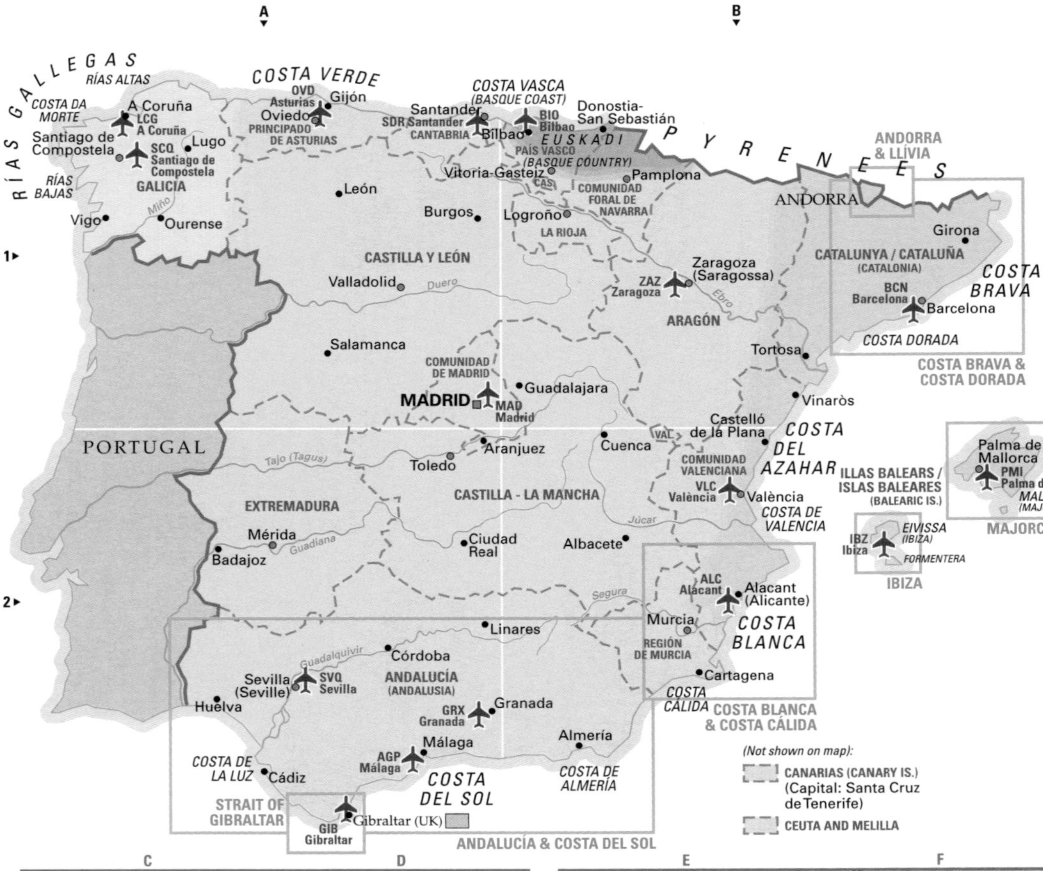

Legend:
- – – – Autonomous community boundary
- ● Autonomous community capital

Languages spoken in **Spain**:
- Castilian Spanish

Bilingual areas of Spain:
- Basque (spoken by a significant & increasing minority)
- Catalan* (spoken by 50-70% of people)
- Galician (spoken by over 90% of people)

Languages spoken in the **rest of Iberia**:
- Portuguese
- English
- Catalan is the official language in Andorra

300 km / 150 miles

*Catalan, an official EU language since 1990, is often called Valencian in Comunidad Valenciana
Local spellings are used in bilingual areas. Where more than one version is shown, the Castilian spelling appears after the local spelling.

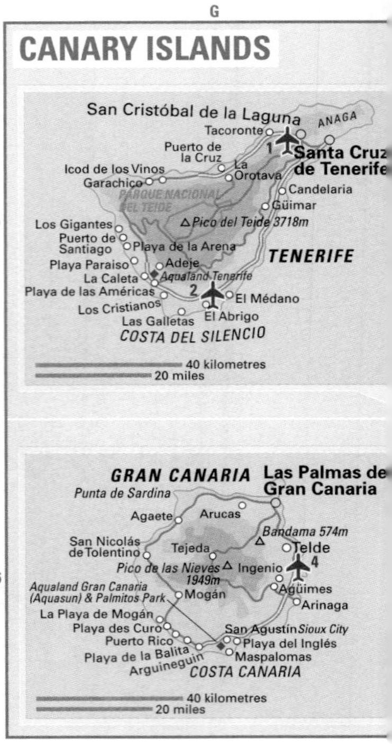

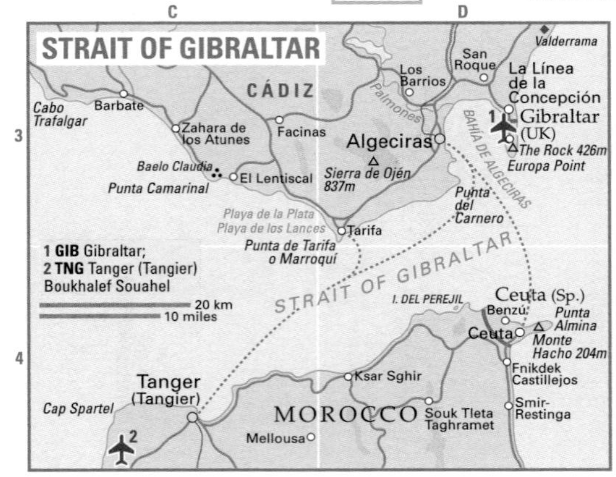

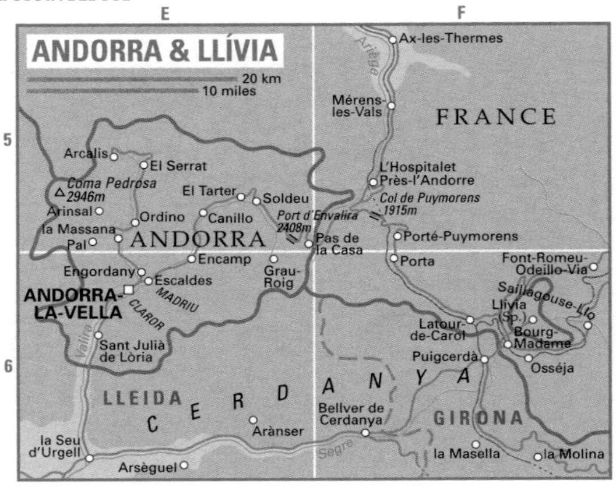

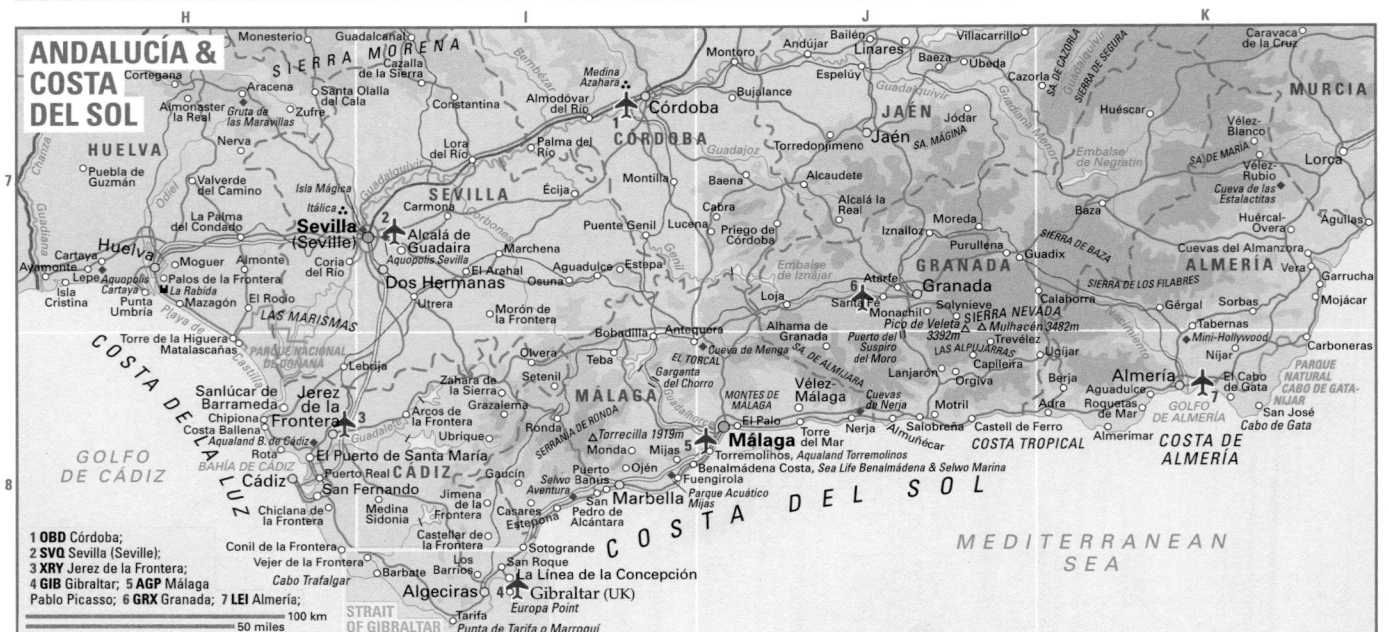

CANARY ISLANDS

STRAIT OF GIBRALTAR
1 GIB Gibraltar;
2 TNG Tanger (Tangier)
Boukhalef Souahel

ANDORRA & LLÍVIA

ANDALUCÍA & COSTA DEL SOL
1 OBD Córdoba;
2 SVQ Sevilla (Seville);
3 XRY Jerez de la Frontera;
4 GIB Gibraltar; 5 AGP Málaga
Pablo Picasso; 6 GRX Granada; 7 LEI Almería;

(Not shown on map):
- CANARIAS (CANARY IS.) (Capital: Santa Cruz de Tenerife)
- CEUTA AND MELILLA

The listings above refer to a selection of related themes.
For more information, see the Contents (2-5).

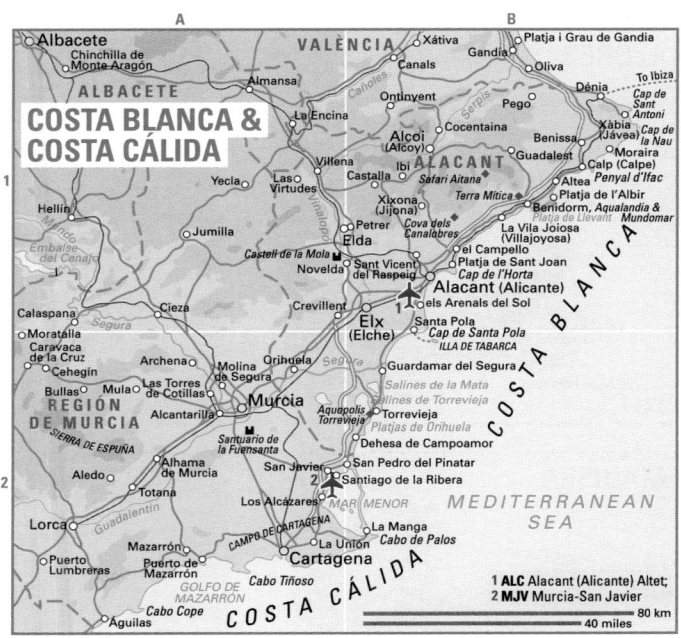

COSTA BLANCA & COSTA CÁLIDA

1 **ALC** Alacant (Alicante) Altet;
2 **MJV** Murcia-San Javier

80 km / 40 miles

COSTA BRAVA & COSTA DORADA

1 **REU** Reus; 2 **BCN** Barcelona
El Prat de Llobregat;
3 **GRO** Girona Costa Brava

80 km / 40 miles

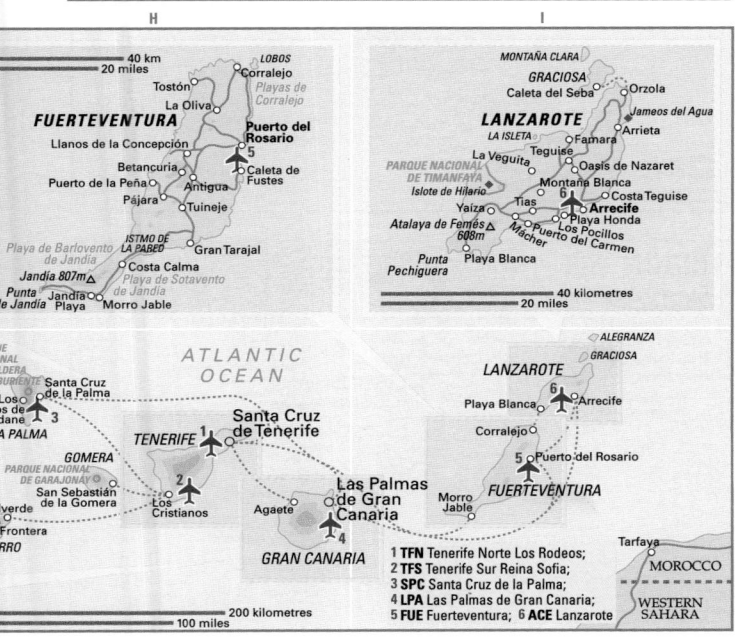

1 **TFN** Tenerife Norte Los Rodeos;
2 **TFS** Tenerife Sur Reina Sofia;
3 **SPC** Santa Cruz de la Palma;
4 **LPA** Las Palmas de Gran Canaria;
5 **FUE** Fuerteventura; 6 **ACE** Lanzarote

40 km / 20 miles
40 kilometres / 20 miles
200 kilometres / 100 miles

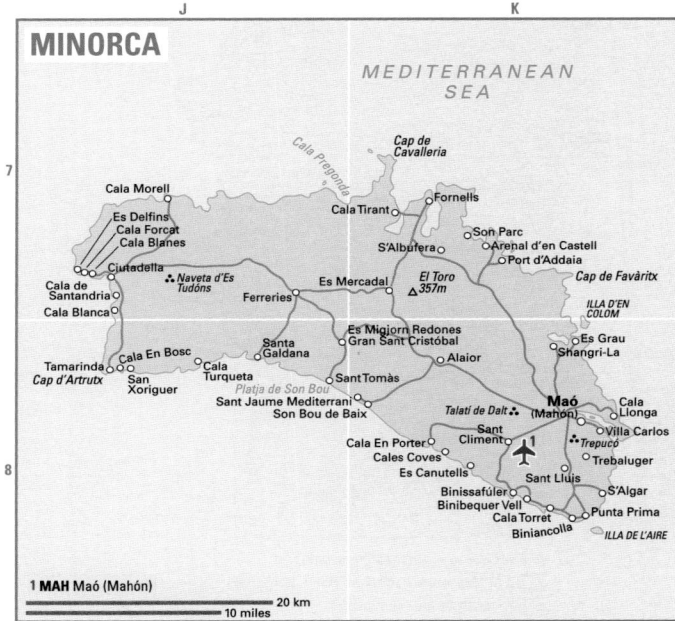

MINORCA

1 **MAH** Maó (Mahón)

20 km / 10 miles

IBIZA

1 **IBZ** Eivissa (Ibiza)

20 km / 10 miles

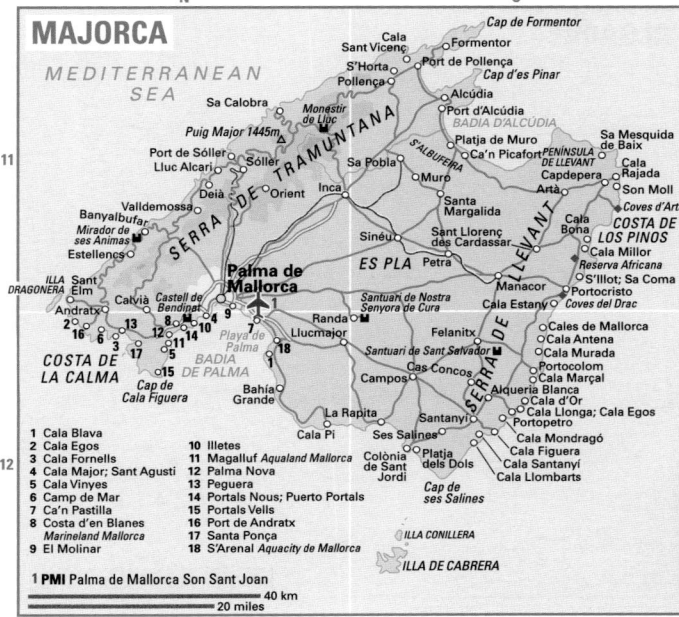

MAJORCA

1 Cala Blava
2 Cala Egos
3 Cala Fornells
4 Cala Major; Sant Agustí
5 Cala Vinyes
6 Camp de Mar
7 Ca'n Pastilla
8 Costa d'en Blanes
  Marineland Mallorca
9 El Molinar
10 Illetes
11 Magalluf Aqualand Mallorca
12 Palma Nova
13 Peguera
14 Portals Nous; Puerto Portals
15 Portals Vells
16 Port d'Andratx
17 Santa Ponça
18 S'Arenal Aquacity de Mallorca

1 **PMI** Palma de Mallorca Son Sant Joan

40 km / 20 miles

1000 metres
500 metres
Sea level

▶ **See also...** Contents (2-5) – this country features in many thematic and regional maps throughout the *BTEC First Travel Atlas*.

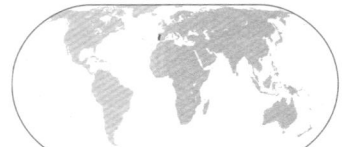

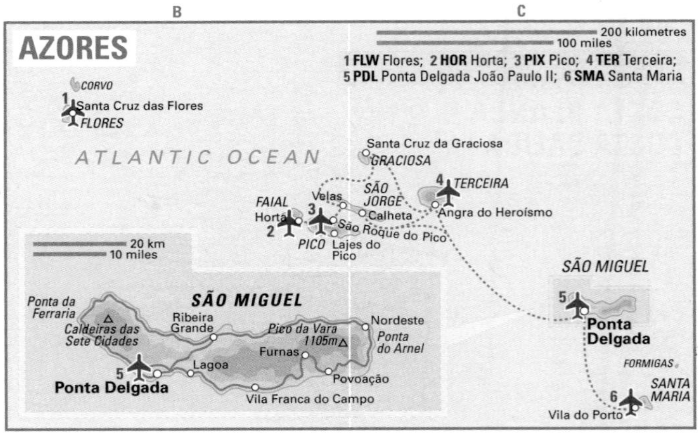

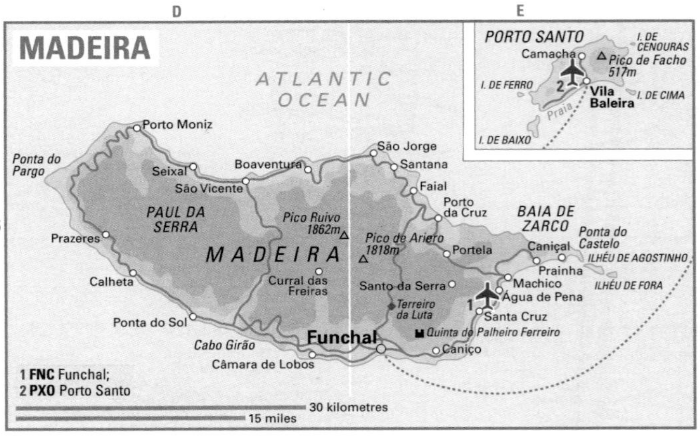

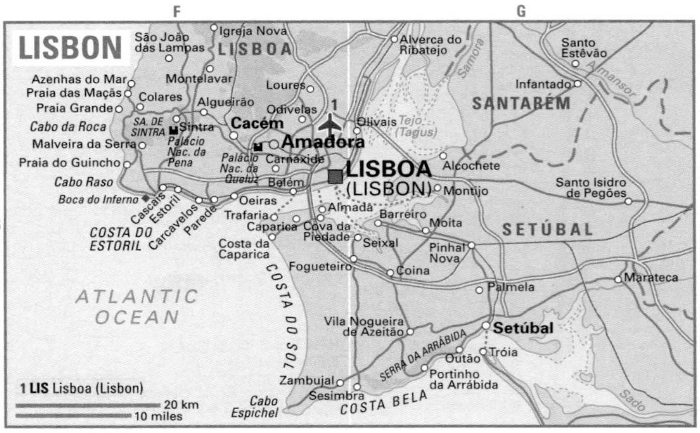

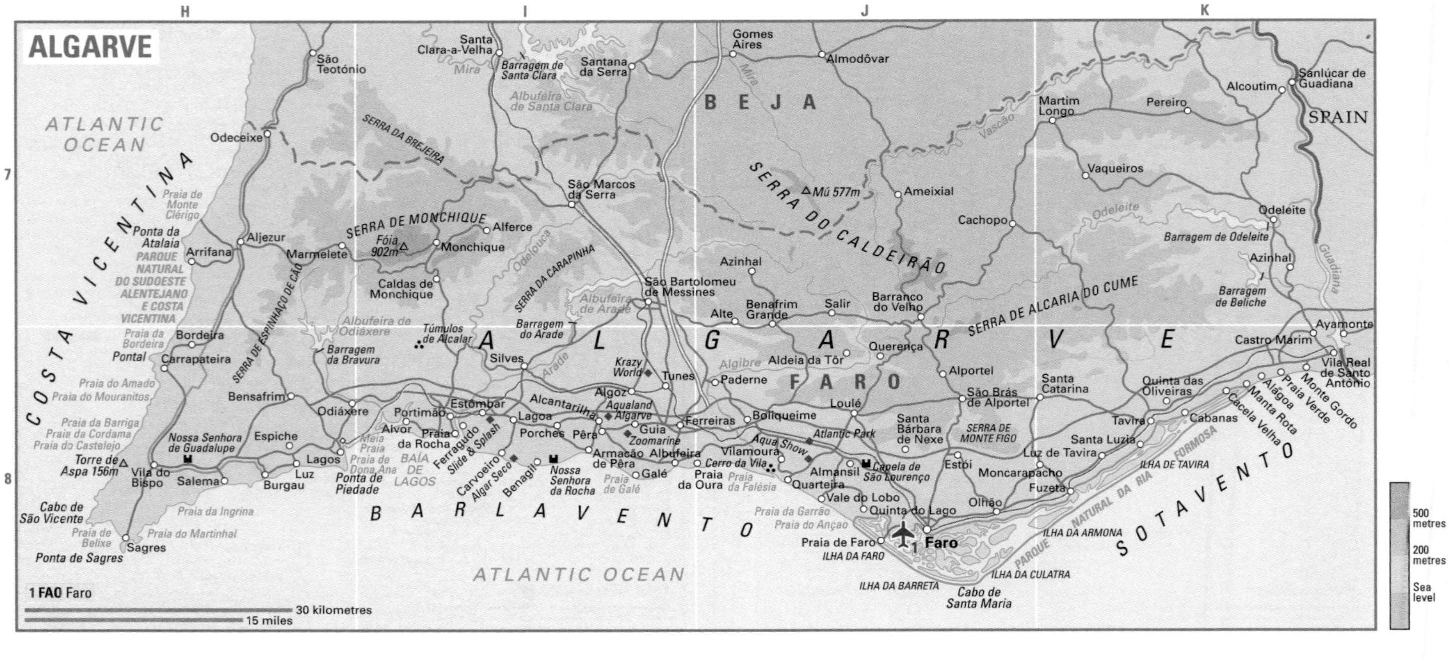

AZORES

1 **FLW** Flores; 2 **HOR** Horta; 3 **PIX** Pico; 4 **TER** Terceira;
5 **PDL** Ponta Delgada João Paulo II; 6 **SMA** Santa Maria

MADEIRA

1 **FNC** Funchal;
2 **PXO** Porto Santo

LISBON

1 **LIS** Lisboa (Lisbon)

ALGARVE

1 **FAO** Faro

District boundary
District capital

(Not shown on map) AUTONOMOUS REGIONS OF:
AÇORES (AZORES) (Capital: Ponta Delgada)
MADEIRA (Capital: Funchal)

Lambert Equal Area Projection   Blue boxes indicate focus map coverage

200 kilometres
100 miles

▶ *See also...* Winter Sports (57); The Alps (88–89);
The Mediterranean (94)

*The listings above refer to a selection of related themes.
For more information, see the Contents (2–5).*

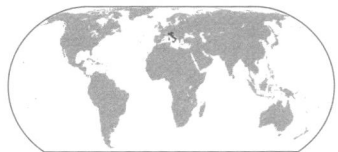

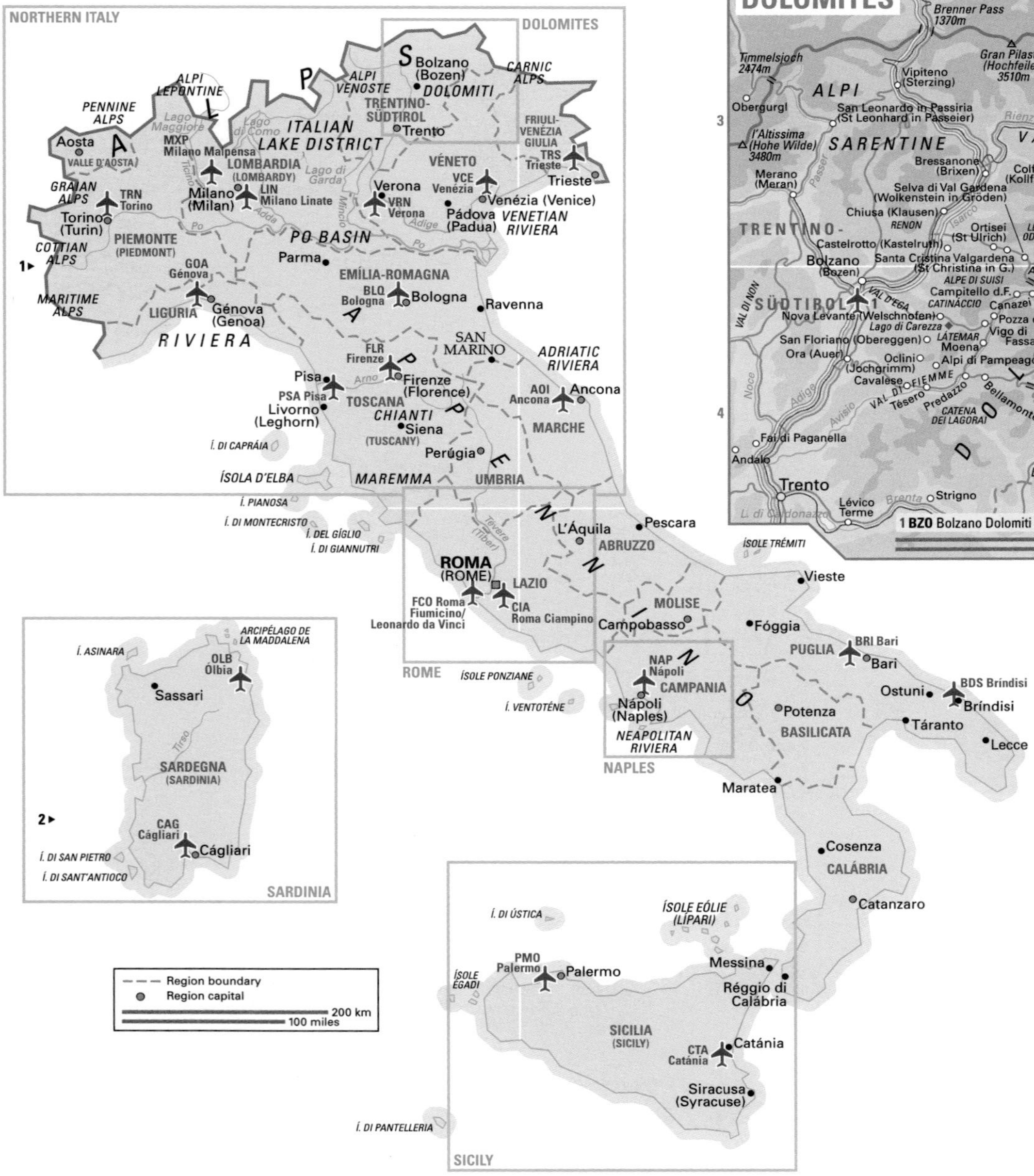

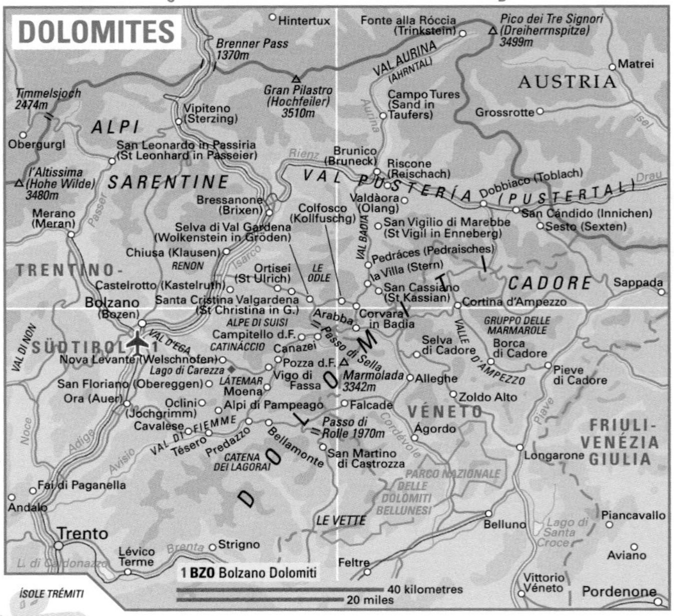

NORTHERN ITALY

PENNINE ALPS · ALPI LEPONTINE · GRAIAN ALPS · COTTIAN ALPS · MARITIME ALPS · VALLE D'AOSTA · PIEMONTE (PIEDMONT) · LOMBARDIA (LOMBARDY) · ITALIAN LAKE DISTRICT · Lago Maggiore · Lago di Como · Lago di Garda · TRENTINO-SÜDTIROL · DOLOMITI · ALPI VENOSTE · CARNIC ALPS · FRIULI-VENEZIA GIULIA · VÉNETO · VENETIAN RIVIERA · PO BASIN · EMÍLIA-ROMAGNA · LIGURIA · RIVIERA · TOSCANA (TUSCANY) · CHIANTI · MAREMMA · UMBRIA · MARCHE · SAN MARINO · ADRIATIC RIVIERA · APENNINES

Aosta · Torino (Turin) · Génova (Genoa) · Milano (Milan) · Verona · Pádova (Padua) · Venézia (Venice) · Trieste · Trento · Bolzano (Bozen) · Parma · Bologna · Ravenna · Pisa · Livorno (Leghorn) · Firenze (Florence) · Siena · Perúgia · Ancona

MXP Milano Malpensa · LIN Milano Linate · TRN Torino · GOA Génova · VRN Verona · VCE Venézia · BLQ Bologna · FLR Firenze · PSA Pisa

Í. DI CAPRÁIA · Í. PIANOSA · Í. DI MONTECRISTO · ÍSOLA D'ELBA · Í. DEL GÍGLIO · Í. DI GIANNUTRI

DOLOMITES

Hintertux · Brenner Pass 1370m · Fonte alla Róccia (Trinkstein) · Pico dei Tre Signori △ Dreiherrnspitze 3499m · Matrei · AUSTRIA · Timmelsjoch 2474m · Vipiteno (Sterzing) · Gran Pilastro (Hochfeiler) 3510m · Campo Tures (Sand in Taufers) · Grossrotte · Obergurgl · St Leonard in Passeier · Brunico (Bruneck) · Riscone (Reischach) · San Cándido (Innichen) · Sesto (Sexten) · l'Altissima (Hohe Wilde) 3480m · Merano (Meran) · Bressanone (Brixen) · Valdáora (Olang) · San Vigílio di Marebbe (St Vigil in Enneberg) · Sappada · VAL PUSTÉRIA (PUSTERTAL) · Chiusa (Klausen) · Colfosco (Kollfuschg) · Selva di Val Gardena (Wolkenstein in Gröden) · Pedráces (Pedraisches) · la Villa (Stern) · CADORE · Castelrotto (Kastelruth) · Ortisei (St Ulrich) · Santa Cristina Valgardena (St Christina in G.) · San Cassiano (St Kassian) · Corvara in Badia · Cortina d'Ampezzo · Bolzano (Bozen) · ALPE DI SUISI · San Floriano (Obereggen) · Lago di Carezza · Canazei · Pozza d.F. · Selva di Cadore · Borca di Cadore · Pieve di Cadore · Ora (Auer) · Moena · Vigo di Fassa · Marmolada 3342m · Zoldo Alto · Cavalese · Predazzo · Alpi di Pampeágo · Falcade · Ágordo · VÉNETO · Bellamonte · San Martino di Castrozza · Longarone · FRIULI-VENEZIA GIULIA · Fái di Paganella · Andalo · LE VETTE · Belluno · Piancavallo · Trento · Lévico Terme · Strigno · Feltre · Vittório Véneto · Aviano · Pordenone

1 **BZO** Bolzano Dolomiti

40 kilometres · 20 miles

JAN 31st Fiera di Sant'Orso (**Aosta**)
FEB Festa del Mandorlo in fiore: almond blossom festival (**Agrigento**)
before Lent Carnevale (**Venice** and countrywide)
ASH WEDNESDAY Il Pranzo del Purgatori: Purgatory Dinner (**Grádoli**, Lazio)
GOOD FRIDAY Processions (Southern Italy and Sicily)
EASTER SUNDAY Il Scoppio del Carro: fireworks (**Florence**)
MAR-APR La Festa di Primavera: Spring Festival (**Rome**)
MAY 1st Festa di Sant'Efisio (**Cágliari**)
MAY Festa di San Domenico Abate (Cocullo, **L'Aquila**)
MAY Festa di San Gennaro (**Naples**); also Sep 19th and Dec 16th
MAY Sagra di San Nicola (**Bari**)
MAY 15th Corso dei Ceri: 'candle' race (**Gúbbio**)
MAY Cavalcata Sarda: Sardinian Cavalcade (**Sassari**)
MAY La Festa della Sensa: Wedding to the Sea (**Venice**)
JUN Luminaria: Festival of Lights; Gioco del Ponte: tug-of-war; historical regatta (**Pisa**)
JUN Corpus Christi Procession (**Orvieto**)
JUN La Festa di San Giovanni and Gioco di Calcio Storico: football match in medieval costume (**Florence**)
JUN-JUL Festival dei Due Mondi: arts festival (**Spoleto**)
JUN-SEP Biennale (**Venice**); every two (odd) years
JUL 2nd Palio delle Contrade: horse races (**Siena**); also AUG 16th
JUL La Festa del Redentore: Feast of the Redeemer (**Venice**)
JUL-AUG International Opera Festival (**Verona**)
JUL-SEP Estate Romana: Roman Summer arts festival (**Rome**)
AUG La Festa del Redentore: Feast of the Redeemer (**Nuoro**)
AUG-SEP International Film Festival (**Venice** Lido)
SEP La Giostra del Saracine: jousting tournament (**Arezzo**)
SEP La Regatta Storico: historical regatta (**Venice**)
SEP Douja d'Or: wine festival; Festival delle Sagre; Palio (**Asti**)
SEP La Partita a Scacchi: living chess (**Maróstica**); every two (even) years
SEP 19th La Festa di San Gennaro (**Naples**)
OCT Festa dell'uva: Grape Festival (**Merano**)
OCT-DEC **Rome** Jazz Festival
NOV La Festa della Madonna della Salute (**Venice**)

ROME

ROMA (ROME) · LAZIO · ABRUZZO · MOLISE · CAMPANIA · NEAPOLITAN RIVIERA · FCO Roma Fiumicino/Leonardo da Vinci · CIA Roma Ciampino · NAP Nápoli · L'Áquila · Pescara · Vieste · Fóggia · Campobasso · Nápoli (Naples) · ÍSOLE PONZIANE · Í. VENTOTÉNE · ÍSOLE TRÉMITI

NAPLES

SARDINIA

ARCIPÉLAGO DE LA MADDALENA · Í. ASINARA · OLB Ólbia · Sassari · SARDEGNA (SARDINIA) · CAG Cágliari · Cágliari · Í. DI SAN PIETRO · Í. DI SANT'ANTIOCO

Region boundary · ● Region capital · 200 km · 100 miles

SARDINIA

STRAIT OF BONIFACIO · Capo Testa · la Maddalena · ÍSOLA MADDALENA · ÍSOLA CAPRERA · Santa Teresa di Gallura · Porto Rafael · Palau · Porto Cervo · GOLFO DI MARINELLA · Arzachena · ÍSOLA ASINARA · GOLFO DELL' ASINARA · Báia Sardínia · Golfo Aranci · COSTA SMERALDA · ÍSOLA TAVOLARA · Capo del Falcone · Stintino · Castelsardo · Porto Rotondo · Ólbia · ÍSOLA MÓLARA · Porto Tórres · LA NURRA · Santíssima Trinità di Saccargia · Sássari · ANGLONA · Porto Conte · Grotta di Nettuno · Alghero · LOGUDORO · Ozieri · Posada · la Caletta · RIVIERA DEL CORALLO · Bosa · Siniscóla · BARÓNIA · Capo Comino · Necrópoli di S. Ándria Priu · Oroséi · Cala Liberotto · Monte Ferru 1050m · Núoro · Oliéna · Villaggio nuragico di Serra Órrios · Santa Caterina di Pittinuri · Macomér · Dorgali · GOLFO DI OROSEI · MONTI DEL GENNARGENTU · SINIS · Thárros · Oristano · SARDEGNA · Árbatax · Punta La Mármora 1834m · MEDITERRANEAN SEA · GOLFO DI ORISTANO · Terralba · Gúspini · Barúmini · Ússasi · Tortolì · COSTA VERDE · Su Nuraxi di Barúmini · Sanluri · TYRRHENIAN SEA · CAMPIDANO · Villacidro · Villaputzu · COSTA REI · IGLESIENTE · Iglésias · Portoscuso · Carbónia · Muravera · Capo Boi · ÍSOLA DI SAN PIETRO · Carloforte · Calasetta · Sant'Antioco · Quartu Sant'Elena · Villasímius · Capo Carbonara · ÍSOLA DI SANT'ANTIOCO · Cágliari · GOLFO DI CÁGLIARI · PINETA · Pula · Nora · GOLFO DI PALMAS · Santa Margherita di Pula · Forte Village Resort · Chia · Bíthia · Capo Spartivento · COSTA DEL SUD

1 **AHO** Alghero Fertília;
2 **OLB** Ólbia Costa Smeralda;
3 **CAG** Cágliari Élmas

100 km · 50 miles

SICILY

TYRRHENIAN SEA · Í. STRÓMBOLI · ÍSOLE EÓLIE O LÍPARI (AEOLIAN OR LIPARI IS.) · Í. PANÁREA · from Naples · Í. FILICUDI · Í. SALINA · Í. ALICUDI · Í. LÍPARI · Í. VULCANO · ÍSOLA DI ÚSTICA · Mondello · Capo d'Orlando · Sant'Ágata di Militello · Milazzo · Tyndaris · Villa San Giovanni · Messina · San Vito lo Capo · Castellammare del Golfo · PMO Palermo · GOLFO DI TÉRMINI IMERESE · Cefalù · VAL DEMONE · Réggio di Calábria · Érice · Segesta · Partinico · Monreale · Bagheria · Stretto di Messina · Trápani · Partanna · VAL DI MAZARA · Castelvetrano · Jato · MADONIE · Randazzo · Taormina · Giardini-Naxos · Marsala · Selinunte · Menfi · MADONIE · Bronte · Monte Etna 3350m · Mazzarò · ÍSOLE ÉGADI · Í. MARETTIMO · Í. FAVIGNANA · Í. DELLA LÉVANZO · Mazara del Vallo · SICILIA · Paterno · Riposto · MEDITERRANEAN SEA · Sciacca · Eraclea Minoa · Morgantina · Lentini · Aci Trezza · Acireale · Agrigento · Porto Empédocle · Villa Romana del Casale · Piazza Armerina · Caltanissetta · Enna · Catánia · GOLFO DI CATÁNIA · Valle dei Templi · Canicattì · Caltagirone · Palazzolo · Augusta · Licata · Gela · Naro · VAL DI NOTO · Siracusa (Syracuse) · GOLFO DI GELA · Vittória · Cómiso · Ragusa · Módica · Avola · Noto · GOLFO DI NOTO · Pozzallo · Cava d'Íspica · Capo Pássero · Páchino

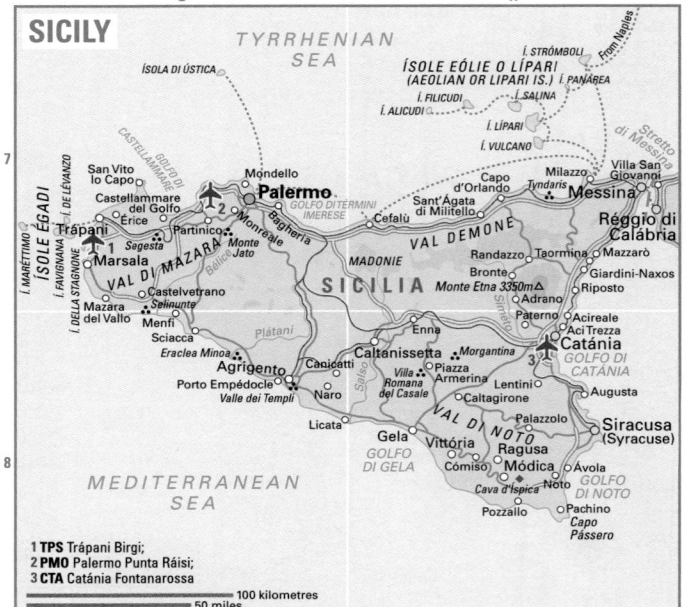

1 **TPS** Trápani Birgi;
2 **PMO** Palermo Punta Ráisi;
3 **CTA** Catánia Fontanarossa

100 kilometres · 50 miles

2300 metres · 1000 metres · Sea level

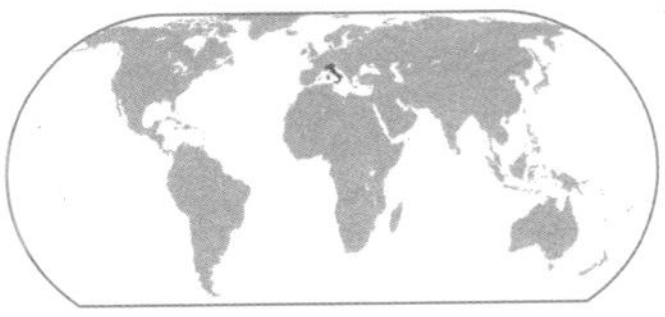

See also... Winter Sports (57); The Alps (88-89); The Mediterranean (94)

The listings above refer to a selection of related themes. For more information, see the Contents (2-5).

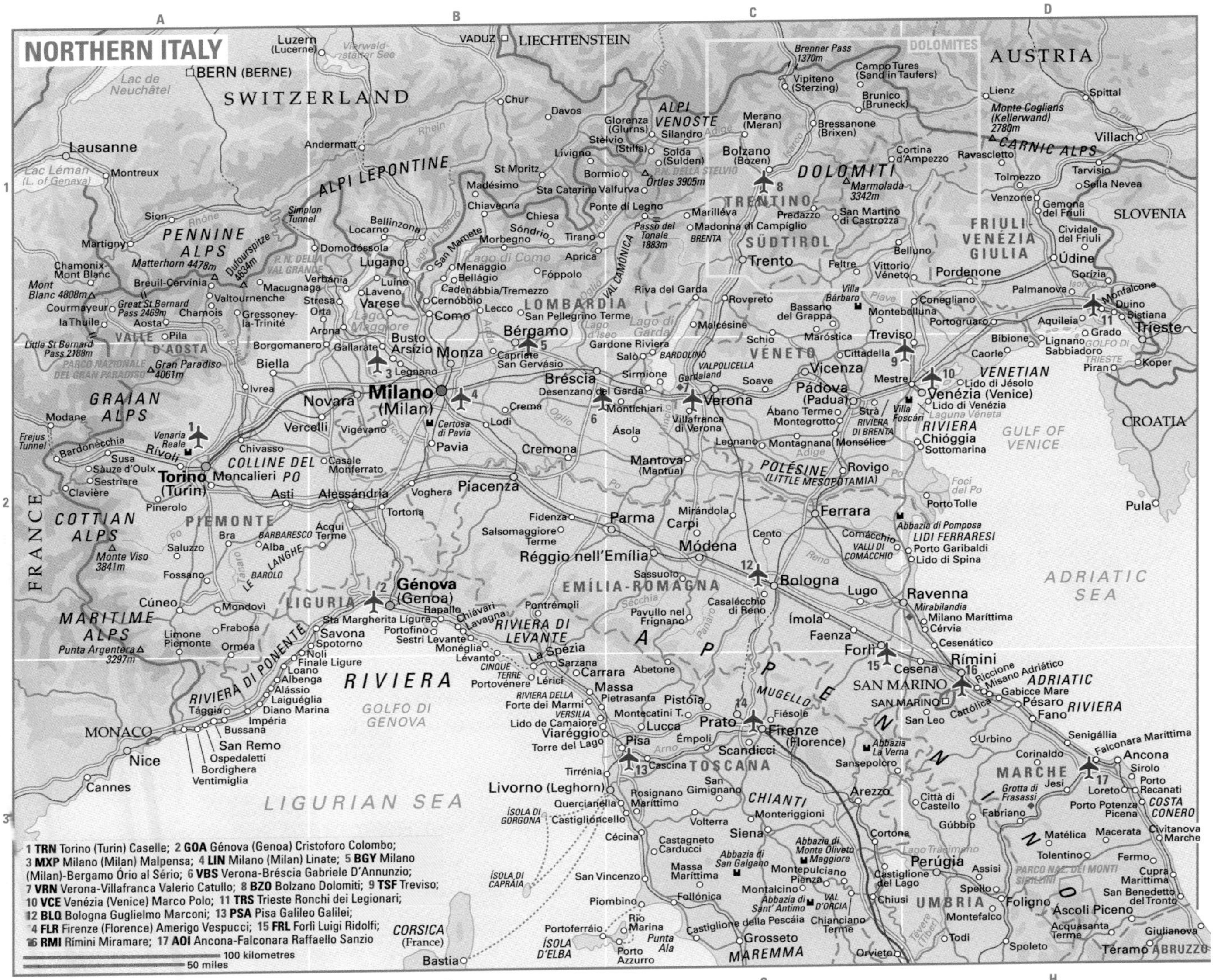

NORTHERN ITALY
SWITZERLAND
AUSTRIA
SLOVENIA
CROATIA
FRANCE
LIECHTENSTEIN
MONACO
SAN MARINO
CORSICA (France)
BERN (BERNE)
Milano (Milan)
Torino (Turin)
Génova (Genoa)
Venézia (Venice)
Bologna
Firenze (Florence)
Verona
Trieste
DOLOMITI
ALPI LEPONTINE
PENNINE ALPS
GRAIAN ALPS
COTTIAN ALPS
MARITIME ALPS
CARNIC ALPS
LOMBARDIA
VÉNETO
PIEMONTE
LIGURIA
EMÍLIA-ROMAGNA
TOSCANA
UMBRIA
MARCHE
FRIULI-VENÉZIA GIULIA
TRENTINO
SÜDTIROL
RIVIERA
RIVIERA DI PONENTE
RIVIERA DI LEVANTE
LIGURIAN SEA
ADRIATIC SEA
GULF OF VENICE
APPENNINO
1 TRN Torino (Turin) Caselle; 2 GOA Génova (Genoa) Cristoforo Colombo;
3 MXP Milano (Milan) Malpensa; 4 LIN Milano (Milan) Linate; 5 BGY Milano
(Milan)-Bergamo Ório al Sério; 6 VBS Verona-Bréscia Gabriele D'Annunzio;
7 VRN Verona-Villafranca Valerio Catullo; 8 BZO Bolzano Dolomiti; 9 TSF Treviso;
10 VCE Venézia (Venice) Marco Polo; 11 TRS Trieste Ronchi dei Legionari;
12 BLQ Bologna Guglielmo Marconi; 13 PSA Pisa Galileo Galilei;
14 FLR Firenze (Florence) Amerigo Vespucci; 15 FRL Forlì Luigi Ridolfi;
16 RMI Rímini Miramare; 17 AOI Ancona-Falconara Raffaello Sanzio
100 kilometres
50 miles

ROME
ROMA (ROME)
VATICAN CITY
LAZIO
UMBRIA
ABRUZZO
SABINA
APPENNINO ABRUZZESE
TYRRHENIAN SEA
GOLFO DI GAETA
60 km
30 miles
1 FCO Roma (Rome) Fiumicino/
Leonardo da Vinci;
2 CIA Roma (Rome) Ciampino

International arrivals (millions)
1980
1985
1990
1995
2000
2005
0
10
20
30
40
Source: World Tourism Organisation

NAPLES
Nápoli (Naples)
CAMPANIA
PUGLIA
Caserta
Salerno
Benevento
Avellino
Pompeii
Vesuvio (Vesuvius)
TYRRHENIAN SEA
GOLFO DI NÁPOLI
GOLFO DI SALERNO
NEAPOLITAN RIVIERA
COSTIERA AMALFITANA
1 NAP Nápoli (Naples) Capodichino
40 kilometres
20 miles

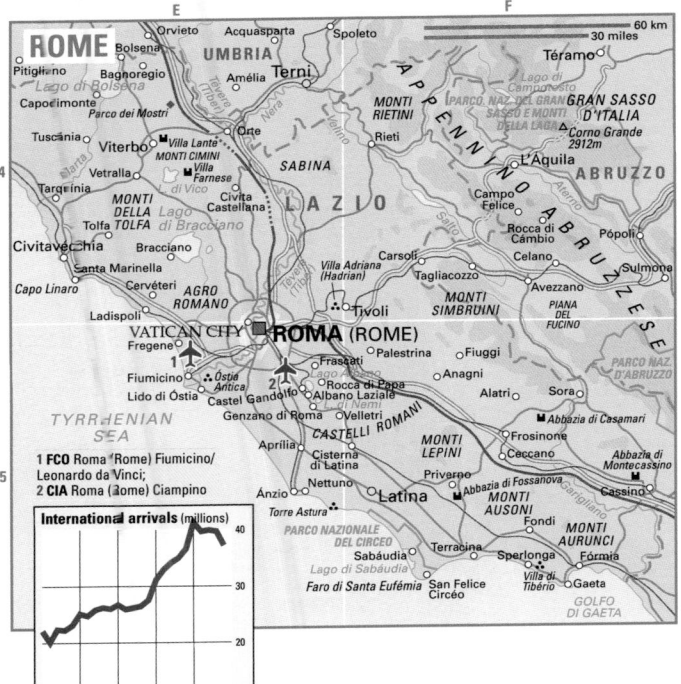

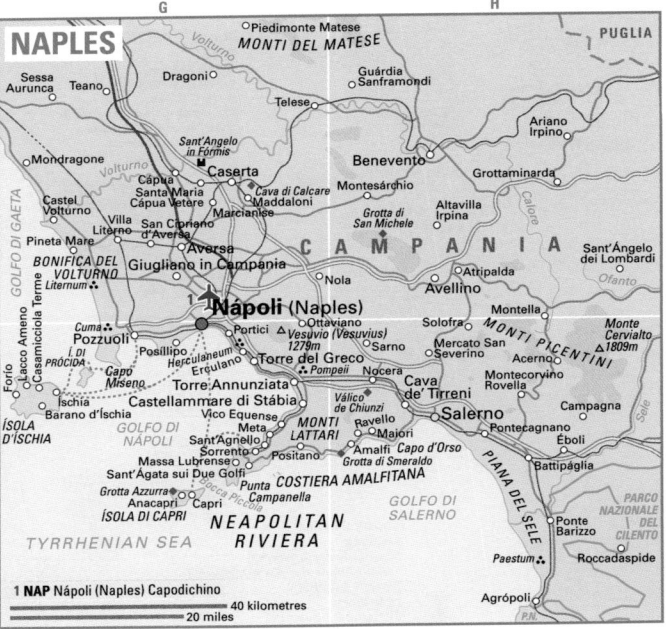

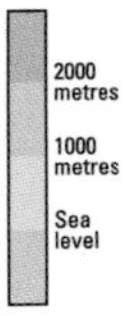

2000 metres
1000 metres
Sea level

▶ **See also...** Attractions in UK (64), Belgium (67), Netherlands (69), Germany (73), France (77) and Iberia (79)

The listings above refer to a selection of related themes. For more information, see the Contents (2-5). See also the Columbus Tourist Attractions and Events of the World.

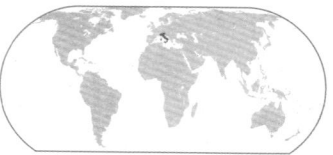

Legend:
- Theme park, leisure park
- Museum, gallery
- Religious building
- Park, reserve, zoo, etc.
- Historic/notable building
- Water-related attraction
- Other place of interest

Attractions in cities marked in red are listed around the map

200 km
100 miles

Milano (Milan)
- Il Cenacolo (Last Supper)
- Civico Museo di Arte Contemporanea
- Museo Civico di Archeologico
- Museo Nazionale della Scienza e Tecnica Leonardo da Vinci
- Museo Poldi-Pezzoli
- Pinacoteca Ambrosiana
- Pinacoteca di Brera
- Duomo
- Santa Maria presso San Satiro
- Giardini Pubblici
- Castello Sforzesco
- Galleria Vittorio Emanuele II
- Teatro alla Scala
- Quadrilatero d'Oro
- Stadio Meazza (San Siro)

Torino (Turin)
- Galleria Civica d'Arte Moderna e Contemporanea
- Galleria Sabauda
- Museo dell'Automobile
- Museo Egizio
- Museo Nazionale del Cinema
- Pinacoteca Giovanni e Marella Agnelli
- Palazzo Reale
- Basilica di Superga
- Duomo di San Giovanni
- Piazza San Carlo

Verona
- Arche Scaligari
- Basilica di San Zeno Maggiore
- Chiesa di Sant'Anastasia
- Arena
- Casa di Giulietta
- Castelvecchio
- Piazza delle Erbe
- Piazza dei Signori

Bologna
- Museo Civico Archeologico
- Museo Civico Medievale e del Rinascimento
- Pinacoteca Nazionale
- Basilica di San Petronio
- Piazzale Maggiore e del Nettuno
- Torre Pendenti

Venézia (Venice)
- Ca d'Oro
- Collezione Peggy Guggenheim
- Galleria dell'Accademia
- Museo Correr
- Museo Diocesano
- Museo Vitrario di Murano
- Basilica di San Marco
- Chiesa di Santa Maria della Salute
- Chiesa di Santa Maria Gloriosa dei Frari
- Chiesa di San Zaccaria
- Palazzo Ducale
- Scuola di San Giorgio degli Schiavoni
- Scuola di San Rocco
- Villa Fóscari (at Malcontenta)
- Canal Grande
- Museo Storico Navale
- Ponte di Rialto
- Ponte dei Sospiri (Bridge of Sighs)
- Arsenale
- Burano
- Ghetto
- Murano
- Piazza San Marco

Firenze (Florence)
- Galleria degli Uffizi
- Galleria dell'Accademia
- Museo Archeologico
- Museo dell'Opera del Duomo
- Museo di San Marco
- Museo di Storia della Scienza
- Palazzo e Museo Nazionale del Bargello
- Palazzo Medici-Riccardi
- Palazzo Pitti
- Chiesa di San Lorenzo
- Chiesa di Santa Croce
- Chiesa di Santa Maria del Carmine
- Chiesa di Santa Maria Novella
- Chiesa di Santo Spirito
- Piazza del Duomo
- Giardino di Boboli
- Orsanmichele
- Palazzo Vecchio
- Ponte Vecchio

Trieste
- Castello di Miramare
- Colle di San Giusto
- Piazza dell'Unità d'Italia

Pádova (Padua)
- Basilica di Sant'Antonio
- Capella degli Scrovegni
- Chiesa degli Eremitani
- Villa Pisani, Strà
- Orto Botanico

Ravenna
- Basilica di Sant'Apollinare in Classe
- Basilica di San Vitale
- Mausoleo di Galla Placidia
- Domus dei Tappeti di Pietra

Úrbino
- Galleria Nazionale delle Marche
- Palazzo Ducale

Gúbbio
- Palazzo dei Consoli
- Città Vecchia

Perúgia
- Galleria Nazionale dell'Umbria
- Museo Archeologico Nazionale dell'Umbria
- Chiesa di San Pietro
- Piazza 4 Novembre

Assisi
- Basilica di San Francesco
- Chiesa di Santa Chiara
- Eremo delle Carceri
- Rocca Maggiore

Génova (Genoa)
- Galleria Nazionale di Palazzo Spinola
- Museo di Arte Orientale
- Palazzo Bianco
- Palazzo Rosso
- Cattedrale di San Lorenzo
- Casa Mazzini
- Acquario di Génova
- Centro Storico
- Gran Bigo
- Lanterna

Roma (Rome) & **Vatican City**
- Luneur
- Galleria Borghese
- Galleria Doria Pamphili
- Museo Capitolino
- Museo del Palazzo dei Conservatori
- Museo Nazionale di Villa Giulia
- Museo Nazionale Romano
- Musei Vaticani e Cappella Sistina
- Palazzo Barberini
- Basilica di San Giovanni in Laterano
- Basilica di San Paolo Fuori le Mura
- Basilica di San Pietro
- Chiesa del Gesù
- Chiesa di Santa Maria Maggiore
- Chiesa di Santa Maria della Vittoria
- Giardini Vaticani
- Castel Sant'Angelo
- Colosseo
- Keats-Shelley Memorial House
- Pantheon
- Fontana di Trevi
- Campidoglio
- Catacombe
- Fori Imperiali
- Foro Romano
- Palatino
- Piazza Navona
- Piazza del Popolo
- Piazza di San Pietro
- Piazza del Spagna & Spanish Steps
- Terme di Caracalla

Nápoli (Naples)
- Edenlandia
- Museo Archeologico Nazionale
- Palazzo e Galleria Nazionale di Capodimonte
- Certosa di San Martino
- Castel Nuovo
- Catacombe di San Gennaro
- Porto di Santa Lucia

Palermo
- Museo Archeologico Regionale
- Museo Etnografico Pitrè
- La Martorana
- Palazzo dei Normanni

Map labels (regions, cities and attractions):

VALLE D'AOSTA · Aosta · Parco Naz. del Gran Paradiso · Funivie Mont-Blanc · Isole Borromee · Sacri Monti · Sacra di San Michele · Varallo · Venaria Reale · Vercelli · Novara · **Torino** (Turin) · PIEMONTE (PIEDMONT) · Cuneo · Alessándria · Abbazia di Vezzolano · Certosa di Pavia · Pavia · Basilica di Sant'Andrea · Monza · **Milano** (Milan) · Bérgamo · Accademia Carrara · Città Alta · Como · Duomo · Lago di Como · LOMBARDIA (LOMBARDY) · Parco Naz. della Val Grande · Tremezzo · Villa Carlotta · Lago Maggiore · Villa Táranto · Bellágio · Villa Serbelloni · Villa Melzi · Sondrio · Val Camónica · Parco Nazionale Dello Stelvio · Merano (Meran) · Passeggiate · Bolzano (Bozen) · TRENTINO-SÜDTIROL · Trento · Cortina · Tofana di Mezzo · Tondi di Faloria · Bressanone (Brixen) · Abbazia di Novacella · Plose · FRIULI-VENÉZIA GIULIA · Cividale del Friuli · Museo Archeologico Nazionale · Tempietto · Údine · Piazza della Libertà · Pordenone · VÉNETO · Vicenza · La Rotonda · Treviso · Piazza dei Signori · Gardaland · Lago di Garda · Lago d'Iseo · Cremona · Piazza del Comune · Mantova (Mantua) · Palazzo Ducale · Palazzo Tè · Piacenza · Palazzo del Commune · Parma · Galleria Nazionale · Centro Episcopale · Réggio nell'Emília · Modena · Galleria Estense · Duomo · Ferrara · Duomo · Palazzo dei Diamanti · Abbazia di Pomposa · EMÍLIA-ROMAGNA · **Bologna** · Mirabilandia · LIGÚRIA · Savona · Parco Naturale di Portofino · Albenga · Cattedrale · San Remo · La Spézia · Cinque Terre · Pistóia · Piazza del Duomo · Prato · Duomo · Lucca · Museo Nazionale Guinigi · Chiesa di San Michele in Foro · Duomo · Pisa · Campo dei Miracoli · Museo Nazionale di San Matteo · Chiesa di Santa Maria della Spina · Livorno (Leghorn) · Forlì · Fiabilandia · Rímini · SAN MARINO · Rocca Gualta · San Leo · Forte · Ancona · MARCHE · Conero Riviera · Loreto · Santuario della Santa Casa · Tolentino · Basilica di San Nicola · Firenze (Florence) · TOSCANA (TUSCANY) · Arezzo · Chiesa di San Francesco · Cortona · Piazza del Duomo · Montepulciano · Madonna di San Biagio · Piazza Grande · Pienza · Volterra · Piazza dei Priori · San Gimignano · Piazza della Cisterna · Piazza del Duomo · Siena · Ospedale di Santa Maria della Scala · Pinacoteca · Duomo · Palazzo Pubblico · Piazza del Campo · Massa Maríttima · Piazza Garibaldi · Grosseto · Orvieto · Duomo · Todi · Piazza del Popolo · Parco dei Mostri · UMBRIA · Parco Nazionale dei Monti Sibillini · Áscoli Piceno · Piazza del Popolo · L'Aquila · Basilica di San Bernardino · Fontana delle 99 Cannelle · Parco Nazionale del Gran Sasso · ABRUZZO · Abbazia di San Clemente a Casauria · Monte Capanne · ÍSOLA D'ELBA · ÍSOLA PIANOSA · ÍSOLA DEL GÍGLIO · ÍSOLA DI MONTECRISTO · ÍSOLA DI CAPRÁIA · Tarquínia · Necropoli Etrusca · Cervéteri · Necropoli della Banditaccia · Civitavécchia · Villa Farnese · VATICAN CITY · ROMA (ROME) · Ostia Antica · Tívoli · Villa Adriana · Villa d'Este · Castelli Romani · Parco Nazionale d'Abruzzo · Parco Nazionale della Maiella · MOLISE · Campobasso · Vieste · Parco Nazionale del Gargano · Monte Sant'Angelo · Santuario di San Michele · Trani · Cattedrale · Bari · Basilica di San Nicola · Abbazia di Casamari · Abbazia di Montecassino · Abbazia di Fossanova · Parco Nazionale del Circeo · Benevento · Museo Sannio · Arco di Traiano · Castel del Monte · PUGLIA · Grotte di Castellana · Alberobello · Trulli · Bríndisi · Lecce · Museo Sigismundo Castromediano · Basilica di Santa Croce · Piazza del Duomo · Táranto · Museo Nazionale · Caserta · La Reggia · CAMPANIA · **Nápoli** (Naples) · Vesuvio · Ercolano · Herculaneum · Isola d'Ischia · Pompeii · Sorrento · Salerno · Duomo · Isola di Capri · Paestum · Amalfi · Ravello · Grotta dello Smeraldo · Costiera Amalfitana · Villa Cimbrone · Villa Rufolo · BASILICATA · Potenza · Matera · Sassi · Maratea · CALÁBRIA · Cosenza · La Sila · Parco Nazionale della Calábria · Crotone · Lamézia · Catanzaro · Strómboli · ÍSOLE EÓLIE (LÍPARI) · Aspromonte · Messina · Réggio di Calábria · Museo Nazionale · Taormina · Teatro Greco · Monte Etna · Catánia · Militello in Val di Catánia · Late Baroque towns of the Val di Noto · Siracusa (Syracuse) · Museo Archeologico Regionale · Zona Archeologica · Noto · Scicli · Módica · Ragusa · Palazzolo · Agrigento · Valli dei Templi · Caltagirone · Caltanissetta · Enna · Castello di Lombardia · SICILIA (SICILY) · Cefalù · Cattedrale · Monreale · Duomo · Palermo · Trápani · Segesta · ÍSOLE ÉGADI · ÍSOLA DI ÚSTICA · ÍSOLE PONZIANE · ÍSOLA DI PANTELLERIA · ÍSOLE TRÉMITI

Sardegna / Sardinia:
ÍSOLA ASINARA · ARCIPÉLAGO DE LA MADDALENA · Costa Smeralda · Ólbia · Porto Tórres · Santíssima Trinità di Saccargia · Sassari · Alghero · Grotta di Nettuno · Nuoro · Museo Etnografico · SARDEGNA (SARDINIA) · Oristano · Su Nuraxi du Barúmini · **Cágliari** · Museo Nazionale Archeologico · Strada di Muravera · ÍSOLA DI SAN PIETRO · ÍSOLA DI SANT'ANTIOCO

See also... Contents (2-5) – these countries feature in many thematic and regional maps throughout the *BTEC First Travel Atlas*.

Lambert Equal Area Projection

100 kilometres
100 miles
200 kilometres

BOHEMIA

CENTRAL SOUTHERN POLAND

1 KLV Karlovy Vary (Karlsbad);
2 PRG Praha (Prague) Ruzyne

1 KTW Katowice; 2 KRK Kraków (Cracow) John Paul II Balice

100 kilometres
50 miles

60 km
30 miles

1000 metres
500 metres
Sea level

▶ **See also...** Winter Sports (57); Germany (70-73);
France (74-77); Italy (83-86); Central Europe: South (90)

The listings above refer to a selection of related themes.
For more information, see the Contents (2-5).

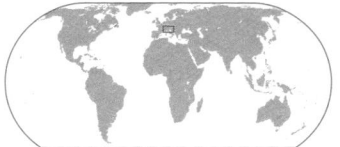

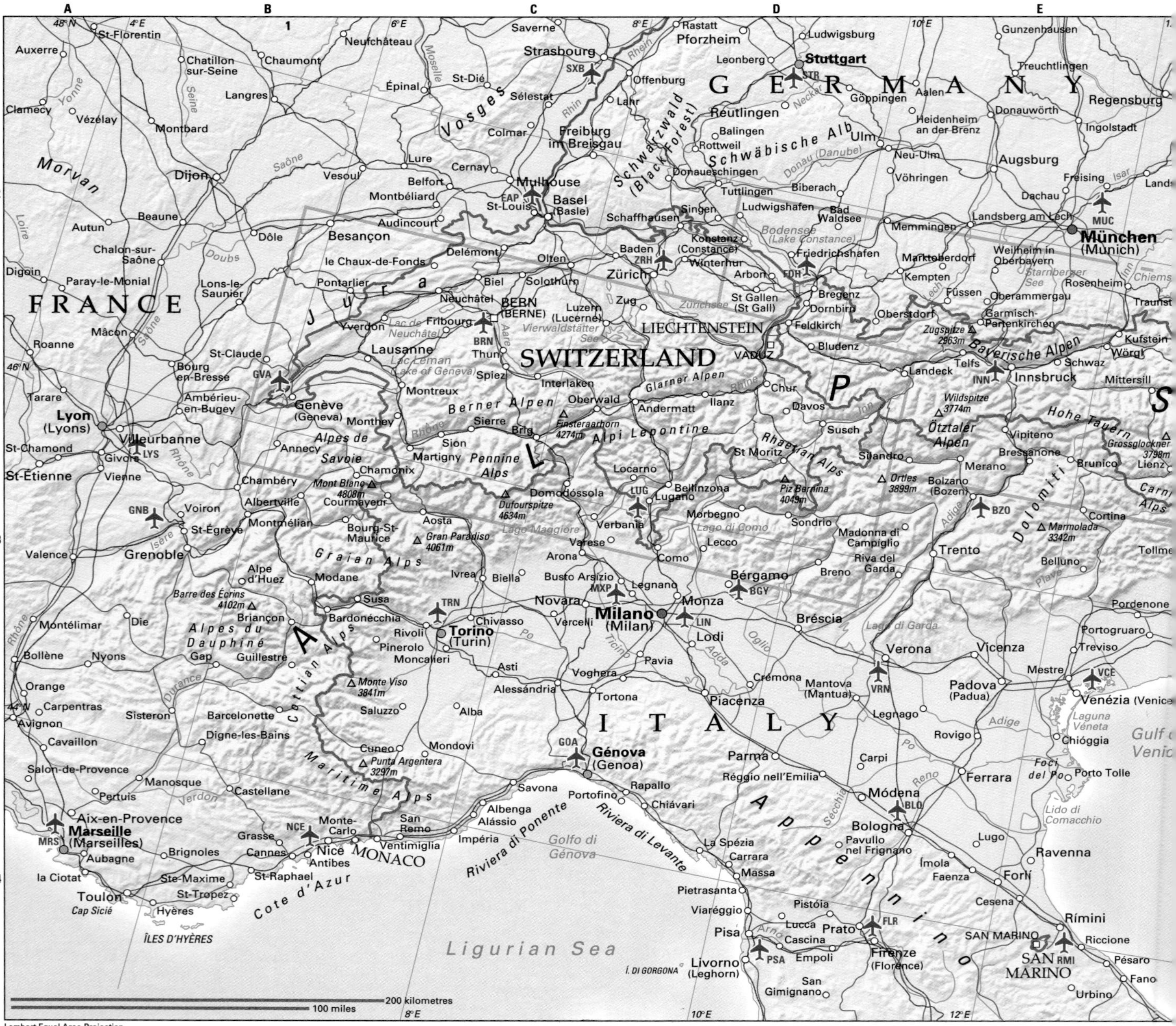

Lambert Equal Area Projection

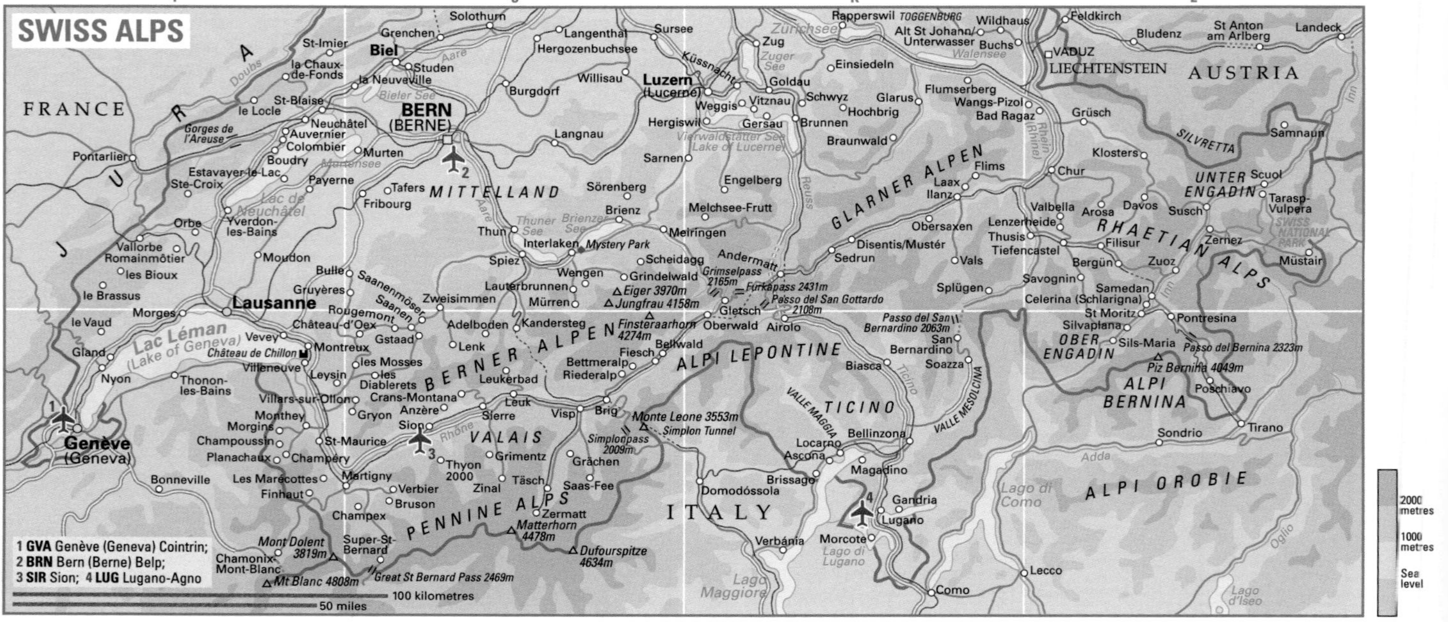

SWISS ALPS

1 **GVA** Genève (Geneva) Cointrin; 2 **BRN** Bern (Berne) Belp; 3 **SIR** Sion; 4 **LUG** Lugano-Agno

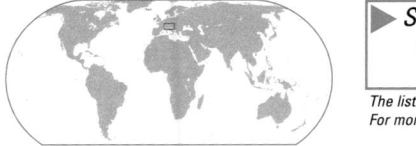

► See also... Winter Sports (57); Germany (70-73); France (74-77); Italy (83-86); Central Europe: South (90)

The listings above refer to a selection of related themes.
For more information, see the Contents (2-5).

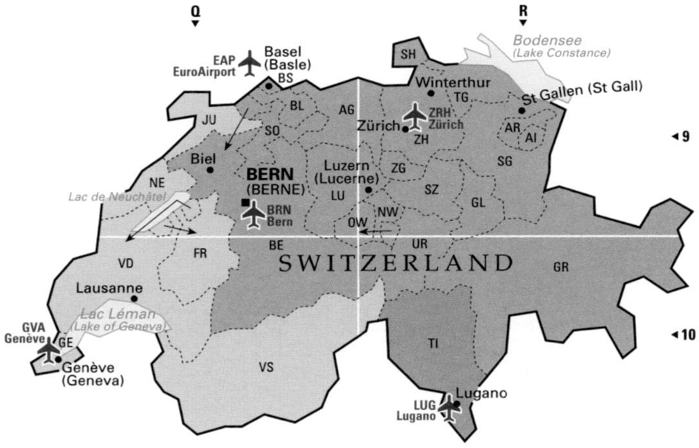

Map (Central Europe)

F 14°E G 16°E H

CZECH REPUBLIC

Cham · Strakonice · Pisek · Tábor · Bohemian Forest · Straubing · Regen · Prachatice · Deggendorf · Vilshofen · Jindřichuv Hradec · Třebíč · Olomouc · Brno · BRQ · Vilshofen · Passau · an der Isar · Cesky Krumlov · Gmünd · Znojmo · Dyje · Morava · Břeclav · Eggenfelden · Brauneu am Inn · ...ried im Innkre s · Linz · Freistadt · Krems an der Donau · Hollabrunn · Mistelbach · Malacky · Trnava · SLOVAK REP. · LNZ · Wels · Melk · Tulln · WIEN (VIENNA) · Pezinok · Senec · BRATISLAVA · VIE · BTS · Šamorín · Vöckla bruck · Attersee · Gmunden · Steyr · Amstetten · St Pölten · Mödling · Baden · Traunsee · Waidhofen an der Ybbs · Wiener Neustadt · Neusiedler See · Mosonmagyaróvár · Salzburg · SZG · Bad Ischl · Mariazell · Neunkirchen · Sopron · Csorna · Győr · Hallein · Bischofs hofen · Enns · Rottenmann · Mürzzuschlag · Köszeg · Raba · Pápa

AUSTRIA · Niedere Tauern · Leoben · Knittelfeld · Bruck an der Mur · Szombathely · Sárvár · St Michael im Langau · Mur · Judenburg · Graz · GRZ · Fürstenfeld · Zalaegerszeg · HUNGARY · Köflach · Raab · Wildon · ...ttal-an der Glan · Villach · St Veit an der Glan · Wolfsberg · Leibnitz · Tapolca · Balaton · Velden · KLU · Klagenfurt · Völkermarkt · Murska Sobota · Keszthely · Fonyód · ...mona · Jesenice · Julijske Alpe · Kranj · LJU · Trbovlje · Drava · Maribor · Nagykanizsa · Kaposvár · ...al Friuli · ...dine · LJUBLJANA · SLOVENIA · Ribnica · Celje · Varaždin · Koprivnica · Trieste · Koper · Novo Mesto · ZAGREB · ZAG · Poreč · Opatija · Rijeka · Karlovac · Sisak · ...rni · ISTRA · Ogulin · Crikvenica · CROATIA · Pula · PUY · CRES · KRK · Senj · Bosanski Novi · Bosanska Krupa · Bihać · BOSNIA-HERZ. · RAB · PAG · Gospić · Gračac · Bosanski Petrovak · Adriatic Sea · Zadar · Knin · DUGI OTOK · Velebit · Dinara

48°N · 46°N

International arrivals (millions)

Austria · Switzerland

1980 · 1985 · 1990 · 1995 · 2000 · 2005

Source: World Tourism Organisation

Switzerland map

Q · R · Bodensee (Lake Constance)

Basel (Basle) · EAP EuroAirport · BS · SH · Winterthur · St Gallen (St Gall) · JU · BL · AG · TG · ZRH Zürich · ZH · AR · AI · SO · Biel · Zürich · Luzern (Lucerne) · ZG · SG · NE · BERN (BERNE) · BRN Bern · LU · SZ · GL · Lac de Neuchâtel · OW · NW · UR · GR · VD · FR · BE · SWITZERLAND · Lausanne · Lac Léman (Lake of Geneva) · TI · GVA Genève · GE · VS · Genève (Geneva) · LUG Lugano · Lugano · 9 · 10

Cantons where the majority of the population speak:

☐ French ☐ German ☐ Italian

AG	AARGAU	NW	NIDWALDEN
AI	APPENZELL-INNER RHODEN	OW	OBWALDEN
AR	APPENZELL-AUSSER RHODEN	SG	ST GALLEN
BE	BERN	SH	SCHAFFHAUSEN
BL	BASEL-LAND	SO	SOLOTHURN
BS	BASEL-STADT	SZ	SCHWYZ
FR	FRIBOURG	TG	THURGAU
GE	GENÈVE	TI	TICINO
GL	GLARUS	UR	URI
GR	GRAUBÜNDEN	VD	VAUD
JU	JURA	VS	VALAIS
LU	LUZERN	ZG	ZUG
NE	NEUCHÂTEL	ZH	ZÜRICH

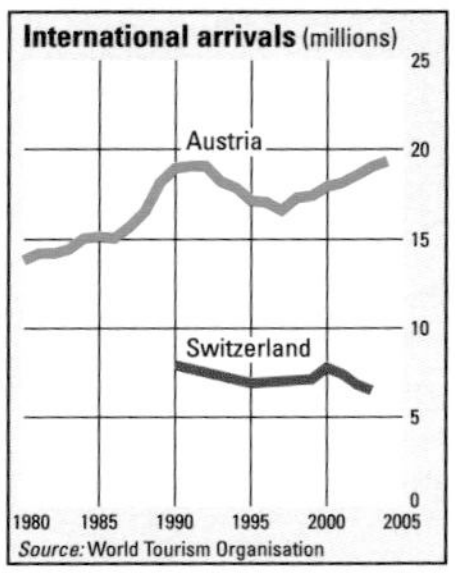

Austria map

S · T · Gmünd · Krems an der Donau · Donau (Danube) · Wachau · WIEN (VIENNA) · Bodensee (Lake Constance) · LNZ Linz · St Pölten · WIEN · VIE Wien · OBERÖSTERREICH (UPPER AUSTRIA) · NIEDERÖSTERREICH (LOWER AUSTRIA) · Bregenz · Salzburg · SZG Salzburg · Eisenstadt · Neusiedler See · VORARLBERG · LIECHTENSTEIN · INN Innsbruck · Innsbruck · SALZBURG · NIEDERE TAUERN · AUSTRIA · Bruck an der Mur · BURGENLAND · TIROL · HOHE TAUERN · STEIERMARK (STYRIA) · GRZ Graz · ÖTZTALER ALPEN · Mur · Graz · KÄRNTEN (CARINTHIA) · KLU Klagenfurt · Villach · Drau · Klagenfurt · KARAWANKEN · 11

AUSTRIAN ALPS

M · N · O · P

Überlingen · Ammersee · Starnberger See · Chiemsee · Oberndorf · Irrsdorf · Vöcklabruck · Gmunden · Konstanz (Constance) · Ravensburg · Memmingen · Kaufbeuren · Weilheim · Traunstein · Salzburg · Mondsee · Attersee · Friedrichshafen · Kempten · GERMANY · Rosenheim · St Gilgen · St Wolfgang · Bad Ischl · Bodensee (Lake Constance) · BAYERISCHE ALPEN · Bad Tölz · Erl · Berchtesgaden · Hallein · Gosau · Bad Goisern · Bad Aussee · St Gallen (St Gall) · Bregenz · Füssen · Kufstein · Kirchdorf · SALZKAMMERGUT · Halstatt · Obertraun · Lindau · Jungholz · Garmisch-Partenkirchen · KAISER-GEBIRGE · St Johann in Tirol · Fieberbrunn · SALZBURGER ALPEN · DACHSTEIN · Dornbirn · Schwarzenberg · Reutte · Zugspitze 2963m · Söll · Ellmau · Kitzbühel · Saalbach · Bischofshofen · Schladming · VORARLBERG · Au · Oberstdorf · Lermoos · WETTERSTEIN · Seefeld in Tirol · Westendorf · Alpbach · Oberau · Saalfelden · St Johann im Pongau · Wagrain · Flachau · NIEDERE TAUERN · Damüls · Mittelberg · Riezlern · Ehrwald · KARWENDEL · Rattenberg · Niederau · Fügen · Zell am See · Mittersill · Dorfgastein · Altenmarkt · Feldkirch · Schröcken · Warth · Holzgau · Imst · Telfs · Hall in Tirol · Schwaz · KITZBÜHELER ALPEN · Krimml · Kaprun · Bad Hofgastein · Obertauern · LIECHTENSTEIN · Bürserberg · Lech · Zürs · St Anton am Arlberg · Arlbergpass 1793m · Mutters · Igls · INNSBRUCK · Zell am Ziller · Gerlos · Bad Gastein · St Michael im Langau · VADUZ · GR. WALSERTAL · Bludenz · St Christoph · Landeck · OBER-INNTAL · STUBAIER ALPEN · Fulpmes · Mayrhofen · Finkenberg · HOHE TAUERN · Sportgastein · Tauerntunnel · Katschberg-tunnel · Walensee · Malbun · Brand · Schruns · Ischgl · St Anton · Axamer Lizum · Neustift · ZILLERTALER ALPEN · Grossglockner 3798m · Badgastein · NORISCHE ALPEN · Chur · Gargellen · Partenen · Gaschurn · Galtür · SAMNAUN · Hochsölden · Steinach · Hintertux · Heiligenblut · Obervellach · Obertauern · SILVRETTA · Serfaus · ÖTZTALER ALPEN · Sölden · Brenner Pass 1370m · St Jakob in Defereggen · Millstatt · Davos · Nauders · 3774m Wildspitze · Hochgurgl · Timmelsjoch 2474m · Vipiteno (Sterzing) · Matrei in Osttirol · KÄRNTEN · Obergurgl · TIROL · Brunico (Bruneck) · Lienz · Oberdrauburg · Spittal an der Drau · Millstätter See · SWITZERLAND · ITALY · Bressanone (Brixen) · GAILTALER ALPEN · Drau · Merano (Meran) · Adige · Rienz · Kellerwand 2780m · Hermagor · Villach · CARNIC ALPS

1 INN Innsbruck Kranebitten;
2 SZG Salzburg W.A. Mozart

100 kilometres
50 miles

2000 metres
1000 metres
Sea level

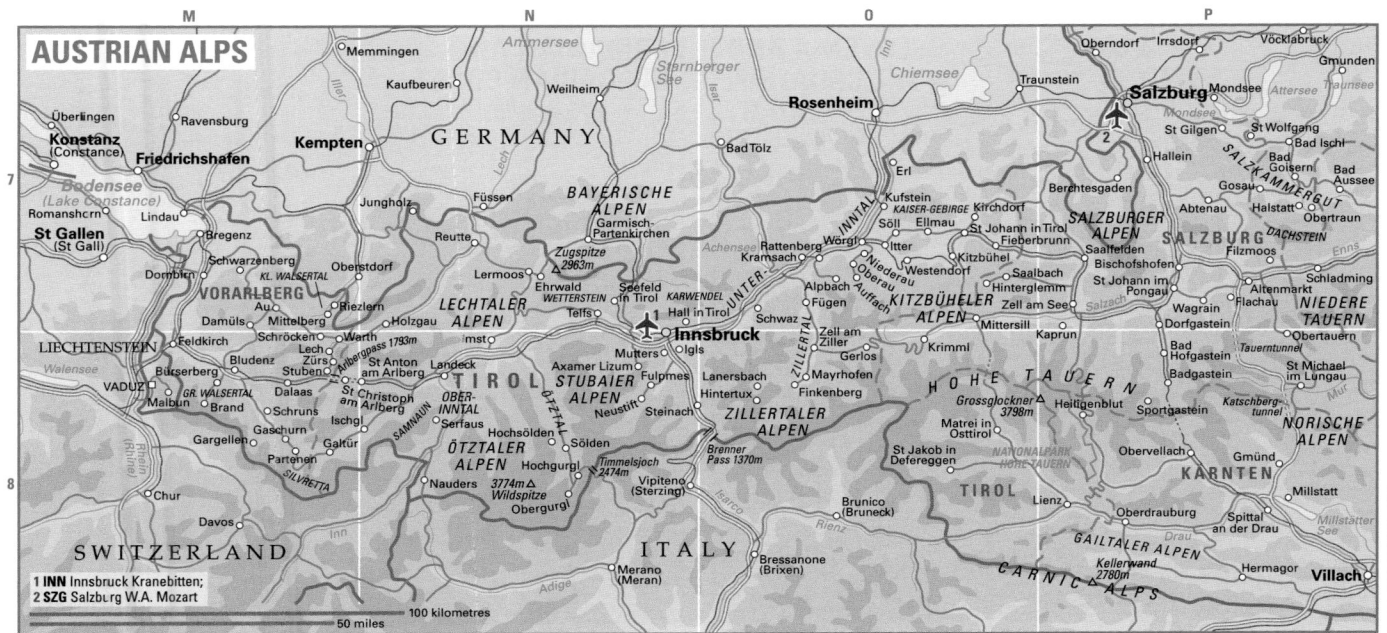

▶ *See also...* Contents (2-5) — these countries feature in many thematic and regional maps throughout the *BTEC First Travel Atlas*.

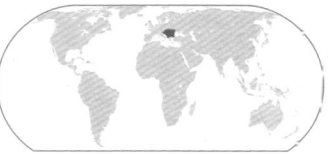

SLOVENIA AND THE CROATIAN COAST

1 **LJU** Ljubljana Brnik; 2 **ZAG** Zagreb Pleso;
3 **PUY** Pula; 4 **ZAD** Zadar; 5 **SPU** Split;
6 **DBV** Dubrovnik; 7 **SJJ** Sarajevo Butmir

ROMANIAN AND BULGARIAN COAST

1 **OTP** Bucharest Otopeni;
2 **BBU** Bucharest Eneasa;
3 **CND** Constanta Mihail Kogalniceanu;
4 **VAR** Varna; 5 **BOJ** Burgas

Lambert Equal Area Projection

150 miles   300 kilometres

1000 metres	
500 metres	
Sea level	

For more information, see the Contents (2-5).

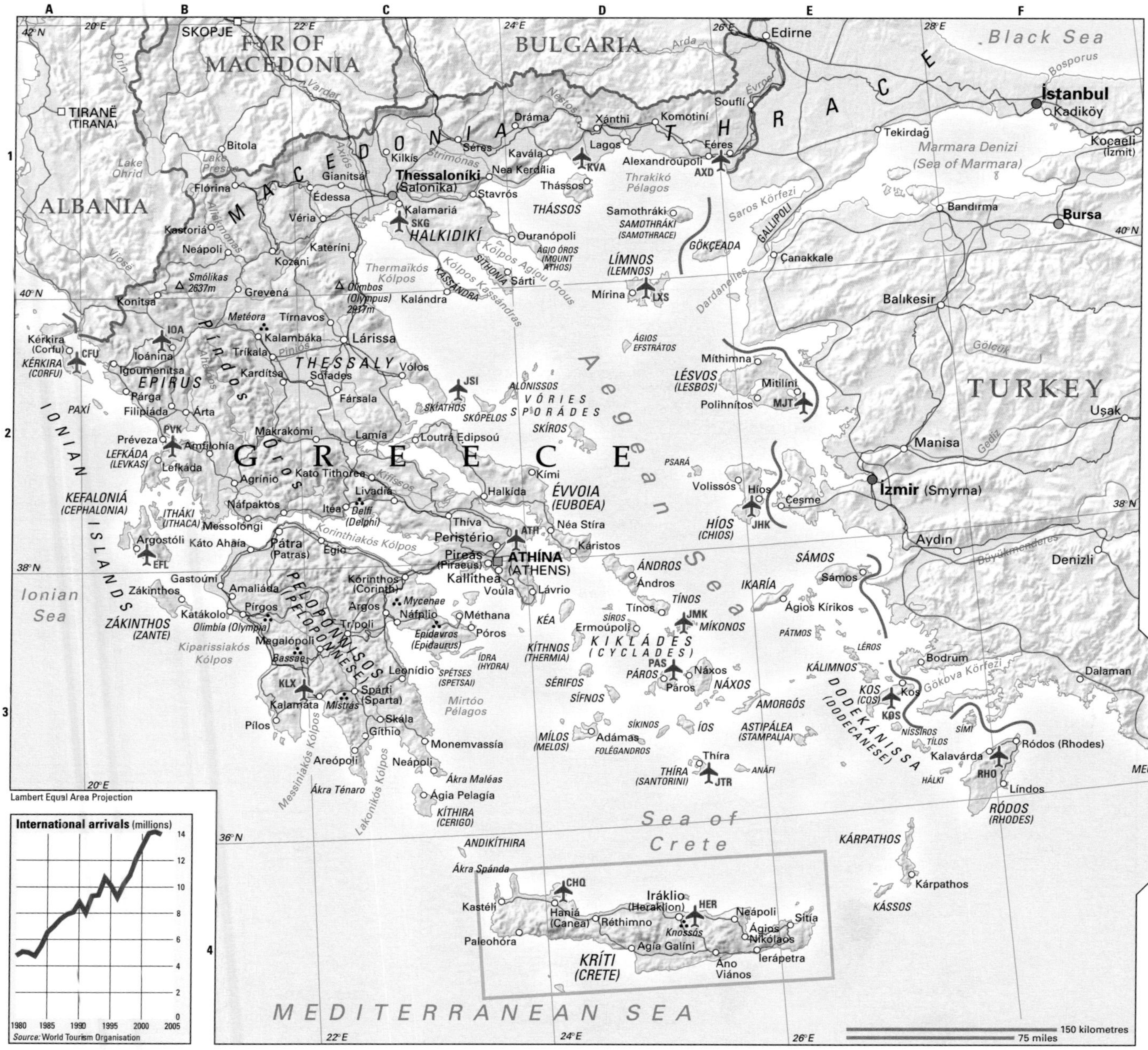

JAN 6th Blessing of the Waters (**Piraeus** & all coastal towns)
before Lent Carnival (**Patras** & countrywide)
MAR 25th Liberation Day (countrywide)
APR 23rd Feast of St George (**Cos**)
MAY Anastenaria Firewalking Festival (**Agía Eléni**, near **Séres**)
MAY Week of prose and art (**Lesbos**)
MAY Kariaskaki: folklore celebration (**Karditsa**)

MAY-SEP Sound and Light (**Athens** & **Rhodes**)
JUN-JUL Epidaurus Theatre Festival
JUL Santoríni Jazz Festival
JUL Rockwave Festival (**Athens**)
JUL-SEP Athens Festival (Odeon amphitheatre)
OCT St Demetrius Festival (**Thessaloníki**)
NOV **Athens** Marathon
NOV **Thessaloníki** International Film Festival

International arrivals (millions)

1980 1985 1990 1995 2000 2005
Source: World Tourism Organisation

Lambert Equal Area Projection

150 kilometres
75 miles

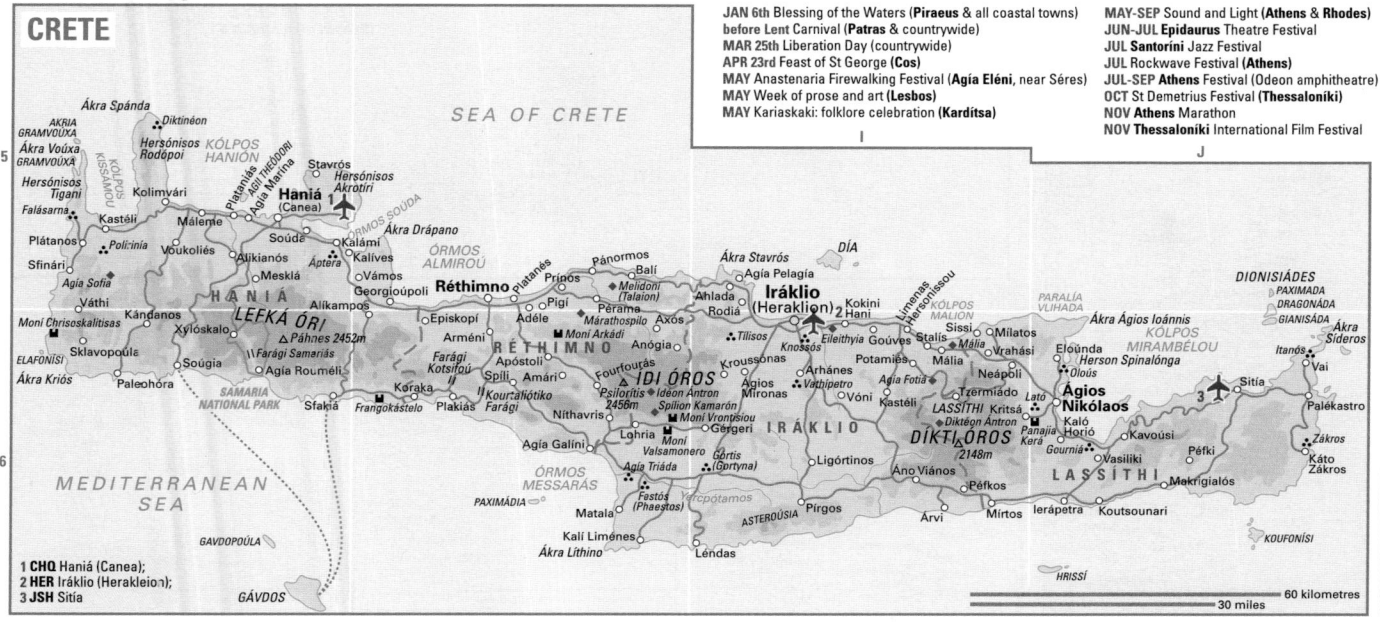

CRETE

1 **CHQ** Haniá (Canea);
2 **HER** Iráklio (Herakleion);
3 **JSH** Sitía

60 kilometres
30 miles

1000 metres
500 metres
Sea level

See also... The Mediterranean (94)

The listings above refer to a selection of related themes.
For more information, see the Contents (2-5).

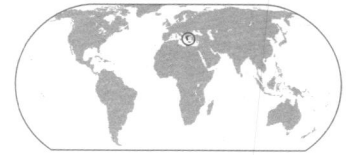

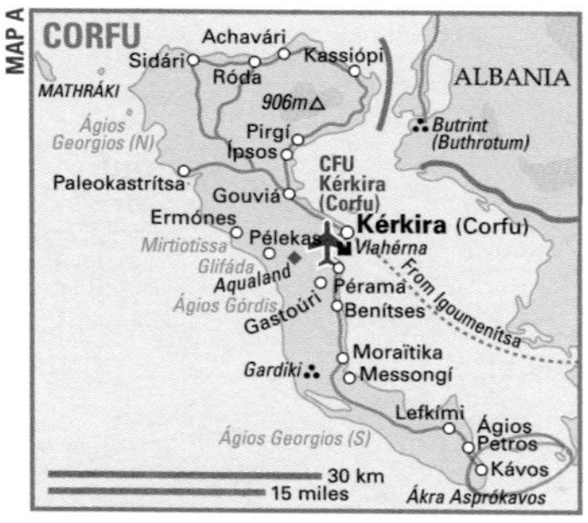

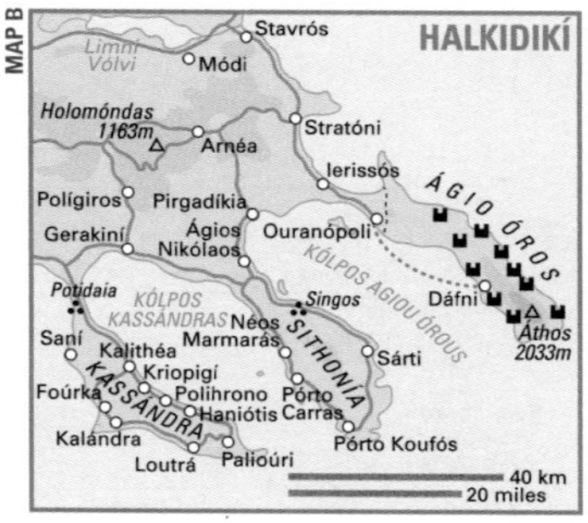

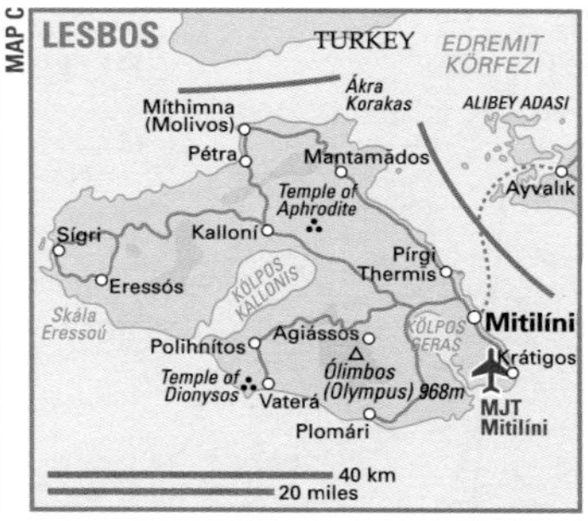

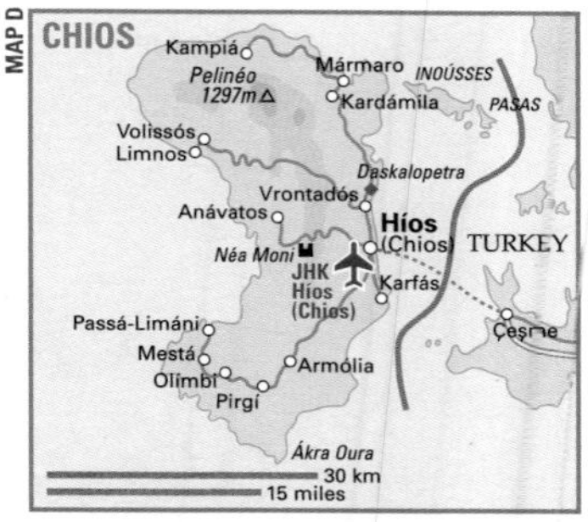

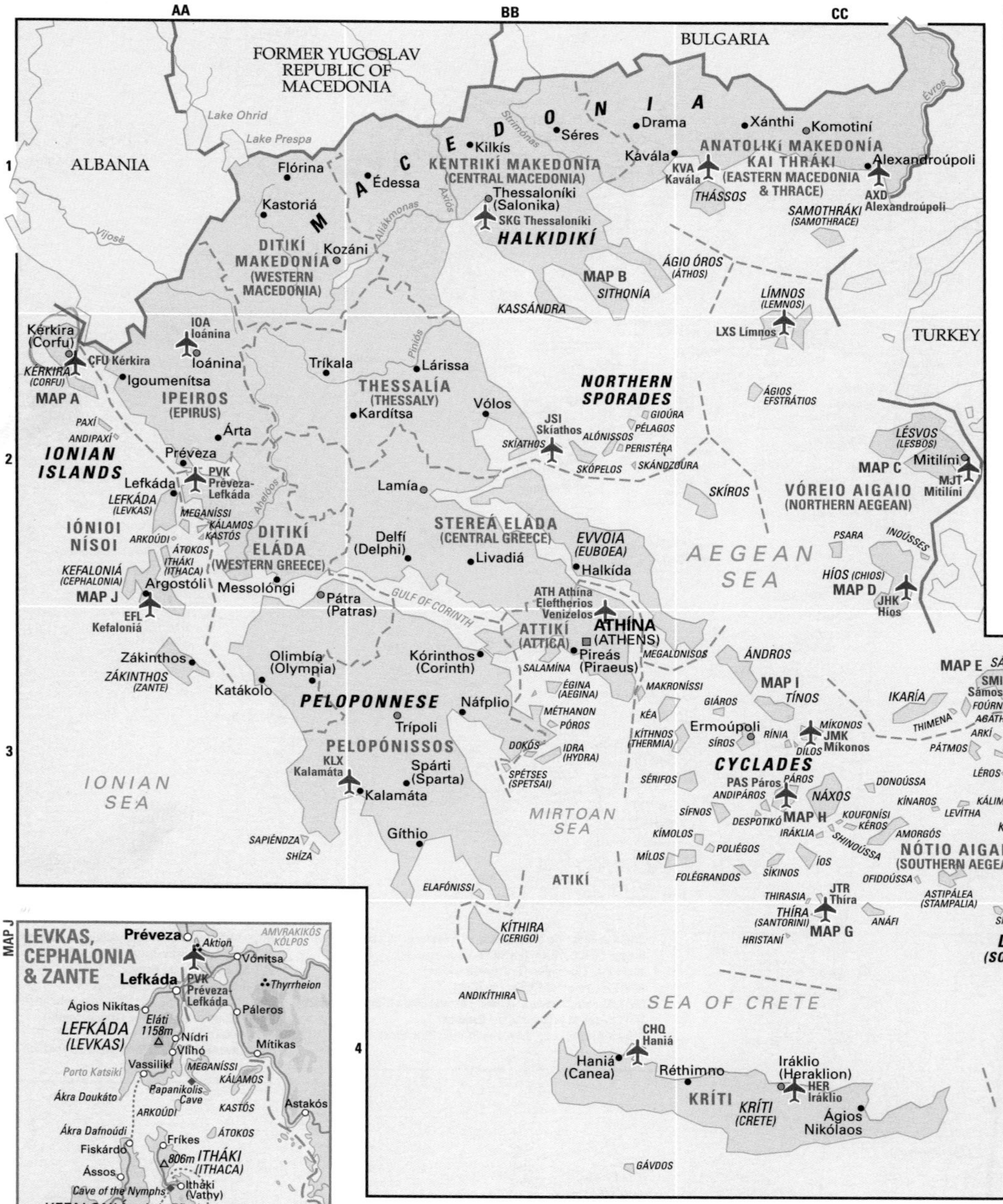

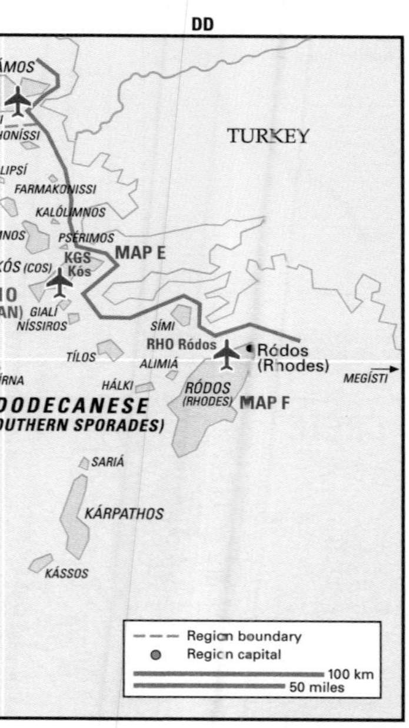

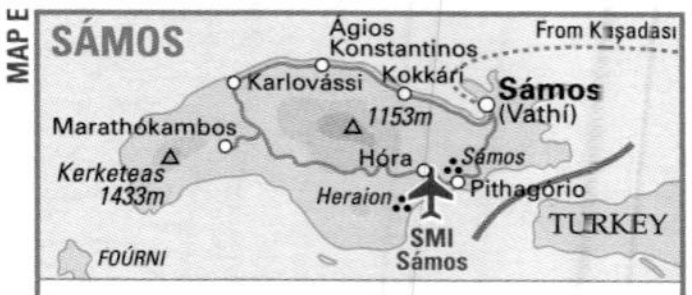

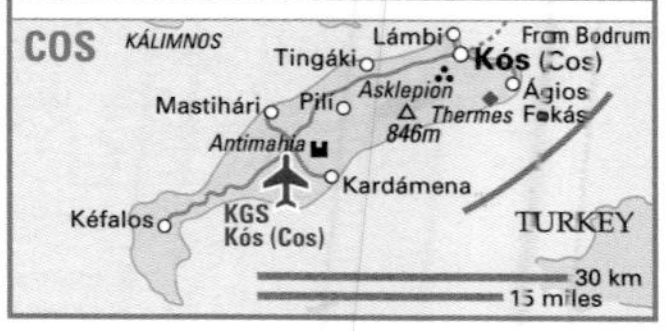

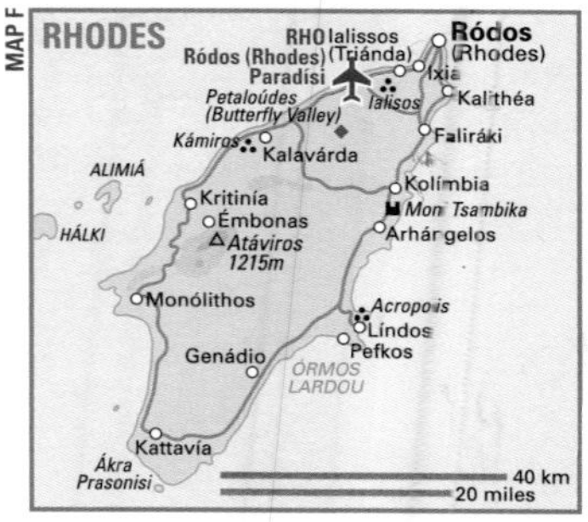

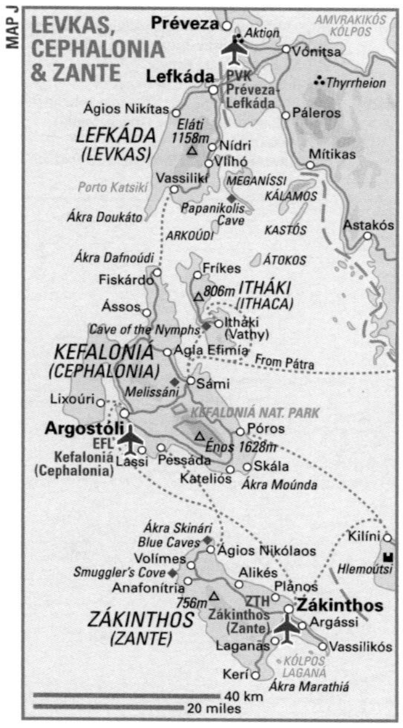

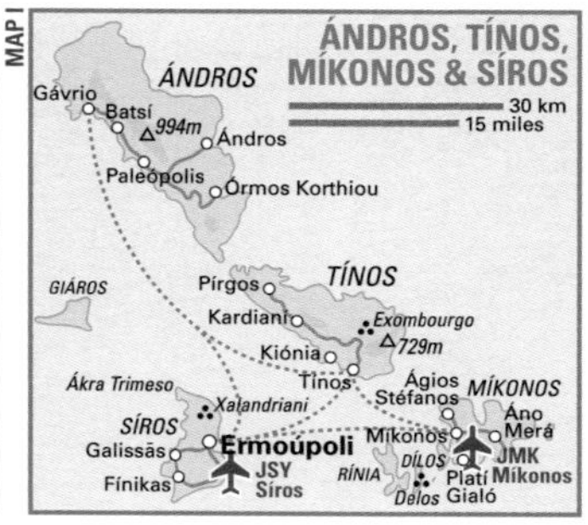

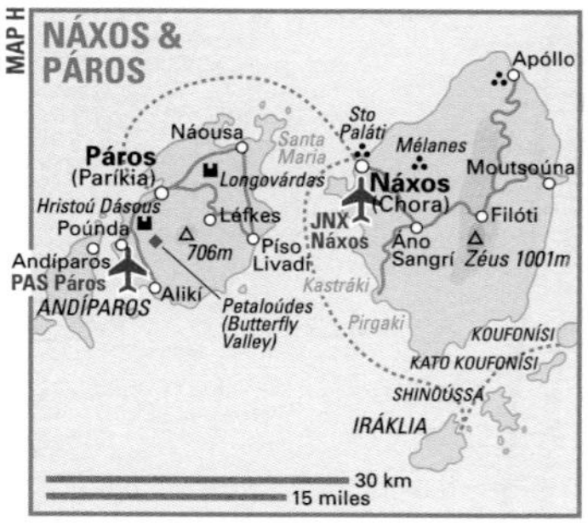

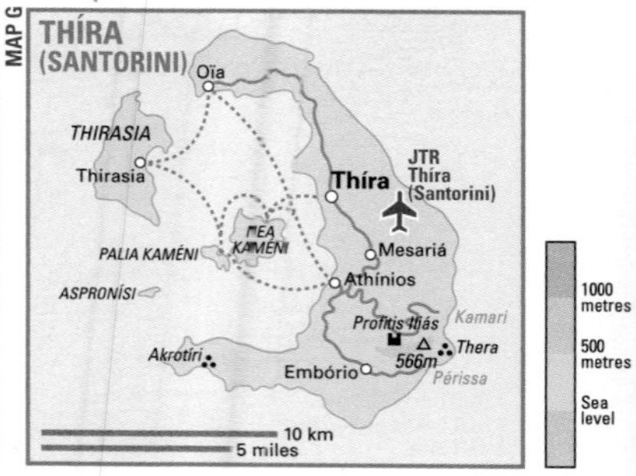

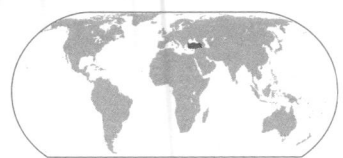

▶ *See also...* The Mediterranean (94)

The listings above refer to a selection of related themes.
For more information, see the Contents (2-5).

Lambert Equal Area Projection

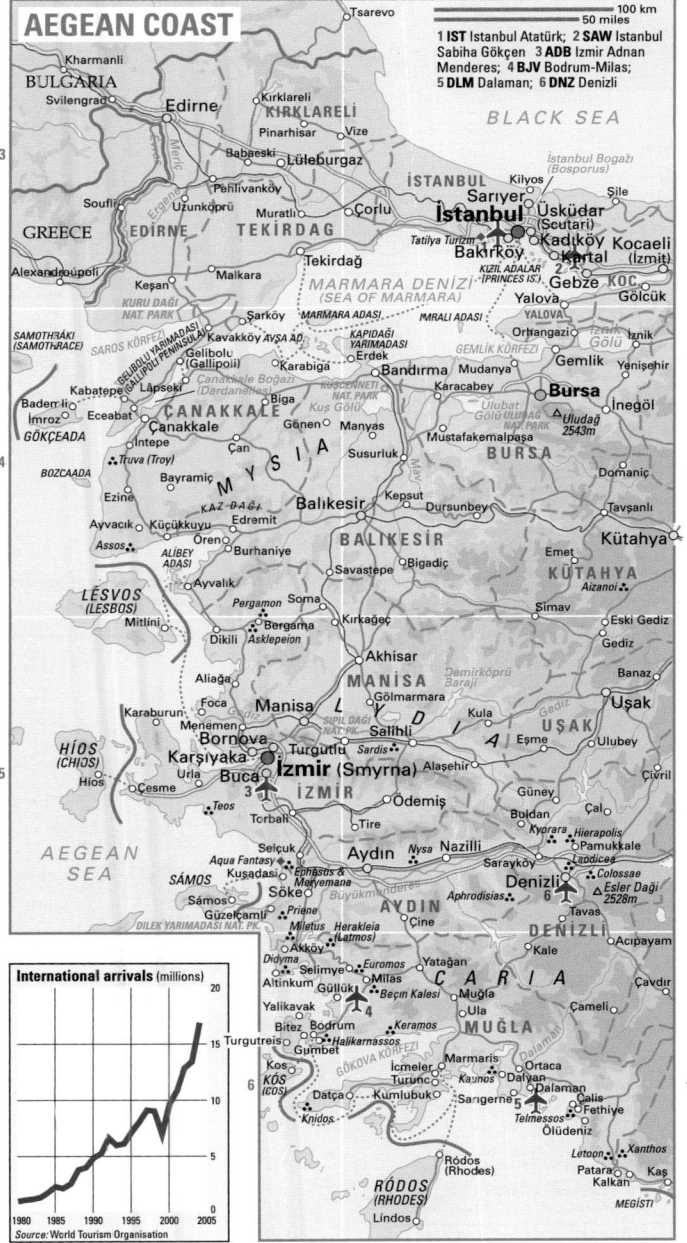

AEGEAN COAST

1 **IST** Istanbul Atatürk; 2 **SAW** Istanbul
Sabiha Gökçen 3 **ADB** Izmir Adnan
Menderes; 4 **BJV** Bodrum-Milas;
5 **DLM** Dalaman; 6 **DNZ** Denizli

International arrivals (millions)

Source: World Tourism Organisation

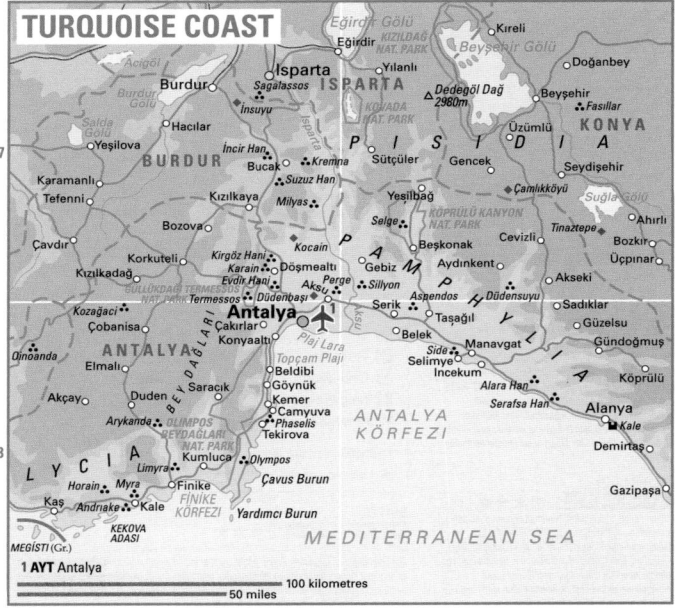

TURQUOISE COAST

1 **AYT** Antalya

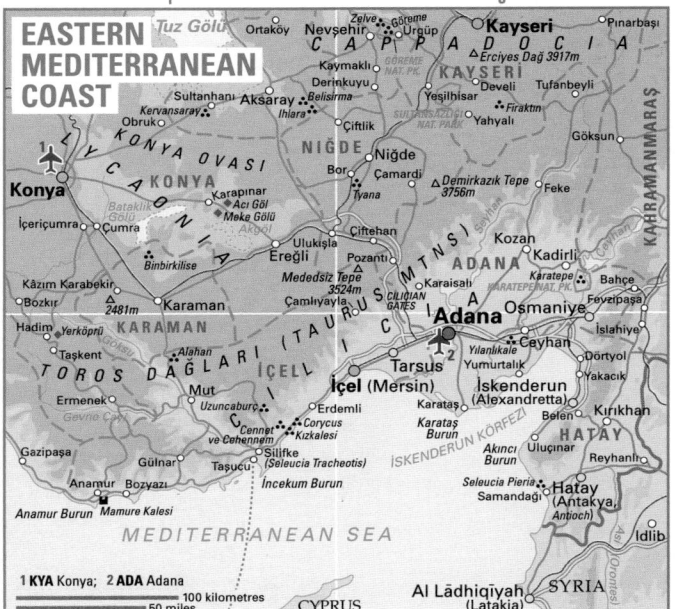

EASTERN MEDITERRANEAN COAST

1 **KYA** Konya; 2 **ADA** Adana

The listings above refer to a selection of related themes.
For more information, see the Contents (2-5).

This map shows the principal diving destinations in the Mediterranean Sea and the main underwater attractions including the existence of soft corals or sea fans, cliffs and caves and shipwrecks (including submerged aircraft). The diver may encounter turtle and dolphin at any time, shark and rays less often, but only those places where regular sightings occur are indicated here. Whales are now exceedingly rare.

Diving facilities for each destination, including availability of scuba diving equipment and related support services, are graded as limited, good or excellent. It must be emphasised that these grades are a general reflection on the overall availability of everything required by the visiting scuba diver and are not an interpretation of the standards found within any one facility or organisation.

Each diving destination provides every level of depth from the very shallow to the extremely deep.

FRANCE: SOUTH COAST ★
1 2 3 4 D S T W ★

Dive sites all along the coast; main facilities in Marseilles, Nice and Toulon
Shipwreck 'Liban' off Cap Croisette and submarine 'Rubis' off Cap Camarat are outstanding; the diving infrastructure on mainland France is rather limited, largely because French divers favour the club system for diving; PADI is, however, opening up new shops and facilities all the time and it is worth requesting a PADI Centre List before departure

FRANCE: CORSICA
1 2 3 4 D S T W ★

Dive sites all around the island; main facilities in Ajaccio, Calvi and Sagone
British Vickers Viking, Canadian CL215 and US B17 bomber provide three very unusual aircraft wrecks off the west coast

ITALY: MAINLAND
1 2 3 4 D S T W ★★★

Dive sites all around the coast; facilities in all major towns, especially Genoa and Portofino
Diving is very popular in Italy; there are numerous shipwrecks, both ancient and modern, although many lie in very deep waters; cave systems on the Adriatic coast and steep underwater cliffs everywhere; away from the busy industrial ports, water clarity is very good

ITALY: SARDINIA
1 2 3 4 D S T W ★★

Dive sites all around the island; facilities centred on Bosa, Cágliari, Orosei and Palau
Several shipwrecks including 'Romagna'; at least one aircraft plus several cave systems including the Nereo Caves off Cape Caccia

ITALY: WESTERN ISLANDS
(Capráia, Elba, Giannutri, Gíglio, Montecristo)
1 2 3 4 D S T W ★

Dive sites all around the islands; some facilities on Elba but generally very limited on the islands – best nearby mainland facilities at Portofino
Spectacular vertical cliffs with outstanding seafans, red coral and large shoals of tuna; a few very exciting shipwrecks, such as the vehicle ferry 'Nasim II' off Giannutri

ITALY: SICILY
1 2 3 4 D S T W ★★

Dive sites all around the island; facilities centred on Catánia, Messina and Palermo
Shipwreck 'Amerique' on the northern tip of the island; Sicily attracts large pelagics and large shoals of tuna at certain times of the year

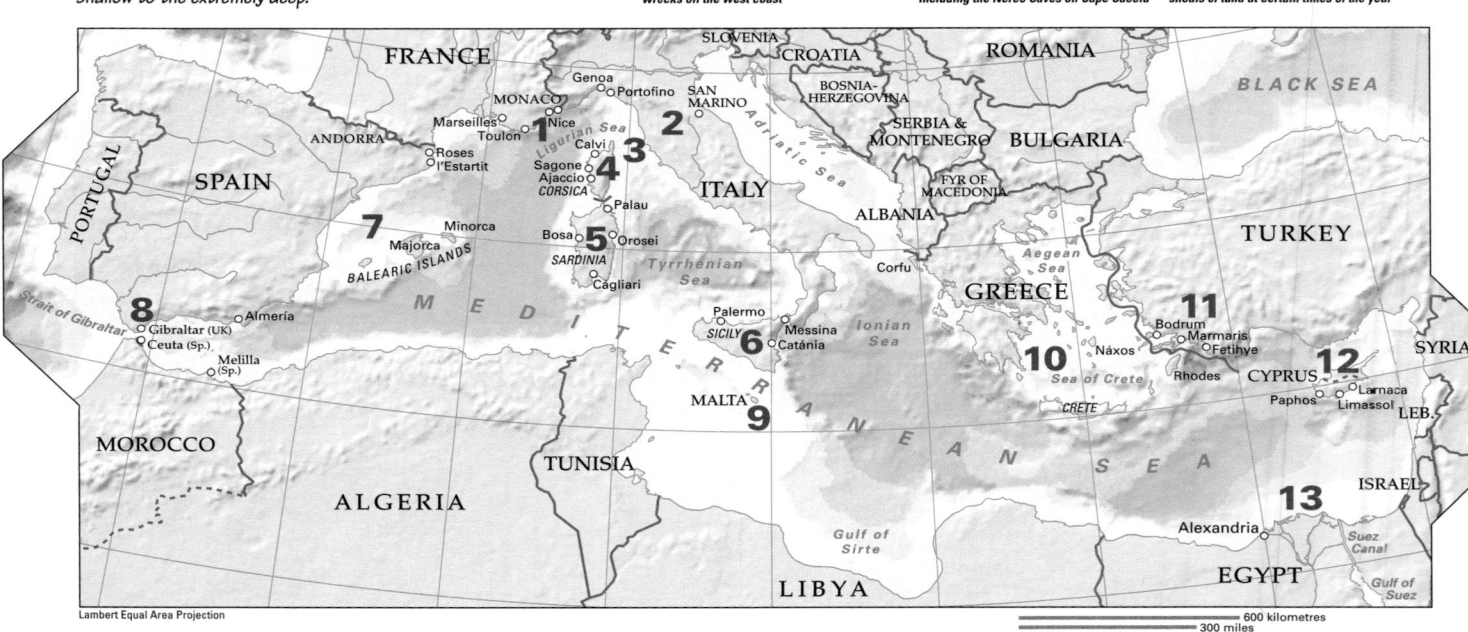

Lambert Equal Area Projection

600 kilometres
300 miles

SPAIN
1 2 3 4 D S T W ★★✓

Main dive areas Balearic Islands and Costa Brava; best facilities at l'Estartit and Roses (Costa Brava), Almeria, Majorca, Minorca
Submarine cave system 'Pont en Gill' holds outstanding examples of submerged stalactites and stalagmites; the Medes Islands (off l'Estartit) are a protected marine reserve where the flora and fauna is quite prolific

GIBRALTAR
1 2 3 4 D S T W ★★★

Main dive sites off the western and southern coastlines; facilities in Gibraltar town
Shipwrecks 'Excellent' and 'Rosslyn' just outside Gibraltar Harbour are outstanding; there is also ongoing artificial reef programme which involves the sinking of small vessels near Rosia Bay

Dive sites:
1 Soft corals / sea fans
2 Steep underwater cliffs
3 Cave diving
4 Shipwrecks
White square: not present

Regular sightings of:
D Dolphins
S Sharks / rays / pelagics
T Turtles
W Whales
White square: not regularly seen

Facilities for the diver:
★ Limited ★★ Good ★★★ Excellent

MALTA
1 2 3 4 D S T W ★★★

Dive sites all around the islands; facilities in all resort towns
Diving is very popular here although a valid medical certificate and proof of diving experience/qualifications are required; outstanding submarine arches, walls, reefs, tunnels and caves plus some new and very exciting shipwrecks deliberately sunk for divers

GREECE
1 2 3 4 D S T W ★★

Main dive areas Corfu, Crete, Náxos and Rhodes; best facilities on Crete
Until recently, Greece frowned upon scuba divers; today, however, new centres are opening all the time and there are several sites of ancient amphora where the diver is allowed to look but not touch; there are also spectacular submarine cave systems

CYPRUS
1 2 3 4 D S T W ★★★

Main dive sites off the southern and western coastlines; facilities centred on Larnaca, Limassol and Paphos
12,000 tonne ro-ro ferry 'Zenobia' sank off Larnaca in 1980 and is the largest shipwreck in the Mediterranean; the seas are very warm but Cyprus suffers from severe over-fishing
The Turkish Republic of Northern Cyprus has less opportunities for divers and limited facilities

TURKEY
1 2 3 4 D S T W ★★✓

Dive sites all along the coast; facilities centred on the southwest coast, in particular at Bodrum, Fetihye and Marmaris
Many ancient amphora wrecks available for inspection and new diving areas are being explored all the time before being opened to visitors

EGYPT: NORTH COAST
1 2 3 4 D S T W ★

Main dive sites and facilities at Alexandria
Not as popular as Egypt's Red Sea coast and often overlooked; the remains of Cleopatra's Palace were recently found in Alexandria Harbour
For Egypt's Red Sea dive sites, see page 109

Data compiled by Ned Middleton, all rights reserved
email: ned@nedmiddleton.demon.co.uk

Sea level
-200 metres
-1000 metres
-2000 metres

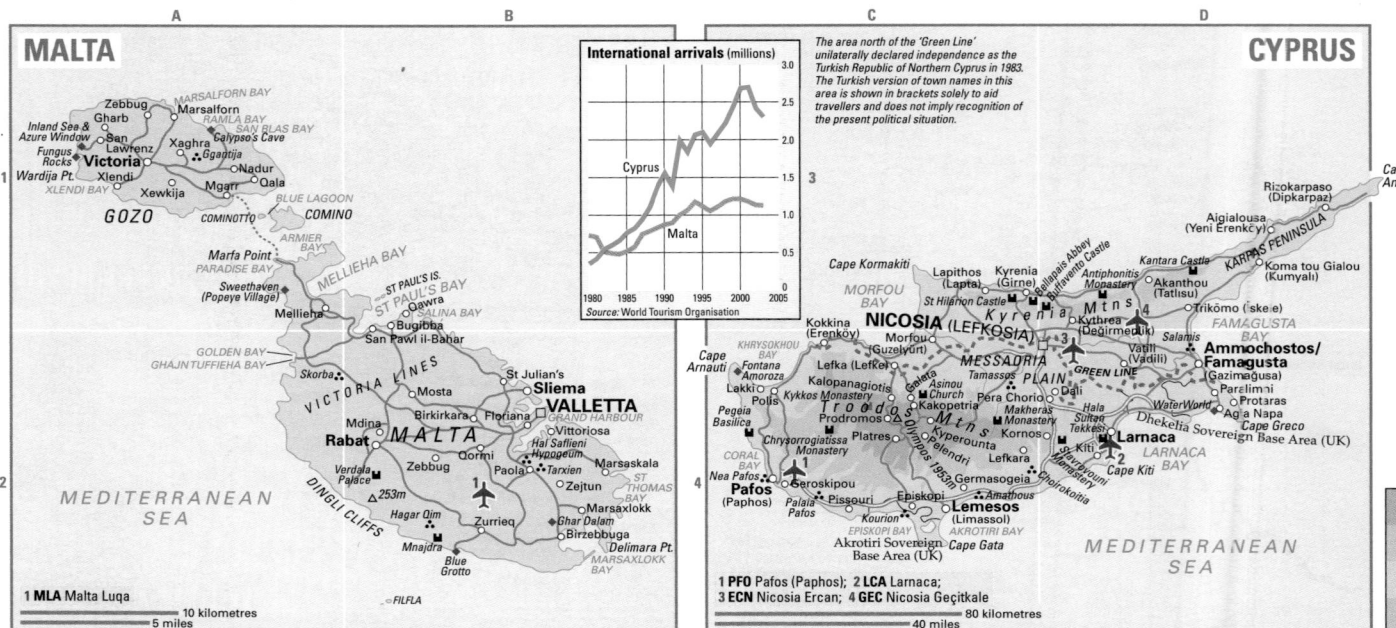

MALTA

International arrivals (millions)
Cyprus
Malta
1980 1985 1990 1995 2000 2005
Source: World Tourism Organisation

CYPRUS

The area north of the 'Green Line' unilaterally declared independence as the Turkish Republic of Northern Cyprus in 1983. The Turkish version of town names in this area is shown in brackets solely to aid travellers and does not imply recognition of the present political situation.

1 **MLA** Malta Luqa

10 kilometres
5 miles

1 **PFO** Pafos (Paphos); 2 **LCA** Larnaca;
3 **ECN** Nicosia Ercan; 4 **GEC** Nicosia Geçitkale

80 kilometres
40 miles

1000 metres
500 metres
Sea level

See also... 96-97 for more on Scandinavia; 98 for more on the Baltic States

The listings above refer to a selection of related themes. For more information, see the Contents (2-5).

Europe **95**

Scandinavia, Iceland & the Baltic States

Modified Lambert Equal Area Projection

300 kilometres
150 miles

▶ **See also...** Contents (2–5) – these countries feature in many thematic and regional maps throughout the *BTEC First Travel Atlas.*

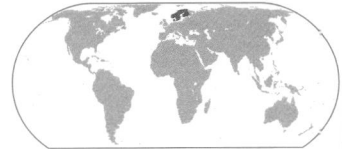

NORWAY
FEB **Holmenkollen** Ski Festival
MAY-JUN **Bergen** International Festival
MAY-JUN **Bergen** Night Jazz Festival ('Nattjazz')
JUN Midsummer Eve
JUL **Forde** Folk Music Festival
JUL **Molde** International Jazz Festival
JUL Riddu Riddu Festival (**Kåfjord, nr Alta**)
JUL-AUG **Notodden** International Blues Festival
AUG Elvefestivalen (**Vormsund**)
AUG **Oslo** Jazz Festival
AUG International Chamber Music Festival (**Stavanger**)
AUG Norwegian International Film Festival (**Haugesund**)

DENMARK
MAY 21st **Aalborg** Carnival
JUN **Skagen** Festival
JUN Midsummer Eve
JUN-JUL Viking Festival (**Frederikssund**)
JUN-JUL **Roskilde** Festival
JUL **Copenhagen** Jazz Festival
JUL 4th US Independence Festival (**Rebild**)
AUG Fire Festival Regatta (**Silkeborg**)
AUG Denmark Tattoo (**Varde**, every 3 years)
AUG **Copenhagen** International Ballet Festival
AUG Baltic Sail (**Helsingør**)
AUG **Esbjerg** International Chamber Music Festival
AUG European Medieval Festival (**Horsens**)
AUG-SEP **Århus** Festival

SWEDEN
JAN-FEB **Kiruna** Snow Festival
APR 30th Walpurgis Night (countrywide)
MAY **Drottningholm** Court Theatre
JUN 6th Swedish National Day (**Stockholm** & countrywide)
JUN Midsummer Eve
JUN-JUL Musik van Siljan (**Lake Siljan**)
JUN-JUL **Östhammar** Music Week
JUL **Falun** Folkmusik Festival ('Ethno')
JUL Trästock Festival ('Woodstock') (**Skellefteå**)
AUG **Stockholm** Water Festival
AUG Göteborgskalaseti: **Gothenburg** Party
AUG Medieval Week (**Gotland**)
SEP **Stockholm** Beer & Whisky Festival
NOV **Stockholm** International Film Festival
DEC 10th Nobel Prize ceremony (**Stockholm**)
Peace Prize awarded in Oslo
DEC 13th St Lucia Day (countrywide)

FINLAND
MAR Tar Skiing Race (**Oulu**)
JUN Midsummer Eve
JUN Midnight Sun Film Festival (**Sodankylä**)
JUN-JUL **Kuopio** Dance & Music Festival
JUL **Savonlinna** Opera Festival
JUL **Pori** Jazz Festival
JUL Tammerfest (**Tampere**)
JUL **Kotka** Maritime Festival
AUG-SEP **Helsinki** Festival
DEC 6th Finland Independence Day

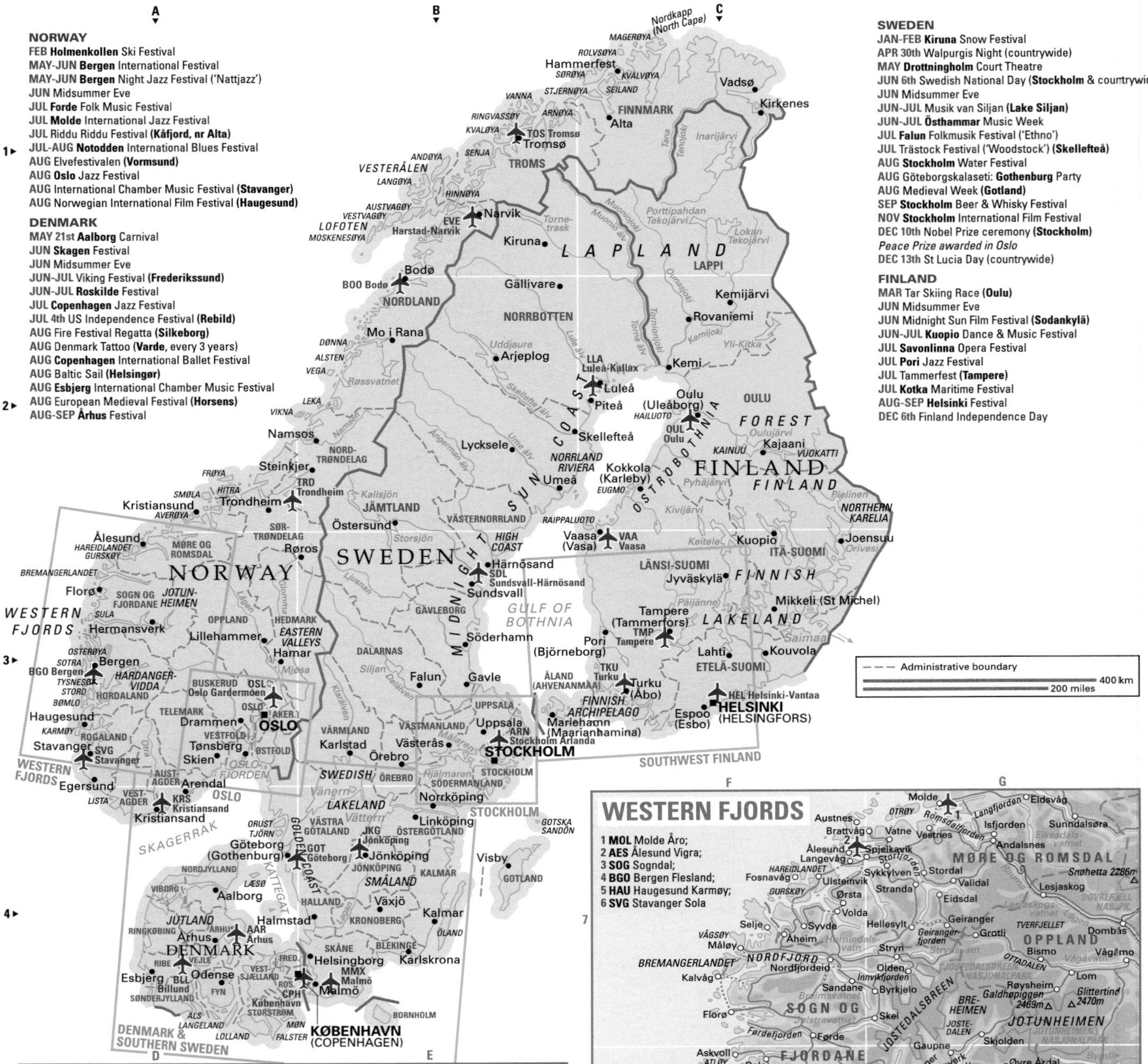

--- Administrative boundary
400 km
200 miles

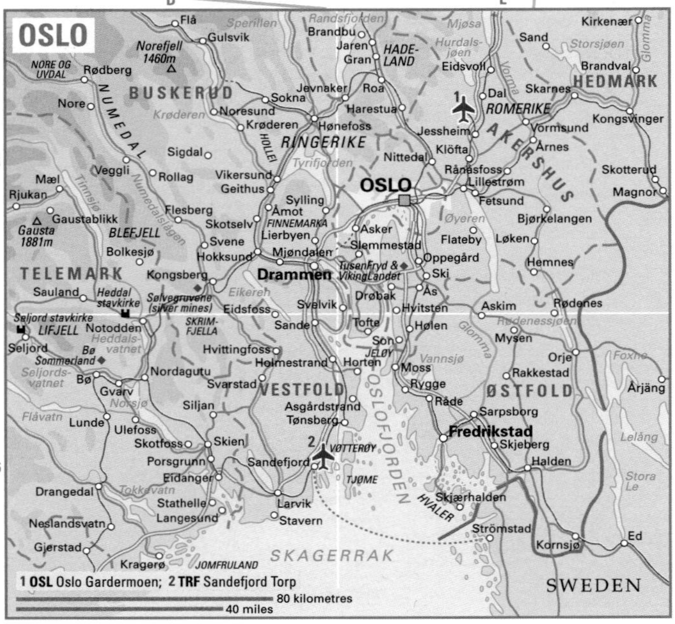

WESTERN FJORDS
1 **MOL** Molde Åro;
2 **AES** Ålesund Vigra;
3 **SOG** Sogndal;
4 **BGO** Bergen Flesland;
5 **HAU** Haugesund Karmøy;
6 **SVG** Stavanger Sola

OSLO
1 **OSL** Oslo Gardermoen; 2 **TRF** Sandefjord Torp

80 kilometres
40 miles

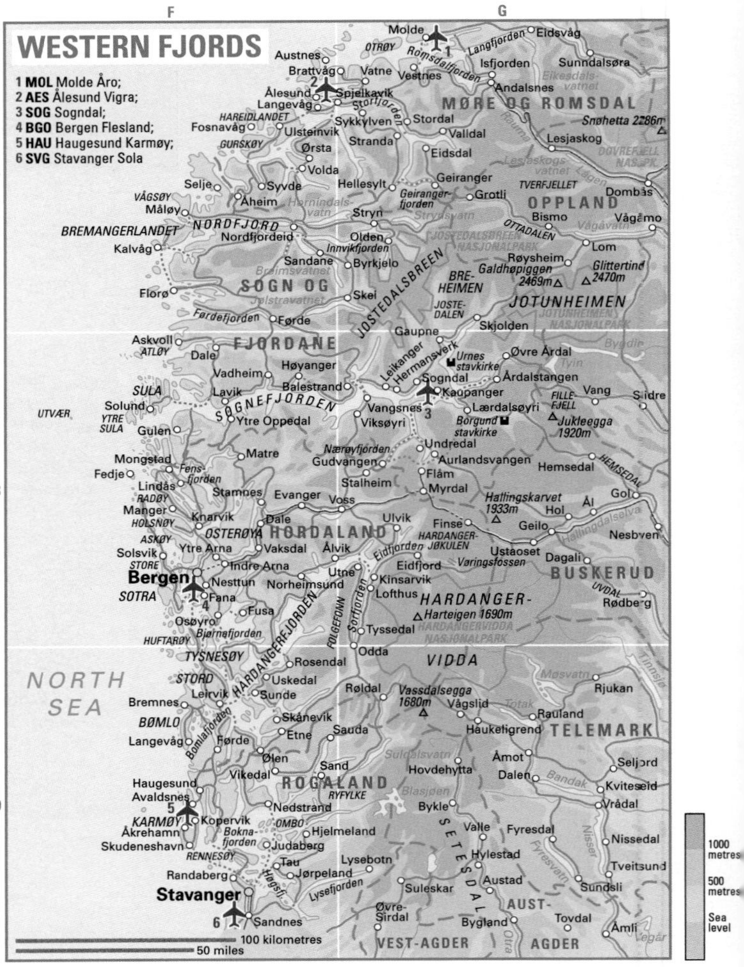

100 kilometres
50 miles

1000 metres
500 metres
Sea level

See also... Contents (2-5) – these countries feature in many thematic and regional maps throughout the *BTEC First Travel Atlas*.

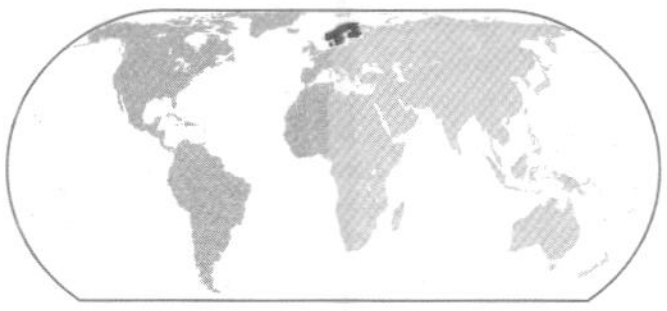

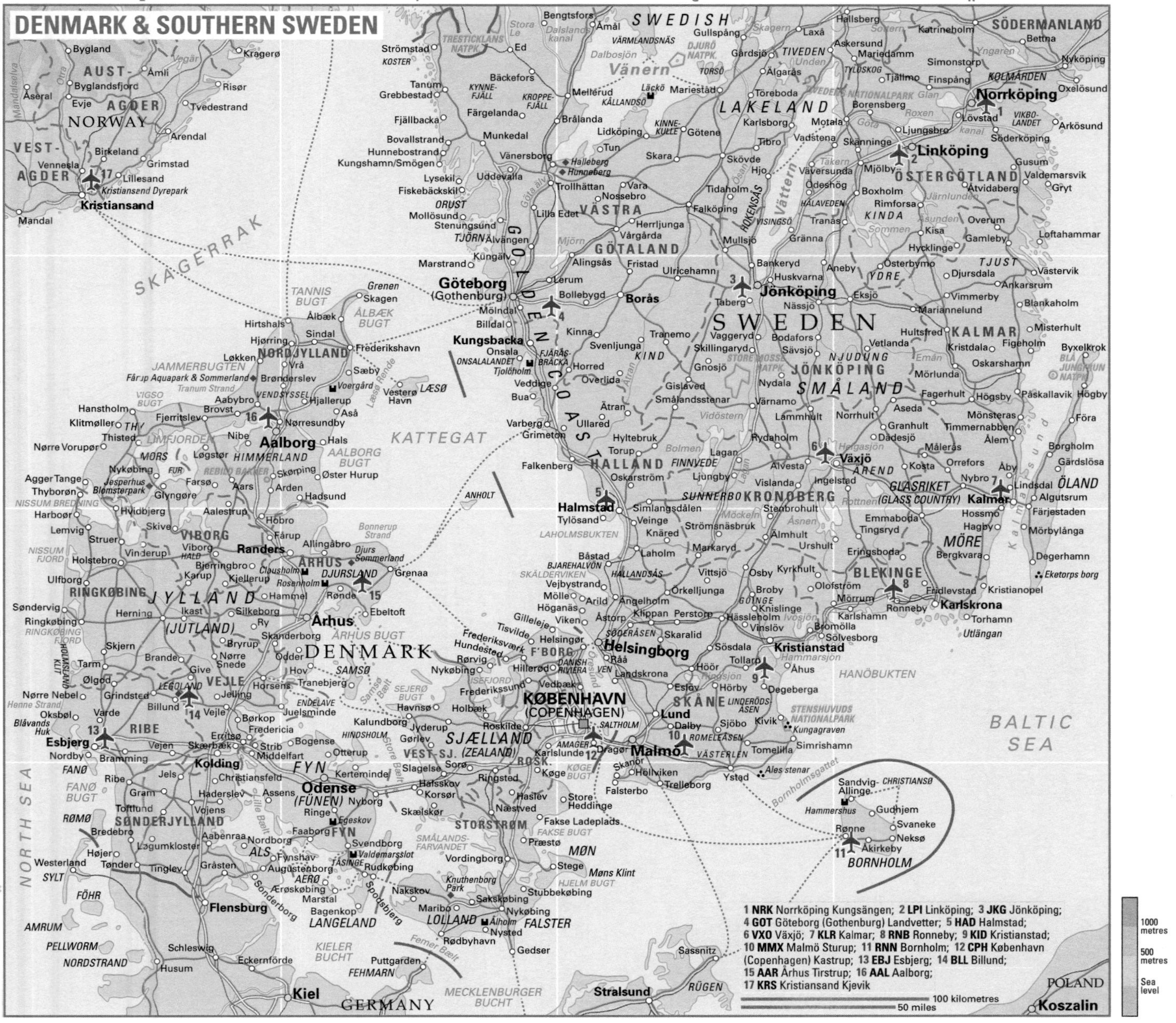

Europe 97

Scandinavia

STOCKHOLM

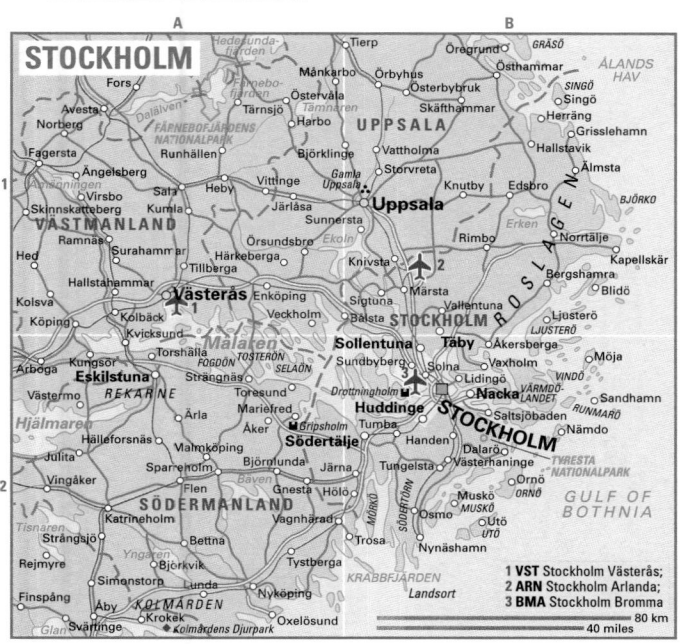

1 VST Stockholm Västerås;
2 ARN Stockholm Arlanda;
3 BMA Stockholm Bromma

80 km
40 miles

SOUTHWEST FINLAND

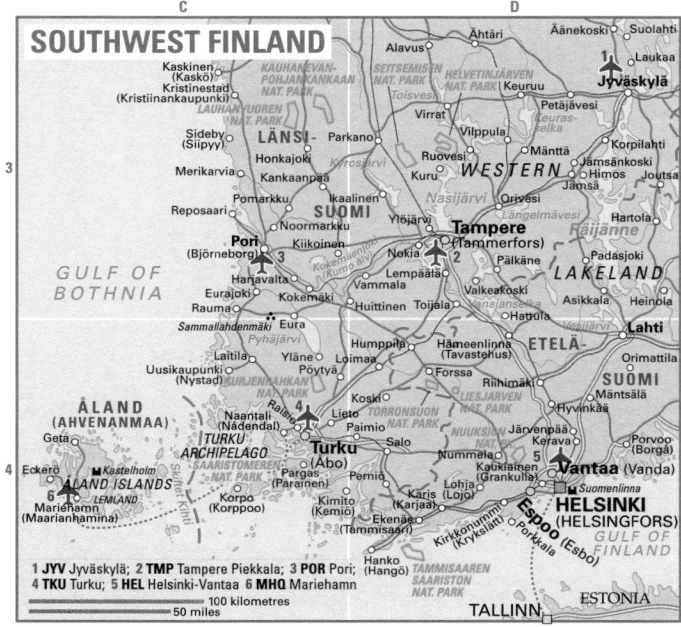

1 JYV Jyväskylä; 2 TMP Tampere Piekkala; 3 POR Pori;
4 TKU Turku; 5 HEL Helsinki-Vantaa 6 MHQ Mariehamn

100 kilometres
50 miles

DENMARK & SOUTHERN SWEDEN

1 NRK Norrköping Kungsängen; 2 LPI Linköping; 3 JKG Jönköping;
4 GOT Göteborg (Gothenburg) Landvetter; 5 HAD Halmstad;
6 VXO Växjö; 7 KLR Kalmar; 8 RNB Ronneby; 9 KID Kristianstad;
10 MMX Malmö Sturup; 11 RNN Bornholm; 12 CPH København
(Copenhagen) Kastrup; 13 EBJ Esbjerg; 14 BLL Billund;
15 AAR Århus Tirstrup; 16 AAL Aalborg;
17 KRS Kristiansand Kjevik

100 kilometres
50 miles

1000 metres
500 metres
Sea level

See also... Contents (2-5) – these countries feature in many thematic and regional maps throughout the *BTEC First Travel Atlas*.

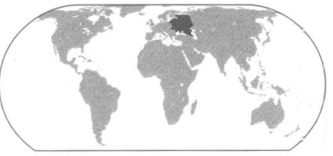

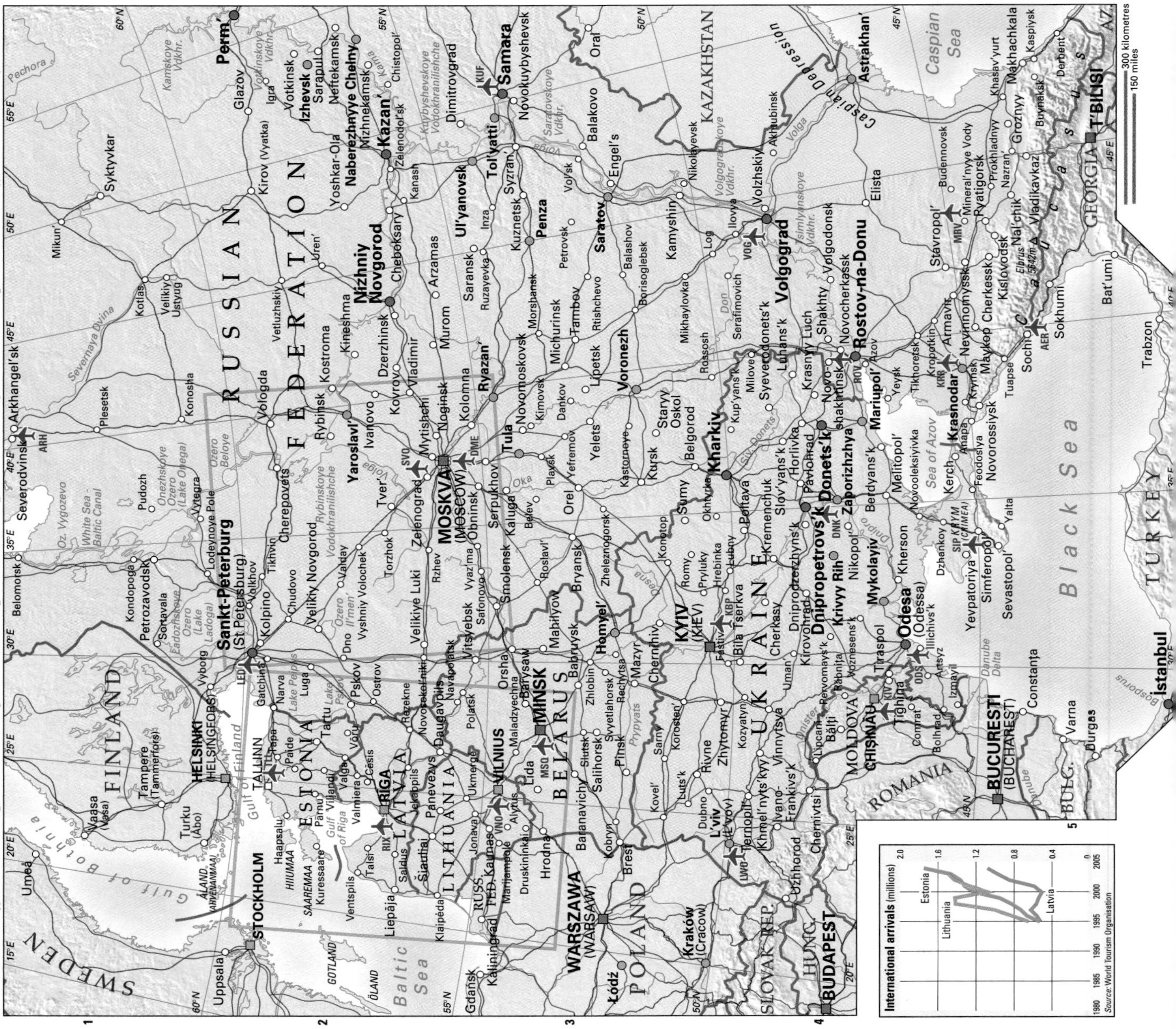

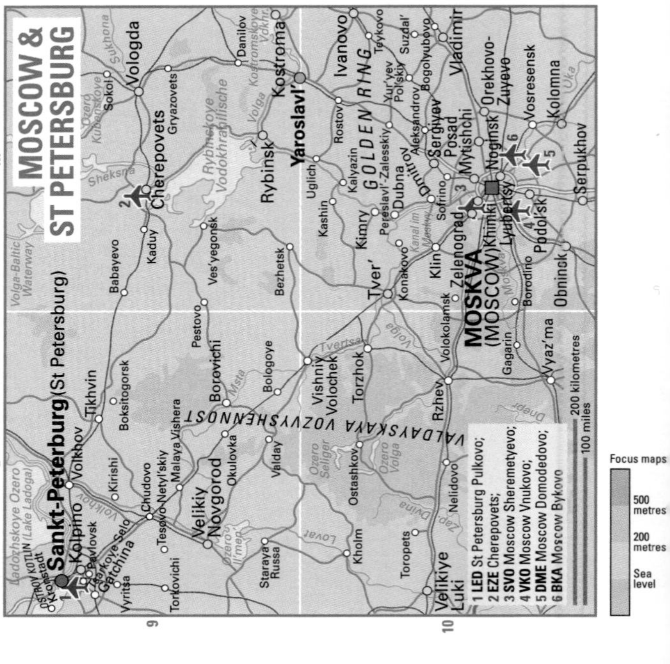

300 kilometres
150 miles

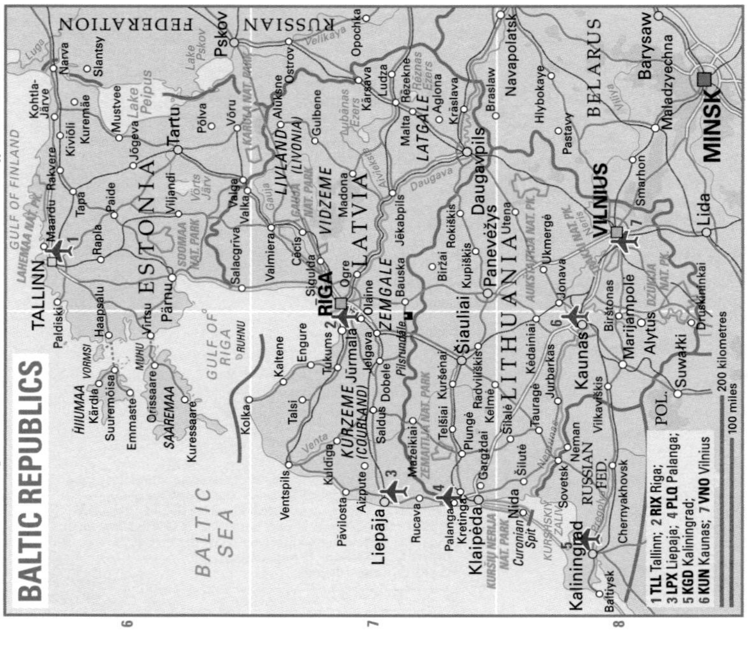

BALTIC REPUBLICS

1 TLL Tallinn; 2 RIX Riga;
3 LPX Liepāja; 4 PLQ Palanga;
5 KGD Kaliningrad;
6 KUN Kaunas; 7 VNO Vilnius

200 kilometres
100 miles

MOSCOW & ST PETERSBURG

1 LED St Petersburg Pulkovo;
2 ZZE Cherepovets;
3 SVO Moscow Sheremetevo;
4 VKO Moscow Vnukovo;
5 DME Moscow Domodedovo;
6 BKA Moscow Bykovo

200 kilometres
100 miles

International arrivals (millions)
Source World Tourism Organisation

Estonia
Lithuania
Latvia

1980 1985 1990 1995 2000 2005

Focus maps

500 metres
200 metres
Sea level

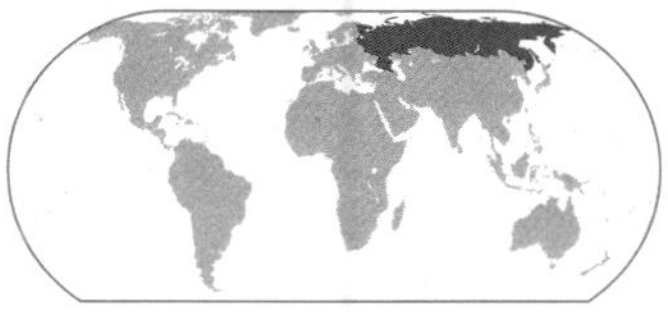

The listings above refer to a selection of related themes.
For more information, see the Contents (2-5).

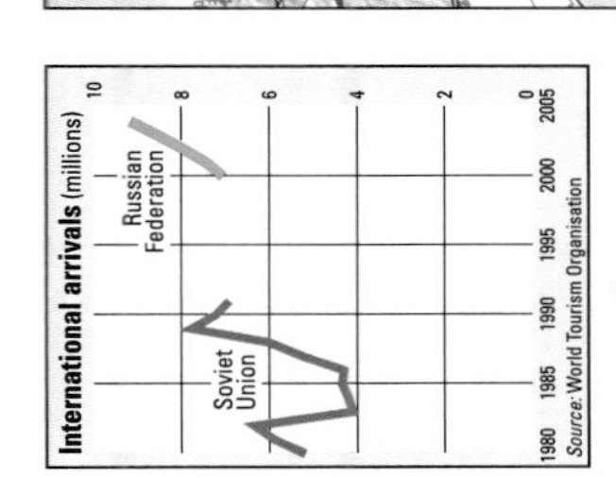

TRANS-SIBERIAN RAILWAY

	Moscow	Vladimir	Nizhniy Novgorod	Kirov	Perm'	Yekaterinburg	Omsk	Novosibirsk	Krasnoyarsk	Irkutsk	Ulan-Ude	Chita	Belogorsk	Karymskoye	Khabarovsk	Ussuriysk	Nakhodka	Vladivostok
Km		210	461	917	1,397	1,778	2,676	3,303	4,065	5,152	5,608	6,266	7,622	6,165	6,261	7,613	7,834	8,492
Miles		130	286	570	868	1,105	1,663	2,052	2,526	3,201	3,485	3,894	4,736	3,831	3,890	4,730	4,868	5,277

9,148 9,258
5,683 5,842 5,753

Distances from Moscow ▲

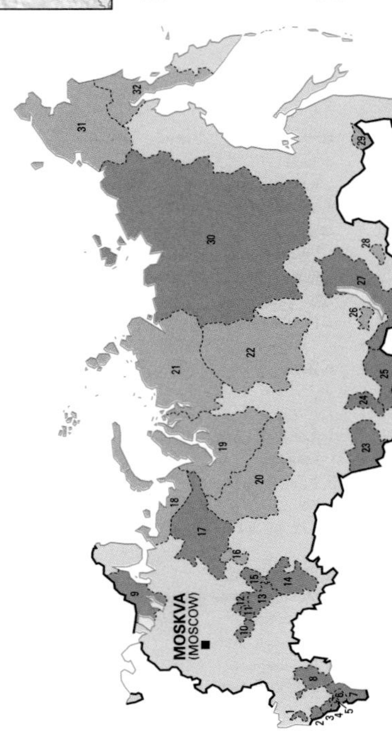

Lambert Equal Area Projection

1000 kilometres
500 miles

REPUBLIC

1 ADYGEYA
2 KARACHAY-CHERKESSIA
3 KABARDINO-BALKARIA
4 NORTH OSSETIA (ALANIA)
5 INGUSHETIA
6 CHECHNYA
7 DAGESTAN
8 KALMYKIA
9 KARELIA
10 MORDOVIA
11 CHUVASHIA
12 MARI-EL
13 TATARSTAN
14 BASHKORTOSTAN
15 UDMURTIA
16 Komi-Permyak
17 KOMI

Autonomous Area or Region

18 Nenets
19 Yamalo-Nenets
20 Khanty-Mansi
21 Taymyr
22 Evenki
23 ALTAY
24 KHAKASSIA
25 TUVA
26 Ust-Ordyn-Buryat
27 BURYATIA
28 Agin-Buryat
29 Jewish Autonomous Region
30 SAKHA (YAKUTIA)
31 Chukot
32 Koryak

International arrivals (millions)

Russian Federation

Soviet Union

Source: World Tourism Organisation

1980 1985 1990 1995 2000 2005

See also... World Physical (26-27)

The listings above refer to a selection of related themes.
For more information, see the Contents (2-5).

1: Geographical Definitions

The following list covers a number of the main geographical terms which are used to describe areas of the world. In many cases there is no officially adopted definition. Different industries, cultures and international bodies will use their own definitions which are, if consistently applied, as valid of those used by any other. The definitions of the continents, for example, are often not those which have been used in this atlas. Some of these ambiguities are referred to here.

Arabian Peninsula
Geographical region comprising: Bahrain, Kuwait, Oman, Qatar, Saudi Arabia, United Arab Emirates, Yemen.

Australasia
Geographical region comprising: Australia, New Caledonia, New Zealand, Solomon Islands, Vanuatu and the island of New Guinea including all of Papua New Guinea. Often described as equivalent to all of Oceania between the Equator and 47°S. The term is not commonly used in Australia and New Zealand because of confusion with Australia itself.

Bahama Islands
Group of islands in the Atlantic Ocean comprising the Commonwealth of The Bahamas and the Turks and Caicos Islands.

Balkans, The
The Balkan Peninsula, which is bordered by the Adriatic and Ionian Seas to the west, the Aegean and Black Seas to the east and the Mediterranean Sea to the south. The countries occupying this peninsula are described as Balkan states: Albania, Bosnia-Herzegovina, Bulgaria, Croatia, Greece, Former Yugoslav Republic of Macedonia, Romania, Slovenia, Serbia, Montenegro and the European part of Turkey.

Borneo
Island in the Malay Archipelago (qv) divided between Brunei, Indonesia (the provinces of Central, East, South and West Kalimantan) and Malaysia (the states of Sabah and Sarawak).

British Isles
Geographical region comprising: United Kingdom (qv), Republic of Ireland, Isle of Man, Channel Islands.

Caribbean
General tourist destination term used to describe the West Indies (qv) and sometimes the countries with coastlines on the Caribbean Sea (such as Venezuela and Eastern Mexico).

Caroline Islands
Archipelago in the west Pacific Ocean. Islands comprise the Federated States of Micronesia and Palau.

Celebes
Island in the Malay Archipelago (qv), Sulawesi in Indonesian.

Central America
Geographical region comprising: Belize, Costa Rica, El Salvador, Guatemala, Honduras, Nicaragua, Panama. Sometimes considered part of the North American (qv) continent.

Ceylon
Island off the southeast coast of India, officially Sri Lanka.

Channel Islands
Group of islands comprising Jersey, Guernsey, Alderney, Sark and Herm, situated off the northwest coast of France. They are possessions of the British Crown and not officially part of the United Kingdom (qv).

East Indies
General geographical term sometimes applied loosely to India, Indochina and the Malay Archipelago (qv). Often used as alternative to the Malay Archipelago or the Republic of Indonesia itself. The term is now rarely used.

Europe
Continent. Northern boundary formed by Arctic Ocean. Eastern boundary formed by Ural Mountains, Ural River and Caspian Sea. Southern boundary formed by Caucasus Mountains, Black Sea, Bosporus, Aegean Sea and Mediterranean Sea. Western boundary formed by Atlantic Ocean. Includes Iceland, Svalbard and area of Turkey west of the Bosporus.

Far East
General geographical term describing east and South-East Asia: Brunei, Cambodia, China, Indonesia, Japan, Democratic People's Republic of Korea (North Korea), Republic of Korea (South Korea), Laos, Malaysia, Myanmar (Burma), the Philippines, Singapore, Taiwan, Thailand, Vietnam. Sometimes extended to include Mongolia and eastern Siberian region of the Russian Federation.

Formosa
Island off the southeast coast of the People's Republic of China, known variously as Taiwan, the Republic of China, Taiwan (RoC) or China (Taiwan) .

Great Britain
Geographical region comprising: England, Scotland, Wales.

Greater Antilles
Group of Caribbean islands comprising: Cayman Islands, Cuba, Hispaniola, Jamaica, Puerto Rico.

Hispaniola
Island in the Greater Antilles (qv) divided between the Dominican Republic and Haiti.

Iberia
Peninsula in southwest Europe occupied by Spain, Portugal, Andorra and Gibraltar.

Indochina
Geographical region comprising: Cambodia, Laos, Peninsular Malaysia, Myanmar, Singapore, Thailand, Vietnam.

Isle of Man
An island in the Irish Sea between Great Britain (qv) and Ireland. It is a possession of the British Crown and not officially part of the United Kingdom (qv).

Latin America
Defined either as: the Spanish- and Portuguese-speaking countries of the Americas (sometimes also including French-speaking Haiti); or all of the Americas south of the United States. This latter, more general, definition is the one used in this atlas.

Lesser Antilles
Group of Caribbean islands comprising: Leeward Islands (qv), Windward Islands (qv), Aruba, Barbados, Bonaire, Curaçao, Trinidad and Tobago. Also includes the chain of small Venezuelan islands east of Bonaire.

Leeward Islands
Group of Caribbean islands comprising: Anguilla, Antigua and Barbuda, Dominica, Guadeloupe, Montserrat, Saba, St Eustatius, St Kitts and Nevis, St Maarten/St Martin, Virgin Islands.

Low Countries
Geographical region comprising: Belgium, Luxembourg, The Netherlands.

Maghreb
Arabic name for northwest Africa and, in the Moorish period, Spain. Algeria, Morocco and Tunisia are described as Maghreb countries.

Malay Archipelago
The largest island group in the world, off the southeast coast of Asia and between the Indian and Pacific Oceans. Major islands include Borneo (qv), Sulawesi (Celebes, qv), Jawa (Java), New Guinea and Sumatera (Sumatra). Countries within this archipelago: Brunei, Indonesia, East Malaysia, Papua New Guinea, the Philippines.

Mediterranean
General tourist destination term used to describe the islands of the Mediterranean Sea and the countries bordering it.

Melanesia
Collective name for the islands in the southwest Pacific Ocean, south of the Equator and northeast of Australia. Includes: Fiji Islands, Nauru, New Caledonia, Papua New Guinea (excluding New Guinea mainland), Solomon Islands, Vanuatu.

Micronesia
Collective name for the islands in the west Pacific Ocean, north of the Equator and east of the Philippines. Includes: Guam, Kiribati (west), Marshall Islands, Federated States of Micronesia, Northern Mariana Islands, Palau.

Middle East
General geographical term describing a loosely defined area comprising: countries of the Arabian Peninsula (qv), Egypt, Iran, Iraq, Israel, Jordan, Lebanon, Syria. Sometimes extended to include Algeria, Cyprus, Libya, Morocco, Sudan, Tunisia and Turkey

Near East
Rarely used general geographical term describing an area of SW Asia: the Arabian Peninsula, Cyprus, Israel, Jordan, Lebanon, Syria, Turkey. Often extended to Egypt and Sudan.

Netherlands Antilles
Islands of the West Indies administered by The Netherlands, comprising: Bonaire, Curaçao, Saba, St Eustatius, St Maarten. Aruba, formerly part of the Netherlands Antilles, is a separate part of the Kingdom of the Netherlands.

New Guinea
Island in the Malay Archipelago (qv) divided between Papua New Guinea and the Indonesian province of Irian Jaya.

North America
Continent comprising: USA, Canada, Mexico, Bermuda, West Indies (qv). Usually considered to also include Greenland and (less commonly) Central America.

Oceania
General geographical term describing the islands of the central and south Pacific Ocean, including Melanesia, Micronesia and Polynesia. Sometimes extended to include Australia, New Zealand and the Malay Archipelago (qv).

Polynesia
Collective name for the islands of the central and south Pacific Ocean. Includes: American Samoa, Cook Islands, Easter Island, French Polynesia, Hawaii, Kiribati (east), New Zealand, Niue, Pitcairn Islands, Samoa, Tokelau, Tonga, Tuvalu, Wallis & Futuna.

Scandinavia
Geographical region comprising: Denmark, Norway, Sweden. Generally extended to include Finland and (less commonly) Iceland.

South America
Continent comprising: countries on mainland south of Panama Falkland Islands, Galapagos Islands.

South-East Asia
Geographic region comprising Maynmar, Laos, Thailand, Vietnam, Cambodia, Malaysia, Singapore, Brunei and the Philippines. Sometimes taken to include Indonesia, Taiwan, Macau, Hong Kong and the southern coastal areas of China.

Ulster
Geographical region comprising Northern Ireland plus the counties of Cavan, Donegal and Monaghan in the Republic of Ireland. It is often used (incorrectly) as an unofficial term to describe Northern Ireland.

United Kingdom
Country comprising Great Britain (qv) and Northern Ireland. The Isle of Man and the Channel Islands are Crown dependencies and not officially part of the UK.

West Indies
Islands enclosing the Caribbean Sea, comprising: Bahama Islands (qv), Greater Antilles (qv), Lesser Antilles (qv).

Windward Islands
Group of Caribbean islands comprising: Grenada, Martinique, St Lucia, St Vincent and The Grenadines.

2: Highest & Lowest

Name	Metres	Feet	Country
AFRICA			
▲ **Kilimanjaro (Kibo)**	5,895	19,340	Tanzania
▼ **Lake Assal**	–155	–509	Djibouti
ANTARCTICA			
▲ **Vinson Massif**	4,897	16,066	Antarctica
▼ **(ice covered)**	–2,538	–8,327	Antarctica
ASIA			
▲ **Everest (Qomolangma Feng/ Sagarmatha)**	8,850	29,035	China-Nepal
▼ **Dead Sea**	–411	–1,349	Israel-Jordan-Palestine
AUSTRALASIA & OCEANIA			
▲ **Aoraki (Cook)**	3,754	12,315	New Zealand
▼ **Lake Eyre**	–16	–52	Australia
EUROPE & RUSSIAN FEDERATION			
▲ **Elbrus**	5,642	18,510	Russian Fed.
▼ **Caspian Sea**	–28	–92	Russia-C. Asia-Caucasus
NORTH AMERICA			
▲ **McKinley (Denali)**	6,194	20,321	Alaska, USA
▼ **Death Valley**	–86	–282	California, USA
SOUTH AMERICA			
▲ **Aconcagua**	6,960	22,834	Argentina
▼ **G. Bajo de S. Julián**	–105	–344	Argentina

Name	Metres	Feet	Country
SOME OTHER NOTABLE MOUNTAINS			
K2 (Chogori/ Qogir Feng)	8,611	28,250	China-Kashmir
Kangchenjunga	8,586	28,170	India-Nepal
Makalu	8,463	27,766	China-Nepal
Dhaulagiri	8,167	26,795	Nepal
Nanga Parbat	8,126	26,660	Kashmir
Annapurna	8,091	26,545	Nepal
Gosainthan (Xixabangma Feng)	8,013	26,289	China
Qullai Garmo	7,495	24,590	Tajikistan
Ojos del Salado	6,908	22,664	Argentina-Chile
Huascarán	6,768	22,205	Peru
Logan	5,959	19,550	Yukon, Canada
Damavand	5,681	18,638	Iran
Citlaltépetl (Orizaba)	5,610	18,405	Mexico
Kenya (Kirinyaga)	5,199	17,057	Kenya
Ararat	5,165	16,946	Turkey
Mont Blanc	4,808	15,774	France-Italy
Ras Dashen	4,533	14,872	Ethiopia
Whitney	4,418	14,495	California, USA
Kinabalu	4,094	13,432	Malaysia
Fuji	3,776	12,388	Japan

3: The World's Longest Rivers

Local names are shown in square brackets.

River	Length: (km)	(miles)	Source(s) and outflow
Nile Luvironza-Ruvuvu-Kagera-White Nile	6,825	4,240	Lake Victoria region – Mediterranean Sea
Amazon Apurimac-Ene-Tambo-Ucayali	6,516	4,049	Peruvian Andes – Atlantic Ocean
Chang Jiang (Yangtze) [Tuotuo-Tongtian-Jinsha]	6,380	3,964	Tanggula Shan, China – East China Sea
Mississippi-Missouri Red Rock-Beaverhead	5,969	3,709	SW Montana – Gulf of Mexico
Ob-Irtysh [Ertix]	5,568	3,459	Altay Mountains, China – Kara Sea
Yenisey Selenga-Angara	5,550	3,448	Western Mongolia – Kara Sea
Huang He (Yellow)	5,464	3,395	Bayan Har Shan, China – Yellow Sea
Congo Lualaba	4,667	2,900	Katanga Plateau, Congo D.R. – Atlantic Ocean
Paraná Río de la Plata	4,500	2,796	Serra da Mantiquera, Brazil – Atlantic Ocean
Mekong [Za-Lancang]	4,425	2,749	Tanggula Shan, China – South China Sea
Amur Kerulen-Argun	4,416	2,744	Eastern Mongolia – Sea of Japan
Lena Kirenga	4,400	2,734	Baikal Mtns, Russian Fed., – Laptev Sea
Mackenzie Finlay-Peace-Slave	4,241	2,635	Omineca Mtns, BC, Canada – Beaufort Sea
Niger [Joliba/Kworra]	4,184	2,599	Guinea/Sierra Leone border – Gulf of Guinea
Murray-Darling	3,750	2,330	Gt. Dividing Range, Australia – Southern Ocean

4: Conversions (Kilometres/ Miles; Metres/Feet; Centimetres/Inches; Centigrade/Fahrenheit)

Kms	**10**	**20**	**30**	**40**	**50**	**60**	**70**	**80**	**90**	**100**
Mi	6.2	12.4	18.6	24.9	31.1	37.3	43.5	49.7	55.9	62.1
M	**10**	**20**	**30**	**40**	**50**	**60**	**70**	**80**	**90**	**100**
Ft	33	66	98	131	164	197	230	262	295	328

Cms	**10**	**20**	**30**	**40**	**50**	**60**	**70**	**80**	**90**	**100**
Ins	3.9	7.9	11.8	15.7	19.7	23.6	27.6	31.5	35.4	39.4
°C	**-10**	**-5**	**0**	**5**	**10**	**15**	**20**	**25**	**30**	**35**
°F	14	23	32	41	50	59	68	77	86	95

The listings above refer to a selection of related themes.
For more information, see the Contents (2-5).

5: Glossary of Foreign Geographical Terms

The following list provides the English equivalents for some of the most common foreign geographical terms used in this and other international atlases.

Term	Language	Meaning
Å, -å	Danish, Norwegian	Stream
Abar, Abyar	Arabic	Wells
Açude	Portuguese	Reservoir
Adalar	Turkish	Islands
Adasi	Turkish	Island
Agía, Ágios	Greek	Saint
Aiguille(s)	French	Peak(s)
Aïn, Aïn	Arabic	Spring, well
-air	Indonesian	Stream
Ákra, Akrotírion	Greek	Cape, point
Ala-	Finnish	Lower
A'lá	Arabic	Upper
Alt-	German	Old
Alta, Alto	Italian, Portug., Spanish	Upper
Altiplanicie	Spain	High plain, mesa
Älv, -älven	Swedish	River
am, an	German	On, upon
Áno	Greek	Upper
Anse	French	Bay
Ao	Chinese, Thai	Bay
'Aqabat	Arabic	Pass
Arrecife	Spanish	Reef
Arroio/Arroyo	Portuguese/Spanish	Watercourse
Archipiélago	Spanish	Archipelago
Aust-	Norwegian	East, eastern
Austral	Spanish	Southern
'Ayn	Arabic	Spring, well
Baai	Afrikaans	Bay
Bab	Arabic	Strait
Bach	German	Stream
Bad	German	Spa
Badiyat	Arabic	Desert
Bælt	Danish	Strait
Baharu	Malay	New
Bahía	Spanish	Bay
Bahiret	Arabic	Lagoon
Bahr	Arabic	Bay, canal, lake
Bahra/Bahrat	Arabic	Lagoon/Lake
Baia/Baie	Portuguese/French	Bay
Baixo	Portuguese	Lower
Baja, Bajo	Spanish	Lower
Bala	Persian	Upper
Ban	Cambodian, Laotian, Thai	Village
-bana	Japanese	Cape, point
Bañado	Spanish	Marshy land
Banc/Banco	French/Spanish	Sandbank
Bandao	Chinese	Peninsula
Bandar	Arabian, Malay, Persian	Inlet, port
-bando	Korean	Peninsula
Baraj, Baraji	Turkish	Dam
Barat	Indonesian, Malay	West, western
Barqa	Arabic	Hill
Barra	Portuguese	Sandbank
Barracão	Portuguese	Dam, weir
Barragem	Portuguese	Reservoir
Baruun	Mongolian	Western
Bas, Basse	French	Lower
Bassin	French	Basin
Batin, Batn	Arabic	Depression
Becken	German	Basin
Beek	Flemish	Stream
bei	German	At, near
Bei	Chinese	North, northern
Beinn, Ben	Gaelic	Mountain
Belogor'ye	Russian	Mountain
Bereg	Russian	Bank, shore
-berg	Norwegian, Swedish	Mountain
Berg(e)	German	Mountain(s)
Besar	Indonesian, Malay	Big, great
Bir, Bîr/Bi'ar	Arabic	Well/Wells
Birkat, Birket	Arabic	Pool, well
-bjerg	Danish	Hill
Boca	Portuguese, Spanish	Mouth
Bocche	Italian	Estuary, mouths
Bodden	German	Bay, gulf
Bogazi	Turkish	Strait
Bogen	Norwegian	Bay
Bois	French	Woods
Boloto	Russian	Bog, marsh
Bol'sh-aya, -iye, -oy, -oye	Russian	Big
-bong	Korean	Mountain
Boquerón	Spanish	Pass
Bor	Polish	Forest
-botn/-botten	Norwegian/Swedish	Valley floor
Bouche	French	Estuary, mouth
-bre, -breen	Norwegian	Glacier
Bredning	Danish	Bay
Bron	Afrikaans	Spring, well
-brønn	Norwegian	Spring, well
Bucht/Bugt	German/Danish	Bay
Buhayrat, Buheirat	Arabic	Lake
Bukhta	Russian	Bay
Bukit	Malay	Hill
Bukt, Bukten	Norwegian, Swedish	Bay
Bulag	Mongolian	Spring
Bulak	Russian, Uighur	Spring
Burg	German	Castle
Burun, Burnu	Turkish	Cape, point
Büyük	Turkish	Big
Cabeço	Portuguese	Summit
Cabeza	Spanish	Summit
Cabo	Portuguese, Spanish	Cape, headland
Cachoeira	Portuguese	Waterfall
Cala/Caleta	Catalan/Spanish	Inlet
Cañada	Spanish	Ravine
Cañadón	Spanish	Gorge
Canal	Portuguese, Spanish	Channel
Cañe	Spanish	Stream
Cañon	Spanish	Canyon
Cap/Capo	Catalan, French/Italian	Cape, headland
Catarata	Spanish	Waterfall
Cayo(s)	Spanish	Islet(s), rock(s)
Cerro	Spanish	Hill, peak
Chaco	Spanish	Plain
Chaîne	French	Mountain chain
Chalb	Arabic	Watercourse
Chapada	Portuguese	Hills, uplands
Chebka	Arabic	Hill
-chedo	Korean	Archipelago
Chenal	French	Channel
Chiang	Thai	Town
-ch'on	Korean	River
Chong	Thai	Bay
Chott	Arabic	Marsh, salt lake
Chuluu	Mongolian	Mountain
Chute	French	Waterfall
Ci	Indonesian	Stream
Ciénaga	Spanish	Marshy lake
Cima/Cime	Italian/French	Summit
Città/Ciudad	Italian/Spanish	City, town
Co	Tibetan	Lake
Col	French	High pass
Collado	Spanish	Hill, saddle
Colle	Italian	Pass
Collina	Italian	Hill
Colline(s)	French	Hill(s)
Combe	French	Valley
Conca	Italian	Hollow
Cordillera	Spanish	Mountain chain
Corne/Corno	French/Italian	Peak
Costa	Italian, Portug., Spanish	Coast, shore
Côte	French	Coast, slope
Coteau(x)	French	Hill(s)
Cove	Catalan	Cave
Cuchilla	Spanish	Mountain chain
Cuenca	Spanish	River basin
Cueva	Spanish	Cave
Cun	Chinese	Village
Da	Chinese	Big
Dag/Dagh	Turkish/Persian	Mountain
Daglar	Turkish	Mountain
-dake	Japanese	Peak
-dal	Afrikaans, Danish, Norwegian, Swedish	Valley
Danau	Indonesian	Lake
Dao	Chinese	Island
Darreh	Persian	Valley
Daryacheh	Persian	Lake
Dasht	Persian, Urdu	Desert
Davaa	Mongolian	Pass
Denizi	Turkish	Sea
Dhar	Arabic	Hills, mountain
-diep	Flemish	Channel
Djebel/Djibâl	Arabic	Mountain/Mtns.
-do	Korean	Island
Dolina	Russian	Valley
Dolna/Dolní	Bulgarian/Czech	Lower
Dolny	Polish	Lower
Dong	Chinese	East, eastern
Dong	Thai	Mountain
-dong	Korean	Village
Donja, Donji	Serbo-Croat	Lower
Dorf	German	Village
-dorp	Afrikaans	Village
Dür	Arabic	Mountains
Dzüün	Mongolian	East, eastern
Eiland(en)	Afrikaans, Flemish	Island(s)
-elv, -elva	Norwegian	River
Embalse	Spanish	Reservoir
Embouchure	French	Estuary
Ensenada	Spanish	Bay
Erg	Arabian	Desert & dunes
Eski	Turkish	Old
Estero	Spanish	Inlet, estuary, swamp
Estrecho	Spanish	Strait
Estreito	Portuguese	Strait
Étang	French	Lake, lagoon
Fajj	Arabic	Watercourse
Fels	German	Rock
Feng	Chinese	Peak
Fiume	Italian	River
-fjäll, -fjället	Swedish	Mountain
-fjärden	Swedish	Fjord
-fjell, -fjellet	Norwegian	Mountain
-fjord, -fjorden	Danish, Norwegian	Fjord, lagoon
Fleuve	French	River
Foce	Italian	River-mouth
-fonn	Norwegian	Glacier
Förde	German	Inlet
Forêt/Forst	French/German	Forest
-foss	Norwegian	Waterfall
Fuente	Spanish	Source, well
-gan	Japanese	Rock
Gang	Chinese	Harbour
Garet	Arabic	Hill
Gardaneh	Persian	Pass
Gat	Flemish	Channel
-gata	Japanese	Inlet, lagoon
Gau	German	District
Gave	French	Torrent
-gawa	Japanese	River
Gebel	Arabic	Mountain
Gebergte	Afrikaans	Mountain range
Gebiet	German	District, region
Gebirge	German	Mountains
Gedigi	Turkish	Pass
Geziret/Gezâir	Arabic	Island/Islands
Ghadfat	Arabic	Watercourse
Ghadir	Arabic	Well
Ghard	Arabic	Sand dunes
Ghubbat	Arabic	Bay
Gipfel	German	Peak
Gletscher	German	Glacier
Gobi	Mongolian	Desert
Gol	Mongolian	River
Göl, Gölü	Turkish	Lake
Golfe	French	Bay, gulf
Golfete	Spanish	Bay
Golfo	Italian, Spanish	Bay, gulf
Gora	Bulgarian	Forest
Gora/Góra	Russian, Serbo-Croat/Polish	Mountain
Górka	Polish	Hill
Gornja, Gornji	Serbo-Croat	Upper
Gory/Góry	Russian/Polish	Mountains
Goulet	French	Narrow entrance
Grabean	German	Ditch, trench
-grad	Bulgarian, Russian, Serbo-Croat	Town, castle
Grand, Grands	French	Big
Grat	German	Crest, ridge
Greben'	Russian	Ridge
-gród	Polish	Town, castle
Groot	Afrikaans	Big
Gross, -e, -en, -er	German	Big
Grotta/Grotte	Italian/French	Cave, grotto
Grund	German	Ground, valley
Gryada	Russian	Ridge
Guan	Chinese	Pass
Guba	Russian	Bay
Guelta	Arabic	Well
-gunto	Japanese	Island group
Gunung	Indonesian, Malay	Mountain
Hadabat	Arabic	Plain
Hadh, Hadhat	Arabic	Sand dunes
-haehyop	Korean	Strait
Hafar	Arabic	Wells
Hafen	German	Harbour, port
Haff	German	Bay
Hai	Chinese	Sea
Halbinsel	German	Peninsula
-halvøya	Norwegian	Peninsula
Hamad-a, -et	Arabic	Plateau
Hammad-ah, -at	Arabic	Plain, rocky plateau
-hamn	Norwegian, Swedish	Harbour
Hamun	Persian	Marsh
-hanto	Japanese	Peninsula
Hardt	German	Wooded hills
Harrat	Arabic	Lava fields
Hassi, Hasy	Arabic	Well
-haug	Norwegian	Hill
Haut, -e	French	Upper
Hawr	Arabic	Lake
-havn	Danish, Norwegian	Harbour
Hazm	Arabic	Plateau
He	Chinese	River
-hede	Danish, Norwegian	Heath
-hegység	Hungarian	Mountains
-hei/Heide	Norwegian/German	Heath, moor
Hersónisos	Greek	Peninsula
Higashi-	Japanese	East, eastern
-hisar-	Turkish	Castle
Hisn	Arabic	Fort
-hø	Norwegian	Peak
Hoch/Hoë	German/Afrikaans	High
Hoek	Flemish	Cape, point
Hög/-høg(d)	Swedish/Norwegian	High, height
Höhe, Hohen-	German	Height

The listings above refer to a selection of related themes.
For more information, see the Contents (2-5).

Term	Language	Meaning
Hoog	Flemish	High
-høoj	Danish	Hill
Hora/Hory	Czech	Mountain/Mtns
Horn	German	Peak, summit
Horní	Czech	Upper
Hot	Mongolian	Town
-høy	Norwegian	Height
-hrad	Czech	Castle
Hu	Chinese	Lake
Hügel	German	Hill
Idd	Arabic	Well
Idhan	Arabic	Sand dunes
'Idwet	Arabic	Mountain
Île(s)/Ilha(s)	French/Portuguese	Island(s)
Illa, Illes	Catalan	Island, islands
im, in	German	In
Inférieur, -e	French	Lower
Insel(n)	German	Island(s)
Irmak	Turkish	Large river
'Irq	Arabic	Sand dunes
Isla(s)/Isle	Spanish/French	Island(s)
Islote	Spanish	Small island
Iso	Finnish	Big
Ísola, Isole	Italian	Island, islands
Istmo	Spanish	Isthmus
Jabal	Arabic	Mountain
-järvi	Finnish	Lake
-jaure, -javrre	Lappish	Lake
Jazirat/Jaza'ir	Arabic	Island/Islands
Jbel, Jebel	Arabic	Mountain
Jezero/Jezioro	Serbo-Croat/Polish	Lake
Jiang	Chinese	River
Jiao	Chinese	Point, reef
Jibal	Arabic	Mountains
-jima	Japanese	Island
-joki/-jokka	Finnish/Lappish	River
-jøkulen	Norwegian	Glacier
-jökull	Icelandic	Glacier
Jun	Arabic	Bay
Kaap	Afrikaans	Cape
-kai	Japanese	Sea, bay, inlet
Kali	Indonesian	River
Kamm	German	Crest, ridge
Kampung	Indonesian, Malay	Village
Kanaal/Kanal	Flemish/German, Russian	Canal
-kapp	Norwegian	Cape
Karif	Arabic	Well
Kathib	Arabic	Sand dunes
Káto	Greek	Lower
-kawa	Japanese	River
Kecil	Indonesian, Malay	Small
Kepulauan	Indonesian	Archipelago
Kereb	Arabic	Hill, ridge
Keski-	Finnish	Central, middle
Khalig, Khalij	Arabic	Bay, gulf
Khao	Thai	Peak
Khashm	Arabic	Mountain
Khawr, Khor/Khowr	Arabic/Persian	Inlet
Khrebet	Russian	Mountain range
Kis-	Hungarian	Small
Kita-	Japanese	North, northern
Klamm	German	Ravine
Klein	Afrikaans, German	Small
Klint/Klit	Danish	Cliff/Dunes
Klong	Thai	Canal, creek
Kloof	Afrikaans	Gorge
Ko/Koh	Thai/Cambodian	Island
-ko	Japanese	Lake, inlet
Kólpos	Greek	Gulf
Koog	German	Polder
Kop/Kopf	Afrikaans/German	Hill
Körfezi	Turkish	Bay, gulf
Kotlina	Czech, Polish	Basin, depression
Kotlovina	Russian	Depression
-köy	Turkish	Village
Kraj	Czech, Polish, Serbo-Croat	Region
Kray	Russian	Region
Kreis	German	District
Kryazh	Russian	Ridge
Kuala	Malay	Estuary
Küçük	Turkish	Small
Kuduk	Russian	Spring, well
Kuh	Persian	Mountain
Kul'	Russian	Lake
Kület	Arabic	Hill
Kum	Russian	Sandy desert
-kundo	Korean	Island group
-kylä	Finnish	Village
Lac	French	Lake
Laem	Thai	Point
Lago	Italian, Portug., Spanish	Lake
Lagoa	Portuguese	Lagoon
Laguna	Spanish	Lagoon, lake
Lam	Thai	Stream
Län	Swedish	Province
Land	German	Province, area
Lande	French	Heath, sandy moor
Las/Les	Polish/Czech, Russian	Forest, wood
Laut	Indonesia	Sea
Lednik	Russian	Glacier
lès, lez	French	Beside, near
Liedao	Chinese	Island group
Lille	Danish, Norwegian	Small
Liman	Russian	Bay, gulf
Liman, Limani	Turkish	Harbour, port
Límni	Greek	Lake, lagoon
Ling	Chinese	Mountain range
Llano	Spanish	Plain, prairie
Loma	Spanish	Hill
-luoto	Finnish	Rocky island
-lyng	Danish	Heath
Macizo	Spanish	Massif
Madinat	Arabic	City, town
Mae Nam	Thai	River
Mala/Malé	Serbo-Croat/Czech	Small
Malaya, -oye, -yy	Russian	Small
-man	Korean	Bay
Manâqîr	Arabic	Hills
Mar	Portuguese, Spanish	Sea
Marais	French	Marsh, swamp
Mare	Italian/Romanian	Sea/Big
Marsá	Arabic	Anchorage, inlet
Marsch	German	Fen, marsh
Masabb	Arabic	Estuary
Mashâsh	Arabic	Well
Massif	French	Mountains, upland
Mayor	Spanish	Higher, larger
Meer	Afrikaans, Flemish, German	Lake, sea
Méga, Megál-a, -i, -o	Greek	Big
Menor	Portuguese, Spanish	Lesser, smaller
Mer	French	Sea
Mersa	Arabic	Anchorage, inlet
Mesa, Meseta	Spanish	Tableland
Mesto	Czech, Serbo-Croat	Town
Mezzo	Italian	Middle, mid-
Miasto	Polish	Town
Mic/Mikr-í, ón	Romanian/Greek	Small
Mina'	Arabic	Harbour, port
Minami-	Japanese	South, southern
Minqâr	Arabic	Hill
-misaki	Japanese	Cape, point
Mishâsh, Mushâsh	Arabic	Well
Miti	Greek	Cape
Mittel-, Mitten-	German	Central, middle
Mjesto	Serbo-Croat	Town
Monasterio/Moni	Spanish/Greek	Monastery
Mont/Monte	French/Italian, Portuguese, Spanish	Mountain
Montagne(s)	French	Mountain(s)
Monti	Italian	Mountains
Moor	German	Bog, moor, swamp
Moos	German	Bog, moss
More	Russian	Sea
Mörön	Mongolian	River
Morro	Portuguese	Hill, mountain
-mose	Danish	Bog, moor
Moyen, -ne	French	Middle, mid-
Muara	Indonesian	Estuary
Mudiriyat	Arabic	Province
Muntii	Romanian	Mountains
-myr	Norwegian, Swedish	Moor, swamp
Mys	Russian	Cape
na	Bulgarian, Russian, Serbo-Croat	On
nad	Czech, Polish, Russian	Above, over
-nada	Japanese	Gulf, sea
Nádrz	Czech	Reservoir
-naes	Danish	Cape, point
Nafud	Arabic	Desert, dune
Nagor'ye	Russian	Highland, uplands
Nagy-	Hungarian	Big, great
Nahr	Arabic	River
Nakhon	Thai	Town
Nam	Korean, Vietnamese	South, southern
Nam	Burmese, Thai, Vietnamese	River
Nan	Chinese	South, southern
Naqb	Arabic	Pass
Nasb	Arabic	Hill, mountain
Né-a, -on, -os	Greek	New
Neder-	Flemish	Lower
Nehri	Turkish	River
Nei	Chinese	Inner
-nes	Icelandic, Norwegian	Cape, point
Neu-/Neuf, Neuve	German/French	New
Nevado	Spanish	Peak
-ni	Korean	Village
Nieder-	German	Lower
Nieu	Afrikaans	New
Nieuw-, -e, -en, -er	Flemish	New
Nishi	Japanese	West, western
-nísi	Greek	Island
Nizhn-eye, -iy, -iye, -yaya	Russian	Lower
Nízina/Nizni	Czech	Lowland/Lower
Nizmennost'	Russian	Lowland
Noord-	Flemish	North, northern
Nord	Danish, French, German	North, northern
Nordre, Nørre	Danish	Northern
Norra	Swedish	Northern
Norte	Portuguese, Spanish	North
Nos	Bulgarian, Russian	Point, spit
Nótios	Greek	Southern
Nou	Romanian	New
Nouv-eau, -elle	French	New
Nova	Italian	New
Nova, Novi	Bulgarian, Serbo-Croat	New
Nova, Novo	Portuguese	New
Nová, Nové, Novy	Czech	New
Nov-aya, -o, -oye, -yy, -yye	Russian	New
Nowa, Nowe, Nowy	Polish	New
Nudo	Spanish	Mountain
Nueva, Nuevo	Spanish	New
Nuruu	Mongolian	Mountains
Nusa	Indonesian	Island
Nuur	Mongolian	Lake
Ny-	Danish, Norwegian, Swedish	New
-ö, -ön/-ø	Swedish/Danish	Island
-oaivi, -oaivve	Lappish	Hill, mountain
Ober-	German	Upper
Oblast'	Russian	Province
Occidental	Spanish	Western
-odde	Danish, Norwegian	Cape, point
Ogla, Oglet	Arabic	Well
Okrug	Russian	District
Ömnö-	Mongolian	South, southern
Onder	Flemish	Lower
Öndör-	Mongolian	Upper
-oog	German	Island
Oost, -er, -elijk	Flemish	East, eastern
Orasu	Romanian	Town
Oriental, -e	French, Romanian, Spanish	Eastern
Ormani	Turkish	Forest
Órmos	Greek	Bay
Óros/Óri	Greek	Mountain/Mtns.
Ost-/Øster-	German/Danish, Norweg.	East, eastern
Ostan	Persian	Province
Östra	Swedish	East, eastern
Ostrov(a)	Russian	Island(s)
Otok/Otoci	Serbo-Croat	Island/Islands
Oud, -e, -en, -er	Flemish	Old
Oued	Arabic	Dry river-bed
Ovasi	Turkish	Plain
Over-	Danish, Flemish	Upper
Över-, Övre-	Norwegian, Swedish	Upper
-øy, -a	Norwegian	Island
Ozero, Ozera	Russian	Lake, lakes
-pää	Finnish	Hill
Palai-á, -ó, Palió	Greek	Old
Parbat	Urdu	Mountain
Parc	French	Park
Pas	French	Low pass, strait
Paso	Spanish	Pass, strait
Pass/Passo	Spanish/Italian	Pass
Pays	French	Region
Pegunungan	Indonesian	Mountain range
Pélagos	Greek	Sea
Peña(s)	Spanish	Cliff(s), rocks(s)
Pendi	Chinese	Basin
Penisola	Italian	Peninsula
Peñon	Spanish	Cliff
Pereval	Russian	Pass
Perv-o, -yy	Russian	First
Peski	Russian	Sands, desert
Petit, -e, -es	French	Little
Pic	French, Spanish	Peak, summit
Pico/Picacho	Portuguese, Spanish	Peak, summit
Pik	Russian	Peak, summit
Pingyuan	Chinese	Plain
Pizzo	Italian	Peak, summit
-plaat	Dutch	Sandbank, shoal
Plage	French	Beach
Plaine/Planicie	French/Spanish	Plain
Plaj(i)	Turkish	Beach(es)
Planalto	Portuguese	Plateau
Planina	Bulgarian, Serbo-Croat	Mountains
Platja/Playa	Catalan/Spanish	Beach
Plato	Afrikaans, Bulg., Russian	Plateau
Platte	German	Plateau, plain
Plosina	Czech	Tableland
Ploskogor'ye	Russian	Plateau
pod	Czech, Russian	Under
Pohor-í, -ie	Czech	Mountain range
Pointe	French	Cape, point
Poluostrov	Russian	Peninsula
Pólwysep	Polish	Peninsula
Pongo	Spanish	Water gap
Ponta, Pontal	Portuguese	Point
Portile	Romanian	Gate
Portillo	Spanish	Gap, pass
Porto	Catalan, Italian, Portug.	Harbour, port
Pradesh	Hindi	State
Praia	Portuguese	Beach, shore
près	French	Near
Presqu'île	French	Peninsula
Pri-	Russian	Near
Proliv	Russian	Strait

The listings above refer to a selection of related themes.
For more information, see the Contents (2-5).

Term	Language	Meaning
Protoka	Russian	Channel
Prusmyk	Czech	Pass
Przelecz	Polish	Pass
Pubu	Chinese	Waterfall
Pueblo	Spanish	Village
Puente	Spanish	Bridge
Puerta	Spanish	Narrow pass
Puerto	Spanish	Harbour, port
Puk-	Korean	North, northern
Pulau	Indonesian, Malay	Island
Puna	Spanish	Desert plateau
Punta	Catalan, Italian, Spanish	Cape, point
Puntjak	Indonesian	Mountain
Puy	French	Peak
Qa	Arabic	Depression
Qalamat, Qalib	Arabic	Well
Qanat	Arabic, Persian	U'ground conduit
Qararat	Arabic	Depression
Qâret	Arabic	Hill
Qiao	Chinese	Bridge
Qiuling	Chinese	Hills
Qoz	Arabic	Hill
Qu	Tibetan	Stream
Quan	Chinese	Spring
Quedas	Portuguese	Rapids
Qulban	Arabic	Wells
Qum	Persian	Sand
Qundao	Chinese	Archipelago
Qûr, Qurayyat	Arabic	Hills
Qurnat	Arabic	Peak
Quwayrat/Qurûn	Arabic	Hill/Hills
Ramlat	Arabic	Sands
Râs/Ra's	Arabic/Arabic, Persian	Cape, point
Raso	Portuguese	Upland
Ravnina/Razlivy	Russian	Plain
Região	Portuguese	Region
Represa	Portuguese	Dam
Reshteh	Persian	Mountain range
-retto	Japanese	Island chain
-rev	Norwegian	Cliff, reef
Ri	Tibetan	Mountain
-ri	Korean	Village
Ria/Ría	Portuguese/Spanish	River-mouth
Ribeirão	Portuguese	River
Ribeiro	Portuguese	Stream
Rio/Río	Portuguese/Spanish	River
Rivier/Rivière	Afrikaans/French	River
Rocher	French	Cliff, rock
Rocque	French	Rock
Rt	Serbo-Croat	Cape, point
Rücken	German	Ridge
Rud, Rudkhaneh	Persian	River
Rudohorie	Czech	Mountains
-saari	Finnish	Island
Sabkhat	Arabic	Salt-flat
Sagar, Sagara	Hindi	Lake
Sahl	Arabic	Plain
Sahra	Arabic	Desert
-saki	Japanese	Cape, point
Salada/Salar,		
Salina	Spanish	Salt lake/Salt pan
Salto	Portuguese, Spanish	Waterfall
-san	Japanese, Korean	Mountain
-sanchi	Japanese	Mountainous area
Saniyat	Arabic	Well
Sanmaek	Korean	Mountain range
-sanmyaku	Japanese	Mountain range
San	Italian, Portug., Spanish	Saint
Sankt/Sant	German/Catalan	Saint
Santa, Santo	Italian, Portug., Spanish	Saint
São	Portuguese	Saint
Satu	Romanian	Village
Schloss	German	Castle, mansion
Schutzgebiet	German	Reserve
Sebkra	Arabic	Salt-flat
See	German	Lake
-sehir	Turkish	Town
Selat	Indonesian	Channel, strait
Selatan	Indonesian, Malay	South, southern
-selkä	Finnish	Open water, ridge
Selo	Russian, Serbo-Croat	Village
Selva	Spanish	Forest, wood
-sen	Japanese	Mountain
Serra/Serrania	Catalan, Portug. /Span.	Mountain range
-seto	Japanese	Channel, strait
Sever-naya,		
-noye, -nyy, -o	Russian	North, northern
Sfintu	Romanian	Saint
Shahr	Persian	Town
Sha'ib, -an	Arabic	Watercourse
Shamo	Chinese	Desert
Shan	Chinese	Mountain(s)
Shandi	Chinese	Mountainous area
Shang	Chinese	Upper
Shankou	Chinese	Pass
Shanmai	Chinese	Mountain range
Sharm	Arabic	Cove, inlet
Shatt	Arabic	River, river-mouth
-shima/-shoto	Japanese	Island/Island group
Shuiku	Chinese	Reservoir
Sierra	Spanish	Mountain range
Silsilesi	Turkish	Mountain range
Sint	Afrikaans, Flemish	Saint
-sjø/sjön	Norwegian/Swedish	Lake
Skala, Skaly	Czech	Cliff, rock
-skog	Norwegian	Woods
-slette	Norwegian	Plain
Sliabh, Slieve	Gaelic	Mountain, upland
Sloboda	Russian	Suburb, large village
Sø	Danish, Norwegian	Lake
Söder-, Södra	Swedish	Southern
Solonchak	Russian	Salt lake
Sommet	French	Peak, summit
Sønder-	Danish	Southern
Søndre	Danish, Norwegian	Southern
Sopka	Russian	Hill
Sør	Norwegian	Southern
sous	French	Under
Spitze	German	Peak
Sredn-a, -i	Bulgarian	Central, middle
Sredn-e, -eye,		
-iy, -yaya	Russian	Central, middle
-stad	Afrikaans, Norwegian, Swedish	Town
-stadt	German	Town
Stara, Stari	Serbo-Croat	Old
Stará, Staré	Czech	Old
Star-aya, oye,		
-yy, -yye	Russian	Old
Stausee	German	Reservoir
Stenó	Greek	Pass, strait
Step'	Russian	Steppe
Stít	Czech	Peak
Stor-, Stora/Store	Swedish/Danish	Big
Strand	Gaelic, German	Beach
-strand	Danish, Norwegian, Swedish	Beach
Strasse	German	Road
-strede	Norwegian	Passage, strait
Strelka	Russian	Spit
Stretto	Italian	Strait
Sud	French	South
Süd(er)	German	South (southern)
Suhul	Arabic	Plain
Suid	Afrikaans	South
-suido	Japanese	Channel, strait
Sul	Portuguese	South
sul, sull'	Italian	On
Sund	Swedish	Sound, strait
Sungai	Indonesian, Malay	River
-suo	Finnish	Marsh, swamp
Supérieur/Superior	French/Spanish	Upper
Sur	Spanish	South
sur	French	On
Sveti	Serbo-Croat	Saint
Szent-	Hungarian	Saint
-take	Japanese	Peak
Tal	German	Valley
Tall(ât)	Arabic	Hill(s)
Tang	Persian	Pass, strait
Tanjung	Indonesian, Malay	Cape, point
Taraq	Arabic	Hills
Tasek	Malay	Lake
Tau	Russian	Mountain(s)
Tekojärvi	Finnish	Reservoir
Tell	Arabic	Hill
Teluk	Indonesian	Bay
Tengah	Indonesian	Middle
Teniet	Arabic	Pass
Tepe, Tepesi	Turkish	Hill, peak
Tepeler, Tepeleri	Turkish	Hills, peaks
Terre/Tierra	French/Spanish	Land
Thale	Thai	Lake
Tilat	Arabic	Hill
Timur	Indonesian	East, eastern
-tind, -tinderne	Norwegain	Peak, peaks
Tir'at	Arabic	Canal
-tji	Indonesian	Stream
-to	Japanese	Island
-toge	Japanese	Pass
-tong	Korean	Village
Tonle	Cambodian	Lake
-topp	Norwegian	Peak
Torrente	Spanish	Rapids
Travesía	Spanish	Desert
Tulul	Arabic	Hills
Túnel	Spanish	Tunnel
über	German	Above
-udden	Swedish	Cape, point
Új-	Hungarian	New
Ujung	Indonesian	Cape, point
-umi	Japanese	Inlet
Unter-	German	Lower
'Uqlat	Arabic	Well
-ura	Japanese	Inlet
'Urayq	Arabic	Sand ridge
'Uruq	Arabic	Area of dunes
Ust'ye	Russian	Estuary
Utara	Indonesian	North, northern
Uttar	Hindi	Northern
Uul	Mongolian	Mountains
Uval	Russian	Hill
'Uyun	Arabic	Springs
-vaara(t)	Finnish	Hill(s)
-vaart	Flemish	Canal
-våg	Norwegian	Bay
Val, Vall	Italian, Spanish	Valley
Vale	Portuguese, Romanian	Valley
Valle/Vallée	Italian, Spanish/French	Valley
Vallon	French	Small valley
-vann	Norwegian	Lake
-város	Hungarian	Town
-varre	Norwegian	Mountain
Väster, Västra	Swedish	Western
-vatn	Icelandic, Norwegian	Lake
-vatnet	Norwegian	Lake
-vatten, vattnet	Swedish	Lake
Vaux	French	Valleys
Vecchio	Italian	Old
Vechi	Romanian	Old
Velha, Velho	Portuguese	Old
Velik-a, -i	Serbo-Croat	Big
Velik-aya, -iy, -iye	Russian	Big
Vel'k-á, -é, -y	Czech	Big
Verkhn-e, -eye,		
-iy, -yaya	Russian	Upper
-vesi	Finnish	Lake, water
Vester	Danish	Western
Vest, Vestre	Norwegian	West, western
-vidda	Norwegian	Plateau
Vieja, Viejo/		
Vieux	Spanish/French	Old
Vig/-vik	Danish/Norwegian	Bay
Vila	Portuguese	Small town
Ville	French	Town
Víztároló	Hungarian	Reservoir
Vodokhranilishche	Russian	Reservoir
Volcán	Spanish	Volcano
Vorota	Russian	Channel, strait
Vostochn-aya,		
-oye, -yy	Russian	Eastern
Vozvyshennost'	Russian	Uplands
Vpadina	Russian	Depression
Vrch(y)	Czech	Mountain(s)
Vrchovina	Czech	Mountainous area
Vysocina	Czech	Upland
Vysok-aya, -oye	Russian	Upper
Wad	Flemish	Sand-flat
Wâdi, Wadi	Arabic	Watercourse
Wahat	Arabic	Oasis
Wai	Chinese	Outer
Wald	German	Forest
Wan/-wan	Chinese/Japanese	Bay
Wand	German	Cliff
Wasser	German	Lake, water
Wes-	Afrikaans	West
West, Wester	Flemish, German	West
Wielk-a, -i, -ie, -o	Polish	Big
Wysok-a, -i, -ie	Polish	Upper
Xi	Chinese	Stream, west
Xia	Chinese	Gorge, lower
Xian	Chinese	County
Xiao	Chinese	Small
Xu	Chinese	Islet
-yama	Japanese	Mountain(s)
Yang	Chinese	Ocean
Yarimadasi	Turkish	Peninsula
Yeni	Turkish	New
Yli-	Finnish	Upper
Ytre-	Norwegian	Outer
Ytter-	Norwegian, Swedish	Outer
Yuan	Chinese	Spring
Yugo-	Russian	Southern
Yunhe	Chinese	Canal
Yuzhn-aya, -o, -oye, -yy	Russian	South, southern
-zaki	Japanese	Cape, point
Zalew	Polish	Bay, inlet, lagoon
Zaliv	Russian	Bay
-zan	Japanese	Mountain
Zapadn-aya, -o, -oye, -yy	Russian	West, western
Zatoka	Polish	Gulf
-zee	Flemish	Sea
Zemlya	Russian	Land
-zhen	Chinese	Town
Zhong	Chinese	Middle
Zhou	Chinese	Islet
Zui	Chinese	Point, spit
Zuid	Flemish	South
Zuid-elijk, er	Flemish	Southern

See also... Climate maps (30,45); Appendix 5: Glossary of Foreign Geographical Terms (101-103)

The listings above refer to a selection of related themes. For more information, see the Contents (2-5).

6: Glossary of Regional Climate Terms

An alphabetical list of the main climate terms used in various parts of the world.

Benguela Current *Africa*
A cold current flowing north along the west coast of South Africa, cooling the coastal region.

Berg Wind *Africa*
A hot dry wind which blows from the interior to the coastal regions of Namibia and South Africa.

Bora *Europe*
A cold dry wind which blows from the N and NE, affecting the Adriatic coastlines of Croatia, Italy and Slovenia.

California Current *North America*
A cold current which flows south along the west coast of California and Mexico, cooling the coastal region, and responsible for the frequent sea fogs particularly during the summer.

Canary Current *Africa*
An extension of the North Atlantic Drift (qv), flowing south along the NW Africa coast and moderating temperatures in the coastal region.

Chinook *North America*
A warm dry wind which blows down the eastern slopes of the Rockies, rapidly melting lying snow.

Crachin *Asia*
Light rain in the northern mountains and coastal regions of Vietnam.

Cyclone *Asia*
Tropical cyclones (qv) in the SW Indian Ocean are simply called cyclones. The season lasts from November to May.

El Niño *South America*
A change in the ocean-atmosphere system in the Pacific, increasing water temperatures in the central and eastern equatorial Pacific Ocean and bringing rain to the NW coast of South America. A periodic phenomenon, it often affects the western coast of America as far north as California. In some years the weather pattern of the whole American continent can be disrupted, and in exceptional years its effects can be experienced worldwide.

Etesian Wind / Meltemi *Europe*
A wind blowing from the N and NW in the eastern Mediterranean and the Aegean, often creating rough seas.

Föhn *Europe*
A wind which blows down Alpine valleys, warming as it descends, and melts snow rapidly.

Garúa *South America*
A heavy mist on the Pacific slope of the Andes in a normally very dry part of the coast.

Ghibli *Africa*
Local name for the Sirocco (qv) in Libya.

Guinea Monsoon *Africa*
Warm humid winds blowing from the SW in West Africa between April and September, associated with the rainy season.

Gulf Stream *North America*
A warm current which flows NE from the Gulf of Mexico. After passing Newfoundland, it divides and follows three separate routes: 1. northwest towards Europe (the North Atlantic Drift (qv)); 2. southeast; 3. recirculating around an area north of Bermuda.

Harmattan *Africa*
A dry and dusty NE wind in West Africa blowing from the Sahara, associated with the dry season; cool at night and warm in the day. Opposite of the Guinea Monsoon (qv).

Hurricane *North America*
The name used for a tropical cyclone (qv) in the N Atlantic and NE Pacific Oceans. The Atlantic hurricane season lasts from June to November, the peak period being August to October. The NE Pacific season is from June to October. For more information on N Atlantic hurricanes, see the N America climate page. (The term is also used in the Beaufort Scale of wind speed: force 12 and above).

Kharif *Asia*
The rainy season in northern India and Arab countries.

Khamsin / Sharav *Africa*
A hot dry wind blowing from the S and SE in the eastern Mediterranean, warming the coastal region and helping to create dust storms and a hazy atmosphere.

Labrador Current *North America*
A cold current flowing south along the east coast of Canada, carrying icebergs and keeping the coastal region relatively cool druing the summer; fogs are caused off the Newfoundland coast where the current meets the warmer Gulf Stream flowing NE from the Gulf of Mexico.

La Niña *South America*
The opposite phenomenon to El Niño. Warm surface water flows towards Asia and colder water from the ocean depths moves to the surface in the eastern equatorial Pacific. Evaporation decreases and rainfall in the region is reduced. Often La Niña occurs the year after El Niño, with drought affecting the areas which experienced flooding the year before.

Leveche *Europe*
A hot, dry and dusty wind in southern Spain which blows from the Sahara.

Mistral *Europe*
A strong cold dry wind blowing from the north in southern France; known as Cers in Aude département.

Monsoon Winds *Asia*
Seasonal winds which change direction during the year; during the dry season in India the NE monsoon blows dry air from the land and during the wet season the SW monsoon blows humid air from the ocean, bringing heavy rain (**Monsoon Rains**). The term is also used in Africa and Australasia.

Mozambique Current / Agulhas Current *Africa*
A warm current flowing south and west along the coast of Mozambique and eastern South Africa, warming the coastal region.

North Atlantic Drift *Europe*
An extension of the Gulf Stream (qv) which helps to maintain relatively mild winters in the British Isles and along the Norwegian coast.

Peru Current / Humboldt Current *South America*
A cold current flowing north along the west coast of South America and cooling the coastal region as far as the Equator.

Severe Cyclonic Storm *Asia*
The name used for a tropical cyclone (qv) in the N Indian Ocean, most likely to occur in May-June & Oct-Nov (Arabian Sea) and Apr-May & Oct-Dec (Bay of Bengal).

Severe Tropical Cyclone *Asia*
The name used for a tropical cyclone (qv) in the SW Pacific Ocean, peak period December to March and the SE Indian Ocean, where it is also known as a Willy-Willy (qv), peak period January-March.

Shamal *Africa*
A hot dry wind which blows from the NW in Iraq and The Gulf.

Sirocco *Europe*
A hot dusty wind blowing towards Europe from north Africa. Known as the Ghibli (qv) in Libya and Leveche (qv) in Spain. Its origins are the same as the Khamsin (qv) or Sharav (qv). On the northern Mediterranean coast, particularly in southern Italy, the wind is moist after crossing the Mediterranean.

Tropical Cyclone *Asia and North America*
A storm with low atmospheric pressure at the centre and strong winds blowing around it, accompanied by a great deal of precipitation. It rotates anticlockwise in the northern hemisphere and clockwise in the southern. The central area has light winds and higher temperatures (the 'eye'), feeling oppresive after the strong winds preceding it, but is soon followed by even stronger winds in the opposite direction. Temperate cyclones are much less violent and are usually called depressions or lows. Tropical cyclones which reach winds of at least 17 metres/second (39mph) they are called tropical storms and assigned a name. If winds reach 33 metres/second (74mph) they are called in different parts of the world: hurricane, typhoon, severe tropical cyclone, severe cyclonic storm, willy-willy or simply cyclone.

Typhoon *Asia*
The term for a tropical cyclone (qv) in the NW Pacific and the China Seas. The typhoon season lasts from May to January but most occur between July and October.

Willy-Willy *Asia*
The name used for a tropical cyclone (qv) affecting the coasts of northern Australia. Likely to occur between December to April, the peak period is January to March.

7: The World's Major Urban Areas

The list shows the world's largest urban agglomerations, with UN estimates of their population in 2005. The UN defines the term 'urban agglomeration' as a contiguous area inhabited at a density regarded as urban, ignoring administrative boundaries.

The ten largest cities in 1900 and in 1800 are listed at the foot of the page.

Urban area & country	Pop. ('000)
Tokyo-Kawasaki-Yokohama, Japan	35,327
Mexico City, Mexico	19,013
New York-Newark, NY, USA	18,498
Mumbai (Bombay), India	18,336
São Paulo, Brazil	18,333
Delhi, India	15,334
Kolkata (Calcutta), India	14,299
Buenos Aires, Argentina	13,349
Jakarta, Indonesia	13,194
Shanghai, China	12,665
Dhaka, Bangladesh	12,560
Los Angeles-Long Beach-Santa Ana, CA, USA	12,146
Karachi, Pakistan	11,819
Rio de Janeiro, Brazil	11,469
Osaka-Kobe, Japan	11,286
Cairo, Egypt	11,146
Lagos, Nigeria	11,135
Beijing, China	10,849
Metro Manila, the Philippines	10,677
Moscow, Russian Fed.	10,672
Paris, France	9,854
Istanbul, Turkey	9,760
Seoul, Rep. of Korea	9,592
Tianjin, China	9,346
Chicago, IL, USA	8,711
Lima, Peru	8,180
London, United Kingdom	7,615
Bogotá, Colombia	7,594
Tehran, Iran	7,352
Hong Kong, China	7,182
Chennai (Madras), India	6,915
Bangkok, Thailand	6,604
Rhine-Ruhr North, Germany	6,559
Bochum-Dortmund-Duisburg-Essen	
Bangalore, India	6,532
Lahore, Pakistan	6,373
Hyderabad, India	6,145
Wuhan, China	6,003
Baghdad, Iraq	5,910
Kinshasa, Dem. Rep. of Congo	5,717
Santiago, Chile	5,623
Riyadh, Saudi Arabia	5,514
Miami, FL, USA	5,380
Philadelphia, PA, USA	5,325
St Petersburg, Russian Fed	5,315
Belo Horizonte, Brazil	5,304
Ahmadabad, India	5,171
Madrid, Spain	5,145
Toronto, OT, Canada	5,060
Ho Chi Minh City, Vietnam	5,030
Chongqing, China	4,975
Shenyang, China	4,916
Dallas-Fort Worth, TX, USA	4,612
Khartoum, Sudan	4,495
Pune (Poona), India	4,485
Barcelona, Spain	4,424
Sydney, NS, Australia	4,388
Singapore	4,372
Boston, MA, USA	4,313
Atlanta, GA, USA	4,284
Houston, TX, USA	4,283
Washington, DC, USA	4,190
Chittagong, Bangladesh	4,171
Hanoi, Vietnam	4,147
Yangon (Rangoon), Myanmar	4,082
Bandung, Indonesia	4,020
Milan, Italy	4,007

Urban area & country	Pop. ('000)
Detroit, MI, USA	3,980
Ankara, Turkey	3,953
Guadalajara, Mexico	3,905
Guangzhou, China	3,881
Jeddah, Saudi Arabia	3,807
Pôrto Alegre, Brazil	3,795
Alexandria, Egypt	3,760
Casablanca, Morocco	3,743
Rhine-Main, Germany	3,700
Frankfurt-Darmstadt-Wiesbaden	
Surat, India	3,671
Melbourne, VI, Australia	3,663
Busan, Rep. of Korea	3,527
Recife, Brazil	3,527
Monterrey, Mexico	3,517
Abidjan, Côte d'Ivoire	3,516
Montréal, QU, Canada	3,511
Chengdu, China	3,478
Phoenix-Mesa, AZ, USA	3,393
San Francisco-Oakland, CA, USA	3,342
Brasília, Brazil	3,341
Salvador, Brazil	3,331
Berlin, Germany	3,328
Rhine-Ruhr Middle, Germany	3,325
Düsseldorf-Mönchenglad.-Wuppertal	
Johannesburg, South Africa	3,288
Kabul, Afghanistan	3,288
Pyongyang, DPR of Korea	3,284
Caracas, Venezuela	3,276
Fortaleza, Brazil	3,261
Algiers, Algeria	3,260
Xi'an, China	3,256
Athens, Greece	3,238
Medellín, Colombia	3,236
Nagoya, Japan	3,189
Cape Town, South Africa	3,103
Changchun, China	3,092
Rhine-Ruhr South, Germany	3,084
Bonn-Cologne-Leverkusen	
East Rand (Ekurhuleni), S. Africa	3,043
Kanpur, India	3,040
Tel Aviv-Yafo, Israel	3,025
Seattle, WA, USA	2,959
Katowice, Poland	2,914
Naples, Italy	2,905
Addis Ababa, Ethiopia	2,899
Harbin, China	2,898
Kano, Nigeria	2,884
Curitiba, Brazil	2,871
Luanda, Angola	2,839
San Diego, CA, USA	2,818
Fukuoka-Kitakyushu, Japan	2,815
Nanjing, China	2,806
Jaipur, India	2,796
Zibo, China	2,775
Surabaya, Indonesia	2,735
Dalian, China	2,709
Stuttgart, Germany	2,705
Hamburg, Germany	2,686
Dar es Salaam, Tanzania	2,683
Jinan, China	2,654
Durban, South Africa	2,643
Incheon, Rep. of Korea	2,642
Campinas, Brazil	2,640
Rome, Italy	2,628
Kiev, Ukraine	2,623
Lucknow, India	2,589
Cali, Colombia	2,583
Faisalabad, Pakistan	2,533

1900:

London, United Kingdom	6,500
New York, USA	4,200
Paris, France	3,300
Berlin, Germany	2,700
Chicago, USA	1,700
Vienna, Austro-Hungarian Empire	1,700
Tokyo, Japan	1,500
St Petersburg, Russia	1,400
Manchester, United Kingdom	1,400
Philadelphia, USA	1,400

1800:

Peking, China	1,100
London, Great Britain	900
Canton, China	800
Tokyo (Edo), Japan	700
Constantinople, Ottoman Empire	600
Paris, France	550
Naples, Kingdom of Naples	450
Hangchow, China	400
Osaka, Japan	380
Kyoto, Japan	380

▶ *See also...* UNESCO Heritage (48-49)

*The listings above refer to a selection of related themes.
For more information, see the Contents (2-5).*

8: The World's Tallest Buildings

Height is measured from the street level of the main entrance to the structural or architectural top of the building, including spires but excluding antennae and flag poles. The list shows the world's tallest traditional buildings (structures intended primarily for human habitation with the great majority of their height divided into occupiable levels). Buildings under construction, TV-tower hybrids and other structures not recognised as traditional buildings are excluded. The world's tallest freestanding structure is Toronto's CN Tower (553m).

Name & location	*Height (m)*	*Date*
Taipei 101, Taipei, Taiwan	509	2004
Petronas Tower 1, Kuala Lumpur, Malaysia	452	1998
Petronas Tower 2, Kuala Lumpur, Malaysia	452	1998
Sears Tower, Chicago, IL, USA	442	1974
Jin Mao Tower, Shanghai, China	421	1998
Two International Finance Cent., Hong Kong, China	415	2003
CITIC Plaza, Guangzhou, China	391	1997
Shun Hing Square, Shenzhen, China	384	1996
Empire State Building, New York, NY, USA	381	1931
Central Plaza, Hong Kong, China	374	1992
Bank of China Tower, Hong Kong, China	367	1990
Emirates Office Tower, Dubai, UAE	355	2000
Tuntex Sky Tower, Kaohsiung, Taiwan	348	1997
Aon Center, Chicago, IL, USA	346	1973
The Centre, Hong Kong, China	346	1998
John Hancock Center, Chicago, IL, USA	344	1969
Shimao International Plaza, Shanghai, China	333	2005
Wuhan International Securities Bldg, Wuhan, China	331	2005
Ryugyong Hotel, Pyongyang, DPR of Korea	330	1992
Q1 Tower, Surfers Paradise, QL, Australia	323	2005
Burj al Arab, Dubai, UAE	321	1999
Chrysler Building, New York, NY, USA	319	1930
Nina Tower I, Hong Kong, China	319	2005
Bank of America Plaza, Atlanta, GA, USA	312	1992
US Bank Tower, Los Angeles, CA, USA	310	1989
Menara Telekom, Kuala Lumpur, Malaysia	310	2001
Jumeirah Emirates Towers Hotel, Dubai, UAE	309	2000
AT&T Corporate Center, Chicago, IL, USA	307	1989
JPMorganChase Tower, Houston, TX, USA	305	1982
Baiyoke Tower II, Bangkok, Thailand	304	1997
Two Prudential Plaza, Chicago, IL, USA	303	1990
Kingdom Centre, Riyadh, Saudi Arabia	302	2002
First Canadian Place, Toronto, ON, Canada	298	1976
Yokohama Landmark Tower, Yokohama, Japan	296	1993
Wells Fargo Plaza, Houston, TX, USA	296	1983
311 South Wacker Drive, Chicago, IL, USA	293	1990
SEG Plaza, Shenzhen, China	292	2000
American International, New York, NY, USA	290	1932
Key Tower, Cleveland, OH, USA	289	1991
Plaza 66, Shanghai, China	288	2001
One Liberty Place, Philadelphia, PA, USA	288	1987
Bank of America Tower, Seattle, WA, USA	285	1985
Tomorrow Square, Shanghai, China	285	2003
Chongqing World Trade Centre, Chongqing, China	283	2005
Cheung Kong Centre, Hong Kong, China	283	1999
The Trump Building, New York, NY, USA	283	1930
Bank of America Plaza, Dallas, TX, USA	281	1985
OUB Centre, Singapore	280	1986
Republic Plaza, Singapore	280	1995
UOB (United Overseas Bank) Plaza One, Singapore	280	1992
Citicorp Center, New York, NY, USA	279	1977
Hong Kong New World Tower, Shanghai, China	278	2002
Scotia Plaza, Toronto, ON, Canada	275	1988
Williams Tower, Houston, TX, USA	275	1983
Wuhan World Trade Tower, Wuhan, China	273	1998
Renaissance Tower, Dallas, TX, USA	270	1974
Dapeng International Plaza, Guangzhou, China	269	2004
21st Century Tower, Dubai, UAE	269	2003
Al Faisaliyah Center, Riyadh, Saudi Arabia	267	2000
900 North Michigan Avenue, Chicago, IL, USA	265	1989

9: The World's Longest Bridge Spans

Name & location	*Type*	*Length (m)*	*Date*
Akashi Kaikyo, Kobe–Akashi Island, Japan	Suspension	1,991	1998
Storebælt East, Fyn (Fünen)–Sjælland (Zealand), Denmark	Suspension	1,624	1998
Runyang South, Yangtze River, Zhenjiang, Jiangsu, China	Suspension	1,490	2005
Humber, Kingston upon Hull, England, UK	Suspension	1,410	1981
Jiangyin, Yangtze River, Jiangsu, China	Suspension	1,385	1999
Tsing Ma, Lantau Island–Tsing Yi Island, Hong Kong, China	Suspension	1,377	1997
Verrazano Narrows, Brooklyn–Staten Island, NY, USA	Suspension	1,298	1964
Golden Gate, San Francisco Bay, CA, USA	Suspension	1,280	1937
Höga Kusten (High Coast), Ångermanälven R., Kramfors, Sweden	Suspension	1,210	1997
Mackinac Straits, Mackinaw City–St Ignace, MI, USA	Suspension	1,158	1957
Minami Bisan-Seto, Kojima–Sakaide [Honshu–Shikoku], Japan	Suspension	1,100	1988
Bosporus II (Fatih Sultan Mehmet), Turkey	Suspension	1,090	1988
Bosporus I (Atatürk), Turkey	Suspension	1,074	1973
George Washington, Hudson River, NJ-NY, USA	Suspension	1,067	1931
Kurushima Kaikyo 3;2, Onomichi–Imabari [Honshu–Shikoku], Japan	Suspension	1,030;1,020	1999
Ponte 25 de Abril, Tagus River, Lisbon, Portugal	Suspension	1,013	1966
Forth Road, Edinburgh, Scotland, UK	Suspension	1,006	1964
• LONGEST BRIDGE SPANS OF OTHER TYPES:			
Tatara, Onomichi – Imabari [Honshu – Shikoku], Japan	Cable-stayed	890	1999
Pont de Normandie, Seine River, Le Havre, France	Cable-stayed	856	1995
Pont de Québec, St Lawrence River, QC, Canada	Cantilever Truss	549	1917
Forth Rail, Edinburgh, Scotland, UK	Cantilever Truss	521	1890
Lupu, Huangpu River, Shanghai, China	Steel Arch	550	2003
New River Gorge, Fayetteville, WV, USA	Steel Arch	518	1977

10: The World's Longest Tunnels

Name & location (excludes metro tunnels)	*Type*	*Length (km)*	*Date*
Seikan, Tsugaru Strait [Honshu–Hokkaido], Japan	Rail	53.9	1988
Channel Tunnel, Strait of Dover [England–France]	Rail	50.5	1994
Iwate Ichinohe, Tohoku Shinkansen, Honshu, Japan	Rail	25.8	2002
Lærdal, Lærdal–Aurland, Sogn og Fjordane, Norway	Road	24.5	2000
Shimizu, Joetsu Shinkansen, Honshu, Japan	Rail	22.2	1982
Simplon II; I, Brig, Switzerland–Iselle, Italy	Rail	19.8;19.8	1922; '06
Vereina, Selfranga–Sagliains, Switzerland	Rail	19.1	1999
Shin-Kanmon, Sanyo Shinkansen [Honshu–Kyushu], Japan	Rail	18.7	1975
Appennino, 'Direttissima' Bologna–Florence, Italy	Rail	18.5	1934
Qinling I-II, Xi'an–Ankang Line, Shaanxi, China	Rail	18.5	2002
Gotthard (Road), Göschenen–Airolo, Switzerland	Road	16.9	1980
Rokko, Sanyo Shinkansen [Osaka–Kobe], Honshu, Japan	Rail	16.3	1972
Furka Base, Oberwald–Realp, Switzerland	Rail	15.4	1982
Haruna, Joetsu Shinkansen, Honshu, Japan	Rail	15.4	1982
Severomuysk, Baikal-Amur Line, Russian Federation	Rail	15.3	2001
Gorigamine, Hokuriku Shinkansen, Japan	Rail	15.2	1997
Monte Santomarco, Páola–Cosenza, Italy	Rail	15.0	1987
Gotthard (Rail), Andermatt–Airolo, Switzerland	Rail	15.0	1882
Nakayama, Joetsu Shinkansen, Japan	Rail	14.9	1982
Mount Macdonald, Rogers Pass, Glacier Nat. Park, BC, Canada	Rail	14.7	1988
Lötschberg, Kandersteg–Goppenstein, Switzerland	Rail	14.6	1913
Romeriksporten, Oslo–Gardermoen Airport, Norway	Rail	14.6	1999
Dayaoshan, Hengyang–Guangzhou Line, Guangdong, China	Rail	14.3	1987
Arlberg, Langen–St Anton, Austria	Road	14.0	1978

11: World Monuments Fund

The World Monuments Fund (http://wmf.org) is a New York-based non-profit organisation dedicated to the conservation of culturally and historically significant works of art and architecture around the world. The Fund calls attention to imperiled cultural heritage sites by publishing a list every two years of the world's 100 most endangered sites. The 2006 list is shown below.

• UNITED STATES & CANADA
Ennis Brown House, Los Angeles, CA
Hanging Flume, Montrose County, CO
Bluegrass cultural landscape, central KY
Cyclorama Center, Gettysburg, PA
Mount Lebanon Shaker Village, New Lebanon, NY
Dutch Reformed Church, Newburgh, NY
2 Columbus Circle, New York, NY
Ellis Island Baggage and Dormitory Building, New York, NY

• LATIN AMERICA & THE CARIBBEAN
Pimería Alta Missions, Sonora, Mexico
San Nicolás Obispo, Morelia, Mexico
Mexico City historic centre, Mexico
Chalcatzingo, Morelos, Mexico
San Juan Bautista Cuauhtinchan, Puebla, Mexico
Naranjo, El Petén, Guatemala
San Miguel Arcangel and Santa Cruz de Roma, Oanchimalco and Huizucar, El Salvador
Panama Canal area, Panama
Finca Vigia (Hemingway's House), San Francisco de Paula, Cuba
La Guaira historic city, Venezuela
Túcume archaeological site, Lambayeque, Peru
Cajamarquilla, Lima, Peru
Presbítero Maestro Cemetery, Lima, Peru
Quinta Heeren, Lima, Peru
Revash funerary complex, near Chachapoyas, Peru
Convent of San Francisco and Historic Olinda, Olinda, Brazil
Cerros Pintados, Tarapacá, Chile
Tulor Village, Antofagasta, Chile

• EUROPE (including Turkey)
Sandviken Bay, Bergen, Norway
Helsinki-Malmi Airport, Finland
St Vincent's Street Church, Glasgow, Scotland
St Mary's Church, Stow, Lincolnshire
Wonderul Barn, Kildare, Ireland
Segovia Aqueduct, Spain
Teatro Capitolio, Lisbon, Portugal
Santa Maria in Stelle Hypogeum, Verona, Italy
Civita di Bagnoregio, Bagnoregio, Italy
Cimitero Acattolico, Rome, Italy
Temple of Portunus, Rome, Italy
Academy of Hadrian's Villa, Tivoli, Italy
Portici Royal Palace, Naples, Italy
Murgia del Trulli, Puglia, Italy
Jerusalem Hospital of the Teutonic Order, Malbork, Poland
Mausoleum of Karol Scheibler, Lodz, Poland
Lednicke-Rovne Historical Park, Slovak Republic
Novi Dvori Castle, Zapresic, Croatia
St Blaise Church, Dubrovnik, Croatia
Mehmed-Pasha Sokolovic Bridge, Visegrad, Bosnia-Herzegovina
Subotica Synagogue, Serbia
Prizren historic centre, Serbia
Treskavec Monastery and Church, FYR of Macedonia
Oradea Fortress, Romania
Helike archaeological site, Achaia, Greece
Little Hagia Sophia, Istanbul, Turkey
Aphrodisias, near Denizli, Turkey
Riga Cathedral, Latvia

• RUSSIAN FEDERATION
Melnikov's House-Studio, Moscow
Narkomfin Building, Moscow
Semenovskoe-Otrada, Moscow region

• AFRICA
Sabil Ruqayya Dudu, Cairo, Egypt
Tarabay al-Sharify, Cairo, Egypt
Suakin, Sudan
Luxor West Bank, Egypt
Asmara historic city centre and theatre, Eritrea
Massawa historic town, Eritrea
Kidane-Mehret Church, Senafe, Eritrea
Tarrafal Concentration Camp, Cape Verde
Chinguetti Mosque, Mauritania
Old Fourah Bay College, Freetown, Sierra Leone
Benin City earthworks, Nigeria
Bafut Palace, Bafut, Cameroon
Mtwapa heritage site, Kilifi, Kenya
Richtersveld cultural landscape, northern Cape Province, South Africa

• ASIA
Amrit archaeological site, Syria
Shayzar Castle, Syria
Tell Mozan (Ancient Urkesh), NE Syria
Tripoli International Fairground, Lebanon
Chehabi Citadel, Hasbaya, Lebanon
Tell Balatah (Shechem or Ancient Nablus), Nablus, Palestine NRA
Jvari Monastery, Mtshekta, Georgia
Cultural heritage sites countrywide, Iraq
Bam, Iran
Haji Piyada Mosque, Balkh, Afghanistan
Thatta monuments, Pakistan
Mian Nasir Mohamed Graveyard, Dadu district, Pakistan
Guru Lhakhang and Sumda Chung Temples, Ladakh, India
Dhangkar Gompa, Himachal Pradesh, India
Watson's Hotel, Mumbai, India
Dalhousie Square, Kolkata, India
Sonargaon-Panam City, Bangladesh
Patan Royal Palace complex, Nepal
Tianshui traditional houses, Gansu, China
Qikou Town, Shanxi, China
Cockcrow Post Town, Huailai, Hebei, China
Lu Mansion, Dongyang, Zhejiang, China
Stone Towers of southwest China, China
Tuanshan Historical Village, Yunnan, China
Chom Phet cultural landscape, Luang Prabang, Laos
Omo Hada, Nias, Indonesia

• AUSTRALASIA & OCEANIA
Dampier Rock Art Complex, Burrup Peninsula, WA, Australia
Pulemelei Mound, Palauli, Letolo Plantation, Samoa

• ANTARCTICA
Sir Ernest Shackleton's Expedition Hut

The listings above refer to a selection of related themes.
For more information, see the Contents (2-5).

12: City Nicknames

Thousands of cities world-wide have a nickname, and many have more than one. This list has limited itself to a selection of important cities, and to a maximum of four nicknames for each.

Nicknames can have several origins. Some date back centuries, while others are recent and often fanciful inventions by marketing companies or tourist offices. Many refer to a real or imagined pre-eminence in agricultural or industrial production, others to qualities of architecture, location or nightlife that the city sees itself as possessing. Some may have been given to one city by another in a spirit of rivalry, friendly or otherwise. These are often obscure to anyone not from that area, and occasionally strikingly offensive, and so have generally not been included here. Apologies to any city where a particularly uncomplimentary nickname has slipped in by mistake.

Two of the most popular types of nicknames are, firstly, a comparison with a more famous city such as Athens, Paris or Venice because of similar characteristics; and secondly, the claim to be the 'World capital of...' In some cases this refers more to past glory than present reality. The world capitals which have not been included here include those of fruitcake, hubcaps, rhubarb pie, snacks, polar bears, fire hydrants, curtains, gumboots, horseradish sauce and barbed wire. Whatever the reason for a nickname, and however accurate it may be, each gives a clue as to how a city sees itself, or how it would wish others to do so.

Aberdeen, Scotland	Granite City; Silver City
Abidjan, Côte d'Ivoire	Paris of Africa
Adelaide, SA, Australia	City of Churches
Akron, OH, USA	Rubber City
Albuquerque, NM, USA	Duke City
Alexandria, Egypt	Pearl of the Mediterranean
Allentown, PA, USA	Cement Town; Truck Capital of the World
Alleppey, India	Venice of the East
Amsterdam, The Netherlands	Venice of the North; Gateway to Europe
Anchorage, AK, USA	City of Lights; Anchortown; The End of the World
Ancona, Italy	Princess of the Adriatic; Doric City
Annapolis, MD, USA	Crabtown; Sailing Capital of the World; Naptown
Aosta, Italy	The Rome of the Alps
Århus, Denmark	World's Smallest Metropolis
Asheville, NC, USA	Paris of the South
Atlanta, GA, USA	Athens of the South; Phoenix City of the South; Gate City of the South; Dogwood City
Auckland, New Zealand	City of Sails, Queen City; Big Smoke
Augusta, GA, USA	Home of the Masters; Garden City
Austin, TX, USA	Live Music Capital of the World; City of the Violet Crown
Ávila, Spain	City of Saints and Stones
Bacolod, the Philippines	City of Smiles
Baguio, the Philippines	Summer Capital of the Philippines; City of Pines
Baltimore, MD, USA	Monument City; Charm City; City That Reads; Mob Town
Bangalore, India	India's Silicon Valley; City of Gardens
Bangkok, Thailand	Venice of the East
Bangor, Wales	Athens of Wales
Bari, Italy	Small Paris
Barranquilla, Colombia	The Sandy, Curramba the Beautiful
Basra, Iraq	Venice of the Middle East
Bayamón, Puerto Rico	City of the Cowboys
Beijing, China	The Forbidden City
Beirut, Lebanon	Paris of the Middle East
Belgrade, Serbia	White City
Benares, India	Luminous City
Bérgamo, Italy	City of Garibaldi's Thousand
Berkeley, CA, USA	Athens of the West
Berlin, Germany	Spree-Athens; Grey City
Berne, Switzerland	Zürich West
Billings, MT, USA	Star of the Big Sky Country; Magic City; City Beneath the Rimrocks
Birmingham, AL, USA	Magic City; Pittsburgh of the South
Birmingham, England	Venice of the North; Brum; City of a Thousand Trades
Bogotá, Colombia	Athens of South America
Boise, ID, USA	City of Trees
Bologna, Italy	The Fat One; The Learned One; The Red One
Bolzano, Italy	Door to the Dolomites
Bordeaux, France	Wine Capital of the World
Boston, MA, USA	Puritan City; Cradle of Liberty; Athens of America; Beantown
Braga, Portugal	City of the Bishops
Brandon, MN, Canada	Paris of the Prairies
Bremen, Germany	Key to the World
Bréscia, Italy	Lioness of Italy
Bridgeport, CT, USA	Park City
Brighton, England	Liberal City
Brisbane, QL, Australia	River City; Brisvegas
Bruges, Belgium	Venice of the North
Bucharest, Romania	Little Paris
Budapest, Hungary	Pearl of the Danube
Buenos Aires, Argentina	Paris of Latin America; Queen of the Plata
Buffalo, NY, USA	Bison City; Nickel City; Queen City of the Great Lakes; City of Good Neighbors
Bydgoszcz, Poland	Venice of the North
Caguas, Puerto Rico	Country City
Calgary, AL, Canada	Stampede City; Canada's Oil Capital; Cowtown; Gateway to the Rockies
Cali, Colombia	The Sultaness of the Valley
Cambridge (and area), England	Silicon Fen
Cambridge, MA, USA	Moscow on the Charles
Campbell River, BC, Canada	Salmon Capital of the World
Campinas, Brazil	Brazilian Silicon Valley
Canberra, AC, Australia	Bush Capital
Cape Town, South Africa	Mother City
Carolina, Puerto Rico	Giant City
Caserta, Italy	Versailles of Italy
Casper, WY, USA	Oil Capital of the Rockies; Ghost Town
Cebu, the Philippines	Queen City of the South
Cedar Rapids, IA, USA	City of Five Seasons
Charleston, SC, USA	Palmetto City; America's Most Historic City; Marina City; Holy City
Charleston, WV, USA	Chemicalville
Charlotte, NC, USA	Queen City; Hornet's Nest
Chattanooga, TN, USA	Scenic City; Dynamo of Dixie
Chengdu, China	Brocade City; City of Hibiscus
Cheyenne, WY, USA	Magic City of the Plains
Chicago, IL, USA	Windy City; Second City; City of Big Shoulders; Hog Butcher to the World
Christchurch, New Zealand	Garden City
Cincinnati, OH, USA	Queen City of the West; Porkopolis
Clarksville, TN, USA	Gateway to the New South; Queen City; ClarksVegas
Clearwater, FL, USA	Lightning Capital of the World
Cleveland, OH, USA	Forest City; Mistake on the Lake
Cody, WY, USA	Rodeo Capital of the World
Colorado Springs, CO, USA	Pikes Peak City
Columbus, IN, USA	Athens of the Prairie
Columbus, OH, USA	Crossroads of Ohio; Cowtown
Coober Pedy, SA, Australia	Opal Capital of the World
Corpus Christi, TX, USA	Sparkling City by the Sea
Coventry, England	Concrete Block
Cracow, Poland	Royal Capital City
Cuernavaca, Mexico	City of Eternal Springs
Dakar, Senegal	Paris of Africa
Dalian, China	Hong Kong of the North
Dallas, TX, USA	The Texas Star; Big D; Cowtown
Dallas-Fort Worth, TX, USA	Metroplex
Dayton, OH, USA	Gem City; Birthplace of Aviation
Denver, CO, USA	Mile-High City; Gateway to the Rockies; Queen City of the Plains; Convention City
Detroit, MI, USA	Motor City (Motor-Town/Motown); Hitsville USA; Amityville; Hockeytown
Dodge City, KS, USA	Cowboy Capital of the World
Dresden, Germany	Florence on the Elbe
Dublin, Ireland	Fair City; The Pale
Dubrovnik, Croatia	Pearl of the Adriatic
Dunedin, New Zealand	Edinburgh of the South
Durham, NC, USA	Bull City; City of Medicine
Edinburgh, Scotland	Athens of the North; Auld Reekie
Edmonton, AL, Canada	Nashville of the North; City of Champions; Gateway to the North; Canada's Festival City
El Paso, TX, USA	Sun City Texas; City with a Legend
Erfurt, Germany	Thuringian Rome
Eskilstuna, Sweden	Smith City
Florence, Italy	City of Lilies; Athens of Italy
Fort Lauderdale, FL, USA	Venice of America; Fort Leatherdale
Fort Wayne, IN, USA	Summit City; City of Churches
Fort Worth, TX, USA	Where The West Begins; Cowtown
Frankfurt, Germany	Mainhattan; Bankfurt
Fredericton, NB, Canada	City of Stately Elms
Fresno, CA, USA	Garden of the Sun; California's New Frontier; Raisin Capital of the World
Gaeta, Italy	Venice of the Tyrrhenian
Galway, Ireland	Venice of the West; City of the Tribes
Genoa, Italy	The Superb
Ghadamis, Libya	Pearl of the Desert
Glasgow, Scotland	Second City of the Empire; Shipbuilding Capital of the World; Dear Green Place
Gothenburg, Sweden	Little London
Grand Rapids, MI, USA	Furniture City; Valley City
Green Bay, WI, USA	Titletown USA
Guadalajara, Mexico	The Tapatian Pearl
Hague, The, The Netherlands	City of Peace and Justice
Hamburg, Germany	Gateway to the World; Venice of the North
Hamilton, New Zealand	Hamiltron
Hamilton, OT, Canada	Steeltown
Harbin, China	Paris of the East
Havana, Cuba	Paris of the Caribbean
Helsinki, Finland	White City of the North
Hershey, PA, USA	Chocolate Town USA; The Sweetest Place on Earth
Ho Chi Minh City, Vietnam	Paris of the Orient
Hollywood (West), CA, USA	Boystown; Creative City
Hollywood, CA, USA	Tinseltown; Showbusiness Capital of the World; Hollyweird
Hong Kong, China	Pearl of the Orient; Asia's World City
Houston, TX, USA	Magnolia City; Space City; Bayou City; Oil Capital of the World
Hyderabad, India	Cyberabad
Indianapolis, IN, USA	Crossroads of America; Naptown; Railroad City; Circle City
Isfahan, Iran	Half of the World
Jackson, MS, USA	Chimneyville
Jacksonville, FL, USA	Bold New City of the South; River City by the Sea; Where Florida Begins
Japiur, India	Pink City
Jeddah, Saudi Arabia	Paris of Arabia
Jerusalem, Israel	City of David; City of Peace; Holy City
Jodhpur, India	Blue City
Johannesburg, South Africa	Egoli (City of Gold)
Jönköping, Sweden	Jerusalem of Småland
Kansas City, MO, USA	City of Fountains; Heart of America; Cowtown
Knoxville, TN, USA	Marble City
Kolkata (Calcutta), India	City of Love; City of Palaces
Kristianstad, Sweden	Little Paris

The listings above refer to a selection of related themes.
For more information, see the Contents (2-5).

Kuching, Malaysia	Cat City
Lahti, Finland	Finland's Chicago
Las Vegas (downtown), NV, USA	The Strip; Glitter Gulch
Las Vegas, NV, USA	Entertainment Capital of the World; City of Lights; America's Playground; Sin City
León, Mexico	Shoe Capital of Mexico
Lexington, KY, USA	Horse Capital of the World
Lima, Peru	City of the Kings
Lisbon, Portugal	White City; City with a Future
Little Rock, AR, USA	City of Roses
Livingston (and area), Scotland	Silicon Glen
London (City of), England	The City; The Square Mile
London, England	Big Smoke; Great Wen
London, OT, Canada	Forest City
Londonderry, Northern Ireland	Maiden City
Los Angeles, CA, USA	Big Orange; City of the Angels; Entertainment Capital of the World; City of Flowers & Sunshine
Louisville, KY, USA	Derby City; Falls City; River City; City of Beautiful Churches
Lubbock, TX, USA	Hub of the Plains
Macau, China	Monte Carlo of the East
Madison, WI, USA	Four Lake City; Mad City
Madurai, India	Athens of the East
Manchester, England	Venice of the North
Manchester, NH, USA	Queen City
Manila, the Philippines	Pearl of the Orient; City by the Bay
Mar del Plata, Argentina	Queen of the Coast; La Feliz (The Happy)
Mayagüez, Puerto Rico	Sultan of the West
Mazatlán, Mexico	Pearl of the Pacific
Medellín, Colombia	Orchid City; La Bella Villa
Melbourne, VI, Australia	Paris on the Yarra
Memphis, TN, USA	Home of the Blues; Birthplace of Rock 'n' Roll; Bluff City; River City
Mérida, Mexico	White City
Mexicali, Mexico	City That Captured the Sun
Mexico City, Mexico	City of Palaces
Miami Beach, FL, USA	America's Riviera; Sun and Fun Capital of the World
Miami, FL, USA	Little Cuba; Gateway to the Americas; Capital of Latin America; Magic City
Milan, Italy	Fashion Capital of the World; Factory of the Future; Moral Capital of Italy; Drinkable City
Milwaukee, WI, USA	Cream City; Brew/Beer City; City of Festivals; Flour City
Minneapolis, MN, USA	City of Lakes; Minneapple; Mill City; Flour City
Minneapolis-St Paul, MN, USA	Twin Cities
Mobile, AL, USA	Azalea City; City of Five Flags
Moncton, NB, Canada	Hub City; Monkeytown
Monterrey, Mexico	Sultaness of the North
Montréal, QU, Canada	City of Saints
Mopti, Mali	Venice of Mali
Moscow, Russian Federation	The Third Rome; Big Village
Munich, Germany	Village of a Million Inhabitants; World City with Heart
Nantes, France	Venice of the West
Naples, Italy	Capital of the South
Nashville, TN, USA	Music City USA; Country Music Capital of the World; Athens of the South; Protestant Vatican
New Orleans, LA, USA	Big Easy; Crescent City; Queen of the Mississippi; City That Time Forgot
New York (Lower Manhattan), NY, USA	Silicon Alley
New York, NY, USA	Big Apple; Empire City; City That Never Sleeps; Capital of the World
Newark, NJ, USA	Brick City; Renaissance City
Newcastle upon Tyne, England	The Toon; Georgieland (refers to the Tyneside conurbation)
Niagara Falls, OT, Canada	Honeymoon Capital of the World

Nijmegen, The Netherlands	Oldest City of The Netherlands
Norrköping, Sweden	Peking
Nouméa, New Caledonia	Paris of the Pacific
Oakland, CA, USA	Oaktown
Oklahoma City, OK, USA	Renaissance City
Oporto, Portugal	The Invincible
Orange County, CA, USA	Biotech Beach
Orlando, FL, USA	City Beautiful
Ottawa, OT, Canada	Venice of the North; Silicon Valley of the North; Bytown
Oxford, England	City of Dreaming Spires; Silicon Spires
Paris, France	City of Light; City of Love
Pasadena, CA, USA	City of Roses; Crown City
Penang, Malaysia	Pearl of the Orient
Pensacola, FL, USA	City of Five Flags
Perth, WA, Australia	City of Lights
Petra, Jordan	Rose Red City
Philadelphia, PA, USA	City of Brotherly Love; Philly; Quaker City
Phoenix, AZ, USA	Valley of the Sun; Desert Storm
Pittsburgh, PA, USA	Steel City; Iron City; Birmingham of America; City of Champions
Ponce, Puerto Rico	City of the Lions; Senior City
Port Elizabeth, South Africa	Friendly City; Windy City
Portland, ME, USA	Forest City; Hill City
Portland, OR, USA	City of Roses; Rip City; Bridgetown; Little Beirut; Stumptown
Portsmouth, England	Pompey
Prague, Czech Republic	Golden City; City of 100 Spires; Heart of Europe; Rome of the North
Pretoria, South Africa	Jacaranda City
Providence, RI, USA	Beehive of Industry
Puebla, Mexico	City of Angels; City of Sweet Potatoes; City of Tiles
Qom, Iran	Iran's Vatican
Québec, QU, Canada	Gibraltar of North America; Le Grande Village; La Vieille Capital
Queenstown, New Zealand	Extreme Sports Capital of the World
Raleigh, NC, USA	City of Oaks; Raleighwood
Recife, Brazil	Venice of Brazil
Regina, SA, Canada	Queen City
Reno, NV, USA	Biggest Little City in the World; Neon Babylon
Richmond, VA, USA	Capital of the Confederacy; City of Seven Hills; Easy to Love; Fist City
Riga, Latvia	Paris of the East
Rio de Janeiro, Brazil	Marvellous City
Rochester, NY, USA	Flower City; Kodak City; Snapshot City
Rome, Italy	Eternal City; City of the Seven Hills; City of Love; City of Cats
Rosario, Argentina	Chicago of Argentina
Sacramento, CA, USA	Big Tomato; Camelia Capital of the World; Almond Capital of the World; River City
St John, NB, Canada	Port City
St Louis, MO, USA	Gateway to the West; Mound City; City with a Future
St Paul, MN, USA	Moscow on the Mississippi
St Petersburg, Russian Fed.	Venice of the North; Northern Palmyra
Salem, MA, USA	City of Witches
Salem, OR, USA	Cherry City
San Antonio, TX, USA	Alamo City; Mission City; River City; Venice of the West
San Diego, CA, USA	Plymouth of the West; America's Finest City; The Place Where California Began; The First Great City of the 21st Century
San Francisco (southern bay area), CA, USA	Silicon Valley
San Francisco, CA, USA	Golden Gate City; Shaky Town; City by the Bay; Baghdad by the Bay
San Jose, CA, USA	Garden City; Capital of Silicon Valley

São Paulo, Brazil	Brazil's Locomotive; City That Never Sleeps; Land of Fog
Saskatoon, SA, Canada	City of Bridges; Saskabush
Scarborough, England	Queen of the Yorkshire Coast
Seattle, WA, USA	Emerald City; Jet City; Queen City of the Pacific Northwest
Sète, France	Venice of the South
Shanghai, China	Paris of the Orient
Sheffield, England	Steel City; People's Republic of South Yorkshire
Shibam, Yemen	Manhattan of the Desert
Shiraz, Iran	Athens of Iran; Paris of Iran; City of Roses
Singapore	Lion City
Sioux Falls, SD, USA	Gateway to the Plains
Sitka, AK, USA	The Natural Place to Visit; Paris of the Pacific
Spokane, WA, USA	Lilac City; Spokavegas; The Can; Skybridge City
Springfield, MA, USA	City of Firsts; Birthplace of Basketball
Springfield, MO, USA	Gateway to the Ozarks; Birthplace of Route 66
Stockholm, Sweden	Venice of the North; The Oak
Stockton, CA, USA	California's Sunrise Seaport; Asparagus Capital of the World
Suzhou, China	Venice of the East
Sydney, NS, Australia	Harbour City; Emerald City
Syracuse, NY, USA	Salt City; Central City; City of Bridges; Typewriter City
Tabriz, Iran	City of Uprising
Tacoma, WA, USA	City of Destiny; Tacyoma; America's Number One Wired City
Tai O, Hong Kong, China	Venice of Hong Kong
Tampa, FL, USA	America's Next Greatest City
Tampere, Finland	Manchester of the North
Táranto, Italy	City of the Two Seas
Tarpon Springs, FL, USA	Venice of the South
Taxco, Mexico	Silver Capital of the World
Te Puke, New Zealand	Kiwi Fruit Capital of the World
Tehran, Iran	City of 72 Nations
Tel Aviv, Israel	City That Never Stops
Tijuana, Mexico	Television Capital of the World
Tikal, Guatemala	City That Time Forgot
Toledo, OH, USA	Glass City; Frog Town; Corn City
Toronto, OT, Canada	Queen City; Hogtown; Festival City; Hollywood North
Tromsø, Norway	Paris of the North
Tucson, AZ, USA	The Old Pueblo
Tulsa, OK, USA	Oil Capital of the World
Turin, Italy	Capital of the Alps; First Capital of Italy; Regal City
Udaipur, India	Venice of the East
Umeå, Sweden	City of Birches
Ushuaia, Argentina	The End of the World
Vancouver, BC, Canada	Rainy City; Brollywood; Terminal City; VanCity
Västerås, Sweden	Cucumber City
Venice, Italy	Bride of the Sea; Queen of the Adriatic; La Serenissima
Victoria, BC, Canada	Whale-watching Capital of the World; Little England; Garden City
Vilnius, Lithuania	Athens of the North
Warsaw, Poland	Paris of the North; Phoenix City; Biggest Village in Poland
Washington DC, USA	News Capital of the World; Capital City; Our City, Our Future
Wellington, New Zealand	Harbour Capital; Windy City; Wellywood
Wichita, KS, USA	Emerald City; Air Capital of the World
Wilmington, DE, USA	Chemical Capital of the World
Windsor, OT, Canada	Tijuana North; Sin City Canada
Winnipeg, MN, Canada	Winterpeg
Zákinthos, Greece	Venice of the South
Zamboanga, the Philippines	City of Flowers

108 Appendices

Countries A-Z: Afghanistan-Benin

▶ **See also...** pages 116 for notes relating to this section; Contents (2-5) for details of all maps and charts in this Atlas

These pages provide exact data on a variety of themes, some of which are addressed in maps or charts elsewhere in this atlas. Information is provided here for every country in the world, not just for those in Europe. The matter of deciding what is and what is not a country is by no means clear-cut, but no political or other subjective stance has been adopted. Many countries have dependencies, overseas possessions, offshore island groups and the like; for various reasons (mainly connected with the availability, reliability or relevance of statistical data) some have been listed separately, some have had their figures amalgamated with those for their mother country and some have been excluded altogether. As a general, but not infallible, rule, where 'T' appears in the Military Spending column, this indicates that the 'country' has a dependence of some kind on another state (which takes responsibility for its defence).

For more information on countries worldwide and related matters, consult the latest edition of the Columbus *World Travel Atlas*, *World Travel Dictionary* or *World Travel Guide*.

Throughout, n/a means that, at the time of going to press, data was not available, not reliable or not relevant. In the case of mobile telephone lines and internet usage, it may in a few instances also mean that the country did not have a network or service.

Some countries have more than one capital city or have recently changed their capital or its name. These are referred to in the notes at the foot of the chart on page 116. These notes also specify inclusions and exclusions for offshore islands and the like for some of the more important countries.

The *italic* numbers in the second row for each country (preceded by •) give the world ranking for that category in descending order highest figure ranked number 1). The top 10 countries in each category have their ranking figure in **bold**. Countries whose figures are equal according to whatever rounding has been used have been ranked equally. As data is not always available for all 226 countries, the figures at the bottom of the chart give the lowest ranking figure in that category; as this can be shared by two or more countries, it may therefore not always represent the total number of countries covered.

Country (Map Ref)	Code	Capital	Area 000 sq km	Population 000	Pop Density /sq km	Intl Arrivals 1997 000	Intl Arrivals 2004 000	Visitor Receipts US$m	Intl Departures 000	Visitor Expenditure US$m	Hotel Bedrooms 2003	Gross Nat'l Income US$bn	GNI per Person US$	GDP Growth %	Energy Production	Energy Consumption Mill	Energy Consumption /person	Fixed Tel Lines	Mobile Tel Lines	Internet Usage	Agricultural Land %	Total Health Spending %	Life Expectancy	Military Spending %
Afghanistan (M4)	.af	Kabul	652.10 •41	29,929 •38	45.9 •150	n/a	n/a	n/a	n/a	n/a	n/a	5,543 •122	185 •217	15.3 •2	0.21 •131	0.48 •159	0.02 •209	0.20 •220	2.41 •188	0.10 •204	58.3 •44	8.0 •42	41.5 •210	2.8 •40
Albania (J3)	.al	Tirana	28.70 •142	3,563 •130	124.2 •80	19 •192	42 •144	673 •75	n/a	n/a	4,161 •114	6,641 •114	1,864 •136	5.4 •40	1.39 •106	2.44 •119	0.68 •137	8.30 •142	35.80 •88	2.35 •160	39.7 •103	6.1 •87	72.0 •87	1.2 •120
Algeria (J4)	.dz	Algiers	2,381.70 •11	32,532 •37	13.7 •194	635 •85	1,234 •71	n/a	n/a	1,254 •56	n/a	73,676 •49	2,265 •119	4.1 •68	176.64 •16	33.29 •42	1.02 •114	7.08 •149	14.48 •128	2.61 •156	16.8 •170	4.3 •150	70.5 •111	3.3 •31
American Samoa (A6)	.as	Pago Pago	0.20 •211	58 •205	289.4 •40	26 •184	n/a	n/a	n/a	n/a	n/a	500 •191	8,638 •68	n/a	0.00 –	0.21 •176	3.62 •48	25.86 •85	4.14 •174	n/a	24.9 •149	n/a	76.0 •55	T –
Andorra (J3)	.ad	Andorra la Vella	0.45 •196	71 •200	156.8 •65	2,347 •47	2,791 •54	n/a	n/a	n/a	n/a	1,900 •159	26,932 •23	n/a	n/a	n/a	n/a	52.30 •26	61.63 •56	16.42 •81	55.6 •52	6.5 •71	81.0 •4	T –
Angola (J6)	.ao	Luanda	1,246.70 •23	11,827 •69	9.5 •204	45 •174	194 •121	97 •103	n/a	n/a	9,244 •83	14,441 •83	1,221 •148	9.5 •6	48.99 •37	3.37 •111	0.28 •160	0.67 •203	6.68 •156	1.22 •174	46.0 •83	5.0 •124	40.0 •213	4.7 •17
Anguilla (F5)	.ai	The Valley	0.16 •215	13 •219	82.8 •106	43 •177	54 •141	69 •109	n/a	n/a	759 •139	30 •220	n/a	n/a	0.00 –	n/a	n/a	47.69 •39	13.85 •131	n/a	0.0 –	n/a	77.0 •47	T –
Antigua & Barbuda (F5)	.ag	St John's	0.44 •197	69 •202	156.2 •66	240 •129	245 •115	n/a	n/a	n/a	n/a	800 •179	11,641 •59	3.7 •81	0.00 –	0.19 •180	2.75 •68	49.35 •35	70.13 •49	25.97 •58	31.7 •122	4.8 •133	72.5 •77	M –
Argentina (F7)	.ar	Buenos Aires	2,780.40 •8	39,538 •31	14.2 •192	2,764 •41	3,353 •47	2,563 •46	3,088 •39	2,964 •31	174,629 •15	142,338 •35	3,600 •100	2.2 •142	91.17 •25	66.76 •28	1.69 •88	22.76 •96	35.35 •89	16.10 •82	63.7 •25	8.9 •29	74.5 •63	1.2 •120
Armenia (L3)	.am	Yerevan	29.80 •141	2,983 •135	100.1 •92	23 •188	n/a	169 •78	n/a	n/a	n/a	3,424 •142	1,148 •150	7.7 •13	0.95 •110	4.31 •99	1.44 •96	9.09 •140	6.66 •157	4.91 •131	46.9 •77	5.8 •99	68.5 •127	2.7 •45
Aruba (F5)	.aw	Oranjestad	0.18 •213	72 •199	397.6 •22	n/a	650 •81	728 •85	n/a	n/a	7,731 •86	323 •200	4,513 •88	3.6 •85	0.00 –	0.34 •169	4.72 •27	35.03 •60	73.61 •46	33.33 •43	10.4 •188	n/a	79.5 •17	n/a
Australia (P7)	.au	Canberra	7,682.30 •6	20,090 •52	2.6 •220	4,318 •28	5,200 •38	12,952 •9	3,388 •37	9,407 •17	204,461 •17	541,173 •14	26,937 •22	3.6 •36	256.53 •9	128.46 •18	6.39 •16	58.55 •19	82.76 •33	65.28 •8	58.1 •45	9.5 •19	80.5 •15	1.9 •77
Austria (J3)	.at	Vienna	83.90 •115	8,185 •89	97.6 •95	16,647 •11	19,373 •10	15,412 •9	5,060 •27	11,416 •14	282,614 •10	262,147 •22	32,029 •15	2.2 •142	12.37 •63	36.38 •40	4.44 •31	46.20 •41	97.36 •12	47.52 •30	40.5 •100	7.7 •49	79.0 •24	0.8 •144
Azerbaijan (L3)	.az	Baku	86.60 •113	7,912 •91	91.4 •102	306 •120	n/a	n/a	1,376 •53	524 •54	5,034 •107	7,828 •104	989 •161	11.4 •4	22.77 •53	15.86 •66	2.00 •80	12.28 •124	17.44 •125	4.89 •132	54.2 •61	3.7 •167	65.0 •146	1.9 •77
Bahamas (F4)	.bs	Nassau	13.90 •159	302 •175	21.7 •179	1,618 •56	1,561 •64	1,884 •54	n/a	n/a	15,393 •71	4,684 •131	15,521 •42	3.2 •108	0.00 –	1.21 •136	4.01 •41	44.14 •48	58.68 •61	29.34 •49	1.0 •213	6.9 •66	72.0 •87	M –
Bahrain (L4)	.bh	Manama	0.71 •187	688 •161	969.5 •10	1,611 •57	n/a	740 •73	n/a	n/a	n/a	8,834 •99	12,834 •55	5.2 •42	11.19 •67	10.22 •77	14.85 •5	25.92 •84	87.92 •24	20.67 •72	14.1 •176	4.4 •146	74.0 •70	5.1 •15
Bangladesh (N4)	.bd	Dhaka	148.40 •93	144,320 •7	972.5 •9	182 •136	271 •112	67 •110	1,414 •52	n/a	4,565 •110	61,230 •52	424 •188	5.6 •36	10.90 •68	15.37 •67	0.11 •179	0.61 •205	2.03 •193	0.22 •198	61.2 •35	3.1 •179	63.0 •154	1.2 •120
Barbados (F5)	.bb	Bridgetown	0.43 •198	279 •178	648.5 •13	472 •95	552 •95	810 •69	n/a	n/a	6,210 •97	2,507 •151	8,990 •67	2.4 •133	0.08 •141	0.55 •157	1.97 •82	50.09 •31	73.85 •44	55.35 •18	44.2 •88	6.9 •66	74.5 •63	M –
Belarus (K3)	.by	Minsk	207.60 •85	10,300 •78	49.6 •145	254 •126	68 •138	287 •93	n/a	n/a	n/a	20,856 •73	2,025 •131	6.8 •23	2.14 •99	30.76 •45	2.99 •63	32.24 •65	22.73 •114	24.98 •59	43.0 •91	6.4 •75	69.0 •126	1.2 •120
Belgium (J3)	.be	Brussels	30.50 •139	10,364 •77	339.8 •28	6,037 •23	6,710 •23	9,120 •18	7,268 •18	13,954 •11	63,220 •34	322,837 •18	31,149 •18	2.2 •142	12.25 •64	67.02 •27	6.47 •15	46.44 •40	88.32 •23	40.62 •37	49.8 •69	9.1 •26	78.5 •30	1.3 •113
Belize (E5)	.bz	Belmopan	23.00 •150	281 •177	12.2 •196	146 •142	231 •118	231 •118	n/a	n/a	5,050 •105	1,115 •171	3,967 •94	5.7 •35	0.02 •151	0.32 •171	1.14 •107	12.92 •121	35.12 •91	13.41 •86	6.6 •199	5.2 •115	68.0 •131	2.0 •73
Benin (J5)	.bj	Porto Novo	112.60 •100	7,649 •93	67.9 •121	148 •141	n/a	n/a	n/a	n/a	n/a	3,667 •141	479 •184	4.6 •58	0.02 •151	0.64 •153	0.08 •187	1.00 •194	5.33 •161	1.38 •170	29.9 •128	4.7 •137	53.0 •185	1.8 •83

▶ See also... pages 108 & 116 for notes relating to this section; Contents (2-5) for details of all maps and charts in this Atlas

Appendices **109**

Countries A-Z: Bermuda-Congo

Values are shown as *figure* with its world ranking (•rank). Ranking: top 10 in **bold**. n/a: Not available, not relevant or not reliable. T: See note on page 41. M: See note on page 41. For more information, see pages 202 & 210.

Country / Map Ref	Internet code	Capital	Area ('000 sq km)	Population ('000, 2004)	Pop. Density (people/sq km, 2004)	Intl Arrivals 1997 ('000)	Intl Arrivals 2004 ('000)	Visitor Receipts (US$ m, 2004)	Intl Departures ('000, 2004)	Visitor Expenditure (US$ m, 2004)	Hotel Bedrooms (2003)	Gross Nat'l Income (US$ bn, 2004)	GNI per Person (US$, 2004)	GDP Growth (av. annual % 1997-2006)	Energy Production (Mt oil eq, 2004)	Energy Consumption (Mt oil eq, 2004)	Energy Consumption (t oil eq/person, 2004)	Fixed Tel Lines (/100, 2004)	Mobile Tel Lines (/100, 2004)	Internet Usage (subscribers/100, 2004)	Agricultural Land (% area, 2004)	Total Health Spending (% GNI, 2002)	Life Expectancy (years)	Military Spending (% of GNI)
Bermuda F4	.bm	Hamilton	0.05 •221	65 •203	1,307.3 •**6**	380 •104	272 •111	354 •90	n/a –	232 •68	3,100 •122	2,710 •149	41,459 •**4**	n/a –	0.00 –	0.20 •178	3.08 •61	86.15 •**4**	79.03 •37	62.90 •**10**	18.9 •167	n/a –	n/a –	T –
Bhutan N4	.bt	Thimphu	46.50 •131	2,232 •142	48.0 •149	5 •200	9 •152	12 •114	n/a –	n/a –	1,239 •136	677 •186	303 •204	8.2 •12	0.52 •119	0.46 •161	0.21 •167	3.88 •169	2.45 •187	0.04 •207	12.5 •183	4.5 •144	62.5 •155	1.8 •83
Bolivia F8	.bo	note 9	1,098.60 •28	8,858 •86	8.1 •208	355 •112	405 •105	n/a –	672 •61	n/a –	20,611 •58	8,656 •101	977 •163	3.0 •117	8.72 •76	4.70 •93	0.53 •141	6.97 •150	20.07 •116	3.90 •139	33.6 •118	7.0 •62	65.0 •146	1.7 •88
Bosnia-Herzegovina J3	.ba	Sarajevo	51.10 •127	4,430 •119	86.7 •104	76 •160	190 •122	490 •82	n/a –	126 •73	n/a –	7,841 •103	1,770 •138	9.1 •**7**	4.36 •84	5.51 •89	1.24 •102	22.17 •97	27.40 •106	5.38 •127	41.5 •95	9.2 •24	72.5 •77	2.9 •35
Botswana K7	.bw	Gaborone	581.70 •47	1,640 •147	2.8 •218	607 •88	1,202 •73	549 •77	n/a –	n/a –	3,589 •119	7,490 •107	4,567 •86	5.5 •39	0.58 •116	1.30 •130	0.79 •128	7.96 •145	33.31 •96	3.50 •143	44.7 •87	6.0 •92	36.5 •217	4.1 •26
Brazil G6	.br	Brasília	8,547.40 •**5**	186,113 •**5**	21.8 •177	2,850 •40	4,725 •39	3,222 •42	2,293 •42	2,871 •33	n/a –	552,096 •13	2,966 •103	2.4 •133	178.37 •14	220.81 •**10**	1.19 •106	23.46 •93	36.32 •85	12.18 •90	30.8 •125	7.9 •45	69.5 •123	1.6 •93
British Virgin Is. F5	.vg	Road Town	0.13 •217	23 •214	174.2 •63	n/a –	244 •128	332 •108	n/a –	n/a –	2,705 •126	265 •203	11,703 •57	n/a –	0.00 –	0.02 •204	0.87 •124	50.87 •30	34.78 •93	17.39 •78	58.8 •42	n/a –	76.5 •53	T –
Brunei O5	.bn	Bandar Seri Begawan	5.80 •169	372 •173	64.2 •130	n/a –	n/a –	n/a –	n/a –	n/a –	n/a –	6,842 •111	18,375 •38	2.1 •149	21.78 •54	2.36 •120	6.34 •17	25.57 •86	17.74 •123	15.30 •83	3.3 •206	3.5 •171	77.0 •47	6.1 •11
Bulgaria K3	.bg	Sofia	111.00 •102	7,450 •95	67.1 •122	2,980 •37	4,630 •40	2,168 •49	3,403 •36	963 •45	n/a –	21,326 •71	2,862 •104	3.1 •112	9.73 •74	22.22 •57	2.98 •64	35.13 •59	60.94 •57	28.35 •51	48.0 •74	7.4 •56	72.5 •77	2.6 •47
Burkina H5	.bf	Ouagadougou	274.10 •74	13,492 •63	49.2 •146	n/a –	138 •145	n/a –	n/a –	n/a –	n/a –	4,436 •135	329 •200	5.6 •36	0.04 •146	0.45 •162	0.03 •202	0.61 •205	2.97 •185	0.40 •192	37.9 •109	4.3 •150	45.0 •201	1.3 •113
Burundi K6	.bi	Bujumbura	27.80 •145	7,795 •92	280.4 •42	n/a –	11 •198	n/a –	n/a –	n/a –	n/a –	669 •187	86 •224	2.4 •133	0.04 •146	0.19 •180	0.02 •208	0.34 •212	0.90 •204	0.35 •195	78.0 •**9**	3.0 •182	42.5 •208	5.9 •**9**
Cambodia O5	.kh	Phnom Penh	181.00 •89	13,636 •62	75.3 •116	219 •130	1,055 •79	n/a –	n/a –	n/a –	n/a –	4,430 •136	325 •201	7.0 •19	0.01 •158	0.21 •176	0.02 •210	0.26 •217	3.52 •180	0.28 •196	29.3 •134	12.0 •**2**	53.5 •184	1.5 •102
Cameroon J5	.cm	Yaoundé	475.40 •53	16,988 •58	35.7 •162	42 •178	190 •130	n/a –	n/a –	n/a –	n/a –	13,138 •89	773 •156	4.2 •66	4.83 •83	1.91 •125	0.11 •178	0.59 •207	9.43 •148	1.02 •175	19.3 •166	4.6 •140	47.5 •196	1.5 •102
Canada D2	.ca	Ottawa	9,970.60 •**2**	32,805 •35	3.3 •214	17,669 •**9**	19,150 •11	12,843 •12	17,739 •**10**	16,017 •**9**	n/a –	905,629 •**8**	27,606 •21	2.5 •128	460.91 •**5**	337.11 •**7**	10.28 •**9**	64.27 •15	46.72 •75	62.56 •12	6.8 •198	9.6 •16	80.0 •**10**	1.2 •120
Cape Verde H5	.cv	Praia	4.00 •172	418 •171	104.6 •90	45 •175	157 •124	109 •102	109 •102	78 •75	5,127 •104	852 •177	2,037 •130	7.2 •17	0.00 –	0.06 •195	0.14 •173	15.56 •110	13.94 •130	5.30 •129	17.4 •169	5.0 •124	70.0 •116	0.7 •147
Cayman Is. E5	.ky	George Town	0.26 •205	44 •208	170.3 •64	381 •103	260 •103	n/a –	n/a –	n/a –	n/a –	1,391 •166	31,421 •16	n/a –	0.00 –	0.13 •185	2.95 •65	86.36 •**3**	38.64 •81	22.50 •64	11.6 •186	n/a –	80.0 •**10**	T –
Central African Rep. K5	.cf	Bangui	622.40 •43	4,238 •121	6.8 •210	27 •182	17 •193	n/a –	n/a –	n/a –	n/a –	1,226 •169	289 •206	1.6 •159	0.02 •151	0.15 •184	0.04 •200	0.26 •217	1.53 •198	0.23 •197	8.3 •193	3.9 •161	42.5 •208	1.3 •113
Chad J5	.td	Ndjaména	1,284.00 •21	9,657 •82	7.5 •209	n/a –	27 •182	n/a –	n/a –	n/a –	156 •80	2,277 •154	236 •213	8.4 •**10**	2.03 •100	0.07 •191	0.07 •191	0.15 •222	1.39 •201	0.68 •184	37.9 •109	6.5 •71	45.5 •198	1.4 •109
Channel Is. I3	.gg, .je	note 10	0.20 •212	156 •190	780.2 •11	n/a –	n/a –	n/a –	n/a –	n/a –	n/a –	6,190 •119	39,669 •**7**	n/a –	0.00 –	n/a –	n/a –	86.00 •**5**	83.33 •32	42.00 •35	0.0 –	n/a –	80.0 •**10**	T –
Chile F7	.cl	Santiago	736.90 •39	15,981 •60	21.7 •180	1,644 •55	1,785 •61	1,091 •61	2,100 •47	892 •47	52,362 •39	78,407 •48	4,906 •82	4.1 •68	8.39 •77	27.59 •49	1.73 •86	21.53 •99	62.08 •54	27.90 •54	20.2 •161	6.1 •99	77.0 •47	3.5 •30
China O4	.cn	Beijing	9,536.10 •**3**	1,306,314 •**1**	137.0 •73	23,770 •**6**	41,761 •**4**	25,739 •**7**	20,222 •**9**	19,100 •**7**	992,804 •**4**	1,676,846 •**6**	1,284 •146	8.4 •**10**	1,102.52 •**2**	1,137.06 •**2**	0.87 •123	23.98 •91	25.76 •110	7.23 •113	57.9 •47	5.8 •99	71.5 •95	2.3 •60
China: Hong Kong SAR[1] O4	.hk	–	1.10 •180	6,899 •98	6,271.5 •**4**	11,273 •13	21,811 •**7**	9,007 •19	4,428 •29	13,258 •12	42,936 •44	183,516 •29	26,602 •25	3.1 •112	0.00 –	21.82 •61	3.16 •59	54.42 •25	118.77 •**2**	50.32 •21	6.4 •201	n/a –	79.5 •17	n/a –
China: Macau SAR[1] O4	.mo	–	0.02 •222	449 •167	22,459.9 •**1**	3,836 •33	8,323 •24	7,452 •22	156 •80	n/a –	9,185 •84	6,717 •113	14,953 •44	n/a –	0.00 –	0.66 •151	1.47 •95	37.38 •56	92.94 •17	32.24 •45	0.0 •**1**	n/a –	82.0 •**1**	n/a –
Colombia F5	.co	Bogotá	1,141.70 •26	42,954 •29	37.6 •159	639 •84	744 •84	1,032 •63	1,177 •57	1,290 •41	54,820 •38	90,626 •44	2,110 •128	2.2 •142	76.55 •29	28.83 •47	0.67 •138	17.14 •108	22.95 •113	8.94 •103	40.2 •101	8.1 •40	72.5 •77	4.4 •18
Comoros L6	.km	Moroni	1.90 •177	671 •162	353.3 •26	26 •184	26 •184	n/a –	n/a –	n/a –	n/a –	489 •180	328 •199	2.4 •133	0.00 –	0.04 •198	0.06 •192	1.66 •185	0.25 •211	1.01 •176	78.9 •**7**	2.9 •183	64.0 •151	3.0 •34
Congo J6	.cg	Brazzaville	341.80 •63	3,602 •128	10.5 •200	27 •182	n/a –	n/a –	n/a –	n/a –	n/a –	2,974 •147	826 •165	3.5 •91	13.11 •61	0.38 •165	0.11 •180	0.36 •211	10.05 •147	0.94 •178	29.9 •128	2.2 •187	54.0 •183	1.4 •109

*: Ranking (top 10 in **bold**). n/a: Not available, not relevant or not reliable. T: See note on page 41. M: See note on page 41. For more information, see pages 202 & 210.

110 Appendices

Countries A-Z: Congo, DR-French Guiana

▶ *See also...* pages 108 & 116 for notes relating to this section; Contents (2-5) for details of all maps and charts in this Atlas

Each cell shows the indicator value over its ranking (● Ranking, top 10 in bold).

Country	Map Ref. (pp14-15)	Internet code	Capital	Area 000 sq km	Population 000 (2004)	Population Density people/sq km (2004)	International Arrivals 000 (1997)	International Arrivals 000 (2004)	Visitor Receipts US$ million (1997)	International Departures 000 (2004)	Visitor Expenditure US$ million (2004)	Hotel Bedrooms (2003)	Gross Nat'l Income US$ million (2004)	GNI per Person US$ (2004)	GDP Growth Av. annual % 1997-2006	Energy Production Mil toe (2004)	Energy Consumption Mil toe (2004)	Energy Consumption toe/person (2004)	Fixed Tel. Lines /100 (2004)	Mobile Tel. Lines /100 (2004)	Internet Usage Subscribers/100 (2004)	Agricultural Land % of area (2004)	Total Health Spending % of GNI (2004)	Life Expectancy Years (2004)	Military Spending % of GNI (2003)
Congo, Dem. Rep.	K6	.zr	Kinshasa	2,344.90 / 12	60,764 / 20	25.9 / 174	30 / 179	30 / 148	1 / 117	n/a / –	n/a / –	5,829 / 100	6,416 / 117	106 / 223	0.9 / 169	2.78 / 94	2.01 / 122	0.03 / 204	0.02 / 223	1.89 / 194	0.09 / 205	9.7 / 189	4.0 / 159	44.5 / 205	1.0 / 134
Cook Is.	A6	.ck	Avarua	0.23 / 210	21 / 215	93.0 / 99	50 / 171	83 / 136	n/a / –	10 / 90	n/a / –	1,152 / 137	531 / 189	24,827 / 27	n/a / –	0.00 / –	0.02 / 204	0.95 / 119	29.52 / 73	7.14 / 155	17.14 / 79	n/a / –	4.6 / 140	71.0 / 99	– / T
Costa Rica	E5	.cr	San José	51.10 / 128	4,016 / 123	78.6 / 112	811 / 74	1,453 / 67	1,357 / 58	373 / 70	404 / 58	35,003 / 52	18,969 / 78	4,723 / 84	4.5 / 59	2.22 / 97	4.25 / 100	1.06 / 109	31.62 / 69	21.73 / 115	23.54 / 61	56.1 / 50	9.3 / 21	77.5 / 41	– / M
Côte d'Ivoire	I5	.ci	note 11	320.80 / 68	17,298 / 57	53.9 / 142	274 / 122	n/a / –	n/a / –	n/a / –	841 / 48	n/a / –	13,263 / 88	767 / 168	1.0 / 168	3.40 / 90	2.53 / 117	0.15 / 171	1.43 / 188	9.07 / 149	1.78 / 165	23.6 / 155	6.2 / 81	45.5 / 198	1.5 / 102
Croatia	J3	.hr	Zagreb	56.50 / 126	4,496 / 117	79.6 / 111	4,178 / 31	7,912 / 25	6,973 / 23	7,912 / 25	n/a / –	77,113 / 29	29,700 / 61	6,606 / 75	3.6 / 85	4.32 / 85	9.95 / 78	2.21 / 79	42.74 / 51	58.37 / 63	29.51 / 48	55.6 / 52	7.4 / 56	74.5 / 63	2.1 / 66
Cuba	F4	.cu	Havana	110.90 / 103	11,347 / 72	102.3 / 91	1,153 / 63	2,017 / 58	n/a / –	113 / 82	n/a / –	43,696 / 43	25,501 / 66	2,247 / 123	3.7 / 81	3.76 / 88	11.78 / 74	1.04 / 111	6.78 / 151	0.67 / 206	1.32 / 171	60.1 / 39	7.5 / 55	77.0 / 47	n/a / –
Cyprus [2]	K4	.cy	Nicosia	9.30 / 166	780 / 158	83.9 / 105	2,088 / 52	2,349 / 55	2,096 / 50	629 / 63	208 / 70	46,706 / 41	13,633 / 85	17,475 / 40	3.5 / 91	0.00 / –	2.83 / 114	3.63 / 47	51.84 / 27	79.37 / 36	36.93 / 41	1.1 / 212	7.0 / 62	78.5 / 30	1.5 / 102
Czech Rep.	J3	.cz	Prague	78.90 / 117	10,241 / 79	129.8 / 76	4,976 / 27	6,061 / 33	4,169 / 37	36,074 / 5	2,271 / 39	97,282 / 23	93,155 / 42	9,096 / 66	2.2 / 142	28.70 / 49	43.46 / 38	4.24 / 37	33.58 / 62	105.64 / 5	49.97 / 25	54.2 / 61	7.0 / 62	75.5 / 59	2.2 / 63
Denmark	J3	.dk	Copenhagen	43.10 / 133	5,432 / 108	126.0 / 78	2,158 / 51	3,358 / 46	5,669 / 29	5,564 / 25	n/a / –	41,729 / 45	219,422 / 27	40,392 / **6**	2.0 / 153	29.41 / 47	22.17 / 27	4.08 / 39	64.46 / 14	95.51 / 15	60.41 / 14	61.9 / 31	8.8 / 31	77.5 / 41	1.5 / 102
Djibouti	L5	.dj	Djibouti	23.20 / 149	477 / 165	20.5 / 181	20 / 191	20 / 191	n/a / –	n/a / –	n/a / –	n/a / –	739 / 183	1,550 / 141	2.2 / 142	0.00 / –	0.66 / 151	1.38 / 100	1.63 / 186	5.07 / 164	1.32 / 171	56.1 / 50	6.3 / 77	54.5 / 182	4.3 / 20
Dominica	F5	.dm	Roseau	0.75 / 184	69 / 201	92.0 / 100	65 / 167	65 / 167	n/a / –	n/a / –	n/a / –	n/a / –	261 / 204	3,781 / 98	4.9 / 48	0.01 / 158	0.05 / 197	0.72 / 135	29.40 / 74	58.68 / 61	28.75 / 50	29.3 / 134	6.4 / 75	73.5 / 75	– / M
Dominican Republic	F5	.do	Santo Domingo	48.40 / 130	9,050 / 84	187.0 / 57	2,211 / 50	3,450 / 45	3,180 / 43	321 / 72	n/a / –	56,378 / 35	18,443 / 79	2,038 / 129	4.0 / 73	0.35 / 125	7.27 / 83	0.80 / 127	10.65 / 134	28.82 / 101	9.10 / 102	76.3 / 12	6.1 / 87	68.5 / 127	1.1 / 129
East Timor	P6	.tp	Dili	14.60 / 158	1,041 / 155	71.3 / 119	n/a / –	n/a / –	n/a / –	n/a / –	n/a / –	n/a / –	506 / 190	486 / 181	n/a / –	n/a / –	n/a / –	n/a / –	n/a / –	n/a / –	n/a / –	19.6 / 162	9.7 / 13	58.0 / 176	n/a / –
Ecuador	F6	.ec	Quito	275.80 / 73	13,364 / 64	48.5 / 148	529 / 89	793 / 83	367 / 89	613 / 64	391 / 59	38,237 / 47	28,783 / 63	2,154 / 127	2.6 / 126	24.69 / 50	9.73 / 80	0.73 / 134	12.22 / 126	26.86 / 108	4.73 / 133	29.7 / 130	4.8 / 133	71.0 / 99	2.4 / 57
Egypt	K4	.eg	Cairo	997.70 / 30	77,506 / 15	77.7 / 114	3,656 / 34	7,051 / 26	6,125 / 26	3,644 / 34	1,257 / 43	136,510 / 18	90,129 / 45	1,163 / 149	4.9 / 48	67.62 / 32	58.06 / 29	0.75 / 132	13.52 / 117	10.92 / 143	5.57 / 126	3.4 / 205	4.9 / 128	67.0 / 137	2.6 / 47
El Salvador	E5	.sv	San Salvador	21.00 / 152	6,705 / 99	319.3 / 32	387 / 102	966 / 80	337 / 91	940 / 58	240 / 67	4,578 / 109	15,613 / 81	2,329 / 117	2.5 / 128	0.89 / 111	2.98 / 113	0.44 / 146	13.42 / 119	27.71 / 105	8.88 / 104	81.0 / 5	8.0 / 42	70.0 / 116	0.7 / 147
Equatorial Guinea	J5	.gq	Malabo	28.10 / 144	529 / 164	18.8 / 185	n/a / –	n/a / –	n/a / –	n/a / –	n/a / –	n/a / –	323 / 201	611 / 171	34.8 / **1**	11.47 / 66	1.24 / 134	2.34 / 75	1.77 / 181	10.95 / 142	0.99 / 177	11.9 / 185	1.8 / 191	51.0 / 190	2.5 / 53
Eritrea	K5	.er	Asmara	93.70 / 109	4,670 / 115	49.8 / 144	410 / 100	87 / 134	n/a / –	73 / 106	365 / 61	4,139 / 115	806 / 178	173 / 219	1.4 / 163	0.00 / –	0.24 / 175	0.05 / 196	9.30 / 139	4.74 / 168	11.84 / 91	61.7 / 32	5.1 / 119	59.5 / 169	19.4 / **1**
Estonia	K3	.ee	Tallinn	45.20 / 132	1,333 / 151	29.5 / 169	730 / 77	1,750 / 63	806 / 70	2,075 / 48	n/a / –	12,445 / 74	9,435 / 98	7,079 / 71	6.5 / 25	3.07 / 92	5.59 / 87	4.19 / 38	33.95 / 61	96.00 / 13	51.22 / 20	15.4 / 173	5.1 / 119	71.0 / 99	1.9 / 77
Ethiopia	L5	.et	Addis Ababa	1,104.30 / 27	73,053 / 16	66.2 / 126	139 / 144	184 / 141	n/a / –	n/a / –	n/a / –	3,497 / 120	7,747 / 105	106 / 222	4.4 / 61	0.52 / 119	1.94 / 123	0.03 / 207	0.63 / 204	0.25 / 211	0.16 / 201	27.1 / 141	5.7 / 107	50.0 / 192	4.3 / 20
Falkland Is.	G8	.fk	Stanley	12.20 / 160	3 / 225	0.2 / 225	n/a / –	n/a / –	n/a / –	n/a / –	n/a / –	n/a / –	32 / 217	10,785 / 61	n/a / –	0.00 / –	0.01 / 207	3.33 / 55	80.00 / **6**	n/a / –	50.00 / 23	92.8 / **1**	n/a / –	0.0 / –	– / T
Faroe Is.	I2	.fo	Tórshavn	1.40 / 179	47 / 207	33.5 / 164	n/a / –	n/a / –	n/a / –	n/a / –	n/a / –	n/a / –	1,008 / 173	21,464 / 32	n/a / –	0.02 / 151	0.26 / 173	5.53 / 22	49.76 / 34	85.78 / 28	66.47 / **5**	2.1 / –	n/a / –	79.5 / 17	– / T
Fiji Is.	P6	.fj	Suva	18.30 / 155	893 / 156	48.8 / 147	359 / 110	507 / 99	n/a / –	n/a / –	n/a / –	6,142 / 98	2,281 / 153	2,553 / 108	2.5 / 128	0.16 / 134	0.68 / 148	0.76 / 131	12.35 / 123	13.31 / 134	7.20 / 114	25.1 / 147	4.2 / 158	68.5 / 127	2.2 / 63
Finland	K2	.fi	Helsinki	338.10 / 64	5,223 / 111	15.4 / 189	1,832 / 54	2,840 / 53	n/a / –	5,585 / 24	n/a / –	55,767 / 37	171,024 / 30	32,742 / 14	3.6 / 85	10.49 / 70	30.48 / 46	5.84 / 20	45.40 / 44	95.63 / 14	63.00 / **9**	6.6 / 199	7.3 / 59	78.5 / 30	1.2 / 120
France [3]	J3	.fr	Paris	549.10 / 49	60,656 / 21	110.5 / 85	66,591 / **1**	75,121 / **1**	n/a / –	17,426 / 11	28,636 / **5**	603,279 / **7**	1,858,731 / **5**	30,644 / 19	1.7 / 156	128.38 / 21	281.05 / **8**	4.63 / 28	56.04 / 28	73.72 / 45	41.37 / 36	54.3 / 59	9.7 / 13	80.0 / **10**	2.6 / 47
French Guiana	G5	.gf	Cayenne	85.50 / 114	196 / 184	2.3 / 222	68 / 164	n/a / –	n/a / –	n/a / –	n/a / –	n/a / –	2,282 / 152	11,672 / 58	n/a / –	0.00 / –	0.36 / 167	1.84 / 84	30.22 / 72	53.55 / 67	20.77 / 70	0.3 / 215	n/a / –	77.5 / 41	n/a / –

● : Ranking (top 10 in **bold**). **n/a**: Not available, not relevant or not reliable. **T**: See note on page 41. **M**: See note on page 41. For more information, see pages 202 & 210.

▶ See also... pages 108 & 116 for notes relating to this section; Contents (2-5) for details of all maps and charts in this Atlas

Appendices | **111**

Countries A-Z: French Polynesia-Israel

Country (Map Ref pp 14-15)	Capital	Internet code	Military Spending % of GNI (2003)	Life Expectancy Years (2004)	Total Health Spending % of GNI (2004)	Agricultural Land % of national area (2004)	Internet Usage Subscribers/100 people (2004)	Mobile Tel. Lines /100 people (2004)	Fixed Tel. Lines /100 people (2004)	Energy Consumption Tonnes oil equiv./person (2004)	Energy Consumption Mil tonnes oil equiv. (2004)	Energy Production Mil tonnes oil equiv. (2004)	GDP Growth Av. annual % 1997-2006	GNI per Person US$ (2004)	Gross Nat'l Income US$ (2004)	Hotel Bedrooms (2003)	Visitor Expenditure US$ million (2004)	International Departures '000 (2004)	Visitor Receipts US$ million (2004)	International Arrivals 2004 '000	International Arrivals 1997 '000	Population Density people/sq km (2004)	Population '000 (2004)	Area '000 sq km
French Polynesia (B7)	Papeete	.pf	T –	76.0 •55	n/a –	10.8 •187	18.15 •75	29.24 •100	21.48 •100	1.00 •115	0.27 •172	0.02 •151	n/a –	14,027 •50	3,794 •138	3,221 •121	n/a –	n/a –	n/a –	212 •119	180 •137	64.4 •129	270 •180	4.20 •171
Gabon (J6)	Libreville	.ga	0.3 •162	57.5 •177	4.3 •150	19.3 •165	2.96 •153	36.20 •86	3.17 •173	0.70 •136	0.98 •140	13.30 •59	4.7 •53	3,884	5,415 •123	n/a –	n/a –	236 •75	n/a –	n/a –	167 •139	5.2 •212	1,394 •150	267.70 •76
Gambia, The (H5)	Banjul	.gm	0.6 •152	57.5 •177	7.3 •59	63.2 •27	3.35 •146	11.97 •138	2.89 •177	0.06 •189	0.10 •188	0.00 –	4.7 •53	260 •208	414 •193	n/a –	n/a –	n/a –	n/a –	n/a –	85 •156	149.1 •70	1,595 •148	10.70 •164
Georgia (L3)	Tbilisi	.ge	1.1 •129	71.0 •99	3.8 •163	43.1 •90	3.46 •144	16.57 •126	13.47 •118	0.75 •133	3.49 •109	1.96 •101	6.0 •30	1,001 •159	4,683 •132	n/a –	n/a –	n/a –	n/a –	n/a –	313 •118	67.1 •123	4,677 •114	69.70 •121
Germany (J3)	Berlin	.de	1.4 •109	79.0 •24	10.9 •7	47.5 •75	42.67 •33	86.42 •27	66.15 •12	4.32 •34	356.03 •5	132.43 •19	1.2 •165	30,194 •20	2,488,974 •3	892,302 •5	72,271 •1	74,600 •1	27,657 •5	20,137 •9	15,837 •12	230.9 •50	82,431 •14	357.00 •62
Ghana (I5)	Accra	.gh	0.7 •147	58.5 •175	5.6 •109	61.5 •33	1.72 •166	7.93 •152	1.47 •187	0.14 •174	3.14 •112	1.53 •105	4.8 •50	369 •197	8,090 •102	n/a –	n/a –	n/a –	n/a –	n/a –	325 •115	92.0 •101	21,946 •50	238.50 •81
Gibraltar (I4)	Gibraltar	.gi	T –	80.0 •10	n/a –	0.0 •216	22.14 •65	35.00 •92	87.50 •2	47.14 •2	1.32 •129	0.00 –	n/a –	17,860 •39	498 •192	n/a –	n/a –	n/a –	n/a –	n/a –	n/a –	4,647.3 •5	28 •213	0.01 •225
Greece (K4)	Athens	.gr	4.1 •26	78.5 •30	9.5 •19	64.0 •23	17.81 •77	84.77 •29	57.84 •20	3.33 •54	35.57 •41	10.38 •71	3.4 •98	17,239 •41	183,917 •28	330,970 •9	2,874 •32	n/a –	12,872 •11	13,787 •16	10,070 •16	80.8 •107	10,668 •75	132.00 •96
Greenland (G2)	Nuuk	.gl	T –	n/a –	n/a –	0.1 •216	66.32 •6	35.15 •90	44.69 •46	3.57 •49	0.20 •178	0.00 –	n/a –	13,552 •53	764 •181	n/a –	n/a –	n/a –	n/a –	n/a –	n/a –	0.0 •226	56 •206	2,166.10 •14
Grenada (F5)	St George's	.gd	M	67.5 •135	5.7 •107	37.6 •111	7.77 •110	42.05 •78	31.75 •68	1.00 •115	0.09 •189	0.00 •189	3.4 •98	4,436 •89	397 •194	1,758 •131	n/a –	n/a –	n/a –	134 •126	111 •148	263.2 •46	90 •196	0.34 •202
Guadeloupe (F5)	note[12]	.gp	n/a –	78.0 •39	n/a –	28.2 •139	17.83 •76	71.04 •48	48.73 •36	1.49 •94	0.67 •149	0.00 –	n/a –	13,385 •54	6,006 •120	7,603 •90	n/a –	n/a –	n/a –	n/a –	660 •89	263.9 •45	449 •168	1.70 •178
Guam (Q5)	Agaña	.gu	T –	78.5 •30	n/a –	40.1 •102	47.88 •29	19.29 •119	50.89 •29	5.92 •19	1.00 •139	0.00 –	n/a –	18,509 •36	3,120 •146	7,227 •93	n/a –	n/a –	n/a –	n/a –	1,382 •60	312.2 •33	169 •188	0.54 •191
Guatemala (E5)	Guatemala City	.gt	0.5 •156	66.5 •140	4.8 •133	41.4 •97	5.97 •123	25.02 •111	8.94 •141	0.36 •151	4.35 •97	1.95 •102	3.3 •103	2,243 •124	26,945 •64	17,519 •64	649 •50	658 •62	770 •72	1,182 •72	576 •89	110.3 •86	12,014 •68	108.90 •104
Guinea (I5)	Conakry	.gn	2.9 •35	46.5 •197	5.8 •99	49.8 •69	0.53 •186	1.44 •199	0.34 •212	0.06 •193	0.56 •156	0.11 •137	3.7 •81	389 •195	3,681 •140	n/a –	n/a –	n/a –	30 •111	45 •143	17 •193	38.4 •158	9,453 •83	245.90 •78
Guinea-Bissau	Bissau	.gw	3.1 •32	45.0	6.3 •77	45.1 •85	1.99 •164	0.10 •215	0.82 •196	0.09 •183	0.13 •185	0.00 –	-0.3 •175	177 •218	250 •207	n/a –	n/a –	n/a –	n/a –	n/a –	n/a –	39.2 •156	1,413 •149	36.10 •137
Guyana (G5)	Georgetown	.gy	0.9 •138	62.5 •155	5.6 •109	8.1 •194	18.90 •73	13.64 •132	13.39 •120	0.78 •129	0.60 •155	0.00 –	1.1 •167	1,000 •160	765 •180	n/a –	n/a –	n/a –	n/a –	122 •127	76 •160	3.6 •213	765 •160	215.00 •84
Haiti (F5)	Port-au-Prince	.ht	0.9 •138	53.0 •185	7.6 •52	57.3 •48	6.09 •122	4.87 •166	1.71 •182	0.08 •188	0.67 •149	0.06 •144	0.9 •169	416 •192	3,380 •143	n/a –	n/a –	n/a –	n/a –	n/a –	149 •140	292.1 •39	8,122 •90	27.80 •146
Honduras (E5)	Tegucigalpa	.hn	0.4 •159	67.0 •137	6.2 •81	26.1 •143	3.18 •152	10.10 •146	5.57 •157	0.35 •154	2.52 •118	0.44 •121	3.4 •98	1,021 •157	7,321 •108	18,590 •62	210 •69	277 •73	396 •87	672 •87	307 •109	63.9 •131	7,168 •96	112.10 •101
Hungary (J3)	Budapest	.hu	1.8 •83	72.5 •77	7.8 •48	63.1 •28	26.74 •56	86.43 •26	35.43 •58	2.68 •69	26.86 •50	9.73 •74	4.0 •73	8,326 •70	83,315 •46	64,091 •33	2,864 •34	14,283 •14	4,061 •38	12,212 •17	2,887 •39	107.6 •87	10,007 •81	93.00 •110
Iceland (I2)	Reykjavik	.is	M	80.0 •10	9.9 •11	22.1 •159	77.00 •2	99.00 •10	65.01 •13	11.78 •8	3.50 •108	2.50 •95	n/a –	37,740 •8	11,199 •96	7,330 •92	n/a –	372 •88	n/a –	836 •82	202 •132	2.9 •217	297 •176	103.00 •105
India[19] (M4)	New Delhi	.in	2.1 •66	61.5 •158	6.1 •87	55.1 •55	3.24 •151	4.37 •170	4.07 •167	0.32 •156	350.75 •6	253.66 •11	6.0 •30	624 •170	674,580 •11	91,720 •25	5,072 •24	5,351 •26	4,739 •35	3,457 •44	2,374 •45	352.5 •27	1,080,264 •2	3,065.00 •7
Indonesia (O6)	Jakarta	.id	1.5 •102	66.5 •140	3.2 •177	23.3 •156	6.52 •120	13.48 •133	4.49 •162	0.49 •144	117.97 •20	216.96 •12	2.7 •124	1,025 •156	248,007 •23	263,014 •11	3,507 •28	4,798 •34	4,798 •34	5,322 •37	5,185 •25	126.1 •77	241,974 •4	1,919.40 •16
Iran (L4)	Tehran	.ir	3.8 •28	69.5 •123	6.0 •92	37.1 •112	7.88 •108	6.16 •158	21.97 •98	2.22 •78	150.98 •16	281.68 •6	4.8 •50	2,264 •120	153,984 •33	n/a –	n/a –	n/a –	n/a –	n/a –	764 •76	41.3 •153	68,018 •18	1,648.00 •18
Iraq (L4)	Baghdad	.iq	n/a –	55.5 •180	1.5 •192	23.0 •157	0.14 •202	2.22 •191	4.00 •168	0.94 •120	24.40 •53	71.44 •31	n/a –	#VALUE!	n/a –	n/a –	n/a –	n/a –	n/a –	n/a –	15 •197	59.5 •137	26,075 •44	438.30 •58
Ireland (I3)	Dublin	.ie	1.0 •134	78.5 •30	7.3 •59	62.7 •29	29.63 •47	93.49 •16	49.94 •33	3.78 •44	15.20 •68	0.88 •112	7.7 •13	34,306 •12	137,761 •37	n/a –	5,200 •23	4,929 •28	4,279 •36	6,982 •24	5,587 •24	57.1 •139	4,016 •124	70.30 •120
Israel[20] (K4)	Jerusalem	.il	9.1 •4	80.0 •10	9.1 •26	25.6 •145	46.63 •32	105.25 •6	43.72 •49	3.55 •50	22.28 •56	0.20 •132	n/a –	18,819 •34	118,124 •37	46,368 •42	2,976 •30	3,299 •38	2,383 •47	1,506 •65	2,010 •53	286.6 •41	6,277 •101	21.90 •151

*: Ranking (top 10 in **bold**).   n/a: Not available, not relevant or not reliable.   **M:** See note on page 41.   **T:** See note on page 41.   For more information, see pages 202 & 210.

112 **Appendices**

Countries A-Z: Italy-Mali

▶ **See also...** pages 108 & 116 for notes relating to this section; Contents (2-5) for details of all maps and charts in this Atlas

Country / Map Ref.	Capital	Internet code	Area 000 sq km	Population 000 (2004)	Pop. Density people/sq km (2004)	Int'l Arrivals 1997 000	Int'l Arrivals 2004 000	Visitor Receipts US$ m 2004	Int'l Departures 000 (2004)	Visitor Expenditure US$ m (2004)	Hotel Bedrooms (2003)	Gross Nat'l Income US$ bn (2004)	GNI per Person US$ (2004)	GDP Growth Av. % 1997-2006	Energy Production Mil. toe (2004)	Energy Consumption Mil. toe (2004)	Energy Consumption toe/person (2004)	Fixed Tel. Lines /100 (2004)	Mobile Tel. Lines /100 (2004)	Internet Usage /100 (2004)	Agricultural Land % (2004)	Total Health Spending % GNI (2004)	Life Expectancy yrs (2004)	Military Spending % of GNI (2003)
Italy — J3	Rome	.it	301.30 •71	58,103 •23	192.8 •55	34,692 •4	37,071 •5	35,658 •4	26,817 •7	20,544 •6	999,722 •3	1,503,562 •7	25,878 •26	1.2 •165	31.19 •45	199.05 •12	3.43 •52	44.75 •45	108.19 •4	49.78 •26	51.2 •67	8.5 •35	81.0 •4	1.9 •77
Jamaica — F5	Kingston	.jm	11.40 •162	2,736 •138	240.0 •49	1,192 •62	1,415 •68	1,437 •57	n/a	287 •64	20,827 •57	7,738 •106	2,829 •106	1.3 •164	0.05 •145	3.84 •106	1.40 •99	14.60 •113	82.21 •34	39.87 •38	46.7 •81	6.0 •92	72.5 •77	0.4 •159
Japan — P4	Tokyo	.jp	377.80 •61	127,417 •10	337.3 •29	4,218 •30	6,138 •32	11,294 •13	13,296 •15	38,129 •4	1,562,867 •2	4,749,910 •2	37,278 •9	0.9 •169	98.56 •23	560.53 •4	4.40 •33	46.00 •43	71.58 •47	50.20 •22	13.7 •177	7.9 •45	81.5 •2	1.0 •134
Jordan — J4	Amman	.jo	91.90 •111	5,760 •61	62.7 •133	1,127 •64	2,853 •52	826 •67	1,533 •51	826 •67	19,698 •61	11,629 •85	2,019 •132	4.4 •61	0.37 •123	5.96 •85	1.03 •112	11.00 •131	28.41 •104	10.69 •98	12.8 •181	9.3 •21	71.0 •99	8.9 •6
Kazakhstan — M3	Astana	.kz	2,717.30 •9	15,186 •61	5.6 •211	—	1,471 •59	n/a	2,374 •41	n/a	11,104 •77	33,780 •60	2,224 •125	7.1 •18	104.38 •22	52.22 •33	3.44 •51	16.23 •109	17.91 •122	2.60 •157	76.1 •13	3.5 •171	61.5 •158	1.1 •129
Kenya — K5	Nairobi	.ke	582.60 •46	33,830 •34	58.1 •138	907 •70	1,132 •77	495 •81	n/a	n/a	n/a	14,987 •82	443 •186	2.8 •123	1.00 •108	3.84 •106	0.11 •177	0.92 •195	7.85 •153	4.63 •135	45.6 •84	4.9 •128	49.5 •193	1.7 •88
Kiribati — A6	Bairiki	.ki	0.72 •186	103 •195	143.2 •71	5 •200	5 •200	n/a	n/a	n/a	n/a	95 •215	922 •164	4.2 •66	0.00 •108	0.01 •207	0.10 •182	5.11 •158	0.59 •207	2.35 •160	48.1 •73	8.0 •42	64.5 •150	T
Korea, DPR (North) — P3	Pyongyang	.kp	122.80 •98	22,912 •47	186.6 •58	193 •134	236 •117	n/a	n/a	n/a	n/a	11,047 •97	482 •183	n/a	20.45 •55	22.04 •59	0.96 •118	4.10 •166	n/a	n/a	22.4 •158	4.6 •140	66.5 •140	n/a
Korea, Rep. (South) — P4	Seoul	.kr	99.40 •107	48,641 •36	489.3 •19	3,908 •32	5,818 •35	5,697 •28	7,086 •19	9,499 •16	56,196 •36	673,036 •12	13,837 •52	4.7 •53	33.93 •42	215.84 •11	4.44 •32	55.31 •23	76.09 •41	65.68 •7	19.5 •163	5.0 •124	76.5 •53	2.5 •53
Kuwait — L4	Kuwait City	.kw	17.80 •156	2,336 •140	131.2 •75	79 •159	91 •132	180 •98	2,286 •43	n/a	n/a	43,052 •58	18,433 •37	3.0 •117	130.29 •20	23.45 •54	10.04 •10	19.47 •103	78.34 •38	23.50 •62	8.5 •191	3.8 •163	77.5 •41	9.0 •5
Kyrgyzstan — M3	Bishkek	.kg	199.90 •86	5,146 •112	25.7 •175	87 •155	165 •123	n/a	n/a	n/a	n/a	2,050 •157	398 •193	5.6 •36	3.46 •89	4.63 •94	0.90 •122	8.18 •144	5.17 •162	5.16 •130	54.3 •59	4.3 •150	63.5 •152	2.9 •35
Laos — O5	Vientiane	.la	236.80 •82	6,217 •102	26.3 •173	403 •104	894 •81	119 •101	n/a	n/a	12,289 •76	2,239 •155	360 •198	6.2 •28	1.11 •107	1.24 •134	0.20 •168	1.30 •190	3.53 •179	0.36 •194	7.9 •195	2.9 •183	59.0 •172	2.1 •66
Latvia — K3	Riga	.lv	64.60 •124	2,290 •141	35.5 •163	635 •85	1,080 •78	267 •94	n/a	377 •60	7,618 •89	12,570 •73	5,489 •80	6.8 •23	0.54 •118	3.90 •103	1.70 •87	28.45 •62	67.22 •38	n/a	38.3 •99	5.1 •119	71.0 •99	1.7 •88
Lebanon — K4	Beirut	.lb	10.50 •165	3,826 •126	364.4 •25	558 •90	1,278 •70	n/a	n/a	n/a	16,202 •69	22,668 •69	5,925 •78	3.0 •117	0.26 •129	5.74 •86	1.50 •93	17.75 •105	25.01 •112	16.90 •80	31.5 •124	11.5 •3	70.0 •116	4.3 •20
Lesotho — K7	Maseru	.ls	30.40 •140	2,031 •144	66.8 •124	144 •143	304 •116	n/a	n/a	n/a	n/a	1,336 •167	658 •169	2.0 •153	0.09 •139	0.17 •183	0.08 •186	2.07 •180	8.83 •150	2.39 •159	76.9 •11	6.2 •81	37.5 •216	2.6 •47
Liberia — I5	Monrovia	.lr	99.10 •108	2,900 •136	29.3 •170	n/a	n/a	n/a	n/a	n/a	n/a	391 •196	135 •221	0.06 •190	0.00 •182	0.18 •182	0.06 •190	0.21 •200	1.40 •200	0.03 •208	26.6 •142	2.1 •188	41.5 •210	7.5 •8
Libya — J4	Tripoli	.ly	1,775.50 •17	5,766 •104	3.2 •215	88 •155	n/a	n/a	n/a	n/a	12,405 •75	25,257 •68	4,381 •90	3.5 •91	83.91 •26	18.15 •65	3.15 •60	13.56 •116	2.30 •189	3.62 •141	8.7 •190	3.3 •175	63.5 •152	2.0 •73
Liechtenstein — J3	Vaduz	.li	0.16 •216	34 •210	210.7 •52	57 •170	50 •142	n/a	50 •171	57 •170	591 •141	1,252 •168	37,133 •10	n/a	0.00 •182	n/a	n/a	67.22 •38	n/a	n/a	56.3 •49	n/a	79.5 •17	T
Lithuania — K3	Vilnius	.lt	65.30 •123	3,597 •129	55.1 •140	1,012 •67	1,800 •60	817 •68	3,502 •35	639 •51	7,694 •87	19,727 •75	5,485 •81	5.9 •32	4.63 •81	10.95 •75	3.04 •62	23.80 •92	99.29 •9	28.09 •52	53.4 •65	5.9 •96	72.0 •87	1.6 •93
Luxembourg — J3	Luxembourg	.lu	2.60 •174	469 •166	180.2 •60	778 •75	874 •81	3,666 •41	n/a	3,347 •29	7,626 •88	25,302 •67	53,998 •1	5.2 •42	0.04 •146	4.46 •96	9.51 •13	79.75 •9	119.38 •1	59.00 •15	24.0 •152	6.2 •81	79.0 •24	0.9 •138
Macedonia, FYR — K3	Skopje	.mk	25.70 •148	2,045 •143	79.6 •110	121 •147	165 •123	72 •107	n/a	n/a	6,825 •94	4,855 •127	2,374 •113	2.4 •133	1.56 •104	2.77 •115	1.35 •101	25.19 •89	37.23 •82	7.70 •111	48.3 •72	6.8 •69	72.0 •87	2.5 •53
Madagascar — L8	Antananarivo	.mg	587.00 •45	18,040 •56	30.7 •167	101 •151	229 •120	n/a	n/a	n/a	9,325 •85	5,181 •124	287 •207	3.2 •108	0.14 •136	0.92 •144	0.05 •197	0.33 •214	1.87 •195	0.50 •187	46.9 •77	2.1 •188	57.0 •179	1.4 •109
Malawi — K6	Lilongwe	.mw	118.50 •99	12,707 •65	107.2 •88	207 •131	414 •104	72 •107	n/a	n/a	20,871 •56	1,922 •158	151 •220	5.9 •32	0.32 •126	0.61 •154	0.05 •198	0.75 •200	1.80 •196	0.37 •193	36.2 •114	9.8 •12	35.0 •219	0.8 •144
Malaysia — O5	Kuala Lumpur	.my	329.80 •66	23,953 •46	72.6 •117	6,211 •22	15,703 •13	8,198 •20	32,201 •6	n/a	144,380 •16	117,132 •38	4,890 •83	4.4 •61	93.04 •24	57.85 •30	2.42 •73	17.38 •106	57.12 •66	38.62 •40	23.9 •153	3.8 •163	72.5 •77	2.8 •40
Maldives — M6	Malé	.mv	0.30 •204	349 •174	1,163.7 •8	366 •108	617 •90	479 •83	44 •87	n/a	8,557 •85	752 •182	2,154 •126	6.9 •20	0.00 •145	0.85 •145	2.44 •72	9.60 •138	34.53 •94	5.79 •124	43.6 •89	5.8 •99	65.0 •146	5.5 •13
Mali — I5	Bamako	.ml	1,248.60 •22	11,415 •71	9.1 •205	75 •162	113 •129	n/a	n/a	n/a	3,907 •116	4,335 •137	380 •196	5.2 •42	0.17 •133	0.38 •165	0.03 •203	0.68 •202	3.60 •177	0.45 •190	28.0 •140	4.5 •144	45.0 •201	1.9 •77

*: *Ranking* (top 10 in **bold**). **n/a:** Not available, not relevant or not reliable. **T:** See note on page 41. **M:** See note on page 41. For more information, see pages 202 & 210.

► See also... pages 108 & 116 for notes relating to this section; Contents (2-5) for details of all maps and charts in this Atlas

Appendices **113**

Countries A-Z: Malta-Niue

Note: values shown as "value •rank" (ranking; top 10 in **bold**).

Country / Map Ref.	Internet code	Capital	Area 000 sq km (2004)	Population 000 (2004)	Pop. Density /sq km (2004)	Int'l Arrivals 1997 000	Int'l Arrivals 2004 000	Visitor Receipts US$m (2004)	Int'l Departures 000 (2004)	Visitor Expenditure US$m (2004)	Hotel Bedrooms (2003)	Gross Nat'l Income US$bn (2004)	GNI per Person US$ (2004)	GDP Growth av.% 1997-2006	Energy Production Mtoe (2004)	Energy Consumption Mtoe (2004)	Energy Consumption toe/person (2004)	Fixed Tel Lines /100 (2004)	Mobile Tel Lines /100 (2004)	Internet Usage /100 (2004)	Agricultural Land % (2002)	Total Health Spending % of GNI (2002)	Life Expectancy yrs (2004)	Military Spending % of GNI (2003)
Malta J4	.mt	Valletta	0.32 •203	399 •172	1,245.4 •**7**	1,111 •66	1,156 •76	779 •71	174 •77	256 •65	n/a	4,913 •126	12,328 •56	2.5 •128	0.00 •–	0.98 •140	2.46 •71	51.63 •28	76.52 •40	75.25 •**4**	31.6 •123	9.6 •16	78.5 •30	0.7 •147
Marshall Is. R5	.mh	Majuro	0.18 •214	59 •204	328.2 •30	6 •199	7 •153	n/a	n/a	n/a	n/a	142 •210	2,404 •112	n/a	0.00 •–	note 1	n/a	8.27 •143	1.11 •203	3.51 •142	77.3 •**10**	10.6 •**8**	61.5 •158	T •–
Martinique F5	.mq	Fort-de-France	1.10 •181	433 •170	393.5 •24	513 •93	471 •100	n/a	n/a	n/a	6,766 •95	6,346 •118	14,659 •47	n/a	0.00 •–	0.72 •146	1.66 •90	44.47 •47	74.78 •43	27.09 •55	30.0 •127	n/a	79.0 •24	n/a
Mauritania I5	.mr	Nouakchott	1,030.70 •29	3,087 •133	3.0 •216	24 •187	n/a	n/a	n/a	n/a	n/a	1,210 •170	392 •194	7.4 •15	0.01 •158	1.25 •133	0.40 •147	1.31 •189	17.53 •124	0.47 •189	38.6 •106	3.9 •161	50.5 •191	1.6 •93
Mauritius L7	.mu	Port Louis	2.00 •176	1,231 •152	615.3 •15	536 •91	719 •86	853 •66	161 •79	255 •66	9,647 •81	5,730 •121	4,656 •85	5.0 •45	0.03 •150	1.30 •130	1.06 •110	28.69 •75	41.36 •79	14.60 •84	55.4 •54	3.5 •171	72.5 •77	0.2 •163
Mayotte L6	.yt	Dzaoudzi	0.37 •200	194 •185	523.3 •18	n/a	n/a	n/a	n/a	n/a	n/a	881 •175	4,550 •87	n/a	0.00 •–	n/a	n/a	6.24 •154	28.80 •102	n/a	n/a	n/a	74.5 •63	T •–
Mexico D4	.mx	Mexico City	1,967.20 •15	106,203 •11	54.0 •141	19,351 •**8**	20,618 •**8**	10,753 •14	11,044 •17	6,959 •22	496,292 •**8**	703,080 •**10**	6,620 •74	3.5 •91	254.19 •**10**	169.79 •13	1.60 •91	17.22 •107	36.64 •84	13.38 •87	54.9 •56	6.1 •87	74.5 •63	0.5 •156
Micronesia, Fed. States Q5	.fm	Palikir	0.70 •188	108 •194	154.4 •67	17 •193	19 •150	95 •104	n/a	135 •71	n/a	252 •206	2,331 •115	n/a	0.00 •–	0.02 •204	2.22 •77	10.81 •133	11.52 •140	10.81 •97	67.1 •21	6.5 •71	69.5 •123	T •–
Moldova K3	.md	Chisinău	33.70 •138	4,455 •118	132.2 •74	21 •190	24 •149	n/a	67 •85	n/a	2,559 •127	2,563 •150	575 •175	3.3 •103	0.09 •140	4.34 •98	0.97 •117	20.25 •101	18.46 •121	9.52 •100	75.0 •14	7.0 •62	67.0 •137	0.4 •159
Monaco J3	.mc	Monaco-Ville	0.002 •226	32 •211	16,204.5 •**2**	259 •124	246 •114	n/a	n/a	n/a	2,212 •130	870 •176	26,844 •24	n/a	0.00 •–	n/a	n/a	105.31 •**1**	60.31 •59	50.00 •23	0.0 •–	11.0 •**6**	81.5 •**2**	T •–
Mongolia O3	.mn	Ulan Bator	1,565.00 •19	2,791 •137	1.8 •223	82 •157	n/a	403 •86	n/a	87 •74	2,749 •125	1,484 •165	532 •179	4.4 •61	1.72 •103	2.35 •121	0.84 •126	5.62 •156	12.98 •136	7.60 •112	83.4 •**3**	6.3 •77	65.5 •145	2.1 •66
Montserrat F5	.ms	Plymouth[13]	0.10 •219	9 •222	93.4 •98	5 •200	10 •151	n/a	n/a	n/a	n/a	21 •221	2,248 •122	n/a	0.00 •–	0.02 •204	2.22 •77	14.62 •112	11.54 •139	0.02 •209	29.4 •133	7.6 •52	79.0 •24	T •–
Morocco I4	.ma	Rabat	458.50 •55	32,726 •36	71.3 •118	3,072 •36	5,501 •36	3,921 •40	1,694 •50	568 •53	75,284 •30	46,518 •56	1,421 •143	3.3 •103	0.32 •127	12.39 •92	0.38 •150	4.38 •164	31.23 •98	11.71 •92	42.6 •92	4.6 •140	71.0 •99	4.2 •24
Mozambique K7	.mz	Maputo	799.40 •35	19,407 •54	24.3 •176	189 •135	n/a	95 •104	n/a	134 •72	n/a	4,710 •130	243 •211	8.5 •**9**	3.92 •86	4.16 •102	0.21 •164	0.42 •209	3.73 •176	0.73 •182	60.6 •36	5.8 •99	45.0 •201	1.3 •113
Myanmar (Burma) N4	.mm	Yangon[14]	676.60 •40	46,997 •26	69.5 •120	189 •135	242 •116	136 •100	n/a	n/a	17,039 •65	13,785 •84	293 •205	n/a	10.14 •72	4.58 •95	0.10 •181	0.79 •198	0.17 •214	0.12 •203	16.1 •172	2.2 •188	59.5 •169	2.3 •60
Namibia J7	.na	Windhoek	824.30 •34	2,031 •181	2.5 •221	502 •94	n/a	n/a	78 •84	n/a	2,749 •125	4,813 •128	2,370 •114	3.5 •91	0.36 •124	1.26 •132	0.62 •139	6.36 •153	14.23 •129	3.73 •140	47.1 •76	6.7 •70	51.5 •189	2.8 •40
Nauru R6	.nr	Yaren District	0.02 •223	13 •220	652.4 •12	n/a	n/a	n/a	n/a	n/a	n/a	32 •218	2,452 •110	n/a	0.00 •–	0.06 •195	4.62 •29	n/a	n/a	n/a	0.0 •–	7.6 •52	61.5 •158	T •–
Nepal N4	.np	Kathmandu	140.80 •95	27,677 •40	196.6 •54	422 •97	360 •107	258 •74	n/a	n/a	20,063 •60	6,538 •116	236 •212	3.7 •81	0.57 •117	1.55 •128	0.06 •194	1.69 •183	0.47 •208	0.48 •188	34.2 •116	5.2 •115	60.5 •166	1.6 •93
Netherlands J3	.nl	Amsterdam[15]	41.50 •134	16,407 •59	395.4 •23	7,841 •18	9,646 •20	10,081 •16	16,463 •12	16,539 •**8**	88,146 •26	515,148 •15	31,397 •17	2.3 •139	63.20 •34	100.47 •22	6.12 •18	48.44 •38	91.21 •18	61.63 •13	46.9 •77	8.8 •31	78.5 •30	1.6 •93
Netherlands Antilles F5	.an	Willemstad	0.80 •183	220 •181	274.9 •43	705 •78	n/a	919 •64	n/a	477 •57	n/a	2,154 •156	9,793 •63	1.7 •156	0.00 •–	3.87 •105	17.59 •**4**	37.23 •57	90.09 •17	n/a	8.3 •192	n/a	76.0 •55	T •–
New Caledonia R7	.nc	Nouméa	18.60 •154	216 •182	11.6 •199	105 •149	100 •130	n/a	n/a	n/a	n/a	3,158 •145	14,587 •48	n/a	0.08 •142	0.70 •147	3.24 •58	22.98 •95	50.19 •69	n/a	13.4 •178	n/a	74.0 •70	T •–
New Zealand R7	.nz	Wellington	270.50 •75	4,035 •122	14.9 •191	1,497 •58	2,348 •56	4,951 •33	1,374 •54	2,360 •38	20,072 •59	82,465 •47	20,435 •33	3.1 •112	17.12 •56	21.87 •60	5.42 •23	46.11 •42	77.52 •39	81.95 •**1**	63.7 •25	8.5 •35	79.5 •17	1.1 •129
Nicaragua E5	.ni	Managua	130.70 •97	5,465 •107	41.8 •151	358 •111	615 •91	167 •115	562 •65	n/a	4,418 •112	4,452 •134	815 •166	3.8 •79	0.22 •130	1.60 •127	0.29 •159	3.77 •171	13.00 •135	2.20 •162	58.0 •46	7.9 •45	70.5 •111	0.9 •138
Niger J5	.ne	Niamey	1,186.40 •25	12,163 •66	10.3 •201	44 •176	44 •176	19 •221	n/a	40 •163	1,472 •133	2,836 •148	233 •214	3.6 •85	0.11 •137	0.40 •163	0.03 •205	0.19 •221	1.19 •202	0.19 •199	13.0 •180	4.0 •159	41.5 •210	1.1 •129
Nigeria J5	.ng	Abuja (9)	923.80 •32	128,766 •**9**	139.4 •72	611 •87	611 •87	21 •112	n/a	81 •51	n/a	53,983 •54	419 •191	4.1 •68	140.10 •18	24.62 •51	0.19 •169	0.81 •197	7.20 •154	1.39 •169	78.2 •**8**	4.7 •137	45.5 •198	1.2 •120
Niue A6	.nu	Alofi	0.26 •206	2 •226	8.3 •207	2 •204	3 •154	n/a	n/a	n/a	n/a	4 •224	1,847 •137	n/a	0.00 •–	0.00 •211	0.50 •143	55.00 •24	20.00 •117	n/a	30.4 •126	9.7 •15	71.0 •99	T •–

*: Ranking (top 10 in **bold**). n/a: Not available, not relevant or not reliable. M: See note on page 41. T: See note on page 41. For more information, see pages 202 & 210.

114 **Appendices**

Countries A-Z: N. Mariana Is-San Marino

▶ *See also...* pages 108 & 116 for notes relating to this section; Contents (2-5) for details of all maps and charts in this Atlas

Values shown as "value •rank"; — = not ranked; n/a = not available/not relevant/not reliable; T / M = see note on page 41.

Country (code, Map Ref)	Capital	Military Spending % of GNI (2003)	Life Expectancy Years (2004)	Total Health Spending % of GNI (2004)	Agricultural Land % of national area (2004)	Internet Usage Subscribers/100 (2004)	Mobile Tel. Lines /100 (2004)	Fixed Tel. Lines /100 (2004)	Energy Consumption t oil equiv./person (2004)	Energy Consumption Mt oil equiv. (2004)	Energy Production Mt oil equiv. (2004)	GDP Growth Av annual % 1997-2006	GNI per Person US$ (2004)	Gross Nat'l Income US$ million (2004)	Hotel Bedrooms (2003)	Visitor Expenditure US$m (2004)	International Departures '000 (2004)	Visitor Receipts US$m (2004)	International Arrivals '000 (2004)	International Arrivals '000 (1997)	Population Density /sq km (2004)	Population '000 (2004)	Area '000 sq km
Northern Mariana Is. (.mp, O5)	Saipan	T –	76.0 •55	n/a –	28.4 •138	n/a –	3.75 •175	26.25 •82	n/a –	n/a –	0.00 –	n/a –	1,456 •142	117 •212	4,231 •113	n/a –	n/a –	n/a –	525 •97	685 •79	174.7 •62	80 •198	0.46 •194
Norway (.no, J2)	Oslo	2.0 •73	79.5 •17	9.6 •16	3.2 •207	39.37 •39	90.89 •19	48.64 •37	9.69 •12	44.51 •36	260.06 •8	3.0 •117	51,904 •2	238,398 •25	67,114 •32	8,428 •19	2,588 •40	3,087 •44	3,600 •42	2,702 •42	14.2 •193	4,593 •116	323.80 •67
Oman (.om, L5)	Muscat	12.2 •2	74.0 •70	3.4 •174	3.5 •204	10.14 •99	33.32 •95	10.05 •136	3.25 •57	9.75 •79	59.36 •36	4.0 •73	6,832 •72	20,508 •74	6,473 •96	n/a –	n/a –	n/a –	n/a –	376 •105	9.7 •203	3,002 •134	309.50 •70
Pakistan (.pk, M4)	Islamabad	4.4 •18	62.0 •157	3.2 •177	34.1 •117	1.31 •173	3.29 •182	2.95 •176	0.29 •158	47.69 •35	31.62 •43	4.5 •59	558 •176	90,663 •43	36,451 •49	1,275 •42	n/a –	186 •97	648 •89	375 •106	204.0 •53	162,420 •6	796.10 •36
Palau (.pw, P5)	Koror	T –	68.0 •131	9.1 •26	17.7 •168	n/a –	5.00 •165	33.50 •63	n/a –	n/a –	n/a –	n/a –	6,748 •73	137 •211	n/a –	n/a –	n/a –	n/a –	89 •133	74 •163	39.8 •155	20 •217	0.51 •192
Palestine NAR[4] (.ps, K4)	Jerusalem[16]	n/a –	72.5 •77	n/a –	61.5 •33	4.34 •138	26.44 •109	9.70 •137	n/a –	n/a –	n/a –	4.1 •68	1,002 •158	3,771 •139	5,919 •99	n/a –	n/a –	n/a –	n/a –	201 •133	606.8 •16	3,762 •125	6.20 •168
Panama (.pa, E5)	Panama City	1.2 •120	75.5 •59	8.9 •29	29.5 •132	9.46 •101	26.98 •107	11.85 •129	1.59 •92	4.99 •90	0.72 •115	3.4 •98	4,289 •91	13,468 •86	16,766 •68	n/a –	227 •76	685 •74	652 •88	421 •98	41.6 •152	3,140 •132	75.50 •118
Papua New Guinea (.pg, Q6)	Port Moresby	0.6 •152	60.5 •166	4.3 •150	2.3 •209	2.91 •154	0.27 •210	1.13 •193	0.21 •166	1.17 •137	2.95 •93	0.6 •174	588 •173	3,262 •144	2,830 •124	n/a –	n/a –	18 •113	59 •140	66 •166	12.0 •198	5,545 •106	462.80 •54
Paraguay (.py, G7)	Asunción	0.9 •138	72.0 •87	8.4 •38	61.0 •36	2.49 •158	29.38 •99	4.73 •160	1.68 •89	10.64 •76	13.13 •60	1.7 •156	1,064 •155	6,752 •112	4,899 •108	n/a –	153 •81	70 •108	309 •109	395 •101	15.6 •188	6,348 •100	406.80 •59
Peru (.pe, F6)	Lima	1.3 •113	70.5 •111	4.4 •146	24.4 •151	11.61 •93	14.75 •127	7.39 •147	0.51 •142	14.22 •69	10.04 •73	3.9 •76	2,329 •116	65,043 •50	123,252 •19	620 •59	889 •59	1,078 •62	1,203 •72	649 •82	21.7 •178	27,926 •39	1,285.20 •20
Philippines (.ph, P5)	Manila	0.9 •138	68.0 •131	2.9 •183	40.7 •99	5.32 •128	39.85 •80	4.16 •165	0.36 •153	31.30 •44	10.63 •69	3.8 •79	1,103 •154	96,930 •41	21,409 •55	1,315 •40	1,803 •49	2,012 •52	2,291 •57	2,223 •49	292.9 •38	87,857 •12	300.00 •72
Poland (.pl, J3)	Warsaw	2.0 •73	75.0 •62	6.1 •87	58.7 •43	23.35 •63	59.91 •60	31.85 •67	2.37 •74	91.20 •23	75.82 •30	3.5 •91	6,027 •77	232,398 •26	68,588 •31	3,906 •27	38,730 •4	5,828 •27	14,290 •15	19,520 •7	123.3 •81	38,558 •32	312.70 •69
Portugal[5] (.pt, I3)	Lisbon	2.1 •66	77.5 •41	9.3 •21	44.9 •86	28.03 •53	98.41 •11	40.25 •55	2.64 •70	27.92 •48	4.58 •82	2.5 •128	14,176 •34	149,790 •34	105,986 •21	2,767 •35	n/a –	7,788 •21	11,617 •19	10,172 •15	115.0 •82	10,566 •76	91.90 •112
Puerto Rico (.pr, F5)	San Juan	T –	n/a –	n/a –	32.8 •120	22.12 •66	68.82 •50	28.53 •76	3.34 •53	13.07 •71	0.07 •143	n/a –	1,142 •152	4,468 •133	12,788 •73	499 •56	1,272 •55	3,024 •45	3,541 •43	3,242 •35	439.5 •21	3,911 •125	8.90 •167
Qatar (.qa, L4)	Doha	10.0 •3	74.5 •63	3.1 •179	6.2 •202	22.00 •67	65.38 •52	25.45 •87	14.37 •6	12.40 •72	77.43 •27	9.9 •5	22,583 •30	19,490 •80	3,858 •117	n/a –	498 •80	n/a –	n/a –	435 •96	75.7 •115	863 •157	11.40 •163
Réunion (.re, L7)	Saint-Denis	n/a –	74.5 •63	n/a –	19.5 •163	26.08 •57	75.51 •42	41.04 •53	1.42 •98	1.10 •138	0.15 •135	n/a –	11,268 •60	8,755 •100	2,910 •123	n/a –	333 •71	448 •85	430 •103	374 •107	310.8 •34	777 •159	2.50 •175
Romania (.ro, K3)	Bucharest	2.4 •57	71.5 •95	6.3 •77	62.2 •30	20.76 •71	47.13 •73	20.25 •101	1.89 •83	42.12 •39	29.02 •48	2.4 •133	2,862 •105	63,910 •51	97,320 •22	512 •55	6,497 •20	505 •79	3,739 •41	2,957 •38	94.5 •97	22,330 •49	236.40 •83
Russian Federation (.ru, M2)	Moscow	4.3 •20	65.0 •146	6.2 •81	12.7 •182	11.10 •95	51.61 •68	27.47 •78	5.07 •25	726.61 •3	1,230.03 •2	6.4 •26	3,398 •101	487,335 •16	177,200 •14	15,730 •10	20,468 •8	5,226 •31	9,164 •21	17,463 •10	8.4 •206	143,420 •8	17,075.40 •1
Rwanda (.rw, K6)	Kigali	2.8 •40	44.5 •205	5.3 •114	70.2 •16	0.45 •190	1.64 •197	0.27 •215	0.04 •199	0.34 •169	0.02 •151	4.7 •16	222 •215	1,875 •160	n/a –	n/a –	n/a –	n/a –	n/a –	104 •150	320.9 •31	8,441 •88	26.30 •147
St Helena (.sh, I7)	Jamestown	T –	78.0 •39	n/a –	29.3 •134	7.14 •115	n/a –	31.43 •70	1.43 •97	0.01 •207	0.00 –	n/a –	2,413 •111	18 •222	n/a –	n/a –	n/a –	n/a –	n/a –	n/a –	62.2 •134	7 •223	0.12 •218
St Kitts & Nevis (.kn, F5)	Basseterre	M –	70.5 •111	5.5 •112	38.2 •108	21.41 •68	20.00 •117	50.00 •32	1.03 •113	0.04 •198	0.00 –	3.2 •108	9,164 •65	357 •197	3,749 •118	n/a –	n/a –	n/a –	n/a –	88 •154	149.8 •69	39 •209	0.26 •207
St Lucia (.lc, F5)	Castries	M –	72.0 •87	5.0 •124	32.5 •124	36.67 •42	62.00 •55	31.95 •55	0.78 •130	0.13 •185	0.00 –	2.1 •149	4,245 •92	706 •184	n/a –	n/a –	n/a –	325 –	298 •110	248 •127	288.2 •44	166 •189	0.62 •190
St Pierre et Miquelon (.pm, G3)	St Pierre	T –	70.0 •116	n/a –	12.4 •184	n/a –	n/a –	68.57 •11	4.29 •35	0.03 •202	0.01 •158	n/a –	15,402 •43	108 •214	n/a –	n/a –	n/a –	n/a –	n/a –	n/a –	29.2 •171	7 •224	0.24 •208
St Vincent & the Gren. (.vc, F5)	Kingstown	M –	70.0 •116	5.9 •96	41.1 •98	6.61 •119	47.07 •74	13.72 •115	0.59 •140	0.07 •191	0.02 •151	3.3 •103	3,369 •102	396 •195	1,680 •132	n/a –	n/a –	n/a –	87 •134	65 •167	301.4 •37	118 •191	0.39 •199
Samoa (.ws, S6)	Apia	T –	68.5 •127	6.2 •81	46.3 •82	3.33 •147	5.76 •160	7.29 •148	0.40 •148	0.07 •191	0.00 –	3.3 •103	1,878 •135	333 •198	939 •138	n/a –	n/a –	n/a –	98 •131	68 •164	63.3 •132	177 •187	2.80 •173
San Marino (.sm, J3)	San Marino	T –	81.0 •4	7.7 •49	16.4 •171	49.31 •27	57.93 •65	71.03 •9	n/a –	n/a –	0.00 –	n/a –	22,611 •29	653 •188	683 •140	n/a –	n/a –	n/a –	42 •146	28 •181	481.3 •20	29 •212	0.06 •220

*•: Ranking (top 10 in **bold**). n/a: Not available, not relevant or not reliable. T: See note on page 41. M: See note on page 41. For more information, see pages 202 & 210.*

▶ See also... pages 108 & 116 for notes relating to this section; Contents (2-5) for details of all maps and charts in this Atlas

Appendices 115

Countries A-Z: São Tome-Tonga

Table columns are given in the chart's left-to-right order. Each data cell shows the value followed by its ranking in italics (top-10 rankings are shown in **bold**).

Country (Map Ref.)	Capital	Internet code	Military Spending % of GNI (2003)	Life Expectancy Years (2004)	Total Health Spending % of GNI (2004)	Agricultural Land % of national area (2002)	Internet Usage Subscribers/100 (2004)	Mobile Tel. Lines /100 (2004)	Fixed Tel. Lines /100 (2004)	Energy Consumption t oil equiv./person (2004)	Energy Consumption Mt oil equiv. (2004)	Energy Production Mt oil equiv. (2004)	GDP Growth Av. annual % 1997-2006	GNI per Person US$ (2004)	Gross Nat'l Income US$ billion (2004)	Hotel Bedrooms (2003)	Visitor Expenditure US$ m (2004)	International Departures 000 (2004)	Visitor Receipts US$ m (2004)	International Arrivals 2004 000	International Arrivals 1997 000	Population Density /sq km (2004)	Population 000 (2004)	Area 000 sq km
São Tomé e Príncipe (J6)	São Tomé	.st	0.8 *144*	59.0 *172*	11.1 ***5***	54.9 *56*	12.20 *89*	3.17 *183*	4.59 *161*	0.21 *165*	0.04 *198*	0.00 *–*	3.3 *103*	320 *202*	60 *216*	n/a	n/a	n/a	n/a	n/a	5 *200*	187.4 *56*	187 *186*	1.00 *182*
Saudi Arabia (L4)	Riyadh	.sa	8.7 ***7***	71.0 *99*	4.3 *150*	41.5 *95*	6.36 *121*	36.82 *83*	14.83 *111*	5.39 *24*	142.30 *17*	580.17 ***4***	3.4 *98*	9,167 *64*	242,180 *24*	81,197 *28*	4,406 *26*	4,104 *31*	6,542 *24*	8,580 *22*	n/a	12.0 *197*	26,418 *43*	2,200.00 *13*
Senegal (I5)	Dakar	.sn	1.5 *102*	55.5 *180*	5.1 *119*	54.7 *58*	4.66 *134*	10.85 *144*	2.37 *179*	0.14 *175*	1.64 *126*	0.04 *146*	5.4 *40*	595 *172*	6,967 *109*	10,268 *80*	n/a	n/a	n/a	363 *106*	314 *117*	59.7 *136*	11,706 *70*	196.20 *87*
Serbia & Montenegro [22] (K3)	Belgrade	.yu	4.2 *24*	72.5 *77*	8.1 *40*	15.4 *173*	18.61 *74*	58.01 *64*	32.94 *64*	1.78 *85*	19.23 *63*	13.34 *58*	2.0 *153*	2,005 *133*	21,715 *70*	37,101 *48*	n/a	n/a	220 *95*	580 *92*	298 *121*	106.0 *89*	10,829 *74*	102.20 *106*
Seychelles (L6)	Victoria	.sc	1.8 *83*	72.0 *87*	5.2 *115*	39.0 *105*	24.69 *60*	60.78 *58*	26.16 *83*	4.94 *26*	0.40 *163*	0.00 *–*	0.7 *173*	8,437 *69*	685 *185*	2,435 *129*	55	50 *86*	172 *99*	121 *128*	130 *146*	176.5 *61*	81 *197*	0.46 *195*
Sierra Leone (I5)	Freetown	.sl	1.7 *88*	38.0 *215*	2.9 *183*	3.0 *208*	0.19 *199*	2.28 *190*	0.48 *208*	0.06 *191*	0.35 *168*	0.00 *–*	5.0 *45*	190 *216*	1,113 *172*	1,457 *134*	n/a	13 *88*	n/a	44 *144*	23 *188*	80.0 *108*	5,867 *103*	73.30 *119*
Singapore (O5)	Singapore	.sg	5.2 *14*	61.5 *158*	4.3 *150*	49.6 *71*	56.12 *16*	89.47 *21*	43.20 *50*	9.92 *11*	43.92 *37*	0.00 *–*	n/a	23,724 *28*	104,994 *39*	35,930 *50*	7,744 *21*	4,221 *30*	5,090 *32*	8,328 *23*	6,531 *21*	6,808.8 ***3***	4,426 *120*	0.65 *189*
Slovak Rep. (K3)	Bratislava	.sk	1.9 *77*	74.0 *70*	5.9 *96*	24.9 *149*	42.27 *34*	79.39 *35*	23.22 *94*	3.69 *46*	20.04 *62*	7.07 *79*	4.1 *68*	6,427 *76*	34,907 *59*	35,853 *51*	745 *49*	408 *68*	901 *65*	1,401 *69*	814 *72*	110.8 *84*	5,431 *109*	49.00 *129*
Slovenia (J3)	Ljubljana	.si	1.5 *102*	77.0 *47*	8.3 *39*	4.2 *203*	47.96 *28*	87.09 *25*	40.68 *54*	3.82 *43*	7.68 *82*	7.55 *78*	3.6 *85*	14,696 *46*	29,555 *62*	15,534 *70*	911 *46*	2,114 *46*	1,630 *55*	1,499 *66*	974 *68*	99.1 *94*	2,011 *146*	20.30 *153*
Solomon Is. (R6)	Honiara	.sb	M *–*	71.0 *99*	4.8 *133*	69.1 *19*	0.61 *185*	0.31 *209*	1.31 *190*	0.13 *176*	0.07 *191*	0.00 *–*	-0.5 *176*	483 *182*	260 *205*	n/a	n/a	n/a	4 *116*	16 *196*	16 *196*	18.9 *184*	538 *163*	28.40 *143*
Somalia note[17] (L5)	Mogadishu	.so	n/a *–*	44.0 *207*	n/a *–*	81.7 ***4***	1.67 *167*	4.17 *173*	1.67 *184*	0.03 *206*	0.26 *173*	0.00 *–*	n/a *–*	#VALUE!	n/a *–*	n/a	n/a	n/a	n/a	n/a	n/a	13.5 *195*	8,592 *87*	637.70 *42*
South Africa note[17] (K7)	—	.za	1.6 *93*	49.0 *194*	8.7 *33*	59.8 *40*	7.89 *107*	43.13 *77*	10.40 *135*	2.76 *67*	122.54 *19*	147.89 *17*	3.1 *112*	3,728 *99*	165,326 *31*	52,329 *40*	2,668 *36*	5,692 *23*	5,648 *30*	6,678 *29*	5,170 *26*	36.2 *161*	44,344 *27*	1,224.70 *24*
Spain [6] (I4)	Madrid	.es	1.2 *120*	79.5 *17*	7.6 *52*	36.0 *115*	33.18 *22*	89.46 *22*	41.52 *52*	3.82 *42*	154.30 *15*	37.99 *39*	3.1 *112*	21,710 *31*	875,817 ***9***	740,747 ***6***	12,156 *13*	4,094 *32*	45,248 ***2***	53,599 ***2***	39,553 ***3***	79.9 *109*	40,341 *29*	504.80 *51*
Sri Lanka note[18] (N5)	—	.lk	2.7 *45*	71.5 *95*	3.7 *167*	53.4 *64*	1.44 *168*	11.37 *141*	5.10 *159*	0.24 *161*	4.90 *91*	0.75 *114*	4.7 *53*	978 *162*	19,618 *76*	16,973 *66*	296 *62*	561 *66*	513 *78*	566 *93*	366 *108*	305.9 *36*	20,065 *53*	65.60 *122*
Sudan (K5)	Khartoum	.sd	2.4 *57*	59.5 *169*	4.9 *128*	0.5 *214*	3.30 *150*	3.04 *184*	2.98 *175*	0.09 *185*	3.46 *110*	12.85 *62*	8.7 ***8***	452 *185*	18,152 *80*	n/a	n/a	n/a	n/a	n/a	30 *179*	16.0 *187*	40,187 *30*	2,505.80 ***10***
Surinam (G5)	Paramaribo	.sr	0.7 *147*	66.0 *143*	8.6 *34*	80.1 ***6***	6.83 *118*	48.48 *71*	18.52 *104*	2.24 *76*	0.98 *140*	0.96 *109*	3.2 *108*	2,276 *118*	997 *174*	n/a	n/a	n/a	n/a	138 *125*	61 *169*	2.7 *219*	438 *169*	163.80 *91*
Swaziland (K7)	Mbabane	.sz	1.7 *88*	34.5 *220*	6.0 *92*	7.0 *197*	3.32 *148*	10.43 *145*	4.43 *163*	0.47 *145*	0.53 *158*	0.28 *128*	2.9 *122*	1,633 *140*	1,859 *162*	1,339 *135*	n/a	n/a	n/a	459 *101*	289 *123*	65.4 *127*	1,138 *153*	17.40 *157*
Sweden (J2)	Stockholm	.se	1.8 *83*	80.5 ***7***	9.2 *24*	36.9 *113*	75.46 ***7***	108.47 ***3***	71.54 ***8***	5.78 *21*	52.01 *34*	30.27 *46*	2.7 *124*	35,704 *11*	321,401 *17*	96,372 *24*	10,123 *15*	12,579 *16*	6,167 *25*	3,003 *49*	2,388 *44*	20.0 *182*	9,002 *85*	450.00 *56*
Switzerland (J3)	Bern	.ch	1.0 *134*	80.5 ***7***	11.2 ***4***	74.3 *53*	47.20 *31*	84.63 *31*	70.97 ***10***	4.25 *36*	31.86 *43*	15.97 *57*	1.5 *160*	47,541 ***3***	356,052 *16*	139,989 *17*	8,797 *18*	n/a	10,309 *15*	6,578 *30*	10,600 *14*	182.2 *59*	7,489 *94*	41.10 *135*
Syria (K4)	Damascus	.sy	7.1 ***9***	71.5 *95*	5.1 *119*	25.0 *148*	4.39 *137*	12.87 *137*	14.60 *113*	1.13 *108*	22.69 *55*	36.99 *40*	3.0 *117*	1,145 *151*	21,125 *72*	16,966 *67*	n/a	3,997 *33*	2,220 *48*	3,032 *48*	891 *71*	99.6 *93*	18,449 *55*	185.20 *88*
Taiwan (P4)	Taipei	.tw	2.6 *47*	77.0 *47*	5.6 *109*	29.7 *175*	53.81 *19*	100.31 ***8***	59.63 *18*	4.56 *30*	104.43 *21*	11.89 *65*	4.3 *65*	13,849 *51*	317,070 *20*	21,896 *54*	8,170 *20*	5,923 *22*	4,040 *39*	2,950 *50*	2,372 *46*	632.4 *14*	22,894 *48*	36.20 *136*
Tajikistan (M4)	Dushanbe	.tj	2.2 *63*	61.0 *165*	3.3 *175*	42.4 *93*	0.08 *206*	0.73 *205*	3.75 *172*	0.90 *121*	6.45 *84*	3.92 *86*	7.4 *15*	248 *210*	1,779 *163*	n/a	n/a	n/a	n/a	n/a	2 *204*	50.1 *143*	7,164 *97*	143.10 *94*
Tanzania (K6)	Dodoma	.tz	2.1 *66*	45.0 *201*	4.9 *128*	39.3 *104*	0.88 *179*	4.35 *172*	0.42 *209*	0.05 *195*	1.94 *123*	0.79 *113*	6.4 *26*	314 *203*	11,560 *93*	10,525 *79*	n/a	n/a	595 *76*	566 *93*	347 *113*	38.9 *157*	36,766 *33*	945.00 *31*
Thailand (O5)	Bangkok	.th	1.3 *113*	70.0 *116*	4.4 *146*	63.9 *24*	11.25 *94*	44.18 *76*	10.97 *132*	1.22 *104*	78.09 *25*	39.81 *38*	2.6 *126*	2,473 *109*	158,703 *32*	n/a	4,517 *25*	2,152 *45*	10,034 *17*	11,651 *18*	7,294 *20*	125.1 *79*	64,186 *19*	513.10 *50*
Togo (I5)	Lomé	.tg	1.6 *93*	52.0 *187*	10.5 ***9***	69.5 *18*	4.41 *136*	4.40 *169*	1.21 *192*	0.48 *159*	0.48 *159*	0.00 *–*	2.3 *139*	346 *199*	1,868 *161*	4,480 *111*	n/a	n/a	n/a	83 *136*	92 *153*	95.1 *96*	5,400 *110*	56.80 *125*
Tonga (S6)	Nuku'alofa	.to	M *–*	71.0 *99*	6.9 *66*	—	2.88 *155*	3.38 *181*	11.29 *130*	0.36 *152*	0.04 *198*	0.00 *–*	2.1 *149*	1,654 *139*	186 *208*	n/a	n/a	n/a	n/a	41 *147*	26 *184*	149.9 *68*	112 *192*	0.75 *185*

116 | Appendices

Countries A-Z: Trinidad & Tobago-Zimbabwe

▶ **See also...** pages 108 for notes relating to this section; Contents (2-5) for details of all maps and charts in this Atlas

Country (Map Ref)	Internet code	Capital	Area 000 sq km	Population 000 (2004)	Population Density people/sq km (2004)	International Arrivals 000 (1997)	International Arrivals 000 (2004)	Visitor Receipts US$ million (2004)	International Departures 000 (2004)	Visitor Expenditure US$ million (2004)	Hotel Bedrooms (2003)	Gross Nat'l Income US$ million (2004)	GNI per Person US$ (2004)	GDP Growth Av. annual % 1997-2006	Energy Production Mil tonnes oil equiv. (2004)	Energy Consumption Mil tonnes oil equiv. (2004)	Energy Consumption Tonnes oil equiv./person (2004)	Fixed Tel. Lines lines/100 people (2004)	Mobile Tel. Lines lines/100 people (2004)	Internet Usage Subscribers/100 people (2004)	Agricultural Land % of national area (2004)	Total Health Spending % of GNI (2002)	Life Expectancy Years (2004)	Military Spending % of GNI (2003)
Trinidad & Tobago (F5)	.tt	Port of Spain	5.10 •170	1,075 •154	210.8 •51	324 •116	443 •102	n/a •–	n/a •–	n/a •–	5,378 •102	11,360 •94	10,567 •62	6.9 •20	31.51 •44	13.28 •70	12.35 •7	24.58 •90	49.82 •70	12.24 •88	25.9 •144	3.7 •167	70.0 •116	0.6 •152
Tunisia (J4)	.tn	Tunis	154.50 •92	10,075 •80	65.2 •128	4,263 •29	5,998 •34	1,910 •53	2,274 •44	326 •62	110,009 •20	26,301 •65	2,611 •107	5.0 •45	6.25 •80	8.56 •81	0.85 •125	12.11 •127	35.86 •87	8.40 •106	59.7 •41	5.8 •99	72.0 •87	1.6 •93
Turkey (K4)	.tr	Ankara	779.50 •37	69,661 •17	89.4 •103	9,040 •17	16,826 •12	15,888 •8	5,928 •21	2,524 •37	201,510 •13	268,741 •21	3,858 •97	3.9 •76	22.81 •52	83.32 •24	1.20 •105	26.45 •81	47.99 •72	14.13 •85	53.5 •63	6.5 •71	70.5 •111	4.9 •16
Turkmenistan (L4)	.tm	Ashgabat	488.10 •52	4,952 •113	10.1 •202	257 •125	n/a •–	n/a •–	n/a •–	n/a •–	n/a •–	6,615 •115	1,336 •145	11.7 •7	65.16 •33	18.46 •64	3.73 •45	7.73 •146	0.19 •213	0.73 •182	66.8 •22	4.3 •150	60.5 •166	2.9 •35
Turks & Caicos Is. (F4)	.tc	Cockburn Town	0.50 •193	21 •216	41.1 •154	93 •152	n/a •–	n/a •–	n/a •–	n/a •–	2,473 •128	117 •213	5,692 •79	n/a •–	0.00 •–	0.01 •207	0.24 •163	27.14 •80	8.10 •151	n/a •–	2.3 •209	n/a •–	74.5 •63	T •–
Tuvalu (R6)	.tv	Funafuti	0.02 •224	12 •221	581.8 •6	1 •206	1 •155	n/a •–	n/a •–	n/a •–	n/a •–	13 •223	1,117 •153	n/a •–	0.00 •–	n/a •–	n/a •–	5.83 •155	n/a •–	10.83 •96	0.0 •–	4.4 •146	61.5 •158	M •–
Uganda (K5)	.ug	Kampala	241.00 •80	27,269 •41	113.2 •83	175 •138	512 •98	n/a •–	n/a •–	n/a •–	n/a •–	6,911 •110	253 •209	5.8 •34	0.44 •122	0.94 •143	0.03 •201	0.27 •215	4.36 •171	0.75 •181	51.1 •68	7.4 •56	48.5 •195	2.3 •60
Ukraine (K3)	.ua	Kyiv (Kiev)	603.70 •44	46,997 •25	77.8 •113	7,558 •19	15,629 •14	1,141 •60	14,795 •13	996 •44	32,572 •53	60,297 •53	1,283 •147	4.8 •50	76.81 •28	156.41 •14	3.33 •56	25.22 •88	28.52 •103	7.79 •109	68.6 •20	4.7 •137	67.5 •135	2.9 •35
United Arab Emirates (L4)	.ae	Abu Dhabi	83.70 •116	2,563 •139	30.6 •168	2,476 •43	6,394 •31	1,593 •56	n/a •–	n/a •–	38,402 •46	48,007 •55	18,729 •35	6.2 •28	178.24 •15	54.19 •31	21.14 •3	27.32 •79	84.71 •30	31.85 •46	7.3 •196	3.1 •179	73.5 •75	3.1 •32
United Kingdom[7] (I3)	.uk	London	243.50 •79	60,441 •22	248.2 •48	25,515 •5	27,755 •6	27,299 •6	61,424 •2	55,930 •3	n/a •–	2,016,393 •4	33,361 •13	2.3 •139	265.24 •7	245.87 •9	4.07 •40	56.35 •21	102.16 •7	62.88 •11	69.8 •17	7.7 •49	78.5 •30	2.8 •40
United States of America[8] (D3)	.us	Washington DC	9,372.60 •4	295,734 •3	31.6 •165	47,752 •2	46,082 •2	74,481 •1	56,175 •3	65,635 •1	4,415,696 •1	12,150,931 •1	41,087 •5	2.2 •142	1,762.39 •1	2,471.07 •1	8.36 •14	60.60 •17	62.11 •53	55.58 •17	42.0 •94	14.6 •1	77.5 •41	3.8 •28
United States Virgin Is. (F5)	.vi	Charlotte Amalie	0.35 •201	109 •193	310.6 •35	411 •99	544 •96	n/a •–	n/a •–	n/a •–	5,044 •106	1,602 •164	14,737 •45	0.00 •–	0.00 •–	5.52 •88	50.64 •1	63.86 •16	n/a •–	n/a •–	28.8 •137	n/a •–	79.0 •24	T •–
Uruguay (G7)	.uy	Montevideo	176.20 •90	3,416 •131	19.4 •183	2,316 •48	1,756 •62	455 •84	495 •67	400 •69	18,160 •63	13,414 •87	3,927 •95	1.5 •160	2.19 •64	4.20 •101	1.23 •101	30.85 •69	18.51 •120	20.98 •69	84.5 •2	10.0 •10	75.5 •59	1.6 •93
Uzbekistan (M3)	.uz	Tashkent	447.40 •57	26,851 •42	60.0 •135	960 •69	n/a •–	n/a •–	n/a •–	n/a •–	7,332 •91	11,860 •91	442 •187	3.5 •91	61.64 •35	53.54 •32	1.99 •81	6.70 •152	2.05 •192	3.32 •148	60.5 •38	5.5 •112	66.0 •143	0.5 •156
Vanuatu (R6)	.vu	Port Vila	12.20 •161	206 •183	16.9 •186	50 •171	61 •139	n/a •–	n/a •–	n/a •–	10,793 •78	287 •202	1,395 •144	1.5 •160	0.00 •–	0.03 •202	0.15 •172	3.11 •174	4.84 •167	3.46 •144	13.3 •179	3.8 •163	68.0 •131	T •–
Venezuela (F5)	.ve	Caracas	916.50 •33	25,375 •45	27.7 •172	814 •72	n/a •–	n/a •–	832 •60	n/a •–	82,366 •27	104,958 •40	4,136 •93	2.1 •149	188.88 •13	72.88 •26	2.87 •66	12.78 •122	32.17 •97	8.84 •105	23.7 •154	4.9 •128	74.0 •70	1.3 •113
Vietnam (O5)	.vn	Hanoi	331.70 •65	83,536 •13	251.8 •47	1,114 •65	2,928 •51	n/a •–	n/a •–	n/a •–	n/a •–	45,082 •57	540 •178	6.9 •20	36.46 •41	24.62 •51	0.29 •157	12.28 •124	6.01 •159	7.12 •116	21.9 •160	5.2 •115	71.0 •99	2.6 •47
Wallis & Futuna (S6)	.wf	Matu Utu	0.24 •209	16 •218	66.8 •125	n/a •–	n/a •–	n/a •–	n/a •–	n/a •–	n/a •–	32 •219	1,997 •134	0.00 •–	0.00 •–	0.00 •–	n/a •–	11.88 •128	n/a •–	5.63 •125	n/a •–	n/a •–	n/a •–	T •–
Western Sahara (I4)	.eh	al-Aioun	252.10 •77	273 •179	1.1 •224	n/a •–	n/a •–	n/a •–	n/a •–	n/a •–	n/a •–	159 •209	582 •174	0.00 •–	0.00 •–	0.09 •189	0.33 •155	0.73 •201	n/a •–	n/a •–	15.1 •175	n/a •–	n/a •–	n/a •–
Yemen (L5)	.ye	San'a	555.00 •48	20,727 •48	37.3 •160	80 •158	n/a •–	n/a •–	n/a •–	n/a •–	13,280 •72	11,218 •95	541 •177	3.9 •76	23.42 •51	3.88 •104	0.19 •170	3.85 •170	5.17 •163	0.87 •180	33.0 •119	3.7 •167	59.0 •172	7.1 •9
Zambia (K6)	.zm	Lusaka	752.60 •38	11,262 •73	15.0 •190	341 •114	515 •125	n/a •–	n/a •–	n/a •–	5,202 •103	4,748 •129	422 •190	3.6 •85	2.25 •96	2.71 •116	0.24 •162	0.79 •198	2.75 •186	2.11 •163	46.9 •77	5.8 •99	39.0 •214	0.6 •152
Zimbabwe (K6)	.zw	Harare	390.70 •60	12,161 •67	31.1 •166	1,281 •61	1,853 •59	194 •96	n/a •–	n/a •–	5,766 •101	5,150 •125	423 •189	-4.3 •177	3.40 •90	4.71 •92	0.39 •149	2.67 •178	3.56 •178	6.90 •117	52.6 •66	8.5 •35	36.5 •217	2.1 •66
• Lowest rank			•226	•226	•226	•206	•161	•117	•90	•77	•141	•224	•224	•158	•177	•211	•211	•223	•215	•209	•216	•192	•220	•163

NOTES:

1 Special Administrative Region of China.
2 Figures exclude Northern Cyprus.
3 All figures exclude overseas Départements and other dependencies listed separately here.
4 National Autonomous Region.
5 All figures include Madeira and the Azores.
6 All figures include Balearic and Canary Islands.
7 All figures exclude the Channel Islands and the Isle of Man.
8 All figures exclude overseas possessions and other dependencies listed separately here.
9 La Paz (seat of government); Sucre (judicial).
10 St Peter Port (Guernsey) & St Helier (Jersey).
11 Yamoussoukro (official); Abidjan (administrative & commercial).
12 Basse-Terre (administrative) & Pointe-à-Pitre (commercial).
13 Plymouth was largely destroyed in 1997 by volcanic eruption. A temporary administrative centre has been established at Brades.
14 Formerly called Rangoon.
15 Amsterdam (capital); The Hague (seat of government).
16 East Jerusalem has been declared the capital by the Palestinian Authority. Currently, the legislature is in Ramallah and the Palestinian Authority executive is is Gaza City.
17 Pretoria (City of Tshwane) (administrative), Cape Town (legislative), Bloemfontein (judicial). This arrangement is currently under review.
18 Colombo (administrative & commercial); Sri Jayawardenepura Kotte (legislative).
19 Population and area figures exclude the disputed territory of Jammu & Kashmir.
20 Population and area figures include the Golan Heights and East Jerusalem.
21 Population and area figures exclude Western Sahara.

21 As a result of a referendum held on 21 May 2006, Montenegro declared independence from Serbia & Montenegro on 3 June 2006, so completing the dissolution of the former state of Yugoslavia. Figures have been included in this chart for the combined republic. Montenegro has an area of 13,812 sq km and a population of 670,000. Its capital is Podgorica.

*: Ranking (top 10 in **bold**). **n/a:** Not available, not relevant or not reliable. **T:** See note on page 41. **M:** See note on page 41. For more information, see pages 202 & 210.

Index

INDEX TO THE ATLAS

The index lists all locations and features which appear in Europe (including the Russian Federation, Turkey and Cyprus). For countries outside Europe, refer to the 'Countries A-Z' section, which gives grid references to the World Political map on pages 28-29. The following special-subject maps and map pages are not indexed:

- World climate
- World sport
- World time
- World tourism
- Airports*
- Flight times
- Cruising
- Europe climate
- European Union
- Europe airports & high-speed rail
- Europe rail & ferries
- Europe museums & art galleries*
- London airports & connections
- UK attractions
- Belgium attractions
- The Dutch vs the Sea
- The Netherlands attractions
- Germany attractions
- France attractions
- Spain & Portugal attractions
- Italy attractions

Maps marked * include a list of locations on the page itself

GENERAL ABBREVIATIONS

Arch.	Archaeological
Hist.	Historic/Historical
I.	Island, Ile and equivalents
Int.	International
Is.	Islands, Iles and equivalents
Mem.	Memorial
Mon.	Monument
Mt	Mount/Mont
Mtn	Mountain/Montagne
Mtns	Mountains/Monts
Nac.	Nacional
Nat.	National
Naz.	Nazionale
Prov.	Provincial
St	Saint/Sankt/Sint

(all 'St' entries are treated as if spelt 'Saint' and are located in the index accordingly)

Ste	Sainte

(all 'Ste' entries are treated as if spelt 'Sainte' and are located in the index accordingly)

Vdkhr.	Vodokhranilishche

Countries and significant dependencies and possessions are shown in CAPITALS

Hyphens and some accents have been removed in certain cases for consistency and ease of viewing. The correct form appears on the maps themselves.

The following names, which appear in bold, indicate the entry is a featured location on one of the special subject maps:

Beach	Beach map
Heritage C	UNESCO map (cultural site)
Heritage N	UNESCO map (natural site)
Park L	Leisure/Theme park map
Park N	National Park map
Russ Adm	Russian administrative map
W Front	Western Front map

The following abbreviations appear occasionally to distinguish features with the same name:

[Adm]	Administrative region
[Apt]	Airport
[Riv]	River

Answers to Quizzes

Answers for UK Quiz 1

Question	Answer
1	F
2	I
3	C
4	A
5	E
6	G
7	B
8	D
9	J
10	H

Answers for UK Quiz 2

Fact	Resort
1	Brighton
2	Aberystwyth
3	St. Austell
4	Blackpool
5	Southend
6	Pwllheli
7	Ballycastle
8	St. Ives
9	Sandown
10	Scarborough

Answers for UK Quiz 3

Area	Gateway
1	D
2	G
3	I
4	B
5	C
6	G
7	A
8	E
9	F
10	J

Answers for UK Quiz 4

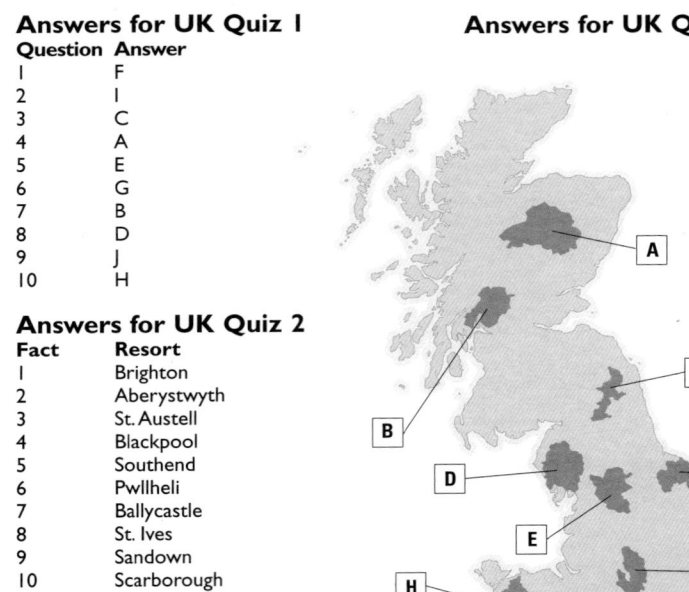

Answers for UK Quiz 5

	Airport	3-letter code
1	London Heathrow	LHR
2	Londonderry	LDY
3	Edinburgh	EDI
4	London Stansted	STN
5	Leeds Bradford	LBA
6	Birmingham	BHX
7	Cardiff	CWL
8	Glasgow International	GLA
9	Belfast City	BHD
10	Bournemouth	BOH

Answers for UK Quiz 6

Seaport	Destination
1	F
2	I
3	B
4	E
5	G
6	A
7	J
8	H
9	C
10	D

Answers for Europe Quiz 1

	Resort	Island	Country	Sea/Ocean
1	Lindos	Rhodes	Greece	Aegean
2	Kavos	Corfu	Greece	Ionian
3	Paphos	Cyprus	Greece	Mediterranean
4	Kyrenia	Cyprus	Turkey	Mediterranean
5	Alcudia	Majorca	Spain	Mediterranean
6	Funchal	Madeira	Portugal	Atlantic
7	Sliema	Malta	Malta	Mediterranean
8	Alghero	Sardinia	Italy	Mediterranean
9	Porto Vecchio	Corsica	France	Tyrrhenian
10	Molyvos	Lesbos	Greece	Aegean

Answers for Europe Quiz 2

Open-ended

Answers for Europe Quiz 3

	Airport	Nearby City	Airlines (correct at time of press)
1	Ciampino	Rome	Easyjet, Ryanair, Thomson Fly, Air Berlin, Wizz Air
2	Bratislava	Vienna	Ryanair, Easyjet, Sky Europe, Lufthansa, Czech Airlines
3	Sabiha Gokcen	Istanbul	Easyjet, Air Arabia, Condor, Pegasus, Turkish Airlines, Germanwings
4	Brescia	Verona	Ryanair, Air Alps Aviation, Gandalf Airlines
5	Beauvais	Paris	Ryanair, Blue Air, Sterling European Airlines, Wizz Air, Braathens
6	Reus	Barcelona	Ryanair, Iberia, Thompson Flights, My Travel, Air Berlin, First Choice
7	Mulhouse	Basel	Easyjet, Air France British Airways, Lufthansa, Luxair
8	Schonefeld	Berlin	Ryanair, Easyjet, Aer Lingus, Virgin Express, Germanwings
9	Treviso	Venice	Ryanair
10	Torp	Oslo	Ryanair, Coast Air, KLM

Answers for Europe Quiz 4

	Port	Body of water
1	Bergen	Norwegian Sea
2	Crete	Mediterranean Sea
3	Dubrovnik	Adriatic Sea
4	Porto	Atlantic Ocean
5	Palma de Mallorca	Mediterranean Sea
6	Istanbul	Bosporus
7	Stockhlom	Baltic Sea
8	Tromso	Norwegian Sea
9	Tallinn	Baltic Sea
10	Gibraltar	Mediterranean Sea

Answers for Europe Quiz 5

	Airport	3-letter code
1	Paris Orly	ORY
2	Faro	FAO
3	Palma, Majorca	PMI
4	Cork	ORK
5	Mikonos	JMK
6	Malaga	AGP
7	Izmir	ADB
8	Larnaca	LCA
9	Prague	PRG
10	Krakow	KRK

Answers for Europe Quiz 6

Seaport	UK destination
1	E
2	F
3	A
4	H
5	B
6	J
7	D
8	C
9	G
10	I